by Linda Lambert Litteral

Boobies, Iguanas, & Other Critters

Biosphere Reserve Series

American Kestrel Press • Steamboat Springs, CO

Boobies, Iguanas, & Other Critters:
Nature's Story in the Galápagos

is the first book in the
Biosphere Reserve Series.

Look for the upcoming titles:

Volcano and Wildlife Watching:
Nature's Story on the Island of Hawaii

From Island Forest to Ocean Reef:
Nature's Story in St. John, United States
Virgin Islands

Galloping 'Gators, Soaring Buzzards,
& Other Critters:
Nature's Story in the Florida Everglades

Step into the Outback:
Nature's Story in Uluru, Australia

Ten percent of all profits on Biosphere Reserve
Books will be made available for scientific and
educational research in Biosphere Reserves.

Book Design by Nan Goggin

Illustrations by Isabella Blumberg,
Nan Goggin, and Timothy Baker.

Photography Credits:
All photography is by Linda Lambert Litteral
©1994, except those by Thomas Litteral
©1994: p. 3 (2nd from top), p. 9 (bottom), p. 19,
p. 29 (top right), p. 58 (middle), and p. 71.

ISBN 1-883966-01-9
Copyright © 1994
Linda Lambert Litteral.
All rights reserved.

CIP information may be found on page 70.
Summary: describes the wildlife, ecology,
and geology of the Galápagos Islands as
well as Darwin's theory of evolution, bird
behavior, and recent scientific study.

Also available in Spanish,
ISBN 1-883966-02-7

Printed in Hong Kong
Published 1994

10 9 8 7 6 5 4 3 2 1

American Kestrel Press
Dept. 10
P.O. Box 774723
Steamboat Springs, CO 80477-4723

CONTENTS

For Russell Szmulewitz
who inspired me to write for young readers

Boobies, Iguanas, & Other Critters is especially written for the needs of young readers. It incorporates ideas and research to make the information interesting and meaningful for young readers. The writing style and design concept for this book result from my teaching experiences, writing and editing experiences, and educational research in reading, writing and design.

Looking at the overall book design, the first thing you will probably notice is that it is generously illustrated with color photographic images. Most of these images have captions with important information. The photographs get the attention of all readers, who will then usually read the captions. This is an important feature for motivating youngsters who are not avid science readers. For the avid science reader, the photographs and captions compliment the rest of the written material. In addition, written information and related illustrations are always located on facing pages. There is never a need to read about something and then have to turn a page to see an illustration or photograph.

Another feature about this book is that it presents general background as well as in-depth information. The material is appealing for those who have a general interest in the subject material and helpful for those readers who are doing research or other school projects. Also, the book includes a special section that will help students write a science report.

Boobies, Iguanas, & Other Critters is a natural history book, which means that it includes information about wildlife, habitats, animal behavior, and geology. In addition, information is given about the history of the islands and their role as a biosphere reserve. Biosphere reserves are places designated by UNESCO (United Nations Educational, Scientific, and Cultural Organization) as representative ecosystems that should be preserved for all times. This book is the first in the Biosphere Reserve Series published by American Kestrel Press.

An important feature of all Biosphere Reserve Series books is that they include the description of at least one recent scientific study conducted in the region. Scientific observations and scientific reasoning are discussed to show how scientists go about the job of being scientists, how they reason, and how they make conclusions. Another important feature of the series is to show human cultures as being *a part* of the ecosystem rather than *apart* from the ecosystem.

Boobies, Iguanas, & Other Critters will make a wonderful addition to a young reader's library and also to school and public libraries. Ten percent of the profits from the sale of this book will be provided for educational and scientific projects in the Galápagos Islands Biosphere Reserve. *Boobies, Iguanas, & Other Critters* is also available in Spanish.

Linda Litteral

The Galápagos– Islands of Surprise

A wide-eyed sea lion pup soaks up the sun waiting for its mother to return from her feeding journey.

Have you ever wished you

Have you ever wished you could get very close to a wild animal without having it run away? Maybe you have tried to look at an animal eye-to-eye, but just couldn't get close enough to do so. There is a place, though, where you can do just this. In a wild place called the Galápagos Islands, the animals are not afraid of humans. You can get very close to almost all of the animals.

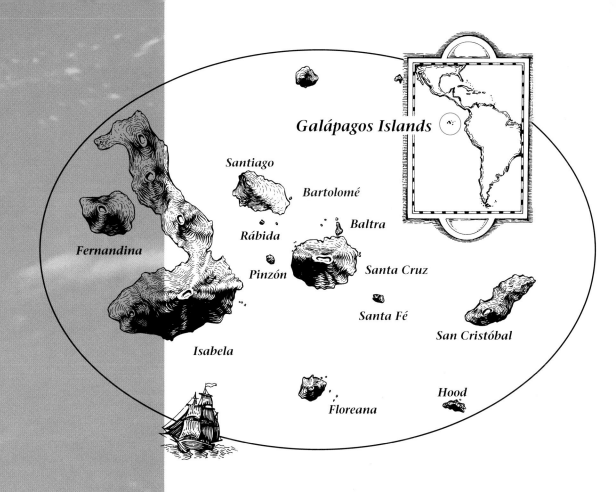

Galápagos Islands

Santiago

Bartolomé

Fernandina

Rábida

Baltra

Pinzón

Santa Cruz

Santa Fé

San Cristóbal

Isabela

Hood

Floreana

could get very close to a wild animal without having it run away?

The animals here are protected from harm and from too much human contact. You are not allowed to pet the animals. However, the animals are allowed to pet you! So, don't be surprised if the wet nose of a sea lion pup gives you a gentle nudge.

The Galápagos Islands belongs to the country of Ecuador. The islands are located about 700 miles off the coast of this South American country. There are 13 large islands, 6 smaller islands, and over 40 tiny islands. Some of these islands are shown on the map.

The cormorant is a bird that eats fish. There are many kinds of cormorants in the world. However, the Galápagos cormorant is different from other cormorants because its wings are so small that flying is impossible.

Many of the plants and animals in the Galápagos are found nowhere else in the world. Also, the animals have special habits that are very different from the habits of their relatives. For example, only in the Galápagos are there lizards that swim in the ocean to find their food. Other examples of plants and animals that are only found in the Galápagos or that have special habits are shown in the illustrations on these pages.

Rare plants and animals are often in danger of dying out until no more exist. So, concerned people around the world try to protect these special living things. Sometimes people think that plants and animals can be saved simply by preventing people from harming them. But this is not enough. The place where the plants and animals live must also be protected. For example, suppose an animal has a special plant that it must eat to live. If that plant can only grow in a special place, then that place must also be protected.

Some plants such as this lava cactus are found nowhere else. The lava cactus is one of the few plants that grow on new lava. You can tell when the cactus is actively growing because younger cactus spines are lighter in color than older spines.

This bird is a Darwin's finch. It is one of several kinds of small finches found only on islands in the Galápagos.

The marine iguana is a lizard. It uses the flat side of its tail as a paddle to help it swim. Unlike any other kind of lizard, the Galápagos iguana searches for its food in the ocean.

The Galápagos Islands is a place where many special plants and animals rely on each other. So, in the Galápagos, the plants and the animals and the places where they live are all protected from harm. However, this has not always been so. Many years ago, from the late 1500s to the early 1700s, pirates, whale hunters, and other sailors visited the islands. They discovered great numbers of land turtles, which are also called tortoises.

The tortoises became an important food source for the sailors for two reasons. First, tortoise meat is both good tasting and nutritious. Second, since there were no refrigerators, fresh meat could not be kept on long voyages. However, tortoises can live for long periods of time without food and water. In fact, the sailors could keep the tortoises alive without feeding or watering them for as long as a year. So, the tortoise was an ideal source for fresh meat for the sailors. Unfortunately, the sailors took too many tortoises away—as many as 100,000 or more.

Not all of the Galápagos tortoises were the same. Different kinds of giant tortoises were found on different islands. Since the sailors took so many tortoises away, some kinds of tortoises became too few in number to survive

Not all of the Galápagos

Sailors of the 1600s captured tortoises to use for food on long voyages. Tortoises can go for long periods without food and water because they are reptiles. Reptiles are cold-blooded, which means they do not have to use food energy to keep their bodies at a constant temperature. Therefore, they require very little food to stay alive. Furthermore, when drinking water is not available, the tortoise can use stored body fat to make water.

and their groups died out. Although all the different kinds of tortoises are protected today, there is no way to replace the special kinds that used to be. They are gone forever.

tortoises were the same.

G. e. becki

G. e. darwini

G. e. porteri

G. e. vicina

G. e. chathamensis

G. e. ephippium

G. e. elephantopus (extinct)

The different types of tortoises (Geochelone elephantopus ssp.) have different shapes to their shells. Different tortoises are found on different islands. Some islands have more than one type of tortoise. Some of the different types no longer exist. They are extinct.

CHAPTER TWO

The Galápagos Islands–
A Scientific Laboratory

One of the four different species of mockingbirds lives on Hood Island.

Another mockingbird species lives on Fernandina Island.

This iguana from Hood Island is distinctly red.

The word *galápagos* is the Spanish name for tortoises. The Galápagos Islands was famous for these tortoises and was named after them. The tortoise also helped make the islands famous for another reason. The tortoises played a noteworthy role in the development of an important scientific theory—the Theory of Evolution by Natural Selection. This theory was proposed by Charles Darwin.

In 1835, the young scientist named Charles Darwin arrived in the Galápagos Islands from England. He was traveling around the world to study and collect plants and animals. Darwin thought that each Galápagos island would have the same kinds of plants and animals as the other islands. So, he did not record the exact place where each plant or animal was found.

One day, Darwin was speaking with someone who lived on one of the islands. The local man said he could tell which island a tortoise belonged to just by looking at its shell. Now Darwin realized he needed to keep more accurate records. So, he started writing down exactly where each plant and animal came from. He soon saw a pattern. He saw that the plants and animals from separate islands showed small but definite differences. For example, Darwin was surprised to find that there were different kinds of mockingbirds on the different islands. The iguanas also differed from island to island. Of course, Darwin also saw that the tortoises were different.

Darwin's Theory of Evolution

Darwin wondered why each island should have its own special type of animal. Why wouldn't you find the same kind of mockingbird only 50 miles away? Darwin thought about this question for many years. Finally, he decided that the closely related species did not arrive on the islands in their present form. Darwin thought that the closely related species on different islands had the same ancestor. However, the plants and animals changed in slightly different ways on each island. They changed in different ways because the food and climate were somewhat different on each island. Over many thousands of years the plants and animals showed the obvious changes we see today. Some of the plants and animals changed enough to be called a new species. Some other plants and animals have changed but not enough to be called a new species. They are called subspecies (ssp.).

Darwin's idea about how animals and plants change over time is called the theory of evolution by natural selection. The phrase *evolution by natural selection* means that *nature selects,* or determines, how a group of organisms will *evolve*. To evolve is to change. So, the conditions of nature, such as the type of available food or the amount of rainfall, influence which organisms in a group can survive. Over a long period of time, the characteristics of the organisms change slowly. At first, the changes in the organisms are hardly noticeable. Eventually, the organisms look somewhat different from their ancestors.

The idea for the theory started when Darwin learned that the tortoises on each island were not quite the same. He spent many years studying his animal and plant collections. He also did many experiments to test his idea. Only after many studies did he state his theory. Darwin's theory is one of the most important theories in science today.

Can you tell how this iguana from Fernandina Island differs from the Hood Island iguana?

It has a different color.

Darwin's theory of evolution by natural selection explains why these finches look so much alike, but also look different.

As Darwin's theory explains, the tortoises changed slowly over thousands of years. How they changed depended on the place where they landed. The type of change depended on the local environment. Tortoises in a wet environment changed differently from those in a dry environment.

Most scientists agree that the tortoises have not changed enough to be called separate species. Therefore, the different types of tortoises are called subspecies. Someday, it is possible that the different tortoise groups will change enough to be called separate species.

Darwin's theory explains how the Galápagos plants and animals changed over time, but it does not explain how their ancestors arrived on these islands. Darwin and other scientists have also tried to explain the arrival of the plants and animals.

How did the first Plants and Animals Arrive in the Galápagos?

Some tortoises landed in hot, dry places with few plants.

Tortoises on dry islands eat cactus pads and grasses. They have long necks and long legs. The shell is curved up in the front. The curved shell allows the tortoise to stretch its neck up and reach the cactus pads.

Some tortoises landed in cool, wet places with many plants. The tortoises in wetter areas have short legs and a short neck. They do not need to reach high to get food. Their shell is better adapted to protect them as they push through thick vegetation.

How did the first plants and animals arrive? To answer a question, scientists try to make direct observations whenever possible. Sometimes this is not possible, though. For example, you can't tell how a particular plant arrives unless you are there to see it happen. Plants and animals of the Galápagos may have started to arrive as long as 3 million or more years ago. At that time there were no humans to see or record their arrival.

When direct observations cannot be made, scientists answer questions in other ways. For example, scientists believe that the way things happen today is the same way things happened in the past. Today, plants such as ferns arrive in the Galápagos when their spores are carried by the wind. Since this happens today, scientists think it also happened long ago. Some of the ways that plants get from place to place are shown in the pictures on this page.

How Plants Get from Place to Place

Fern spores are so tiny they can only be seen with a microscope. They float high in the sky to their new home. The spores grow into fern plants.

A few kinds of seeds, such as the coconut, can survive after floating in salty sea water.

Some plants have "wings" that help carry them in the wind.

Mud on birds' feet carries seeds. Fleshy fruits such as berries are eaten by birds. The soft part is digested but not the seed. The seed passes out of the bird and is ready to grow.

Sometimes scientists use observations from experiments as clues. Then, they reason how the clues fit together to answer a question. For example, Darwin and other scientists noticed that many birds have mud on their feet. Furthermore, this mud often contains plant seeds. So, scientists reason that some plants arrive in the Galápagos on the feet of birds.

A few plants like *Sesuvium* and the seeds of mangrove trees are not killed by salt water. They probably drifted to their new home across the ocean. Humans, too, have brought large numbers of plants in recent years. However, using all the clues, scientists believe that the birds and wind brought most of the plants to the Galápagos.

This iguana walks in the *Sesuvium*. *Sesuvium* can tolerate salt water and salt spray. It grows close to the sea shore.

Seeds wa[sh]
ashore to for[m]
mangrove swamp[s]
along the coa[st]

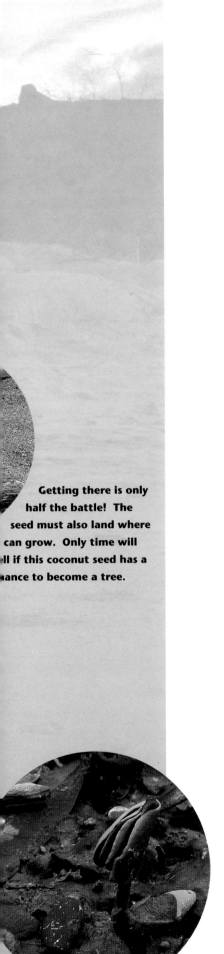

Getting there is only
half the battle! The
seed must also land where
can grow. Only time will
ll if this coconut seed has a
ance to become a tree.

Most animals came to the
Galápagos from South America.
Other animals are believed to have
come from North America, Central
America, and the Caribbean.

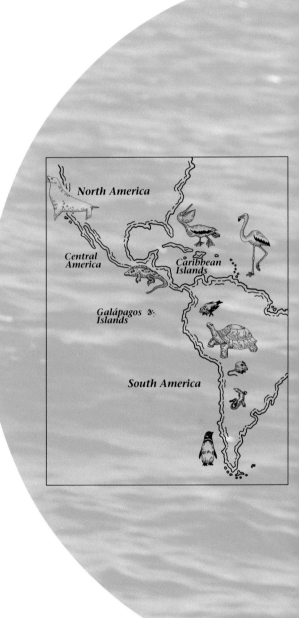

North America

Central
America

Caribbean
Islands

Galápagos
Islands

South America

Sea birds are strong fliers. They arrive under their own power.

Insects probably arrived on wind currents. Some insects arrived when mats of vegetation floated across the ocean from South America. Small birds such as Darwin's finches may have been blown to the islands by storms with strong winds. Some of the ways other animals arrived on the islands are shown in the pictures on these pages.

Some animals like penguins (left) and the sea lion (above) are good swimmers. They arrived by swimming in strong ocean currents.

The tortoise came to the Galápagos long before humans arrived.

The tortoise came to the Galápagos long before humans arrived. The first tortoises probably traveled to the Galápagos Islands on large rafts. The rafts formed when trees and other vegetation clumped together along the banks of large rivers of South America. Then, the clump of vegetation broke loose and floated down the river to the ocean. Finally, this newly formed raft slowly floated across the sea. Many living plants and animals were trapped on the raft. Tortoises and other cold-blooded reptiles were able to survive the long voyage. Warm-blooded mammals (animals with fur) could not easily survive the long journey. Even today there are only a few mammals in the Galápagos.

Although no one knows for sure, scientists think that tortoises landed first on San Cristóbal Island. Then, they spread out to the other islands. Slowly over many centuries, the shapes of the tortoises' shells changed. How they changed depended on the place where they lived.

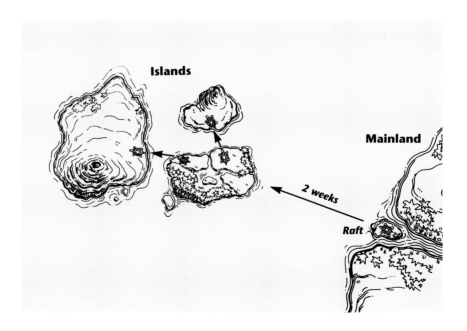

CHAPTER THREE

Current Scientific Studies in the Galápagos

Charles Darwin was only in the Galápagos Islands for five weeks. Even though his visit was short, he came to realize the value of the islands in explaining the process of evolution. Other scientists also see their value. Today, the interest in studying evolution in the Galápagos is very high. Many experiments have been made since Darwin's time and many are in progress now.

Convergent Evolution

Some current experiments have to do with studying *convergent evolution*. Generally speaking, convergent evolution means that two unrelated organisms come to look like one another. They come to look alike because they have similar needs. For example, a slim bill is useful to birds that capture insects for food. So, different species of insect-eating birds often have slim bills.

The following example explains how convergent evolution occurred for finches and warblers in South America. There are many small birds called warblers that feed on flying insects. They usually have slim bills. Finches, however, are birds that usually have thick bills and strong jaw muscles. These features allow the finch to crack seeds open and eat them.

Insect-eating warblers and seed-eating finches lived on the continent of South America thousands of years ago. However, none of the warblers landed on the Galápagos Islands. Only seed-eating finches landed there.

Since there were no warblers on the islands to eat the insects, there was a good food supply of insects available to the finches. Some, but not all, of the finches in the group ate insects. Scientists believe that finches with slightly slimmer bills had the best chance of catching and eating insects. So, the finches with slimmer bills had plenty of food and therefore lived to have many offspring. They passed the trait for slimmer bills to their offspring.

For a long period of time, nature selected for slimmer and slimmer bills in this group of insect-eating finches. Eventually, there was a large group of finches with slim bills. Today, these finches with slim bills look very much like warblers. The changes in the appearance of the finches to look like warblers are a result of convergent evolution.

In summary, we know that South American warblers and Galápagos finches have a similar need—to eat insects. Scientists believe that their feeding needs were solved in a similar way. They both evolved a slim bill. So, they came to look alike. Their evolution has come to a similar point, or *converged*. It is important to remember, though, the warbler is still a warbler and the finch is still a finch. The finch comes to look like a warbler but does not become a warbler.

Divergent Evolution

The concept of convergent evolution explains how warbler and finch bills came to look alike. At the same time, another event also occurred. The finch bills also became different from the thick shape of the original finch group.

When a certain character evolves to look differently from the original, scientists say that *divergent evolution* occurs. So, in this example, the bill shape of one group becomes different, or *diverges,* from the bill shape of the original group.

This graph illustrates the concepts of divergent and convergent evolution in bill shape for two groups of birds: the warblers and the finches. The finch ancestors in South America (upper left) were seed eaters and had thick bills. Some of their offspring continued to be seed eaters (red line). The flatness of the line shows that bill shape stayed the same. Some finches on the Galápagos came to eat insects (purple-blue line). Their bill shape became slimmer over time. Where the purple line splits from the red line shows where bill shapes started to change. That is, the bill shapes of the two groups became different, or diverged, from one another. The steepness of the purple-blue line shows there is change in bill shape.

In comparison, the warbler ancestors in South America (lower left) were insect eaters. They already had slim bills. The flatness of the light blue line shows that their bill shape has not changed over time. However, the bill shape of insect-eating finches approaches the bill shape of the warblers as seen where the purple line comes close to the light blue line. That is, the bill shapes of the two finch groups come to look alike, or converge. Notice that the purple-blue line never actually touches the light blue line. This is because the finch is still a finch; it never becomes a warbler.

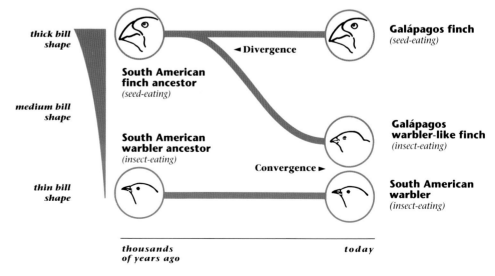

Convergent and Divergent Evolution in the Bill Shape of Warblers and Finches

thick bill shape

medium bill shape

thin bill shape

South American finch ancestor *(seed-eating)*

◄ Divergence

Galápagos finch *(seed-eating)*

South American warbler ancestor *(insect-eating)*

Convergence ►

Galápagos warbler-like finch *(insect-eating)*

South American warbler *(insect-eating)*

thousands of years ago

today

Convergent Evolution for Sea Lions and Marine Iguanas

You might ask how sea lions and marine iguanas could possibly be alike. The example with the finch and the warbler shows how animals can come to look alike. Scientists think that *behaviors* can also come to be alike, or converge. Remember that convergent evolution starts with two unrelated animals. A recent study has looked at the behavior of two very unrelated animals—the sea lion and the marine iguana. Both of these animals have a similar mating behavior.

The mating behavior occurs when the male defends a certain space. This means he tries to keep all other males out of his space. Eventually, several females will come into his space to rest. The male lets all females stay in his space. So, one male will have several female mates.

The scientists Fritz and Krisztina Trillmich studied the mating behavior of both sea lions and marine iguanas. They have proposed a way to explain how a defended space for mating evolved in both groups. To start with, they think this behavior can only occur in areas with plenty of food and few enemies. There are not many places in the world where these conditions exist. However, the Galápagos is such a place.

The next three sections describe the observations, scientific reasoning, and conclusions made by Fritz and Krisztina Trillmich.

Sea Lion Beaches
Sea lions don't move easily over large boulders. They prefer sandy beaches or beaches with small boulders.

Iguana Beaches
Iguanas find it easy to scramble over rocks. They prefer beaches that are close to a food source. Their food grows on underwater rocks close to the shore.

Aggregation—The Behavior of Sea Lion and Marine Iguana Ancestors

Scientists give the name *aggregation* to the act of gathering together by chance. For example, suppose you are walking in a park. Suddenly it begins to rain. Just ahead there is a shelter. You decide to sit under the shelter until the rain stops. It's a nice place to get out of the rain. After a while other people also sit under the shelter because it's a good place to escape the rain. The people came to sit in the shelter because it was a convenient place to gather, or aggregate.

Female sea lions of the Galápagos are able to rest on the beach without fear because they have no enemies. They do not have to find places to hide. At first, a long time ago, many females probably came to the same beach because it was a convenient place to rest.

There was no special reason for the females to be together in the same place. The beach just happened to have some feature the female sea lions liked. It was a nice beach to stop at. So, many female sea lions happened to gather there by chance. That is, they aggregated on the beach.

The scientists also believe that female iguanas used to gather, or aggregate, on certain beaches. However, the beaches that the iguanas liked were different from the beaches that sea lions liked.

The Trillmiches wondered what it was that made a beach attractive to female sea lions and to female iguanas. After observing the habits of each, they decided sea lions and iguanas had different needs. Therefore, they aggregated on beaches for different reasons. For example, newborn sea lion pups can not stay in the water for long periods of time. So, female sea lions found beaches where their pups had an easy place to get out of the water. The female sea lions gathered, or aggregated, on these beaches.

On the other hand, the scientists rejected the idea that female iguanas gathered on beaches to raise their young. The scientists observed that the iguanas leave the beaches where they lay their eggs. The females do not stay on these beaches to raise their young. Instead, they gather on other beaches where they can feed. The scientists concluded that iguanas originally gathered, or aggregated, on beaches for the purpose of feeding.

Female sea lions try to get warm by squeezing between other females on the beach.

The Evolution of Gregarious Behavior

The scientists believe that female aggregation occurred first. Eventually, this led to *gregarious* behavior.

Gregarious means that the animal actively looks for others to be with. For example, suppose that you plan a picnic. You tell everyone to meet you at the shelter in the park. Now the people will look for others and join them. The people are being gregarious. They meet on purpose, not by chance.

Sea lions catch fish in the ocean when they feed. The scientists observed that female sea lions did not come out of the ocean and just lie down anywhere. The female would try to lie down by squeezing between two other sea lions. She would not lie down in an equally good but empty space. This suggests that the sea lion was joining the others on purpose, or showing gregarious behavior. Other observations showed that when the temperature is high, the sea lions soon spread out. The scientists also knew that sea lions lose body heat while feeding in cold ocean water. So, they concluded that the sea lion squeezed between the other females on purpose to help get warm. When all the females were warm enough, they spread apart.

Iguanas feed in the oceans, too. However, they are cold-blooded. So, they become cold even faster than the warm-blooded sea lions. Scientists believe that iguanas like the sea lions gather on purpose to keep warm. However, iguanas face a problem that sea lions do not. They have an enemy, the Galápagos hawk. So, it is possible that by gathering in a large group, a particular female has less chance of becoming a meal for the hawk. The scientists concluded that female iguanas show gregarious behavior when they gather on purpose to keep warm. Gregarious behavior may also help protect an individual iguana from its enemy.

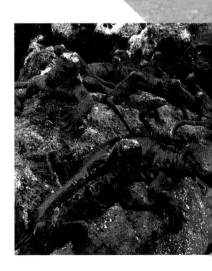

Female iguanas seek others for warmth. This behavior would also help males keep warm. The larger males join the females in sun-soaking only when the mating season is over. During the mating season males are too busy to sit in the sun. They are busy chasing other males away. The males are much larger than the females.

The Evolution of Behavior to Defend a Space

So far we have seen that female sea lions and iguanas probably gathered by chance at first. Next, the females started to gather on purpose. Finally, this gathering of females in one area started to happen on a regular basis. So, the area became a good place for a male to find a mate. A male that defends this area against other males will have more mates and more offspring. In order to have many mates, he must have the best ability to keep the other males away. His offspring will inherit his ability. In this way, nature selects for males with the best ability to defend a breeding space.

Two things help a male defend his space. One is fierceness and the other is size. The fiercer and larger the male is, then the easier he can chase other males away. As a result, evolution has favored fierce, large males. The males are much larger than the females. This is true for both sea lions and marine iguanas.

Conclusion

In conclusion, we see that the behavior of sea lions and iguanas have converged along similar lines. Female aggregation, a gathering by chance, was followed by female gregariousness, a gathering on purpose. Gregarious behavior was followed by a male defense of a mating area. Male defense of a mating area allowed fierce large males to evolve.

Male sea lions defend their breeding space by swimming back and forth in the water along the beach. The male on the right recognizes the female on the left by smell. Females are allowed to stay but males are chased away. A male sea lion is larger than a female and can be identified by the "bump" on his forehead.

A rapid up and down movement of the head along with an open mouth is a way iguanas show fierceness.

CHAPTER FOUR

Seabirds–
Studies on Behavior

Scientific studies about evolution are commonly done in the Galápagos, but there are other studies, too. Scientists also study animal behavior. The behavior of seabirds is especially interesting and has been well studied. Seabirds are those birds that make their living from the sea. That is, they get most of their food from the sea.

The way a bird feeds is one type of behavior that scientists study. One thing seems to be sure. No two animals living in the same area feed in exactly the same way. There can be similarities in feeding, but there are also differences. For example, two different kinds of birds might both feed on fish, but they feed on different kinds of fish. Another possibility is that both feed on the same kind of fish, but one feeds during the day and the other feeds at night. Thus, neither bird directly interferes with the feeding of the other. In the following discussions, notice that each group of birds has a different way of feeding than the others.

All animals must mate and raise young, if the species is to survive. Therefore, scientists also study seabirds for mating and chick-raising behaviors. These behaviors can be described as *rituals*. That is, the behavioral action of one animal causes a certain reaction in another animal of the same species. The set of behaviors is always the same; it never changes. For example, if a booby chick pecks its parent's bill, then the parent automatically feeds the chick. If the chick cried out instead of pecking its parent's bill, it would not get fed. There is only one proper set of behaviors in a ritual. Each species has its own rituals.

Not all behaviors are part of a ritual. Some behaviors are actions that help a bird survive on a day-to-day basis. For example, birds living on hot islands need ways to keep from overheating. Some behaviors that prevent overheating are shown here.

Behaviors That Are Part of a Ritual

Pecking the bill of a parent is one way the masked booby chick begs for food.

Masked boobies often nest on steep slopes. A mating couple jabs each other as part of a greeting ritual. It is the booby way to say, "Hello."

Swallow-tailed gulls have a behavior that looks like choking. The bird "chokes" when it wants to show that it owns this site. Choking behavior is followed by *foot-looking* as seen here. Scientists do not know what foot-looking means.

Behaviors That Are Not Part of a Ritual

Penguins are usually found in cold climates. The feet of cold climate penguins are used to absorb the heat of sunlight. Galápagos penguins have adapted to their hot environment by keeping their feet shaded. In this way they do not take in extra heat.

This masked booby shades its chick during the first week of life. Chicks this young have no way of cooling down by themselves.

The adult blue-footed booby gets rid of extra heat by opening its mouth to pant. Heat also escapes when the feathers on the back are lifted.

Frigatebirds—Acrobats and Pirates of the Sea

Frigatebirds are called the acrobats of the sky. They are acrobatic because they have a light body suspended between very long wings. The specialty of the frigatebird is that of a pirate. It steals food from others. First, the frigate will fly after a bird that has caught a fish. Next, the frigate grabs the other bird's tail feathers. The frigate repeats this behavior several times. Finally, the other bird drops its fish to avoid being attacked again. As the fish drops, the acrobatic frigate catches it in midair.

The mating behavior of the frigate is part of a ritual. During the mating season, the male frigatebird settles on a tree to attract a mate. Next, he inflates a red flap of skin on his neck. This makes the frigate look like it has a bright red balloon under his chin. Then, the male rests his bill on the red pouch. When a female flies overhead, he spreads his wings out and shakes them. If the male is successful in attracting a female, they will mate.

The couple builds its nest in trees or shrubs. Both the male and the female take turns sitting on the single egg. After about two months the egg hatches. The young bird sits on its nest of twigs for five months before it is ready to fly. Learning the acrobatic flying skills of a frigatebird is not easy. While learning to fly, the young frigate cannot catch enough food for itself. So, the parents continue to feed their youngster for six more months. Only then is the young bird skilled enough to get food by itself. From the time mating behavior begins until the young bird can feed itself is 15 to 18 months.

Frigatebirds have an eight foot wing span to help them float on wind currents. They are very acrobatic. Their acrobatic skills allow them to steal food from other birds.

The male and female frigatebirds often embrace during courtship. It takes about 20–30 minutes to inflate the male's red pouch. The red pouch will disappear after courtship.

A young frigatebird sits in its nest of twigs for five months before it is ready to fly. You can easily tell the difference between a young frigate chick and a young booby because the frigate has a sharp hook on its bill and the booby does not.

The swallow-tailed gull stays with its chick during the day (above). The parents leave the nest at night to feed (below). Like most sea-birds, the parents carry food to the nest in their stomachs. The young chick pecks at the white spot on the base of its parent's bill to get fed. Then the parent empties its stomach of fish into the mouth of the chick.

Gulls and Tropicbirds

The swallow-tailed gull is perhaps the most beautiful gull in the world. During the breeding season its large eye has a beautiful red ring around it. The large size of the eye is a special adaptation for seeing better at night. The large opening lets more light into the eye than a smaller opening would. The swallow-tailed gull is the only gull in the world to feed at night. Occasionally this gull can be seen bringing food back to its nest during the day. But the food is almost always stolen by a frigatebird during a daytime flight. Scientists suggest that piracy by frigatebirds may be the reason that a nighttime feeding behavior has evolved in swallow-tailed gulls.

Tropicbirds fly far out to sea to get their food. They feed by day and dive beneath the surface of the water to catch fish. Tropicbirds are also pestered by frigatebirds to give up their fish dinners. Sometimes the frigatebird does get a free meal. Much of the time, though, the tropicbird is quick enough to get away.

This young tropicbird waits for its parents to return from the sea with fish. Tropicbirds feed so far from land that young birds must be good fliers before they leave the nest to fish on their own. Once the young bird leaves, it leaves for good. It does not come back to the nest to be fed by the parents.

Boobies

Some of the most interesting seabirds are those called boobies. The name *booby* means someone or something that is easy to fool. As we have seen, birds that live on ocean islands have few, if any, predators. So, they have not evolved a behavior to fear others. When people first arrived on the ocean islands, boobies did not fear them. The birds were easy to capture. So, the people called them boobies.

There are three kinds of boobies on the Galápagos Islands. The two that are most easily seen by visitors are the masked booby and the blue-footed booby. Both species of boobies tend to feed on flying fish and squid. However, they do not interfere with each other's feeding because they feed in different locations. The blue-footed booby feeds close to shore and the masked booby feeds farther from shore.

The distance each kind of booby has to travel to get food affects its chick-raising behavior. Since the blue-footed booby feeds closer to shore, it can bring food to its young more often than the masked booby can. As a result, the blue-footed booby can raise two chicks at a time. The masked booby can only raise one chick because it takes the parents too long to get enough food for two chicks.

The blue-footed chick that hatches first is older, larger, and stronger than the second chick.

The masked booby chick on the right is only a few days old. A second egg has not yet hatched. Even though the chick can barely lift its head it will try to destroy the egg. In this way, the chick has a better chance to survive.

The larger blue-footed chick often chases the smaller chick away, especially when the food supply is low.

Blue-footed boobies can raise two chicks. The eggs hatch about three to five days apart. If there is plenty of food, both chicks survive. If there is not a good food supply, the older chick will chase the younger chick away. The younger chick will then die from the cold of the night or from a lack of shade during the hot day.

Masked boobies usually lay two eggs but only one survives. This is true even during years with plenty of food. The second chick will hatch and survive only if the first egg is damaged or the first chick dies.

Blue-footed booby

Both birds are about six weeks old. Notice that the blue-footed booby chick already has black flight feathers but the masked booby chick does not. This is because the blue-footed booby gets more food and grows faster than the masked booby.

Masked booby

Only one masked booby chick survives past the first few days. This is a normal behavior that best allows the parents to successfully raise a chick. The parents cannot bring enough food for two chicks.

CHAPTER FIVE

Nature as Artist

The mystery and magic of the Galápagos is more than its wonderful collection of plants and animals. The landscape also adds to the power and magnificence of this special place. Volcanoes appear as large scoops of ice cream topped with chocolate sauce and clouds of whipped cream. Other places have a more rugged appearance. Some places give you the illusion of walking among the craters of the moon.

The artistic beauty of the landscape is a result of natural events. Much of its design results from volcanic action. For example, the steep sides of mountains are made when a volcano grows. Growth occurs deep beneath the earth when a chamber fills with melted rock. As the chamber grows larger, it pushes the earth up to form a mound. Occasionally, the melted rock forces its way to the surface and flows down the sides. The melted rock, called lava, soon hardens. The layers of lava can be dozens of feet thick. The build-up of many layers of lava adds to the height and beauty of the volcano.

The volcanoes of the Galápagos have steep sides compared to other volcanoes of the world. The tops of the tallest volcanoes are frequently hidden by clouds. What appears as chocolate sauce running down the side is really lava.

The Birth of a Volcano

**The red-orange color shows hot,
liquid rock. When the
hot, liquid rock is beneath the
earth's surface it is
called magma. When the
hot, liquid rock is on the
earth's surface it is called
lava. As the hot liquid cools,
it hardens and turns black.
This hardened black rock is
also called lava.**

Lava

Magma

A Galápagos-type volcano takes millions of years to form and grow. The volcano will pass through a series of stages. The drawings on these pages show the stages in the growth cycle of a volcano. First, the volcano swells, erupts, empties, and collapses. Then, these events repeat themselves over millions of years.

Formation and Growth of a Volcano

1. Hot, liquid rock rises from deep within the earth where it makes and fills a chamber. This causes the earth to bulge at the surface. The increasing pressure of the magma causes the rocks above the chamber to crack.

The shorter Island of Daphne Major does not have a cloudy top. Like most Galápagos volcanoes it has a relatively flat top because the top of the volcano falls inward.

2. Magma flows through the cracks and rises to the surface at many places. Some of the magma pours out from a circle of openings at the top of the volcano. However, most of it flows sideways through tunnels within the volcanic mountain.

3. As the magma erupts, the chamber starts to empty. An empty space now exists where the magma used to be.

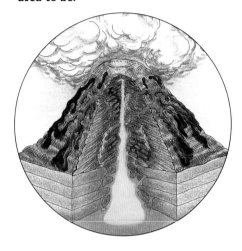

4. Next, the top of the volcano drops into the empty space of the chamber. The volcano collapses forming a large pit called a caldera. In 1968, a caldera on Fernandina Island dropped an amazing 1100 feet (350 meters) in only 9 days.

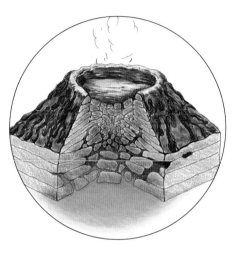

A large pit called a caldera forms when the top of the volcano falls inward. The floor of the caldera on Daphne Major is flat. The dark spots seen on the floor are nesting birds.

Special Features of the Volcanic Landscape

Volcanic activity forms the large structure of the volcanic mountain. It also forms other interesting features of the landscape. These pages show some of these volcanic features.

Spatter Cones

Most volcanic activity in the Galápagos occurs as quiet flows of lava. Sometimes, though, the hot liquid rock meets water as it moves up to the earth's surface. The water changes to steam and the lava explodes. The exploding lava produces lumps of different sizes. These lumps land on each other to make spatter cones such as these on Bartolomé Island.

Fumeroles

Lava cools and hardens when it reaches the surface of the earth. Many feet below, though, the lava is still hot and liquid. In this picture you can see what looks like "smoke" on the crater walls. The "smoke" is really steam. At first, water soaks through the many holes of the hardened lava. When the water meets hot lava, the water changes to steam and rises to the surface. The place where the steam comes out is called a fumerole.

Hornitos

When lava flows over a bit of surface water, the water turns to steam and explodes. The steam tosses up bits of lava which make a small cone called a hornito. Hornitos are small. They are usually less than three feet (one meter) tall.

Lava Channels

Lava flows downhill like a river and takes the easiest pathway. The lava on the two outside edges of the flow cools first and then hardens. Now, thin hardened walls of lava form a channel where the liquid lava can flow. Sometimes lava overflows the channel and quickly hardens. This happens many times until thicker walls are formed. Finally, when the lava flow stops, the very last bit of lava drains out of the channel leaving the walls behind.

Lava Crust

When lava begins to cool down, the top hardens first to form a bendable crust. The thick liquid lava underneath the crust keeps flowing, though. This flow causes the thin crust on top to wrinkle into many beautiful patterns.

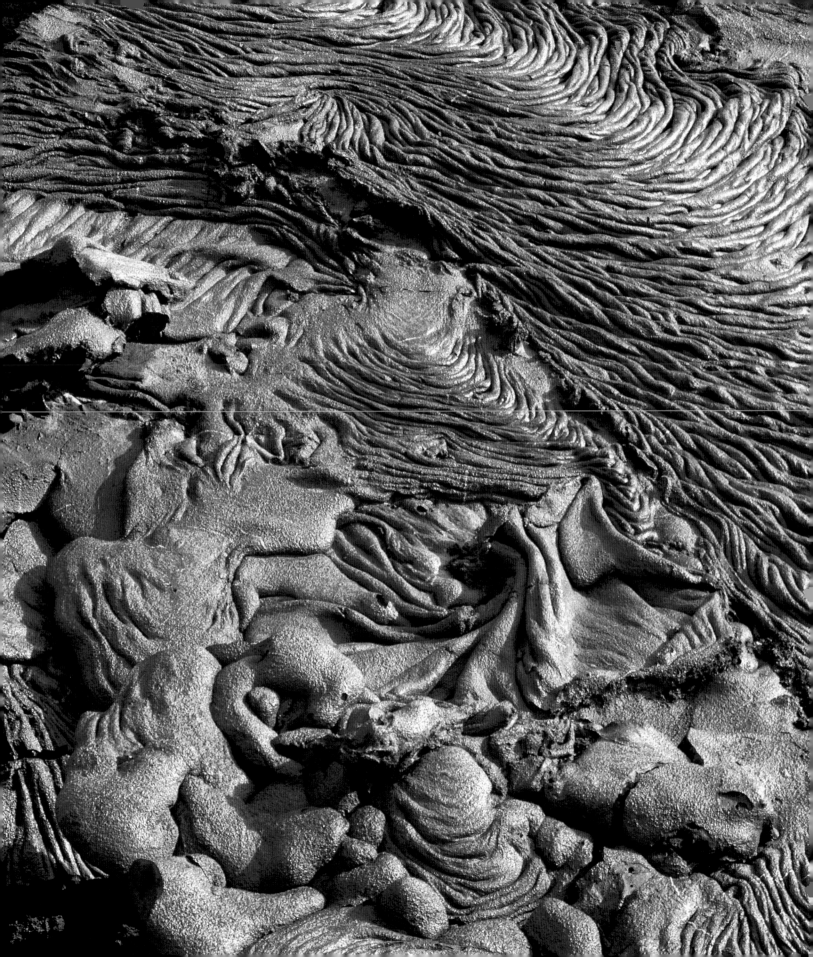

Very small particles thrown from the volcano are called ash. The ash settles on the ground in many layers. The particles weld together to form a rock called tuff.

Volcanoes also produce very small particles called ash. The volcano explodes and throws the ash high into the air. Then the ash rains down upon the land. Eventually, the ash becomes so thick that cliffs can form on the ocean's edge.

Waves carved the tuff cliff on Isabela Island to make a cave.

The layers of tuff can be so thick that high cliffs form. Wave action carves tuff cliffs into many other interesting designs.

Lava cactus is about the only thing that can start to grow on the new lava.

Hardened lava is a rock. So, you can imagine how difficult it must be for a plant to start to grow here. Plant roots cannot easily poke through the lava rock. Dust particles must first collect in the cracks before most plants can grow.

Although volcanic action is responsible for the creation of much of the landscape, other forces are also at work. For example, waves can make caves. Waves can also make sand. The waves that beat against the rocky shore break the rocks apart and make sand the color of the rock. So, beach sand can also be black, green, and even red.

The beach sand on Rábida is red. The waves smashed into the red cliffs slowly crushing its rocks to make sand.

This Galápagos Hawk has carried its food onto a beach made of broken pieces of coral that have washed ashore.

Some fish can also make sand. For example, certain fishes eat sea animals called corals. The hard white skeletons of the corals are chewed into small sand-sized pieces. However, they cannot be digested by the fish. Instead, they pass through the fish and out of its body. Eventually, they wash ashore to make white sandy beaches.

A Sally lightfoot crab walks along a green beach. The green color comes from the mineral olivine, which is found in rocks.

Parrotfish live in the coral reef. They eat the coral animals and their hard skeletons. The skeletal remains help make the white sand found on the ocean bottom and on some of the shores.

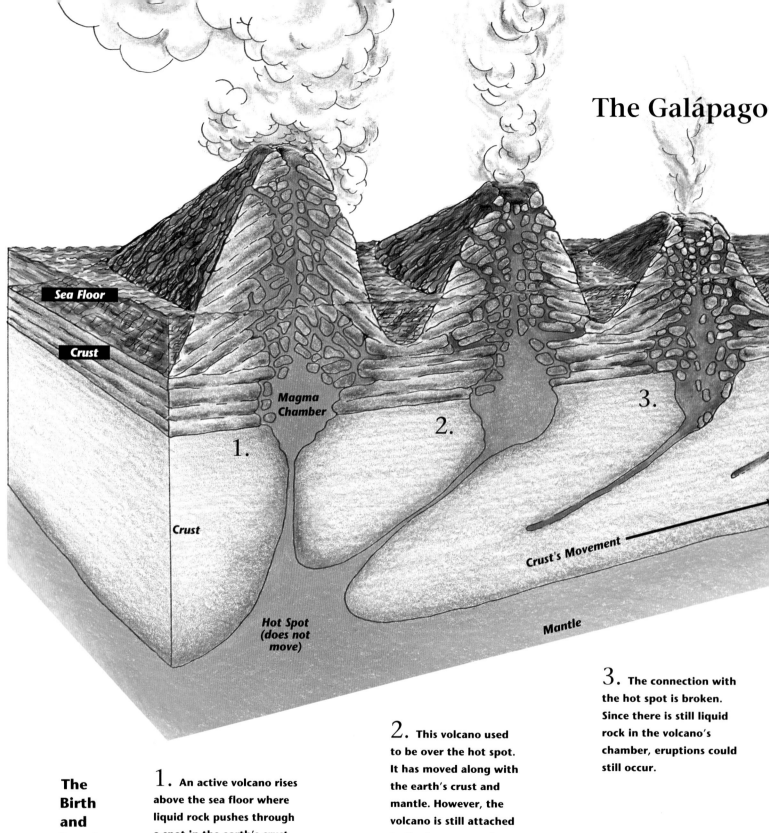

The Galápago

Sea Floor

Crust

Magma
Chamber

1.

2.

3.

Crust

Hot Spot
(does not
move)

Crust's Movement

Mantle

3. The connection with
the hot spot is broken.
Since there is still liquid
rock in the volcano's
chamber, eruptions could
still occur.

2. This volcano used
to be over the hot spot.
It has moved along with
the earth's crust and
mantle. However, the
volcano is still attached
to the hot spot and
continues to erupt.

**The
Birth
and
Death
of a
Volcano**

1. An active volcano rises
above the sea floor where
liquid rock pushes through
a spot in the earth's crust.
The spot is called a hot
spot. Over many thousands
of years, the volcano gets
taller and taller.

s a Very Hot Spot to Be

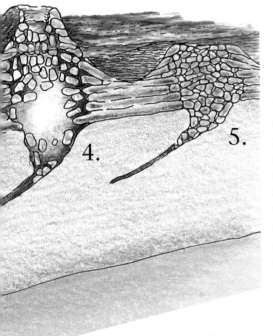

The earth's crust including the volcano floats on top of the mantle. The mantle moves sideways. As the mantle moves, the volcano will move with it. However, the hot spot does not move.

4. **This old volcano has no more liquid rock in its chamber. The volcano cannot erupt any more; it is extinct. Wind and rain erode the volcano down. The volcano gets shorter and shorter. The empty chamber cannot support the weight of the heavy rock layers above it. The earth collapses into the chamber.**

5. **Eventually, the old volcano is completely eroded down to the surface of the ocean. Now waves can wash over its surface. Wave erosion results in a very flat underwater surface.**

The Galápagos is a Very Hot Spot to Be

The upper part of the earth is made up of hot fluid rock called the mantle. A thin crust of solid earth rests on top of the mantle. This crust makes up the part of the earth we walk on. It also makes up the floor of the ocean.

The crust is not a single continuous sheet of solid material. Instead, it has several large moving *plates.* The movement of these plates explains why some Galápagos islands are older than others. At certain spots called hot spots, the liquid mantle of the earth breaks through to form a volcano. The hot spot stays in the same place, but the plate keeps on moving. The first volcano that forms eventually breaks away from the hot spot as it moves along. Now a new volcano can begin to form at the same hot spot. After a very long time, a string of many volcanic mountains stretch across the ocean.

Some of the volcanoes in the Galápagos are over 5,000 feet (1,500 meters) above sea level. However, part of the volcano is also below the ocean's surface. The part below the surface adds another 9,000 feet (2,800 meters) to the total height of the volcano. In other words, the volcano grew 14,000 feet (4,300 meters) above the sea floor.

Volcanoes do not grow at a steady rate. Rather they grow in spurts. First, there will be a rapid increase in size. This is followed by a long quiet period when no new growth occurs. Then a rapid growth period occurs again. The cycle repeats itself many times over thousands of years.

Here and There–
This and That

Scientists are not the only ones who can learn about the interesting features of the Galápagos. You can visit the Galápagos Islands and see them, too. On your visit, you will go from here to there. You will get to see a little bit of this and a little bit of that. This chapter talks about other sights you can see in the Galápagos.

Biosphere Reserves

Most of the Galápagos Islands is part of a national park that belongs to Ecuador. The area is also a *biosphere reserve.* Biosphere reserves are special places in the world. The places are special because they are good examples of the kinds of ecosystems found on earth today. Concerned people around the world wish to protect these places so that they will always be here in the future. In a biosphere reserve, both the education of visitors from around the world and scientific study are important. Conservation and the needs of local people are also important.

Biosphere reserves are often divided into three zones—a special use zone, a buffer zone, and a core zone. Local people live in the special use zone where they build homes and raise food. The buffer zone is an area that surrounds and protects another area. The buffer zone has many things of scientific, cultural, and educational interest. The buffer zone is usually a place that is not seriously damaged when large numbers of people visit it. These areas are especially good for educating visitors.

The buffer zone protects the core of the biosphere reserve. The core zone is more fragile than the other zones. Although some scientists occasionally enter the core zone, most visitors cannot. Thus, the plants and animals in the core zone have a chance to live and grow and evolve as they naturally would.

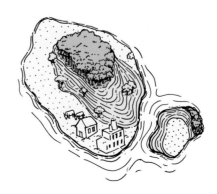

Arrangement of biosphere reserve zones on oceanic islands
The special use zone is used for farming and building homes. The buffer zone provides a spot for educational and scientific activities. Core zones protect habitats and wildlife; humans do not interfere.

Florida Everglades

Volcanoes National Park, Hawaii

Uluru, Australia

There are over 190 biospheres reserves throughout the world. The four reserves shown on this page will be the subject for the next books featured in the Biosphere Reserve Series.

St. John, U. S. Virgin Islands

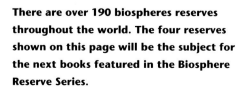

47

Habitats of the Galápagos

The Galápagos have many different habitats. A habitat is a particular place where certain plants and animals live together. Some habitats include humans and their activities. Some habitats are moist and cool with many plants. Others are dry and hot with few plants. Some habitats are located on the coast and have plants and animals that are specially adapted to grow there. Some habitats including the coral reef are part of the surrounding ocean waters. The photographs on these and the following pages show some of the organisms of the Galápagos and their habitats.

The Human Habitat

The people of the Galápagos make their living from fishing, farming, and working in the tourist industry. Humans use the resources of many habitats in the special use zone. Some of the native animals can benefit from human activities as well.

many different habitats.

Moist Habitats

Volcanoes can erupt in different ways. Sometimes they flow with lava. At other times they violently explode and produce ash particles that rain down upon the land. In areas where these particles land, they form a loose soil. Plants have an easier time growing on this volcanic soil than on hard lava. Plants grow quickly in places with loose soil and plenty of rain. You can tell where these places are because you will see a gently rolling landscape with lush vegetation.

Particles thrown from the volcano form a layer of loose dirt. In moist regions, plants soon cover the landscape.

Dry Habitats

Most of the land in the Galápagos has a very dry climate. Only the tops of the volcanoes have moisture at all times of the year. The lowlands only have moisture during the rainy season. During the dry season, some plants lose their leaves, which helps prevent water loss.

In other dry areas, much of the vegetation is the type found in deserts. For example, some plant leaves are small to prevent the loss of water. Other leaves, such as cactus pads, are specially adapted to store water for the plant.

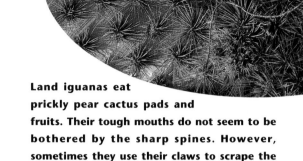

Land iguanas eat prickly pear cactus pads and fruits. Their tough mouths do not seem to be bothered by the sharp spines. However, sometimes they use their claws to scrape the spines away.

The giant prickly pear cactus can grow to three or four times the height of a person. This habitat is the home for the land iguana.

The land iguana can reach a length of 3 feet (1 meter) and a weight of 25 pounds (11 kilograms). It can live for up to 60 years.

Within the forest, widely scattered vegetation indicates a dry habitat. *Scalesia* is the scientific name of the short green plant in the picture. It is in the same plant group as the sunflower and dandelion. There are about twenty different kinds of *Scalesia* found in different habitats of the Galápagos Islands. Some, like this one are small shrubs. Others are woody and grow into trees.

The Galápagos dove eats cactus seeds and insects. It is found in dry areas of the islands. Wild house cats are enemies to these doves.

As you climb up a mountain in the Galápagos, you may pass through what looks like a dead forest. Actually, the trees have lost their leaves. They lose their leaves during the dry season. When the rainy season comes, leaves will grow and give a greener look to the landscape. 51

Habitats of the Ocean and Coast

The coastal area includes the habitats where the land meets the ocean. The kinds of plants and animals found along the shore are much different from those found in the deep oceans. Coastal habitats are greatly affected by tides. Tides raise and lower the height of water along the shore. So, sometimes the land is covered with sea water and other times the land is uncovered. Living in a habitat that is soaked in salt water part of the day and baked in sunlight part of the day is difficult to do. In areas where the tide goes in and out, only specially adapted organisms can survive. The coastal area below is found on Bartolomé Island.

A young pelican rests at the water's edge. The brown pelican feeds by flying over the water, plunging into the water, and scooping up fish in its huge pouch.

Brown pelicans are found in many places around the world. Only the Galápagos pelican would let you get as close to it as this. This pelican was interested in watching a group of people as they got out of a swamped boat. The bird was trembling and the people thought it might be afraid of them. They thought the bird might be injured and couldn't fly away. However, when all the people were safely on shore and it was calm, the bird flew away.

This American oystercatcher doesn't eat oysters! Rather, it feeds on crabs, mussels, and worms. This bird probes the soft mud with its long bill when the tide goes out. Oysters do not live in this type of habitat.

A sea lion feeds her pup. The pups stay on the beach while their mothers return to the ocean to feed on fish. She needs to feed so that she can produce milk for her pup. The pups may feed on milk for up to three years. Since pups can be born once a year, one mother may be feeding two different sized pups at the same time.

The Sally lightfoot crab got its name because it can skip across the surface of the water for short distances. Perhaps you have been on a scavenger hunt where you collect a little bit of this and a little bit of that. The Sally lightfoot crab makes its living as a scavenger. That is, it eats a little bit of everything that washes in with the tide.

The striped heron is a fish eater found in the mangrove swamp.

The Mangrove Swamp Habitat

Places where trees grow in the water are called swamps. Swamps along the salty waters of the coasts are mangrove swamps. Many animals take shelter among the roots of the mangrove trees. The leaves of these trees drop into the water and start to decay. The decayed material is an important source of nutrients for plants and animals of the ocean.

The Beach Habitat

Beaches are areas where the land meets the sea. These beaches often provide places where animals can rest, mate or nest. Some beaches are used by sea lions or iguanas. Others are used by sea turtles.

A mating pair of green sea turtles are seen here next to a mangrove swamp. Each weighs from 100 to 200 pounds. The turtles' shells are black in color, but they have green fat. So, the green turtle gets its name because of the color of its fat. The green sea turtles that feed, mate, and lay eggs in the Galápagos do not usually travel long distances across the ocean as other green sea turtles do.

This mangrove swamp of the Galápagos Islands is home to many different plants and animals.

The marine iguana can find shelter among the roots of mangrove trees.

Young turtles usually hatch at night. They cross the sand and make their way to the sea. Young turtles make an easy meal for birds of prey like the Galápagos hawk.

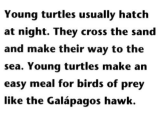

Eggs are usually laid at night. The turtle then leaves the nesting site in the early morning to return to the sea.

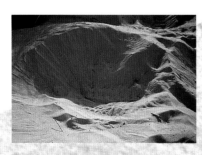

Female turtles leave the ocean to lay their eggs. Here, turtle tracks lead away from the ocean and go to the tops of sand dunes.

Where would you look for turtle eggs? If you guessed they are laid in the pit, you would be wrong. The eggs are in the area behind the pit. The turtle used sand from the pit to cover its eggs.

55

Dolphins are found in the open ocean. Although they look like fish, this is the result of convergent evolution (see pages 20 and 21). They are actually mammals that have hair, breathe at the surface of the water, and feed milk to their young.

A rocky coast swept by crashing waves is a difficult habitat to live in. This particular area is a place where unmated male sea lions gather to come ashore and rest.

Rocky Coasts and Open Ocean Habitats

Rocky coasts are also difficult places in which to survive. Here the waves are a powerful force with which to deal. Yet, not far away, calm ocean waters shelter animals such as corals and fish.

Green algae grow on the rocks of the shore. Like all plants, they make their own food. The algae plants are food for marine iguanas and other animals.

A school of yellow-tailed surgeon fish pass over the coral reef. Here, they feed on plants called green algae.

White-tipped sharks are predators of the sea. They feed on other fish.

The Galápagos Islands is indeed a special place to visit. It represents a living laboratory where scientists can learn new things and test their ideas. It is also a place where interested visitors can watch the animals at close range and see beautiful sights. Special efforts by the government of Ecuador and the international community are helping to preserve the Galápagos.

Good management allows for its use by scientists, visitors, and residents. In this way, the Galápagos will remain a good place to visit for many decades to come. Perhaps one day you will travel to the Galápagos. Then, you can swim with a sea lion, climb a volcano, walk with a tortoise, and look at a booby—eye to eye.

CHAPTER SEVEN

Writing a
Science Report

If you are reading this book because you need to write a science report, this section will help you. A science report is different from a book report. In a book report, you usually write a summary of the content of the book. However, in a science report, you will use several references to fully develop a topic or answer a question. Usually your teacher will suggest a general topic for you to write about. Then, you need to find a specific topic to develop. Your teacher may also give some "rules" for writing your report. Always use these rules if they are different from the suggestions listed here.

Getting Started

First, decide what the general topic of the report will be about. For example, perhaps your teacher wants you to write about animal behavior. Since this is a very general topic to talk about, you should decide on a more specific subject. For example, you might want to decide on a particular animal whose behavior interests you. You may already have an idea from this book that you are interested in or you may want to look through other books to get other ideas.

Next, see if you can make the topic even more specific. For example, perhaps you will want to talk only about feeding behaviors or mating rituals of a particular animal. Once you have thought about your specific topic, write a one sentence summary of your purpose or write a question that you will answer in your report.

Boobies, Iguanas, & Other Critters has many topics that could be used for reports. Some of the topics are listed in the colored box on the next page. This list does not cover every possible topic, but it may help you think of a topic that interests you. Remember a good report will mix and arrange information from several references. Do not use just one resource.

Sample Topics

What scientific evidence did Darwin gather to support his Theory of Evolution By Natural Selection? (a general topic)

How does behavior evolve? (a general topic)

Compare the evolution of mating behavior of iguanas and sea lions. (a specific topic)

How does ritualistic behavior differ from non-ritualistic or learned behavior? (a general topic)

How did plants and animals arrive and then evolve on the Galápagos Islands? (a specific topic)

What is convergent evolution? (a general topic)

How does the behavior of aggregation differ from gregarious behavior? (a specific topic)

Compare and contrast the feeding behavior of sea birds. (a general topic)

How did feeding behaviors of sea birds evolve to reduce the competition for food? (a specific topic)

What is the life cycle of the frigatebird (booby, etc.)? (a specific topic)

How do volcanic hot spots form? (a general topic)

How do Hawaiian and Galápagos volcanoes compare with one another? (a specific topic)

How do other volcanic eruptions differ from Galápagos-type eruptions? (a general topic)

How are the land forms of a volcanic landscape created? (a general topic)

Describe the habitats of the Galápagos Islands. (a general topic)

Once you have determined a purpose for your science report, you will want to do two things. First, check with your teacher to make sure the topic is appropriate. Second, go to the library and look for other books that you could use for your report. If you can't find other resources about your topic, change your topic. The section called *For Further Reading* (pages 66–67) may help you find some references for your paper.

Gathering Information

Use books, magazines, and other resources to find information to help you write your report. As you read and take notes, you may notice that the information you are collecting can be organized into several groups. For example, if you are writing about the behavior of a frigate bird, you might see that there are several categories of behavior— behaviors such as mating, feeding, and chick-raising. You may want to start placing this type of information into groups as you take your notes.

Organizing the Report

There are several ways to start writing a report. Many teachers recommend that you start with an outline. To make an outline you first organize facts and details into groups of general ideas. Then, subdivide the large groups into smaller specific groups. You will want to organize the larger and smaller groups into an appropriate sequence. Then, you can use your outline as a guide to write sentences and paragraphs. Do not think of this outline as your first, last, and only outline. Good writers often find that they think of new ways to say things or organize things as they write. *Good writers will change their outlines several times before they are done.*

Your report will have several parts:

Introduction

Body

Summary or Conclusion

Introduction

The introduction will only be a few paragraphs long. Use the first paragraph of the introduction to grab the readers attention. You can do this by introducing and discussing an interesting detail or by asking a question that makes the reader want to read further to find the answer. Next, use the introduction to help the readers understand what topic you are writing about or what question you are trying to answer.

Body

The body of your report should provide enough details so your readers will understand the topic. The body of the report should be organized so that ideas flow in a logical order. If you use words that are similar to or exactly like a particular author or authors, then you should give them credit in your report. If the information is general information you do not need to quote the author, but you should use your own words when writing.

Summary or Conclusion

You should have a paragraph at the end of the report that either summarizes the main ideas in the report or draws a conclusion about the information in the report. If you have written your report based on a question, the last paragraph can be used to answer that question in a short and accurate manner. Sometimes, writers have trouble thinking of what to put in the concluding paragraph. One way to get an idea for the last paragraph is to read the first paragraph or first page. The first paragraph or page will often provide ideas for writing the last paragraph.

Try This Tip

Here is one way to make sure you use your own words while writing a paragraph.

1. Only use one or two key words to help you remember each idea you want to talk about in your paragraph. Place the words in a logical order.

2. Next, think how you would explain each idea to your teacher or classmates during a conversation. Then, write the sentence or sentences down.

3. Finally, reread each paragraph and ask yourself these questions:
- Does this paragraph have a main idea that I want the reader to know about?
- Have I given details to explain the main idea?
- Have I come to a conclusion or logical ending?
- Are there any sentences that do not relate to the main idea (if there are, rewrite the paragraph)?
- Does each sentence follow in a logical order?

Writing the Report

As you start writing the body of your report, you will write sentences and paragraphs. There is more than one way to write a paragraph. However, one pattern that works well is suggested here:

1. Write a beginning sentence that describes the main idea.

2. Add sentences that explain the main idea or give reasons that support the main idea.

3. Add words or phrases that will show the reader your organization. You might use words such as *first, next, then, finally, therefore, in conclusion, if...then, the problem is...,* and so on.

There are also other ways to structure paragraphs. These are listed below and briefly described:

Use Logic.
First, make a claim or statement. Then, support the claim using valid reasons or facts. At the end of the paragraph, you may want to restate the original claim or state a conclusion about the original claim.

Describe a Topic.
Start with the most general ideas first. Then, write about more specific ideas.

Compare Ideas.
Show similarities and differences between two or more ideas.

Show Cause and Effect.
Describe an event and then show how the event causes a particular response or effect.

Discuss a Problem and Its Solution.
State a problem and suggest a solution for the problem. This writing structure is often developed using logic *(see above)*.

After writing several paragraphs, look for places you can add words or sentences to show how the paragraphs are related to one another.

Improving Your Report

Many students make the mistake of turning their first attempt at writing into their teachers as the final product. However, you can make the report much better if you take the time to write more than one draft. Good writers will often write many drafts before they feel the report is good enough. Good writers also ask others to read their report and give them comments about it.

Of course, you will want to use correct grammar for your report. However, the organization of your report is probably the most important aspect of good writing. So, when you revise your report, look for better ways of organizing it. You can also ask classmates and adults to give you comments about your report. It is best to ask them to answer specific questions. Here are some questions and instructions I give people to help me revise:

- Is there anything you would add to make this report easier to understand?

- Do you think any of the sentences or paragraphs should be in a different order?

- Please mark any sentences or paragraphs you do not understand.

- Is there anything you would want to know more about to make the report more interesting?

- Are there any sentences or paragraphs that seem to be unrelated to the rest of the report?

Review the suggestions your readers have made. Decide which ones will make your report better. Then, write a new draft of your report.

Making a Final Check

When you evaluate your work, you should first review your original purpose. Then, answer these questions.

- Did you accomplish your goal or answer your question completely?

- Is your report well organized and focused on the original purpose?

- Do your main ideas flow in a logical order? You might want to make a new outline from your final draft. Then, review the outline to see if all the topics are properly related to one another.

- Did you start with a paragraph designed to catch the reader's attention?

- Did you draw a final conclusion?

When you have made all the necessary changes, you are ready to hand the report in to your teacher. Congratulations for doing a great job!

Books about the Galápagos
(*see also* Advanced Reader References)

McCormick, Maxine. 1989. *Galapagos.*

Selsan, Millicent E. 1977. *Land of the Giant Tortoise: The Story of the Galápagos.*

Books about Darwin
(*see also* Advanced Reader References)

Gallant, Ray A. 1972. *Charles Darwin: The Making of a Scientist.*

Hyndley, Kate. 1989. *The Voyage of the Beagle.*

Ralling, Christopher. 1986. *The Voyage of Charles Darwin: His Autobiographical Writings.*

Shapiro, Irwin. 1977. *Darwin and the Enchanted Islands.*

Skelton, Renee. 1987. *Charles Darwin and the Theory of Evolution.*

Books about Evolution

Attenborough, David. 1981. *Life on Earth: A Natural History*

Burton, John. 1988. *Close to extinction.*

Hitching, Francis. 1983. *The Neck of the Giraffe: Darwin, Evolution and the New Biology.*

Moore, Ruth. 1969. *Evolution.*

Patent, Dorothy H. 1977. *Evolution Goes on Every Day.*

Raham, Gary. 1988. *Dinosaurs in the Garden: An Evolutionary Guide to Backyard Biology.*

Stein, Sara. 1986. *The Evolution Book.*

Taylor, Ron. 1981. *The Story of Evolution.*

Books about Animals

Bare, Colleen, S. 1986. *Sea Lions.*

Carr, Archie. 1969. *The Reptiles.*

Cook, Joseph J. & Ralph W. Schreiber. 1974. *Wonders of the Pelican World.*

Evans, Phyllis Roberts. 1986. *The Sea World Book of Seals and Sea Lions.*

Hosking, Eric & Ronald M. Lockley. 1984. *Seabirds of the World.*

Johnson, Sylvia A. 1975. *Penguins.*

Patent, Dorothy. 1990. *Seals, Sea Lions and Walruses.*

Rabinowich, Ellen. 1980. *Seals, Sea Lions, and Walruses.*

Rahn, Joan. 1983. *Keeping Warm, Keeping Cool.*

Saunders, David. 1973. *Sea Birds.*

Sibbald, Jean H. 1986. *Strange Eating Habits of Sea Creatures.*

Stidworthy, John. 1989. *Reptiles and Amphibians.*

Strange, Ian. 1981. *Penguin World.*

Todd, Frank. 1981. *The Sea World Book of Penguins.*

Wexo, John B. 1988. *Penguins.*

Books about Animal Behavior

Callahan, Philip S. 1979. *Birds and How They Function.*

Gravelle, Karen & Anne Squire. 1988. *Animal Talk.*

Patent, Dorothy. 1990. *How Smart Are Animals?*

Pringle, Lawrence. 1985. *Animals at Play.*

Sparks, John. 1970. *Bird Behavior.*

Books about Plants And Seeds

Hutchins, Ross, E. 1965. *The Amazing Seeds.*

Overbeck, Cynthia. 1982. *How seeds Travel.*

Books about Earth Science—Geology, Oceanography, and Volcanology

(*see also* Advanced Reader References)

Aylesworth, T.G. 1990. *Moving Continents: Our Changing Earth.*

Bramwell, Martyn. 1989. *Oceanography.*

Daniels, George G. (ed.). 1982. *Volcano.* (Time-Life Books)

Fodor, R. V. 1981. *Earth Afire! Volcanoes and their Activity.*

Gallant, Roy A. 1986. *Our Restless Earth.*

Lambert, David. 1988. *A Field Guide to Geology.*

Lambert, David. 1988. *Seas and Oceans.* (Our World)

Lauber, Patricia. 1986. *Volcano: The Eruption and Healing of Mount St. Helens.*

National Geographic. 1978. *The Ocean Realm.*

Rogers, Daniel. 1991. *Waves, Tides, & Currents.*

Smith, Sandra. 1981. *Discovering the Sea.*

Sotnak, Lewann. 1989. *Hawaii Volcanoes.*

Polking, Kirk. 1983. *Oceans of the World.*

Poynter, Margaret. 1980. *Volcanoes: The Fiery Mountains.*

Rhodes, Frank. 1972. *Geology*

Rossbacher, Lisa. 1986. *Recent Revolutions in Geology.*

Rublowsky, John. 1981. *Born in Fire: A Geological History of Hawaii.*

Thomas, G. & Virginia L. Leswork. 1983. *The Mt. St. Helen's Disaster: What We've Learned.*

Van Rose, Susanna. 1992. *Volcano & Earthquakes.* (Eyewitness Books)

ADVANCED READER REFERENCES

Decker, Robert & Barbara Decker. 1980. *Volcano Watching.*

Jackson, Michael. 1985. *Galapagos: A Natural History Guide.*

Moorehead, Alan. 1969. *Darwin and the Beagle.*

Perry, R. (ed.). 1984. *Galapagos.* (Key Environments)

Steadman, David & Steven Zousmer. 1989. *Galápagos: Discovery on Darwin's Islands.*

Stephenson, Marylee. 1989. *The Galapagos Islands: The Essential Handbook for Exploring, Enjoying, & Understanding Darwin's Enchanted Island.*

Trillmich, Fritz and Krisztina G. K. Trillmich. 1984. The mating systems of pinnipeds and marine iguanas: convergent evolution of polygyny. *Biol. J. of the Linnean Society 21:* 209-216.

Acknowledgments

The author wishes to thank the many young readers who read and commented on the text and photographs. She would also like to thank adult readers for their comments especially Sue Stoller, Librarian, Lake Park High School, Roselle, IL; Lynn Snell, Board of Education, Oak Grove Middle School, Libertyville, IL; Dr. Leslie Edmunds, Director of Youth Services and Family Literacy, St. Louis Public Library, MO; Dr. Donna Ogle, Reading Specialist, National Lewis College of Education, Evanston, IL; and Dr. Bonnie Armbruster, Reading Specialist, University of Illinois, Urbana/Champaign.

Library of Congress Cataloging-in-Publication Data

Litteral, Linda Lambert, 1949–
      Boobies, iguanas & other critters : nature's story in the
Galápagos / by Linda Lambert Litteral.
         p. cm. -- (Biosphere reserve series)
      Includes bibliographical references and index.
      ISBN 1-883966-01-9 (alk. paper) : $23.00
      1. Natural history--Galapagos Islands--Reserva Biosferica en los
Galápagos-- Juvenile literature. 2. Reserva Biosferica en los
Galápagos (Galapagos Islands)--Juvenile literature. [1. Natural
history--Galapagos Islands--Galapagos Islands Biosphere Reserve.
2. Galapagos Islands Biosphere Reserve (Galapagos Islands)]
I. Title. II. Title: Boobies, iguanas, and other critters.
III. Series.
QH198.G3L57 1994
508.866'5--dc20

93-5745

*The paper used in this publication meets the
minimum requirements of American National
Standard for Information Sciences—Permanence
of Paper for Printed Library Materials, ANSI
Z39.48-1984.*

Dr. Linda Lambert Litteral

grew up in the greater Chicagoland area and now lives in northwestern Colorado with her husband Thomas Litteral. When not travelling and writing, Linda is an outdoor enthusiast and enjoys skiing, tennis, hiking, backpacking, nature photography, and in-line roller skating. She has been the recipient of the Illinois Governor's Master Teacher Award, Exemplary Educator Award, and numerous awards for nature photography. She holds degrees as a Doctor of Education from University of Illinois and as a Bachelor of Science and Master of Arts in Biology. Linda taught biology and science at the Jr. High and High School level for 17 years. She has also taught biology, earth science, and education courses at the college level and worked as a science/health editor and contributor for a major publishing company.

Look for the next titles in the **Biosphere Reserve Series:**

Volcano and Wildlife Watching:
Nature's Story on the Island of Hawaii

From Island Forest to Ocean Reef:
Nature's Story in St. John, United States Virgin Islands

Galloping 'Gators, Soaring Buzzards, & Other Critters:
Nature's Story in the Florida Everglades

Step into the Outback:
Nature's Story in Uluru, Australia

Would you like to order a copy of *Boobies, Iguanas & Other Critters* or be on our mailing list to receive information about future books? Please send your name and address to:

American Kestrel Press
Dept. 10
P. O. Box 774723
Steamboat Springs, CO 80477-4723

Printed in Hong Kong.

TREATISE ON
INVERTEBRATE PALEONTOLOGY

Prepared under the Guidance of the
Joint Committee on Invertebrate Paleontology

Paleontological Society	Society of Economic Paleontologists and Mineralogists	Palaeontographical Society

Directed and Edited by

RAYMOND C. MOORE
Assisted by CHARLES W. PITRAT

Part I
MOLLUSCA 1

MOLLUSCA—GENERAL FEATURES
SCAPHOPODA
AMPHINEURA
MONOPLACOPHORA
GASTROPODA—GENERAL FEATURES
ARCHAEOGASTROPODA AND SOME (MAINLY PALEOZOIC)
CAENOGASTROPODA AND OPISTHOBRANCHIA

J. BROOKES KNIGHT, L. R. COX, A. MYRA KEEN, A. G. SMITH, R. L. BATTEN,
E. L. YOCHELSON, N. H. LUDBROOK, ROBERT ROBERTSON, C. M. YONGE, and
R. C. MOORE

GEOLOGICAL SOCIETY OF AMERICA
and
UNIVERSITY OF KANSAS PRESS

1960

Library of Congress Catalogue Card
Number: 53-12913

Printed in the U.S.A. by
THE UNIVERSITY OF KANSAS PRESS
Lawrence, Kansas

Illustrations and Offset Lithography
MERIDEN GRAVURE COMPANY
Meriden, Connecticut

Binding
RUSSELL-RUTTER COMPANY
New York City

Address all communications to The Geological Society of America, 419 West 117 Street, New York 27, N.Y.

The *Treatise on Invertebrate Paleontology* has been made possible by (1) a grant of funds from The Geological Society of America through the bequest of Richard Alexander Fullerton Penrose, Jr., for preparation of illustrations and partial defrayment of organizational expense; (2) contribution of the knowledge and labor of specialists throughout the world, working in co-operation under sponsorship of The Palaeontographical Society, The Paleontological Society, and The Society of Economic Paleontologists and Mineralogists; and (3) acceptance by the University of Kansas Press of publication without cost to the Societies concerned and without any financial gain to the Press.

JOINT COMMITTEE ON INVERTEBRATE PALEONTOLOGY

RAYMOND C. MOORE, University of Kansas, *Chairman*

G. ARTHUR COOPER, United States National Museum, *Executive Member*

NORMAN D. NEWELL, Columbia University and American Museum of Natural History, *Executive Member*

C. J. STUBBLEFIELD, Geological Survey of Great Britain, *Executive Member*

Representing THE PALAEONTOGRAPHICAL SOCIETY

L. BAIRSTOW, British Museum (Natural History)

O. M. B. BULMAN, Sedgwick Museum, Cambridge University

C. P. CHATWIN, Geological Survey of Great Britain (retired)

L. R. COX, British Museum (Natural History)

T. NEVILLE GEORGE, Glasgow University

H. L. HAWKINS, University of Reading

R. V. MELVILLE, Geological Survey of Great Britain

H. M. MUIR-WOOD, British Museum (Natural History)

C. J. STUBBLEFIELD, Geological Survey of Great Britain

H. DIGHTON THOMAS, British Museum (Natural History)

Representing THE PALEONTOLOGICAL SOCIETY

G. ARTHUR COOPER, United States National Museum

CARL O. DUNBAR, Yale University

B. F. HOWELL, Princeton University

A. K. MILLER, State University of Iowa

R. R. SHROCK, Massachusetts Institute of Technology

F. M. SWARTZ, Pennsylvania State College

H. E. VOKES, Tulane University

A. SCOTT WARTHIN, JR., Vassar College

J. W. WELLS, Cornell University

W. P. WOODRING, United States Geological Survey

Representing THE SOCIETY OF ECONOMIC PALEONTOLOGISTS AND MINERALOGISTS

CARL C. BRANSON, University of Oklahoma

DON L. FRIZZELL, Missouri School of Mines

H. V. HOWE, Louisiana State University

J. BROOKES KNIGHT, Longboat Key, Florida

C. G. LALICKER, Wichita, Kansas

STUART A. LEVINSON, Humble Oil & Refining Company

N. D. NEWELL, Columbia University; American Museum of Natural History

F. W. ROLSHAUSEN, Humble Oil & Refining Company

H. B. STENZEL, Shell Development Company

J. M. WELLER, University of Chicago

GEOLOGICAL SOCIETY OF AMERICA

H. R. ALDRICH, *Editor-in-Chief*   AGNES CREAGH, *Managing Editor*

UNIVERSITY OF KANSAS PRESS
CLYDE K. HYDER, *Editor*

iv

TREATISE ON INVERTEBRATE PALEONTOLOGY

Directed and Edited by

RAYMOND C. MOORE

Assisted by CHARLES W. PITRAT

PARTS

The indicated Parts (excepting the first and last) are to be published at whatever time each is ready. All may be assembled ultimately in bound volumes. In the following list, already published Parts are marked with a double asterisk (**) and those in press or nearing readiness for press are marked with a single asterisk (*). Each is cloth bound with title in gold on the cover. Copies are available on orders sent to the Geological Society of America at 419 West 117th Street, New York 27, N.Y., at prices quoted, which very incompletely cover costs of producing and distributing them but on receipt of payment the Society will ship copies without additional charge to any address in the world.

The list of contributing authors is subject to change.

(A)—INTRODUCTION.

B—PROTISTA 1 (chrysomonads, coccolithophorids, diatoms, etc.).

C—PROTISTA 2 (foraminifers).

**D—PROTISTA 3 (radiolarians, tintinnines) (xii+195 p., 1050 figs.). $3.00.

**E—ARCHAEOCYATHA, PORIFERA (xviii + 122 p., 728 figs.). $3.00.

**F—COELENTERATA (xvii + 498 p., 2,700 figs.). $8.00.

**G—BRYOZOA (xii + 253 p., 2,000 figs.). $3.00.

H—BRACHIOPODA.

**I—MOLLUSCA 1 (chitons, scaphopods, gastropods) (this volume).

J—MOLLUSCA 2 (gastropods).

K—MOLLUSCA 3 (nautiloid cephalopods).

**L—MOLLUSCA 4 (ammonoid cephalopods) (xxii + 490 p., 3,800 figs.). $8.50.

M—MOLLUSCA 5 (dibranchiate cephalopods).

N—MOLLUSCA 6 (pelecypods).

**O—ARTHROPODA 1 (trilobitomorphs) (xix+560 p., 2880 figs.). $10.50.

**P—ARTHROPODA 2 (chelicerates, pycnogonids) (xvii + 181 p., 565 figs.). $3.50.

Q—ARTHROPODA 3 (ostracodes).

R—ARTHROPODA 4 (branchiopods, cirripeds, malacostracans, myriapods, insects).

S—ECHINODERMATA 1 (cystoids, blastoids, edrioasteroids, etc.).

T—ECHINODERMATA 2 (crinoids).

U—ECHINODERMATA 3 (echinozoans, asterozoans).

**V—GRAPTOLITHINA (xvii + 101 p., 358 figs.). $3.00.

W—MISCELLANEA (worms, conodonts, problematical fossils.

ADDENDA (index).

CONTRIBUTING AUTHORS

AGER, D. V., Imperial College of Science and Technology, London, England.

AMSDEN, T. W., Oklahoma Geological Survey, Norman, Okla.

†ARKELL, W. J., Sedgwick Museum, Cambridge University, Cambridge, Eng.

BAIRSTOW, LESLIE, British Museum (Natural History), London, Eng.

BARKER, R. WRIGHT, Shell Development Co., Houston, Tex.

BASSLER, R. S., U.S. National Museum, Washington, D.C.

BATTEN, ROGER, L., University of Wisconsin, Madison, Wisconsin.

BAYER, FREDERICK M., U.S. National Museum, Washington, D.C.

BENSON, R. H., University of Kansas, Lawrence, Kans.

BERDAN, JEAN M., U.S. Geological Survey, Washington, D.C.

BOARDMAN, R. S., U.S. Geological Survey, Washington, D.C.

BOLD, W. A. VAN DEN, Louisiana State University, Baton Rouge, La.

BOSCHMA, H., Rijksmuseum van Natuurlijke Historie, Leiden, Netherlands.

BOWSHER, ARTHUR L., Sinclair Oil & Gas Co., Tulsa, Okla.

BRAMLETTE, M. N., Scripps Institution of Oceanography, La Jolla, California.

BRANSON, CARL C., University of Oklahoma, Norman, Okla.

BROWN, D. A., University of Otago, Dunedin, N.Z.

BULMAN, O. M. B., Sedgwick Museum, Cambridge University, Cambridge, Eng.

CAMPBELL, ARTHUR S., St. Mary's College, St. Mary's College, Calif.

CARPENTER, FRANK M., Biological Laboratories, Harvard University, Cambridge, Mass.

CASEY, RAYMOND, Geological Survey of Great Britain, London, Eng.

CASTER, K. E., University of Cincinnati, Cincinnati, Ohio

CHAVAN, ANDRÉ, Chantemerle à Seyssel (Ain), France.

COLE, W. STORRS, Cornell University, Ithaca, N.Y.

COOPER, G. ARTHUR, U.S. National Museum, Washington, D.C.

COX, L. R., British Museum (Natural History), London, Eng.

CURRY, DENNIS, Pinner, Middlesex, Eng.

†DAVIES, L. M., Edinburgh, Scot.

DECHASEAUX, C., Laboratoire de Paléontologie à la Sorbonne, Paris, France.

DOUGLASS, R. C., U.S. National Museum, Washington, D.C.

DURHAM, J. WYATT, Museum of Palaeontology, University of California, Berkeley, Calif.

EAMES, F. E., Anglo-Iranian Oil Company, London, Eng.

ELLIOTT, GRAHAM F., Iraq Petroleum Company, London, Eng.

EMERSON, W. K., American Museum of Natural History, New York, N.Y.

ERBEN, H. K., Universität Bonn, Bonn, West Ger.

EXLINE, HARRIET, Rolla, Mo.

FELL, H. BARRACLOUGH, Victoria University College, Wellington, N.Z.

FISCHER, ALFRED G., Princeton University, Princeton, N.J.

FISHER, D. W., New York State Museum, Albany, N.Y.

FLOWER, ROUSSEAU H., New Mexico Institute of Mining and Technology, Socorro, N.Mex.

FRIZZELL, DONALD L., Missouri School of Mines, Rolla, Mo.

FURNISH, WILLIAM M., State University of Iowa, Iowa City, Iowa.

GARDNER, JULIA, U.S. Geological Survey, Washington, D.C.

GEORGE, T. NEVILLE, Glasgow University, Glasgow, Scot.

HAAS, FRITZ, Chicago Natural History Museum, Chicago, Ill.

HANAI, TETSURO, University of Tokyo, Tokyo, Japan.

HANNA, G. DALLAS, California Academy of Sciences, San Francisco, Calif.

HÄNTZSCHEL, WALTER, Geologisches Staatsinstitut, Hamburg, Ger.

HARRINGTON, H. J., Tennessee Gas Transmission Company, Houston, Tex.

†HASS, WILBERT H., U.S. Geological Survey, Washington, D.C.

HATAI, KOTORA, Tohoku University, Sendai, Japan.

HAWKINS, H. L., Reading University, Reading, Eng.

HEDGPETH, JOEL, College of the Pacific, Dillon Beach, Calif.

HENNINGSMOEN, GUNNAR, Paleontologisk Museum, University of Oslo, Oslo, Norway.

HERTLEIN, L. G., California Academy of Sciences, San Francisco, Calif.

HESSLAND, IVAR, Geologiska Institutet, University of Stockholm, Stockholm, Swed.

HILL, DOROTHY, University of Queensland, Brisbane, Queensl.

HOLTHUIS, L. B., Rijksmuseum van Natuurlijke Historie, Leiden, Netherlands.

HOWE, HENRY V., Louisiana State University, Baton Rouge, La.

HOWELL, B. F., Princeton University, Princeton, N.J.

HYMAN, LIBBIE H., American Museum of Natural History, New York, N.Y.

JAANUSSON, VALDAR, Paleontological Inst., Uppsala, Sweden.

JELETZKY, J. A., Geological Survey of Canada, Ottawa, Can.

KAMPTNER, ERWIN, Naturhistorisches Museum, Wien, Aus.

KEEN, MYRA, Stanford University, Stanford, Calif.

KESLING, ROBERT V., Paleontological Museum, University of Michigan, Ann Arbor, Mich.

KIER, PORTER, U. S. National Museum, Washington, D.C.

KNIGHT, J. BROOKES, Longboat Key, Fla.

KUMMEL, BERNHARD, Museum of Comparative Zoology, Harvard University, Cambridge, Mass.

LA ROCQUE, AURÈLE, Ohio State University, Columbus, Ohio.

†LAUBENFELS, M. W. DE, Oregon State College, Corvallis, Ore.

LECOMPTE, MARIUS, Institut Royal des Sciences Naturelles, Bruxelles, Belg.

LEONARD, A. BYRON, University of Kansas, Lawrence, Kans.

LEVINSON, S. A., Humble Oil & Refining Company, Houston, Tex.

LOCHMAN-BALK, CHRISTINA, New Mexico Institute of Mining and Technology, Socorro, N.Mex.

LOEBLICH, A. R., JR., California Research Corporation, La Habra, Calif.

LOEBLICH, HELEN TAPPAN, University of California, Los Angeles, Calif.

LOHMAN, KENNETH E., U.S. Geological Survey, Washington, D.C.

LOWENSTAM, HEINZ A., California Institute of Technology, Pasadena, Calif.

LUDBROOK, N. H., Department of Mines, Adelaide, S.Austral.

MARWICK, J., New Zealand Geological Survey, Wellington, N.Z.

MELVILLE, R. V., Geological Survey and Museum, London, Eng.

MILLER, ARTHUR K., State University of Iowa, Iowa City, Iowa.

MONTANARO-GALLITELLI, EUGENIA, Istituto di Geología e Paleontología, Università, Modena, Italy.

MOORE, RAYMOND C., University of Kansas, Lawrence, Kans.

MORRISON, J. P. E., U.S. National Museum, Washington, D.C.

MUIR-WOOD, HELEN M., British Museum (Natural History), London, Eng.

NEWELL, NORMAN D., American Museum of Natural History (and Columbia University), New York, N.Y.

OKULITCH, VLADIMIR J., University of British Columbia, Vancouver, B.C.

OLSSON, AXEL A., Coral Gables, Florida.

PALMER, KATHERINE VAN WINKLE, Paleontological Research Institution, Ithaca, N.Y.

PECK, RAYMOND E., University of Missouri, Columbia, Mo.

PETRUNKEVITCH, ALEXANDER, Osborn Zoological Laboratory, Yale University, New Haven, Conn.

POULSEN, CHR., Universitetets Mineralogisk-Geologiske Institut, København, Denm.

POWELL, A. W. B., Auckland Institute and Museum, Auckland, N.Z.

PURI, HARBANS, Florida State Geological Survey, Tallahassee, Fla.

RASETTI, FRANCO, Johns Hopkins University, Baltimore, Md.

RASMUSSEN, H. W., Universitets Mineralogisk — Geologiske Institut, København, Denm.

REGNÉLL, GERHARD, Paleontologiska Institution, Lunds Universitets, Lund, Swed.

REHDER, HARALD A., U.S. National Museum, Washington, D.C.

REICHEL, M., Bernouillanum, Basel University, Basel, Switz.

REYMENT, RICHARD A., University of Stockholm, Stockholm, Swed.

†RICHTER, EMMA, Senckenberg Natur-Museum, Frankfurt-a.-M., Ger.

†RICHTER, RUDOLF, Universität Frankfurt-a.-M., Frankfurt-a.-M., Ger.

ROBERTSON, ROBERT, Museum of Comparative Zoology, Harvard University, Cambridge, Mass.

ROWELL, A. J., Nottingham University, Nottingham, Eng.

SCHINDEWOLF, O. H. Geologisch-paläontologisches Institut der Universität Tűbingen, Tűbingen, Ger.

SCHMIDT, HERTA, Senckenbergische Naturforschende Gesellschaft, Frankfurt-a.-M., Ger.

SCOTT, HAROLD W., University of Illinois, Urbana, Ill.

SDZUY, KLAUS, Senckenbergische Naturforschende Gesellschaft, Frankfurt-a.-M., Ger.

SHAVER, ROBERT, State Geological Survey, Bloomington, Indiana.

SIEVERTS-DORECK, HERTHA, Stuttgart-Möhringen, Ger.

SINCLAIR, G. W., Geological Survey of Canada, Ottawa, Can.

SMITH, ALLYN G., California Academy of Sciences, San Francisco, Calif.

SOHN, I. G., U.S. Geological Survey, Washington, D.C.

†SPENCER, W. K., Crane Hill, Ipswich, Suffolk, Eng.

†STAINBROOK, MERRILL A., Brandon, Iowa.

STEHLI, F. G., Tulsa, Okla.

STENZEL, H. B., Shell Development Co., Houston, Tex.

STOVER, LEWIS E., Tulsa, Okla.

STØRMER, LEIF, Paleontologisk Institutt, University of Oslo, Oslo, Nor.

STRUVE, WOLFGANG, Senckenbergische Naturforschende Gesellschaft, Frankfurt-a.-M., Ger.

STUBBLEFIELD, C. J., Geological Survey and Museum, London, Eng.

STUMM, ERWIN C., Museum of Paleontology, University of Michigan, Ann Arbor, Mich.

SWAIN, FREDERICK M., University of Minnesota, Minneapolis, Minn.

SYLVESTER-BRADLEY, P. C., University of Sheffield, Sheffield, Eng.

TASCH, PAUL, University of Wichita, Wichita, Kans.

TEICHERT, CURT, U.S. Geological Survey, Federal Center, Denver, Colo.

THOMPSON, M. L., Illinois Geological Survey, Urbana, Ill.

THOMPSON, R. H., University of Kansas, Lawrence, Kans.

†TIEGS, O. W., University of Melbourne, Melbourne, Victoria, Austral.

TRIPP, RONALD P., Seven Oaks, Kent, Eng.

UBAGHS, G., Université de Liège, Liège, Belg.

VOKES, H. E., Johns Hopkins University, Baltimore, Md.

†WANNER, J., Scheidegg (Allgäu), Bayern, Ger.

WEIR, JOHN, Glasgow University, Glasgow, Scot.

WELLER, J. MARVIN, University of Chicago, Chicago, Ill.

WELLS, JOHN W., Cornell University, Ithaca, N.Y.

WHITTINGTON, H. B., Museum of Comparative Zoology, Harvard University, Cambridge, Mass.

WILLIAMS, ALWYN, Queens University of Belfast, Belfast, N.Ire.

WILLS, L. J., Romsley, Eng.

†WITHERS, T. H., Bournemouth, Eng.

WRIGHT, A. D., Queens University of Belfast, Belfast, N. Ire.

WRIGHT, C. W., Kensington, Eng.

†WRIGLEY, ARTHUR, Norbury, London, Eng.

YOCHELSON, ELLIS L., U.S. Geological Survey, Washington, D.C.

YONGE, C. M., University of Glasgow, Glasgow, Scot.

---

†—Deceased.

viii

EDITORIAL PREFACE

The aim of the *Treatise on Invertebrate Paleontology,* as originally conceived and consistently pursued, is to present the most comprehensive and authoritative, yet compact statement of knowledge concerning invertebrate fossil groups that can be formulated by collaboration of competent specialists in seeking to organize what has been learned of this subject up to the mid-point of the present century. Such work has value in providing a most useful summary of the collective results of multitudinous investigations and thus should constitute an indispensable text and reference book for all persons who wish to know about remains of invertebrate organisms preserved in rocks of the earth's crust. This applies to neozoologists as well as paleozoologists and to beginners in study of fossils as well as to thoroughly trained, long-experienced professional workers, including teachers, stratigraphical geologists, and individuals engaged in research on fossil invertebrates. The making of a reasonably complete inventory of present knowledge of invertebrate paleontology may be expected to yield needed foundation for future research and it is hoped that the *Treatise* will serve this end.

The *Treatise* is divided into parts which bear index letters, each except the initial and concluding ones being defined to include designated groups of invertebrates. The chief purpose of this arrangement is to provide for independence of the several parts as regards date of publication, because it is judged desirable to print and distribute each segment as soon as possible after it is ready for press. Pages in each part will bear the assigned index letter joined with numbers beginning with 1 and running consecutively to the end of the part. When the parts ultimately are assembled into volumes, no renumbering of pages and figures is required.

The outline of subjects to be treated in connection with each large group of invertebrates includes (1) description of morphological features, with special reference to hard parts, (2) ontogeny, (3) classification, (4) geological distribution, (5) evolutionary trends and phylogeny, and (6) systematic description of genera, subgenera, and higher taxonomic units. In general, paleoecological aspects of study are omitted or little emphasized because comprehensive treatment of this subject is being undertaken in a separate work, prepared under auspices of a committee of the United States National Research Council. A selected list of references is furnished in each part of the *Treatise.*

Features of style in the taxonomic portions of this work have been fixed by the Editor with aid furnished by advice from the Joint Committee on Invertebrate Paleontology representing the societies which have undertaken to sponsor the *Treatise.* It is the Editor's responsibility to consult with authors and co-ordinate their work, seeing that manuscript properly incorporates features of adopted style. Especially he has been called on to formulate policies in respect to many questions of nomenclature and procedure. The subject of family and subfamily names is reviewed briefly in a following section of this preface, and features of *Treatise* style in generic descriptions are explained.

A generous grant of $35,000 has been made by the Geological Society of America for the purpose of preparing *Treatise* illustrations. Administration of expenditures has been in charge of the Editor and most of the work by photographers and artists has been done under his direction at the University of Kansas, but sizable parts of this program have also been carried forward in Washington and London.

FORM OF ZOOLOGICAL NAMES

Many questions arise in connection with the form of zoological names. These include such matters as adherence to stipulations concerning Latin or Latinized nature of words accepted as zoological names, gender of generic and subgeneric names, nominative or adjectival form of specific names, required endings for some family-group names, and numerous others. Regulation extends to capitalization, treatment of particles belonging to modern patronymics, use of neo-Latin letters, and approved methods for converting diacritical marks. The magnitude and complexities of nomenclature problems surely are enough to warrant the

ix

complaint of those who hold that zoology is the study of animals rather than of names applied to them.

CLASSIFICATION OF ZOOLOGICAL NAMES

In accordance with the "Copenhagen Decisions on Zoological Nomenclature" (London, 135 p., 1953), zoological names may be classified usefully in various ways. The subject is summarized here with introduction of designations for some categories which the *Treatise* proposes to distinguish in systematic parts of the text for the purpose of giving readers comprehension of the nature of various names together with authorship and dates attributed to them.

CO-ORDINATE NAMES OF TAXA GROUPS

Five groups of different-rank taxonomic units (termed *taxa,* sing., *taxon*) are discriminated, within each of which names are treated as co-ordinate, being transferrable from one category to another without change of authorship or date. These are: (1) Species Group (subspecies, species); (2) Genus Group (subgenus, genus); (3) Family Group (tribe, subfamily, family, superfamily); (4) Order/Class Group (suborder, order, subclass, class); and (5) Phylum Group (subphylum, phylum). In the first 3 of these groups, but not others, the author of the first-published valid name for any taxon is held to be the author of all other taxa in the group which are based on the same nominate type and the date of publication for purposes of priority is that of the first-published name. Thus, if author A in 1800 introduces the family name X-idae to include 3 genera, one of which is *X-us;* and if author B in 1850 divides the 20 genera then included in X-idae into subfamilies called X-inae and Y-inae; and if author C in 1950 combines X-idae with other later-formed families to make a superfamily X-acea (or X-oidea, X-icae, etc.); the author of X-inae, X-idae and X-acea is A, 1800, under the Rules. Because taxonomic concepts introduced by authors B and C along with appropriate names surely are not attributable to author A, some means of recording responsibility of B and C are needed. This is discussed later in explaining proposed use of *"nom. transl."*

The co-ordinate status of zoological names belonging to the species group is stipulated in Art. 11 of the present Rules; genus group in Art. 6 of the present Rules; family group in paragraph 46 of the Copenhagen Decisions; order/class group and phylum group in paragraphs 65 and 66 of the Copenhagen Decisions.

ORIGINAL AND SUBSEQUENT FORMS OF NAMES

Zoological names may be classified according to form (spelling) given in original publication and employed by subsequent authors. In one group are names which are entirely identical in original and subsequent usage. Another group comprises names which include with the original subsequently published variants of one sort or another. In this second group, it is important to distinguish names which are inadvertent changes from those constituting intentional emendations, for they have quite different status in nomenclature. Also, among intentional emendations, some are acceptable and some quite unacceptable under the Rules.

VALID AND INVALID NAMES

Valid names. A valid zoological name is one that conforms to all mandatory provisions of the Rules (Copenhagen Decisions, p. 43-57) but names of this group are divisible into subgroups as follows: (1) *"inviolate names,"* which as originally published not only meet all mandatory requirements of the Rules but are not subject to any sort of alteration (most generic and subgeneric names); (2) *"perfect names,"* which as they appear in original publication (with or without precise duplication by subsequent authors) meet all mandatory requirements and need no correction of any kind but which nevertheless are legally alterable under present Rules (as in changing the form of ending of a published class/order-group name); (3) *"imperfect names,"* which as originally published and with or without subsequent duplication meet mandatory requirements but contain defects such as incorrect gender of an adjectival specific name (for example, *Spironema recta* instead of *Spironema rectum*) or incorrect stem or form of ending of a family-group name (for example, Spironemidae instead

of Spironematidae); (4) *"transferred names,"* which are derived by valid emendation from either of the 2nd or 3rd subgroups or from a pre-existing transferred name (as illustrated by change of a family-group name from -inae to -idae or making of a superfamily name); (5) *"improved names,"* which include necessary as well as somewhat arbitrarily made emendations allowable under the Rules for taxonomic categories not now covered by regulations as to name form and alterations that are distinct from changes that distinguish the 4th subgroup (including names derived from the 2nd and 3rd subgroups and possibly some alterations of 4th subgroup names). In addition, some zoological names included among those recognized as valid are classifiable in special categories, while at the same time belonging to one or more of the above-listed subgroups. These chiefly include (7) *"substitute names,"* introduced to replace invalid names such as junior homonyms; and (8) *"conserved names,"* which are names that would have to be rejected by application of the Rules except for saving them in their original or an altered spelling by action of the International Commission on Zoological Nomenclature in exercising its plenary powers to this end. Whenever a name requires replacement, any individual may publish a "new name" for it and the first one so introduced has priority over any others; since newness is temporary and relative, the replacement designation is better called substitute name rather than new name. Whenever it is considered desirable to save for usage an otherwise necessarily rejectable name, an individual cannot by himself accomplish the preservation, except by unchallenged action taken in accordance with certain provisions of the Copenhagen Decisions; otherwise he must seek validation through ICZN.

It is useful for convenience and brevity of distinction in recording these subgroups of valid zoological names to introduce Latin designations, following the pattern of *nomen nudum, nomen novum,* etc. Accordingly, the subgroups are (1) *nomina inviolata* (sing., *nomen inviolatum,* abbr., *nom. inviol.*); (2) *nomina perfecta* (sing., *nomen perfectum,* abbr., *nom. perf.*); (3) *nomina imperfecta* (sing., *nomen imperfectum,*

abbr., *nom. imperf.*); (4) *nomina translata* (sing., *nomen translatum,* abbr., *nom. transl.*); (5) *nomina correcta* (sing., *nomen correctum,* abbr., *nom. correct.*); (6) *nomina substituta* (sing., *nomen substitutum,* abbr., *nom. subst.*); (7) *nomina conservata* (sing., *nomen conservatum,* abbr., *nom. conserv.*).

Invalid names. Invalid zoological names consisting of originally published names that fail to comply with mandatory provisions of the Rules and consisting of inadvertent changes in spelling of names have no status in nomenclature. They are not available as replacement names and they do not preoccupy for purposes of the Law of Homonomy. In addition to *nomen nudum,* invalid names may be distinguished as follows: (1) *"denied names,"* which consist of originally published names (with or without subsequent duplication) that do not meet mandatory requirements of the Rules; (2) *"null names,"* which comprise unintentional alterations of names; and (3) *"vain or void names,"* which consist of invalid emendations of previously published valid or invalid names. Void names do have status in nomenclature, being classified as junior synonyms of valid names.

Proposed Latin designations for the indicated kinds of invalid names are as follows: (1) *nomina negata* (sing., *nomen negatum,* abbr., *nom. neg.*); (2) *nomina nulla* (sing., *nomen nullum,* abbr., *nom. null.*); (3) *nomina vana* (sing., *nomen vanum,* abbr., *nom. van.*). It is desirable in the *Treatise* to identify invalid names, particularly in view of the fact that many of these names (*nom. neg., nom null.*) have been considered incorrectly to be junior objective synonyms (like *nom. van.*), which have status in nomenclature.

SUMMARY OF NAME CLASSES

Partly because only in such publications as the *Treatise* is special attention to classes of zoological names called for and partly because new designations are now introduced as means of recording distinctions explicitly as well as compactly, a summary may be useful. In the following tabulation valid classes of names are indicated in boldface type, whereas invalid ones are printed in italics.

Definitions of Name Classes

nomen conservatum (nom. conserv.). Name otherwise unacceptable under application of the Rules which is made valid, either with original or altered spelling, through procedures specified by the Copenhagen Decisions or by action of ICZN exercising its plenary powers.

nomen correctum (nom. correct.). Name with intentionally altered spelling of sort required or allowable under the Rules but not dependent on transfer from one taxonomic category to another ("improved name"). (*See* Copenhagen Decisions, paragraphs 50, 71-2-a-i, 74, 75, 79, 80, 87, 101; in addition, change of endings for categories not now fixed by Rules.)

nomen imperfectum (nom. imperf.). Name that as originally published (with or without subsequent identical spelling) meets all mandatory requirements of the Rules but contains defect needing correction ("imperfect name"). (*See* Copenhagen Decisions, paragraphs 50-1-b, 71-1-b-i, 71-1-b-ii, 79, 80, 87, 101.)

nomen inviolatum (nom. inviol.). Name that as originally published meets all mandatory requirements of the Rules and also is uncorrectable or alterable in any way ("inviolate name"). (*See* Copenhagen Decisions, paragraphs 152, 153, 155-157).

nomen negatum (nom. neg.). Name that as originally published (with or without subsequent identical spelling) constitutes invalid original spelling and although possibly meeting all other mandatory requirements of the Rules, is not correctable to establish original authorship and date ("denied name"). (*See* Copenhagen Decisions, paragraph 71-1-b-iii.)

nomen nudum (nom. nud.). Name that as originally published (with or without subsequent identical spelling) fails to meet mandatory requirements of the Rules and having no status in nomenclature, is not correctable to establish original authorship and date ("naked name"). (*See* Copenhagen Decisions, paragraph 122.)

nomen nullum (nom. null.). Name consisting of an unintentional alteration in form (spelling) of a previously published name (either valid name, as *nom. inviol., nom. perf., nom. imperf., nom. transl.;* or invalid name, as *nom. neg., nom. nud., nom. van.,* or another *nom. null.*) ("null name"). (*See* Copenhagen Decisions, paragraphs 71-2-b, 73-4.)

nomen perfectum (nom. perf.). Name that as originally published meets all mandatory requirements of the Rules and needs no correction of any kind but which nevertheless is validly alterable ("perfect name").

nomen substitutum (nom. subst.). Replacement name published as substitute for an invalid name, such as a junior homonym (equivalent to "new name").

nomen translatum (nom. transl.). Name that is derived by valid emendation of a previously published name as result of transfer from one taxonomic category to another within the group to which it belongs ("transferred name").

nomen vanum (nom. van.). Name consisting of an invalid intentional change in form (spelling) from a previously published name, such invalid emendations having status in nomenclature as junior objective synonyms ("vain or void name"). (*See* Copenhagen Decisions, paragraphs 71-2-a-ii, 73-3.)

Except as specified otherwise, zoological names accepted in the *Treatise* may be understood to be classifiable either as *nomina inviolata* or *nomina perfecta* (omitting from notice *nomina correcta* among specific names) and these are not discriminated. Names which are not accepted for one reason or another include junior homonyms, a few senior synonyms classifiable as *nomina negata* or *nomina nuda,* and numerous junior synonyms which include both objective *(nomina vana)* and subjective (all classes of valid names) types; effort to classify the invalid names as completely as possible is intended.

NAME CHANGES IN RELATION TO GROUP CATEGORIES

SPECIFIC AND SUBSPECIFIC NAMES

Detailed consideration of valid emendation of specific and subspecific names is unnecessary here because it is well understood and relatively inconsequential. When the form of adjectival specific names is changed to obtain agreement with the gender of a generic name in transferring a species from one genus to another, it is never needful to label the changed name as a *nom. transl.* Likewise, transliteration of a letter accompanied by a diacritical mark in manner now called for by the Rules (as in changing originally published *brőggeri* to *broeggeri*) or elimination of a hyphen (as in changing originally published *cornuoryx* to *cornuoryx* does not require *"nom. correct."* with it. Revised provisions for emending specific and subspecific names are stated in the report on Copenhagen Decisions (p. 43-46, 51-57).

GENERIC AND SUBGENERIC NAMES

So rare are conditions warranting change of the originally published valid form of generic and subgeneric names that lengthy discussion may be omitted. Only elimi-

nation of diacritical marks of some names in this category seems to furnish basis for valid emendation. It is true that many changes of generic and subgeneric names have been published, but virtually all of these are either *nomina vana* or *nomina nulla*. Various names which formerly were classed as homonyms are not now, for two names that differ only by a single letter (or in original publication by presence or absence of a diacritical mark) are construed to be entirely distinct. Revised provisions for emendation of generic and subgeneric names also are given in the report on Copenhagen Decisions (p. 43-47).

Examples in use of classificatory designations for generic names as previously given are the following, which also illustrate designation of type species, as explained later.

Kurnatiophyllum THOMSON, 1875 [*K. concentricum;* SD GREGORY, 1917] [=*Kumatiophyllum* THOMSON, 1876 *(nom. null.); Cymatophyllum* THOMSON, 1901 *(nom. van.); Cymatiophyllum* LANG, SMITH & THOMAS, 1940 *(nom. van.)*].

Stichophyma POMEL, 1872 [*Manon turbinatum* RÖMER, 1841; SD RAUFF, 1893] [=*Stychophyma* VOSMAER, 1885 *(nom. null.); Sticophyma* MORET, 1924 *(nom. null.)*].

Stratophyllum SMYTH, 1933 [*S. tenue*] [=*Ethmoplax* SMYTH, 1939 *(nom. van. pro Stratophyllum); Stratiphyllum* LANG, SMITH & THOMAS, 1940 *(nom. van. pro Stratophyllum* SMYTH*) (non Stratiphyllum* SCHEFFEN, 1933)].

Placotelia OPPLIGER, 1907 [*Porostoma marconi* FROMENTEL, 1859; SD DELAUBENFELS, herein] [=*Plakotelia* OPPLIGER, 1907 *(nom. neg.)*].

Walcottella DELAUB., *nom. subst.,* 1955 [*pro Rhopalicus* SCHRAMM., 1936 *(non* FÖRSTER, 1856)].

Cyrtograptus CARRUTHERS, 1867 [*nom. correct.* LAPWORTH, 1873 *(pro Cyrtograpsus* CARRUTHERS, 1867), *nom. conserv.* proposed BULMAN, 1955 (ICZN pend.)]

FAMILY-GROUP NAMES; USE OF *"NOM. TRANSL."*

The Rules now specify the form of endings only for subfamily (-inae) and family (-idae) but decisions of the Copenhagen Congress direct classification of all family-group assemblages (taxa) as co-ordinate, signifying that for purposes of priority a name published for a unit in any category and based on a particular type genus shall date from its original publication for a unit in any category, retaining this priority (and

authorship) when the unit is treated as belonging to a lower or higher category. By exclusion of -inae and -idae, respectively reserved for subfamily and family, the endings of names used for tribes and superfamilies must be unspecified different letter combinations. These, if introduced subsequent to designation of a subfamily or family based on the same nominate genus, are *nomina translata,* as is also a subfamily that is elevated to family rank or a family reduced to subfamily rank. In the *Treatise* it is desirable to distinguish the valid emendation comprised in the changed ending of each transferred family group name by the abbreviation *"nom. transl."* and record of the author and date belonging to this emendation. This is particularly important in the case of superfamilies, for it is the author who introduced this taxon that one wishes to know about rather than the author of the superfamily as defined by the Rules, for the latter is merely the individual who first defined some lower-rank family-group taxon that contains the nominate genus of the superfamily. The publication of the author containing introduction of the superfamily *nomen translatum* is likely to furnish the information on taxonomic considerations that support definition of the unit.

Examples of the use of *"nom. transl."* are the following.

Subfamily STYLININAE d'Orbigny, 1851

[*nom. transl.* EDWARDS & HAIME, 1857 (*ex* Stylinidae D'ORBIGNY, 1851]

Superfamily ARCHAEOCTONOIDEA Petrunkevitch, 1949

[*nom. transl.* PETRUNKEVITCH, herein (*ex* Archaeoctonidae PETRUNKEVITCH, 1949)]

Superfamily CRIOCERATITACEAE Hyatt, 1900

[*nom. transl.* WRIGHT, 1952 (*ex* Crioceratitidae HYATT, 1900)]

FAMILY-GROUP NAMES; USE OF *"NOM. CORRECT."*

Valid emendations classed as *nomina correcta* do not depend on transfer from one category of family-group units to another but most commonly involve correction of the stem of the nominate genus; in addition, they include somewhat arbitrarily chosen modification of ending for names of tribe

or superfamily. Examples of the use of *"nom. correct."* are the following.

Family STREPTELASMATIDAE Nicholson, 1889

[*nom. correct.* WEDEKIND, 1927 (*ex* Streptelasmidae NICHOLSON, 1889, *nom. imperf.*)]

Family PALAEOSCORPIIDAE Lehmann, 1944

[*nom. correct.* PETRUNKEVITCH, herein (*ex* Palaeoscorpionidae LEHMANN, 1944, *nom. imperf.*)]

Family AGLASPIDIDAE Miller, 1877

[*nom. correct.* STØRMER, herein (*ex* Aglaspidae MILLER, 1877, *nom. imperf.*)]

Superfamily AGARICIICAE Gray, 1847

[*nom. correct.* WELLS, herein (*ex* Agaricioidae VAUGHAN & WELLS, 1943, *nom. transl. ex* Agariciidae GRAY, 1847)]

FAMILY-GROUP NAMES; USE OF *"NOM. CONSERV."*

It may happen that long-used family-group names are invalid under strict application of the Rules. In order to retain the otherwise invalid name, appeal to ICZN is needful. Examples of use of *nom. conserv.* in this connection, as cited in the *Treatise,* are the following.

Family ARIETITIDAE Hyatt, 1874

[*nom. correct.* HAUG, 1885 (*pro* Arietidae HYATT, 1875), *nom. conserv.* proposed ARKELL, 1955 (ICZN pend.)]

Family STEPHANOCERATIDAE Neumayr, 1875

[*nom. correct.* FISCHER, 1882 (*pro* Stephanoceratinen NEUMAYR, 1875, invalid vernacular name), *nom conserv.* proposed ARKELL, 1955 (ICZN pend.)]

FAMILY-GROUP NAMES; REPLACEMENTS

Family-group names are formed by adding letter combinations (prescribed for family and subfamily but not now for others) to the stem of the name belonging to genus (nominate genus) first chosen as type of the assemblage. The type genus need not be the oldest in terms of receiving its name and definition, but it must be the first-published as name-giver to a family-group taxon among all those included. Once fixed, the family-group name remains tied to the nominate genus even if its name is changed by reason of status as a junior homonym or junior synonym, either objective or subjective. According to the Copenhagen Decisions, the family-group name requires replacement only in the event that the nominate genus is found to be a junior homonym, and then a substitute family-group name is accepted if it is formed from the oldest available substitute name for the nominate genus. Authorship and date attributed to the replacement family-group name are determined by first publication of the changed family-group name.

The aim of family-group nomenclature is greatest possible stability and uniformity, just as in case of other zoological names. Experience indicates the wisdom of sustaining family-group names based on junior subjective synonyms if they have priority of publication, for opinions of different workers as to the synonymy of generic names founded on different type species may not agree and opinions of the same worker may alter from time to time. The retention similarly of first-published family-group names which are found to be based on junior objective synonyms is less clearly desirable, especially if a replacement name derived from the senior objective synonym has been recognized very long and widely. To displace a much-used family-group name based on the senior objective synonym by disinterring a forgotten and virtually unused family-group name based on a junior objective synonym because the latter happens to have priority of publication is unsettling. Conversely, a long-used family-group name founded on a junior objective synonym and having priority of publication is better continued in nomenclature than a replacement name based on the senior objective synonym. The Copenhagen Decisions (paragraph 45) take account of these considerations by providing a relatively simple procedure for fixing the desired choice in stabilizing family-group names. In conformance with this, the *Treatise* assigns to contributing authors responsibility for adopting provisions of the Copenhagen Decisions.

Replacement of a family-group name may be needed if the former nominate genus is transferred to another family-group. Then the first-published name-giver of a family-group assemblage in the remnant taxon is to be recognized in forming a replacement name.

FAMILY-GROUP NAMES; AUTHORSHIP AND DATE

All family-group taxa having names

based on the same type genus are attributed to the author who first published the name for any of these assemblages, whether tribe, subfamily, or family (superfamily being almost inevitably a later-conceived taxon). Accordingly, if a family is divided into subfamilies or a subfamily into tribes, the name of no such subfamily or tribe can antedate the family name. Also, every family containing differentiated subfamilies must have a nominate *(sensu stricto)* subfamily, which is based on the same type genus as that for the family, and the author and date set down for the nominate subfamily invariably are identical with those of the family, without reference to whether the author of the family or some subsequent author introduced subdivisions.

Changes in the form of family-group names of the sort constituting *nomina correcta,* as previously discussed, do not affect authorship and date of the taxon concerned, but in publications such as the *Treatise* it is desirable to record the authorship and date of the correction.

ORDER/CLASS-GROUP NAMES; USE OF *"NOM. CORRECT."*

Because no stipulation concerning the form of order/class-group names is given yet by the Rules, emendation of all such names actually consists of arbitrarily devised changes in the form of endings. Nothing precludes substitution of a new name for an old one, but a change of this sort is not considered to be an emendation. Examples of the use of *"nom. correct."* as applied to order/class-group names are the following.

Order DISPARIDA Moore & Laudon, 1943

[*nom. correct.* MOORE, 1952 (*ex* Disparata MOORE & LAUDON, 1943)]

Suborder FAVIINA Vaughan & Wells, 1943

[*nom. correct.* WELLS, herein (*ex* Faviida VAUGHAN & WELLS, 1943)]

Suborder FUNGIINA Verrill, 1865

[*nom. correct.* WELLS, herein (*ex* Fungiida DUNCAN, 1884, *ex* Fungacea VERRILL, 1865)]

TAXONOMIC EMENDATION

Emendation has two measurably distinct aspects as regards zoological nomenclature. These embrace (1) alteration of a name itself in various ways for various reasons, as has been reviewed, and (2) alteration of taxonomic scope or concept in application of a given zoological name, whatever its hierarchical rank. The latter type of emendation primarily concerns classification and inherently is not associated with change of name, whereas the other type introduces change of name without necessary expansion, restriction, or other modification in applying the name. Little attention generally has been paid to this distinction in spite of its significance.

Most zoologists, including paleozoologists, who have signified emendation of zoological names refer to what they consider a material change in application of the name such as may be expressed by an importantly altered diagnosis of the assemblage covered by the name. The abbreviation *"emend."* then may accompany the name, with statement of the author and date of the emendation. On the other hand, a multitude of workers concerned with systematic zoology think that publication of *"emend."* with a zoological name is valueless because more or less alteration of taxonomic sort is introduced whenever a subspecies, species, genus, or other assemblage of animals is incorporated under or removed from the coverage of a given zoological name. Inevitably associated with such classificatory expansions and restrictions is some degree of emendation affecting diagnosis. Granting this, still it is true that now and then somewhat radical revisions are put forward, generally with published statement of reasons for changing the application of a name. To erect a signpost at such points of most significant change is worth while, both as aid to subsequent workers in taking account of the altered nomenclatural usage and as indication that not-to-be-overlooked discussion may be found at a particular place in the literature. Authors of contributions to the *Treatise* are encouraged to include records of all specially noteworthy emendations of this nature, using the abbreviation *"emend."* with the name to which it refers and citing the author and date of the emendation.

In Part G (Bryozoa) and Part D (Protista 3) of the *Treatise,* the abbreviation *"emend."* is employed to record various sorts of name emendations, thus conflicting with usage of *"emend."* for change in taxonomic application of a name without alteration of the name itself. This is objectionable. In Part E (Archaeocyatha, Porifera) and later-issued divisions of the *Treatise,* use of *"emend."* is restricted to its customary sense, that is, significant alteration in taxonomic scope of a name such as calls for noteworthy modifications of a diagnosis. Other means of designating emendations that relate to form of a name are introduced.

STYLE IN GENERIC DESCRIPTIONS

DEFINITION OF NAMES

Most generic names are distinct from all others and are indicated without ambiguity by citing their originally published spelling accompanied by name of the author and date of first publication. If the same generic name has been applied to 2 or more distinct taxonomic units, however, it is necessary to differentiate such homonyms, and this calls for distinction between junior homonyms and senior homonyms. Because a junior homonym is invalid, it must be replaced by some other name. For example, *Callopora* HALL, 1851, introduced for Paleozoic trepostome bryozoans, is invalid because GRAY in 1848 published the same name for Cretaceous-to-Recent cheilostome bryozoans, and BASSLER in 1911 introduced the new name *Hallopora* to replace HALL's homonym. The *Treatise* style of entry is:

Hallopora BASSLER, 1911 [*pro Callopora* HALL, 1851 (*non* GRAY, 1848)].

In like manner, a needed replacement generic name may be introduced in the *Treatise* (even though first publication of generic names otherwise in this work is avoided). The requirement that an exact bibliographic reference must be given for the replaced name commonly can be met in the *Treatise* by citing a publication recorded in the list of references, using its assigned index number, as shown in the following example.

Mysterium DELAUBENFELS, *nom. subst.* [*pro Mystrium* SCHRAMMEN, 1936 (ref. 40, p. 60) (*non* ROGER, 1862)] [*Mystrium porosum SCHRAMMEN, 1936].

For some replaced homonyms, a footnote reference to the literature is necessary. A senior homonym is valid, and in so far as

the *Treatise* is concerned, such names are handled according to whether the junior homonym belongs to the same major taxonomic division (class or phylum) as the senior homonym or to some other; in the former instance, the author and date of the junior homonym are cited as:

Diplophyllum HALL, 1851 [*non* SOSHKINA, 1939] [**D. caespitosum*].

Otherwise, no mention of the existence of a junior homonym is made.

CITATION OF TYPE SPECIES

The name of the type species of each genus and subgenus is given next following the generic name with its accompanying author and date, or after entries needed for definition of the name if it is involved in homonymy. The originally published combination of generic and trivial names for this species is cited, accompanied by an asterisk (*), with notation of the author and date of original publication. An exception in this procedure is made, however, if the species was first published in the same paper and by the same author as that containing definition of the genus which it serves as type; in such case, the initial letter of the generic name followed by the trivial name is given without repeating the name of the author and date, for this saves needed space. Examples of these 2 sorts of citations are as follows:

Diplotrypa NICHOLSON, 1879 [**Favosites petropolitanus* PANDER, 1830].

Chainodictyon FOERSTE, 1887 [**C. laxum*].

If the cited type species is a junior synonym of some other species, the name of this latter also is given, as follows:

Acervularia SCHWEIGGER, 1819 [**A. baltica* (=*Madrepora ananas LINNÉ, 1758)].

It is judged desirable to record the manner of establishing the type species, whether by original designation or by subsequent designation, but various modes of original designation are not distinguished.

Original designation of type species. The Rules provide that the type species of a genus or subgenus may be recognized as an original designation if only a single species was assigned to the genus at the time of first publication (monotypy), if the author of a generic name employed this same name for one of the included species (tautonymy), if one of the species was named *"typus," "typicus,"* or the like, if the original author explicitly indicated the species chosen as the type, or if some other stipulations were met. According to convention adopted in the *Treatise,* the absence of any indication as to manner of fixing the type species is to be understood as signifying that it is established by original designation, the particular mode of original designation not being specified.

Subsequent designation of type species; use of "SD" and "SM." The type species of many genera are not determinable from the publication in which the generic name was introduced and therefore such genera can acquire a type species only by some manner of subsequent designation. Most commonly this is established by publishing a statement naming as type species one of the species originally included in the genus, and in the *Treatise* fixation of the type species in this manner is indicated by the letters "SD" accompanied by the name of the subsequent author (who may be the same person as the original author) and the date of publishing the subsequent designation. Some genera, as first described and named, included no mentioned species and these necessarily lack a type species until a date subsequent to that of the original publication when one or more species are assigned to such a genus. If only a single species is thus assigned, it automatically becomes the type species and in the *Treatise* this subsequent monotypy is indicated by the letters "SM." Of course, the first publication containing assignment of species to the genus which originally lacked any included species is the one concerned in fixation of the type species, and if this named 2 or more species as belonging to the genus but did not designate a type species, then a later "SD" designation is necessary. Examples of the use of "SD" and "SM" as employed in the *Treatise* follow.

Hexagonaria Gürich, 1896 [*Cyathophyllum hexagonum* Goldfuss, 1826; SD Lang, Smith & Thomas, 1940].

Muriceides Studer, 1887 [*M. fragilis* Wright & Studer, 1889; SM Wright & Studer, 1889].

SYNONYMS

Citation of synonyms is given next following record of the type species and if 2 or more synonyms of differing date are recognized, these are arranged in chronological order. Objective synonyms are indicated by accompanying designation "(obj.)," others being understood to constitute subjective synonyms. Examples showing *Treatise* style in listing synonyms follow.

Calapoecia Billings, 1865 [*C. anticostiensis;* SD Lindström, 1833] [=*Columnopora* Nicholson, 1874; *Houghtonia* Rominger, 1876].

Staurocyclia Haeckel, 1882 [*S. cruciata* Haeckel, 1887] [=*Coccostaurus* Haeckel, 1882 (obj.); *Phacostaurus* Haeckel, 1887 (obj.)].

A synonym which also constitutes a homonym is recorded as follows:

Lyopora Nicholson & Etheridge, 1878 [*Palaeopora? favosa* M'Coy, 1850] [=*Liopora* Lang, Smith & Thomas, 1940 (*non* Girty, 1915)].

Some junior synonyms of either objective or subjective sort may take precedence desirably over senior synonyms wherever uniformity and continuity of nomenclature are served by retaining a widely used but technically rejectable name for a generic assemblage. This requires action of ICZN using its plenary powers to set aside the unwanted name and validate the wanted one, with placement of the concerned names on appropriate official lists. In the *Treatise* citation of such a conserved generic name is given in the manner shown by the following example.

Tetragraptus Salter, 1863 [*nom. correct.* Hall, 1865 (*pro Tetragrapsus* Salter, 1863), *nom. conserv.* proposed Bulman, 1955, ICZN pend.] [*Fucoides serra* Brongniart, 1828 (=*Graptolithus bryonoides* Hall, 1858].

ABBREVIATIONS

A few author's names and most stratigraphic and geographic names are abbreviated in order to save space. General principles for guidance in determining what names should be abbreviated are frequency of repetition, length of name, and avoidance of ambiguity. Abbreviations used in this division of the *Treatise* are explained in the following alphabetically arranged list.

xvii

Aalen., Aalenian
Abhandl., Abhandlungen
Abt., Abteilung, -en
Acad., Academia, Académie, Academy
Afr., Africa, -an
Agric., Agriculture, -al
Akad., Akademie
Ala., Alabama
Alb., Albian
Alba., Alberta
Am., America, -n
Anat., Anatomie
Anis., Anisian
Ann., Annal, -s, Annual
Antarct., Antarctic
App., Appendix
Apt., Aptian
Arch., Archipelago, Archiv
Arct., Arctic
Arenig., Arenigian
Arg., Argentina
Argov., Argovian
Ariz., Arizona
Ark., Arkansas
Årssk., Årsskrift
Art., Article
Assoc., Association
Atl., Atlantic
Auctt., Auctores
Aus., Austria
Austral., Australia
Baj., Bajocian
Barrem., Barremian
Bathon., Bathonian
B.C., British Columbia
Belg., Belgique, Belgium
Biol., Biological, Biology
Blackriv., Blackriveran
Bol., Boletín, Bolivia
Brit., Britain, British
Bull., Bulletin
Bur., Bureau
Burdigal., Burdigalian
C., Central
ca., circa
Cab., Cabinet
Calif., California
Callov., Callovian
Cam., Cambrian
Campan., Campanian
Can., Canada
Carb., Carboniferous
Carib., Caribbean
Carn., Carnian
Cenom., Cenomanian
c.f., confero (compare)
chirur., chirurgisch
Coll., Collection, -s; College
Colo., Colorado
Comp., Comparative
Conch., Conchology
Conchyl., Conchyliologie
Coniac., Coniacian
Contr., Contribution, -s
cosmop., cosmopolitan

cour., courant
Cret., Cretaceous
Czech., Czechoslovakia
Dan., Danian
Denkschr., Denkschriften
Denm., Denmark
Dept., Department, -s
deutsch., deutschen
Dev., Devonian
Dict., Dictionnaire
E., East
ed., edition, editor
e.g., exempli gratia (for example)
Eng., England
Eoc., Eocene
Ergebn., Ergebnisse
Est., Estonia
etc., et cetera
Eu., Europe
expériment., expérimentale
Explor., Exploration
f., för, für
F., Formation
Fac., Facultad, Faculté, Faculty
fasc., fascicle
fig., figure, -s
Fla., Florida
Förhandl., Förhandlingar, -er
Fortschr., Fortschritte
Fr., France, Française, -e, French
Fysiogr., Fysiografiska
G.Brit., Great Britain
Geogr., Geographic, -al
Geol., Geologiá, Geological, Geológico, Geologie, Geologisch, Geologiska, Geology
Géol., Géologie, Géologique
Ger., Germany
Gesell., Gesellschaft
Gotl., Gotland
Gr., Group
Greenl., Greenland
Handb., Handbuch
Handl., Handlingar
Havunders., Havundersøgelser
Hemi., Hemisphere
Hist., Histoire, -ia; Historia, History
Hofmus., Hofmuseums
Hung., Hungarica, Hungary
I.(Is.), Island, -s
ICZN, International Commission on Zoological Nomenclature
i.e., id est (that is)
Ill., Illinois
illus., illustration, -s
in., inches
Ind., Indiana
Inst., Institut, Institute, Institutet, Institution, Instituto, Instituut
intermed., intermediate
Ire., Ireland
Jahrb., Jahrbuch
Jahrg., Jahrgang
Jour., Journal
Jur., Jurassic

K., Kaiserlich
Kais., Kaiserlich
Kan., Kansas
Kimm., Kimmeridgian
Kgl., Königlich
Komm., Kommissionen
kön., königlich
Kungl., Kongliga
Ky., Kentucky
L., Lower, Land
Ladin., Ladinian
Landesanst., Landesanstalt
lat., lateral
Lias., Liassic
Lief., Lieferung, -en
Linn., Linnean, Linnéene
livr., livre, -s
Ls., Limestone
M., Middle
Maastricht., Maastrichtian
Mag., Magazine
Malac., Malacological
Malacol., Malacology
malak., malakologisch
Man., Manitoba, Manual
Mass., Massachusetts
Md., Maryland
Med., Medicine, Medizin
Meddel., Meddelelser
Medit., Mediterranean
Mem., Memoir, -s, Memoria
Mém., Mémoire, -s
Mex., Mexico
Micr., Microscopical
Mineral., Mineralogical, Minrale, Mineralogisch, -e
Minn., Minnesota
Mio., Miocene
Misc., Miscellaneous
Miss., Mississippi, Mississippian
Mitteil., Mitteilungen
mm., millimeter
Mo., Missouri
Mon., Monograph
Morphol., Morphology, -ie
MS., Manuscript
Mus., Musée, Museo, Museum
n., new
N., North
N.Am., North America
Nat., Natural; Naturale, -s; Naturali; Naturelle, -s
Natl., National
naturforsch., naturforschende
Naturhist., Naturhistorie, -ischen
Naturwiss., Naturwissenschaft, -liche
NC., North Central
N.Car., North Carolina
NE., Northeast
Neb., Nebraska
Neocom., Neocomian
Neog., Neogene
Nev., Nevada
Newf., Newfoundland

no., number, -s; numéro, -s; número, -s
nom. correct., nomen correctum
nom. nov., nomen novum
nom. null., nomen nullum
nom. subst., nomen substitum
nom. transl., nomen translatum
Nor., Norway
N.S.W., New South Wales
NW., Northwest
N.Y., New York
N.Z., New Zealand
obj., objective
Okla., Oklahoma
Oligo., Oligocene
Ont., Ontario
Ord., Ordovician
Oxford., Oxfordian
p., page, -s
Pa., Pennsylvania
Pac., Pacific
Paläont., Paläontologie, Paläontologisch
Palaeont., Palaeontologia
Palaeontogr., Palaeontographia, Palaeontographica, Palaeontographical
Paleoc., Paleocene
Paléont., Paléontologie
pend., pending
Penn., Pennsylvanian
Perm., Permian
philomat., philomathique
Philos., Philosophical
Phys., Physique, Physikalische
pl., plates, -s
Pleist., Pleistocene
Plio., Pliocene
Portland., Portlandian
Preuss., Preussische
Proc., Proceedings
pt., part, -s
Pub., Publication

Pubbl., Pubblicazioni
Publ., Publication
Quart., Quarterly
Que., Quebec
Queensl., Queensland
Raurac., Rauracian
Rec., Recent
reconstr., reconstructed, -ion
ref., reference
Reichsanst., Reichsanstalt
Rept., Report, -s
Rhaet., Rhaetian
Roy., Royal, -e
Russ., Russia
S., South; Sea
S.Am., South America
Sarmat., Sarmatian
SC., South Central
Sci., Sciences, Scientifique
Scot., Scotland
SD, subsequent designation
SE., Southeast
sec., seciton, -s
Selsk., Selskabs
Senon., Senonian
ser., series, serial
sér., série
Sib., Siberia
Sil., Silurian
Sitzungsber., Sitzungsberichte
Skr., Skrifter
Smithson., Smithsonian
Soc., Sociedad, Società, Société, Society
Sp., Spain
sp., species
spp., species (plural)
Spec., Special
s.s., sensu stricto
SSSR, Soiuz Sovetskikh Sotsialisticheskikh Respublik
Staz., Stazione

subtrop., subtropical
Suppl., Supplement
SW., Southwest
Swed., Sweden, Swedish
Switz., Switzerland
Tasm., Tasmania
tech., technical
Tenn., Tennessee
Tert., Tertiary
Tex., Texas
Tithon., Tithonian
Tournais., Tournaisian
Trans., Transactions
transv., transverse
Trias., Triassic
trop., tropical
Turon., Turonian
u., und
U., Upper
Univ., Universidad, Università, Université, Universitets, University
U.S., United States
USA, United States (America)
USSR, Union of Soviet Socialist Republics
v., volume, -s
Va., Virginia
Ver., Verein
Verhandl., Verhandlung, -en
Vetenskapsak., Vetenskapsakademiens
Videnskab., Videnskabernes
Vt., Vermont
W., West
Wis., Wisconsin
Wiss., Wissenschaften
Wyo., Wyoming
z., zone
Zeitschr., Zeitschrift
Zool., Zoologi, Zoologia, Zoological, Zoologie, Zoologisch, Zoologiska

REFERENCES TO LITERATURE

Each part of the *Treatise* is accompanied by a selected list of references to paleontological literature consisting primarily of recent and comprehensive monographs available but also including some older works recognized as outstanding in importance. The purpose of giving these references is to aid users of the *Treatise* in finding detailed descriptions and illustrations of morphological features of fossil groups, discussions of classifications and distribution, and especially citations of more or less voluminous literature. Generally speaking, publications listed in the *Treatise* are not original sources of information concerning taxonomic units of various rank but they tell the student where he may find them; otherwise it is necessary to turn to such aids as the *Zoological Record* or NEAVE's *Nomenclator Zoologicus*. References given in the *Treatise* are arranged alphabetically by authors and accompanied by index numbers which serve the purpose of permitting citation most concisely in various parts of the text; these citations of listed papers are inclosed invariably in parentheses and are distinguishable from dates because the index numbers comprise no more than 3 digits. Ordinarily, index numbers for literature references are given at the end of generic or family diagnoses.

SOURCES OF ILLUSTRATIONS

At the end of figure captions an index number is given to supply record of the author of illustrations used in the *Treatise,* reference being made to an alphabetically arranged list of authors' names which follows. The names of authors, but generally not individual publications, are cited. Illustrations consisting of exact copies of previously published figures (except for possible change of scale) are distinguished by the use of an asterisk (*) with the index number, and previously unpublished illustrations are marked by the letter "n" (signifying "new") with the index number; all other indications of the sources of illustrations are construed to mean "after" the cited author or authors, that is, embodying some degree of change. Addition of the abbreviation "mod." denotes appreciable alteration of the source figure.

STRATIGRAPHIC DIVISIONS

Classification of rocks forming the geologic column as commonly cited in the *Treatise* in terms of units defined by concepts of time is reasonably uniform and firm throughout most of the world as regards major divisions (e.g., series, systems, and rocks representing eras) but it is variable and unfirm as regards smaller divisions (e.g., substages, stages, and subseries), which are provincial in application. Users of the *Treatise* have suggested the desirability of publishing reference lists showing the stratigraphic arrangement of at least the most commonly cited divisions. Accordingly, a tabulation of European and North American units, which broadly is applicable also to other continents, is given here.

Generally Recognized Divisions of Geologic Column

EUROPE	NORTH AMERICA
ROCKS OF CENOZOIC ERA	**ROCKS OF CENOZOIC ERA**
NEOGENE SYSTEM[1]	**NEOGENE SYSTEM**[1]
Pleistocene Series (including Recent)	Pleistocene Series (including Recent)
Pliocene Series	Pliocene Series
Miocene Series	Miocene Series
PALEOGENE SYSTEM	**PALEOGENE SYSTEM**
Oligocene Series	Oligocene Series
Eocene Series	Eocene Series
Paleocene Series	Paleocene Series
ROCKS OF MESOZOIC ERA	**ROCKS OF MESOZOIC ERA**
CRETACEOUS SYSTEM	**CRETACEOUS SYSTEM**
Upper Cretaceous Series	**Gulfian Series (Upper Cretaceous)**
Maastrichtian Stage[2]	Navarroan Stage
Campanian Stage[2]	Tayloran Stage
Santonian Stage[2]	Austinian Stage
Coniacian Stage[2]	
Turonian Stage	
Cenomanian Stage	Woodbinian (Tuscaloosan) Stage
	Comanchean Series (Lower Cretaceous)
	Washitan Stage
Lower Cretaceous Series	
Albian Stage	Fredericksburgian Stage
	Trinitian Stage
Aptian Stage	
	Coahuilan Series (Lower Cretaceous)

Barremian Stage[3]
Hauterivian Stage[3]
Valanginian Stage[3]
Berriasian Stage[3]

JURASSIC SYSTEM

Upper Jurassic Series
Portlandian Stage[4]
Kimmeridgian Stage
Oxfordian Stage

Middle Jurassic Series
Callovian Stage
Bathonian Stage
Bajocian Stage

Lower Jurassic Series (Liassic)
Toarcian Stage
Pliensbachian Stage
Sinemurian Stage
Hettangian Stage

TRIASSIC SYSTEM

Upper Triassic Series
Rhaetian Stage[5]
Norian Stage
Carnian Stage

Middle Triassic Series
Ladinian Stage
Anisian Stage (Virglorian)

Lower Triassic Series
Scythian Series (Werfenian)

ROCKS OF PALEOZOIC ERA

PERMIAN SYSTEM

Upper Permian Series
Tartarian Stage[6]

Middle Permian Series
Kazanian Stage [7]
Kungurian Stage
Artinskian Stage[8]

Lower Permian Series
Sakmarian Stage

CARBONIFEROUS SYSTEM

Upper Carboniferous Series
Stephanian Stage

Westphalian Stage

Namurian Stage

Nuevoleonian Stage

Durangoan Stage

JURASSIC SYSTEM

Upper Jurassic Series
Portlandian Stage
Kimmeridgian Stage
Oxfordian Stage

Middle Jurassic Series
Callovian Stage
Bathonian Stage
Bajocian Stage

Lower Jurassic Series (Liassic)
Toarcian Stage
Pliensbachian Stage
Sinemurian Stage
Hettangian Stage

TRIASSIC SYSTEM

Upper Triassic Series
(Not recognized)
Norian Stage
Carnian Stage

Middle Triassic Series
Ladinian Stage
Anisian Stage

Lower Triassic Series
Scythian Stage

ROCKS OF PALEOZOIC ERA

PERMIAN SYSTEM

Upper Permian Series
Ochoan Stage

Middle Permian Series
Guadalupian Stage

Leonardian Stage

Lower Permian Series
Wolfcampian Stage

PENNSYLVANIAN SYSTEM

Kawvian Series (Upper Pennsylvanian)
Virgilian Stage
Missourian Stage
Oklan Series (Middle Pennsylvanian)
Desmoinesian Stage
Bendian Stage
Ardian Series (Lower Pennsylvanian)
Morrowan Stage

MISSISSIPPIAN SYSTEM

Tennesseean Series (Upper Mississippian)

Lower Carboniferous Series
Viséan Stage

Tournaisian Stage
Strunian Stage

DEVONIAN SYSTEM

Upper Devonian Series
Famennian Stage

Frasnian Stage

Middle Devonian Series
Givetian Stage

Couvinian Stage

Lower Devonian Series
Coblenzian Stage

Gedinnian Stage

SILURIAN SYSTEM
Upper Silurian Series
Ludlovian Stage

Middle Silurian Series
Wenlockian Stage

Llandoverian Stage (upper part)
Lower Silurian Series
Llandoverian Stage (lower part)

ORDOVICIAN SYSTEM

Upper Ordovician Series
Ashgillian Stage
Caradocian Stage (upper part)

Middle Ordovician
Caradocian Stage (lower part)

Llandeilian Stage
Llanvirnian Stage

Lower Ordovician Series
Arenigian Stage
Tremadocian Stage[9]

CAMBRIAN SYSTEM
Upper Cambrian Series

Chesteran Stage

Meramecian Stage
Waverlyan Series (Lower
Mississippian)
Osagian Stage
Kinderhookian Stage

DEVONIAN SYSTEM
Chautauquan Series (Upper
Devonian)
Conewangoan Stage
Cassadagan Stage
Senecan Series (Upper Devonian)
Chemungian Stage
Fingerlakesian Stage

Erian Series (Middle Devonian)
Taghanican Stage
Tioughniogan Stage
Cazenovian Stage

Ulsterian Series (Lower Devonian)
Onesquethawan Stage
Deerparkian Stage
Helderbergian Stage

SILURIAN SYSTEM
Cayugan Series (Upper Silurian)
Keyseran Stage
Tonolowayan Stage
Salinan Stage

Niagaran Series (Middle Silurian)
Lockportian Stage
Cliftonian Stage
Clintonian Stage

Medinan Series (Lower Silurian)
Alexandrian Stage

ORDOVICIAN SYSTEM
Cincinnatian Series (Upper
Ordovician)
Richmondian Stage
Maysvillian Stage
Edenian Stage

Champlainian Series (Middle
Ordovician)
Mohawkian Stage
Trentonian Substage
Blackriveran Substage
Chazyan Stage

Canadian Series (Lower Ordovician)

CAMBRIAN SYSTEM
Croixian Series (Upper Cambrian)
Trempealeauan Stage
Franconian Stage

Middle Cambrian Series
Lower Cambrian Series

EOCAMBRIAN SYSTEM
ROCKS OF PRECAMBRIAN AGE

Dresbachian Stage
Albertan Series (Middle Cambrian)
Waucoban Series (Lower Cambrian)

EOCAMBRIAN SYSTEM
ROCKS OF PRECAMBRIAN AGE

---

[1] Considered by some to exclude post-Pliocene deposits.
[2] Classed as division of Senonian Subseries.
[3] Classed as division of Neocomian Subseries.
[4] Includes Purbeckian deposits.
[5] Interpreted as lowermost Jurassic in some areas.

[6] Includes some Lower Triassic and equivalent to upper Thuringian (Zechstein) deposits.
[7] Equivalent to lower Thuringian (Zechstein) deposits.
[8] Equivalent to upper Autunian and part of Rotliegend deposits.
[9] Classed as uppermost Cambrian by some geologists.

RAYMOND C. MOORE

PART I

MOLLUSCA 1

———

MOLLUSCA—GENERAL FEATURES
SCAPHOPODA
AMPHINEURA
MONOPLACOPHORA
GASTROPODA—GENERAL FEATURES
ARCHAEOGASTROPODA AND SOME (MAINLY PALEO-
ZOIC) CAENOGASTROPODA AND OPISTHOBRANCHIA

By J. Brookes Knight, L. R. Cox, A. Myra Keen, A. G. Smith, R. L. Batten,
E. L. Yochelson, N. H. Ludbrook, Robert Robertson, C. M. Yonge
and R. C. Moore

———

CONTENTS

———

INTRODUCTION

By Raymond C. Moore

This volume of the *Treatise,* introducing invertebrate phylum Mollusca, has been guided in organization by Dr. L. R. Cox, of the British Museum (Natural History), London. He assisted in arranging for the introductory chapter on general characters of Mollusca, contributed by Prof. C. M. Yonge, of the University of Glasgow, making helpful suggestions in connection with paleontological aspects of this subject. Early-made plans called for treatment next of the minor classes, Scaphopoda and Amphineura, the latter at least being recognized as distinctly primitive in various morphological

features. The mollusks that now are distinguished as an independent class, termed Monoplacophora, formerly were classified as an archaic group of gastropods characterized by the bilateral symmetry of their low cap-shaped shells and multiple muscle scars on the inner side of the shell for attachment of soft parts. Except for having a single shell, they suggest the amphineurans in structural organization and correspondingly differ from typical snails. The discovery (first reported in 1957) of living forms *(Neopilina)* of the same sort, which demonstrate correspondence to the Amphineura in having multiple pairs of gills along sides of the mantle cavity, as well as in other characters of soft-parts anatomy, supports separation of such mollusks as a group distinct from both gastropods and amphineurans; they have been defined (1952) as a class named Monoplacophora and in this volume are described in a section following that devoted to the Amphineura.

It is not to be understood that the sequence of molluscan classes as arranged in the *Treatise* reflects judgment as to order of their evolutionary differentiation or even as to the relative complexity of their morphological characters, taking account both of hard and soft parts. The present volume, designated as Mollusca 1, contains systematic descriptions of (1) Scaphopoda, (2) Amphineura, (3) Monoplacophora, and (4) the geologically oldest kinds of Gastropoda, which chiefly are classified as Archaeogastropoda; predominantly younger gastropod main groups, comprising the Caenogastropoda (subclass Prosobranchia) and representatives of the subclasses Opisthobranchia and Pulmonata, which together are far more numerous than the archaeogastropods, are assigned to the volume Mollusca 2 (in preparation). Then follow divisions of the Cephalopoda (Mollusca 3-5), of which only the Ammonoidea so far has been completed (1957), and finally the Pelecypoda (Mollusca 6). This surely is not intended to imply that the bivalve mollusks are the most highly developed or "advanced" class of the phylum; on the other hand, as now understood, they are interpreted to include very specialized, rather than prevailingly simple and therefore inferentially "primitive" mollusks. About all

that can be said is that the allocated divisions of Mollusca in the *Treatise* are arranged in measurably arbitrary manner, but their respective taxonomic delimitations fairly well reflect utilitarian purposes in studies by paleontologists. Among volumes devoted to the Mollusca, the present one may seem to meet specifications of utility least acceptably, because only a fraction of the Gastropoda is included and this fraction is not defined neatly along taxonomic lines. Opposed to such a view is the advantage from stratigraphic viewpoints of treating together all known groups of Paleozoic gastropods, some being placed in a Supplement for the purpose of republishing them in proper taxonomic position with units belonging to Caenogastropoda and other main divisions assigned to Mollusca 2. This arrangement has been adopted as result of strong recommendations to the director-editor of the *Treatise* by Dr. J. Brookes Knight.

The oldest known mollusks are monoplacophorans and helcionellacean gastropods from Lower Cambrian deposits. At least two genera *(Helcionella, Coreospira)* are firmly identified as representatives of the gastropods having this age, whereas the supposed monoplacophorans from the Lower Cambrian *(Scenella, Cambridium, Stenothecoides)* are as yet somewhat doubtfully included in this class. Thus, the Gastropoda have slightly the better claim to rank as the most ancient molluscan class recorded by fossil remains. Upper Cambrian strata contain at least three unquestioned members of the Monoplacophora *(Palaeacmaea, Proplina, Hypseloconus)*. These are numerically much outweighed by at least 16 known genera of gastropods classified in 9 families and representing three suborders (Bellerophontina, Macluritina, Pleurotomariina) (Fig. 88,*1*). The purpose of making these observations is to point out features of the early fossil record that distinguish monoplacophorans and gastropods from other mollusks, none of which are recognized without question in rocks older than Lower Ordovician (Tremadocian), even though all (excepting doubtful occurrence of scaphopods below the Devonian) appear to have become well established and strongly differentiated in Ordovician time.

GENERAL CHARACTERS OF MOLLUSCA

By C. M. Yonge[1]

CONTENTS

DEFINITION OF MOLLUSCA

The Mollusca, or "soft-bodied" animals, constitute a large and most important group of invertebrates which occupy many habitats in the sea, in fresh water, and on land. Although conforming to the criterion of a phylum in the possession of a highly characteristic common structural plan, mollusks are exceptionally diverse in outward appearance and in habits. Apart from the recently discovered monoplacophoran, *Neopilina galatheae* (LEMCHE, 1957), they are not segmented and include, in the Cephalopoda, the most highly organized nonsegmented animals. Except in *Neopilina,* the coelom is small, consisting of the pericardium and the cavity of the gonads with paired ducts to the exterior.

The animal is divisible into four regions, (1) a usually well-developed **head** with tentacles and eyes, although in the bivalves it is lost, (2) a ventral and muscular **foot,** probably provided primitively with a broad "sole" on which the animal crawled on hard surfaces, but capable of very great modification and seldom lost, (3) a dorsal **visceral mass** (coiled in Gastropoda), in which the internal organs are concentrated, (4) an overgrowing sheet of tissue, the **mantle** (or **pallium**), which secretes a calcareous shell with an organic matrix. The shell assumes many forms, is usually in one piece (including most bivalves where the two valves and the connecting ligament together form the shell), although consisting of eight plates in the Polyplacophora. It may become enclosed by the mantle, reduced, or lost.

A space, usually at the posterior end of the visceral mass between the mantle and underlying tissues and known as the **mantle cavity,** constitutes the respiratory chamber. In it lie the highly characteristic paired molluscan **gills** (or **ctenidia**) By means of cilia they create an inhalant current of water ventrally and an exhalant current that leaves the cavity dorsally. Except in certain Gastropoda and Aplacophora where the primitive condition is lost, the anus and the excretory and reproductive systems all open into this cavity where their products are removed with the outgoing, exhalant current. The **mouth,** commonly with jaws, leads into a buccal cavity that usually contains the characteristic **radula** (or **lingual ribbon**), a horny structure bearing teeth and capable of wide modification. Both jaws and radula are absent in the bivalves. Into the stomach open blind-ended tubules or digestive diverticula. Most recent evidence (1959) indicates that these may have been primitively concerned with extracellular digestion.

The **nervous system** consists of nerve centers in connection with the head, where

[1] Professor of Zoology, University of Glasgow, Glasgow, Scotland.

there is a loop around the anterior end of the gut, viscera, foot, and mantle. Where, as in most modern mollusks, the nerve cells are locally concentrated, these are known respectively as the cerebral, visceral, pedal, and pleural (or pallial) ganglia. They are united by way of commissures.

The **circulatory system** consists of a heart, usually with two auricles which receive blood from the ctenidia, together with a median and more muscular ventricle (elongated and double in *Neopilina*), from which blood is forced anteriorly and posteriorly through arteries opening into large blood sinuses or haemocoels. Only the highly evolved Cephalopoda possess capillaries. The blood may be colorless or contain haemocyanin.

The **excretory system** consists of kidneys, which are mesodermal tubes opening from the pericardium into the mantle cavity. Pericardial glands having an excretory function may also occur.

The **reproductive system** consists of gonads, primitively paired, discharging their products by way of the kidneys. Secondary gonoducts have usually been acquired. Although most often separate in sexes, the Mollusca exhibit a widespread tendency to hermaphroditism, particularly protandry. Development, except where secondarily it has become direct, is by way of a trochophore followed by a veliger larva.

AFFINITIES

The discovery in deep water in the eastern Pacific of the living monoplacophoran, *Neopilina galatheae* LEMCHE (13), has profoundly affected understanding of the relationship of the Mollusca to other phyla. It is no longer true to declare that in adult structure the Mollusca show no obvious affinities with other phyla. In general it may be said that their bilateral symmetry (lost in the Gastropoda) places them in the Bilateria, and the presence of a coelom, which arises by splitting of the mesoderm, indicates relationship with other schizocoelous phyla. Moreover, the fertilized egg develops by spiral cleavage in very much the same manner as in the polyclad Turbellaria, Nemertina, and Annelida. Particular association with the last named had been indicated by the presence in both of a trochophore larva, suggesting common descent from the Radiata. Although previously separation of

these phyla, now clearly very widely separated, had been regarded as having preceded the appearance of segmentation, preliminary accounts of the structure of *Neopilina* show that this undoubted mollusk *is* segmented. In addition to the shell muscles, previously known to have consisted of a series of pairs in the fossil Monoplacophora, it is now established that the auricles, the kidneys, and possibly the gonads are serially repeated. There is also a series of pallial outgrowths, which appear to be segmentally arranged. Now, no doubt remains that the Mollusca must have separated from the Annelida *after* the appearance of segmentation; the affinities between the two phyla are much closer than was previously suspected.

GENERAL FEATURES

The following account of the Mollusca aims only at consideration of some aspects of structure from the functional standpoint; few papers are cited, but these carry extensive reference lists. Classification is taken from THIELE (22), although emendations to this are occasionally suggested. Demonstration of the common structural plan behind the diversity of appearance and habits in the Mollusca represents a major achievement of comparative anatomy, but those who made this analysis of structure did not appreciate all reasons for the great plasticity of the molluscan form. Much light is thrown on this problem when it is realized that primitively a mollusk is divisible into (1) the body consisting of the head and (behind this) the ventral foot with the visceral mass concentrated in a hump dorsal to it, and (2) the shell-secreting mantle, which represents an overlying cap upon the visceral hump. Of these, the body is bilaterally symmetrical, with an anteroposterior axis of growth, but the mantle-and-shell, which grows by marginal increment around a central dorsoventral axis, is radially or, more correctly, owing to the influence of the body, biradially symmetrical. Taking the foot as the one fixed point, mid-ventral, the mantle-and-shell with the visceral mass may revolve through an angle of 180 degrees in the horizontal plane (Gastropoda), or the mantle-and-shell alone may revolve through a similar angle in the vertical plane (Pelecypoda: Tridacnidae). These are but two in-

stances of the independence of regions of the body and of the mantle-and-shell.

Although now liable to revision when the full account of the segmented Monoplacophora becomes available, fundamental aspects of the structure of the type of primitive mollusks, from which members of all other existing classes probably arose, may be noted briefly by reference to Figure 1, representing the views of GOODRICH (9). The presence of ectodermal excretory organs in the form of a pair of protonephridia in larval stages of prosobranch and pulmonate Gastropoda and of Pelecypoda furnishes indication of the presence of similar organs in the primitive mollusk. But in addition, there were paired coelomic cavities opening to the exterior by coelomoducts. The cavities separated into anterior genital and posterior pericardial chambers and the ducts, originally serving solely as genital ducts, acquired an excretory function, their inner openings becoming the renoperi-cardial funnels while the ducts dilated, forming renal chambers. Meanwhile, the nephridia were lost in the adult, although retained in the larvae. The two pericardial chambers fused to form a single pericardium, the contained heart consisting of a single ventricle with an auricle opening into it on either side. This primitive arrangement, with gonads opening into the pericardium and the coelomoducts serving the dual function of gonoducts and excretory organs, becomes modified in the course of evolution within the Mollusca, with notable effects upon both habit and habitat, especially within the Gastropoda.

GOODRICH indicates a straight gut running the length of the body, with radular sac and associated salivary (mucous) glands and paired masses of digestive diverticula opening into the stomach. To this should be added (Fig. 2) the probability of glandular esophageal pouches secreting carbohydrate-splitting enzymes, digestion of protein and fats being carried out intracellularly in the tubules of the digestive diverticula, possibly also in blood phagocytes that migrated into the lumen of the gut. The stomach itself probably early contained a ciliated sorting region, an area of cuticle forming a gastric shield, and a "style-sac" region initially concerned with the consolidation of fecal material—a matter of prime importance when

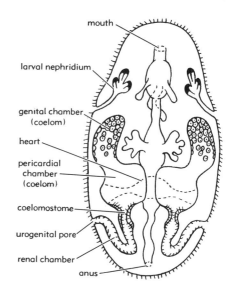

FIG. 1. Diagram of a primitive mollusk, dorsal view (9). Each of the paired coelomic sacs has a genital and a pericardial chamber and a coelomoduct with coelomostome and renal chamber.

the gut opened into the respiratory (i.e., mantle) cavity. Lengthening of the gut posterior to the stomach was also associated with the formation of firm fecal pellets.

As indicated in Figure 2, the foot in primitive Mollusca is envisaged as having a broad muscular sole, the original habit being one of creeping on a hard substratum (the habit of *Neopilina galatheae,* which lives on abyssal ooze, being certainly secondary) and feeding by scraping with a broad multiseriate radula. It was attached to the shell by a series of paired pedal or shell muscles, as in existing and extinct Monoplacophora, e.g., *Neopilina* (13), and fossil Tryblidiacea (12). Such a condition could be regarded as ancestral to that in both the Polyplacophora and the Pelecypoda and, following torsion which involves previous reduction to one pair of shell muscles, to that in the Gastropoda.

The mantle-and-shell must originally have formed a domelike cap over the visceral mass, although the animal could not have been withdrawn inside it. The limpet form (found also in *Neopilina*), in which the mantle-and-shell are pulled down over the body, secured by the sucker-like foot, appears

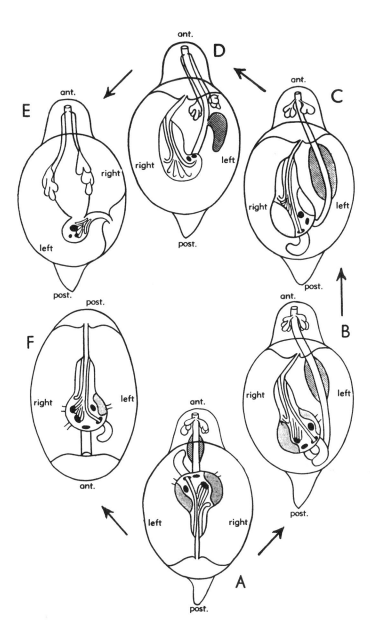

Fig. 2. Possible evolutionary scheme of molluscan gut (11).——*A*. Hypothetical primitive condition showing salivary glands, esophageal glands (hatched), stomach with right and left ducts from digestive diverticula, coiled caecum to left of esophageal opening, into which passes major typhlosole, ciliary sorting region
between this and minor typhlosole, cuticular gastric shield covering much of stomach wall.——*B*. Gastropod, esophagus now opens posteriorly into stomach.——*C*. Archaeogastropod such as *Monodonta*, esophagus
migrating anteriorly.——*D*. Neogastropod such as *Nucella*, greater simplification of stomach.——*E*. Tectibranch or pulmonate, stomach reduced to caecal appendage, esophagus dilated forming crop, esophageal
glands lost.——*F*. Pelecypod (posterior end at top), salivary and esophageal glands lost but stomach retaining primitive features.

too specialized to be primitive. It has been evolved many times independently in the Gastropoda (more than once each in Archaeogastropoda, Mesogastropoda [Caenogastropoda, *partim*], and Pulmonata) but certainly in these cases without subsequent evolutionary advance.

Special interest attaches to the mantle cavity, primitively a respiratory chamber and so remaining throughout the Mollusca (except in the relatively few instances where it has been lost), despite its added functions as a feeding organ in some Gastropoda and almost all Pelecypoda and an organ of jet propulsion in most Cephalopoda and a few Pelecypoda. Although consisting in *Neopilina* (but not necessarily in all Monoplacophora) of narrow pallial grooves with a series of ctenidia or ctenidia-like outgrowths, it is here considered to have been reduced to a relatively deep posterior cavity with a single pair of ctenidia before the other molluscan classes (including the Polyplacophora with multiplied and certainly true ctenidia) were evolved. It is therefore necessary to consider in some detail the organization and functioning of the pallial complex enclosed within this posterior cavity. In this matter deductions from conditions in modern representatives of these classes appear of greater significance than those from conditions in *Neopilina,* although future study of the mantle cavity of this animal in life should prove of great interest.

The pallial complex of ctenidia, osphradia, and hypobranchial glands may be considered in that order. Apart from *Neopilina,* where the precise status of the pallial outgrowths awaits detailed description, the characteristic molluscan gills, or ctenidia, persist in all classes except the Scaphopoda. It would appear that primitively each consisted of a central axis with filaments disposed alternately on the two sides. The condition now found in *Haliotis* (Fig. 3) probably indicates the primitive state. Down the axis run muscles, nerves, and blood vessels. Each filament bears four sets of cilia. The current-producing lateral cilia on the two sides of the filaments create a current of water that moves upward between adjacent filaments. Particles borne in suspension are caught in the currents created by the frontal cilia and so carried to the tip of the filaments and thence, by the agency of long

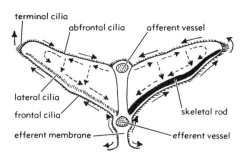

FIG. 3. Lateral view of two filaments with the axis shown in section of *Haliotis tuberculata* and indicating the probable primitive structure of the molluscan ctenidium (29). Lateral cilia shown on left filament only, skeletal rod on right only. Arrows show direction of respiratory current created by lateral cilia and of cleansing currents, dotted arrows course of blood flow within filaments.

terminal cilia, either on to the hypobranchial gland on the roof of the mantle cavity, or else, by way of the abfrontal cilia, to the upper surface of the axis, where they are conveyed to the distal end of the ctenidium and there expelled from the mantle cavity. Buckling of the soft filament is prevented by chitinous supporting rods, which extend within the filaments beneath the zone of lateral cilia. Internally, blood enters by an afferent vessel that runs the length of the axis on the "upper" or "abfrontal" surface and flows from this into each filament, circulating there in the opposite direction to the flow of water created by the beat of the lateral cilia. Respiratory efficiency is thus insured. Blood is re-collected in the efferent vessel that runs along the other surface of the axis and dilates terminally to form the auricle. Throughout the Mollusca the relations of the afferent and efferent vessels are constant and it is advisable to refer to the afferent (abfrontal or dorsal) and efferent (frontal or ventral) surfaces of the ctenidia. For varying distances from their point of origin, the ctenidia are attached to the pallial wall by afferent and efferent membranes. Primitively, as in existing zygobranchous Gastropoda, the efferent membrane was probably the greater, but in some the afferent membrane may be as long (e.g., Gastropoda: Trochacea), or it may entirely replace the efferent membrane (Pelecypoda). So organized, the paired ctenidia

constitute a functional partition dividing the mantle cavity into ventral inhalant and dorsal exhalant cavities.

Certain consequences follow from this (Fig. 4). The sensory osphradium associated with each ctenidium lies in the inhalant cavity in the path of the incoming current where larger particles tend to fall out of suspension. This fact, together with the histology of these receptors in modern Gastropoda, gives strength to the view that they are tactile organs concerned with the estimation of sediment carried in the respiratory current and not, at any rate exclusively, chemoreceptors as they are usually considered. The third component of the pallial complex, the hypobranchial mucous glands, are situated in the roof of the mantle cavity. By the secretory action of these glands particles of sediment are consolidated before being removed, by ciliary action, from the mantle cavity. Fouling with sediment represents the major danger to the efficiency of the respiratory chamber and the activities of osphradia, hypobranchial glands, and all cilia (apart from the lateral tracts) on both ctenidia and mantle surface are concerned with cleansing. Moreover, both the alimentary and the reno-reproductive systems open into the exhalant chamber, so that their products are carried out in the exhalant current without fouling the ctenidia. These facts are fundamental to the understanding of future developments in the form and functioning of the mantle cavity and the contained pallial complex throughout the Mollusca.

The circulatory system is simple, the two auricles (more in *Neopilina* and duplicated in Polyplacophora and in *Nautilus*) and the single ventricle (double in *Neopilina*) into which they open lie in the pericardium. Blood flows into anterior and posterior aortas and so into the haemocoels. Apart from circulation, these play an essential role in Mollusca, notably Gastropoda and Pelecypoda, in which foot and head are protruded, as a result of hydrostatic pressure.

Conditions in *Neopilina* and in the Polyplacophora give the best indication of the primitive condition of the nervous system, there being little accumulation of nerve cells in ganglia. But there was probably an early tendency for such accumulations in centers within the head, foot, mantle, and

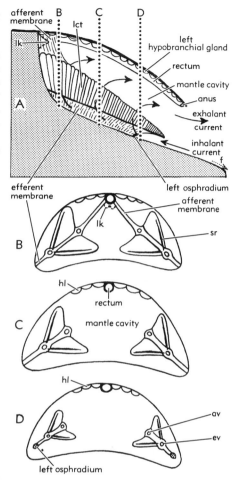

Fig. 4. Diagrams showing probable arrangement of the pallial organs in the pretorsional ancestors of Gastropoda. Mantle cavity viewed from the left side, the dotted lines *(B, C, D)* indicating the position of the three similarly lettered sections, each drawn as viewed from the posterior. (Explanation: *av*, afferent blood vessel; *ev*, efferent blood vessel; *f*, surface of foot with backward directed ciliary currents; *hl*, left hypobranchial gland; *lct*, left ctenidium; *lk*, left kidney aperture; *sr*, skeletal rod in ctenidial filament.)

viscera, with production respectively of cerebral, pedal, pleural, and visceral ganglia connected by way of commissures. Apart from the striking crossing of the visceral loop (streptoneury) in prosobranch Gastropoda, the major changes are the loss (or

great reduction) of the cerebral ganglia (and the head itself) in Pelecypoda and the tendency for concentration of all ganglia in the head in pulmonate Gastropoda and especially Cephalopoda.

From a bilaterally symmetrical primitive mollusk with uncoiled univalve shell and posterior mantle cavity, the evolution of all existing molluscan classes, except the Monoplacophora, may be deduced. The differences between them are to a large extent due to whether the body or the mantle-and-shell has the dominant influence on form.

Class MONOPLACOPHORA

Until the discovery of *Neopilina galatheae,* this recently erected class consisted solely of extinct Paleozoic mollusks characterized by the presence of a series of pairs of muscle scars. Quoting from the only existing account to date of the one modern species[1] so far discovered (13), the class may be defined as follows: "Almost bilaterally symmetrical mollusks with internal metamerism. A single piece of shell covers the pallium which extends all over the dorsum. Anus posteromedian. Coelomic cavities well developed. The metamerically arranged, paired auricles deliver the blood to the two symmetrical, long ventricles, each on either side of the intestine. Metamerically arranged nephridia arise from the coelomic sacs to open on the surface in the pallial furrow. Gonads symmetrically arranged, possibly metameric, opening through the nephridia. Nervous system primitively orthoneurous."

Neopilina galatheae was taken by the *Galathea* expedition west of Central America at Station 716 (9° 23′ N, 89° 32′ W) on May 6, 1952, at a depth of 3,590 meters on a dark muddy clay bottom. LEMCHE suggests that it lives with the almost circular limpet shell undermost and that it is a filter feeder. However, this posture seems inherently unlikely (36), and the animal would seem more probably a deposit feeder (the gut contains radiolarians). Possibly it collects organic debris from the bottom by means of frilled organs, which may be ciliated, situated at the margins of the mouth and which could be analogous, possibly even homologous, with the palp proboscides in the Nuculidae and Nuculanidae (protobranchiate Pelecypoda).

Class POLYPLACOPHORA

[Subclass Polyplacophora of class Amphineura]

In the chitons, which comprise this class Polyplacophora, also known as the Loricata, the mantle-and-shell may be said to dominate the much-flattened body over which, including the head, devoid of tentacles and eyes, it extends. Receptors are confined to the subradular organ, a chemoreceptor that "tests" the ground over which the mouth slowly moves, megalaesthetes (probably receptors of light) on the surface of the shell plates and sensory streaks, homologous or analogous to osphradia, in the mantle cavity. The characteristic subdivision of the shell into eight articulating plates is foreshadowed by the monoplacophoran *Archaeophiala* (12) with six (or ?eight) pairs of muscle scars. Lengthening of the body, together with subdivision of the shell into the linear series of articulating plates, permits these animals to conform to irregular hard surfaces and, if torn off by heavy seas, to curl up with the underside of the body, including the important pallial grooves, protected so that the animals can be rolled about without damage. They are typically inhabitants of rocky, surf-beaten shores and have retained, and indeed developed, the primitive habit of attachment by a broad foot to a hard substratum; in form and habit they are essentially elongated limpets.

The body retains primitive characters in the absence of accumulations of nerve cells forming conspicuous ganglia and in the symmetrical arrangement of the renal and reproductive systems and the general character of the gut. But the gonads have lost connection with the pericardium and are usually fused, although with paired ducts opening into the pallial grooves anterior to the renal pores. Sexes are separate and fertilization is usually external, but one case of viviparity is known. Lunar periodicity in spawning occurs. The kidneys extend forward, although their external openings, almost on a line with the renopericardial pores, are posterior. The heart is unusual in possessing two pairs of auricles opening into

---

[1] Subsequent to the preparation of Professor YONGE's typescript on general characters of Mollusca for the *Treatise,* A. H. CLARK, JR., & R. J. MENZIES, of the Lamont Geological Laboratory, Columbia University, in New York have reported (*Science,* 17 April 1959) the discovery of another monoplacophoran described as a new subgenus and species named *Neopilina (Vema) ewingi.* It was dredged from the sea bottom about 140 miles west of Chicama, Peru, at a depth of 3,200 fathoms.—ED.

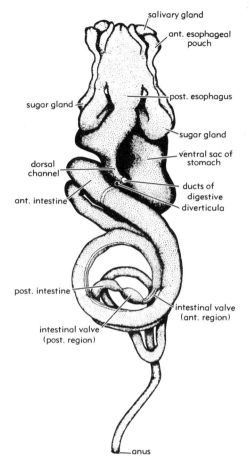

FIG. 5. Alimentary canal of *Lepidochitona cinereus* (6).

of both stomach and intestine, but there is apparently no intracellular digestion, only absorption, in the digestive diverticula. The intestine is divisible into four parts, (1) an anterior intestine, from which fluid products of digestion are squeezed into the ducts of the digestive diverticula, (2) a valve, controlling passage of material into the very long and glandular (3) posterior intestine, which is followed by (4) a short, nonglandular rectum. Regions (3) and (4) are concerned exclusively with elaboration and consolidation of fecal pellets. The anus opens into the posterior end of the mantle cavity.

This cavity and its contained organs are profoundly influenced by the complete overgrowth of the body by the mantle-and-shell and the general flattening of the entire animal. Between the foot and the encircling pallial girdle, also normally in contact with the substratum and a structure of great sig-

the invariably single ventricle. The gut (Fig. 5), described in detail by FRETTER (6), has many primitive features. In keeping with the habit of browsing (primarily on plant material) on hard substrata, there is a long and broad radula, each tooth row possessing 17 teeth, lubricated by mucus from salivary glands. The primitive esophageal glands are here represented by small anterior and large posterior pouches, the latter being sugar glands that secrete amylase. Cilia in the stomach, more restricted than in most Gastropoda and essentially all Pelecypoda, are confined to tracts in a dorsal channel, into the posterior end of which open the ducts of the bilobed digestive diverticula that secrete protease. Phagocytes are numerous in the epithelium and lumen

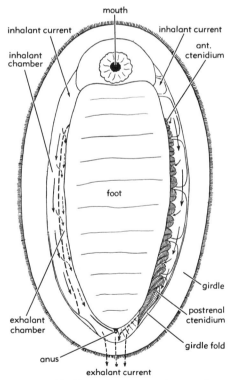

FIG. 6. *Lepidochitona cinereus*, ventral aspect, drawn from life; ctenidia and boundaries of shell plate shown in left pallial groove, division between inhalant and exhalant chambers (denoted by broken line) in right pallial groove (27).

nificance, extend the narrow pallial grooves representing the anterior extension of the much-reduced posterior mantle cavity (Fig. 6). The problem presented by this change in form of the respiratory chamber is met by multiplication of the ctenidia, which continue to divide the mantle cavity into inhalant and exhalant chambers. The ctenidia vary greatly in number (4 to 80 pairs), and the series may be holobranch or merobranch according to whether they occupy all or only part of the pallial grooves. Each one (Fig. 7) has the structure already outlined, but the filaments are characteristically short and deep, with a very broad band of lateral cilia. The unique feature is the presence of a broad band of long cilia on the sides of the filaments (corresponding to the tip of the more characteristic filaments shown in Fig. 3); these cilia interlock with those of the filaments of adjacent ctenidia so as to form the functional division between inhalant and exhalant chambers.

The ctenidia are attached to the roof of the pallial grooves and hang down with the efferent (or frontal) surface facing outward. Hence the respiratory current is drawn inward against the side of the foot. Separation of the outer (ventral) inhalant chamber and the inner (dorsal) exhalant chamber is completed posteriorly by the bridging

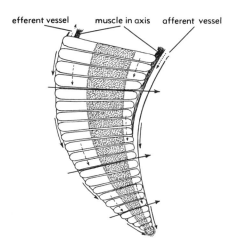

efferent vessel   muscle in axis   afferent vessel

Fɪɢ. 7. *Lepidochitona cinereus,* posterior aspect of a ctenidium from the left pallial groove, drawn from life. Stippled area that of long attaching cilia on filaments. Arrows indicate direction of ciliary currents (large arrows respiratory current), dotted arrows showing flow in afferent blood vessel.

of the pallial grooves in the region of the girdle folds (Fig. 6), by the last (postrenal) ctenidia in the Chitonida and by the adanal ctenidia in the Lepidopleurida (27).

The effect of anterior extension of the mantle cavity, together with ctenidial multiplication and changed disposition, has been to displace the inhalant streams from the posterior end. They now have no fixed position. Wherever the girdle is raised, anterior to the girdle fold, water inevitably enters to be carried through the ctenidia. The renal and reproductive pores open into the exhalant chamber between ctenidia and foot, their products being carried posteriorly to leave, together with feces, in the mid-line posteriorly between the last pair of ctenidia (Fig. 6). Strips of mucous and sensory epithelium occur in the pallial grooves or on the ctenidial axes, some being possibly homologous, and all probably analogous, with the hypobranchial glands and osphradia, respectively.

The Polyplacophora constitute a well-defined and homogeneous group in which the primitive molluscan habit of crawling on hard substrata has been developed to permit life on uneven surfaces. Extension and overlap of the body by the mantle-and-shell with dorsoventral flattening and subdivision of the single valve into an articulating linear series, and finally, the modification of the mantle cavity with multiplication of the ctenidia all tend to this end. Since rocky surfaces are intertidal or in shallow depths, it seems reasonable to assume that the Polyplacophora evolved in shallow, possibly intertidal, waters. Of the two existing orders,[1] the Chitonida are almost exclusively shore-dwelling and occur in all seas. They have a more efficient respiratory system and more complex shell plates than the Lepidopleurida, now represented by only four genera, few species of which live intertidally, although extending into deep, even abyssal, seas. They have a poorer respiratory system but consolidate sediment in the inhalant chamber— not, as in the Chitonida, in the exhalant chamber. This doubtless assists them to live in muddier substrata and may explain

their survival after the more efficient Chitonida had established themselves on the shore.

Class APLACOPHORA

This small group of wormlike Mollusca can receive only passing reference. It has been included by some authors with the Polyplacophora in the class Amphineura, but appears better treated as a separate class. In many respects the animals are more specialized, although less successful, than the Polyplacophora. In place of a shell, a thick cuticle, in which spicules may be embedded, is secreted by a mantle, which almost or completely surrounds the body. In the former case, a much-reduced foot with associated mucous glands occupies a narrow ventral groove. A reduced radula may be present and the gut is straight, with only salivary glands opening into it. The animals are carnivorous, usually feeding on coelenterates, but the shortened gut is probably associated with lack of danger of fouling the respiratory chamber, which, if present at all, represents a small posterior cloacal chamber. What appear to be ctenidia are present in _Chaetoderma_. The majority are hermaphroditic, at least one protandric, the gonads (or gonad) opening into the pericardium, which communicates with the exterior by paired ducts carrying spermathecae and serving solely as gonoducts. They are not excretory and have been claimed to be ectodermal. There are well-developed ganglia in the nervous system. These sluggish animals extend from shallow water to great depths, usually on muddy substrata.

Class GASTROPODA

GENERAL DESCRIPTION

This class, the most diverse group in the Mollusca, is characterized by having suffered torsion now or in the past. The Gastropoda must have arisen from primitive mollusks in which the mantle-and-shell did not elongate and spread over the flattened body as in the _Amphineura_ but deepened to contain the viscera compacted into a rounded mass. The single pair of shell muscles possibly represents reduction from a primitively greater number found in the Monoplacophora for instance, or both condi-

tions could have arisen by the concentration (or splitting up) of a more primitive band of muscles on each side. The mantle cavity deepened as the shell became more conical and instead of the mantle-and-shell spreading over head and foot, these could be withdrawn within the shelter of the deepening shell by contraction of the shell muscles, later extrusion being due to hydrostatic pressure.

Solution to the problem presented by increasing height of the shell was found in coiling, brought about by growth of the mantle-and-shell out of the plane of the generating curve (as it exists at any moment), such growth being greatest around the posterior margin (19) and producing a planispiral shell with the apex directed forward (i.e., exogastric). This enabled the lengthening visceral mass to be disposed in the most compact manner. It is impossible to say to what extent coiling preceded torsion, with which it was certainly _not_ connected. KNIGHT (12) thinks that _Latouchella_ with the spire of the shell curved only through some 90 degrees, may have been the "first bellerophont and first prosobranch." It seems possible, however, that greater coiling than this did precede torsion, although certainly without asymmetry.

These matters of conjecture are of minor importance; it is agreed that there was no internal asymmetry, although the gonads may have been the exception. In no existing gastropod are they paired, even where the pallial organs, auricles, and kidneys (although asymmetrical) are paired. The solitary gonad, which may represent fusion of the original pair (as occurs in the Polyplacophora), opens primitively by way of the renal duct on the right (_post-torsional_) side. The pretorsional right gonad may have been lost or have become fused with the left gonad, which alone retained communication with the kidney duct (Fig. 8).

The remarkable process of torsion comprises displacement of the mantle-and-shell with the enclosed visceral mass moving in a counter-clockwise direction in the horizontal plane through an angle of 180 degrees in relation to the head and foot. The mantle cavity, in consequence, becomes anterior. Torsion can be observed during larval development in Archaeogastropoda such

as *Haliotis, Acmaea, Trochus,* and *Patella,* and in *Viviparus* (5, 29). Initial asymmetry of larval shell muscles causes torsion when they are able to contract, although the time taken in different species to complete torsion varies greatly, judging from available observations. The many hypotheses concerning the possible origin of torsion re-

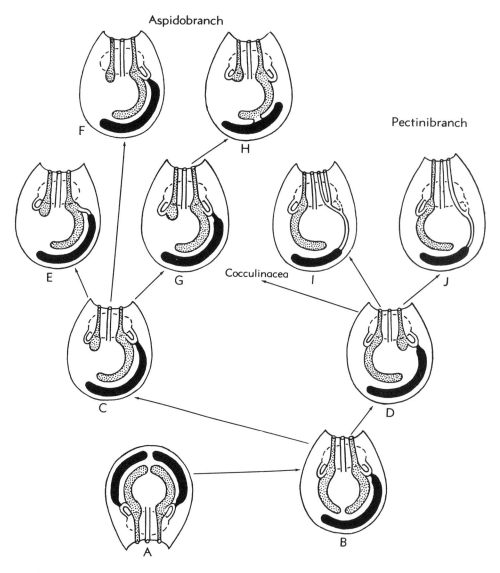

Fig. 8. Diagrams showing arrangement of kidneys and gonads throughout the Prosobranchia (kidneys and ducts stippled, gonad black, pericardium indicated by broken line, anus shown between urinogenital ducts opening into mantle cavity) (29).——*A*. Hypothetical primitive condition.——*B*. Loss of left post-torsional gonad (may have occurred before or after torsion).——*C*. Reduction of left and retention of right kidney, ancestral to conditions in *E, Pleurotomaria* and *Haliotis, F, Diodora* (Fissurellidae), *G, Puncturella* and Trochidae, *H,* Patellacea, i.e., all Archaeogastropoda except Neritacea *(I)* and Cocculinacea.——*D*. Reduction of right and retention of left kidney, ancestral to conditions in Neritacea *(I)* and in all remaining Prosobranchia.

viewed by Naef (17) and Crofts (4) may be summarized (29) in the form of postulates that torsion occurred:

(i) originally by stages in the adult;
(ii) in the embryo due to antagonism between the growth of the foot and that of the shell;
(iii) in the embryo but essentially to meet needs of the adult;
(iv) rapidly in postlarval life to meet the needs of adult life;
(v) rapidly in embryonic life to meet purely embryonic needs.

The last-stated hypothesis, which is associated with the name of Garstang (8), is much the most probable. A larval mutation involving torsion would have survival value because, as shown in Figure 9, before torsion the foot is adjacent to the mantle cavity, so that the delicate and all-important velum—responsible for both locomotion and feeding—cannot be withdrawn. But after torsion the head and velum can be pulled back into the now anterior mantle cavity followed by the foot, the protection of which was enhanced by the appearance, on the dorsal surface posteriorly, of an operculum which closed the opening. It does appear probable that post-torsional veliger larvae would be selected in preference to those in which torsion had not occurred. The other hypotheses (apart from ii, associated with Boutan, which postulates no advantage to either embryo or adult) all assume that the adult benefits by torsion and involve either teleological assumptions or the inheritance of acquired characters. But a larval mutation bringing immediate advantage to the embryo and involving a process still exhibited in the development of Gastropoda with pelagic larvae is much more credible. Moreover, it accounts for the absence of intermediate forms. So far from being of immediate benefit to the adult, torsion raised major problems that only subsequent evolution has solved. With the reduction and final loss of the shell in the Opisthobranchia, detorsion occurs, the mantle cavity moving to the right, the roof then folding back so that the cavity disappears.

The immediate effect of torsion in the adult is to place the mantle cavity behind the head and to twist both gut and nervous system. The anus now opens in the mid-line above the head, while the tube of the gut is twisted to the left in the region of the esophagus. The visceral loop, which connects pleural and visceral ganglia, becomes twisted into the streptoneurous condition. But these asymmetries are internal; so long as the

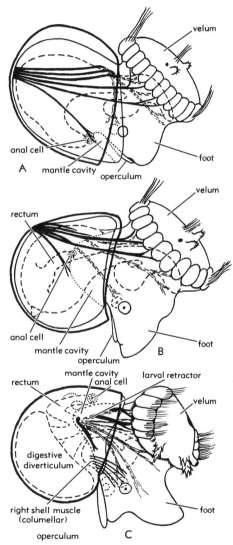

Fig. 9. *Patella vulgata,* reconstruction of veliger larva (5).——*A.* At 70 hours, ready for torsion, viewed from right side, showing lateral retractor cells *(A-F).*——*B.* At 76 hours, with 90 degrees torsion, showing rectum and anal cell with mantle cavity on right side.——*C.* With 180 degrees torsion (3½ to 4 days old), showing final position of rectum, anal cell, and mantle cavity.

shell remained symmetrical there would be no asymmetry in the mantle cavity.

The immediate problem, as first stressed by GARSTANG (1928), would be one of sanitation. Renal and reproductive products and feces would be carried forward over the head of the animal in the exhalant current. The marginal slit or shell apertures present in existing pleurotomariids and in other zygobranchous genera (e.g., *Scissurella, Haliotis, Diodora, Emarginula, Puncturella*) enable the exhalant current to be directed dorsally, away from the head. All fossil shells possessing a marginal slit or sinus (e.g., the "bellerophonts") were those of gastropods; before torsion there was no reason for such a slit. As shown by KNIGHT (1947) for *Sinuites* and *Bellerophon,* such animals possessed a single pair of symmetrical shell muscles, each one being "attached to the opposite end of the columella about one-half whorl within the aperture, a position that would enable them to serve effectively as pedal retractors." There is no evidence that they possessed opercula. But the earliest gastropods would have had no marginal slit, and KNIGHT (12) may be correct in considering that the Coreospiridae, which he includes with the Bellerophontacea, were such animals.

With the bellerophonts the effects of torsion were partially offset by the presence of a marginal slit. The mantle-and-shell, and so the organs in the mantle cavity, remained symmetrical; internally there was asymmetry of the gut and nervous system, possibly also of the reproductive system. Asymmetry of the mantle-and-shell came when a turbinate-spiral replaced a planispiral form owing to changes in growth gradients around the margin of the mantle-and-shell (19). The spire of the shell now projected to the right in a dextral shell and to the left in a sinistral one. This change brought about a more compact arrangement of the viscera and a rearrangement of the shell in relation to the foot, on which it came to rest obliquely instead of longitudinally.

The course of this process, outlined by NAEF (17), is shown in Figure 10. The original transverse axis of coiling became directed posteriorly while the apex was turned up so that balance was restored, with the first whorl resting on the dorsal surface of the foot where, then or subsequently,

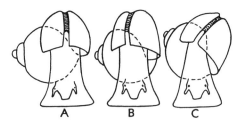

FIG. 10. Diagrams illustrating regulation of position of gastropod shell following asymmetrical coiling (17).——*A.* Shell before regulation.——*B.* Original transverse axis of coiling directed posteriorly ("regulatory detorsion").——*C.* Spire of shell directed upward, so restoring balance, the first whorl resting on the operculum ("inclination").

the operculum was formed. The first process NAEF calls "regulatory detorsion," the second "inclination." The effect of this (coiling being dextral) was to compress the right side of the mantle cavity; hence the pallial organs on the left were enlarged, while the marginal slit and anus were moved from the mid-line to the right. Asymmetry of the mantle-and-shell led to asymmetry of the pallial organs, but, as shown in existing pleurotomarians, paired ctenidia, osphradia, and hypobranchial glands persisted and the respiratory circulation in the mantle cavity was unaltered.

A fundamental dichotomy arose in connection with the reno-reproductive system. Either the right kidney was enlarged and the left one reduced—as in all aspidobranchiate Gastropoda except the Neritacea and Valvatacea (Fig. 8)—or the left kidney alone remained. While the loss of the right kidney could be associated with that of the right ctenidium and auricle, the loss or reduction of the left kidney in the Archaeogastropoda, where the pallial organs on that side persist, is difficult to understand. But the consequences are clear. Where the right kidney persists, the solitary gonoduct—invariably on the post-torsional right—must open via the ureter. If the left kidney is retained, the right ureter persists to form part of the gonoduct. Important consequences follow. Throughout the Archaeogastropoda, egg and sperm are shed freely; there is no penis and, in the female, no accessory glands, except to a minor extent in certain Trochacea such as *Calliostoma.* Development is larval; in consequence, the Archaeogastropoda are confined to the sea.

In the remaining Prosobranchia, which include the Neritacea and Cocculinacea (contained by THIELE in the Archaeogastropoda), there is no such restriction to internal fertilization and the elaboration of yolky eggs with protective capsules. The male possesses a penis, the female has oviducal glands, which, like the penis, are of pallial origin. With internal fertilization and direct development, leading in some cases to ovoviviparity, these animals were able to invade fresh waters and the land. This is true not only of the higher Prosobranchia (Mesogastropoda and Neogastropoda) but of the Neritacea, which, in the opinion of the author, should be raised to the status of an order. So possibly should the Cocculinacea, where also the right kidney is lost but which, possibly in association with their deep-sea habitat, are hermaphroditic.

The ctenidia may continue to be paired (zygobranchous) or only the left ctenidium may persist (retaining the aspidobranch form with filaments alternating from each side of the axis, or with reduction to the pectinibranch condition having a single row of filaments on the right side and the axis adherent to the pallial wall). Reduction to one ctenidium is accompanied by loss of one osphradium and hypobranchial gland; with the change to the pectinibranch condition the position of the osphradium alters, for it continues to lie in the direct line of the current entering the mantle cavity, suspended matter impinging upon it. In certain cases (e.g., Patellacea, *Caecum*) the osphradium, but never the hypobranchial gland, may persist after the ctenidium is lost.

Subclass PROSOBRANCHIA

Order ARCHAEOGASTROPODA

The aspidobranch condition is retained in all Archaeogastropoda, as well as in the Valvatacea among the Mesogastropoda. It takes the following forms:

(i) *Asymmetrical shell with two ctenidia,* i.e., zygobranchous Pleurotomariidae, Scissurellidae, and Haliotidae, the last a highly successful and specialized family in which the limpet character has been attained without complete loss of asymmetrical coiling of the shell.

(ii) *Secondarily symmetrical shell with two ctenidia,* i.e., the zygobranchous Fissurellidae, which form the bulk of living zygobranchs and contain many genera. In these limpets the shell is symmetrical, as are the pallial organs, although not the reno-reproductive system. The exhalant current issues either by way of a marginal slit (e.g., *Emarginula*) or, more usually, through a single apical aperture (e.g., *Diodora, Puncturella, Scutus*).

(iii) *Asymmetrical shell with loss of right ctenidium.* This condition, accomplished with loss of the shell aperture, has been achieved independently by the Trochacea, Neritacea, and Valvatacea. A left-right respiratory circulation is developed, the anus moving to the right side, one of the major disadvantages of torsion thus being overcome. This becomes apparent when the numerous and widespread Trochacea are compared with the scanty remnants of the Pleurotomariidae, from which they differ essentially only in loss of the right pallial organs and of the slit in the shell. An important point in the mantle cavity of the Trochacea is the enlargement of the solitary left ctenidium supported by the forward extension of the originally short afferent ("dorsal") membrane. While achieving its immediate object, this produces a pocket between the ctenidial membranes and the left wall of the mantle cavity (Fig. 11C). This pocket is readily blocked with sediment so that, although the Trochacea are universally distributed on hard substrata between tide marks and in shallow water, they do not invade muddy areas.

In the Neritacea, the aspidobranch ctenidium is unsupported, has very short filaments, and bends to the right. Resemblance to the Trochacea is superficial. Reno-reproductive arrangements are different in the two groups, and although the Neritacea and Trochacea have the same environmental limitations in the sea (confined to hard substrata), the Neritacea have spread into fresh waters and onto land.

The Valvatacea, which are asymmetrically shelled mesogastropods lack-

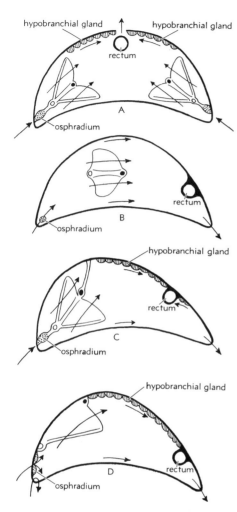

Fig. 11. Diagrams illustrating relations between ctenidia, osphradia, and hypobranchial glands in gastropods (29).——*A.* Zygobranchous archaeogastropod.——*B. Patelloida* (Acmaeidae), i.e., Patellacea with single aspidobranch ctenidium. Inhalant and exhalant currents indicated, also respiratory currents on ctenidia and direction of cleansing currents in mantle cavity (anteriorly directed current conveying material out through *inhalant* opening in *D*).

ing the right ctenidium, are referred to in describing the Mesogastropoda.

(iv) Secondarily symmetrical shell with loss of one or both ctenidia. This condition occurs in the Patellacea, also in the Cocculinaea and in *Septaria* amongst the Neritacea. All are limpets and the Patellacea are the most suc-

cessful of the many groups that have independently assumed this form. In contrast with the Fissurellidae, which they resemble in form and in possessing a horseshoe-shaped shell muscle, they have one ctenidium, arising presumably from ancestors in which, as in the Trochacea, the right ctenidium was lost. In Acmaeidae, such as *Patelloida* (Fig. 11*B*), the left ctenidium is well developed and horizontally disposed, producing a respiratory current entering on the left and leaving the pallial grooves in the mid-line posteriorly; in others, such as *Lottia*, secondary pallial gills are also present in the pallial grooves. In the Patellidae these gills alone occur, although conditions in *Patina* appear intermediate between those in *Lottia* and in the supremely successful *Patella,* where the pallial gills provide an ideal mode of respiration under shore conditions and in which sediment is extruded by muscular instead of ciliary agencies (29).

Order MESOGASTROPODA

[=Caenogastropoda *(partim)*]

Except for the Valvatacea all members of the order Mesogastropoda and of the Neogastropoda possess a pectinibranch ctenidium, unless this has been lost (e.g., *Caecum* and some Heteropoda). This permits uninterrupted left-right flow through the mantle cavity and free disposal of sediment by tracts of cleansing cilia on the pallial floor, the ctenidial filaments, and the hypobranchial gland. A major difficulty presented by torsion is thus removed; in contrast to the Archaeogastropoda, the Mesogastropoda can occupy soft substrata. The left kidney is retained, so permitting free elaboration of the gonoducts on the right. Internal fertilization with direct development and in some groups viviparity now occurs. The Mesogastropoda have thus spread into fresh waters and, with loss of the ctenidium, onto land.

The Valvatacea resemble the pectinibranchs (i.e., Mesogastropoda, Neogastropoda) in all but the possession of an hermaphroditic reproductive system and the retention of an aspidobranch ctenidium.

The Mesogastropoda display a striking degree of adaptive radiation. Apart from

the fresh-water and terrestrial Architaenioglossa and Valvatacea, they burrow in mud (e.g., *Turritella, Aporrhais, Struthiolaria*), move actively through sand (e.g., Naticacea), and swim or float in surface waters (Heteropoda and *Janthina,* respectively). Others (e.g., *Littorina*) retain a more primitive habit, but some have become cemented to the substratum (e.g., Vermetidae, which derive from animals with much-coiled shells, and *Hipponyx,* which, like all Calyptraeacea, is a limpet). Although the parasitic Aglossa should probably now be transferred to the Tectibranchia, *Thyca* (Calyptraeacea) remains an undoubted mesogastropod parasite.

Extremes of form are revealed by a comparison between the sessile Vermetidae and the more modified representatives of the highly active pelagic Heteropoda. In the former, the body, with its anteroposterior axis of growth, is completely subordinated to the mantle-and-shell, the rounded foot (with or without an operculum) having no function except as a plug to close the opening of the shell, the mucus from the pedal gland being used in some for food collection. Opposite conditions prevail in heteropods such as *Carinaria,* where the body is elongated with an enlarged head and a laterally compressed foot, the anterior portion of which is used as a fin. The visceral mass and the enclosing mantle-and-shell are greatly reduced, the ctenidium projecting from the small mantle cavity. Greater reduction of the mantle-and-shell occurs in *Pterotrachea* and *Firoloida,* all pallial organs being lost in the latter. The whole process of reduction of the mantle-and-shell and enlargement of the head and foot with elongation of the body is admirably shown in the series *Oxygyrus-Carinaria-Pterotrachea-Firoloida,* just as the reverse process of increasing domination by the mantle-and-shell can be traced from a *Turritella*-like stock feeding with ciliary currents to sessile operculate vermetids feeding in the same way, and so to those without an operculum and feeding by mucous strings (14).

The usually taenioglossid radula would appear more adaptable for a variety of feeding habits than is the scraping rhipidoglossid or docoglossid radula of the Archaeogastropoda. Apart from relatively unspecialized herbivores and omnivores, feeding

habits in the Mesogastropoda are diverse, including groups of differently specialized carnivores such as the Naticacea, Cypraeacea, Tonnacea, and Heteropoda, no less specialized herbivores like *Lambis* and *Strombus* (feeding largely on epiphytic red seaweeds), detritus-feeders such as *Aporrhais* and *Hipponyx,* and ciliary feeders of diverse origin, including some Vermetidae, many Calyptraeidae and some Capulidae, and such forms as *Turritella* and *Viviparus.* In these the filaments of the pectinibranch ctenidium are lengthened and their cleansing frontal and adfrontal cilia together with tracts on the mantle surface are modified for food collection. Within the gut, esophageal glands persist except where, as in the ciliary feeders and some herbivores (e.g., Strombidae) there is a crystalline style (10). In the carnivores, the stomach becomes simpler, with greater development of extracellular digestion.

While many Mesogastropoda are of separate sexes, increasing numbers of hermaphrodites, usually protandric, are reported. The reproductive system (7) is divisible into (1) gonad, (2) gonadial region of duct forming a seminal vesicle in the male, (3) short renal region of duct (formerly right ureter) extending to the posterior end of the mantle cavity, (4) pallial region of duct reaching to the opening of the mantle cavity. In the male this may be a ciliated groove or be closed and has usually an associated prostate gland, the combined secretions passing to a nonretractile penis on the right side of the head. This organ is absent in some (e.g., *Turritella,* Vermetidae) where sperm is received in the inhalant current. The female pallial duct consists of an albumen gland, a capsule or jelly gland, and a bursa copulatrix, where the sperm is initially received and from which it passes by a nonglandular ciliated groove to the receptaculum seminis (Fig. 12). A remarkable diversity of protective capsules are here formed (23). Ovoviviparity occurs (e.g., in *Littorina rudis, Hydrobia jenkinsi, Viviparus viviparus*).

Order NEOGASTROPODA
[=Caenogastropoda (*partim*)]

In these gastropods, as in some of the Mesogastropoda, the mantle margin on the left side of the mantle cavity is extended to

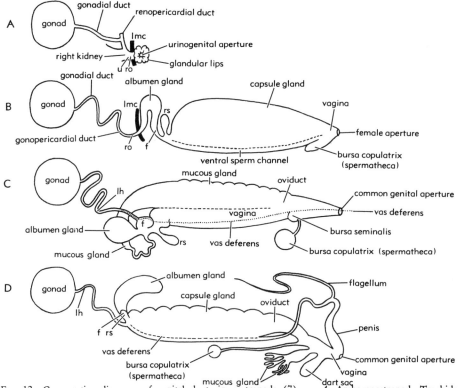

Fig. 12. Comparative diagrams of genital ducts in gastropods (7).——*A.* Archaeogastropod, Trochidae (female).——*B.* Stenoglossid, *Nucella* (female).——*C.* Opisthobranch *Aplysia* (hermaphrodite).——*D.* Pulmonate *Helix* (hermaphrodite). (Explanation: *f*, site of fertilization; *lh*, little hermaphrodite duct (gonadial and renal); *lmc*, limit of mantle cavity; *ro*, renal oviduct; *rs*, receptaculum seminis; *u*, ureter).

form an inhalant siphon, with a corresponding groove in the opening of the shell, which may be greatly prolonged, as in the Muricidae. There is a well-developed proboscis and a narrow radula, rarely lost, with not more than three teeth in a row. There is an unpaired esophageal gland (gland of Leiblein or else poison gland). The nervous system is more concentrated than in the other Prosobranchia. The osphradium is large and bipectinate and with little doubt serves here as a chemoreceptor. The animals are of separate sexes, with a large penis in the male.

These represent the leading characteristics of an order less diverse in form and habit than the Mesogastropoda. Almost all are marine, while most of the characteristic features can be related to a carnivorous or omnivorous scavenging habit. The proboscis, commonly of great length, with the narrow rachiglossid radula, fits them for

eating out the bodies of carrion (e.g., *Buccinum, Nassarius,* and other whelks) or for boring through the shells of living prey such as barnacles or bivalves (e.g., *Nucella, Urosalpinx*). The more specialized Toxoglossa (e.g., *Conus*) kill their prey by means of the long proboscis armed with modified toxiglossid radula and associated poison gland. Possession of a siphon enables Stenoglossa to exploit soft substrata but they are not so restricted to this habitat as are, for instance, the mesogastropod Naticacea. They are well equipped with receptors, nervous system, and large foot, for locating and pursuing or reaching, their prey. Details for the reproductive system (Fig. 12*C*) are the same as in the Mesogastropoda.

Subclass OPISTHOBRANCHIA

The characteristic features of this subclass are the reduction and eventual loss of the shell, with accompanying detorsion. Only

the primitive genus *Acteon* possesses an operculum and can withdraw completely within the shell. The mantle cavity migrates to the right and then posteriorly before opening out. Although in the Notaspida (e.g., *Pleurobranchus*) what has been described as a ctenidium persists, loss of all pallial organs usually accompanies loss of the cavity. Respiratory functions are assumed by undoubted secondary gills in the Nudibranchia, while protection, formerly afforded by the shell, is provided by repugnatorial glands or, in some Nudibranchia, by nematocysts obtained from coelenterate prey. With detorsion, the streptoneurous condition, retained in *Acteon,* gives place to a secondary euthyneury, while nerve ganglia tend to be concentrated around the esophagus; but both conditions occur in some Prosobranchia. The gut straightens (Fig. 2E), and external bilateral symmetry is regained. But the effects of asymmetrical coiling of the shell persist (i.e., the single auricle and asymmetry of renal and reproductive systems). Opening out of the mantle cavity may have to do with the inefficiency of the gills, the resemblance of which to ctenidia is probably only superficial. The radula is multiseriate, teeth being reduced in carnivores as in the Prosobranchia. Neither esophageal glands nor style-sac occurs (except possibly the latter in the thecasomatous Pteropoda). The reduced stomach (Fig. 2E) is associated with the development, probably from the esophagus, of a gizzard (e.g., *Scaphander, Philine*) or of a crop (e.g., *Aplysia*).

The reproductive system (Fig. 12C) is invariably hermaphroditic. Apart from *Acteon,* there is a retractile penis. This must have evolved independently of the pedal outgrowth present in this genus and in higher Prosobranchia (where it is sheltered in the mantle cavity). The pallial region of the hermaphrodite duct is fundamentally similar to that of a female prosobranch but typically divided longitudinally into male and female passages. *Actaeon* is not primitive in this respect but is so in that the pallial ducts do not sink into the haemocoel as they do in the higher Opisthobranchia. The albumen gland is an appendage to the female tract; eggs do not pass through it as they do in the Prosobranchia. Egg capsules are never formed, but the

fertilized eggs are laid in jelly-like masses.

The Opisthobranchia are exclusively marine, their representatives displaying in this environment almost as great a range of adaptive radiation as do the Mesogastropoda. Reduction or loss of the shell proves no disadvantage except for invasion of fresh waters and the land, although the intertidal Onchidiidae have a lung. In habit they range from sand-burrowers, like *Acteon* and *Scaphander,* to herbivorous and carnivorous browsers, like *Aplysia* and many Nudibranchia, to parasitic Pyramidellidae and pelagic Pteropoda. Probably in no comparable group is there such a range of feeding habits, many genera living exclusively on a particular animal or plant (e.g., *Calma* on fish eggs, *Tritonia* on octocorals, and *Pleurobranchus* on simple ascidians). The radula can be highly specialized, notably in the Sacoglossa which suck plant tissues, while ciliary feeding mechanisms—on the epipodia, *not* in the mantle cavity—occur in the thecasomatous Pteropoda. The carnivorous Gymnosomata are the only Gastropoda to possess suckers.

Subclass PULMONATA

The pulmonate gastropods are widespread on land and have invaded fresh waters. Without a ctenidium they retain, with few exceptions, the mantle cavity which acts as a lung. Its reduced and contractile posterior opening forms the pneumostome; a secondary gill occurs in some fresh-water Planorbidae. Usually there is a well-developed shell but only in *Amphibola* an operculum. The radula is primitively multiseriate, but teeth are reduced, as usual, in correlation with the carnivorous habit. Unlike the Prosobranchia with their paired lateral jaws, the Pulmonata possess a single median jaw, which is dorsal. The esophagus lacks secreting pouches. The stomach (Fig. 2E) has lost its primitive ciliary sorting function and, apart from some ellobiids, all trace of the style region. There is typically a gizzard of gastric origin, not of esophageal origin, as in the Opisthobranchia. Extracellular digestion is highly developed, the digestive diverticula being the site both of secretion and of absorption.

The Pulmonata are euthyneurous owing to concentration of all nine nerve ganglia around the esophagus. The auricle is us-

ually anterior, for only in a few detorted genera, such as the carnivorous slug *Testacella,* does it lie behind the ventricle.

Correlated with use of the mantle cavity as a lung, the ureter elongates and typically opens, together with the anus, outside the cavity. All Pulmonata are hermaphroditic, the primitive Ellobiidae being protandrous. In the great majority (*not* in *Helix,* Fig. 12*D*) there are separate male and female openings, the latter representing the original hermaphrodite opening. With the formation of a closed mantle cavity, the female opening comes to lie just in front of the pneumostome. The male opening is on the right side of the head, the penis being retracted into a preputium or penial sac. As in the Opisthobranchia, although for somewhat different reasons, the primitive penis is lost.

Order BASOMMATOPHORA

These pulmonates possess a single pair of noninvaginable tentacles with eyes at the base; all have a shell; the penis is usually removed from the female aperture; there is a veliger stage with reduced velum. The Basommatophora are a somewhat miscellaneous collection of possibly not closely related animals. The Ellobiidae and Otinidae range in habitat from estuarine and intertidal to coastal and inland terrestrial conditions and are certainly primitive. The remainder are divisible into the intertidal marine Amphibolacea and Patelliformia (Siphonariidae and Gadiniidae) and the fresh-water Hygrophila.

Order STYLOMMATOPHORA

There are here two pairs of invaginable tentacles with the eyes borne on the tips of the posterior pair; the male and female apertures usually open into a common vestibule (Fig. 12*D*). There is never a veliger in development. The shell may be reduced to calcareous granules (e.g., *Arion*). This purely terrestrial order (the Onchidiacea are primitive Opisthobranchia) contains very many species displaying great adaptive radiation and exploiting a great range of habitats on land.

The origin of the Pulmonata may be traced with greatest probability through the Ellobiidae (14, 15). But, like the higher Prosobranchia, if not the Opisthobranchia, they must initially have sprung from mono-

tocardiate Archaeogastropoda with, of course, the functional kidney on the left side (i.e., as in Fig. 8*D*). Paleontological evidence indicates that all of these major groups appeared in the Paleozoic,[1] each of them displaying great subsequent adaptive radiation. At the same time the primitive Archaeogastropoda—notably the Patellacea (Docoglossa) and the Trochacea—continued to exploit the possibilities of life on hard substrata in the sea.

Class PELECYPODA

In the evolution of the Pelecypoda the mantle-and-shell presumably first extended and then became laterally compressed, eventually enclosing the body, thus becoming solely responsible for the outward form of the animal. In addition to the symmetrically disposed shell or pedal muscles, there was further attachment by a line of pallial muscles close to the margin of the shell. This may or may not have preceded lateral compression, but the former condition is indicated in Figure 13. Compression was accompanied by subdivision of the mantle into two lateral lobes and a mantle isthmus along the mid-line dorsally. At the same time, anterior and posterior embayments attributable to the mechanical effects of compression shortened the line of the mantle isthmus and so of the ligament which it secreted. Hence the shell consisted of two calcareous valves and a relatively uncalcified uniting ligament. Meanwhile, the valves became united by anterior and posterior adductors representing the local enlargement and cross fusion of the pallial muscles where these came in contact as a result of the bending of the mantle into two lobes along the line of the mantle isthmus (Fig. 13*C*). The contraction of these muscles caused approximation of the two valves, at the same time distorting the ligament by compressing it below the hinge or pivotal axis and subjecting it to tensile stress above this (Trueman, 1951).

Enclosure of the head was accompanied by its reduction, eventually to no more than the site of the mouth opening, devoid of radula and other buccal organs. Food was conveyed from outside the shell, initially

---

[1] Contributors on Paleozoic gastropods to this *Treatise* doubt the recognition of pulmonates in pre-Mesozoic deposits. —Ed.

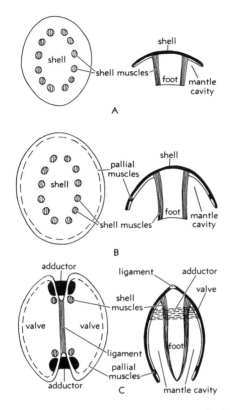

Fig. 13. Diagrams indicating possible stages in the evolution of the Lamellibranchia [Pelecypoda], dorsal view of shell with muscle attachments on left, transverse sections through mantle-and-shell and foot on right (32).——*A.* Primitive mollusk with flattened shell and paired shell muscles.——*B.* Later, with more concave shell overlapping laterally and with additional pallial muscles.——*C.* Compression of shell with two centers of calcification forming valves with ligament between, pallial muscle uniting to form adductors.

probably by palp prosboscides and only later by means of the water currents created by the enlarged ctenidia. The sensory functions of the head were taken over by the mantle margin, now in closest contact with the environment.

The shell (i.e., valves *and* ligament) in the Pelecypoda consists of (1) an external periostracum, (2) an outer, and (3) an inner, calcareous or ligament layer. Of these, the inner calcareous or ligament layer is secreted by the general surface of the lobes and the mantle isthmus, whereas the periostracum and outer calcareous or ligament layer are formed by the mantle edge,

which is thrown into three folds (Fig. 14), outer, middle, and inner, of which the first is solely concerned with formation of the shell. Its outer surface secretes the outer calcareous layer· of the valves and, at the depth of the dorsal embayments, the outer ligament layer. Its inner surface, including the depth of the groove between it and the middle lobe, secretes the noncalcareous periostracum, which covers *all* regions of the shell unless worn away.

The middle fold is largely sensory, being typically extended into tentacles and in some forms (e.g., *Pecten, Spondylus, Cardium*) carrying eyes. It is invariably most developed in the inhalant region, whether this be extensive (as in *Pecten* and *Ostrea*) or restricted to the margin of an inhalant siphon. The inner fold is muscular, controlling entrance into the mantle cavity of the powerful inhalant current created by the enlarged ctenidia in which much sediment may be carried. Where the entrance is widest, as in anisomyarian forms generally, this region is most developed, as in the "velum" or pallial curtains of *Pecten* or *Ostrea;* in siphonate genera it is correpondingly reduced, although here commonly taking the form of interdigitating rows of straining tentacles, as in the Myacea. In this group (as in others) this fold is also well developed around the exhalant opening, forming a membrane that directs the outflow clear of the inhalant stream.

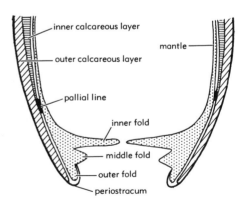

Fig. 14. Pelecypod, margin of mantle-and-shell showing three marginal mantle folds and three shell layers, periostracum being secreted by inner surface of outer mantle fold, outer calcareous layer by outer surface of outer mantle fold, and inner calcareous layer by general surface of mantle.

Complete enclosure of the body within the mantle folds permits the fusion of their margins. As noted above, this occurs initially in the formation of adductors by union of the inner mantle lobes and their contained pallial muscles. Localized fusions around the mantle margins later produce structural divisions between the exhalant and inhalant apertures, and between the latter and the pedal aperture, while in some pelecypods (e.g., Solenacea, Mactracea, Pandoracea) there is a fourth pallial aperture. Fusion is always preceded by local application of the mantle margins; it may take the form of ciliary junctions, cuticular fusion, or complete fusion of tissues. It may involve the inner mantle lobe only, or that together with the middle lobe, or also with the inner surface of the outer lobe, in which case the fused surface is covered with periostracum. Fusion of pallial muscles may lead to the formation of ventral adductors, as in the Tellinacea (30) and Adesmacea (21).

Siphons are formed by local hypertrophy of the mantle margins, being extended by intrinsic or extrinsic means and withdrawn by contraction of siphonal muscles representing local enlargements of the pallial musculature attached correspondingly farther from the edge of the shell. As in other regions of mantle fusion, siphons may be formed from (1) inner, (2) inner with middle, or (3) inner with middle together with inner surface of outer, folds of the mantle margin (YONGE, 1957a). Inhalant and exhalant tubes may be separate, as in the deposit-feeding Tellinacea (30) or, more commonly, be fused (as in the Myacea and Mactracea) where, the inner surface of the outer lobes being involved, the surface is covered with periostracum.

The ligament consists of periostracum (often worn away) with outer and inner ligament layers (Fig. 15). It may be increased in length by secondary extensions due to fusions, at one or both ends, of the inner or periostracum-secreting surface of the outer lobes or of their outer surfaces when a much thicker "fusion layer" is formed, either on the posterior side only, as in *Pinna* (YONGE, 1953b), or on both sides, as in the Pectinidae. The form of the ligament varies greatly, largely owing to bending of the mantle isthmus. The embayments may, however, extend until they meet, so

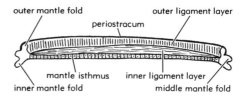

FIG. 15. Pelecypod, semidiagrammatic longitudinal section through ligament region of shell showing how three layers are secreted in the same manner as the three layers forming the rest of the shell.

dividing the shell into two valves, the ligament being lost. This occurs in the Adesmacea, being a prerequisite of the method of boring in these Pelecypoda (not necessarily true of other borers) where the two adductors contract alternately, the valves rocking on rounded dorsal, and in some cases also ventral, articulating surfaces.

Leaving external form until later, the enclosed body is little modified other than by compression. Bilateral symmetry is usually retained, the most notable exceptions being the monomyarians, which come to assume a horizontal posture either attached by byssus or cementation or else becoming secondarily free (32). But the primitive symmetry of the nervous, circulatory, and renal and reproductive systems is little affected, and there is still less effect on the organs in the mantle cavity. The extension both anteriorly and ventrally of the cavity permitted first lengthening and then deepening of the ctenidia. Despite their great modern success, conditions in the protobranchiate Nuculidae are in certain respects primitive and give important aid in following the course of evolution in the Pelecypoda.

As shown in Figure 16, the ctenidia are here restricted to the posterior half of the mantle cavity. They are attached by an elongate afferent membrane. Although increased in numbers, the filaments retain the primitive form; those of each ctenidium are attached by ciliary discs and also by terminal cilia to the filaments of the other ctenidium in the mid-line. Thus they constitute an effective partition between the inhalant and exhalant chambers, the more so because laterofrontal cilia (not present in the primitive filament) assist in preventing the passage of particles upward between the filaments. Nevertheless, sufficient particles

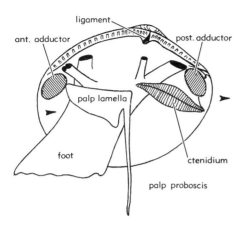

FIG. 16. *Nucula,* mantle cavity viewed from left side; arrows indicate positions of inhalant and exhalant currents.

penetrate for hypobranchial glands to be retained. The inhalant current enters *anteriorly;* this is primitive for the pelecypods, a direct consequence of the forward extension of the mantle cavity (as in the Polyplacophora). In the great majority of the Pelecypoda it has become posterior, ventral to the necessarily posterior exhalant current. This permits burrowing or boring with the anterior end downward or inward, the posterior end maintaining contact with the environment for oxygen and food. Among Eulamellibranchia, only the surface-dwelling or commensal Erycinacea (e.g., *Kellia, Lepton*) and the Lucinacea have an anterior inhalant current.

In *Nucula* the frontal cilia on the ctenidia retain their primitive function of cleansing; particles brought in with the inhalant current are conveyed to the mid-line and then passed forward but then are largely passed to the mantle surface, little being carried to the mouth. This mucus-laden waste material, or pseudofeces, is carried to the mantle margins opposite the base of the foot. There it accumulates for later ejection ventrally following sudden contraction of the adductors. Such accumulation of material, normally posteroventrally, and its periodic ejection from the inhalant chamber occur in all pelecypods. Where the mantle cavity is widely open (e.g., Pectinidae), there is great development of "quick" striated muscle for this purpose. From such cleansing

reactions certain Pectinidae and Limidae have obtained the muscular activity demanded in their swimming movements.

Feeding is by way of the palp proboscides, which extend into the substratum, collecting organic deposits and passing them along a ciliated groove to the area between the palp lamellae. The inner faces of these palp lamellae are grooved and are supplied with diversely beating rows of cilia, which on a quantitative basis select what passes to the mouth. Presumably the labial palps were extended as the head lost contact with the environment while it was gradually enclosed by the mantle-and-shell. At the same time jaws, radula, buccal mass, and salivary and esophageal glands were lost.

Other primitive features of the Nuculidae include the taxodont dentition (but not the condensed ligament), presence of four pairs of pedal (shell) muscles, opening of the gonads into the ureters, and probably mode of life, i.e., burrowing—horizontally when once below the surface—into soft substrata. It is difficult to see how the gradual elongation of the palps could have come about except under such conditions; byssal attachment demands prior establishment of feeding on suspended matter by means of enlarged ctenidia.

Broadly speaking (disregarding the remaining protobranchs and the septibranchs), the pelecypods are ciliary feeders (the wood-boring Teredinidae with an accessory source of carbohydrate). The ctenidium is further elongated until it reaches almost to the mouth, the filaments being extended and bent back on themselves so that the four demibranchs occupy much of the mantle cavity. The palps are reduced to the sorting lamellae. The two arms of each filament are united by interlamellar junctions; in the filibranch condition successive filaments are attached by ciliary junctions but in the eulamellibranch condition by interfilamentary tissue connections. In the former, both blood vessels run along the axis, but in the latter only the afferent vessel; the efferent vessel divides into branches running along the dorsal margins of the demibranchs. In this manner a highly complex lattice-work with great surface area separates the inhalant and exhalant chambers (Fig. 17); the powerful current of water created by

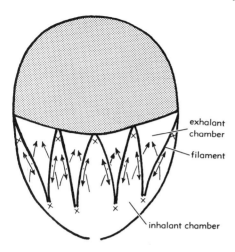

exhalant
chamber

filament

inhalant chamber

FIG. 17. Diagram indicating possible course of currents on the filibranch and eulamellibranch ctenidium; the arms of each of the filaments composing the four demibranchs have been drawn apart the better to indicate flow of water into the exhalant chamber. In different groups, and filaments, frontal cilia may beat dorsalward, ventralward, or both, the site of possible oralward currents being indicated by crosses.

the lateral cilia is effectively sieved, and the originally cleansing frontal cilia convey particles ventrally to the free margins and dorsally (or both ventrally and dorsally) to the axes or dorsal extremities of the demibranchs. There is great diversity in the arrangement of the ciliary patterns (ATKINS, 1936-43), but the end result is the same, passage of smaller mucus-entangled particles to the mouth and rejection of larger masses from ctenidia or palps or both. Mucous glands are abundant. Muscular activity plays an important part in the efficient functioning of the ctenidia.

The typically pelecypod gut (Fig. 2F) is highly adapted for dealing with continuous supplies of finely divided material, primarily of plant origin. Food enters the stomach as it leaves the palps. A crystalline style occurs in all but the protobranchs, where conditions in the gut are probably significantly different from those in the other pelecypods. The mucoid style is fashioned and driven stomachward by cilia; it contains carbohydrate-splitting enzymes continuously released as the head dissolves in the less acid medium of the stomach (25). The

ciliary sorting area in the stomach sends fine particles into the ducts of the diverticula, while large particles, with waste from the diverticula, are carried into the mid-gut. A cuticular region forms a localized gastric shield, against which the head of the style impinges. In the protobranch Nuculidae and Nuculanidae and in the septibranchs it lines much or all of the stomach, which functions as a gizzard. With the possible exception of some protobranchs, absorption and intracellular digestion occur in the tubules of the diverticula, wandering amoebocytes assisting in digestion. The mid-gut and rectum are primarily concerned with consolidation of feces.

Typically, the pelecypod foot is laterally compressed and its frequent and probably primitive use is in plowing slowly through soft substrata, being pushed forward and dilated terminally, contraction of the pedal retractors then pulling the animal forward (Fig. 18). But it is capable of wide modification, in connection with rapid vertical burrowing (as in the Solenidae), with planting byssus threads (as in the Mytilidae), with sucker-like attachment while boring (as in the Adesmacea), or solely with cleansing the mantle cavity (as in certain Pectinidae—e.g., *Spondylus*). Cementation may be accompanied by loss of the foot (e.g., Ostreidae).

The nervous system calls for little comment; there is a single pair of so-called cerebropleural ganglia, in effect largely pleural and reflecting the increased importance of the mantle and effective loss of the head. Where there is concentration of ganglia, as in the Limidae, this takes place posteriorly instead of anteriorly as it does in the Gastropoda and Cephalopoda.

Enclosure of the body within the mantle-and-shell has imposed restrictions on reproduction. With no possibility of internal fertilization, there is no penis and no elaboration of female genital ducts. In either sex the gonad opens by way of a short duct into the exhalant chamber, by way of the ureter in the protobranchs, by way of a common opening with the kidney in filibranchs such as *Pecten,* and separately in the eulamellibranchs. Hermaphroditism of various types is not uncommon, while a probably basic protandry may take the form of alternating hermaphroditism, as in the Ostreidae. In

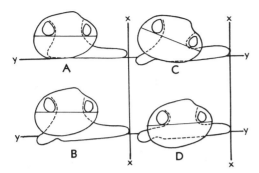

Fig. 18. Diagrammatic representation of shallow digging movements in *Venerupis (Paphia)*; progressive stages indicated in *A-D* (xx and yy being vertical and horizontal lines of reference). (After QUAYLE.)

Xylophaga there is sexual dimorphism, when in the male phase the animal stores sperm for use in the later female phase.

A few pelecypods incubate the eggs in the mantle cavity, usually suprabranchially, except in certain Ostreidae where they are retained in the *inhalant* chamber, having initially to pass through the ctenidium against the water flow, the larvae being eventually expelled ventrally by sudden contraction of the adductor. A parasitic stage in the life history follows incubation in the freshwater Unionacea.

The form of the Pelecypoda is the result of growth of the mantle-and-shell (Fig. 19). Direction of growth at any marginal region of the valve may be resolved (19) into different components: (1) radial, radiating from the umbo and acting in the plane of the generating curve—invariably present and affecting the form of both valves; (2) transverse, acting at right angles to the plane of the generating curve, possibly reduced or absent on one valve, e.g., *Corbula* [*Aloidis*], *Pecten* (but not *Chlamys*), *Pandora*; (3) tangential, acting tangentially to and in the plane of the generating curve, well displayed in *Isocardia* [*Glossus*] and *Chama* but less obviously in *Cardium* and the Mytilidae, although with important consequences in these (34). An invariable effect is anterior splitting and posterior extension of the ligament. The final result of such splitting was seen in the extinct rudistids where the two valves separated, while, owing to absence of a trans-

verse component in the growth of one valve and presence of a most unusually large one in the other, the former valve became essentially an "operculum" closing the deep cavity produced by the latter.

The most convenient way to consider problems of form in the Pelecypoda is by reference to axes or projections from the curved surface of the mantle-and-shell in the sagittal plane, namely, the anteroposterior and median axes of the body with the hinge and demarcation lines of the mantle-and-shell (35). Attempts to compare the form in different pelecypods by means of co-ordinates (THOMPSON, 1942) are possible only if the mantle-and-shell and the body are considered separately; the former may be related by the use of *radial* co-ordinates but the latter only by that of *rectangular* ones. The form finally assumed by any pelecypod is the result of interaction in growth of the mantle-and-shell on the one hand and of the body on the other. For instance, changes in form of the mantle-and-shell (due to changes in growth gradients marginally) affect the disposition but not the proportions of the body (e.g., Solenidae) (Fig. 20*B*). Changes in proportions of the body do occur but only when this is byssally attached, the region of such attachment being a fixed point. The anterior regions of the body may then be reduced (Fig. 20*C*), a condition which, as shown in anisomyarian forms, leads by way of heteromyarianism to monomyarianism (32). This provides another notable instance of the plasticity of the molluscan body. In the Tridacnidae the monomyarian condition has been produced by the mantle-and-shell rotating through an angle of 180 degrees in the sagittal plane in relation to the byssally attached body (32).

Enclosure of the body within the mantle-and-shell has restricted evolutionary potentiality within the Pelecypoda as compared with the Gastropoda, yet this is a supremely successful class. The protective shell is doubtless a factor; only in the commensal, and in one case parasitic, Erycinacea is it enclosed and reduced. But the use of the primitively respiratory ctenidia as organs of feeding, with correlated modification of the gut, is the most important factor. Both soft and hard substrata have been exploited, the latter by byssus attachment and by cementation, the former by burrowing.

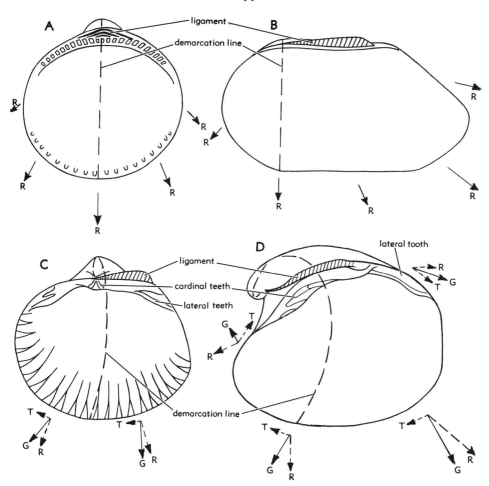

Fig. 19. Diagrams of left valves of pelecypods showing efferent or radial component *(R)* in growth and influence on this of tangential component *(T)* where this occurs, as in *Cardium* and *Isocardia;* the resultant direction of growth at different points around the margin indicated by *G;* demarcation line (i.e., projection on sagittal plane of the line of maximum inflation on each valve) being curved (19).——*A. Glycymeris.* *B. Anodonta.*——*C. Cardium.*——*D. Isocardia.*

Swimming is possible in the Pectinidae and in *Lima,* but as a result of freedom following byssal attachment and by means of mechanisms primarily concerned with cleansing of the mantle cavity. Boring has been achieved in various groups independently and from modification of different initial habits; following byssal attachment, as in the Mytilidae (e.g., *Botula* and *Lithophaga,* boring mechanically and by acid, respectively); following byssal attachment and "nestling," as in *Hiatella* [*Saxicava*]; following deep burrowing, as in *Platyodon*

(Myacea); following burrowing into stiff substrata such as clay, as in the Adesmacea where, especially in the Teredinidae, there is also the capacity for boring in wood, which involves further specialization.

Classification of the Pelecypoda is difficult. To associate the four protobranchiate families comprising the Nuculacea with the Arcacea on the basis largely of the taxodont dentition is certainly unsound. Although in major respects the Nuculidae are primitive (but also very successful), the Malletiidae and Nuculanidae (more suitably

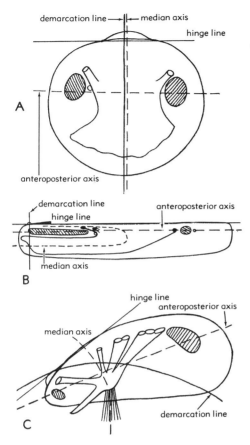

FIG. 20. Symmetry of body and of mantle-and-shell in pelecypods.——A. *Glycymeris,* body and mantle-and-shell both symmetrical in respect of median axis and demarcation line, respectively.——B. Solenidae, mantle-and-shell elongated posteriorly, secondary effects on disposition but not on proportions of body.——C. *Mytilus,* proportions of body affected owing to byssal attachment leading to heteromyarianism, secondary effect on mantle-and-shell.

considered together as one family) have highly specialized pumping ctenidia that in many ways are more elaborate than those of the eulamellibranchs. The protobranchiate ctenidia in the Solemyidae are enlarged for ciliary feeding, this family not possessing palp proboscides (28). It may well prove necessary to divide the Pelecypoda into two subclasses, of which the Protobranchia would be one. The final position of the septibranch families (Poromyidae and Cuspidariidae) also remains to be determined.

Their septa certainly "pump," as do the ctenidia of the Nuculanidae; but they are carnivorous, the palps being reduced (26).

Class SCAPHOPODA

In this small but distinctive class, the body is completely wrapped around by the mantle-and-shell, which, beginning as a cuplike structure, fuses ventrally during early development. There is no compression but the animal is elongated, the head appendages and the foot projecting from the wider anterior opening of the shell, the other end extending above the surface of the soft substratum in which these animals invariably, somewhat obliquely, burrow. There is no ctenidium, a current of water being drawn in posteriorly, partly due to extension of the foot and partly (at least in *Dentalium*) to action of cilia on a series of ridges on the ventral side in front of the anus (Fig. 21). Periodically, water is expelled backward, probably as the foot is being withdrawn, when defecation may also occur. There are no separate inhalant and exhalant apertures as in other Mollusca. The head bears numerous ciliated and prehensile captacula, which collect food particles both from the substratum and from material carried in with the inhalant current which accumulates on the ciliated ridges. These animals are thus deposit feeders. The gut is less reduced than in the Pelecypoda, possessing a dorsal mandible, a short radula with five teeth in each row, and a pair of esophageal pouches. The small size and inactivity of the Scaphopoda are reflected in the great reduction of the circulatory system which contains no heart. The paired kidneys communicate only with the exterior. There are the usual four pairs of nerve ganglia. As in the Polyplacophora there is a subradular organ with an associated ganglion. The animals are of separate sexes and have a single posteriorly extended gonad which opens by way of the right kidney (i.e., corresponding to the left —post-torsional—kidney in the Gastropoda).

Class CEPHALOPODA

In this class of exclusively marine and bilaterally symmetrical animals, the Mollusca attain a degree of structural com-

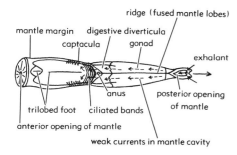

ridge (fused mantle lobes)

mantle margin   digestive diverticula
   captacula   gonad
                              exhalant

anus
                              posterior opening
trilobed foot   ciliated bands   of mantle

anterior opening of mantle

weak currents in mantle cavity

Fig. 21. *Dentalium entalis,* ventral aspect, animal removed from shell and foot withdrawn, showing currents in mantle cavity.

plexity and of metabolic efficiency which represent the summit of evolution in the absence of segmentation. Their living representatives are divisible into the two orders (1) Tetrabranchia, with two pairs of ctenidia and numerous arms and comprising the genus *Nautilus,* and (2) Dibranchia, with one pair of ctenidia and ten or eight arms. The latter consist of three suborders: (a) Decapoda, having four pairs of normal arms and one pair of longer, more or less retractile, "tentacular" arms—the cuttlefishes and squids belong to this suborder; (b) Vampyromorpha (20), comprising the archaic bathypelagic genus *Vampyroteuthis,* in which one of the five pairs of arms consists of long mobile filaments which are retractile into special pockets; and (c) Octopoda, which possess four pairs of arms all similar, apart from some modifications in respect of reproduction.

While all are predacious carnivores, the modern Cephalopoda have exploited the major marine habitats. Squids inhabit surface waters and cuttlefishes and octopods respectively sandy and rocky bottoms in shallow water. Other squids, including *Architeuthis,* the largest of invertebrates, and also certain octopods, are bathypelagic or live on or near the sea floor in abyssal depths. Many of them are strikingly modified, some being so gelatinous as to resemble coelenterates.

Comments on these most elaborately constructed animals can only cover a few aspects of structure chosen to emphasize both their fundamental molluscan nature and at the same time the extent to which the poten-

tialities latent in the molluscan ground plan have been realized in the Cephalopoda.

The manner in which the characteristic form of the modern Cephalopoda has been attained may be briefly outlined. The first stage was probably the cutting off within the domelike shell of the primitive mollusk of first one and then a succession of chambers (Fig. 22). These must have been traversed with a siphuncle through which tissue extended, i.e., unlike the superficially somewhat similar chambering which occurs in some elongated gastropod shells (e.g., the vermetids). At the same time the terminal chamber deepened and was necessarily accompanied by a pronounced ventral flexure of the animal within. The head and the opening into the mantle cavity came to face ventrally, being separated only by the much-reduced foot. Initially in the form of overlapping flaps, eventually as a closed tube or

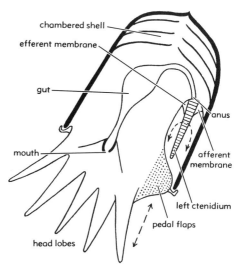

chambered shell
efferent membrane
gut
mouth
                                    anus
                                    afferent
                                    membrane
                        left ctenidium
                   pedal flaps
head lobes

Fig. 22. Possible early stage in evolution of a cephalopod showing chambering of shell with development of head lobes and modification of the foot to form flaps at the entrance to the mantle cavity. With the dorsal elongation of this, the anus has begun to migrate from the primitively dorsal to the primitively ventral (topographically upper) position that it occupies in the Cephalopoda. At the same time, the efferent membrane has been reduced to the size of the afferent membrane, which itself becomes extended in the Dibranchia (Fig. 24). Direction of water flow in the mantle cavity is uncertain depending on the part played by the pedal flaps (cf. *Nautilus*).

funnel, the foot came into functional association with the mantle cavity. Conversion of the shell into a hydrostatic organ enabled the Cephalopoda at some early stage to change from the primitive bottom-living habit to a pelagic or bathypelagic habit, as in the ammonites, while by the same means the modern *Nautilus* may float with the shell breaking the surface. The fact that it was lighter than water permitted elongation without necessary coiling of the shell—not feasible in the benthonic Gastropoda. Such straight-shelled Cephalopoda (e.g., *"Orthoceras"*) indicate how the later belemnites and the modern Dibranchia have evolved. Exogastric coiling also occurred and in a planispiral form (e.g., ammonites and modern *Nautilus*).

In the Cephalopoda, to a much greater extent than in the other molluscan classes, the shell became overgrown by the mantle, so that of modern forms only *Nautilus* has an external shell, although the purely internal shell of the bathypelagic *Spirula* retains the primitive chambered shell with a siphuncle. But in all the Dibranchia, like the extinct belemnites, the shell is enclosed, forming the internal skeleton of the elongated, streamlined decapod squids and cuttlefishes and being reduced almost to a vestige in the paired or unpaired stylets of the more baglike Octopoda with their more varied and often bottom-living habit. Throughout these changes, the fundamental molluscan features remain unchanged, the major elaboration being the appearance of the characteristic prehensile arms surrounding the head. These are organs of feeding, which also assist in locomotion in *Nautilus* and again, secondarily, in Octopoda. They are not here considered to be of pedal origin.

In their most highly evolved form, as exhibited by the modern Dibranchia, the Cephalopoda may be said to have reconciled the conflict between the growth axes of the body and those of the mantle-and-shell. The anterior head and the ventral foot, which forms the funnel, have come to lie side by side. They occupy one end of the elongate animal, with the tip of the visceral mass and of the contained shell at the other. The mantle cavity remains posterior. With the adoption of a horizontal posture, shown most clearly in a cuttlefish or a squid (Fig. 23), the head and the funnel lie in front, with the dorsal extremity behind and the mantle cavity beneath. The major axis of the animal is thus really ventrodorsal, but since anterior head and ventral foot are now associated, this means that in effect the two axes coincide.

This change indicates, at any rate, the structural background which has made possible the speed and power displayed by the Cephalopoda in such marked contrast to other Mollusca. Speed is due above all else to modification of the foot, the agent of jet propulsion. In *Nautilus,* where the mantle wall is not muscular, a water current is created by pulsations of the funnel in which there are both proximal "circular" muscles for expulsion of water and distal longitudinal muscles used for steering by directing the flow of water; these muscles are attached to the shell. In the Dibranchia the outer wall of the mantle cavity, no longer confined within a shell, contains a thick layer of circular muscle, the contraction of which provides a much greater expulsive force than is possible with the gentle funnel movements in *Nautilus.* Longitudinal muscles predominate in the funnel; both sets of muscles are attached to the internal skeleton (i.e., guard, phragmacone, and pro-

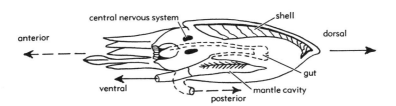

F IG. 23. Dibranchiate cephalopod, diagram showing disposition in life with reconciliation of growth axes of body (anteroposterior) with those of mantle (dorsoventral), also how direction of movement (arrows at extreme left and right) is controlled by direction of jet flow through the funnel.

ostracum) or to its derivatives. With its highly mobile tip, the funnel directs a powerful stream of water to produce so efficient a means of jet propulsion that, over short distances, squids are probably the fastest moving creatures in the sea.

The evolutionary changes within the mantle cavity are of major significance (29). In the primitive condition (Fig. 4), with ctenidium attached by a long efferent and a very short afferent membrane and with anus and urinogenital openings dorsal to it, the respiratory current, created by lateral cilia on the filaments, entered ventrally and left dorsally. In the Dibranchia (Fig. 24) the same organs (apart from osphradia and hypobranchial glands) are present but the ctenidia are attached exclusively by the afferent membrane, and the respiratory current, created by contraction of the pallial musculature, is in the *opposite* direction. But with the anal and other openings now on the efferent side of the ctenidia, their products continue to leave with the exhalant current through the funnel. A hypothetical intermediate stage (Fig. 22) indicates that the mantle cavity has elongated dorsally, the ctenidia at the same time migrating in this direction so that they come to lie on either side of the anus (as do the two pairs of ctenidia in *Nautilus*). The efferent attachment was reduced to the length of the afferent one, so that the ctenidia (again as in *Nautilus*) were only attached proximally. The foot then formed the bilobed flap which must have preceded the formation of the unfused funnel still retained in *Nautilus*. What cannot be determined is whether the respiratory current was produced by lateral cilia, and so followed the primitive course, or whether it was the result of muscular contraction (initially no doubt by movements of the funnel, as in *Nautilus*), in which case it would change direction.

The effects on the organs of the pallial complex have been considerable. At an early stage the hypobranchial glands probably disappeared, the greater respiratory flow rendering them unnecessary. The osphradia may well have been retained wherever blocking of the cavity with sediment represented a danger. In *Nautilus* they are so retained, in association with all four cteni-

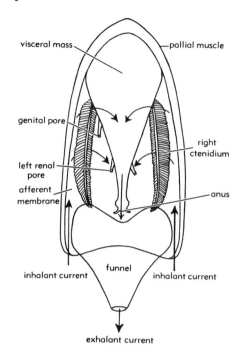

FIG. 24. *Sepia*, disposition of organs in the mantle cavity, viewed from posterior ("under") side (29).

dia, and presumably for this reason, since the respiratory current is relatively gentle, but they are absent in the Dibranchia. The effect on the filaments of change in direction of the respiratory current, now from afferent to efferent side, has been countered by the appearance of secondary skeletal rods on the *afferent* side of the filaments where they arise within a membrane that extends from the afferent surface of the filaments to the afferent membrane by which the ctenidia are now attached. This important distinction between the primitive aspidobranch filament and that of the Cephalopoda is indicated in Figure 25. In addition, the respiratory surface of the filaments is greatly increased by lateral, followed by secondary, foldings. The increasing complexity of this folding can be traced in development; in adults there is increasing complexity in the series *Nautilus*-Decapoda-Octopoda (e.g., *Eledone*). With the adoption of a more passive benthonic life in the Octopoda and eventual change in some deep-sea species to

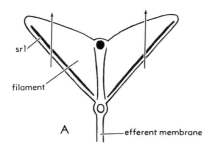

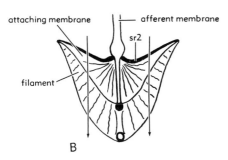

Fig. 25. Comparison between axis seen in section and filaments of *(A)* aspidobranch ctenidium of Gastropoda and *(B)* ctenidium of decapod (e.g. *Sepia*) (29). (Explanation: *sr1*, primitive skeletal rod, efferent side within filament; *sr2*, secondary rod, along free border of membrane which attached filament to afferent membrane. Arrow shows direction of respiration current.)

a medusa-like form of swimming by means of the webbed arms (e.g., Cirromorpha), the opening into the mantle cavity is reduced and so are the ctenidia, which finally become vestigial in the abyssal Vitrelodonellidae, where respiration must be carried on through the general body surface.

Although the elaborate circulatory system is typically molluscan, with a heart consisting of a ventricle and a pair of auricles (two pairs in *Nautilus*) enclosed in a pericardium, there is a notable advance in the substitution, apart from *Nautilus*, of capillaries for sinuses. This applies both to the systematic and the branchial circulation, additional branchial hearts providing the force needed to drive the blood through the ctenidial capillaries.

It is here convenient to refer to the relationship between the Tetrabranchia and the Dibranchia. NAEF (1913, 1926) and others who believe that primitively the Mollusca had two pairs of ctenidia, main-

tain that the tetrabranchiate condition is primitive. This is *not* here maintained. Although the "Tetrabranchia" are the oldest of existing Mollusca, there is no evidence that the primitive nautiloids had two pairs of ctenidia; that is assumed from conditions in *Nautilus*. The early Cephalopoda were probably sluggish animals like other Mollusca and eventual duplication of the ctenidia in the capacious mantle cavity may have been associated with increased activity and heightened metabolism. But this tetrabranchiate condition was only one of two solutions; the other, as shown below, being that achieved in the Dibranchia, which retained the primitive single pair of ctenidia.

Owing to the comparatively low oxygen-carrying powers of their haemocyanin and its slow rate of oxygenation, the increasing respiratory needs of the evolving Cephalopoda could have been met by morphological changes which increased *either* the surface *or* the efficiency of the respiratory system in the following ways: (1) by the maintenance of the primitive circulatory system but increase of the respiratory surface by duplication of the ctenidia, an increased respiratory current being produced by the pulsations of the overlapping pedal folds forming the funnel (i.e., as in *Nautilus*); and (2) by the retention of the single pair of ctenidia but their increased efficiency by acquisition of capillary circulation with accessory branchial hearts; at the same time a much more powerful respiratory current was produced by the pallial musculature under precise nervous control, which developed following the reduction and overgrowth of the shell (i.e., as in Dibranchia).

So far as the mantle cavity was concerned, these two possible lines of cephalopod evolution could have diverged during the Triassic when the belemnites appeared,[1] the Tetrabranchia appearing about the same time. If so, then the ammonites, arising from a more primitive nautiloid stock in the Devonian, need not have possessed two pairs of ctenidia unless, in association with the same metabolic reason, they were independently duplicated. However, it was the second alternative, first exploited possibly by the belemnites, which proved the more

---

[1] Actually, numerous undoubted belemnites now are known from Mississippian rocks in North America.—ED.

successful. It permitted the evolution of rapid locomotion by mechanisms concerned initially with increasing the force of the respiratory current. The acquisition of a mantle cavity of this type, combined with development from the foot of the highly mobile funnel, was clearly a prime factor in the survival of the modern Dibranchia and in their successful colonization of all zones in the sea.

The nervous system which controls the all-important contractions of the pallial musculature and mediates between the elaborate receptors, notably the eye, and these and other effectors, is of great complexity. It is concentrated around the esophagus in a massive "brain," which is protected in a cranium. It is difficult to homologize the various regions with the ganglia of other Mollusca owing to the great length of time since the Cephalopoda diverged and the exceptional evolutionary progress that has since occurred within this class. The central nervous system is divisible into three divisions comprising 14 lobes—namely, the subesophageal ganglia with four lobes, the supraesophageal ganglia with eight and the large optic division with two. The subesophageal lobes consist of the brachial, pedal, palliovisceral, and *lobus magnocellularis,* this so named because in it reside the large cells of the giant nerve fiber system (Fig. 26), which, as shown by YOUNG (37), control the movements of the mantle and the funnel, i.e., the organs largely concerned with the precise capture of active prey. This system is present in all Decapoda but not in the demersal Octopoda, although the *lobus magnocellularis* is retained.

Impulses are set up, often presumably as a result of stimulation from the eye by way of the optic ganglia, in either of these giant cells and so carried to seven pairs of second-order giant neurons in the palliovisceral lobe, the axons of which control the muscles concerned with expulsion of water from the mantle cavity. They run direct to the retractor muscles of the funnel and head and, by way of the stellate ganglia where they make contact with third-order giant fibers, to the pallial muscles. Hence, a single impulse set up in the giant cells brings about a sudden contraction, producing sudden expulsion of water through the funnel and so a darting movement of the animal in the opposite direction to that in which the funnel is pointed. Speed of conduction, made possible by the large axons, is all-important. Other large motor cells in the *lobus magnocellularis* may constitute the center for controlling the composite set of movements—by arms, mantle and funnel—by which prey is seized.

Just as with the respiratory, circulatory, muscular, and nervous systems, that of digestion represents a strikingly efficient development of primitive molluscan features. It has been most thoroughly studied in the squids (2), where the process is so efficient that a complete meal can be digested in four to six hours, *Sepia* taking about twice and *Octopus* about three times as long. Prey seized by the two long arms is carried to the mouth, where it is killed by poison from

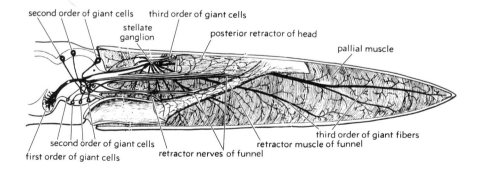

FIG. 26. Diagram of squid, *Loligo pealii,* showing arrangement of giant nerve fibers controlling movements of pallial muscles and retractors of head and funnel (28).

buccal glands; it is then bitten by the jaws and swallowed by aid of the radula. In the Octopoda digestive enzymes may be regurgitated and ejected into the body of the prey (e.g., a crab), and the products of this "extra-intestinal" digestion later are sucked in. The digestive diverticula consist of two distinct glands, the so-called "liver" and "pancreas." Digestion is exclusively and most effectively extracellular, enzymes com-

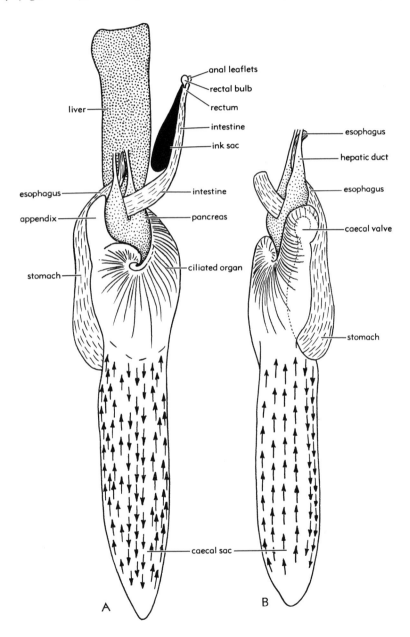

FIG. 27. *Loligo* spp., mid-gut and mid-gut glands, *(A)* ventral view, *(B)* left side (2). Arrows indicate alternative systems of ciliary currents in the caecal sac.

ing from both of these sources although by a common "pancreatic" duct. By a striking parallel with conditions in the vertebrates, digestion occurs in two stages, the first in the actively churning and chitin-lined stomach by the agency of "pancreatic" secretion, and the second by enzymes from the "liver" in the long caecum which extends dorsal to (or "behind") this. As the partly digested food enters the caecum (Fig. 27) from the stomach, it first encounters a ciliated organ—most probably related to the ciliary region in the stomachs of other Mollusca—where solid particles are collected and passed by a groove into the intestine. Absorption of the final products of digestion in the remaining fluid takes place through the walls of the caecum, but also—especially during the breeding season when the caecum may be restricted by the enlarged gonad—in the intestine. The whole process is one of striking efficiency, involving "delicate interplay of the muscular action of the stomach, caecal sac, esophageal,

intestinal, and hepatic sphincters, and hepatopancreatic fold and caecal valve" (2).

The Cephalopoda are invariably of separate sexes, some (e.g., *Argonauta*), displaying marked sexual dimorphism. The gonad, within the large genital coelom, is single, with ducts opening directly into the mantle cavity. These are primitively paired, but in many cases (including *Nautilus*), are reduced to one. Development is direct and fertilization internal. This involves the presence of glands in association with both oviduct and *vas deferens* for the production, respectively, of protective capsules for the eggs and of spermatophores. The latter are conveyed into the mantle cavity of the female at copulation by the agency of a seasonally modified arm (hectocotylus) in the Dibranchia and of the spadix (permanent modification of four arms) in *Nautilus*. In this remarkable way internal fertilization has been retained despite increased enclosure of the female reproductive opening within the mantle cavity.

REFERENCES

Atkins, D.
(1) 1936-43, *On the ciliary mechanisms and interrelationships of lamellibranchs, Parts I-VIII:* Quart. Jour. Micr. Sci. (London), v. 79, p. 339-373, p. 375-421, p. 423-445; v. 80, p. 321-329, p. 331-344, p. 345-436; v. 84, p. 187-256.

Bidder, A. M.
(2) 1950, *The digestive mechanism of the European squids Loligo vulgaris, Loligo forbesii, Alloteuthis media, and Alloteuthis subulata:* Same, v. 91, p. 1-43.

Boettger, C. R.
(3) 1954, *Die Systematik der euthyneuren Schnecken:* Deutsch. zool. Gesell., Verhandl. (Leipzig), p. 253-280.

Crofts, D. R.
(4) 1937, *The development of Haliotis tuberculata, with special reference to the organogensis during torsion:* Roy. Soc. (London), Philos. Trans., ser. B, v. 228, p. 219-268.
(5) 1955, *Muscle morphogenesis in primitive gastropods and its relation to torsion:* Zool. Soc. London, Proc., v. 125, p. 711-750.

Fretter, V.
(6) 1937, *The structure and function of the alimentary canal of some species of Polyplacophora (Mollusca):* Roy. Soc. Edinburgh, Trans., v. 59, p. 119-164.

(7) 1946, *The genital ducts of Theodoxus, Lamellaria and Trivia, and a discussion on their evolution in the Prosobranchs:* Marine Biol. Assoc. United Kingdom (Plymouth), Jour., v. 26, p. 312-351.

Garstang, W.
(8) 1928, *The origin and evolution of larval forms:* Rept. Brit. Assoc. Glasgow, 1928, sec. D, p. 77-98.

Goodrich, E.
(9) 1945, *The study of nephridia and genital ducts since 1895:* Quart. Jour. Micr. Sci. (London), v. 86, p. 113-392.

Graham, A.
(10) 1939, *On the structure of the alimentary canal of style-bearing prosobranchs:* Zool. Soc. London, Proc., ser. B, v. 109, p. 75-112.
(11) 1949, *The molluscan stomach:* Roy. Soc. Edinburgh, Trans., v. 61, p. 737-778.

Knight, J. B.
(12) 1952, *Primitive fossil gastropods and their bearing on gastropod classification:* Smithson. Misc. Coll. (Washington), v. 117, no. 13, p. 1-56.

Lemche, H.
(13) 1957, *A new living deep-sea mollusc of the Cambro-Devonian Class Monoplacophora:* Nature (London), v. 179, p. 413-416.

Morton, J. E.
(14) 1955a, *The evolution of vermetid gastro-*

pods: Pacific Science (Honolulu), v. 9, p. 3-15.

(15)   1955b, *The evolution of the Ellobiidae with a discussion on the origin of the Pulmonata:* Zool. Soc. London, Proc., v. 125, p. 127-168.

(16)   1955c, *The functional morphology of the British Ellobiidae (Gastropoda Pulmonata) with special reference to the digestive and reproductive systems:* Roy. Soc. (London), Philos. Trans., ser. B, v. 239, p. 89-160.

Naef, A.
(17)   1913, *Studien zur generellen Morphologie der Mollusken, 1:* Ergebn. Zool. (Jena), Band 3, p. 73-164.

(18)   1926, *Studien zur generellen Morphologie der Mollusken, 3:* Same, Band 6, p. 27-124.

Owen, G.
(19)   1953, *The shell in the Lamellibranchia:* Quart. Jour. Micr. Sci. (London), v. 94, p. 57-70.

Pickford, G. E.
(20)   1946-49, *Vampyroteuthis infernalis Chun, an archaic dibranchiate cephalopod. I. Natural history and distribution. II. External anatomy:* Dana Reports (Carlsberg Foundation, Copenhagen), nos. 29, 32.

Purchon, R. D.
(21)   1955, *The structure and function of the British Pholadidae (rock-boring Lamellibranchia):* Zool. Soc. London, Proc., v. 124, p. 859-911.

Thiele, J.
(22)   1931-35, *Handbuch der systematischen Weichtierkunde:* Fischer (Jena), v. 1, 2.

Thorson, G.
(23)   1946, *Reproduction and larval development of Danish marine bottom invertebrates:* Meddelelser Kommissionen Danmarks Havundersøgelser, ser. Plankton (København), v. 4, no. 1.

Trueman, E. R.
(24)   1951, *The structure, development and operation of the hinge ligament of Ostrea edulis:* Quart. Jour. Micr. Sci. (London), v. 92, p. 129-140.

Yonge, C. M.
(25)   1926, *Structure and physiology of the organs*

of feeding and digestion in Ostrea edulis: Marine Biol. Assoc. United Kingdom (Plymouth), Jour., v. 14, p. 295-386.

(26)   1928, *Structure and function of the organs of feeding and digestion in the septibranchs, Cuspidaria and Poromya:* Roy. Soc. (London), Philos. Trans., ser. B, v. 216, p. 221-263.

(27)   1939a, *On the mantle cavity and its contained organs in the Loricata (Placophora):* Quart. Jour. Micr. Sci. (London), v. 81, p. 367-390.

(28)   1939b, *The protobranchiate Mollusca: a functional interpretation of their structure and evolution:* Roy. Soc. (London), Philos. Trans., ser. B, v. 230, p. 79-147.

(29)   1947, *The pallial organs in the aspidobranch Gastropoda and their evolution throughout the Mollusca:* Same, v. 232, p. 443-518.

(30)   1949, *On the structure and adaptations of the Tellinacea, deposit-feeding Eulamellibranchia:* Same, v. 234, p. 29-76.

(31)   1952, *Studies on Pacific coast mollusks. IV. Observations on Siliqua patula Dixon and on evolution within the Solenidae:* Univ. California Publ. Zool. (Berkeley), v. 55, p. 421-438.

(32)   1953a, *The monomyarian condition in the Lamellibranchia:* Roy. Soc. Edinburgh, Trans., v. 62, p. 443-478.

(33)   1953b, *Form and habit in Pinna carnea:* Roy. Soc. (London), Philos. Trans., ser. B, v. 237, p. 335-374.

(34)   1955, *Adaptation to rock boring in Botula and Lithophaga (Lamellibranchia, Mytilidae) with a discussion on the evolution of this habit:* Quart. Jour. Micr. Sci. (London), v. 96, p. 383-410.

(35)   1957a, *Mantle fusion in the Lamellibranchia:* Pubbl. Staz. zool. Napoli, v. 29, p. 151-171.

(36)   1957b, *Reflexions on the Monoplacophoran, Neopilina galatheae Lemche:* Nature (London), v. 179, p. 672-673.

Young, J. Z.
(37)   1939, *Fused neurons and synaptic contacts in the giant nerve fibres of cephalopods:* Roy. Soc. (London), Philos. Trans., ser. B, v. 229, p. 465-503.

SCAPHOPODA

By N. H. Ludbrook[1]

Class SCAPHOPODA Bronn, 1862

[=Cirrhobranchiata DE BLAINVILLE, 1825; Lateribranchiata CLARK, 1851; Solenoconchia LACAZE-DUTHIERS, 1857; Prosopocephala BRONN, 1862]

Marine, bilaterally symmetrical mollusks protected by an external elongate, tubular, tapering, calcareous shell, open at both ends and generally somewhat curved. Concave side of shell dorsal, convex side ventral; aperture or anterior opening larger, apex or posterior opening simple or variously slit or notched, some forms with terminal pipe. Shell substance of 3 distinct layers (Fig. 28). Shell secreted by a mantle of same shape, larger (anterior) opening of which is contracted by a muscular thickening of the mantle and gives egress to the long conical foot; smaller (posterior) opening serves as outlet for organic waste and genital products. Mouth furnished with a radula, borne on a cylindrical snout and surrounded by a rosette of lobes; a cluster of threadlike, distally enlarged appendages known as "captacula" springs from its base. No eyes or tentacles; otocysts present. Liver 2-lobed, symmetrical; gut strongly convoluted, anus ventral and somewhat anterior, kidney openings near it. Heart rudimentary; no gills, respiration performed by the general integument. Nervous system with well-developed ganglia united by commissures. Gonad simple, sexes separate, reproduction without copulation. *?Ord., Dev.-Rec.*

Scaphopoda are without exception benthonic marine animals, the described Recent species being approximately equally distributed between the neritic and bathyal realms. Littoral species are few. They live partly embedded in mud or sand on the sea bottom, with only the smaller posterior end protruding into the water. Food consists of Foraminifera or similar organisms captured by the captacula (4, 5, 8).

Earliest geologic record of the Scaphopoda is from the Ordovician of Russia; it is, however, doubtful whether most of the species described therefrom have been correctly placed systematically. None have been recorded from the Silurian, but the class is well represented in the Devonian where three genera are recognized. Generic di-

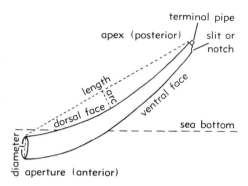

FIG. 28. Morphological features of Scaphopoda.

vergence was gradual during late Paleozoic and early Mesozoic, and modern forms did not appear until early Cretaceous. Maximum development of the class is attained in Recent times, the number of living species being in excess of the total number recorded from the Tertiary (Fig. 29).

Family DENTALIIDAE Gray, 1834

[Antalinae STOLICZKA, 1868; Scaphopoda G. O. SARS, 1878]

Shell generally tapering regularly throughout, sculptured or smooth, diameter greatest at aperture. Animal has conical foot with an encircling sheath expanded laterally and interrupted dorsally. *?Ord., Dev.-Rec.*

Dentalium LINNÉ, 1758 [*D. elephantinum; SD MONTFORT, 1810]. Shell curved and tapering, longitudinally sculptured, smooth or annulated. Embryonic whorls minute, fragile, and lost at an early growth stage. Apex commonly modified by a slit or notch due to absorption. Anterior aperture circular, or oblique, in many forms modified by longitudinal ribbing (4). *M.Trias.-Rec.*, cosmop.

D. (Dentalium) [=*Paradentalium* COTTON & GODFREY, 1933]. Prismatic or decidedly ribbed, especially toward apex where transverse section is polygonal; apex without notch or slit or with a short one (3). *U.Cret.-Rec.*, cosmop.——FIG. 30,4. *D. (D.) elephantinum* LINNÉ, Rec., Asia-E.Indies; ×0.5 (Pilsbry & Sharp, 1897).

D. (Antalis) H.ADAMS & A.ADAMS, 1854 [*non Dentale* DACOSTA, 1778; *nec Antalis* HERMANNSEN, 1846 (ICZN op. 361)] [*D. entalis LINNÉ, 1758; SD PILSBRY & SHARP, 1897] [=*Entalis* GRAY, 1847 (*non* SOWERBY, 1839); *Entaliopsis*

---

[1] Paleontologist, Department of Mines, Adelaide, South Australia.

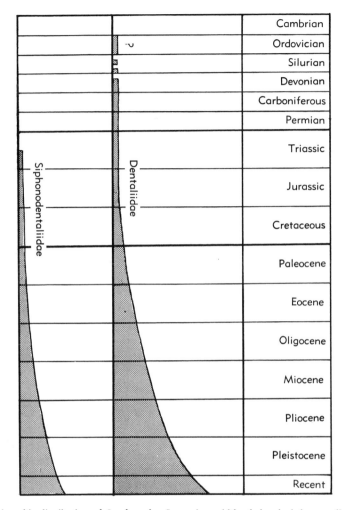

FIG. 29. Stratigraphic distribution of Scaphopoda. Increasing width of the shaded areas diagrammatically indicates expansion in numbers of known genera and subgenera (Ludbrook, n).

NEWTON & HARRIS, 1894]. Less strongly ribbed than *D. (Dentalium),* apical section not polygonal, apex generally with a V-shaped notch on or near convex side and a solid plug with central pipe or orifice (5). *M.Trias.-Rec.,* cosmop.——FIG. 30,5. *D. (A.) entalis* LINNÉ, Plio.-Rec., Eu.-N.Am.; *5a,* side; *5b,c,* posterior extremity; ×1 (5).

D. (Bathoxiphus) PILSBRY & SHARP, 1897 [*D. ensiculus* JEFFREYS, 1877]. Thin, conspicuously compressed laterally, nearly or quite smooth, with broad apical slit on convex side (5). *Rec.,* Eu.-N.Am.-Afr.-E.Indies.

D. (Coccodentalium) SACCO, 1896 [*D. radula* SCHRÖTER, 1784]. Shell with longitudinal, strongly granose ribs. Apex commonly truncate with a small central pipe. *M.Eoc.,* Eu.-E.Indies; *Rec.,* E.Indies.

D. (Compressidens) PILSBRY & SHARP, 1897 [*D. pressum* PILSBRY & SHARP, 1897]. Small, decidedly tapering, conspicuously compressed between convex and concave sides, weakly sculptured, nearly smooth; apex simple (5). *L.Oligo.,* Eu.-C.Am.-E.Indies; *Rec.,* N.Am.-C.Am.-Austral.-E.Indies.

D. (Episiphon) PILSBRY & SHARP, 1897 [*D. sowerbyi* GUILDING, 1834; SD SUTER, 1913]. Small, very slender, rather straight, needle-shaped or truncated, thin and fragile, glossy and smooth; apex with projecting pipe, or simple (5). *L.Jur.-Rec.,* cosmop.

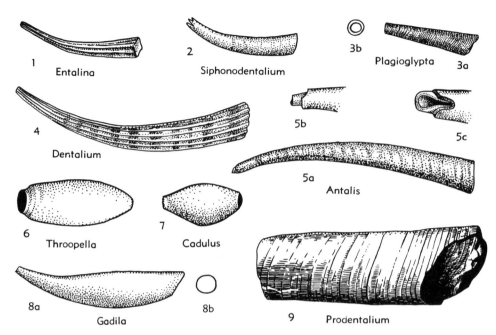

FIG. 30. Genera of the scaphopod families Dentaliidae and Siphonodentaliidae.

D. (**Fissidentalium**) FISCHER, 1885 [*D. ergasti-cum*] [=*Schizodentalium* SOWERBY, 1894]. Large and solid, with many longitudinal riblets, apex typically with a long slit, commonly simple (5). *L.Cret.-Rec., cosmop.*

D. (**Fustiaria**) STOLICZKA, 1868 [*D. circinatum* SOWERBY, 1823; SD PILSBRY & SHARP, 1897]. Arcuate, polished, sculptured with regular en-circling grooves that divide surface of the tube into short, oblique segments. Aperture circular, apex round or ovate, with very long straight linear slit on convex side. *L.Cret.-Tert.,* Eu.-Asia-E.Indies-Afr.-S.Am.; *Rec.,* E.Indies.

D. (**Gadilina**) FORESTI, 1895 [*D. triquetrum* BROCCHI, 1814]. Smooth and slender, imperfectly triangular in section, concave side flattened, con-vex side rounded (5). *L.Mio.,* Eu.-E.Indies-Austral.; *Rec.,* E.Indies.

D. (**Graptacme**) PILSBRY & SHARP, 1897 [*D. ebo-reum* CONRAD, 1846; SD WOODRING, 1925]. Shell with close, fine, deeply engraved longitudinal striae near apex, remainder smooth (5). *L.Eoc.,* Eu.-N.Am.; *Rec.,* cosmop.

D. (**Heteroschismoides**) LUDBROOK, *nom. subst.,* herein [pro *Heteroschisma* SIMROTH, 1895 (non WACHSMUTH, 1893)] [*D. subterfissum* JEFFREYS, 1877; SD PILSBRY & SHARP, 1897 (pro *Hetero-schisma* SIMROTH) herein affirmed pro *Hetero-schismoides*]. Coarsely striate or ribbed longi-tudinally with apical slit on concave side (5). *Rec.,* Atl.

D. (**Laevidentalium**) COSSMANN, 1888 [*D. in-certum* DESHAYES, 1825]. Moderate or large in size, smooth, with growth lines only; circular or slightly oval in section; apex simple or with slight notch on the convex side (5). *M.Trias.-Rec., cosmop.*

D. (**Lobantale**) COSSMANN, 1888 [*D. duplex* DE-FRANCE, 1819]. Slender, compressed, smooth; interior with 2 longitudinal ribs placed laterally one on each side, giving transverse section a bilobed shape (5). *M.Eoc.,* Eu.

D. (**Pseudantalis**) MONTEROSATO, 1884 [*D. rubes-cens* DESHAYES, 1825; SD SACCO, 1897]. Thin, shining, smooth; apex with long, straight, linear slit on the convex side. *L.Cret.-Rec.,* N.Hemi.

D. (**Rhabdus**) PILSBRY & SHARP, 1897 [*D. rec-tius* CARPENTER, 1865]. Nearly straight or slightly curved, shell very thin throughout and glossy, some with annular swellings; surface brilliant, polished, without longitudinal sculpture; aper-ture and apex simple (5). *L.Plio.,* E.Indies; *Rec.,* N.Am.-C.Am.-S.Am.-Asia-E.Indies.

D. (**Tesseracme**) PILSBRY & SHARP, 1898 [*D. quadrapicale* SOWERBY, 1860; SD WOODRING, 1925]. Square at or near apex, with angles on convex, concave, and lateral sides, becoming suborbicular at aperture. Apex with or without a short pipe (5). *M.Eoc.,* N.Am.-C.Am.; *Rec.,* N. Am.-C.Am.-E.Indies-Afr.

Plagioglypta PILSBRY & SHARP, 1897 [*Dentalium undulatum* MÜNSTER, 1844]. Shell tapering, cir-cular or elliptical in section, without longitudinal sculpture, with close and fine obliquely encircling

wrinkles throughout or on anterior portion. Aperture with a fairly long and broad slit. *?L.Ord.*, Russia; *U.Dev.-U.Cret.*, N.Am.-S.Am.-Eu.-Asia.——Fig. 30,*3*. **P. undulata* (MÜNSTER), Trias., Aus.(Tyrol); *3a,b,* side view and transv. sec., ×1 (Kittl, 1891).

Prodentalium YOUNG, 1942 [**P. raymondi*]. Shell with oblique growth lines and fine longitudinal ribs generally with a slightly zigzag alignment. *Dev. - Penn.(U.Carb.),* N.Am.-Eu.-Asia. —— Fig. 30,*9*. **P. raymondi,* Penn., USA(N.Mex.); ×0.5 (Young, 1942).

Family SIPHONODENTALIIDAE Simroth, 1894

[Gadilinae STOLICZKA, 1868; Siphonopoda G. O. SARS, 1878; Siphonopodidae SIMROTH, 1894]

Scaphopoda having the foot either expanded distally in a symmetrical disc with crenate continuous edge and with or without a median, finger-like projection, or simple and vermiform, without developed lateral processes. Shell small and generally smooth, commonly contracted toward mouth (8). *?M.Trias., L.Cret.-Rec.*

Cadulus PHILIPPI, 1844 [*Dentalium ovulum]. Tubular, circular or oval in section; somewhat arcuate, varying from cask-shaped to acicular, more or less bulging or swollen near middle or anteriorly, contracting toward aperture. Surface smooth or delicately striated (5). *L.Cret.,* Eu.-N.Am.-Greenl.; *Tert.-Rec.,* cosmop.

C. (Cadulus). Cask-shaped, short and obese, conspicuously swollen in middle, tapering rapidly toward both ends. Aperture simple. Apex simple, with wide circular callus or ledge within (5). *U.Cret.,* N.Am.; *Tert.,* N. Am.-W. Indies-Eu.; *Rec.,* Eu.-N. Am.-S. Am.-W. Indies-Afr.-E.Indies.——Fig. 30,*7*. **C. (C.) ovulum* (PHILIPPI), Mio.-Rec., Italy; ×4 (Pilsbry & Sharp, 1897).

C. (Dischides) JEFFREYS, 1867 [*Ditrupa polita S.V.WOOD, 1842] [=*Discides* SACCO, 1897]. Rather slender, only slightly bulging, apex cut into ventral and dorsal lobes by 2 deep lateral slits, one on each side (5). *M.Eoc.,* Eu.; *Rec.,* Eu.-E.Indies-Austral.-Oceanica.

C. (Gadila) GRAY, 1847 [*Dentalium gadus MONTAGU, 1803] [=*Helonyx* STIMPSON, 1865; *Loxoporus* JEFFREYS, 1883]. Rather slender and decidedly curved, convex ventrally, concave dorsally; more or less swollen near middle or toward aperture, more tapering toward apex, which lacks callus or has weak callous ring far within. Edges not slit (5). *L.Cret.-Rec., cosmop.*——Fig. 30,*8*. **C. (G.) gadus* (MONTAGU), Rec., Jamaica; *8a,b,* side and transv. sec., ×2 (Pilsbry & Sharp, 1897).

C. (Gadilopsis) WOODRING, 1925 [**Ditrupa dentalina* GUPPY, 1874]. Moderately small, very slender, needle-shaped, slightly swollen very near

aperture; sculptured with oblique growth lines on posterior; apical opening small, unslit. *L.Mio.-L.Plio.,* W.Indies-C.Am.-N.Z.

C. (Platyschides) HENDERSON, 1920 [**C. grandis* VERRILL, 1884]. Shell with 2 or 4 broad apical slits, lobes between low and wide (3). *M.Oligo.-Rec.,* N.Am.-C.Am.-S.Am.-W.Indies.

C. (Polyschides) PILSBRY & SHARP, 1897 [**Siphodentalium tetraschistum* WATSON, 1897]. Only slightly inflated above middle, apex with 4 or more slits (3). *M.Eoc.,* Eu.-N.Am.-W.Indies-C. Am.; *Rec.,* N. Am.-W. Indies - S. Am. - E. Indies-Austral.-Antarctica.

Entalina MONTEROSATO, 1872 [**Dentalium tetragonum* BROCCHI, 1814; SD SACCO, 1897] [=*Eudentalium* COTTON & GODFREY, 1933]. Shell *Dentalium*-like, small, largest at aperture, thence tapering to apex; strongly ribbed, angular in section near apex. Foot expanding distally into disc with digitate periphery, and having a median process or filament (5). *?M.Trias.,* Eu.; *Tert.,* Eu.-E.Indies; *Rec.,* Eu.-Afr.-N. Am.-E. Indies-Austral. —— Fig. 30,*1*. *E. quinquangularis* (FORBES), Rec., Eu.; ×1 (Pilsbry & Sharp, 1897).

Siphonodentalium M.SARS, 1859 [**Dentalium vitreum* M.SARS, 1851 (*non* GMELIN, 1791 =*Dentalium lobatum* SOWERBY, 1860)] [=*Siphodentalium* MONTEROSATO, 1874; *Siphonodontum, Tubidentalium* LOCARD, 1886]. Shell a smooth, arcuate, slightly tapering tube, largest at aperture, section circular or nearly so. Apex rather large, either slit into lobes or simple. Foot capable of expanding into terminal disc (5). *Paleoc.,* Eu.-Asia-Austral.; *Rec.,* Eu.-N.Am.-Arctic-W.Indies-E.Indies-Austral.-Antarctica.

S. (Siphonodentalium). Apex slit into lobes. *M. Eoc.,* Eu.Asia; *Rec.,* Eu.-N.Am.-Arctic-W.Indies-Antarctica.——Fig. 30,*2*. **S. lobatum* (SOWERBY), Rec., Atl.; ×1 (Pilsbry & Sharp, 1897).

S. (Pulsellum) STOLICZKA, 1868 [**S. lofotense* M. SARS, 1864; SD COSSMANN, 1888] [=*Siphonentalis* G.O.SARS, 1878]. Like *Siphonodentalium* but without apical slits. Foot-disc has filiform tentacle in middle. *Paleoc.,* Eu.-Asia; *Rec.,* Eu.-N.Am.-E. Indies-Austral.

INCERTAE SEDIS

?Throopella GREGER, 1933 [**T. typa*]. Shell tapering at each end, posterior more attenuate, anterior end crateriform with oblique, circular opening; collar or peristome in opening folding back on outside. *U.Dev.,* N.Am.——Fig. 30,*6*. **T. typa,* USA(Mo.); ×1 (Greger, 1933). Possibly not a scaphopod.

GENERIC NAMES FOR SUPPOSED SCAPHOPODA BUT BELONGING TO OTHER ORGANISMS

Ditrupa AUCTT. [*non* BERKELEY, 1835]. Vermes.
Gadus AUCTT. [*non* LINNÉ, 1758]. Pisces.

REFERENCES

Deshayes, M. G. P.
(1) 1825, *Anatomie et monographie du genre Dentale:* Soc. Histoire nat., v. 2, p. 322-378, pl. 15-18 (Paris).

Gardner, J. S.
(2) 1878, *On the Cretaceous Dentaliidae:* Geol. Soc. London, Quart. Jour., v. 34, p. 56-65.

Henderson, J. B.
(3) 1920, *A monograph of the East American scaphopod mollusks:* Smithson. Inst. U. S. Natl. Mus., Bull. 111, 177 p., 20 pl.

Lacaze-Duthiers, Henri
(4) 1856, *Histoire de l'organization et du développement du Dentale:* Ann. Sci. nat., ser. 4, Zoologie, v. 6, p. 225-281; v. 7, p. 5-51; 171-225; v. 8, p. 18-44.

Pilsbry, H. A. & Sharp, B.
(5) 1897-98, *Scaphopoda: in* Tryon, G. W., Manual of Conchology, v. 17, 280 p., 39 pl.

Plate, L. H.
(6) 1892, *Über den Bau und die Verwandschaftsbeziehungen der Solenoconchen:* Zool. Jahrb., Abt. für Anatomie und Ontogenie der Thiere, v. 5, p. 301-386.

Richardson, L.
(7) 1906, *Liassic Dentaliidae:* Geol. Soc. London, Quart. Jour., v. 62, p. 573-596.

Simroth, H.
(8) 1894-95, *[Scaphopoda]:* in Bronn, H. G., Klassen und Ordnungen des Thier-Reichs, v. 3, p. 354-467.

AMPHINEURA

By Allyn G. Smith[1]

CONTENTS

INTRODUCTION

The Amphineura are strictly marine mollusks. A living amphineuran has a typical bilaterally symmetrical body with an anterior mouth and a posterior anus. The foot is ventral and adapted for creeping. The animal has a partly or completely enclosed mantle. Internally the alimentary tract is nearly straight, generally with a radula present in a poorly defined head. Gills project into a shallow mantle cavity situated on either side of the foot between it and the mantle edge; they may be paired or many, posterior or lateral. The nervous system consists of an esophageal ring with ganglia and four longitudinal cords, two of which are ventral and two lateral. There are no cephalic eyes, tentacles, or otocysts.

The name Amphineura was proposed first in 1876 by Herman von Ihering as a phylum separate from the Mollusca, to include the classes Placophora (chitons) and Aplacophora (Solenogastres). Until recent years most students of the classification of these marine invertebrates have considered the Amphineura as a class consisting of two orders, Polyplacophora (or Loricata), including the chitons, and Aplacophora, comprising forms without shell covering, known also as Solenogastres. The Amphineura are here considered as a class separate from the Gastropoda and are treated as composed of the subclasses Polyplacophora and Aplacophora.

[1] Research Malacologist, California Academy of Sciences, San Francisco, Calif.

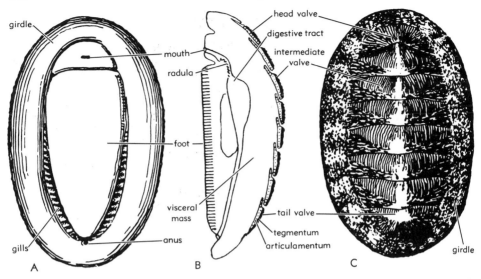

FIG. 31. General features of a modern amphineuran—a moderately large chiton (Polyplacophora), ×1, showing ventral and dorsal aspects *(A,C)* with median longitudinal section *(B)*. (Modified from Moore in Moore, Lalicker & Fischer, "Invertebrate Fossils," copyright 1952, courtesy of McGraw-Hill Book Company, New York.)

The Polyplacophora, or chitons, generally have a series of eight overlapping shells or valves, situated dorsally, and held in place by a tough muscular girdle, which may be either nude or variously ornamented with spicules, scales, bristles, or hairy protuberances. Earliest fossil polyplacophoran remains (generally separate valves) occur in the Upper Cambrian and have been found sparingly in rocks of all geological ages, but they seem to be rarest of all in Mesozoic deposits. The chitons are most prolific at the present day and comprise an extensive world-wide group.

The Aplacophora, or Solenogastres, are wormlike invertebrates representing a specialized and probably degenerate group with definite amphineuran characters. Adults have no shells. No fossil remains have been reported; hence the group is at present of no particular significance to paleontologists.

POLYPLACOPHORA
GENERAL FEATURES

The Polyplacophora, commonly known as chitons, are sluggish crawlers on the sea bottom. They live on or under rocks, in the interstices of coral, in coral holes, and in seaweed holdfasts; a few specialized types occur between the sheaths of certain species

of eel-grass. They are found mostly in the littoral zone but may be present at all depths down to 2,300 fathoms. Species have been described from nearly all seas.

They have an evenly elliptical or elongate outline and their thickness along the median dorsal line is roughly one-fourth of their greatest width (Fig. 31). The body is bilaterally symmetrical. No head is visible from the dorsal side and there are no tentacles or other projections reaching beyond the periphery of the animal. A marginal band of muscular tissue, generally of uniform width, is commonly differentiated from the central portion of the back. This band, called the **girdle,** belongs with the soft parts. Its covering may be nude and leathery, or it may consist of various types of decorative processes, including fine to coarse calcareous spicules or spines, small, rounded imbricate scales, or chitinous hairy projections of simple or dendritic form. The girdles of some species may have these decorations in various combinations, whereas others display conspicuous bunches of spicules, called sutural tufts, that occur at regular intervals (Fig. 32).

The central part of the back consists of a calcareous shell in the form of a series of articulating pieces (normally eight) with

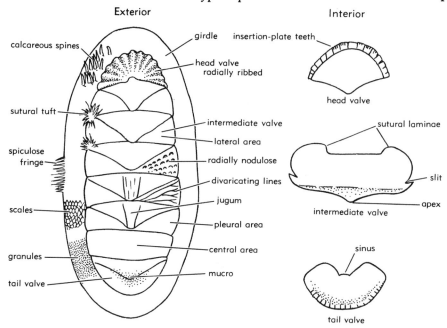

FIG. 32. Morphological features of Polyplacophora. (Modified from F. M. Bayer in R. Tucker Abbott, "American Seashells," copyright 1954, courtesy of D. Van Nostrand Company, Inc., Princeton, N.J.)

joints between them running transverse to the axis of the body. This allows a chiton, when disturbed, to roll up like a pill bug (wood louse), bending at each joint between the shell pieces. The surface of the separate shells may be smooth or variously sculptured with ribs, pustules, or microscopic granules, occurring alone or in combination. This sculpture is invariably in low relief, when present, without the prominent protuberances or projections that are found on some gastropods. In a few species the dorsal shells may be almost or completely buried in an extension of the girdle over them.

The underside of a chiton consists mostly of a broad, flat muscular **foot**, like that of a marine snail. A well-marked groove is visible along the border, for the mantle cavity opens in this position. At one end is the **head**, which is identified merely by a constriction separating it from the foot and by the presence of the mouth opening. The anus is at the opposite extremity.

A chiton of average size is 1 to 3 inches long and its width amounts to about a fourth to a third of its length. Some minute species measure only 0.25 inch long in the adult stage, but the largest known species,

the giant chiton of the West Coast of North America, reaches a length of 13 to 14 inches.

Coloration of the upper part of the shells is quite variable, even between individuals of the same species, although in most species the color pattern is fairly constant. Black, brown, white, and various tints of red and green form the usual color range, some species being quite strikingly maculated or banded.

The food habits of chitons are not well known. Some are wholly herbivorous, feeding on various kinds of marine algae; others feed on bryozoans, hydroids, and even on very young barnacles; still others appear to be more or less omnivorous. Seemingly, a close relationship is discernible between food habits and the ecological niches where chitons normally live. Also, there is evidence that polyplacophorans have homing habits similar to those of limpets, coming out from their hiding places at night in order to feed and then returning to the same spot where they stay during the day.

Breeding seasons vary with species. Eggs are laid in jelly-like strings or masses, similar to those of many gastropods. Most chitons pass through a free-swimming larval

stage of short duration before settling to the bottom to begin development of the parental form. Several species in the Callistoplacidae, however, are reported to be viviparous, brooding their young between the underside of the mantle and the foot until they are fully formed with complete shells.

MORPHOLOGY OF SOFT PARTS

Strange to say, main features of the soft anatomy of chitons are more important in paleontological study than the characters of the hard parts, for a comparison of the internal organization of chitons with the structure of gastropods and other mollusks throws considerable light on the evolutionary significance of the symmetrical or asymmetrical arrangements of the body parts. The shell of chitons furnishes little help in this direction, and accordingly, analysis of its special features merits effort only in proportion to the importance of the group as fossils, which is not great, although it can throw some light on interesting evolutionary development.

The soft parts of a chiton are essentially those of a simplified, perfectly symmetrical prototype mollusk, which has posterior placement of the respiratory apparatus and anus. The chiton does not quite meet these specifications because the gills, though symmetrically paired, are multiplied in number, especially in the more highly developed groups, evidently by proliferation from an original single pair. Some chitons have two gills on each side of the anus but in others the number ranges to 40 on each side, filling most of the anteriorly extended mantle cavities that stretch like grooves along the sides of the body to the head. Whether few or many gills are present, one pair dominates in size; and because this pair is located at or near the rear end of the mantle cavity, it may be interpreted as the primitive initial pair, corresponding to the single pair in primitive marine snails. The gill structure is also the same, having double rows of leaflets.

The alimentary tract is a tube extending from the mouth, on the underside of the head, to the anus located on the mid-line of the body at the rear. Chitons have a hard rasplike mouth structure composed of horny recurved denticles borne on a tough, flexible ribbon. This is the **radula,** which is bilaterally symmetrical and has eight denticles of varying strength and configuration on each side of a central one, or a total of 17 in each transverse row. The strongest of these denticles is the so-called major lateral, which occupies a position second to the right and left of the central row.

The polyplacophoran heart contains two auricles. There are two kidneys. All chitons are unisexual. In most species the gonad is single and median, lying on the dorsal side of the body between the aorta and the intestine. The genital aperture is situated in front of the renal aperture between two of the posterior gills.

The anatomy of the chitons undoubtedly closely approaches the internal organization of the ancient primitive snails, which are characterized by bilateral symmetry of form. Chitons are specialized in the adaptation of their body for longitudinal bending. They have persisted throughout geologic time with extremely little change. The archaic symmetrical gastropods, however, vanished early in Mesozoic time. Moreover, in the modern chitons there is no present indication of continuing degradation of essential parts.

MORPHOLOGY OF HARD PARTS

The discrete calcareous shell elements of chitons ordinarily comprise eight main pieces that somewhat inaptly are called **valves.** Although living specimens have been found occasionally with seven or nine normally formed valves, these are rare deviations. However, what appears to be a perfectly normal seven-valved species has been discovered in the late Ordovician of Scotland, enough examples having been collected to verify its validity. The matrix in which it occurs indicates a sand-dwelling type, which, if true, makes it the only one known with this habitat.

The chiton valves cover the central part of the back. They are formed as transverse thickenings of the dorsal cuticle behind the velum, the upper shell layer being the first to be laid down. All eight valves generally make their appearance simultaneously but in some species the eighth valve is formed later than the others. Until recently, chiton valves were considered to consist of two layers. The upper or dorsal layer, termed

tegmentum (*tegmen*, roof), is relatively soft, being perforated by a labyrinth of fine and coarse pores. The lower or ventral layer, called **articulamentum**, is quite different in structure and appearance, for it is dense, porcelaneous, and laminated. This lower layer projects into the girdle and underlies the valves next in series, like tiles on a roof. Head and tail valves are usually different in shape from the six intermediate valves, the latter commonly being similar in contour. Based on the investigations of KNORRE (1925) and BERGENHAYN (1931), chiton valves have been shown to contain four layers, which are (1) the **periostracum,** an extremely thin outer dorsal layer equivalent to that of other mollusk types; (2) the tegmentum, immediately underlying the periostracum; (3) the **articulamentum** *(sensu stricto),* or layer composing the insertion plates and the sutural laminae of a valve; and (4) the **hypostracum,** or lowest ventral layer underlying the articulamentum and having a somewhat different crystalline structure. In some of the more highly developed chitons another layer, the **mesostracum,** occurs between the articulamentum and the tegmentum. The existence of all or only some of these shell layers in the valves of both Recent and fossil chitons serves as a further indication of evolutionary development and thus is being found helpful in classification of these animals.

MORPHOLOGICAL TERMS APPLICABLE TO POLYPLACOPHORA

The following alphabetically arranged glossary applying to the Polyplacophora defines the terms most commonly used by specialists in descriptions and in systematic keys developed for identification purposes.

aesthete. Sensory organ terminating in the tegmentum of certain chiton species. Larger ones, called *megalaesthetes,* take the form of eyes, with cornea, lens, pigment layer, iris, and retina, and may or may not be accompanied by one or more smaller ones, called *micraesthetes.* The eyes in a living chiton shell, when present, appear as tiny black spots, scattered or in regular lines radiating from the apex of a valve on the dorsal side.

apex. Central point of the posterior edge of an intermediate valve; sometimes termed the beak or umbo of the valve.

apical area. Short part of the periostracum and tegmentum on the head and intermediate valves of all chitons that is adjacent to the posterior

dorsal edge of a valve and which extends over the edge and onto the ventral side.

apophyses (or apophysis plates). *See* sutural laminae.

articulamentum. Formerly used to indicate the inner, usually hard, semiporcelaneous shell layer, generally projecting past the tegmentum on the sides and front of the valves to form the insertion plates and the sutural laminae; recently restricted to indicate the shell layer between tegmentum and hypostracum, called the articulamentum *(sensu stricto)* and composed of several separate components of crystalline shell structure.

beak. Angular projection of the apex of an intermediate valve. A similar projection of the upper surface of the valve anteriorly and between the sutural laminae is termed a *false beak.* Beaked valves are termed *mucronate.*

body valve. See intermediate valve.

central area. Upper surface of an intermediate valve lying centrally, usually differing in sculpture from the lateral areas.

dorsal area. See jugal area.

eaves. Portions of the tegmentum just over the line where the insertion plates and the sutural laminae project from under it.

eave tissue. Composition of the shell material that forms the eaves; this may be porcelaneous or "spongy," i.e., riddled with microscopic tubules.

false beak. See beak.

gills (or ctenidia). Triangular branchial plumes underneath the girdle and protected by the foot, extending from near the tail forward from a fourth to the entire length of the foot; gills are *posterior* (short) in the lower chiton groups, and long *(ambient)* in the more highly developed groups.

girdle. Flexible muscular integument, plain or "leathery," or variously ornamented, in which the valves are imbedded and which holds them in place.

head valve. Anterior valve, numbered *i* in the series.

hypostracum. Lowest ventral calcareous layer of a valve.

insertion plate. Narrow marginal extension of the articulamentum layer in the head and tail valves and at the sides of the intermediate valves, which project into the girdle; sometimes termed the *lamina of insertion.* This structure is absent or nearly obsolete in lower groups of chitons.

intermediate valve. Any one of the valves between head and tail valves; sometimes called *median* or *body valve.* Numbered, in order, *ii* to *vii,* respectively, from the head end of the animal.

jugal angle. Angle formed by the two halves of an intermediate valve.

jugal area (or tract). Upper surface of a valve immediately adjacent to the jugum, sculptured differently from the rest of the surface in some forms; also called *dorsal area.*

jugal sinus. Depression or "bay" between sutural laminae; sometimes called *sutural sinus.*

jugum. Longitudinal ridge of an intermediate valve, when present; may be sharp or rounded.

lamina of insertion. See insertion plate.

lateral area. Portion of upper surface of an intermediate valve, commonly triangular in shape, lying at the side and toward its posterior, usually sculptured diagonally and set off from remainder of upper surface by a diagonal ridge of varying prominence.

lateropleural area. Entire upper portion of the side slopes of an intermediate valve in some species; a term used to denote sculpture of a valve that is much the same, with no particular line of demarcation between the lateral and pleural areas.

median valve. See intermediate valve.

mesostracum. Calcareous shell layer in certain more highly developed living chiton species, lying between the tegmentum and the articulamentum *(s. s.).*

mucro. Point or projection on the tail valve, usually marking a separation between the configuration of the central and posterior areas. The mucro may be prominent or obsolete; anterior, median or posterior in position; elevated or depressed in shape; or rarely may be curved upward.

mucronate valve. *See* beak.

periostracum. Uppermost, extremely thin layer of a valve on top of the tegmentum, composed of organic material.

pleural area. Side slopes of the upper part of a valve, not including the jugal area or lateral areas where the latter are well differentiated.

posterior sinus. Embayment in posterior median line of a tail valve, formed by the tegmentum and in some forms by the articulamentum set.

radula. Bilaterally symmetrical lingual ribbon set with chitinous denticles. There is a simple-cusped central rachidian tooth, on each side of which, in order, are a translucent minor lateral or varying form, a major lateral with a conspicuous black cusp having 1 to 4 denticles (larger than on any other teeth), two bosslike or thickened uncinal plates of irregular shape, a twisted spatulate uncinal, and three scalelike or slightly thickened external uncini—a total of 17 in each transverse row.

scales. Term usually used to denote small calcareous bodies decorating the dorsal side of the girdle in many species; normally, they are closely set or overlapping and of various shapes, smooth or with minute striations.

slit. Abrupt transverse indentation in the insertion plate.

slit ray. Shallow groove or row of pores or pits extending from a slit to the apex of the valve on the ventral side.

spicules (or spines). Dorsal girdle decorations varying widely with species in size, shape, and frequency. They may be closely set, sparse, gathered into scattered conspicuous bunches, or a combination of these. Both scales and spicules may occur together.

sutural laminae. Sharp, platelike anterior projections of the articulamentum varying in prominence, extending from either side of an intermediate or tail valve. When present, they are lobe-shaped, project into the girdle, and are overlapped by the posterior portion of the preceding valve when in normal position. These two laminae may be separated by a sinus or partially joined by a laminar extension of the articulamentum. (Also called apophysis plates.)

sutural plate. Lamina of articulamentum across the jugal sinus of intermediate and tail valves, extending between the sutural laminae. This is usually thin, when present, and may be finely denticulated and notched at the sides.

sutural sinus. See jugal sinus.

tail valve. Posterior valve.

teeth. Portions of articulamentum between slits, usually most prominent in the tail valve. Teeth may be *pectinated* (crenulated or finely cut like a comb) or *propped* (with edges thickened on the outside); they are sharp and smooth in many species. This term applies to the valves of a chiton and should not be confused with the denticles of the radula, also called teeth.

tegmentum. Outer, usually softer and somewhat porous calcareous layer of a valve just below the periostracum; this shell layer, together with the mesostracum (when present) and articulamentum layers, corresponds to the *ostracum* of gastropods and pelecypods.

terminal area. Upper surface of head or tail valve. Tail valves in some species are separated into a central area and a posterior area by two dividing lines on either side of the valve radiating from the mucro.

uncinal plate. *See* radula.

valve. One of the discrete shells or "plates" of chiton skeleton; commonly numbered *i* to *viii* beginning with the head valve to indicate the exact position.

valve coverage (or overlap). When two contiguous valves lie in such a relation to each other that the rear edge of one covers the whole front edge of the one posterior to it, this is termed *complete coverage*. If only a small part of the front edge of the next valve is overlapped, coverage is termed *partial*. If only the apical part of a valve overlaps the next one, this is called *jugal coverage*. The extent of valve coverage in some primitive chiton species is indicated by the degree to which the tegmentum of the apical area extends over the edge of a valve on to the ventral side.

OCCURRENCE AS FOSSILS

Undoubted chiton species have been reported and described from rocks of prac-

tically all ages from Upper Cambrian to Tertiary. In the search for a true ancestral form from which the chitons stemmed, one must look far back in the Precambrian, for such a form must have been extremely ancient.

Most Paleozoic chitons are distinguished from later ones by weak development of imbrication of the valves. These fitted against each other with only a very slight overlap and are characterized by the complete absence of projecting structures such as the insertion plates and sutural laminae of modern forms. In some species the valves are massive and thick with little or no indication of an articulamentum layer. Mesozoic and Cenozoic chitons are much like modern forms and are about the same in size, although an undescribed species from the Permian of Texas has large valves, indicating that the animal was at least 5 inches long. In general, most Paleozoic types of polyplacophorans died out before the Mesozoic. However, one of the more primitive living genera *(Lepidopleurus)* has had an extraordinarily long existence, being reported as far back as the Carboniferous.

The number of described species of fossil chitons has not been exactly determined but must be at least 350. This does not include a number of species, mistaken for chitons and described as such, but which actually belong elsewhere. Some are based on barnacle plates, partial casts of trilobites or other crustaceans, inside casts of portions of the septa of ammonites, and aptychi of ammonites. Certain older patellid gastropods also were originally thought to be chitonoid. A census of the distribution of fossil species of chitons by geological age made by C. T. Berry (1939) showed totals of 90 Paleozoic species, 21 Mesozoic species, and 145 Cenozoic species, 256 in all. Since 1939, numerous additional species have been described but hardly any from the Mesozoic, which emphasizes an apparent scarcity of chitons in this part of the column that is noteworthy. Chitons exhibit an almost explosive development in Recent time, as evidenced by the fact that no less than 500 species and subspecies have been described. A compilation of data made by me, in which *nomina nuda* and synonymized species are excluded but which takes account of unnamed species reported in the literature shows distribution of presently known fossil

polyplacophorans as follows: Ordovician, 9; Silurian, 8; Devonian, 16; Carboniferous and Permian, 40 (Paleozoic, 73, amounting to 22 per cent of total); Triassic, 6; Jurassic, 18; Cretaceous, 7 (Mesozoic, 31, amounting to 9 per cent of total); Eocene, 20; Oligocene, 8; Miocene, 93; Pliocene, 67; Pleistocene, 50; Tertiary undifferentiated, 10 (Cenozoic, 248, amounting to 69 per cent of total). In this tabulation species known also from the Recent include: Miocene, 2; Pliocene, 14; Pleistocene, 40; Tertiary undifferentiated, 3.

Normally, only the disarticulated valves of fossil chitons are found, but there are instances in which all eight valves have been discovered together. Only two instances are known of the fossil occurrence of other chiton parts. One from the Ordovician clearly shows a mass of spicules in what once was the girdle of a complete individual (Fig. 33,2). The other from Middle Pennsylvanian rocks carries the impression of at least eight rows of denticles in the radula (Fig. 33,1). Theoretically, in any adequate sample of disarticulated valves, the end valves should be found in the ratio of one to three intermediate valves. This may not hold true for certain species having massive tail valves that are less liable to destruction or disintegration. The spongy tegmentum layer also often is lost in fossilization, leaving little on which to base a firm identification. While girdle scales, spicules or other girdle processes have not been reported except in one instance, this does not mean that they should not be diligently looked for when microscopic work is done on the washings of marine sediments. A single girdle scale or spicule of characteristic form could easily be sufficient for generic identification.

CLASSIFICATION

Classification of chitons is in a "fluid" state and probably will continue for some time. Most present-day systems stem largely from Pilsbry's magnificent work published in the *Manual of Conchology,* volumes 14 and 15 (1892-94), and are based on valve and girdle configuration and characters. The radula, though used by Thiele and others for systematic arrangement, has not proved adequate by itself. The chiton classification most useful to paleontologists must

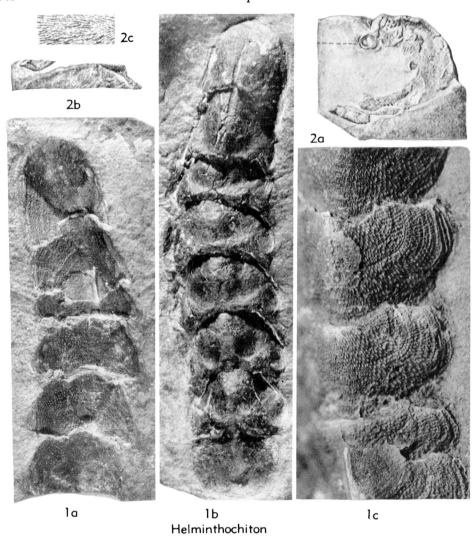

2c

2b

2a

1a   1b   1c

Helminthochiton

Fig. 33. Paleozoic chitons *(Helminthochiton)*. *1. H. concinnus* Richardson, holotype, M.Penn.(Desmoines.), Francis Creek Sh., near Coal City, Ill.; *1a,* anterior part of specimen, mold of dorsal side, showing head valve and next-following intermediate valves, ×2.4; *1b,* mold of underside of shell showing all eight valves with impression of radula on head valve (at top) and intermediate valve *ii* behind it, ×2.4; *1c,* intermediate valves showing ornament, ×5 (50). *2. H. thraivensis* Cowper Reed, Ord., Scot.; *2a,* long. sec. of complete individual showing preserved mass of spicules, ×1; *2b,* internal mold of 3 successive valves, side view, ×3; *2c,* enlarged portion of spicular mass, ca. ×5 (Cowper Reed).

of necessity omit girdle characters, important though these may be. For the present, at least, it would seem logical to use Pilsbry's system, based largely on valve configuration, modified where appropriate by a consideration of the valve structure as developed by Knorre and Bergenhayn. The systematic classification of the Polyplacophora used in the following pages has been developed with this in mind, with the view, also, to avoid over-complication. Admittedly

it may be far from an adequate and workable system but should serve the needs of workers on this interesting not-well-known group.

APLACOPHORA
GENERAL FEATURES

The Aplacophora have a subcylindrical or vermiform body without shelly plates or valves, at least in the adult stage. The body is completely invested by a mantle consist-

ing of a spiculose integument, which may be continuous or interrupted by a longitudinal central furrow. The calcareous spicules are of various shapes and in some genera have an internal cavity. The foot is rudimentary or aborted. The mantle cavity terminates in a posterior cloaca containing rudimentary gills in addition to outlets of the anus and nephridia. In one order (Neomeniida) the animals are hermaphrodite, but in the other (Chaetodermatida) the sexes are separate.

Habitats of the Aplacophora range from shallow marine water down to at least 8,000 feet. Some burrow in mud; others are associated with colonial coelenterates. They are found in nearly all seas.

No fossil remains of aplacophorans have been reported so far, although future careful micropaleontological investigations may result in identifying spicules belonging to this group.

CLASSIFICATION

The Aplacophora are divided into 2 orders defined mainly by the presence of a distinct longitudinal ventral groove (Neomeniida) or its absence (Chaetodermatida), but also by the bisexual nature and lack of a differentiated liver in the first and by the unisexual nature and presence of a liver in the second. The Neomeniida generally are grouped in 4 famiiles (67 genera, 160 species), whereas the Chaetodermatida contain a single family (4 genera, 27 species). These are indicated with brief diagnoses in the latter part of the following section devoted to systematic descriptions.

SYSTEMATIC DESCRIPTIONS
Class AMPHINEURA von Ihering, 1876

[=Isopleura LANKESTER, 1883; Aculifera HATSCHEK, 1888]

Aquatic, marine, bilaterally symmetrical mollusks having an external mantle that bears a series of exposed dorsal or, less commonly, internal calcareous plates, or is stiffened by disseminated calcareous spicules. Head partially or not differentiated in form; body oval, elongate, or flattened; foot expanded and developed for creeping or wormlike, with a ventral groove or none. Nervous system consisting of an esophageal ring with ganglia and 4 longitudinal cords, 2 ventral and 2 lateral; no cephalic eyes,

tentacles or otocysts. Gills paired or many, posterior or lateral; mouth anterior, usually with a radula; anus posterior and median. *U.Cam.-Rec.*

Subclass POLYPLACOPHORA de Blainville, 1816

[*nom. correct.* GRAY, 1821 (*ex* Polyplacophores DE BLAINVILLE, 1816), validation proposed L. R. Cox, ICZN pend.] [=Loricata SCHUMACHER, 1817; Crepipoda GOLDFUSS, 1820; Polyplaxiphora FÉRUSSAC, 1821; Polyplaxiphora DE BLAINVILLE, 1824 (*non* FÉRUSSAC, 1821); Lamellata LATREILLE, 1825; Polyplaxiphorae MENKE, 1828; Polyplakiphora DE BLAINVILLE, 1829; Cyclobranchia SWAINSON, 1840 (*non* CUVIER, 1817); Placophora VON IHERING, 1876; Polyplaciphora DALL, 1879; Polybranchiata SPENGEL, 1881; Lepidoglossa THIELE, 1893]

Amphineurans of type commonly called chitons, protected by an encircling girdle in which a dorsal series of calcareous plates or valves, generally 8, is partially or wholly imbedded, valves overlapping in greater or lesser degree; head differentiated; with ventral sole adapted for creeping; gills numerous, occupying a ventral groove between foot and girdle; radula present, heterodont. Sexes separate. *U.Cam.-Rec.*

Order PALEOLORICATA Bergenhayn, 1955

[=Eoplacophora PILSBRY, 1893 (*partim*)]

Primitive chitons with valve structure consisting of periostracum, tegmentum, and hypostracum, lacking articulamentum, and therefore without insertion plates and sutural laminae; valves generally thick and massive. *U.Cam.-U.Cret.*

Suborder CHELODINA Bergenhayn, 1943

Shell composed of 8 valves with tegmentum which may or may not be divided into fairly well-marked areas; sculpture, when present, consisting of fine to coarse transverse growth lines or ridges, generally following configuration of anterior edge of valves. *L.Ord.-U.Cret.*

Family CHELODIDAE Bergenhayn, 1943

Intermediate valves longer than wide; tegmentum not divided into areas, or if present, developed very weakly. *L.Ord.-U.Cret.*

Chelodes DAVIDSON & KING, 1874 [**C. bergmani*] [?=Sagmaplaxus OEHLERT, 1881]. Body fairly large and much elongated; intermediate valves heart- or wedge-shaped, thick and massive, with length of each 1.5 times width, and in longitudinal cross section sloping away from well-developed semicircular or angular transverse ventral ridge

located subcentrally; apical areas long, extending on ventral side of valve to internal ridge; anterior sides of valves may be rolled over edges so as to form narrow channels and a small pocket at apex; valve coverage partial. *L.Ord.-Sil., ?L. Dev.,* Eu.(Swed.-Scot.-?Fr.-Czech.) - N. Am.(Ala.-Minn.).——Fig. 34,5. **C. bergmani* M.Sil.(Gotl.), Swed.; *5a,* reconstr., ×0.75; *5b,c,* valve (type), ×2.25 (8*).

Family GOTLANDOCHITONIDAE Bergenhayn, 1955

Relatively small, with intermediate valves wider than long, approximating those of living chitons in general configuration; tegmentum with weak or clearly developed areas. *Sil.*

Gotlandochiton BERGENHAYN, 1955 [**G. interplicatus*]. Tegmentum areas clearly defined; valve coverage jugal or complete. *Sil.,* Swed.——Fig. 34,4. **G. interplicatus,* Gotl.; reconstr., ×1 (8*).——Fig. 34,7. *G. troedssoni* BERGENHAYN, Gotl.; intermed. valve (type), ×3.4 (8*).——Fig. 34,8. *G. laterodepressus* BERGENHAYN, Gotl.; intermed. valve (type), ×3.5 (8*).

Family SCANOCHITONIDAE Bergenhayn, 1943

Intermediate valves wider than long, nearly semicircular or triangular in shape, with tegmentum divided into distinct areas. *U.Cret.*

Scanochiton BERGENHAYN, 1943 [**S. jugatus*]. Outline of intermediate valves nearly semicircular; tegmentum divided into lateral and pleural areas, and broad, triangular, elevated jugal area; head valve semicircular, lacking well-marked division into tegmentum areas; valve coverage partial. *U. Cret.,* Eu.(Swed.).——Fig. 34,6. **S. jugatus,* Senon.(Mammillatus Z.); *6a,* reconstr., ×1 (8*); *6b,* intermed. valve (type), ×4; *6c,* head valve, ×4 (6*b,c,*42*).

Olingechiton BERGENHAYN, 1943 [**O. triangulatus*]. Intermediate valves triangular; tegmentum divided into a raised rectangular jugal area flanked by 2 rather narrow, unwaved lateral areas, sculptured throughout by minute tubercles and distinct lines of growth; valve coverage jugal; end valves unknown. *U.Cret.,* Eu.(Swed.).——Fig. 34,3. **O. triangulatus,* Senon. (Mammillatus Z.); *3a,* reconstr., ×1 (8*);*3b,* 2 associated intermed. valves (type), ×2.5 (42*).

Haeggochiton BERGENHAYN, 1955 [**H. haeggi*]. Intermediate valves trapezoidal; tegmentum surface divided into 2 distinct lateral areas raised above a depressed and somewhat concave median area; valve coverage jugal; end valves unknown. *U.Cret.,* Eu.(Swed.).——Fig. 34,1. **H. haeggi,* Senon.

(Mammillatus Z.); *1a,* reconstr., ×1 (8*); *1b,* half of intermed. valve, ×6.25 (8*).

Ivoechiton BERGENHAYN, 1955 [**I. levis*]. Intermediate valves rectangular in shape, high-arched and rounded, with jugal angle of about 90°; surface of tegmentum not divided into distinct areas, completely smooth; valve coverage complete; end valves unknown. *U.Cret.,* Eu.(Swed.).——Fig. 34, 2. **I. levis,* Senon. (Mammillatus Z.); *2a,* reconstr., ×1 (8*); *2b,* intermed. valve (type), ×2 (8*).

Suborder SEPTEMCHITONINA Bergenhayn, 1955

Body narrow, wormlike, about 17 times longer than wide, with 7 exposed, long and narrow, overlapping dorsal valves. *U.Ord.*

Family SEPTEMCHITONIDAE Bergenhayn, 1955

Surface of tegmentum of all valves divided into distinct areas; valve coverage complete. *U.Ord.*

Septemchiton BERGENHAYN, 1955 [**S. vermiformis*]. Head and intermediate valves with triangular anterior area bounded by 2 lateral areas; tail valve with very long triangular central area terminating in a posterior mucro near end of valve, and bounded by very narrow, short posterior area which is perpendicular to valve axis; sides of valves slope rather steeply from a sharp jugal ridge; areas of tegmentum are set off by well-developed ridges decorated with small, closely set tubercles. [Fossils occur in a fine-grained sandstone matrix, leading to supposition that the animal was a sand dweller.] *U.Ord.* Eu.(S.Scot.).——Fig. 35,1. **S. vermiformis; 1a,b,* head and intermed. valves showing sculpture, ×8; *1c-e,* schematic diagrams of valve areas; *1f,* reconstr., ×1.6 (8*).

Order NEOLORICATA Bergenhayn, 1955

Valve structure consisting of periostracum, tegmentum, articulamentum *(s.s.),* and hypostracum layers, some more highly developed groups with mesostracum layer also; except in more primitive families, articulamentum extending out from under tegmentum in form of insertion plates and sutural laminae. *Carb.-Rec.*

Suborder LEPIDOPLEURINA Thiele, 1910

[Eochitonia DALL, 1889 *(partim);* =Eoplacophora PILSBRY, 1893 *(partim);* Protochitonina ASHBY, 1929 *(partim);* Lepidopleurida THIELE, 1931; Gryphochitonida QUENSTEDT, 1932 *(partim);* Isoplacophora COTTON & WEEDING, 1939 *(partim)*]

Tegmentum surface of head valve with a single shell area only, located anteriorly, on intermediate valves divided into a central and 2 lateral areas but on tail valve into central and posterior areas with a mucro (Fig. 36,*1a-c*). *Carb.-Rec.*

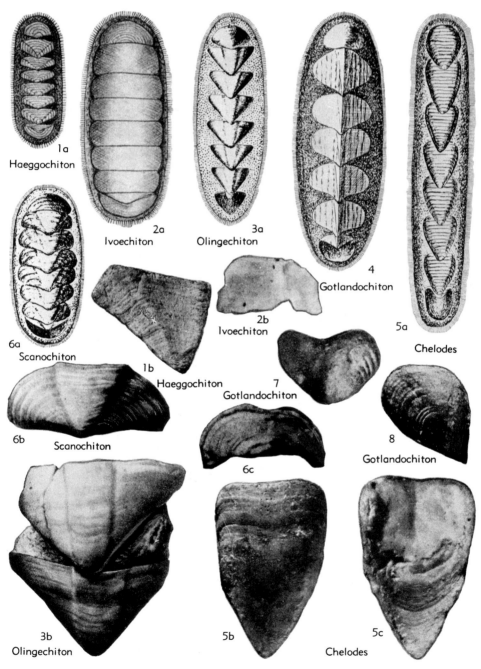

Fig. 34. Paleoloricata; Chelodina (Chelodidae, Gotlandochitonidae, Scanochitonidae) (p. *149-150*).

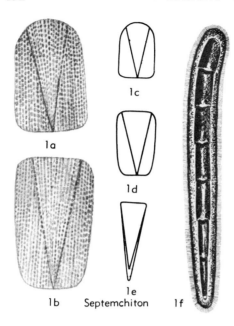

Fig. 35. Paleoloricata; Septemchitonina (Septem-
chitonidae) (p. *150*).

Family LEPIDOPLEURIDAE
Pilsbry, 1892

[=Holochiton Fischer, 1885 (classed as genus); Eochiton Fischer, 1885 (classed as subgenus); Leptochitonidae Dall, 1889 *(partim)*; Gryphochitonidae Pilsbry, 1900 *(partim)*; Protochitonidae Ashby, 1925 *(partim)*]

Relatively small (less than 2 inches long); valves generally sculptured with granules closely set in lines or quincunx; valve coverage complete; girdle narrow, minutely spiculose or scaly; insertion plates lacking, or if present, weak and unslit; articulamentum layer usually consisting only of weakly developed sutural laminae in valves *ii* to *viii*. Gills short, posterior. [Recent species range from shore to 2,300 fathoms.] *Carb.-Rec.*

Lepidopleurus Leach in Risso, 1826 *(non* Carpenter in Dall, 1879) [*Chiton cajetanus* Poli, 1791; SD Gray, 1847] [=*Leptochiton* Gray, 1847; *Deshayesiella* Carpenter in Dall, 1879; *Rhombichiton* DeKoninck, 1883; *Beanella* Thiele, 1893 *(non* Dall, 1882); *Pilsbryella* Nierstrasz, 1905; *Parachiton* Thiele, 1909; *Terenochiton* Iredale, 1914; *Xiphiozona* Berry, 1919; *Belchiton* Ashby & Cotton, 1939]. Elongate-ovate chitons with relatively thin valves, round-backed or with moderately distinct jugal angle; lateral areas of intermediate valves indefinitely marked but in a few species standing out sharply; sculptural features of all valves not at all prominent, generally consisting of an over-all granular background; jugal area usually obscure, not distinct from pleural areas. *Carb.-Rec.;* cosmop. [*Carb.*, Eu.(Belg.-Eng.-Scot.-USSR); *Eoc.*, Eu.(Fr.); *Mio.*, Eu.(Fr.-Ger.-?Italy-Vienna Basin) - Austral.-N. Z.; *Plio.*, Eu. (Italy)-Austral.-N.Z.; *Pleist.*, Eu.(Italy-Norway)-N.Am. (Calif.); *Rec.*, nearly all seas].——Fig. 36,5. *L. laterodepressus* Bergenhayn, Carb. (300 ft. below Hosir Ls.), Scot.; *5a*, reconstr., ×0.5; *5b*, intermed. valve dorsal view, ×1.5; *5c,d*, valve *ii*, dorsal and side view, ×1.5 (42*).——Fig. 36,4. *L. cajetanus* (Poli), Tert.-Rec., living spec., Medit.; *4a,b*, head and intermed. valves dorsal, ×3.2; *4c,d*, intermed. and tail valves, side, ×1 (25*). [In classification adopted by many authors, *Leptochiton, Deshayesiella, Pilsbryella, Parachiton, Terenochiton,* and *Xiphiozona* are accepted as subgenera of *Lepidopleurus.*]

Oldroydia Dall, 1894 [*O. percrassa*]. Valves heavy, strongly sculptured, with irregular transverse ribs that in life are well separated by narrow extensions of girdle reaching to jugum, resulting in coverage that is partial to apical only; articulamentum well developed, unslit; tegmentum with posterior extension between rather large sutural laminae; jugal area prominent, sculptured differently from pleural areas; lateral areas not differentiated. *Rec.*, USA(Calif.).

Protochiton Ashby, 1925 [*Acanthochites (Notoplax) granulosus* Ashby & Torr, 1901]. No insertion plates in head and tail valves, intermediate valves having incomplete unslit insertion plates; articulation well developed; all valves except head valve about as broad as long, strongly sculptured, with rows of elongate granules; articulamentum of tail valve ending in callus, beyond which tegmentum is produced posteriorly almost 0.25 of its total length. *M.Mio.*, Austral.(Victoria).——Fig. 36,7. *P. granulosus* (Ashby & Torr) Balcombian, Balcombe Bay, Victoria; *7a,b*, head valve, dorsal and ventral (×2); *7c*, intermed. valve (holotype, ×2); *7d,e*, tail valve, dorsal and ventral (×2) (1*).

Helminthochiton Salter in M'Coy, 1846 [*H. griffithi*] [=*Gryphochiton* Gray, 1847; *Chonechiton* Carpenter in Dall, 1882; *Glaphurochiton* Raymond, 1910; *Gryptochiton* Zittel (Broili edit.), 1924, and Dechaseaux in Piveteau, 1952 *(errore)*]. Similar to *Lepidopleurus* but generally much larger, with shell areas of articulamentum less developed; head valve with no articulamentum *(s. s.);* intermediate and tail valves with narrow, widely separated sutural laminae and no insertion plates; all valves usually as long as wide, subquadrate; tail valve with subcentral mucro. *L.Ord.-Carb.*, Eu.-N.Am. [*L.Ord.(Arenig.)*, Czech.; *M. Ord.*, Scot.; *Sil.*, Ire.; *L.Carb.(Tournais.)*, Belg.-?USSR; *Miss.*, USA(Ind.); *Penn.*, USA(Pa.-Ill.)].——Fig. 36,3. *H. griffithi*, Sil., Ire.(Galway); *3a,b*, dorsal and side views, posterior part of shell, ×2, ×1 (51*).——Fig. 36,2. *H. priseus* Münster,

L.Carb.(Tournais.), Tournai, Belg.; *2a,* complete specimen, ×1 (49*); *2b-d,* side, dorsal, and ventral views of intermed. valve, ×1 (23*). Also, Fig. 33.]

Pterochiton CARPENTER in DALL, 1882 [**Chiton eburonicus* RYCKHOLT, 1845] [=*Loricites* CARPENTER in DALL, 1882; *Anthracochiton* ROCHEBRUNE, 1883]. Shell elongated, leptoidal; valves

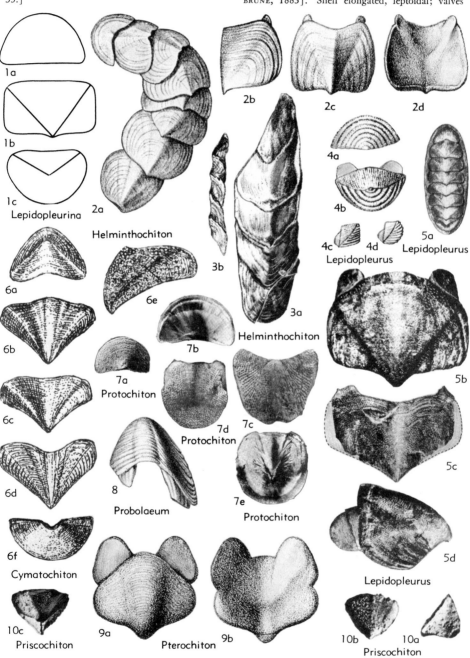

FIG. 36. Neoloricata; Lepidopleurina (Lepidopleuridae) (p. 150-154). [*1a-c.* Divisions of shell areas of Lepidopleurina, schematic; *1a,* head valve; *1b,* intermediate valve; *1c,* tail valve (*Aa*—anterior area, *Ac*—central area, *Al*—lateral area, *Ap*—posterior area).]

laterally excavated, posteriorly acuminate; last valve regular, mucro ischnoidal; anterior valve (?usually) sinuate; apophyses large, sinus wide. *L.Carb.,* Eu.(Belg.-Ire.).——Fɪɢ. 36,9. **P. eburonicus* (Rʏᴄᴋʜᴏʟᴛ), Tournais., Belg.(Visé); *9a,b,* dorsal and ventral views of intermed. valve, ×1 (30*).

Probolaeum Cᴀʀᴘᴇɴᴛᴇʀ in Dᴀʟʟ, 1882 [**Chiton corrugatus* Sᴀɴᴅʙᴇʀɢᴇʀ, 1853 (=*C. subgranosus* Sᴀɴᴅʙᴇʀɢᴇʀ, 1842)]. Shell leptoidal, elongate, largely projecting; central intermediate valve with central area extending in front of jugum; anterior valve sinuate; posterior valve doubtful. *Dev.,* Eu. (Ger.)-?N.Am.(Que.). —— Fɪɢ. 36,8. **P. subgranosus* (Sᴀɴᴅʙᴇʀɢᴇʀ), Ger.(Villmar); ?head valve, ×? (52*).

Cymatochiton Dᴀʟʟ, 1882 [**Chiton loftusianus* Kɪɴɢ, 1848]. Intermediate valves longer than wide, with somewhat elevated, projecting apex, jugum acute; lateral areas flat, not waved; sutural laminae moderately developed, widely spaced, with very broad jugal sinus; valves thrown forward from apex, giving them a triangular aspect. Differs from *Probolaeum* in transverse instead of squared shape of intermediate valves, and in nonwaved end valves. *Perm.,* Eu.(Eng.-Ger.).——Fɪɢ. 36,6. **C. loftusianus* (Kɪɴɢ), Magnesian Ls., Eng.(Durham); *6a,* head valve; *6b-e,* intermed. valves; *6f,* tail valve; all dorsal except *6e,* side view, ×1 (46*).

Priscochiton Dᴀʟʟ, 1882 [**Chiton canadensis* Bɪʟʟɪɴɢs, 1865]. Small, ?head valve rounded, triangular in dorsal aspect, with acute pointed apex; tegmentum of apical area recurved toward ventral side for short distance back of apex forming 2 minute convex plates visible only from ventral side of valve; side view cone-shaped in outline. Known only from 2 ?head valves. *M.Ord.,* N.Am. (Que.).——Fɪɢ. 36,10. **P. canadensis* (Bɪʟʟɪɴɢs), Ottawa F.(Blackriv.) Ottawa River; *10a-c,* side, dorsal, and ventral views of ?head valve, *10c,* showing rolled over tegmentum at apex, ×2 (53*).

Family HANLEYIDAE Bergenhayn, 1955

Head valve with insertion plate lacking slits but roughened at edge; intermediate valves lacking insertion plates; tail valve with or without insertion plates; sutural laminae well developed in intermediate and tail valves, eaves small; girdle with fine spines but usually no pores. *Pleist.-Rec.*

Hanleya Gʀᴀʏ, 1857 [**H. debilis* (=**Chiton hanleyi* Bᴇᴀɴ in Tʜᴏʀᴘᴇ, 1844)] [=*Hanleia* Cᴀʀᴘᴇɴᴛᴇʀ, 1873 *(nom. null.); Hanleyia* Dᴀʟʟ, 1879 *(nom. null.)*] [*non Hanleya* Aᴅᴀᴍs & Aɴɢᴀs, 1864]. Small granulose chitons with jugal angle and flat side slopes; tegmentum areas of lepidopleuroid type; valve structure normal for family but tail valve lacking insertion plate. *Pleist.,* Norway; *Rec.,* sub-Arctic seas.——Fɪɢ. 37,1. **H. hanleyi* (Bᴇᴀɴ), *Rec.,* Norway; *1a,b,* head valve,

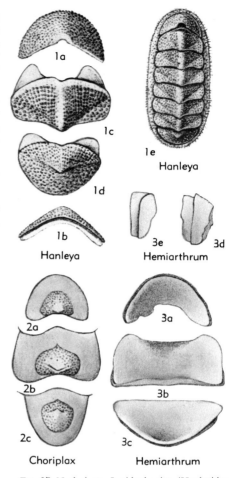

Fɪɢ. 37. Neoloricata; Lepidopleurina (Hanleyidae, Choriplacidae) (p. *I54-I55*).

dorsal and anterior edge; *1c,d,* intermed. and tail valves, dorsal; ×5.4 (25*); *1e,* entire specimen, ×2.7 (25*).

Hemiarthrum Cᴀʀᴘᴇɴᴛᴇʀ in Dᴀʟʟ, 1876 [**H. setulosum*]. Differs from *Hanleya* in presence of insertion plate in tail valve; girdle poriferous, lateral pore tufts small. *Rec.,* Antarctic seas.——Fɪɢ. 37,3. **H. setulosum,* S.Atl.; *3a-c,* head, intermed., and tail valves, ventral; *3d,e,* head and tail valves, side; ×2.25 (25*).

Family CHORIPLACIDAE Cotton & Weeding, 1939

[=Choriplaxidae Bᴇʀɢᴇɴʜᴀʏɴ, 1955]

Elongate chitons of medium size with thin horny girdle covering whole shell like periostracum except for apices of valves, which constitute the tegmentum; articulamentum very large, sutural laminae and

sinus obsolete; insertion plates large, unslit or with obsolete slits; whole shell transparent. *Rec.*

Choriplax PILSBRY, 1894 [**Microplax grayi* ADAMS & ANGAS, 1864] [=*Microplax* ADAMS & ANGAS, 1864 (*non* FIEBER, 1861)]. Shell structure as in family, tegmentum heart-shaped, girdle nude. *Rec., Austral.*——FIG. 37,2. **C. grayi* (ADAMS & ANGAS), Sydney Harbor; *2a-c*, head, intermed., and tail valves, dorsal, ×2.5 (25*).

Suborder ISCHNOCHITONINA Bergenhayn, 1930

[=*Eochitonia* DALL, 1889 (*partim*); *Opsichitonia* DALL, 1889 (*partim*); *Mesoplacophora* PILSBRY, 1893 (*partim*); *Teleoplacophora* PILSBRY, 1893; *Chitonina* THIELE, 1931 (*partim*); *Isoplacophora* COTTON & WEEDING, 1939 (*partim*)]

Chitons ranging in size from small to quite large. Head valve with anterior shell area only; intermediate valves with median and 2 lateral areas; tail valve with separated median and posterior areas; apical areas well developed in valves *i* to *vii*. Lateral and posterior areas sculptured alike, differing in character from that of the median areas. Articulamentum well developed, consisting of insertion plates and sutural laminae, latter lacking only in valve *i*. Insertion plates in all valves divided by varying numbers of slits, forming teeth, which may be smooth and sharp on both sides, strongly or weakly pectinated or buttressed on outside. Slit rays generally present and well developed. Girdle exceedingly variable in width and ornamentation, not encroaching over tops of valves, leaving a large expanse of tegmentum compared with extent of articulamentum layers. *?Trias., Rec.*

Family SUBTERENOCHITONIDAE Bergenhayn, 1930

Shell small, elongate, elevated, and carinated. Articulamentum as in Hanleyidae except that insertion plate in head valve extends somewhat farther around, is multiple-slitted and furnished with slit rays on ventral side. Intermediate and tail valves unslit or with diminutive slit rays. Sculpture simple, generally consisting of quincuncially arranged pustules. Girdle narrow, decorated with small, smooth, imbricating scales. *Rec.*

Subterenochiton IREDALE & HULL, 1924 [**Ischnochiton gabrieli* HULL, 1912]. Characters of family. *Rec., Austral.*——FIG. 38,1. **S. gabrieli* (HULL), holotype; *1a*, entire animal, ×6; *1b-f*, valves, ×9; *1g*, section of girdle, ×12 (11*).

Family ISCHNOCHITONIDAE Dall, 1889

[=Chitonaceae HINDS, 1845 (*partim*); Tonicelloidea SIMROTH, 1894 (*partim*); Callochitonidae THIELE, 1910 (*partim*); Trachydermoninae THIELE, 1910; Lepidochitonidae IREDALE, 1914]

Ovate to elongate chitons of variable size. Tegmentum of intermediate valves divided into lateral and central areas by diagonal rib (commonly indistinct) extending from apex to anterior outer angle of valves on each side. Articulamentum of head and tail valves multiple-slitted, that of intermediate valves with single slit or in some groups with 2 or more slits on each side. Teeth sharp-edged, not pectinated, grooved, or buttressed on outside. Eaves not porous. Sutural laminae sharp and well developed. *Eoc.-Rec.*

Ischnochiton GRAY, 1847 [**Chiton textilis* GRAY, 1828; SD GRAY, 1847]. [=*Lepidochiton* CARPENTER, 1857; *Ischnoradsia* CARPENTER in DALL, 1879; *Beanella* THIELE, 1893 (*non* DALL, 1882): *Lophyriscus, Leptopleura, Stereoplax, Rhodoplax* THIELE, 1893; *Levicoplax* IREDALE & HULL, 1925; *Diktuonus* ASHBY, 1931]. Shell oval or subovate, up to 2 inches in length but generally smaller. Tegmentum sculpture of lateral areas of intermediate valves usually raised, consisting of smooth or beaded radial ribs that vary in strength; on central areas sculpture may be finely granular throughout or consist of longitudinal ribs accompanied in some species by transverse riblets. Tail valve with well-developed mucro. Articulamentum of head and tail valves usually with more than 8 slits in insertion plates, that of intermediate valves typically single-slitted or with 2 or more slits in some groups. [A widespread and variable genus found from shore to depths of 100 fathoms or more.] *U.Eoc.*, Eng.(Isle of Wight); *Oligo.*, USA(Fla.)-N.Z.; *Mio.*, C.Eu.-E.Afr.-Austral.; *Plio.*, USA(N.Car.-Fla.)-Austral.(Victoria); *Pleist.*, USA (Calif.); *Rec.*, cosmop.

I. (**Ischnochiton**). *U.Eoc.-Rec.*, cosmop.——FIG. 38,9. **I. (I.) textilis* (GRAY), Rec., W.Afr.; *9a-c*, head, intermed., and tail valves, dorsal, ×2.5 (41*).——FIG. 38,10. *I. (I.) numantius* COTTON & GODFREY, L.Plio., Victoria; tail valve, ×2 (11*).——FIG. 43,4. *I. (I.) spiculosus* (REEVE), Plio., USA(N.Car.); intermed. valve, dorsal, ×10 (9*). The following additional subgenera based on Recent species have been defined from various localities:

I. (**Stenosemus**) MIDDENDORFF, 1847 (**Chiton albus* LINNÉ, 1767; SD WINCKWORTH, 1926] [=*Lepidopleuroides* THIELE, 1893].

I. (**Ischnoradsia**) SHUTTLEWORTH, 1853 [**Chiton australis* SOWERBY, 1840; SD PILSBRY, 1892] [=*Lepidoradsia* CARPENTER in DALL, 1879].

I. (Heterozona) CARPENTER in DALL, 1879 [*Ischnochiton (H.) cariosus* CARPENTER in PILSBRY, 1892; SD PILSBRY, 1892].

I. (Ischnoplax) CARPENTER in DALL, 1879 [*Chiton pectinatus* SOWERBY, 1840].

I. (Radsiella) PILSBRY, 1892 [*Ischnochiton tridentatus* PILSBRY, 1893].

I. (Lophyropsis) THIELE, 1893 [*Chiton (Ischnochiton) imitator* E.A.SMITH, 1881 (*nom. correct.* A.G.SMITH, herein, *pro L. imitatrix* THIELE, 1893)].

I. (Haploplax) PILSBRY, 1894 [*Lophyrus smaragdinus* ANGAS, 1867] [=*Chartoplax* IREDALE & HULL, 1924; *Radsiella* THIELE, 1893 (*non* PILSBRY, 1892)].

I. (Chondropleura) THIELE, 1906 [*Lophyrus exaratus* G.O.SARS, 1878; SD A.G.SMITH, herein].

I. (Anisoradsia) IREDALE & MAY, 1916 [*Ischnochiton (A.) mawlei*].

I. (Rhombochiton) BERRY, 1919 [*non* LINDSTRÖM, 1884, *nom. null. pro Rhombichiton* DEKONINCK, 1883)] [*Chiton regularis* CARPENTER, 1855].

I. (Tripoplax) BERRY, 1919 [*Trachydermon trifidus* CARPENTER, 1864] [=*Ischnoradsia* CARPENTER in DALL, 1879 (*non* SHUTTLEWORTH, 1853)].

I. (Strigichiton) HULL, 1923 [*Ischnochiton verconis* TORR, 1911].

I. (Autochiton) IREDALE & HULL, 1924 [*Ischnochiton torri* IREDALE & MAY, 1916].

I. (Euporoplax) IREDALE & HULL, 1924 [*Chiton virgatus* REEVE, 1847].

I. (Euretoplax) IREDALE & HULL, 1924 [*Ischnochiton wilsoni* SYKES, 1896].

I. (Isochiton) ASHBY & COTTON, 1934 [*Ischnochiton (I.) bardwelli*].

I. (Ovatoplax) COTTON & WEEDING, 1939 [*Ischnochiton (Haploplax) mayi* PILSBRY, 1895].

Lepidozona PILSBRY, 1892 [*Chiton mertensii* MIDDENDORFF, 1846] [=*Lepidopleurus* CARPENTER in DALL, 1879 (*non* LEACH in RISSO, 1826); *Solivaga* IREDALE & HULL, 1925; *Gurjanovillia* JAKOLEVA, 1952]. Similar to *Ischnochiton* except that valves *ii* to *viii* have a delicately denticulate lamina across sinus, separated from sutural laminae on each side by small notch; insertion teeth sharp, somewhat rugose, fairly thick. Tegmentum sculpture on lateral areas of intermediate and end valves comprising radial rows of pustules or graniferous ribs; central areas sculptured with longitudinal riblets and latticed interstices. Mucro low, inconspicuous, nearly flat, subcentral. Girdle scales strongly convex, smooth or striated. [Modern species found between tides to moderate depths.] *Neogene* (Japan) - *Pleist.*(Calif. - BajaCalif.) - *Rec.* (NW.Pac.-NE.Pac.) —— FIG. 38,*11.* *L. mertensii* (MIDDENDORFF), Pleist., Calif.(SanPedro); *11a,b,* intermed. and tail valve, dorsal, ×1.4 (10*).—— FIG. 38,*8.* *L. californiensis* (BERRY), Pleist. (U.San Pedro), Calif.(San Diego); intermed. valve, dorsal, ×1.5 (10*).

Stenoplax CARPENTER in DALL, 1879 [*Chiton limaciformis* SOWERBY, 1832]. Small to large (4 in.), with elongate body, length as much as 7 times width. Intermediate valves generally low-arched, rounded, with lateral areas ranging from subobsolete to prominently raised above central areas; tail valve large, somewhat more than semicircular, depressed, with inconspicuous subcentral mucro. Insertion plates of end valves with 9 to 15 slits and of intermediate valves with 1 to 3 or more slits. Surface may show smooth polish, over-all minute granulations, or rather strong vermiculate ribs on lateral areas and in some also on central areas. Girdle narrow, decorated with small to extremely minute imbricating scales, smooth and polished or delicately striated. Sutural sinus wide and straight between rather narrow, elongate sutural laminae. [Species live typically under smooth stones buried in sand near low-tide mark but some are adapted to a special habitat in root sheaths of sea grasses, thus accounting for their elongated shape.] U.Eoc. (Auversian), Eng.; ?Plio., Calif.; Pleist., Calif.-BajaCalif.; Rec., NW.Pac.(Japan)-NE.Pac.(Calif.)-Carib.

S. (Stenoplax). U.Eoc., ?Plio., Pleist.-Rec., Eu.-Carib.-W.N.Am.-Japan.——FIG. 38,7. *S. (S.) limaciformis* (SOWERBY), Rec., Carib.; *7a,* entire animal, ×1.5; *7b,* valves *vii, viii,* ×2 (25*).—— FIG. 38,*12. S. (S.) conspicua* (CARPENTER), Pleist., Calif.; *12a,b,* head valve; *12c,d,* intermed. valve; *12e,f,* tail valve; all ×1 (10*). Other subgenera based on Recent species include:

S. (Stenochiton) ADAMS & ANGAS, 1864 [*Stenochiton juloides*] [=*Zostericola* ASHBY, 1919].

S. (Stenoradsia) CARPENTER in DALL, 1879 [*Chiton magdalenensis* HINDS, 1844] [=*Maugerella* DALL, 1879].

Lepidochitona GRAY, 1821 [*Chiton marginatus* PENNANT, 1777 (=*Chiton cinereus* LINNÉ, 1767)] [=*Trachydermon* CARPENTER, 1864; *Craspedochilus* G.O.SARS, 1878; *Leptochitona* PILSBRY, 1893 (*nom. null.*); *Adriella* THIELE, 1893; *Spongioradsia* PILSBRY, 1894; *Lepidochiton* THIELE, 1928, and subseq. authors (*non* CARPENTER, 1857)]. Small to medium-sized, similar to *Ischnochiton*, rather elevated, with subangular jugal ridge. Tail valve usually smaller than head valve; end valves with 9 to 12 slits in insertion plates; intermediate valves single-slitted; eaves generally somewhat spongy. Surface of tegmentum smooth or finely granulose, with little change between central and lateral areas of intermediate valves, lateral areas not prominent. Girdle clothed with minute scale-like processes. ?U.Plio., Italy; Pleist., USA(Calif.)-Norway; Rec., cosmop. (temperate and colder seas).——FIG. 38,*2.* *L. cinerea* (LINNÉ), Rec., North Sea; *2a,* entire animal, ×1; *2b,c,* intermed. valve, ×2 (25*).——FIG. 38,*14.* *L. keepiana* BERRY, Pleist., Calif.; intermed. valve, ×2 (10*).

Oligochiton BERRY, 1922 [*O. lioplax*]. Medium in size. Surface of tegmentum smooth, lateral areas not

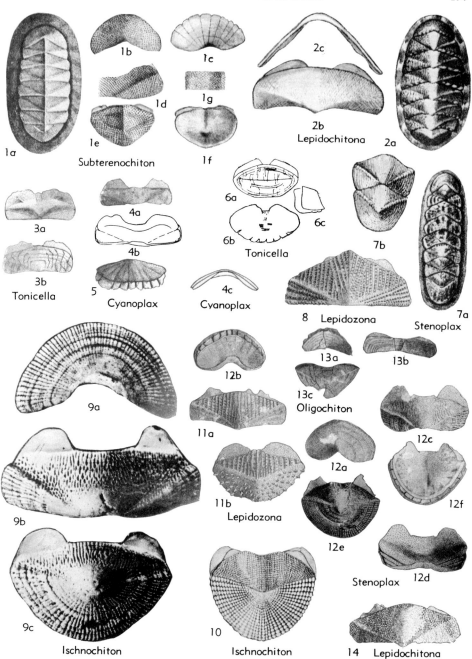

FIG. 38. Neoloricata; Ischnochitonina (Subterenochitonidae, Ischnochitonidae) (p. 155-158).

well defined; insertion plates and teeth present but very short; sutural laminae low and wide, separated by wide, shallow sinus; eaves spongy; slits numerous in end valves, probably 2 or 3 on a side in intermediate valves. *Oligo.*, Can.

(B.C.).——FIG. 38,13. **O. lioplax; 13a-c*, head, intermed., and tail valves, ×1 (10*).

Tonicella CARPENTER, 1873 [*Chiton marmoreus FABRICIUS, 1780] [=*Tonicia* GRAY, 1847; *Platysemus, Stenosemus* MIDDENDORFF, 1847; *Boreo-*

chiton G.O.SARS, 1878; *Toniciella* THIELE, 1893 (*nom. null.*)]. Small to medium-sized, low-arched, with rounded backs. Valve structure generally as in *Ischnochiton* but eaves spongy and intermediate valves single-slitted; lateral areas indistinctly developed. Surface of tegmentum smooth or microgranulose. Girdle appearing nude or with very small scales. *Pleist.,* Eu.(Denm.-Norway)-USA(Calif.)-Mex.(BajaCalif.); *Rec.,* N.Atl.-N.Pac. (shore to 35 fathoms).——FIG. 38,6. *T. marmorea* (FABRICIUS), Rec., Norway; *6a-c,* tail valve, ×1 (48*).——FIG. 38,3. *T. lineata* (WOOD), Pleist., Calif.; *3a,b,* intermed. valve, ventral and dorsal, ×1 (10*). [*Tonicella = Clathropleura* TIBERI, 1877].

Cyanoplax PILSBRY, 1892 [*Chiton hartwegii* CARPENTER, 1855; SD PILSBRY, 1893]. Like *Tonicella* but valves thicker and more solid, somewhat beaked anteriorly. Insertion-plate teeth stout, obtuse, crenulate, and bilobed or trilobed at tips; eaves wide, spongy or pitted. Girdle leathery, minutely papillose. *?Eoc.,* Fr.; *Pleist.,* USA(Calif.)-Mex.(BajaCalif.); *Rec.,* E.Pac. (N.Am.-S.Am. coasts).——FIG. 38,4. *C. hartwegii* (CARPENTER); Pleist., Calif.; *4a-c,* intermed. valve, dorsal, ventral, anterior edge, ×1.5 (10*).——FIG. 38,5. *C. fackenthallae* BERRY, Pleist., Calif.; head valve, ×1.5 (10*). [*Cyanoplax = Mopaliopsis* THIELE, 1893; *Mopaliella* THIELE, 1909].

Basiliochiton BERRY, 1918 [*Mopalia heathii* PILSBRY, 1898] [=*Lophochiton* BERRY, 1925 (*non* ASHBY, 1923); *Ploiochiton* BERRY, 1926]. Small (length 1 in. or less), medium to high-arched, widely carinate, with nearly straight side slopes. Tegmentum minutely granulose, not markedly differentiated into areas, some species with obscure ribbing on lateral areas and tail valve, which is semicircular in posterior outline, with anterior mucro, posterior slope concave. Head valve with 8 slits, intermediate valves single-slitted, and tail valve with regular crescentic insertion plate cut by 5 to 8 slits, insertion plates continuous across sinus of intermediate valves, sinus being moderately to very spongy. Girdle microscopically spiculose, bearing rather long branching bristle at each suture, 2 to 5 in front of head valve and 2 behind tail valve. *Rec.,* NE.Pac.(N.Am. W. coast).

Tonicina THIELE, 1906 [*Chiton zschaui* PFEFFER, 1886]. Shell elongated, relatively small, high-arched, width about 0.5 of length. Tegmentum shining, under magnification showing fine growth striae and minute granulation. Intermediate valves with bluntly angular jugal ridge, somewhat beaked, with central and lateral areas separated by low angle; insertion plates narrow; sutural laminae small; head valve long, tail valve small, distinctly narrower than head valve and notably shorter; slits of insertion plates unknown. Girdle narrow, granulose. *Rec.,* S.Georgia.

Family SCHIZOPLACIDAE Bergenhayn, 1955

[*nom. correct.* A. G. SMITH, herein (*pro* Schizoplaxidae BERGENHAYN, 1955)]

Relatively small, rather elevated, oval-shaped chitons with rounded jugum differing from all others in structure of intermediate valves, which have central jugal slit filled by narrow wedge of horny cartilage, narrowing to point in front, similar in composition to bivalve ligament. *Rec.*

Schizoplax DALL, 1878 [*Chiton brandtii* MIDDENDORFF, 1846]. Shell and girdle like *Tonicella,* tegmentum remarkably porous where exposed at small eaves and jugal sinus. Slit formula: 11-1-11. *Rec.,* Okhotsk Sea-Aleutian I.——FIG. 39,1. *S. brandtii* (MIDDENDORFF), Aleutian I.; *1a,b,* head valves; *1c,d,* intermed. valves; *1e,f,* tail valves; ×2 (25*).

Family CALLOCHITONIDAE Plate, 1899

[*nom. transl.* THIELE, 1910 (*ex* Callochitoninae PLATE, 1899)] [=Ischnochitonidae DALL, 1889 (*partim*); Ischnochitoninae PILSBRY, 1893 (*partim*); Tonicelloidea SIMROTH, 1894 (*partim*); Callochitonidae THIELE, 1910 (*partim*)]

Sutural laminae connected or continuous across shallow jugal sinus. Insertion plates tending to be propped on outside, those of head and tail valves cut into more teeth by multiple slitting than in other groups; intermediate valves generally with 3 or more slits; eaves spongy. Shell eyes present. *Oligo.-Rec.*

Callochiton GRAY, 1847 [*Chiton laevis* MONTAGU, 1803] [=*Clathropleura* TIBERI, 1877 (*partim*); *Trachyradsia* CARPENTER in DALL, 1878; *Collochiton* SARS, 1878 (*nom. null.*); *Stereochiton* CARPENTER in DALL, 1882; *Icoplax* THIELE, 1893; *Eudoxoplax* IREDALE & MAY, 1916; *Paricoplax, Quaestiplax* IREDALE & HULL, 1929; *Acutoplax* COTTON & WEEDING, 1939]. Insertion-plate slits in head valve 14 to 17, in intermediate valves normally 3, in tail valve 11 to 18. Girdle fairly wide, leathery, covered with longitudinally packed minute narrow scales or spicules with only tips showing. *Oligo.,* N.Z.; *L.Mio.,* Eu.(Austr.); *?L.Plio.* Austral. (Victoria); *Rec.,* Antarct.-S.Afr.-Austral.-N.Z.-Medit.-G.Brit.——FIG. 39,7. *C. laevis* (MONTAGU), Rec., North Sea; *7a,b,* intermed. valve, side and dorsal; *7c,* tail valve, ventral, showing slit insertion plates; ×2 (25*). [*Callochiton=Ocellochiton* ASHBY, 1939].

Eudoxochiton SHUTTLEWORTH, 1853 [*Acanthopleura nobilis* GRAY, 1843]. Similar to *Callochiton* but slits in insertion plates more numerous, up to 27 in end valves and 4 to 7 in intermediate valves. Girdle leathery, wide and thin, covered with short,

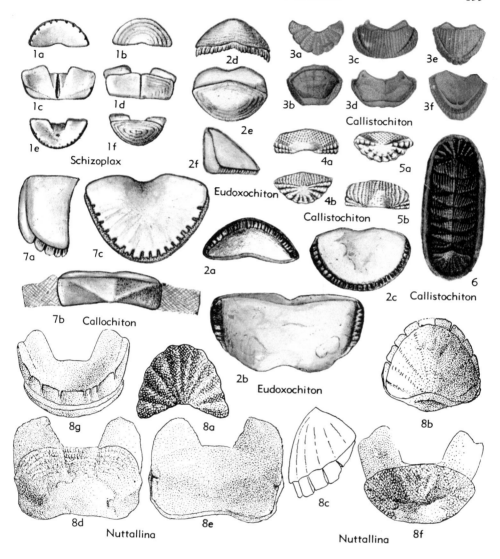

FIG. 39. Neoloricata; Ischnochitonina (Schizoplacidae, Callochitonidae, Callistoplacidae) (p. 158-160).

stiff bristles, sparsely set. *Rec.,* Austral.-N.Z.-Kermadec I.——FIG. 39,2. **E. nobilis* (GRAY), Rec., N.Z.; *2a-c,* head, intermed., tail valves, ventral, showing slit insertion plates, ×1.5; *2d-f,* tail valve, ×1 (25*).

Family CALLISTOPLACIDAE Pilsbry, 1893

[*nom. transl.* DAVIS, 1954 (*ex* Callistoplacinae PILSBRY, 1893)]
[=Callistochitoninae BERRY, 1922; Callistochitonidae IREDALE & HULL, 1923]

Small to medium in size, with strongly sculptured tegmentum usually showing heavy radial ribs on end valves and lateral areas of intermediate valves; insertion plates in all valves cut by teeth that generally correspond in number and position to radial ribs, teeth usually thickened at edges of slits and in some groups peculiarly scalloped. No shell eyes present. Girdle narrow, variously ornamented. *L.Mio.-Rec.*

Callistoplax CARPENTER in DALL, 1882 [**Chiton retusus* SOWERBY, 1832]. Tegmentum sculpture as in family; differs from *Callistochiton* primarily in girdle ornamentation, which is nude except for

series of bristle-bearing pores. *Rec.,* W.S.Am.-W. Mex.

Callistochiton CARPENTER in DALL, 1879 [**C. palmulatus*] [=*Lophochiton* ASHBY, 1923; *Callistelasma* IREDALE & HULL, 1925; *Callistassecla* IREDALE & HULL, 1925]. Tegmentum conspicuously sculptured, central areas smooth in middle, with netted pattern or pitted toward apex, or sculptured throughout with parallel lirae. Insertion plates short, smooth or nearly so, festooned, being curved outward at ribs and slit at rib terminations, thickened outside at edges of slits; end valves multiple-slitted, intermediate valves single-slitted; sinus squared; mucro median, usually depressed. Girdle narrow, poreless, densely set with minute striated or smooth imbricating scales. *L.Mio.,* E.Afr.(Mafia I.); *L.Plio.,* Austral.(Victoria); *Plio.,* USA(Calif.)-Mex.(BajaCalif.); *Rec.,* nearly all temperate seas.——FIG. 39,6. **C. palmulatus, Rec.,* USA(Calif.); entire specimen, ×2 (25*).——FIG. 39,3. *C. crassicostatus* PILSBRY, Pleist. USA(Calif.); *3a,b,* head valve; *3c,d,* intermed. valve; *3e,f,* tail valve; ×2.5 (10*).——FIG. 39,4. *C. inexpectus* ASHBY & COTTON, L.Plio., Austral.(Victoria); *4a,b,* intermed. and tail valves, dorsal, ×2 (4*).——FIG. 39,5. *C. reticulatus* ASHBY & COTTON, L.Plio., Austral.(Victoria); *5a,b,* intermed. and tail valves, dorsal, ×2 (4*).

Nuttallochiton PLATE, 1899 [**Schizochiton hyadesi* ROCHEBRUNE, 1889] [=*Notochiton* THIELE, 1906]. Medium in size, carinated, tegmentum sculptured with ribs or rows of tubercles; sutural laminae short and wide, almost connected across small jugal sinus and extending around sides of intermediate valves. Girdle spiculose, having short thick spicules with single or groups of larger spicules between. *Rec.,* S.Am.-Antarct.

Nuttallina DALL, 1871 [**Chiton scaber* REEVE, 1847 (*non C. scaber* DE BLAINVILLE, 1825) =**Acanthopleura fluxa* CARPENTER, 1864] [=*Nuttalina* FISCHER, 1885 (*nom. null.*); *Nutallina* PALLARY, 1900 (*nom. null.*)]. Elongate, narrow, medium-sized chitons with granulose tegmentum surface, head valve with numerous low radiating ribs, intermediate valves with 2 ribs on lateral areas; mucro somewhat posterior; insertion plates sharp, cut by slits corresponding to dorsal ribs; teeth of tail valve directed forward; sutural laminae well developed, elongate, with deep jugal sinus between. Girdle clothed with minute striated and flattened scales and with marginal row of striated bristles. *Pleist.,* USA(Calif.); *Rec.,* Eu.(Medit.)-Japan-NE.Pac.——FIG. 39,8. *N. californica* (NUTTALL in REEVE), Pleist. USA (Calif.); *8a-c,* head valve; *8d,e,* intermed. valve; *8f,g,* tail valve; ×5 (10*).

Middendorffia CARPENTER in DALL, 1882 [**Chiton polii* PHILIPPI, 1836 (=*C. cinereus* POLI, 1791, *non* LINNÉ, 1767)] [*nom. correct.* FISCHER, 1885 (*pro Middendorfia* CARPENTER in DALL, 1882)] [=*Beania* CARPENTER in DALL, 1879 (*non* JOHN-

STON, 1840); *Beanella* DALL, 1882; *Dawsonia* CARPENTER, 1873 (*non* HARTT, 1868; *nec* NICHOLSON, 1873; *nec* FRITSCH, 1879)]. Like *Nuttallina* except intermediate valves with single slit, insertion-plate teeth more or less thickened at edges. *Neogene,* Eu.(Austr.); *Rec.,* Eu.(Medit.-Adriatic-Sp.).

Ceratozona DALL, 1882 [**Chiton guildingi* REEVE, 1847 (=*Chiton rugosus* SOWERBY, 1841)] [=*Ceratophorus* CARPENTER in DALL, 1882 (*non* DIESING, 1850); *Newcombia* CARPENTER in DALL, 1882]. Oblong, rather convex, with back broadly arched, valves strong and somewhat beaked. Insertion plates of head valve long, sharp, rugose outside, thickened at slits; intermediate valves with similarly propped teeth; tail valve having teeth thick, shorter, rugose; sinus solid; slit formula 7 to 10-1-8 to 10. Girdle tough, bearing peculiar corneous spines, similar in substance to girdle, generally sparsely bunched at sutures, with larger ones not superficial but deeply imbedded. *Rec.,* Carib.-C.Am.

Family CHAETOPLEURIDAE Plate, 1899

[*nom. transl.* BERGENHAYN, 1955 (*ex* Chaetopleurinae PLATE, 1899) [=Chaetopleurae ROCHEBRUNE, 1881 (*partim*); Chaetochitonidae ROCHEBRUNE, 1889 (*partim*); Chaetopleuroidea SIMROTH, 1894]

Valve structure consisting of usual shell layers with addition of a well-developed mesostracum. Tegmentum with complicated microstructure and sculpture consisting generally of radial rows of pustules or nodules on end valves and lateral areas of intermediate valves. Jugal sinus provided with jugal plate across it between sutural laminae. Girdle covered with scales, spicules, or hairy processes. *Mio.-Rec.*

Chaetopleura SHUTTLEWORTH, 1853 [**Chiton peruvianus* LAMARCK, 1819; SD DALL, 1879] [=*Choetopleura* SHUTTLEWORTH, 1856 (*nom. null.*); *Hemphillia* CARPENTER in DALL, 1879 (*non* BLAND & BINNEY, 1872); *Pallochiton* DALL, 1879; *Arthuria* CARPENTER in DALL, 1882; *Helioradsia* THIELE, 1893; *Variolepis* PLATE, 1899; *Pristochiton* CLESSIN, 1903; *Chetopleura* ASHBY, 1929 (*nom. null.*)]. Small to medium-sized, with valves somewhat as in *Ischnochiton,* ventral side porcelaneous, having rather long sharp teeth and squared sinus; eaves solid. Tegmentum usually sculptured with longitudinal beaded riblets on central areas, and pustules or pustulose ribs on lateral areas of intermediate and end valves, pustules being irregularly arranged in some groups. *Mio.,* USA(Md.); *Plio.,* USA(N.Car.-Fla.); *Pleist.,* USA(S.Car.-Calif.)-Mex.(BajaCalif.); *Rec.,* nearly all temperate and warm temperate seas.——FIG. 41,9. *C. apiculata* (SAY), Pleist., USA(S.Car.), *9a,b,* intermed. valve, ×11 (9*).——FIG. 40,2. *C.*

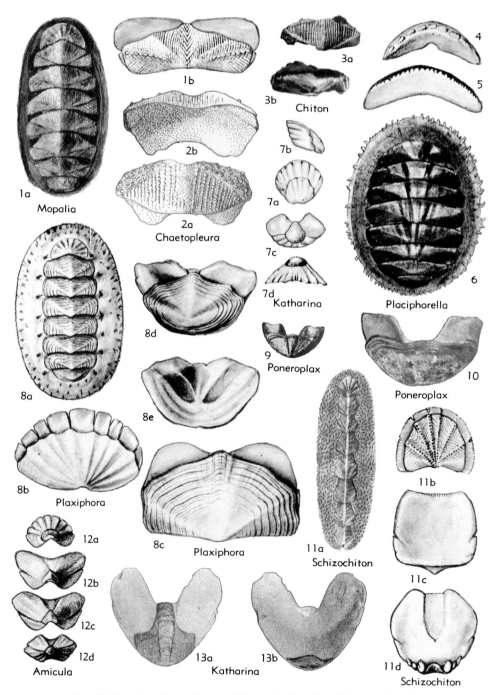

FIG. 40. Neoloricata; Ischnochitonina (Chaetopleuridae, Mopaliidae) (p. 160-163).

gemma CARPENTER in DALL, Pleist., USA(Calif.); *2a,b,* intermed. valve, dorsal, ventral, ×7 (10*).
Dinoplax CARPENTER in DALL, 1882 [*Chiton gigas*

GMELIN, 1788]. Large oval chitons with thick, heavy valves, obtusely angled, lateral areas much elevated. Tegmentum without strongly marked

sculpture, usually eroded smooth in adults. Insertion-plate teeth sharp, smooth, those of tail valve directed forward, slits not corresponding to position of dorsal ribs; sutural laminae rather broadly united across jugal sinus by keystone-shaped lamina; eaves solid; mucro of tail valve posterior. Girdle thick, leathery, with minute scattered bunches of delicate spinelets. *Rec.*, S.Afr.

Calloplax THIELE, 1909 [**Chiton janierensis* GRAY, 1828]. Shell medium-sized, elevated, oblong and rather narrow; lateral areas strongly raised, sculptured with 4 coarse granose ribs; central areas having about 12 granose, acute threads on either side of jugum parallel with it; sutural laminae rounded, with shallow sinus between; slit formula 10-1-9, insertion teeth solid; eaves wide and solid. Girdle with rather wide, ribbed scales and individual spines accompanied by minute spicules. *Rec.*, W. Atl.

Family MOPALIIDAE Dall, 1889

[=Amiculidae DALL, 1889 *(partim)*; Placophoridae DALL, 1889 *(partim)*; Chaetochitonidae ROCHEBRUNE, 1889 *(partim)*; Plaxiphoridae IREDALE, 1915; Mopalidae BERGENHAYN, 1930 *(nom. null.)*; Katharinidae JAKOLEVA, 1952]

Small to large chitons with tegmentum divided into usual lateral and central areas, sculpture combining radial and longitudinal ribs or lirae that vary in strength from low to high relief. Insertion-plate slits in all valves generally corresponding in position with ends of external ribs, teeth not pectinated. Head valve normally with 8 slits but may be smaller or larger by fusion or splitting of one or more teeth, whereas in some forms slits are abnormally multiplied; intermediate and tail valves with single slit on each side, although in one group lacking in tail valve; tail valve with posteromedian sinus; sutural laminae well developed to very large. Girdle more or less hairy or bristly, never with scales, bristles simple or dendritic, in some species growing out of sutural pores, each of which bears one or more hairy bristles. *?U.Oligo., L.Mio.-Rec.*

Mopalia GRAY, 1847 [**Chiton hindsii* SOWERBY in REEVE, 1847; SD GRAY, 1847] [=*Molpalia* GRAY, 1857; *Osteochiton* DALL, 1886]. Valves normal in proportion, transverse, jugal angle acute or almost flat, not beaked; girdle somewhat encroaching at sutures between valves. Sculpture of tegmentum usually furrowed or netted in addition to radial ribbing. Insertion plate of head valve rather long, sharp, slit into nearly smooth teeth that are somewhat thickened at edges of slits, which are normally 8, corresponding in position to external ribs; intermediate valves single-slitted; sinus small; tail valve depressed, with mucro be-

hind center and insertion plate sharp, smooth or roughened, having an oblique slit on each side (rarely doubled) and a larger sinus posteriorly. Girdle wider at sides than in front, leathery, more or less hairy, with or without sutural pores. *Pleist.*, USA(Calif.); *Rec.*, N.Pac.(BajaCalif. to Alaska-Japan).

M. (Mopalia). *Pleist.-Rec.*, W.USA-N.Pac.——FIG. 40,1. **M. (M.) hindsii* (SOWERBY), *Rec.*, Calif.; *1a*, whole animal, ×0.5 (25*); *1b*, intermed. valve, ×1 (25*). Other subgenera (classed by some authors as independent genera) include the following:

M. (Dendrochiton) BERRY, 1911 [**Mopalia (Dendrochiton) thamnopora*], *Rec.*, N.Am.(W. Coast).

M. (Semimopalia) DALL, 1919 [**Mopalia (Semimopalia) grisea*], *Rec.*, S.Am.(CapeHorn).

M. (Hachijomopalia) TAKI, 1954 [**M. (Hachijomopalia) integra*], *Rec.*, Japan.

Placiphorella CARPENTER in DALL, 1879 [**P. velata* DALL, 1879] [=*Euplacophora* VERRILL & SMITH, 1882; *Placphorella* FISCHER, 1885; *Placiphora* DALL, 1889 *(non* FISCHER, 1885*)*; *Placophoropsis* PILSBRY, 1893; *Langfordiella* DALL, 1925]. Medium-sized, with broadly rounded contour, valves very short and wide, middle ones much broader than those toward ends; head valve narrowly crescentic; tail valve much smaller, with shallow posterior sinus and posterior mucro. Tegmentum sculpture subobsolete, lateral areas distinct but very little raised. Insertion plates short and thick, teeth lobed or rugose; sinus small; slits 8 or more in head valve, single-slitted in intermediate valves, and 2 in tail valve (deep-water species with 20 or more slits in head valve and unslit tail valve); eaves spongy. Girdle wide and much extended in front, bearing sparse, scaled hairs or bristles. *Pleist.*, USA(Calif.); *Rec.*, Arctic-NW.Pac.(Japan)-NE.Pac.-NW.Atl.—— FIG. 40,6. **P. velata*, *Rec.*, N.Am.(W.Coast), whole animal, ×1 (25*).——FIG. 40,5. *P. atlantica* (VERRILL & SMITH), *Rec.*, NW.Atl.; head valve showing numerous teeth, ×1 (25*).——FIG. 40,4. *P. blainvillei* (BRODERIP), *Rec.*, Peru; tail valve showing 9 teeth, ×1 (25*).

Plaxiphora GRAY, 1847 [**Chiton carmichaelis* GRAY, 1828 (=**Chiton auratus* SPALOWSKY, 1795)] [=*Euplaxiphora* SHUTTLEWORTH, 1853; *Placiphora* CARPENTER in DALL, 1879 *(nom. null.)*; *Euplaciphora* DALL, 1879; *Plaxifora* FILHOL, 1880 *(nom. null.)*; *Placophora* FISCHER, 1885 *(nom. van.)*; *Euplacifora* JOHNSTON, 1891]. Large, oval chitons with tegmentum sculpture weak or lacking. Head valve normally with 8 indistinct radial ribs and concentric growth wrinkles; intermediate valves with similar indistinct ribs; tail valve with mucro slightly in front of posterior end; insertion plates well developed; head valve usually 8-slitted, intermediate valves single-slitted; tail valve with

smooth insertion plate and unslit or with heavy callus and distinct median sinus. Girdle large, leathery, bearing simple scattered bristles or bristle tufts at sutures. *L.Mio., Austral.*(Victoria); *Rec., Antarctic.* [*Plaxiphora = Euplacophora* FISCHER, 1885 (*non* VERRILL & SMITH, 1882)].

P. (Plaxiphora). *L.Mio.-Rec.,* Austral.-N.Z.-Antarctic.——FIG. 40,*8*. **P. (P.) aurata* (SPALOWSKY), Rec., N.Z.; *8a*, whole animal, ✕0.3; *8b-e*, valves (*8b*, head; *8c*, intermed.; *8d,e*, tail), ✕0.75 (45*). Other subgenera (treated by some authors as independent genera) include:

P. (Guildingia) CARPENTER in DALL, 1882 [**Plaxiphora obtecta* CARPENTER in PILSBRY, 1893; SD PILSBRY, 1893]. *U.Oligo.* or *L.Mio., Rec.,* N.Z.

P. (Diaphoroplax) IREDALE, 1914 [*Chiton biramosus QUOY & GAIMARD, 1835]. *Rec.,* N.Z.

P. (Poneroplax) IREDALE, 1914 [*Chiton costatus DEBLAINVILLE, 1825], *L.Mio.-Rec.,* Austral.—— FIG. 40,*9*. *P. (P.) gellibrandi* ASHBY & TORR, L. Mio., Austral.(Victoria); tail valve, ✕2 (11*). ——FIG. 40,*10*. *P. (P.) concentrica* ASHBY & TORR, L.Mio., Austral.(Victoria); tail valve ✕2 (11*).

P. (Maorichiton) IREDALE, 1914 [*Chiton caelatus REEVE, 1847], *Rec.,* N.Z.-Ceylon-S.Afr.

P. (Aerilamma) HULL, 1924 [**A. primordia*] [=*Vaferichiton* IREDALE & HULL, 1932], *Rec.,* Ceylon-Mozambique-Austral.(Queensl.)

P. (Mercatora) LELOUP, 1942 [**Plaxiphora mercatoris* LELOUP, 1936], *Rec.,* Easter I.

Fremblya H. ADAMS, 1866 [*nom. correct.* DALL, 1882 (*ex Frembleya* H. ADAMS, 1866)] [**Frembleya egregia*] [=*Fremblyia* DALL, 1879 (*nom. null.*); *Streptochiton* CARPENTER in DALL, 1879 (*nom. nud.*); *Frembleyana* ASHBY, 1919 (*nom. van.*); *Kopionella* ASHBY, 1919]. Similar to *Plaxiphora* but smaller, egg-shaped, with more prominent sculpture, tail valve having strongly recurved mucro, concave behind; head valve 8-slitted, teeth grooved with fluted edges. Girdle with sutural tufts. *Rec.,* N.Z.

Katharina GRAY, 1847 [*Chiton tunicatus WOOD, 1815; SD GRAY, 1847] [=*Katherina* CARPENTER, 1857 (*nom. null.*); *Catharina* DUNKER, 1882 (*nom. van.*)]. Large chitons with valves two-thirds covered by smooth black, leathery girdle. Exposed portion of tegmentum divided into jugal and lateral areas. Insertion plates, including sutural laminae, sharp, extremely long, projected forward. Head valve with 7 or 8 slits; tail valve with a wide caudal sinus and several slits on each side, commonly obsolete in part. *Plio.-Pleist.,* USA (Calif.); *Rec.,* NE.Pac.(Alaska to Calif.).——FIG. 40,*7,13*. **K. tunicata* (WOOD); *7a-d* (Rec., Calif.), *7a,b*, head valve, *7c,d*, tail valve, ✕0.75 (25*);

13a,b, (Plio., Calif.), intermed. valve, ✕1.4 (10*). Amicula GRAY, 1847 (June) [*non* GRAY, 1840; *nec* GRAY, 1843 (=*Cryptoconchus* BURROW, 1815)] [*Chiton vestitus BRODERIP & SOWERBY, 1829; SD GRAY, 1847 (Nov.)] [=*Cryptochiton* GRAY, 1847 (June) (*non* MIDDENDORFF, 1847); *Symmetrogephyrus* MIDDENDORFF, 1847; *Stimpsoniella* CARPENTER, 1873; *Chlamydochiton* DALL, 1878; *Chlamydoconcha* PILSBRY, 1893 (*non* DALL, 1884)]. Medium-sized to large chitons with valves almost entirely buried in thick, pilose girdle, leaving very small, heart-shaped tegmentum area exposed at each apex; articulamentum produced backward in rounded sutural laminae at each side, separated by a posterior sinus with tegmentum at its apex; tail valve wtih posterior sinus and single slit on each side. *Pleist.,* Can.; *Rec.,* Arctic (circumboreal).——FIG. 40,*12*. **A. vestita* (BRODERIP & SOWERBY), Rec., Alaska; *12a*, head valve; *12b,c*, intermed. valves; *12d*, tail valve; ✕0.75 (25*).

Family SCHIZOCHITONIDAE Dall, 1889

[=Prochitonidae ROCHEBRUNE, 1889; Loricidae IREDALE & HULL, 1923; Aulacochitonidae COTTON & GODFREY, 1940]

Much elongated or ovate, medium-sized chitons with well-developed tegmentum bearing sculpture of flattened riblets along which are rows of eyes; head valve with 6 to 10 slits; tail valve with deep caudal sinus. Girdle spiculose or scaly. *L.Mio.-Rec.*

Schizochiton GRAY, 1847 [*Chiton incisus SOWERBY, 1841]. Much elongated, valves bearing large eyes along tops of diagonal ribs on all except tail valve; insertion-plate slits in articulamentum correspond in position to ends of diagonal ribs; sinus narrow; head valve wtih 6 to 8 slits; tail valve with deep posterior fissure accompanied by several slits on each side. Girdle bearing small calcareous spinelets, slit behind. *Rec.,* Philippines-N.Austral.—— FIGS. 40,*11*; 41,*1*. **S. incisus* (SOWERBY), SW. Pac.; 40,*11a*, entire animal, ✕1; 40,*11b-d*, valves, ca. ✕2 (25*); 41,*1*, tail valve, ✕2 (25*).

Lorica ADAMS & ADAMS, 1852 [*Chiton cimolius REEVE, 1847] [=*Aulacochiton* SHUTTLEWORTH, 1853; *Protolorica* ASHBY, 1925; *Zelorica* FINLAY, 1927]. Large, elongate-oval, elevated, carinated chitons; tail valve small, with recurved mucro; sculpture of small erect pustules forming radial ribs; eyes small, subobsolete, appearing on intermediate valves only; articulamentum of head valve 8-slitted, slits not corresponding with dorsal ribs, teeth obsoletely pectinated; intermediate valves single-slitted; sutural laminae extending nearly across valves, sinus appearing as small deep gap at jugum only; insertion plates of tail valve reduced to striated callus interrupted by deep

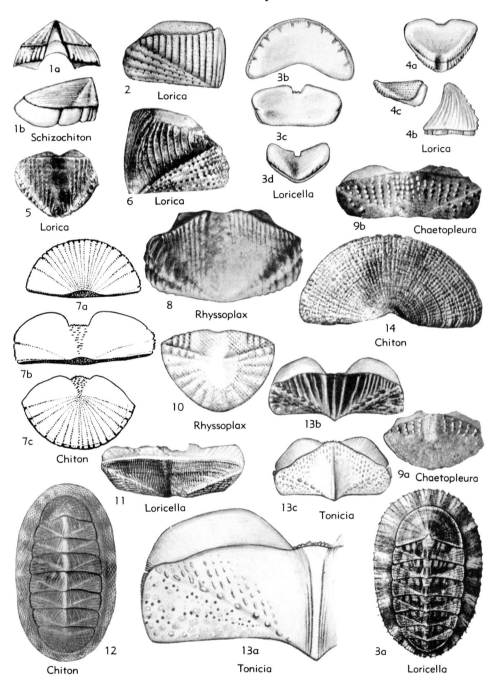

FIG. 41. Neoloricata; Ischnochitonina (Schizochitonidae, Chitonidae) (p. 163-166).

sinus below recurved mucro. Girdle scaly, with slit behind. *L.Mio.*, Tasmania; *M.Mio.*, Austral. (Victoria); *Rec.*, S.Austral.-N.Z.——FIG. 41,2,4.

L. cimolia (REEVE), Rec., Austral.; 2, half of intermed. valve, ×1 (20*); 4a-c, form described as *Chiton volvox* REEVE, 1847 (=*L. cimolia*), Rec.,

Austral., head and tail valves, ×1 (25*).——Fig. 41,5. *L. atkinsoni* (Ashby), L.Mio., Tasmania; tail valve, ×2 (1*).——Fig. 41,6. *L. cudmorei* Ashby, L.Mio., Tasmania, intermed. valve, ×2 (1*).

Loricella Pilsbry, 1893 [*Lorica angasi* H. Adams & Angas, 1864] [=*Squamophora* Nierstrasz, 1905; *Pseudoloricella* Ashby, 1925]. Like *Lorica* but head valve abnormally large. Sutural laminae continuous across intermediate valves in one group but normally with narrow gap under jugum filled with pectinated, spade-shaped forward extension of articulamentum. Tail valve small, with sinuate callus having 2 obscure lateral slits. Girdle also decorated with small spicules. *L.Mio.*, Tasmania; *L.Plio.*, Austral.(Victoria); *Rec.*, Austral.-Celebes. ——Fig. 41,3. *L. angasi* (Adams & Angas), Rec., Austral.; *3a*, whole animal, ×1 (20*); *3b-d*, valves (ventral views), ×1 (25*).——Fig. 41,11. *L. sculpta* Ashby, L.Mio., Tasmania; intermed. valve, ×1.5 (1*).

Family CHITONIDAE Rafinesque, 1815

[*nom. correct.* Gray, 1834 (*pro* family Chitonia Rafinesque, 1815), validation proposed, L. R. Cox, ICZN pend.] [=Gymnoplacidae Gray, 1821; Chitones Férussac, 1821; Chitonacea Menke, 1830; Chitonina Macgillivray, 1843; Chaetopleurae Rochebrune, 1881 (*partim*); Chaetochitonidae Rochebrune, 1889 (*partim*); Placophoridae (*partim*), Lophyridae (*partim*) Dall, 1889; Toniciinae, Chitoninae (*non* Adams & Adams, 1858), Liolophurinae Pilsbry, 1893; Acanthopleurinae Thiele, 1910, Rhyssoplacinae, Amaurochitoninae, Sypharochitoninae, Onithochitoninae Iredale & Hull, 1932; Tonicinae Bergenhayn, 1930]

Small to large chitons with sculpture of tegmentum varying considerably in strength and character; articulamentum consisting of strong insertion plates and sutural laminae. Differ from all other chiton families in well-developed pectination on outside of insertion plates, which ranges from coarsely grooved to fine and comblike. Girdle may be scaly, with short bristles, spines, or spicules, or nude and leathery. *Cret.-Rec.*

The family includes the more highly specialized chitons comprising several diverse groups of species. The well-marked pectination of the insertion plates is considered at present to be the common family character that appears to have developed at least in the Cretaceous and possibly earlier.

Authors have divided the Chitonidae into several subfamilies based largely on type of tegmentum sculpture and variations in girdle ornamentation. As such a division at present can only be provisional in view of the limited knowledge of species relationships within the family, it is not attempted here. Subfamily usage is indicated in the synonymy, the approach to a modern classification dating from Pilsbry, 1893.

Chiton Linné, 1758 [*C. tuberculatus;* SD Dall, 1879] [=*Scuterigulus* Meuschen, 1787; *Lophyrus* Poli, 1791; *Gymnoplax* Gray, 1821; *Lepidopleurus* Leach in Risso, 1826; *Radsia* Gray, 1847; *Trachyodon* Dall, 1892; *Chondroplax, Diochiton, Georgus* Thiele, 1893; *Typhlochiton* Dall, 1921]. Mostly medium-sized to large, usually rather low-arched; intermediate valves with one or more slits and the end valves multiple-slitted; lateral areas generally raised and fairly prominent, their surface smooth to radially or concentrically ribbed, or combining these; central areas may be longitudinally lirated or smooth, or with only jugal area smooth. Girdle usually covered by smooth, large, imbricating scales. [Prior to the work of Dall (1879, 1882) and to some extent subsequently, nearly all polyplacophorans were classified in the genus *Chiton.* This is true of a great many fossil species, a large number of which have been inadequately described and imperfectly or improperly figured because of understandable lack of attention to now-known significant differences in the structure and configuration of chiton shells. Thus, it is impossible to place many fossil species described as *Chiton* in a modern classification without a thorough study of original materials. In the arrangement of Chitonidae here given, only those fossil records are cited that can be referred with some confidence to *Chiton* or other genera of the family group. Other fossil records must be left in the status of *incertae sedis* until relationships of such species can be worked out.] *U.Cret.*, USA(Md.-Tenn.); *Eoc.*, Fr.(Paris Basin)-USA(Ala.); *Mio.-Plio.*, Eu.(Fr.-Aus.-Italy-Eng.); *Pleist.*, Sicily; *Rec.*, cosmop. (nearly all temperate and tropical seas). [*Chiton squamosus* Linné, 1758, herein designated by A. G. Smith as type of *Scuterigulus* Meuschen, 1787.]

C. (*Chiton*). *U.Cret.-Rec.*, cosmop.——Fig. 41,12. *C.* (*C.*) *tuberculatus*, Rec., W.Indies; whole animal, ×1 (25*).——Fig. 41,7. *C.* (*C.*) *albolineatus* Broderip & Sowerby, Rec., Gulf of Calif.; *7a-c*, head, intermed., tail valves showing pectination of insertion plates, ×2 (35*).——Figs. 40,3, 41,14. *C.* (*C.*) *cretaceus* C. T. Berry, U. Cret.; *40,3a,b*, head valve (holotype), USA(Md.), ×2.7; *41,14*, intermed. valve (paratype), USA (Tenn,). ×2.6 (9*). The following names for species groups closely related to *Chiton* as now restricted have been used by recent authors in a sectional or subgeneric sense, and by some as having full generic status. The forms so designated differ from typical *Chiton* in size, characters of tegmentum sculpture, girdle ornamentation, and in what appear to be minor variations in the type of slitting and other feaures of the articulamentum. For convenience they are here treated as having subgeneric rank.

C. (**Rhyssoplax**) Thiele, 1893 [*Chiton janierensis* Gray, 1821; SD Iredale, 1914] [=*Clathropleura* Thiele, 1893 (*non* Tiberi, 1877); *Antho-*

chiton Thiele, 1893]. *Oligo.*, N.Z.; *L.Mio.*, Austral.(Victoria); *Plio.*, Austral.-N.Z.; *Rec.*, Austral.-N.Z.-S.Afr.——Fig. 41,*10. C. (R.) macdonaldensis* (Ashby & Cotton), L.Plio., Victoria (referred to *Anthochiton* by authors); tail valve, ×8.5 (5*).——Fig. 41,*8. C. (R.) relatus* (Ashby & Cotton), U.Plio., S.Austral.; intermed. valve, ×7.5 (11*).

C. (Amaurochiton) Thiele, 1893 [**Chiton olivaceus* Fremly, 1827 (*non* Spengler, 1797), =**Chiton magnificus* Deshayes, 1832; SD Iredale & Hull, 1926 [=*Poeciloplax* Thiele, 1893]. *Rec.*, N.Z.-Tasm.-W.S.Am.

C. (Sypharochiton) Thiele, 1893 [**Chiton pelliserpentis* Quoy & Gaimard, 1835] [=*Triboplax* Thiele, 1893; *Sympharochiton*, Oliver, 1915 (*nom. null.*)]. *Rec.*, N.Z.-E.Austral.

C. (Squamopleura) Nierstrasz, 1905 [**Chiton miles* Carpenter in Pilsbry, 1893; SD Pilsbry, 1893] [=*Sclerochiton* Carpenter in Dall, 1882 (*non* Kraatz, 1859); *Sklerochiton* Nierstrasz, 1905 (*nom. null.*); *Slerochiton* Thiele, 1910 (*errore*)]. Similar to *C. (Chiton)* but teeth of tail valve projecting forward, blunt; sinus smooth, not denticulate. Girdle scales striated and separated, not imbricating. *Rec.*, Ceylon-Indonesia-New Guinea-W.Austral.-N.Caledonia.

C. (Delicatoplax) Iredale & Hull, 1926 [**Chiton translucens* Hedley & Hull, 1909]. *Rec.*, Austral. (NSW-S.Queensl.).

C. (Tegulaplax) Iredale & Hull, 1926 [**Chiton howensis* Hedley & Hull, 1912]. *Rec.*, Red Sea-Ceylon-Maldive Arch.-Molucca I.-N.Austral.

C. (Mucrosquama) Iredale & Hull, 1926 [**Chiton carnosus* Angas, 1867]. *Rec.*, S.Austral.

Tonicia Gray, 1847 (June) [**Chiton elegans* Fremly, 1827 (*non* deBlainville, 1825, *nom. inquir.*); SD Gray, 1847 (Nov.)] [=*Tonichia* Gray, 1840 (*nom. nud.*); *Conicia* Sowerby, 1852 (*nom. null.*); *Fannyia* Gray, 1857; *Fannettia* Dall, 1882 (*pro Fannia* Dall, 1882, *non* Robineau-Desvoidy, 1830); *Tonica* Odhner, 1917 (*nom. null.*)]; *Tonicea* Ashby, 1926 (*nom. null.*)]. Medium-sized (length 1 to 2 in.), surface of tegmentum generally relatively smooth; valve *ii* tending to be noticeably larger than valves *iii* to *viii* and with different sculpture on jugal area; end valves and forward part of lateral areas of intermediate valves with radiating rows or bands of small black eye dots scattered among granules of surface sculpture; eaves not very spongy; insertion-plate teeth pectinated, end valves multiple-slitted, intermediate valves usually with single slit but some with more; sutural laminae separated by squared, denticulate sinus. Girdle leathery, nude or sparsely hairy. *Eoc.-Plio.*, Fr.; *Rec.*, cosmop. (nearly all seas except along W. N.Am. N. of Mex.). [The fossil records are based on the somewhat problematical identifications of Rochebrune, 1883.]——Figs. 41,*13*; 42,*1. *T.

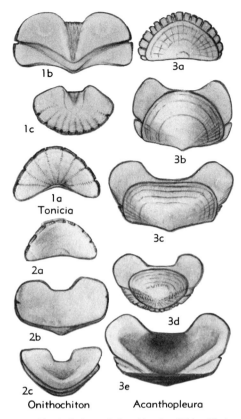

Fig. 42. Neoloricata; Ischnochitonina (Chitonidae) (*p. 166-167*).

elegans (Fremly), Rec., W.S.Am.; 41,*13a-c*, intermed. valves, dorsal view showing eye dots; 42, *1a-c*, head, intermed., tail valves, ventral views; all ×2 except 41,*13a*, ×4 (25*).

Lucilina Dall, 1882 [**Chiton confossus* Gould, 1846] [=*Lucia* Gould, 1862 (*non* Swainson, 1833); *Toniciopsis* Thiele, 1893; *Onithoplax* Thiele, 1910]. Small to medium-sized, elongate-oval, elevated, round-backed or carinated; tegmentum sculpture consisting of pits and nodules; tail valve with prominent, elevated mucro; insertion plates and sutural sinus finely pectinated, posterior insertion plate projecting somewhat forward; slit formula usually 8-1-12. Girdle fleshy, finely spiculose. *Rec.*, Austral.-E.Pac.

Onithochiton Gray, 1847 (June) [**Chiton undulatus* Quoy & Gaimard, 1835 (*non* Wood, 1828) =**Onithochiton neglectus* Rochebrune, 1881] [=*Onythochiton* Gray, 1847 (Nov.) (*nom. null.*); *Ornithochiton* Carpenter in Dall, 1882 (*nom. null.*); *Onitochiton* Rochebrune, 1884 (*nom. null.*); *Pristochiton* Clessin, 1903; *Onithella* Mackay, 1933]. Small to large oval, elevated, round-

backed, polished, somewhat beaked; dorsal sculpture of low nodules and fine longitudinal lirae; tail valve depressed, triangular, with posterior terminal and marginal mucro; eyes well developed in ray on forward part of each lateral area and in numerous rays on head valve; articulamentum as in *Tonicia* but insertion plate of tail valve not slit and reduced to low, smooth, narrow callus; head valve with 8 slits; intermediate valves with single slit; interior of valves porcelaneous. Girdle fleshy, decorated with minute chaffy hairs or spicules, or microscopic scales. *Rec.*, S.Afr.-Austral.-N.Z.——FIG. 42,2. *O. lyelli* (SOWERBY), Austral.; *2a-c*, head, intermed., tail valves, ventral views, showing unslit callused insertion plate of tail valve, ×1.5 (25*).

Acanthopleura GUILDING, 1830 [*Chiton spinosus* BRUGUIÈRE, 1792] [=*Canthapleura* SWAINSON, 1840 *(nom. null.)*; *Corephium* GRAY, 1847 *(non* BROWN, 1827); *Maugeria* GRAY, 1857; *Franciscia* CARPENTER in DALL, 1882; *Rhopalopleura* THIELE, 1893; *Mesotomura, Amphitomura* PILSBRY, 1893; *Acanthozostera* IREDALE & HULL, 1926]. Large, round-backed, depressed, oval, beaked; subobsolete sculpture usually too eroded to be discerned except at valve edges; tegmentum broadly inflexed at posterior valve margins; mucro posterior; eyes small, situated on forward part of lateral areas and scattered among surface granules, usually seen only where unworn new shell growth appears. Valves thick, heavy, generally colored inside; insertion plates deeply grooved and coarsely pectinated, projecting forward. Long teeth of tail valve (more than half length of tegmentum) projecting forward instead of outward, and multiple slitting of intermediate valves characterize genus. Girdle thick and muscular, with dense covering of small to large calcareous spines of varying length. *Pleist.*, S.Am.(Bol.); *Rec.*, E.Afr.-IndoPac.-Austral.-W.S. Am.——FIG. 42,3. *A. spinosa* (BRUGUIÈRE), *Rec.*, Austral.; *3a*, head valve; *3b,c*, intermed. valves; *3d*, tail valve; all dorsal views, ×1.5; *3e*, intermed. valve, ventral view, ×1.5 (25*).

Liolophura PILSBRY, 1893 [*Chiton japonicus* LISCHKE, 1873] [=*Liolopleura* COX, 1893 *(nom. null.)*; *Clavarizona* HULL, 1923]. Like *Onithochiton*, except exterior of valves dull as well as eroded; somewhat raised instead of marginal mucro; distribution of eyes on sides of central areas instead of band on forward part of lateral areas; girdle ornamentation consisting of densely crowded calcareous spines of varying sizes. *Rec.*, Japan-Austral.

Enoplochiton GRAY, 1847 [*Chiton niger* BARNES, 1824]. Like *Onithochiton* except lateral areas of intermediate valves and head valve irregularly studded with minute oval instead of round eyes; articulamentum minutely laminated and punctured in unusual patterns. Girdle fleshy, bearing extremely broad and short, blunt, separately spaced, striated scales. *?Eoc.*, Fr.(Paris Basin); *Rec.*, W.S.Am.

Suborder ACANTHOCHITONINA Bergenhayn, 1930

[=Opsichitonia DALL, 1889 *(partim)*; Mesoplacophora PILSBRY, 1893 *(partim)*; Chitonina THIELE, 1910 *(partim)*; Isoplacophora COTTON & WEEDING, 1939 *(partim)*]

Chitons varying in size from small to largest known, with valves partially to completely buried in girdle; valve coverage ranging from complete to none at all for several posterior valves. Tegmentum surface reduced in area relative to articulamentum, which is highly developed; tegmentum on head valve with anterior area only (FIG. 43,2*a*); on intermediate valves with jugal area having tip at apex of each valve, flanked on both sides by lateropleural areas (FIG. 43,2*b*); tail valve with small triangular jugal area and 2 adjacent subtriangular pleural areas all radiating forward from mucro, and relatively large posterior area behind these (FIG. 43,2*c*). *Oligo.-Rec.*

Family ACANTHOCHITONIDAE Pilsbry, 1893

[*nom. correct.* SIMROTH, 1894 *(pro* Acanthochitidae PILSBRY, 1893)] [=?Acanthochitae ROCHEBRUNE, 1881; Amiculidae DALL, 1889 *(partim)*; Cryptoplacidae, Mopaliidae *(partim)* DALL, 1889; Lophyrochitonidae ROCHEBRUNE, 1889 *(partim)*; Acanthochitinae, Cryptochitoninae PILSBRY, 1893; Cryptoplacinae THIELE, 1910; Cryptoconchidae IREDALE, 1914; Acanthochitoninae ASHBY, 1925; Pseudotonicinae ASHBY, 1928]

This family contains a number of superficially different groups of chitons, all of which seem to be related through division of the tegmentum, when present, into specific shell areas described for the suborder. Encroachment of the girdle over the valves ranges from partial to complete in one genus, which has valves completely buried and no tegmentum layer. Slitting of the insertion plate in the tail valve is an important character and varies from a single slit on each side of a wide, shallow, posterior sinus to multiple-slitted. The head valve in some groups is without dorsal radiating ribs and in others has five such ribs with a correspondingly lobed margin. *L.Oligo.-Rec.*

Recent authors divide this assemblage into subfamilies, which are not recognized here since no approach to unanimity in defining them yet exists. Many genera have been assigned to the family, the tendency having been to raise the status of groups originally

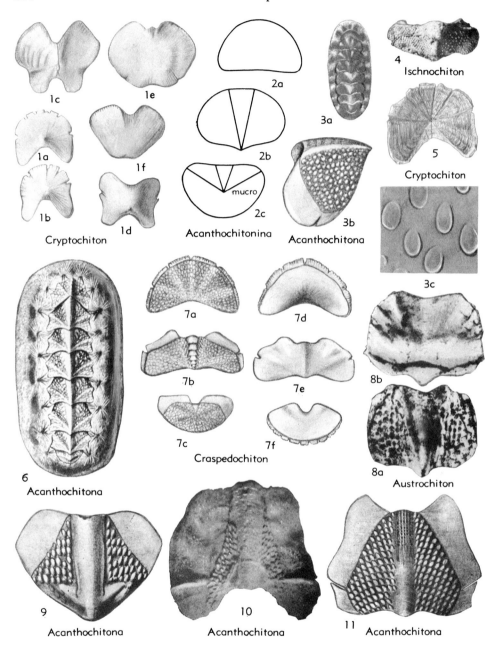

FIG. 43. Neoloricata; Acanthochitonina (Acanthochitonidae) (p. *167-170*).

believed to be only of sectional or subgeneric importance. Because many of these have been segregated on the basis of small differences in tegmentum sculpture and girdle characters, only those appearing to be major generic groups are described in the *Treatise,* what seem to be closely allied group designations being cited in synonymy. Although this arrangement may be regarded by neontologists as somewhat drastic, the classi-

fication is materially simpler for paleontologists, who deal usually only with occasionally found fossil chiton valves.

Acanthochitona GRAY, 1821 [**Chiton fascicularis* LINNÉ, 1766] [=*Chitonellus* DEBLAINVILLE, 1825 (*non* LAMARCK, 1819); *Acanthochites* LEACH in RISSO, 1826; *Phakellopleura* GUILDING, 1830; *Phacellopleura* AGASSIZ, 1846; *Phacelopleura* LOVÉN, 1847 (*nom. null.*); *Platysemus, Hamachiton* MIDDENDORFF, 1848; *Amycula, Strecochiton* A. ADAMS in TAPPARONE-CANEFRI, 1874; *Stectoplax* CARPENTER in DALL, 1882; *Stretochiton* PILSBRY, 1893 (*nom. null.*); *Meturoplax* PILSBRY, 1894; *Acanthochiton* IREDALE, 1915 (*nom. van.*); *Pseudoacanthochiton* ŠULC, 1934; *Eoplax* ASHBY & COTTON, 1936; *Crocochiton* COTTON & WEEDING, 1939; also various misspellings or emendations of *Acanthochites* LEACH in RISSO, 1826: *Acanthochetes* LEACH, 1819 (MS.); *Acanthochistes* COSTA, 1841; *Acanthochaetes* GRAY, 1843; *Acanthochitus* PHILIPPI, 1844; *Acanthochiton* HERRMANNSEN, 1846 (*non Acanthochitona* GRAY, 1821); *Acantoctites* GREGORIO, 1889; *Acanthocites* JOHNSTON, 1891; *Acantochiton* SACCO, 1897; *Acanthochoetes* IREDALE & HULL, 1930]. Small to medium-sized chitons, rather narrow and elongated, tegmentum sculpture consisting of separated nodules or pustules of round to tear-drop shape, generally arranged in radial lines or rows. Valve coverage complete. Tail valves with submedian mucro and no dorsal ribs. Insertion plates generally with 5 slits in head valve, one on each side of intermediate valves, and in tail valve one on each side with a wide shallow sinus between; all teeth sharp and nearly smooth; sutural laminae large. Girdle varying from nude to densely hairy, but invariably with series of bristle-bearing pores (normally 18), situated around head valve with single row on each side at valve sutures. *Mio.*, Eu.(Eng.-Fr.-Aus.) - E. Afr.(Mafia I.) - Austral.(Victoria; *Plio.*, Eu.(Eng.-Fr.-Italy) - USA(Fla.-N. Car.) - Austral.; *Pleist.*, Eu.(Eng.-Sicily)-USA(Calif.); *Rec.*, cosmop. (nearly all seas except N.Pac.).——FIG. 43, 3. **A. fascicularis* (LINNÉ), Rec., Medit.; *3a*, whole animal, ×1; *3b*, intermed. valve, ×3; *3c*, detail of sculpture, ×30 (25*).——FIG. 43,6. *A. crocodilus debilior* IREDALE & HULL, Rec., Austral. (NSW); whole animal, ×2 (20*).——FIG. 43,9. *A. pilsbryoides* ASHBY & COTTON, M.Mio. Austral. (Victoria); intermed. valve, ×14 (11*).——FIG. 43,11. *A. trianguloides* ASHBY & COTTON, L.Plio., Victoria; intermed. valve, ×10 (11*).——FIG. 43, 10. *A. adelaidae* (ASHBY & COTTON), U.Plio., S. Austral. (referred by authors to *Eoplax*); intermed. valve, ×2.8 (11*).——FIG. 43,4. *A. spiculosa* (REEVE), Plio., USA(N.Car.); intermed. valve, ×10 (9*).

Craspedochiton SHUTTLEWORTH, 1853 [**Chiton laqueatus* SOWERBY, 1841; [=*Notoplax* H. ADAMS, 1862; *Phacellopleura, Macandrellus* CARPENTER in

DALL, 1879; *Leptoplax, Spongiochiton, Angasia* (*non* WHITE, 1863) CARPENTER in DALL, 1882; *Augasia* SCUDDER, 1882 (*nom. null.*); *Loboplax* PILSBRY, 1893; *Mecynoplax* THIELE, 1893; *Phacellozona* PILSBRY, 1894 (*pro Angasia* CARPENTER in DALL, 1882, *non* BATE, 1864); *Thaumastochiton, Aristochiton* THIELE, 1909; *Glyptelasma* IREDALE & HULL, 1925; *Craspedoplax* IREDALE & HULL, 1925; *Amblyplax, Lophoplax* ASHBY, 1926; *Bassethullia* PILSBRY, 1928 (*pro Glyptelasma* IREDALE & HULL, 1925; *non* PILSBRY, 1907); *Pseudotonicia* ASHBY, 1928; *Ikedaella* TAKI & TAKI, 1929]. Small to large, generally similar to *Acanthochitona* but nodular sculpture of tegmentum usually more pronounced, head valve having low to prominent ribs, intermediate valves with single rib, and tail valve with or without ribs and subcentral mucro. Animal more or less elongate and tending to be vermiform in some species as result of sponge-living habitat. Insertion plate of head valve 5-slitted, of intermediate valves single-slitted, and of tail valve irregularly with 6 to 10 slits, in some species tending toward replacement with age through degeneration into a callus ridge without slits. Girdle variously spiculose or minutely scaly in addition to sutural tufts (asymmetrical in some species), wider in front than behind. [The genus includes a number of species groups varying in details of surface sculpture, articulamentum structure, and girdle characters, all of which seem to bear close relationship to each other. The dorsal ribbing on the head valve and the multiple-slitted insertion plate of the tail valve seem to be common features that distinguish this genus from *Acanthochitona*.] *L. Oligo.*, N.Z.; *?Mio.*, Eu.(Austr.); *U.Plio.*, N.Z.; *?Tert.*, Eu.(Italy); *Rec.*, IndoPac.-Austral.-N.Z. ——FIG. 43,7. **C. laqueatus* (SOWERBY), Rec., Philippines; *7a-c*, head, intermed., and tail valves, dorsal views; *7d-f*, same, ventral view; ×2 (25*).

Choneplax CARPENTER in DALL, 1882 [**Chiton strigatus* SOWERBY, 1840 (=**Chitonellus latus* GUILDING, 1829)] [=*Chitoniscus* CARPENTER in DALL, 1882 (*?ex* HERRMANNSEN, 1846); *Chnoeplax* PILSBRY, 1894 (*nom. null.*)]. Small to medium-sized, body somewhat vermiform, living in coral holes. Valves subequal in size, with complete valve coverage; mucro of tail valve projecting far backward; insertion plates and sutural laminae all strongly projecting forward, head valve with 3 to 5 shallow slits, others with single slit on each side or none. Girdle minutely setose; sutural tufts may be obsolete. *Rec.*, W.Indies.

Cryptoconchus DEBLAINVILLE in BURROW, 1815 [**Chiton porosus* BURROW; SD GRAY, 1847 (Nov.)] [=*Cryptoconctus* SOWERBY, 1852; *Cryptochoncus* CLESSIN, 1903]. Large, elongate chitons with valves almost completely buried in large, fleshy girdle, only a very small jugal area being exposed. Valves large, valve coverage complete, uncovered tegmentum practically linear in inter-

mediate valves, minute subcircular spot on head valve, and long line on tail valve. Dorsal sculpture consisting of a few small, flattened, somewhat rounded pustules. Articulamentum strong and solid, head valve 5-slitted, intermediate valves single-slitted, tail valve multiple-slitted between 2 major side slits, total number ranging from 5 to 7. Girdle with usual 18 sutural tufts, which grow out of sizeable elevated, rounded pockets. *Rec.*, N.Z.

Cryptochiton MIDDENDORFF, 1847 [*Chiton (Cryptochiton) stelleri;* SD DALL, 1879]. Largest of the chitons, with length up to 10 inches or more. Valves completely buried in tough, thick girdle, lacking tegmentum layer, more or less thinned at edges and crenulated by radial striae, their posterior margins produced backward in a deep lobe on each side, lobes united across median line causing their apices to be removed inward from posterior edge. Head valve with 4 to 7 slits; intermediate valves having subobsolete slits or none; tail valve with slit on each side of deep sinus, mucro posterior or near posterior third. Girdle covered with myriad fascicles of minute spinelets. *Plio.*, USA(Calif.); *Pleist.*, Calif.-Mex.(BajaCalif.); *Rec.*, N.Pac.(N.Japan to Aleutian I. and Calif.).—— FIG. 43,*1,5.* *C. stelleri* (MIDDENDORFF); *1a,b,* head valves; *1c,d,* intermed. valves; *1e,f,* tail valves; all dorsal views, ×0.5, Rec., Calif. (25*); 43,5, ventral view of delaminated head valve, ×0.5, Pleist., Calif. (10*). [*Cryptochiton=Cryptochiton* GRAY, 1847 (*partim*)].

Austrochiton BERGENHAYN, 1945 [*Acanthochites rostratus* ASHBY & TORR, 1901]. Tegmentum of single intermediate valve decorated with oval tubercles arranged in longitudinal rows on lateropleural areas, posterior margin strongly beaked. Maximum width of jugal area about equal to that of lateropleural areas. Articulamentum represented only by sutural laminae, which reach almost to anterior margin of long apical area. *M. Mio.*, Austral.(Victoria).——FIG. 43,*8.* *A. rostratus* (ASHBY & TORR); *8a,b,* intermed. valve (holotype), dorsal and ventral, ×6 (42*).

Cryptoplax DEBLAINVILLE, 1818 [*Chiton larvaeformis* BURROW, 1815; SD HERRMANNSEN, 1852] [=*Chitonellus* LAMARCK, 1819; *Crytoplax* GRAY, 1821; *Chitonella* DESHAYES, 1830 (*nom. null.*); *Oscabrella* BRODERIP, 1835; *Chitoniscus* HERR-MANNSEN, 1846 (*pro Chitenellus* LAMARCK, 1819) (*nom. van.*); *Ametrogephyrus, Phaenochiton, Dichachiton* MIDDENDORFF, 1848; *Dibachiton* PAE-TEL, 1875 (*nom. null.*)]. Medium-sized to large, elongate, almost vermiform chitons with valves well buried in thick, fleshy girdle; valves all in contact in juveniles but with increasing age they tend to separate, separation becoming very wide in valves *v* to *viii.* Tegmentum of head valve circular or more than semicircle; of valve *ii,* irregularly orbicular; of valve *iii,* roundly oval; and of

remainder, elongate-oval. Dorsal sculpture granulose, granules forming longitudinal or radiating lozenge-chains or massing into irregular lines. Jugal area linear, narrow, generally smooth; lateropleural areas not separated. Mucro of tail valve terminal. Articulamentum with large insertion plate in head valve, obsoletely 3-slitted; intermediate valves with large sutural laminae and unslit insertion plates; tail valve also with unslit insertion plate, which generally projects strongly forward but may be directed backward. Girdle densely spiculose, with small sutural tufts, most prominent in living animal. *?L.Mio.(Burdigal.),* Eu. (Austr.); *U.Mio.,* E.Borneo; *Plio.,* Austral.; *Rec.,* Japan-Indo Pac.-Austral.-N. Z.-Tasm. —— FIG. 44, *1a-f.* *C. larvaeformis* (BURROW), Rec., Austral.; *1a,b,* juvenile and adult animals, ×1 (20*); *1c-f,* valves (*1c,* head; *1d,e,* tail, *1f,* juvenile tail), ×2 (20*).——FIG. 44,*1g.* *C. numicus* ASHBY & COT-TON, L.Plio., Victoria; intermed. valve, ×12 (11*). ——FIG. 44,*1h.* *C. pritchardi* HALL, L.Plio., Austral.(Victoria); intermed. valve, ×6.5 (11*).

Suborder AFOSSOCHITONINA Bergenhayn, 1955

Shell areas of tegmentum similar to those in Lepidopleurina, sculpture somewhat resembling *Acanthochitona;* articulamentum represented by sutural laminae only. *M.Mio.*

Family AFOSSOCHITONIDAE Ashby, 1925

[*nom. transl.* BERGENHAYN, 1945 (*ex* Afossochitoninae ASHBY, 1925)]

Characters of the suborder. *M.Mio.*

Afossochiton ASHBY, 1925 [*A. cudmorei*] [?=*Telochiton* ASHBY & COTTON, 1939]. Small chitons having intermediate valves with tegmentum sculpture of large subtriangular tubercles arranged in distinct rows running anteriorly and laterally from posterior margin; sculpture of jugal area undetermined; apical area very narrow; articulamentum as in suborder. Head and tail valves unknown but the latter assumed to have sutural laminae as in intermediate valves. *M.Mio.*, Austral.(Victoria).——FIG. 44,*7.* *A. cudmorei;* intermed. valve, ×6 (42*).

Incertae Sedis
Suborder Uncertain
Family LLANDEILOCHITONIDAE Bergenhayn, 1955

Chitons with shell lacking articulamentum layer. Shape of intermediate valves subquadrate, tegmentum surface divided into 7 areas consisting of 2 side slopes of valve on either side of a peculiarly shaped jugal

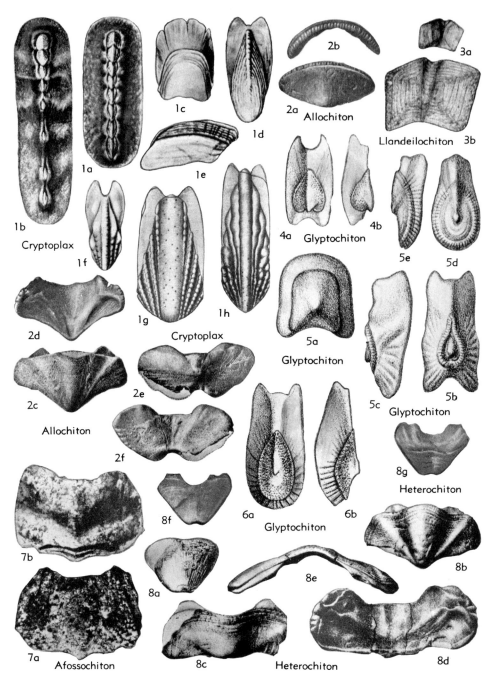

Fig. 44. Neoloricata; Acanthochitonina (Acanthochitonidae); Afossochitonina (Afossochitonidae); Incertae Sedis (Llandeilochitonidae and others) (p. 170-172).

area, which is formed like the lower half of an expanding tube, very narrow posteriorly and gradually enlarging to give the valve a concave dip at middle of the anterior edge; from approximate center of valve 4 indistinct ribs or structural breaks radiate to each

of its corners, thus dividing it into 2 anterior, 2 lateral, and 2 posterior areas, but this division does not affect the channel-like jugal area. *M.Ord.*

Llandeilochiton BERGENHAYN, 1955 [*L. ashbyi*]. Characters of the family. End valves unknown. *M.Ord.*, Austral.——FIG. 44,3. *L. ashbyi*, Llandeilo., Austral., *3a*, intermed. valve (type), ×1.8; *3b*, schematic view of intermed. valve, ×3.6 (8*).

Suborder and Family Uncertain

Allochiton FUCINI, 1912 [*A. gemmellaroi*; SD A.G. SMITH, herein]. Shell not very elongate, tail valve rather large, almost smooth, bilobate, with rounded and beaked posterior apex; insertion plate of head valve with numerous coarse slits, similar in size to those of intermediate valves. [FUCINI states that the genus has some aspects of the Mopaliidae, Acanthochitonidae, and Cryptoplacidae.] *L.Jur.*, Eu.(Sicily).——FIG. 44,2. *A. gemmellaroi*, Montagna di Casale; *2a,b*, head valve; *2c,d*, intermed. valve; *2e,f*, tail valve; all ×2 (15*).

Beloplaxus OEHLERT, 1881 [*Chiton sagittalis* SANDBERGER, 1853]. Chitons with triangular valves having sloping lateral areas, wide median depression, and anterior end with projecting angles and deep indentation at edge; posterior end with narrow insertion surface lying adjacent to lateral edges. [OEHLERT compares this genus with *Sagmaplaxus*, which in the *Treatise* is assigned with some doubt to the Chelodidae.] *Dev.*, Eu.(Villmar-Prussia in Hesse-Nassau).

Glyptochiton DEKONINCK, 1883 [*Chiton? cordifer*, DEKONINCK, 1844]. Elongate, rather small, possibly vermiform chitons with small tegmentum area and much larger articulamentum area, indicating an animal with valves well buried in girdle and almost or entirely separated from each other. Head valve with rounded anterior margin, nearly straight sides, and posterior margin with broad semicircular sinus bounded on either side by rounded marginal valve ends; tegmentum similar in shape, occupying inner 0.7 of dorsal surface except at posterior edge where it coincides with articulamentum; valve subpyramidal in profile with mucro-like apex situated somewhat behind center. Intermediate valves narrow, rather high-arched, twice as long as wide, anterior margin with deep rounded sinus, posterior with a similar but squared sinus, sides somewhat waved, widest about 0.3 of distance behind rounded anterior shell tips, whole valve configuration subquadrate in aspect; tegmentum area of tear-drop or very elongate heart shape, marked by strong crenulated rib, inside of which is a smooth depression with a sizable, raised, elongate pustule at center, and radiating from this rib are rather weak, closely spaced riblike striae that become obsolete at valve margin but do not appear on posterior 0.3 of articulamentum area. Supposed tail valve narrower in front than behind, with somewhat truncated

anterior edge, posterior end oval; tegmentum set off by a similar crenulated ovate rib that occupies more than 0.7 of dorsal area, smooth inside area with prominent subcentral mucro, back of which anterior end slopes away sharply; articulamentum projecting forward from front edge of tegmentum, sloping away from it quite deeply at anterior end of shell and marked with similar radiating striae. Ventral aspect of valves unknown. *L.Carb.*, Eu. (Belg.-Scot.). —— FIG. 44,4. *G. subquadratus* (KIRKBY & YOUNG), Scot.(Ayrshire); *4a,b*, intermed. valve, ×8 (43*).——FIG. 44,5. *G. cordifer* (DEKONINCK), Belg.; *5a-e*, valves (*5a*, head, *5b,c*, intermed., *5d,e*, tail) enlarged (23*).——FIG. 44,6. *G. youngianus* (KIRKBY & YOUNG), Scot. (Ayrshire); *6a,b*, tail valve, ×4 (43*).

Heterochiton FUCINI, 1912 [*H. giganteus*; SD A.G.SMITH, herein]. Shell not very elongate, valves fairly thick and heavy. Tegmentum well developed, sculptured with granules or ribs, or both. Head valve about as long as wide, subpyramidal, widest at anterior edge and narrowing sharply backward; intermediate valves short and wide, generally thrown forward from rounded, projecting apex, with well-marked diagonal rib setting off lateral from pleural areas, which slope upward over rounded jugum. Tail valve solid, shaped like head valve except for fairly deep, rounded sinus anteriorly, apical area extending considerably on to ventral side. Articulamentum of all valves well developed, calloused; insertion plate of head valve slit, of tail valve unslit, and of intermediate valves usually with 2 slits forming rude, rounded teeth; sutural laminae thick, fairly broad, with semicircular or squared sinus between. *L.Jur.*, Eu.(Sicily).——FIG. 44,8. *H. giganteus*, Montagna di Casale; *8a-g*, valves (*8a*, head; *8b-e*, intermed.; *8f,g*, tail), ca. ×2 (15*).——FIG. 45,4. *H. vinassai* FUCINI, Montagna di Casale; *4a,b*, intermed. and tail valves, ca. ×2 (15*).

Lavenachiton COTTON & GODFREY, 1940 [*Ischnochiton (Radsiella) cliftonensis* ASHBY & COTTON, 1939]. Median valve differs from *Ischnochiton* in shape, absence of differentiated lateral areas, and position of sutural laminae; posterior valve characterized by same unique sculpture; bridging of flat irregular ribs forms oblong pits that tend toward a somewhat cuneiform pattern. [The authors think that this genus may belong to the Chitonidae.] *M.Mio.*, Austral.(Victoria).——FIG. 45,7. *L. cliftonensis* (ASHBY & COTTON); intermed. valve, ×3.4 (11*).

Lirachiton ASHBY & COTTON, 1939 [*Acanthochiton (Lirachiton) inexpectus* ASHBY & COTTON, 1931] [=*Molachiton* ASHBY & COTTON, 1939]. Pleural areas decorated with narrow, widely spaced ribs instead of granular ornamentation; in type species sculpture behind mucro and in area corresponding to lateral area of median valve is formed of triangular flat grains; near apex of each is an

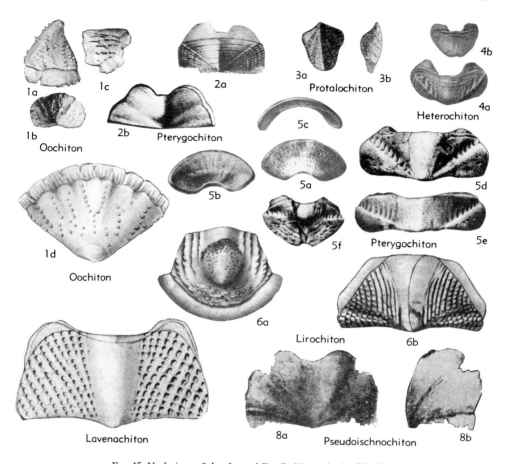

FIG. 45. Neoloricata; Suborder and Family Uncertain (p. *172-174*).

ocellus or sense organ. [Possibly classed in Acanthochitonidae, as provisionally placed by the authors, or in the Afossochitonidae.] *L.Plio.,* Austral.(Victoria).——FIG. 45,6. **L. inexpectus* (ASHBY & COTTON); *6a*, head valve, ×7; *6b*, intermed. valve, ×6.5 (11*).

Oochiton ASHBY, 1929 [**O. halli*]. Very small, high-arched, carinated chitons; valves with steep side slopes. Sculpture of erect, ovate pustules arranged in irregular rows or widely scattered over dorsal surface, each with a minute aperture at summit. Head valve with tegmentum unfolded at apex and well-produced insertion plate with irregularly spaced, broad, and short slits, outside closely grooved but leaving a sharp, beveled edge; intermediate valves with single, broad, deep slit on each side of pectinated insertion plate, sutural laminae joined across median line; tail valve unique, with upturned, greatly thickened extremity and deep sinus immediately behind mucro, tegmentum having an extended fold into sinus.

[Provisionally placed in the Chitonidae by COTTON & GODFREY (1940).] *M.Mio.,* Austral.(Victoria). ——FIG. 45,1. **O. halli; 1a-d,* valves (*1d*, head), enlarged (11*).

Protalochiton ROCHEBRUNE, 1883 [**P. settlensis* (*pro Chiton?* sp. nov. KIRKBY, 1862)]. Shell ovate-elliptical, carinate, head valve semicircular, tail valve elevated; valve *ii* subtriangular, with anterior edge undulate, jugum acute, and posterior edge umbonate; other intermediate valves narrow, elevated, and concave anteriorly. Tail valve cap-shaped, with abruptly acute posterior, reflected apex. Articulamentum, if any, not defined. *L.Carb.,* Eu.(Eng.).——FIG. 45,3. **P. settlensis*, L.Scar Ls., Yorkshire; *3a,b*, ?intermed. valve, ×3 (47*).

Pseudoischnochiton ASHBY, 1930 [**P. wynyardensis*]. Only median valve known, its shell extremely thin and unsculptured except for a strongly raised rib and weak radial ribbing; pleural area unusually broad, tegmentum well bowed for-

ward on either side of jugal sinus; sutural laminae reduced to narrow extension of articulamentum bordering anteriorly bowed tegmentum; insertion plates absent wholly or in part. [ASHBY considers *Pseudoischnochiton* to be a primitive genus belonging either in the Lepidopleuridae or Ischnochitonidae.] *L.Mio.,* Tasmania.——FIG. 45,8. **P. wynyardensis; 8a,b,* intermed. valve, top and side views, ×2, ×3.5 (41*).

Pterygochiton ROCHEBRUNE, 1883 [**Chiton terquemi* DESLONGCHAMPS, 1859; SD A.G.SMITH, herein]. Shell ovate, carinate, strongly arched; valves broad, anterior edge more or less emarginate, sutural laminae broad, rounded, very prominent, and separated by a subquadrate sutural sinus; tail valve elliptical, with very prominent, pointed, straight mucro. *L.Jur.,* Fr.-?Sicily.——FIG. 45,2. **P. terquemi* (DESLONGCHAMPS); *2a,b,* intermed. valve and internal cast, ×? (44*).——FIG. 45,5. *P.? busambrensis* FUCINI, Sicily(Montagna di Casale); *5a-f,* valves (*5a-c,* head; *5d,e,* intermed., *5f,* tail), ca. ×2 (15*).

Doubtful Genera

Several genera considered to represent fossil remains of chitons have been omitted from the systematic account of Polyplacophora because of doubt as to their nature. They include the following:

Duslia JAHN, 1893 [**D. insignis*]. *L.Sil.,* Bohemia.
Permochiton IREDALE & HULL, 1926 [**P. australianus*]. Permo-Carb., Austral.(NSW).
Solenocaris YOUNG & YOUNG, 1868 [**S. solenoides*]. *Sil.,* Scot.
Sulcochiton RYCKHOLT, 1862 [**S. grayi*]. *L.Carb.,* Belg.
Trachypleura JAECKEL, 1900 [**T. triadomarchica*]. *Trias.,* Ger.

Subclass APLACOPHORA von Ihering, 1876

[Treated by VON IHERING as "class" in "phylum" Amphineura of the Vermes] [=Telobranchia KOREN & DANIELSSEN, 1877; Solenogastres GEGENBAUR, 1878; Scolecomorpha LANKESTER, 1883]

Wormlike animals with spiculose integument, adults without covering of shelly plates. *Rec.*

Order NEOMENIIDA Simroth, 1893

[*nom. correct.* A.G.SMITH, herein (*pro* Neomeniina SIMROTH, 1893)] [=Neomeniomorpha PELSENEER in LANKESTER, 1906]

Spiculose integument with distinct longitudinal ventral groove; bisexual, with paired genital glands and lacking a differentiated liver. *Rec.*

Family NEOMENIIDAE von Ihering, 1876

[*nom. correct.* SIMROTH, 1893 (*pro* Neomeniadae VON IHERING, 1876)]

Body short, truncated in front and behind; cloacal orifice transverse; gills present; rather thin integument; no radula. [Contains 43 genera, 96 species.] *Rec.*

Family PRONEOMENIIDAE Simroth, 1893

Body elongate, cylindrical, rounded at both ends; thick integument with acicular spicules; radula polystichous or wanting. [Contains 12 genera, 40 species.] *Rec.*

Family LEPIDOMENIIDAE Pruvot, 1890

Body slender, tapering behind, with subventral cloacal orifice; cuticle thin, without papillae; spicules flattened; no gills.

[Contains 11 genera, 23 species.] *Rec.*

Family GYMNOMENIIDAE Odhner, 1921

Cuticle thin, epidermis a single multicellular layer without papillae; no spicula. [Contains single genus and species.] *Rec.*

Order CHAETODERMATIDA Simroth, 1893

[*nom. correct.* A.G.SMITH, herein (*pro* Chaetodermatina SIMROTH, 1893)] [=Chaetodermorpha PELSENEER in LANKESTER, 1906]

Animals without distinct ventral or pedal groove; gonad unpaired, unisexual; liver differentiated; posterior cloacal chamber with two bipectinate gills. *Rec.*

Family CHAETODERMATIDAE von Ihering, 1876

[*nom. correct.* SIMROTH, 1893 (*pro* Chaetodermata VON IHERING, 1876)]

Characters of the order. [Contains 4 genera, 27 species.] *Rec.*

REFERENCES

POLYPLACOPHORA

The following publications relating to the Polyplacophora have been selected from a much longer list. They are considered to be

the ones most helpful in any study of living and particularly of fossil forms. Some contain extensive reference lists to systematic work on the group that should be consulted for a complete picture of it.

Ashby, Edwin
(1) 1925, *Monograph on Australian fossil Poly-placophora (chitons):* Roy. Soc. Victoria, Proc., new ser., v. 37, pt. 2, p. 170-205, pl. 18-22 (Melbourne).
(2) 1929, *Notes and additions to Australian fossil Polyplacophora (chitons):* Same, v. 41, pt. 2, p. 220-230, pl. 24.
(3) 1929, *New Zealand fossil Polyplacophora (chitons):* New Zealand Inst., Trans. Proc., v. 60, pt. 2, p. 366-369, pl. 32, fig. 1-13a,b (Wellington).
(4) 1939, *Fossil chitons from Mornington, Victoria:* Linn. Soc. London, Proc., 151st session (1938-39), pt. 3, p. 186-189, pl. 3, fig. 1-4.
―――, & Cotton, B. C.
(5) 1936, *South Australian fossil chitons:* South Australian Mus., Records, v. 5, pt. 4, p. 509-512, text fig. (Adelaide).
(6) 1939, *New fossil chitons from the Miocene and Pliocene of Victoria:* Same, v. 6, pt. 3, p. 209-242, pl. 19-21.

Bergenhayn, J. R. M.
(7) 1930, *Kurtze Bemerkungen zur Kenntnis der Schalenstruktur und Systematik der Loricaten:* Kungl. Svenska Vetenskapsak., Handl., ser. 3, v. 9, no. 3, p. 1-54, pl. 1-10 (Stockholm).
(8) 1955, *Die fossilen schwedischen Loricaten nebst einer vorläufigen Revision des Systems der ganzen Klasse Loricata:* Lunds Univ. Årssk., new ser., 2, v. 51, no. 8 (Kungl. Fysiogr. Sallskapets, Handl., new ser., v. 66, no. 8), p. 1-41, pl. 1-2.

Berry, C. T.
(9) 1940, *Some fossil Amphineura from the Atlantic Coastal Plain of North America:* Acad. Nat. Sci. Philadelphia, Proc., v. 91 (1939), p. 207-217, pl. 9-12.

Berry, S. S.
(10) 1922, *Fossil chitons of western North America:* California Acad. Sci., Proc., ser. 4, v. 11, no. 18, p. 399-526, pl. 1-16, text fig. 1-11 (San Francisco).

Cotton, B. C. & Godfrey, F. K.
(11) 1940, *Australian fossil chitons:* Handbook, Molluscs of South Australia, South Australia Mus., pt. 2, p. 569-590, text figs. 577-589 (Adelaide).

Dall, W. H.
(12) 1879, *Report on the limpets and chitons of the Alaskan and Arctic regions, with descriptions of genera and species believed to be new:* U. S. Natl. Mus., Proc., v. 1 (1878), p. 281-344, pl. 1-5; also published, 1879, as Scientific Results, Explor. Alaska, art. 4, p. 63-126, pl. 1-5 (Washington).
(13) 1882, *On the genera of chitons:* U. S. Natl. Mus., Proc., v. 4 (1881), p. 279-291 (Washington).

Dechaseaux, Colette
(14) *Classe des Amphineures:* in PIVETEAU, J., Traité de Paléontologie, v. 2, p. 210-215, fig. 1-4, Masson (Paris).

Fucini, A.
(15) 1912, *Polyplacophora del Lias Inferiore della Montagna di Casale in Sicilia:* Paleontographica Italica, Pisa, v. 18, p. 105-127, pl. 18-19.

Gray, J. E.
(16) 1847, *On the genera of the family Chitonidae:* Zool. Soc. (London), Proc., 1847, p. 63-70.
(17) 1847, *Additional observations on Chitones:* Same, pt. 15, no. 178, p. 126-127.
(18) 1847, *A list of the recent Mollusca, their synonymy and types:* Same, Family Chitonidae, no. 179, p. 168-169.

Hoffman, H.
(19) 1929-30, *Amphineura (Polyplacophora):* in BRONN, H. G., Klassen und Ordnung des Thier-Reichs, v. 3, pt. 1, suppl. 2, p. 135-368 (1929); suppl. 3, p. 369-382, fig. 81-195 (1930); contains long list of references, continuing the list of SIMROTH (in BRONN), 1892-94. (Ref. No. 31).

Iredale, Tom, & Hull, A. F. B.
(20) 1926, *Paleoloricata:* A monograph of the Australian loricates, VIII, App. B, Australian Zool., v. 4, pt. 5, p. 324-328, pl. 45; reprinted, 1927, Roy. Zool. Soc. New South Wales, p. 130-143, pl. 18.

Knorre, Heinrich von
(21) 1925, *Die Schale und die Rückensinnesorgane von Trachydermon (Chiton) cinereus L. und die ceylonischen Chitonen der Sammlung Plate. (Fauna et Anatomica ceylonica, III, nr. 3):* Jenaische Zeitschr. Naturwiss., v. 61 (new ser., v. 54), p. 469-632, pl. 18-35, text fig. 1-17 (Jena).

Koninck, L. G. de
(22) 1857, *Observations on two new species of Chiton from the Upper Silurian 'Wenlock Limestone' of Dudley:* Acad. roy. Sci. Belgique, Bull., ser. 2, v. 3, p. 190-199, pl. 1 (Bruxelles); reprinted in English translation by BAILY, W. H., 1860, Ann. & Mag. Nat. Hist., ser. 3, v. 6, p. 91-98, pl. 2, fig. 1a-d, 2a-c (London).
(23) 1883, *Faune du calcaire carbonifère de la Belgique, pt. 4, Gastéropodes (suite et fin):* Mus. roy. d'Hist. nat. Belgique, Ann., sér. paléont., v. 8, pt. 4, p. 198-213, pl. 50-53 (Bruxelles).

Lindström, G.
(24) 1884, *On the Silurian Gastropoda and Pteropoda of Gotland:* Kungl. Svenska Vetenskap-

sak., Handl., v. 19, no. 6, p. 48-52, pl. 2, fig. 1-28 (Stockholm).

Pilsbry, Henry A.
(25) 1892-94, *Monograph of the Polyplacophora*: Manual of Conchology, v. 14 (1892-93), xxiv+350 p., 68 pl.; v. 15 (1893-94), 133 p., 17 pl. (Philadelphia).
(26) 1900, *Polyplacophora*: in Zittel, K. A., Text-book of Palaeontology (Eastman transl.), p. 433-436, fig. 792-793, Macmillan (London & New York).

Plate, L.
(27) 1897-1901, *Die Anatomie und Phylogenie der Chitonen*: Fauna Chilensis, v. 1, pt. 1, p. 1-243, pl. 1-12 (1897); v. 2, pt. 1, p. 15-216, pl. 2-11 (1899); v. 2, pt. 2, p. 281-600, pl. 12-16 (1901); Zool. Jahrb., Suppl., v. 4 (1898), v. 5 (1902).

Quenstedt, Werner von
(28) 1932, *Die Geschichte der Chitonen und ihre allgemeine Bedeutung*: Paläont. Zeitschr., v. 14, no. 1-2, p. 77-96, fig. 1 (Berlin).

Rochebrune, A. T. de
(29) 1883, *Monographie des espèces fossiles appartenant à la Classe des Polyplaxiphores*: Ann. Sci. géol., v. 14, art. no. 1, p. 1-74, pl. 1-3 (Paris). (The figures are misleading and should be disregarded.)

Ryckholt, Philip de
(30) 1845, *Résumé géologique sur le genre Chiton Lin.*: Acad. roy. Sci. et Belles Lettres, Bull., v. 12, no. 7, pt. 2, p. 36-62, 4 pl. (Bruxelles).

Simroth, H.
(31) 1892-94, *Amphineura*: in Bronn, H. G., Klassen und Ordnung des Thier-Reichs, v. 3 (Mollusca), pt. 1, sec. 1-21, p. 128-355, pl. 1-22, 51 text figs.; excellent bibliography, continued by Hoffman (in Bronn), 1929-30 (Ref. no. 19).

Šulc, Jaroslav
(32) 1936, *Studie über die fossilen Chitonen—I.*

Die fossilen Chitonen im Neogen des Wiener Beckens und der angrezenden Gebiete: Naturhist. Mus. Wien, Ann., v. 47, p. 1-31, text fig. 1-4, pl. 1-2.

Thiele, Johannes
(33) 1893, *Polyplacophora*: in Troschel, F. H., Das Gebiss der Schnecken zur Begründung einer natürlichen Classification, v. 2, p. 353-401, pl. 30-32 (Berlin).
(34) 1909-10, *Revision des Systems der Chitonen*: Zoologica, v. 22, no. 56, p. 1-132, pl. 1-10.
(35) 1929, *Classis Loricata*: Handbuch der systematischen Weichtierkunde, v. 1, pt. 1, p. 1-12, fig. 1-12.

APLACOPHORA

Heath, Harold
(36) 1911, *Reports on the scientific results of the expedition to the tropical Pacific, in charge of Alexander Agassiz, by the U. S. Fish Commission Steamer Albatross, from August 1899 to June 1900, Commander Jefferson F. Moser.–XIV.–The Solenogastres*: Mus. Comp. Zool., Harvard Coll., Mem., v. 45, p. 1-182, pl. 1-40 (Cambridge).
(37) 1918, *Solenogastres from the eastern coast of North America*: Same, v. 45, pt. 2, p. 183-260, pl. 1-14.

Hoffman, H.
(38) 1929, *Aplacophora*: in Bronn, H. G., Klassen und Ordungen des Thier-Reichs, v. 3, pt. 1, p. 1-134, text figs. 1-80 (Leipzig); bibliography of 41 titles.

Pilsbry, H. A.
(39) 1898, *Order Aplacophora v. Ihering*: Man. Conch., Acad. Nat. Sci. Philadelphia, v. 17, p. 281-310.

Simroth, H.
(40) 1893, *Aplacophora*: in Bronn, H. G., Klassen und Ordnungen des Thier-Reichs, v. 3, pt. 1, p. 128-233, pl. 1-4, text figs. 1-12 (Leipzig); bibliography of 40 titles.

SOURCES OF ILLUSTRATIONS

The sources of illustrations for various species in the Polyplacophora are indicated by numbers which in most instances correspond to those assigned to the "List of References" that carry numbers 1-40. Where it has been necessary to select illustrations from sources outside the basic list, these have been assigned numbers above 40, as indicated below. An asterisk(*) associated with an index number signifies that the original figure has been reproduced without alteration except for a possible change in scale.

(41) **Ashby, Edwin**
(42) **Bergenhayn, J. R. M.**
(43) **Etheridge, R., Jr.**
(44) **Eudes-Deslongchamps, J. A.**
(45) **Iredale, Tom & Hull, A. F. B.**
(46) **King, William**
(47) **Kirkby, J. W.**
(48) **Leloup, Eugène**
(49) **Pompeckj, J. F.**
(50) **Richardson, E. S. Jr.**
(51) **Salter, J. W.**
(52) **Sandberger, Guido**
(53) **Wilson, Alice E.**

MONOPLACOPHORA

By J. Brookes Knight[1] and E. L. Yochelson[2]

Class MONOPLACOPHORA Wenz in Knight, 1952

Mollusks with a single shell, cap-shaped, or spoon-shaped to arched, in some groups bilaterally symmetrical, in others longitudinally curved and deviating from symmetry. *L.Cam.-Rec.*

The reader is referred to the general account of the Mollusca prepared by C. M. Yonge, herein, for the basis of erecting this sixth class of mollusks. Briefly, it is based primarily on the absence of torsion in the soft anatomy of a living representative, the pairing of the ctenidia, muscles and other anatomical structures, and the presence of a single shell. The fossil monoplacophorans lived in epicontinental seas, whereas Recent representatives of the class, in contrast, occur in deep oceanic waters, as indicated by specimens obtained at depths ranging from 1,963 to 3,201 fathoms.

Order TRYBLIDIOIDEA Lemche, 1957

Mollusks with a single bilaterally symmetrical shell showing evidence of bilateral symmetry of the soft parts. *L.Cam.-Rec.*

In fossil species there was a more or less elaborate system of shell muscles as evidenced by the symmetrically paired muscle scars in the family Tryblidiidae, where there are five to eight pairs. Tending to support a possible relationship to the Polyplacophora are the numerous fine, branching tubules through the shell of *Tryblidium reticulatum* Lindström. These suggest rather strongly the very similar tubules that carry the aesthetes, or shell eyes, in a number of polyplacophoran genera. It is possible that these extremely fine tubules have been found only in *T. reticulatum* because of its thick shell and the perfect preservation of specimens from Gotland.

Superfamily TRYBLIDIACEA Pilsbry in Zittel-Eastman, 1899

[*nom. transl.* Knight, herein (*ex* Tryblidiidae Pilsbry, 1899)]

Shell cap-shaped, spoon-shaped or slightly arched; with 5 to 8 symmetrical pairs of dorsal muscles. *L.Cam.-Rec.*

Family PALAEACMAEIDAE Grabau & Shimer, 1909

[=Scenellinae Wenz, 1938]

Aperture of shell subcircular; apex commonly subcentral, but position variable among individuals; with several strong rugosities between apex and margin of aperture. *L.Cam.-U.Cam.*

?Scenella Billings, 1872 [**S. reticulata*] [=*Parmorphella* Matthew, 1886]. Low cap-shaped shell with moderately strong concentric wrinkles and fine radiating threads; an early Middle Cambrian species shows 6 (or 7) pairs of dorsal muscle scars. *Cam.*, N.Am.-NE.Asia.——Fig. 46,1. **S. reticulata*, L.Cam., Can.(Newf.); *1a,b*, individuals showing extremes in variation, ×2.7.——Fig. 46,2. *S. sp.* (Rasetti), M.Cam., Can.(B.C.); interior showing muscle scars, ×3.5.

Palaeacmaea Hall & Whitfield, 1872 [**P. typica*]. Low conical shell with subcentral apex; strong concentric rugae; muscle scars unknown. *U.Cam.*, N.Am.-NE.Asia.——Fig. 46,4. **P. typica*, N.Y.; steinkern oblique from above, ×1.3.

Family TRYBLIDIIDAE Pilsbry in Zittel-Eastman, 1899

Most genera with aperture elongate oval; apex distinctly anterior; muscle scars well developed where known. *U.Cam.-Rec.*

Subfamily PROPLININAE Knight & Yochelson, 1958

Shell with apex distinctly overhanging anterior margin; 6 pairs of muscles arranged approximately normal to margin of aperture. *U.Cam.-U.Ord.*

Proplina Kobayashi, 1933 [**Metoptoma cornutaforme* Walcott, 1879]. Apex strongly overhanging anterior end but with no coiling; exterior of shell smooth; 6 muscle scars in shell. *U.Cam.-L. Ord.*, N.Am.-NE.Asia.——Fig. 46,3. **P. cornutaformis* (Walcott); *3a*, U.Cam., N.Y., left side, ×4; *3b*, L.Ord., Mo., steinkern showing muscle scars, ×1.3.

?Vallatotheca Foerste, 1914 [**V. manitoulini*]. Shell relatively deep; ornament sharp concentric lamellae with fine superimposed radiating threads;

[1] Honorary Research Associate, Smithsonian Institution, Washington, D.C.; Longboat Key, Florida.
[2] U.S. Geological Survey, Washington, D.C.

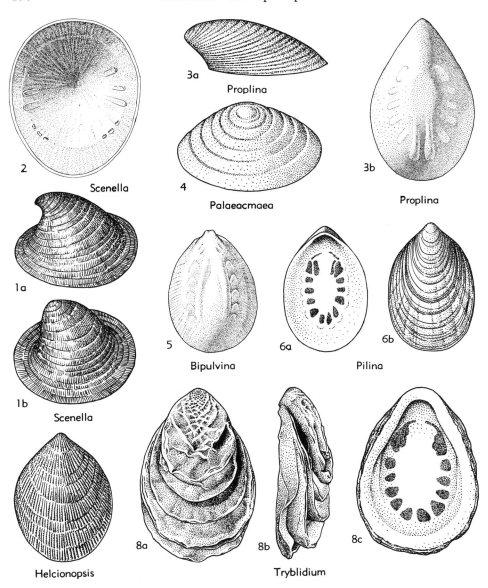

FIG. 46. Tryblidioidea; Tryblidiacea (Tryblidiidae) (p. *177-179*).

muscle scars unknown. *U.Ord.,* N.Am.——FIG. 47. **V. manitoulini,* Can.(Ont.); left side, ×2.

Subfamily TRYBLIDIINAE Pilsbry in Zittel-Eastman, 1899

[*nom. transl.* KNIGHT, herein (*ex* Tryblidiidae PILSBRY, 1899)]

Shell shallow spoon-shaped, with slight arching of margin about 0.3 of distance posteriorly from anterior; with 5 to 8 pairs of muscles, those in front commonly more elaborate. *L.Ord.-M.Sil.*

Bipulvina YOCHELSON, 1958 [**B. croftsae*]. Shell thick, thinning abruptly at margin; at least 5 pairs of muscle scars present; interior of shell flattened for about half its length; ornament unknown. *L.Ord.,* N.Am.——FIG. 46,5. **B. croftsae,* Mo.; steinkern showing muscle scars, ×1.3.

Tryblidium LINDSTRÖM, 1880 [**T. reticulatum;* SD S.A.MILLER, 1889] [=*Triblidium* GRABAU &

Vallatotheca

FIG. 47. Tryblidioidea; Tryblidiacea (Tryblidiidae) —*Vallatotheca manitoulini* Foerste, U.Ord., Can. (Ont.); left side, ×2.

SHIMER, 1909]. Shell interior divided into 4 concentric zones converging under apex, outermost rather thick and rounded around posterior 0.75 of aperture, next inner zone narrow, smooth and gently arched, third zone roughened by muscle scars, and innermost zone smoothed by secondary deposits that cover first-formed parts of muscle scars; scars comprising 6 symmetrical pigmented pairs with scars of anterior pair seemingly compounded of 3 parts; ornament (of type species) consisting of broad, high, thin, frilled lamellae that arise alternately from opposite sides so as to make a reticulate pattern; shell punctured by many microscopic perforations that branch on approaching outer surface in manner suggesting minute openings that carry nerves for aesthetes (or shell eyes) in many Polyplacophora. *?Ord., M.Sil.,* N. Am.-Eu.——FIG. 46,8. **T. reticulatum,* M.Sil., Gotl.; *8a,b,* dorsal and left sides; *8c,* interior showing paired muscle scars (compound scars above); all ×1.3.

Pilina KOKEN, 1925 [**Tryblidium unguis* LINDSTRÖM, 1880]. Like *Tryblidium* in shape and nature of muscle scars but with thinner shell; ornament consisting of concentric growth lines and faint, widely spaced radiating grooves. [A specimen illustrated by LINDSTRÖM (1880, pl. 1, fig. 36) shows a small anterior pit internally, which appears to be the open end of a partially filled protoconch.] *M.Sil.,* Eu.——FIG. 46,6. **P. unguis* (LINDSTRÖM), Gotl.; *6a,* interior showing paired muscle scars; *6b,* dorsal view; ×0.7.

?Helcionopsis ULRICH & SCOFIELD, 1897 [**H. striatum* ULRICH in ULRICH & SCOFIELD, 1897]. Shell with rather wide radiating threads that cross widely spaced growth lines; muscle scars unknown. *U.Ord.,* N.Am.-Eu.——FIG. 46,7. **H. striatum,* Ky.; ×1.3.

Subfamily ARCHAEOPHIALINAE Knight & Yochelson, 1958

Shell deeply cup-shaped, with apex not quite central, offset toward anterior extremity; 6 or 8 muscle scars in shell, anterior ones differentiated from those behind. *M. Ord.-L.Dev.*

Archaeophiala PERNER, 1903 [**Patella antiquissima* HISINGER, 1837; SD KOKEN, 1925] [=*Scapha* HEDSTRÖM, 1923 (*non* HUMPHREY, 1797, *nec* MOTSCHULSKY, 1845, *nec* GRAY, 1847) (obj.); *Scaphe* HEDSTRÖM, 1923 (obj.); *Patelliscapha* TOMLEN, 1929, and *Paterella* HEDSTRÖM, 1930 (*pro Scapha* HEDSTRÖM, 1923) (obj.)]. Shell externally sugarloaf-shaped, with slightly anterior blunt apex; interior cup-shaped, with 6 pairs of pigmented dorsal muscle scars, those of anterior pair being compounded of 3 elements; each principal scar (except anterior) with supplementary shadow scar slightly in front and toward margin; ornament concentric lamellae. *Ord.,* Eu.——FIG. 48,4. **A. antiquissima* (HISINGER), U.Ord., Swed.; *4a,* right side view, ×1.3; *4b,* interior, showing paired muscle scars, compound scars at top, shadow scars outside main circle, ×1.8.

?Micropileus WILSON, 1951 [**M. obesus*]. Shell high cap-shaped, apex rather blunt, slightly anterior; muscle scars and ornament unknown. *M. Ord.,* N.Am.——FIG. 48,2. **M. obesus,* Can. (Ont.); side view of steinkern, ×1 (150).

?Calloconus PERNER, 1903 [**Palaeoscurria (Calloconus) humilis;* SD KNIGHT, 1937]. Shell cap- or cup-shaped, apex subcentral, blunt, pointing anteriorly; muscle scars unknown; ornament, many concentric imbricating lamellae. *L.Dev.,* Eu.—— FIG. 48,1. **C. humilis* (PERNER), Czech.; left side, ×1.3.

Subfamily DRAHOMIRINAE Knight & Yochelson, 1958

Shell low, spoon-shaped; 7 pairs of elongate muscle scars in shell, situated at a high angle to apertural margin. *U.Sil.*

Drahomira PERNER, 1903 [**Tryblidium glaseri* PERNER, 1903]. Like *Trybilidium* and *Pilina* in shape but having 7 pairs of muscle scars, anterior pair larger than others and shaped somewhat like tadpole with tail to the rear and curving inward, next 5 pairs linear and arranged radially on each side of dorsum, posterior pair close together and of irregular pustulose shape; ornament broad, low undulating ribs radiating from the apex (114, p. 23). *U.Sil.,* Eu.——FIG. 48,3. *D. glaseri* (PERNER), Czech.; ×2.7.

Subfamily NEOPILININAE Knight & Yochelson, 1958

Shell low; aperture oval; apex just projecting over anterior margin; 5 or 6 pairs of muscle scars; ornament fine radial striae and growth lines. *Rec.*

Neopilina LEMCHE, 1957 [**N. galatheae*]. Shell exceedingly thin; aperture oval; asymmetrical, coiled protoconch; with bilaterally symmetrical paired muscles and gills, anterior mouth and posterior anus; circular, poorly muscled foot (9, p. 414). [This remarkable living representative of

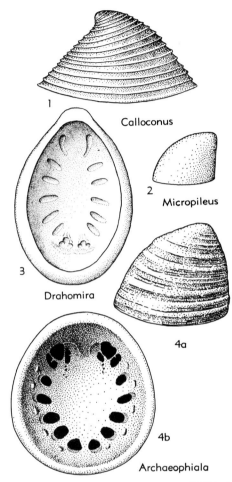

FIG. 48. Tryblidioidea; Tryblidiacea (Tryblidiidae) (p. *179*).

a group supposedly extinct since early Devonian time will be described in detail by LEMCHE and co-workers in the *Galathea* reports. The asymmetrically coiled protoconch is considered a larval adaptation with little taxonomic significance.] *Rec.*, off W. coast of S.Am.

N. (Neopilina). Shell exceedingly thin, smooth and fairly low; protoconch asymmetrically coiled; with anterior mouth and posterior anus, five pairs of gills, and a poorly muscled foot. *Rec.*, off W. coast of C. Amer.——FIG. 48A*1*. *N. (N.) galatheae*: *1a*, apical part of larval shell, ×3.5; *1b,c*, dorsal and ventral views of holotype, ×1, ×1.6; *1d*, ant. part of body, ×1.65 (9).

N. (Vema) CLARKE & MENZIES, 1959 [*N. (Vema) ewingi*]. Shell moderately thin, compressed and fairly high in early growth stages, more similar to typical subgenus at maturity, but lack-

ing coiled protoconch and ornamented by numerous fine radial striae; with 6 pairs of gills (*Science*, 17 April 1959, p. 1026). *Rec.* off W. coast of Peru.——FIG. 48A,*2*. *N. (Vema) ewengi*; *2a-c*, dorsal, lateral, ventral views of paratypes, ×5.3; *2d*, apical part of shell, enlarged (CLARKE & MENZIES, 1959).

Superfamily CYRTONELLACEA Knight & Yochelson, 1958

Shell strongly arched, but not completing one full whorl; apex and anterior margin of shell symmetrical with reference to main body of shell; at least 2 pairs of crescent-shaped shallow muscle scars present in shell. *L.Ord.-M.Dev.*

Family CYRTONELLIDAE Knight & Yochelson, 1958

With the characters of the superfamily. *L.Ord.-M.Dev.*

Cyrtonellopsis YOCHELSON, 1958 [*C. huzzahensis*]. Like *Cyrtonella* in overall shape, but lacking median dorsal crest; muscle scars unknown. *L.Ord.*, N.Am.——FIG. 49,*1*. *C. huzzahensis*, Mo.; *1a,b*, anterior and left side of steinkern, ×1.3.

Cyrtonella HALL, 1879 [*Cyrtolites? mitella* HALL, 1862; SD S.A.MILLER, 1889]. Shell cap-shaped, with apex extending forward about a half circle and marked by an obscure median dorsal crest; ornament rather small concentric lamellae with fine radiating threads between them; 2 symmetrical pairs of dorsal muscle scars are accompanied by 2 pairs of "shadow scars," as in *Archaeophiala*, but presence of other scars anterior to these not established; scars dorsal and quite unlike the single pair of lateral scars on the columella of bellerophonts. *Sil.-Dev.*, N.Am.——FIG. 49,*2*. *C. mitella* (HALL), *M.Dev.*, N.Y.; *2a*, right side; *2b*, dorsal view of steinkern showing 2 pairs of muscle scars with "shadow scars"; ×1.3.

?TRYBLIDIOIDEA INCERTAE SEDIS

Macroscenella WILSON, 1951 [*Metoptoma superba* BILLINGS, 1865]. Shell large, subconical; apex slightly excentric; aperture with slight invagination; muscle scars unknown; ornament cancellate. Shell not a smooth cone, locally with slight indentations and irregularities (150, p. 18). *M.Ord.*, N.Am.

Order ARCHINACELLOIDEA Knight & Yochelson, 1958

Shell shape varied but with apex presumed to be anterior; muscle scar (where known) ring-shaped or an incomplete ring and single pair of discrete muscle scars. *U.Cam.-L.Sil.*

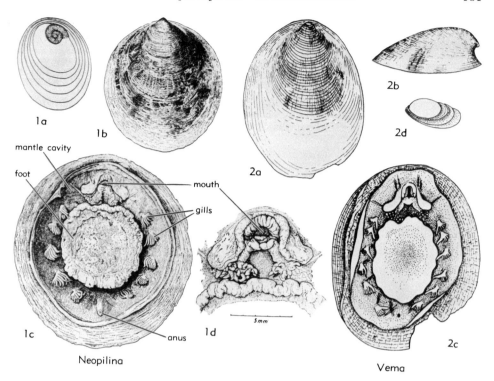

la

lb

2b

2d

mantle cavity

foot

mouth

gills

2a

1c

anus

1d

5mm

2c

Neopilina

Vema

FIG. 48A. Tryblidioidea; Tryblidiacea (Tryblidiidae)—Neopilina, Rec., E.Pac., from deep water (p. *180*).

Superfamily ARCHINACELLACEA Knight, 1956

With characters of the order. *U.Cam.-L.Sil.*

Family ARCHINACELLIDAE Knight, 1956

Shell low, spoon-shaped, apex strongly anterior, just overhanging margin of aperture. *M.Ord.-L.Sil.*

Archinacella ULRICH & SCOFIELD, 1897 [**A. powersi*]. Shell form as in *Pilina* but with muscles forming a continuous scar below apex, possibly open posteriorly with pair of discrete muscles located in the opening; surface marked by widely spaced growth lines. *M.Ord.-L.Sil.*, N.Am.-Eu.——FIG. 50,*1*. **A. powersi*, M.Ord., Wis.; *1a*, left side; *1b*, apertural view; *1c*, posterior side looking obliquely toward aperture; all ×1.3.——FIG. 50, *4. A. patelliformis* (HALL), *M.Ord.*, N.Y.; steinkern showing muscle scar, ×1.3.

?Ptychopeltis PERNER, 1903 [**P. incola*]. Shell thin, saddle-shaped, with greatly convex longitudinal profile and strongly convex transverse profile; apex small, blunt, presumably anterior; muscula-

ture unknown; steinkerns show numerous fine radiating threads near aperture where shell probably is thinnest. *M.Ord.*, Eu.——FIG. 50,*7*. **P. incola*, Czech.; ?left side steinkern, ×1.3.

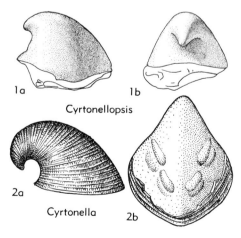

la

lb

Cyrtonellopsis

2a

Cyrtonella

2b

FIG. 49. Tryblidioidea; Cyrtonellacea (Cyrtonellidae) (p. *180*).

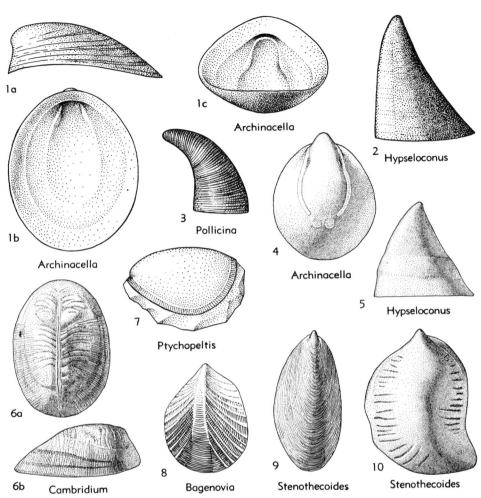

Fig. 50. Archinacelloidea; Archinacellacea (Archinacellidae, Hypseloconidae). Cambridioidea; Cambridiiacea (Cambridiidae) (p. 181-183).

?Family HYPSELOCONIDAE Knight, 1956

Shell a high cone, apex anterior but curved slightly backward; muscle scar believed to be a continuous ring. *U.Cam.-M.Ord.*

Hypseloconus BERKEY, 1898 [*H. recurvus* var. *elongatus*]. Shell thin, with apex above narrow (presumed anterior) extremity and curved slightly backward; form extremely variable; surface marked only by faint, distant growth lines; muscle scars possibly a complete ring. [Although BERKEY reported occurrence of 6 pairs of scars, KNIGHT's examination of his specimens, including those figured as showing muscle scars, fails to confirm this.] *U.Cam.-L.Ord.*, N.Am.——FIG. 50,2. *H. elongatus*, U.Cam., Wis.; ?left side, ×0.7.——50,5. *H.* sp., L.Ord., Mo.; steinkern showing supposed muscle scar, ×1.3.

?Ozarkoconus HELLER, 1954 [1956] [*O. prearcuatus*]. With high, conical slightly curved, cap-shaped shell; aperture oval; ornament longitudinal costae or threads. Muscle scars unknown. *L.Ord.*, N.Am.

?Pollicina HOLZAPFEL, 1895 [*Cyrtolithes corniculum* EICHWALD, 1860 (*pro Cyrtoceras laeve* MURCHISON in EICHWALD, 1842 (*non* SOWERBY, 1839)]]. Shell with rather blunt apex; surface marked by fine concentric threads; muscle scars unknown. *M.Ord.*, Eu.——FIG. 50,3. *P. corniculum* (EICHWALD), Russ.; ?left side, ×1.

?Order CAMBRIDIOIDEA Horný, in Knight & Yochelson, 1958

Shell elongate, with strongly pointed apex, presumably anterior; some shells with marked deviation from bilateral symmetry. *L.Cam.-M.Cam.*

Superfamily CAMBRIDIACEA Horný, 1957

[*nom. transl.* KNIGHT & YOCHELSON (*ex* Cambridiidae HORNÝ, 1957)]

Interior of shell varying in thickness so that numerous ridges and furrows normal to edges of aperture appear on steinkern; muscle scars unknown. *L.Cam.-M.Cam.*

Family CAMBRIDIIDAE Horný, 1957

With characters of superfamily. *L.Cam.-M.Cam.*

Cambridium HOUNÝ, 1957 [**C. nikiforovae*]. Shell symmetrical to asymmetrical, aperture suboval; interior of dorsum with 2 sharp longitudinal ridges, end ridges and furrows curving outward from median part of these ridges; numerous finer ridges and furrows near edges of margin, and essentially normal to margin. *L.Cam.*, N.Asia.——FIG. 50,6. **C. nikiforovae*, Sib.; *6a,b*, dorsal and right side views of steinkern showing internal markings, ×2.

?Bagenovia RADUGIN, 1937 [**B. sajanica* HORNÝ, 1957]. Apex directly above anterior margin; distinct dorsal keel widening posteriorly, ornamented by costae radiating from keel; interior of shell unknown. [According to HORNÝ, may be a bivalve.] *L.Cam.*, C.Asia.——FIG. 50,8. **B. sajanica* HORNÝ, ×2.

Stenothecoides RESSER, 1938 [**Stenotheca elongata* WALCOTT (after HORNÝ)]. Shell distinctly asymmetrical; with a sharp median dorsal crest; ornamented by growth lines only; interior of shell bearing ridges and furrows normal to edges of aperture. *L.Cam.-M.Cam.*, N.Am., Asia.——FIG. 50,9. **S. elongata* (WALCOTT), M.Cam., Nev.; ×5.3.——FIG. 50,10. *S.* sp., M.Cam., Can., steinkern, ×3.3.

REFERENCES

Boettger, C. R.
(1) 1956, *Beiträge zur Systematik der Urmollusken (Amphineura):* Zool. Anzeiger, Suppl. Band, v. 19, p. 223-256 (Leipzig).

Eichwald, Edouard d'
(2) 1842, *Die Urwelt Russlands, durch Abbildungen erläutert:* Nat- und Heilkunde K. med. chirur. Akad. St. Petersburg, Zeitschr., Heft 2, p. 115-210.

Heller, R. L.
(3) 1956, *Stratigraphy and paleontology of the Roubidoux Formation of Missouri:* Missouri Bur. Geol. Survey & Water Resources, ser. 2, v. 35, 118 p., 19 pl. (Rolla). [HELLER's publication did not appear in 1954 as shown on the title page. It was delivered to the Missouri State Geologist on December 20, 1955, but distribution was not begun until January, 1956—J. B. KNIGHT.]

Horný, Radvan
(4) 1955, *Tryblidiinae Pilsbry, 1899 (Gastropoda) from the Silurian of central Bohemia:* Sborník Ústředního ústavu geologického oddíl paleontologický [Service géologique de Tchecoslovaquie, Sec. de paléontologie], v. 22, p. 73-88 (Czech), 90-96 (Russ.), 97-102 (Eng.), pl. 9-12 (Praha).
(5) 1957, *Problematic molluscs (?Amphineura) from the Lower Cambrian of south and east Siberia (U.S.S.R.):* Same, v. 24, p. 397-413 (Czech), 414-422 (Russ.), 423-432 (Eng.), pl. 20-23.

Knight, J. B.
(6) 1941, *Paleozoic gastropod genotypes:* Geol. Soc. America, Spec. Paper 32, 510 p., 96 pl., 32 fig. (New York).
(7) 1952, *Primitive fossil gastropods and their bearing on gastropod classification:* Smithson. Misc. Coll., v. 117, no. 13 (Publ. 4092), 56 p., 2 pl. (Washington).
——, & Yochelson, E. L.
(8) 1958, *A reconsideration of the Monoplacophora and the primitive Gastropoda:* Malac. Soc. London, Proc., v. 33, pt. 1, p. 37-48, pl. 5.

Lemche, Henning
(9) 1957, *A new living deep-sea mollusc of the Cambro-Devonian class Monoplacophora:* Nature, v. 179, p. 413-416, fig. 1-4 (London).

Lindström, G.
(10) 1884, *On the Silurian Gastropoda and Pteropoda of Gotland:* Kungliga Svenska Vetenskaps-Akademiens Handlinger, v. 19, no. 6, p. 1-250, pl. 1-21 (Stockholm).

Perner, Jaroslav
(11) 1903, *Bellerophontidae:* in BARRANDE, JOACHIM, Système silurien du centre de la Bohême, p. 1-164, pl. 1-89 (Praha).
(12) 1907, Same, v. 2, text, p. 1-380, pl. 90-175.
(13) 1911, Same, v. 3, text, p. i-xvii, 1-390, pl. 176-247.

Rasetti, Franco
(14) 1954, *Internal shell structures in the Middle*

Cambrian gastropod Scenella and the prob-lematic genus Stenothecoides: Jour. Paleont., v. 28, no. 1, p. 59-66, pl. 11-12 (Tulsa).

Rusconi, Carlos
(15) 1954, *Fosiles Cambricos y Ordovicos de San Isidro:* Bull. paleontologico de Buenos Aires, no. 30, 4 p.

Wenz, Wilhelm
(16) 1940, *Ursprung und frühe Stammesge-schichte der Gastropoden:* Arch. Mollusken-kunde, v. 72, p. 1-10 (Frankfurt a.M.).
(17) 1938-44, *Gastropoda. Allgemeiner Teil und Prosobranchia:* in O. H. SCHINDEWOLF, ed.,

Handbuch der Paläozoologie, v. 6, pt. 1-7, 1639 p. (Berlin).

Wilson, A. E.
(18) 1951, *Gastropoda and Conularida of the Ottawa Formation of the Ottawa-St. Law-rence Lowland:* Geol. Survey Canada, Bull. 17, 149 p. (Ottawa).

Yochelson, E. L.
(19) 1958, *Some Lower Ordovician monopla-cophoran mollusks from Missouri:* Washing-ton Acad. Sci., Jour., v. 48, no. 1, p. 8-14, fig. 1-13.

GASTROPODA

GENERAL CHARACTERISTICS OF GASTROPODA

By L. R. Cox[1]

CONTENTS

[1] British Museum (Natural History), London, England.

NAME AND DEFINITION OF CLASS

THE NAME "GASTROPODA"

CUVIER in 1797 (27[1]) was the first to recognize the essential characters of this class and the close relationship of its shell-bearing and shell-less forms, which LINNÉ had included respectively in his *Vermes testacea* and *Vermes mollusca*. CUVIER assigned to this group the name "mollusques gastéropodes" or simply "gastéropodes" (Greek γαστήρ, stomach; πούς, ποδός, foot), which appears to have been first rendered in the Latin form "Gastropoda" by DUMÉRIL in 1806 (32). RAFINESQUE (87) gave the name as "Gasteropodia." Early conchologists included the group in their "Univalvia," but this name was gradually abandoned when the heterogeneous composition of the group so designated was recognized. Further synonyms, mostly used only by their authors, are listed on p. *I171*. The Gastropoda, as restricted by the definition given below, are the Gastropoda Anisopleura of LANKESTER (63). ZITTEL (113) used the name Glossophora, then recently introduced by P. FISCHER, as an inclusive term for the Polyplacophora, Scaphopoda, and Gastropoda. FISCHER (35, p. 8, 519, 529, etc.), however, did not intend to apply this term to a single taxonomic group, but used it repeatedly, in groups of differing taxonomic rank, to distinguish radula-bearing forms from forms (Aglossa) without a radula. Some German authors have followed ZITTEL. LANKESTER (63) included all the molluscan classes except the Pelecypoda in the Glossophora.

----

[1] Reference numbers inclosed by parentheses indicate publications cited in the list beginning on p. *I165*.

DEFINITION OF CLASS

The class Gastropoda includes Mollusca with a distinct head, which in unspecialized forms has eyes and tentacles and is more or less fused with the foot, typically solelike and adapted for creeping, but much modified in pelagic and some other forms. A radula normally is present. Cerebral and pleural nerve ganglia are distinct. Organs of the pallial complex are re-oriented (in relation to their positions in a conjectural primitive mollusk) as the result of "torsion," which in some forms is a definite episode observable in early ontogeny, and in others in inferred to have taken place in ancestral forms, although omitted in a condensed ontogeny. Bilateral asymmetry is present to a varying degree in all living representatives, although complete symmetry may have existed in the extinct Bellerophontacea. The shell, if present, is single (univalve), calcareous, closed apically, endogastric when spiral, and not divided regularly into chambers.

The definition just given excludes certain groups which have frequently been included among the gastropods, but in which the orientation of the various organs is (or is inferred to have been) unaffected by "torsion" and in which there is bilateral symmetry. These groups are the Polyplacophora, with their 8-valved shells, and the Monoplacophora with their cap-shaped shells. Excluded also are the shell-less Solenogastres (or Aplacophora), which LANKESTER included with the Polyplacophora in his Gastropoda Isopleura. The systematic position of the bellerophontids, with their bilaterally symmetrical, coiled shells, has been much discussed. J. B. KNIGHT (55, p. 48-55) has reviewed the relevant evidence and concluded that they were forms which were affected by torsion and were true prosobranch gastropods. If they underwent torsion in early ontogeny, an asymmetrical arrangement of their organs must have existed during the course of this episode. Whether perfect symmetry of all soft parts existed on completion of the torsion we have no means of knowing, but the presence of two symmetrically arranged columellar muscle scars can be observed.

All gastropods, with the possible exception of this group, are more or less asymmetrical. The asymmetry is obvious in most forms in which the shell is coiled. In *Patella* and similar genera, the simple conical shell is symmetrical, but asymmetry is displayed by the nervous system and the digestive, excretory, and reproductive organs. In *Fissurella,* although the shell is symmetrical when adult, it is coiled and asymmetrical in an early developmental stage. The pteropods, a group of opisthobranchs modified for a pelagic mode of life, include several genera with bilaterally symmetrical shells, but their digestive, circulatory, and reproductive organs lack symmetry.

Description of the foot as "solelike and adapted for creeping" needs qualification. It is not strictly applicable even to all benthonic gastropods. In the swimming pelagic groups (pteropods and heteropods), the foot is much modified for purposes of propulsion. In some species of the parasitic genus *Stilifer* but not all, the foot is much reduced. It has completely atrophied in the endoparasitic family Entoconchidae. A radula is present in the great majority of gastropods but is obsolete in parasitic families, such as the Eulimidae and Pyramidellidae. Families in which tentacles are absent from the head include the Gadiniidae and Siphonariidae, while eyes are absent in most Cocculinacea, a deep-sea group.

The absence of regular internal septa pierced by a siphuncle distinguishes gastropod shells from those of most Cephalopoda, although irregular septa may sometimes seal off the earliest-formed parts of the shell when the viscera move forward to some extent as it grows.

BIOLOGY

HABITATS AND FOOD

Gastropods inhabit the sea, fresh water, and land. Most marine forms are benthonic, but some are pelagic, and many benthonic species have pelagic larvae. The benthonic forms live on most types of sea bottom, some creeping on solid rock, others living among seaweed, others sheltering beneath stones, and others burrowing into sediment. Some species live near or even above high-water mark and some may occur at very great depths, but the great majority live in comparatively shallow water. Species dredged from the deepest bottoms include representatives of families such as the Trochidae,

Volutidae, and Cassididae, which are common in much shallower seas. One family represented by living forms found only at great depths is the Pleurotomariidae; it is, however, abundantly represented in shallow-water faunas of past eras. In certain cases individual species have a wide depth range. *Natica groenlandica* MØLLER, for example, has been dredged from depths ranging from 2 to 1,290 fathoms. Some marine species, belonging to such genera as *Cerithium* and *Littorina,* can tolerate brackish-water conditions and exist in estuaries, as can also some representatives of typically fresh-water genera, such as *Theodoxus, Melanopsis,* and many Thiaridae. *Hydrobia jenkinsi* SMITH has forsaken brackish water and established itself in fresh water in England within historic times.

Pelagic gastropods are of two types, active swimmers and passive drifters. The pteropods and heteropods are of the first type, while to the second belong *Janthina,* which suspends itself from a raftlike structure or float, to the underside of which its eggs are attached, and *Litiopa,* which lives attached to floating seaweed.

Most gastropods obtain their food direct by means of the mouth and radula, but in a few this mode of feeding is replaced or supplemented by ciliary feeding. Land and fresh-water gastropods are in the main herbivorous, although on occasion slugs and snails will devour animal matter. Of the marine macrophagous forms, some are herbivorous, browsing on seaweed and lichens, and some carnivorous. On the whole, the carnivorous forms are those provided with a long eversible proboscis. Such genera as *Nucella* and *Natica* perforate the shells of other mollusks, particularly pelecypods, in most cases seemingly by the rasping action of the radula, but in the case of *Natica* with the aid also of a chemical secretion; they then extract the soft contents. Parasitic gastropods include species of *Eulima,* which suck the juice of their holothurian or other host by means of a long proboscis. Some Pyramidellidae are parasitic on pelecypods and some on other invertebrates. The living patelliform genus *Thyca* is an ectoparasite, which throughout adult life lives attached to the body of echinoderms. An interesting example of dependence on another organism, although not

strictly describable as parasitism or symbiosis, is that of the Paleozoic genus *Platyceras,* which is sometimes found on the calyx of a crinoid in the neighborhood of the anus, suggesting that it derived nourishment from the feces of the crinoid. Comparable among living gastropods is *Hipponyx,* which associates with *Turbo* and other mollusks and feeds on their feces.

A few gastropods are deposit-feeders. Thus *Aporrhais* uses an extensile proboscis to collect detritus of vegetable origin from the muddy sediment in which it lives. Ciliary feeders, which include some Vermetidae, Siliquariidae, Turritellidae, Calyptraeidae, Capulidae, and Struthiolariidae, feed on finely sifted bottom deposits, which are drawn into the mantle cavity with the inhalant current. The food is collected, consolidated with mucus, and conveyed to the mouth by a variety of processes. A process of ciliary feeding, by which the normal means of feeding can be supplemented, has been demonstrated in a fresh-water snail belonging to the genus *Viviparus.* Details of the food of many gastropods are assembled by GRAHAM (45).

DURATION OF LIFE

The proportion of gastropods that die from old age is probably very small. The majority either become prey to other organisms or perish owing to some external cause such as change in salinity or a falling off in food supply. Some gastropods, particularly among the opisthobranchs and pulmonates, die from exhaustion induced by egg laying. PELSENEER (85, p. 617) and COMFORT (19) have assembled data on the potential duration of life in various species. Some gastropods, especially opisthobranchs and pulmonates, but including certain of the smaller prosobranchs, live only for one year or less. The majority have a longer span of life. Many common land snails live from 5 to 7 years, the maximum recorded age in this group being 9 years (*Helix hortensis* MÜLLER). The maximum recorded longevity of a fresh-water snail, according to data given by PELSENEER, is 10 years, attained by *Viviparus viviparus* (LINNÉ), the usual period for such gastropods being about 5 years. The maximum recorded age for marine prosobranchs is also 10 years, as

recorded of *Littorina littorea* (LINNÉ), *Trochus niloticus* LINNÉ, and probably also *Buccinum undatum* LINNÉ, whereas the average span of life in this group seems to be 3 to 5 years. Data on the great majority of species are still wanting.

MORPHOLOGY OF SOFT PARTS

PARTS PROTRUSIBLE FROM SHELL

In a gastropod with a coiled shell, part **(visceral mass or visceral hump)** remains permanently within the shell, while part is protruded when the creature is active, but in most forms can be withdrawn when necessary into its shelter. The main and often only protrusible part consists of the single sluglike mass **(head-foot mass or cephalopedal mass)** formed by the head and foot (Fig. 51). When this withdraws into the shell the head precedes the foot and if an operculum, borne on the rear dorsal surface of the foot, is present, this completely or partly closes the aperture of the shell.[1] An operculum is present in most prosobranchs, but, with certain exceptions, is absent in pulmonates (which include most land snails) and in opisthobranchs; exceptions are the pulmonate family Amphibolidae and the opisthobranch families Acteonidae and Pyramidellidae. Two tube-like organs, to be discussed later, can also be protruded from the shell in forms in which they are developed. These are the inhalant siphon and the male genital organ **(penis)**. In some gastropods, such as the Cypraeidae and Naticidae, the mantle may extend far beyond the apertural margin, covering the external surface of the shell to a varying extent. Extensions of the foot may also partly cover the shell.

The foot is typically a broad, tough, muscular structure with a flat base applied to the surface over which the mollusk creeps, but in some genera it is greatly modified. In many forms it contains one or more glands. In land snails the **mucous gland** runs longitudinally along the front part of the foot and opens just below the animal's mouth, depositing slime to facilitate its progress over a dry surface. In some marine snails, such as the Cypraeidae, the pedal gland forms a secretion for a similar purpose of lubrication. In many forms the secretion from a pedal gland solidifies to form a thread which is attached to some object and enables the animal to lower itself slowly or ascend again in water or in the air. Species capable of thread-spinning include freshwater snails such as *Lymnaea* and *Planorbis*, many slugs, small marine forms such as *Skeneopsis, Omalogyra, Rissoella, Litiopa,* and *Balcis,* and certain species of prosobranchs belonging to *Cerithidea, Littorina,* and other genera that have half forsaken a marine life and can suspend themselves from mangrove bushes and similar objects. In most Vermetidae long sticky mucous threads from a pedal gland are used to collect plankton for food; *Vermetus gigas* and *V. triqueter* are among the species in which they are best developed. In the female of some advanced Caenogastropoda, such as *Buccinum,* a ventral pedal gland molds and hardens the egg capsules, the material for which has been secreted around the egg mass in the genital ducts. From the oviduct the eggs pass to this gland along a temporary groove along the right side of the foot.

In some gastropods the anterior and posterior parts of the foot, termed respectively the **propodium** and **metapodium** (Fig. 52), are clearly separated by transverse grooves; in some forms it is convenient to term the median region the **mesopodium**. The metapodium bears the operculum, if one is present. In certain genera, such as *Natica, Sinum,* and *Oliva,* which crawl through wet sand, a well-developed, plowlike propodium pushes the sand away to both sides in front of the animal. In many living Archaeogastropoda the foot has a projecting upper border termed the **epipodium;** in some genera, such as *Haliotis* and many Trochidae, this has tentacle-like protrusions. In certain genera of the Thaididae and Muricidae a small **pedal sucker** on the anteroventral part of the foot assists the animal to grip its prey while boring into it. If the foot is examined when the animal is creeping, a series of waves appears to pass along it, the waves being produced by contraction of muscle fibers perpendicular to the creeping surface. Owing to peculiarities in their mode of progression, gastropods of some genera leave very distinctive tracks behind them.

---

[1] In some operculate gastropods, however, the operculum is reduced to a vestige which may have secondary functions.

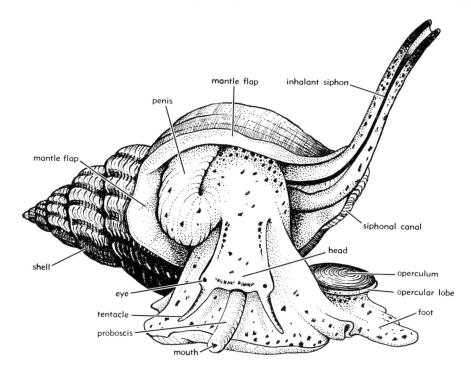

Fig. 51. *Buccinum undatum* Linné (♂) (115n). Shell with protruded head-foot mass; anterior view, ×1.25.

In some opisthobranchs the lateral **parts** of the foot (termed **parapodia**) form broad extensions which, together with the mantle, tend to fold over and cover the shell (Fig. 88). In the pteropods, pelagic forms now classed with the opisthobranchs, the parapodia are finlike structures, and the animal swims with their aid. In the heteropods, pelagic gastropods classified as prosobranchs, the foot is also much modified, forming a fan-shaped, finlike structure in the family Pterotrachaeidae.

The head-foot mass is drawn into the shell by means of the **columellar** (or **retractor**) **muscle** or **muscles**, the only attachment of the soft parts to the shell. The muscle is attached most commonly to the columella some distance back from the aperture (Fig. 53) and passes through the foot to a place of insertion beneath the operculum. In the genus *Haliotis*, with its ear-shaped shell, there are two retractor muscles attached to the interior of the shell; one is very large, cylindrical in shape, and almost median in position, whereas the other is very small and situated near the left-hand margin. In *Scissurella* there are two attachment muscles that differ in size only slightly. The Neritacea and certain Caenogastropods also have two unequal muscles. In the bellerophontids of the Paleozoic two equal muscles existed. In patelliform shells there is a symmetrical, horseshoe-shaped muscle, with an anterior gap.

The head of the gastropod (Fig. 51) bears the animal's most obvious sensory organs. Almost all forms, except certain opisthobranchs, have at least one pair of **cephalic tentacles,** which form hornlike projections pointing obliquely forward. Most gastropods have two eyes which, when (as in most prosobranchs) there is a single pair of tentacles, are situated either on the head at or near the base of the tentacles, or some distance up the latter, although not at their tip. In the Strombidae the eyes are very large and the tentacles are replaced by

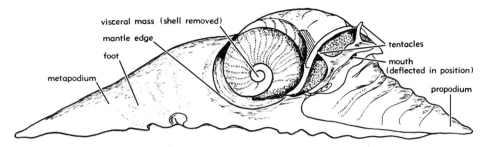

FIG. 52. *Sinum laevigatum* (LAMARCK), showing plowlike propodium and metapodium (a small vestigial operculum is not seen) (132). In this genus the soft parts cannot be fully withdrawn into the shell (not shown in the illustration), ×1.25.

grotesquely enlarged optic peduncles. In the land pulmonates, however, there are two pairs of tentacles, and the eyes are placed at the top of the longer and upper pair, which are capable of retraction by invagination. Two pairs are also present in some opisthobranchs. Apart from their association with the eyes, the tentacles act as tactile organs, while in the case of the pulmonates and opisthobranchs it is believed that the posterior of two pairs are rhinophores (i.e., that they bear olfactory organs). In *Acteon, Scaphander,* and other burrowing opisthobranchs the tentacles form lobes and are used for pushing sand away as the animal moves.

In many gastropods the mouth is a simple opening in the head proper, but in some genera it is placed at the end of a protrusion from the front of the head, ranging from a blunt snout to a long retractible (eversible) **proboscis** (Fig. 54). In some forms, such as *Tonna* and *Mitra,* the proboscis is longer than the rest of the head-foot mass.

MANTLE AND MANTLE CAVITY

The part of the visceral mass termed the **digestive gland** (Fig. 53) extends almost to the apex of a coiled shell, and has a thin, colorless integument. The front portion of the visceral mass, occupying part, commonly most, of the last whorl of the shell, is covered by a thin fleshy hood, known as the **mantle flap**, which is attached at its rear end to the visceral mass. Under the mantle flap, and least developed on the side near the columella, is a space known as the **mantle cavity** (or **pallial cavity**), which plays an important part in the life of the animal.

In many forms the mantle extends forward only as far as the aperture when the animal is extruded from the shell, its margin, which in some forms is a thickened collar, being known as the **mantle edge.** The whole outer surface of the mantle (including that part forming the integument of the visceral mass) contains epithelial cells capable of secreting calcareous shell, but secretion is most active at the mantle edge while forward growth of the shell continues. In gastropods in which the process has been studied, it also has been shown that the periostracum is secreted by the cells along a groove of the mantle edge (**supramarginal groove**). The surmise of some authors that this is the function of a glandular mass found near the mantle edge in *Buccinum* and some other forms is thus probably incorrect. In some groups the mantle flap, as already seen, extends well beyond the aperture, covering part of the outer surface of the shell and depositing a smooth shelly

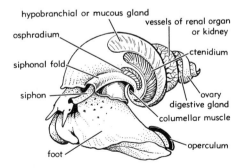

FIG. 53. *Buccinum undatum* LINNÉ (♀), with head-foot mass protruded but with shell treated as transparent to show positions of various organs, ×0.5 (115n).

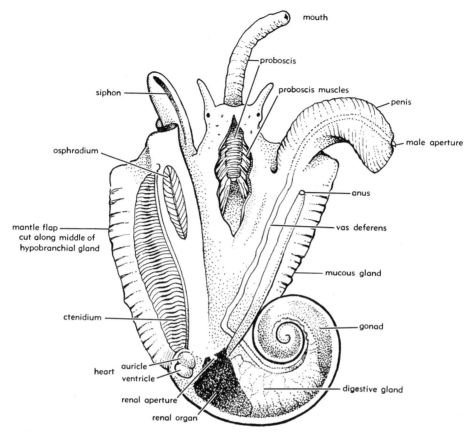

Fig. 54. *Buccinum undatum* Linné (♂) (115n). The organs in the mantle cavity have been exposed by making a median longitudinal incision along the mantle flap and folding the two sides of the latter back; the proximal end of the proboscis and its muscles have been revealed by a further incision, ×1.25.

layer upon it. At sexual maturity it may develop one or more very narrow, shell-secreting protrusions, which give rise to digitations of the outer lip, as in the Aporrhaidae. In *Oliva* there is a long, cordlike appendage of the mantle which coils round the shell, fitting into a groove along the suture. Small tentacles project from the mantle edge in some genera. In *Turritella* and *Vermicularia* a series of pinnately branched tentacles, directed into the mantle cavity from the mantle edge, acts as a screen that prevents detritus from being carried into the cavity with the inhalant current (Fig. 55). In *Valvata* a ciliated pallial tentacle assists in creating a respiratory current.

The most important protrusion of the mantle in many species, however, is a nar-

row fold known as the **inhalant siphon** (usually merely **siphon**), a flexuous, tube-like organ along which the inhalant current of water, containing oxygen necessary for respiration, is drawn into the mantle cavity. The siphon is, on the whole, best developed in carnivorous forms with a long proboscis, and it may be extruded from a notch in the apertural margin or else extend along and be extruded from a narrow extension of the aperture, known as the **siphonal canal.** There are forms, such as *Aporrhais,* in which the siphon is represented only by a very short extension of the mantle, and many others in which no siphon is present, the inhalant current being drawn directly into the mantle cavity. The siphon appears also to have sensory functions in some species. In *Trivia,* a carnivorous genus feeding

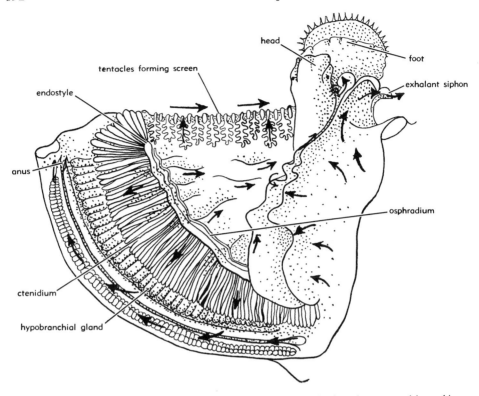

FIG. 55. *Turritella communis* Risso (42). The organs in the mantle cavity have been exposed by making a longitudinal incision along the right side of the mantle flap and folding the latter back to the left; arrows indicate the course of ciliary currents, ×10.

on zooids, it has been observed to feel round for the mouth of the prey, as if searching for the best spot for the proboscis to start its activities. It has also been suggested that the siphon bears chemoreceptors, organs which test the chemical contents of the water drawn through it.

A short **exhalant siphon,** forming an outlet for the exhalant current, is present in various genera belonging to unrelated groups. In the opisthobranch *Acteon* it is a large mammiform protrusion situated near the mantle edge by the right-hand margin of the foot, and occupies the adapical corner of the aperture when the animal is fully extruded from the shell. In *Turritella* an exhalant siphon is formed by a fold of the skin of the head-foot mass. In *Viviparus* such a fold combines with the adjacent part of the mantle to form an exhalant siphon. In *Fissurella* a short exhalant siphon projects through the apical orifice, and in *Emarginula* through the marginal slit.

The mantle cavity (Figs. 54-56) is primarily a respiratory chamber. Within it, in the majority of gastropods, lie the **ctenidium, osphradium,** and the **hypobranchial (or mucous) gland** (these structures are paired in the Zygobranchia, referred to below). Into it are discharged the excreta from the anus and renal opening, while it also contains the female genital opening and houses the male genital organ when this is not protruded.

The inhalant current (Figs. 56*A*), created by the movement of cilia borne by filaments of the ctenidium, enters the mantle cavity, either directly or through a siphon, on the left-hand side of the head-foot mass when there is a single ctenidium. It impinges first upon the osphradium. This organ, situated low on the left side of the mantle flap, is essentially a specialized part of the inner epithelium of the latter. Its size and form vary considerably. It is most complex in the advanced Caenogastropoda,

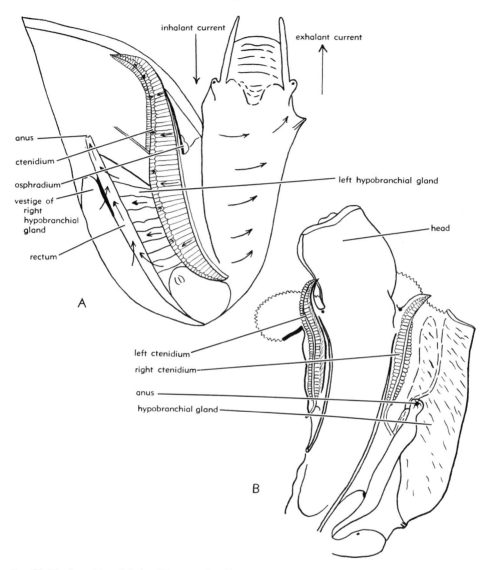

inhalant current

exhalant current

anus

ctenidium

osphradium

vestige of right hypobranchial gland

rectum

left hypobranchial gland

A

head

left ctenidium

right ctenidium

anus

hypobranchial gland

B

FIG. 56. Mantle cavities of *(A) Calliostoma zizyphinum* (LINNÉ), ✕5; *(B) Mikadotrochus beyrichi* (HIL-GER), ✕0.85 (111). As in Figs. 54, 55, the pallial organs have been exposed by appropriate longitudinal incisions along the mantle flap; arrows in *(A)* indicate the course of ciliary currents and in *(B)* attention may be called to the presence of paired ctenidia.

and in *Buccinum,* for example, is a conspicuous plumelike structure superficially resembling a bipectinate gill. In many genera it is a long, narrow, longitudinal ridge. An osphradium has its own nerve, connected with one of the parietal ganglia, and its function is generally considered to be to test the amount of fine sediment in the inhalant current, although, since it is most

complex in carnivorous forms, the suggestion has also been made that it may serve to detect live prey.

In most prosobranchs there is a single respiratory organ, the ctenidium, which lies entirely or for the greater part on the left-hand side of the mantle cavity, usually within the last half-whorl of the shell; it is **monopectinate,** that is, its flexible leaflets

are arranged on one side only of a main axis. The direction of the latter is usually more or less longitudinal, but is oblique or even transverse in some forms. Two ctenidia, left and right, each accompanied by an osphradium, are, however, present in the most primitive living suborder of the prosobranchs, the Pleurotomariina, the Recent species of which belong to the families Pleurotomariidae (Fig. 56*B*), Haliotidae, Scissurellidae, and Fissurellidae. With one exception (the right-hand one in the Scissurellidae), moreover, paired ctenidia are **bipectinate,** that is, they have two rows of leaflets diverging from a median axis. In the Fissurellidae, in which the shell is patelliform and symmetrical, the two ctenidia are equal and symmetrically disposed. In the conispiral Pleurotomariidae and in the Scissurellidae the left-hand ctenidium is slightly the larger. In the Haliotidae, which are depressed and auriform, the inequality of the ctenidia is more marked, the left-hand one being again the larger. The single ctenidium present in species of the Trochacea, Neritacea, and Turbinidae and in the genus *Valvata* is also bipectinate. In all other forms a single ctenidium is monopectinate. In *Valvata* the ctenidium projects from the mantle cavity and shell.

The ctenidium, upon which the inhalant current impinges after testing by the osphradium, serves to aerate the animal's blood. The deoxygenated water then passes (in most prosobranchs) along the right-hand side of the mantle cavity, to form the exhalant current, which is discharged to the right of the animal's head.

The hypobranchial gland, which is a conspicuous organ in many prosobranchs, occupies the middle part of the roof of the mantle cavity, lying on the right-hand side of the ctenidium. It consists of deep transverse folds of the inner wall of the mantle, containing gland cells that produce a very adhesive secretion, by which fine sediment brought into the mantle cavity with the inhalant current is consolidated ready for rejection. Another mucus-secreting organ, concerned with the consolidation of phytoplankton in ciliary feeders such as the Calyptraeidae and some species of *Turritella,* is the **endostyle,** which extends on the wall of the mantle cavity along the entire base of the ctenidium, that is, on the opposite

side of the latter to the hypobranchial gland.

Yonge (112) showed that in most prosobranchs three distinct sets of ciliary currents are concerned with the disposal of suspended matter in the inhalant current. The largest particles, which tend to settle at once, are dealt with by cilia on the margin of the inhalant region and ejected by way of the inhalant opening. Medium-sized particles, which settle farther within the mantle cavity, are carried by cilia on its floor to its right-hand side, where they are caught up in the exhalant current. The lightest particles are carried by a current produced by frontal cilia on the ctenidium across the roof of the mantle cavity to the hypobranchial gland, where they become entangled in mucus and consolidated; they are then carried to the right-hand side to be removed by the exhalant current. The exhalant current also serves to convey away the excreta discharged into the mantle cavity from the anus and the renal aperture. The former is situated near the front of the cavity on the right-hand side, while the renal aperture is a pore at the rear of the cavity.

In the Pleurotomariina, which, as already noted, have two ctenidia, the courses taken by the respiratory currents differ somewhat from those described above. Thus, the exhalant current, instead of emerging to the right-hand side of the animal's head, passes out either through a slit in the apertural margin situated at or near the periphery of the shell *(Pleurotomaria, Emarginula),* or through one or more orifices (or tremata) in the shell wall at its periphery *(Haliotis),* or, in the case of the patelliform *Fissurella,* through an orifice at the apex of the shell. In these forms the anus lies well back from the aperture, in such a position that excreta are also discharged through the slit or orifices. In this way fouling of the inhalant current is avoided. The respiratory currents in these genera are described by Yonge (112). The inferred paths of the currents in the bellerophontid genus *Knightites* are shown in Figure 57. Although primitive in some respects, the Trochacea and Neritacea possess the mechanism, normal in the higher prosobranchs, for discharge of the exhalant current to the right-hand side of the animal's head.

An entirely different type of respiratory apparatus is found in the family Patellidae,

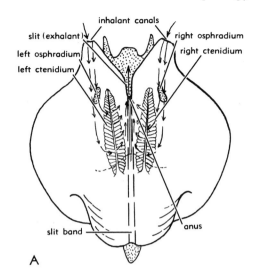

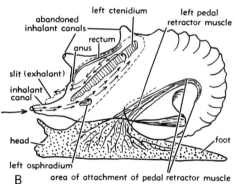

FIG. 57. *Knightites multicornutus* MOORE, restoration of pallial organs, arrows indicating the inferred courses of ciliary respiratory currents, *(A)* dorsal and *(B)* left lateral views, ×2.5 (55).

referred to the suborder Patellina of the Prosobranchia. The whole mantle edge, which adjoins the margin of the conical shell, is here fringed with a circlet of gill-lamellae. These are of secondary origin and not homologous with the ctenidia of normal prosobranchs. Two small osphradia, situated on the neck of the animal, probably indicate the presence of paired ctenidia in its ancestors. In *Patella* itself gentle inhalant and exhalant currents cross the mantle margin all around its circumference, and solid matter is ejected by muscle contractions at the middle of the right-hand side of the margin. The mechanism differs somewhat

in other genera of the family. In the Acmaeidae, patelliform gastropods also included in the Patellina, a true ctenidium is developed on the left-hand side and secondary gill-lamellae are absent. In some of the smaller prosobranchs a tendency toward simplification of the organs of respiration appears. Thus, in the marine genera *Omalogyra* and *Rissoella* both osphradium and ctenidium, and in *Caecum* the ctenidium only, have been lost, respiration taking place through the epithelium of the mantle itself. The exhalant current is created by strips of ciliated epithelium and the inhalant current enters to compensate for the outflowing water. In the land prosobranch families Helicinidae and Pomatiasidae the ctenidium is absent or reduced to a few folds of epithelium, the mantle itself acting as the main respiratory organ. In the amphibious prosobranch family Ampullariidae the mantle cavity is divided by an incomplete fleshy partition into two compartments, the left-hand one containing a normally functioning ctenidium and the right serving as a lung for air-breathing. On the left-hand side is a long siphon which can be extended so as to reach above the surface of the water when the animal is immersed and admit air to the pulmonary chamber. In *Siphonaria,* now classified as a pulmonate, there is also a ctenidium as well as a pulmonary chamber.

These forms are intermediate between normal gill-breathing gastropods and the air-breathing pulmonates proper, and show how gastropods may have succeeded in adapting themselves to a terrestrial habitat. In the great majority of pulmonates a ctenidium is absent and the mantle cavity is no longer freely open to the exterior, but is converted into a respiratory chamber (or **pulmonary sac**) by fusion of the mantle edge with the integument of the head-foot mass. The chamber can be enlarged by the contraction of muscles on its floor, and air is admitted by a narrow aperture (**pneumostome** or **pulmonary orifice**) on the right-hand side. The roof of the chamber is lined with a network of blood vessels and it is here that the blood is oxygenated. Many aquatic pulmonates rise periodically to the surface to admit air into the pulmonary sac, but it is probable that such forms are also capable of respiration through their skin. Secondary or adaptive branchiae are, how-

ever, present in some aquatic pulmonates. They consist of a simple supra-anal lobe in the Ellobiidae, but are intricately folded structures outside the mantle cavity in the Planorbidae and Ancylidae.

Among the opisthobranchs a ctenidium is present in the tectibranchs, lying on the right-hand side and partly projecting from the mantle cavity. The organ is absent in the Pyramidellidae, as also in some other small shell-bearing groups, circulation in and out of the mantle cavity being effected by an exhalant current produced by ridges of ciliated epithelium near the hypobranchial gland. Some nudibranchs have no special breathing organs and respire through the integument, but the majority have developed secondary leaflike gills carried on the back in an exposed position. Few pteropods have a ctenidium of the normal type, but in some an accessory posterior gill is developed. Others respire only through the integument. In the opisthobranch genera *Acteon, Scaphander,* and *Akera,* there is a narrow cordlike extension of the mantle cavity, termed the **pallial caecum,** which is wound around the whorls of the visceral hump on the interior of the shell almost to the tip of the spire. It is thought to be part of a highly developed pallial cleansing apparatus.

CIRCULATORY SYSTEM

In most gastropods the blood is colorless or else faintly blue, owing to presence of the oxygen-carrier haemocyanin. The heart lies within a chamber known as the **pericardial cavity,** situated to the right of the median line in the majority of forms, between the kidney and the digestive gland, and close to the ctenidium. It consists of a ventricle and either one or two auricles. There are two auricles in all gastropods included in the Archaeogastropoda except the Patellina and the Helicinidae; that is, in all forms with bipectinate ctenidia. In other gastropods only the left auricle is present. The auricle adjoins the ctenidium if this is present, and receives from it the efferent branchial vessel (Fig. 58); in the pulmonates, such as *Helix,* it faces the network of blood vessels in the roof of the mantle cavity, and receives the pulmonary vein to which the vessels converge. The ctenidium lies in front of the heart in the Prosobranchia and behind it in most of those Opisthobranchia in which it is developed, as the names for these subclasses imply. In the pulmonates the respiratory chamber is in front of the heart.

Details of the circulatory system differ in various gastropods. The ventricle gives off

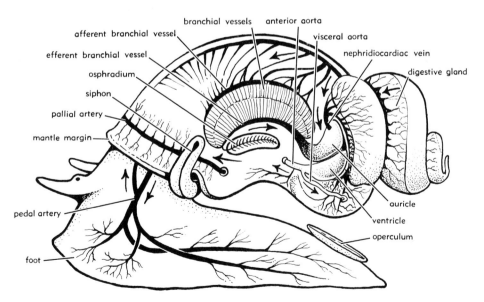

Fig. 58. *Buccinum undatum* Linné, diagrammatic representation of respiratory system, slightly enlarged (115n).

the main aorta, which then subdivides to supply the arterial systems of various parts of the body. In some genera *(Haliotis, Fissurella)* it also gives off directly an artery supplying the mantle. The arteries, which in some forms cannot be traced far from the pericardium, lead to irregular spaces or **lacunae** in the connective tissue of all parts of the body, and the blood from these, when de-oxygenated, collects in other blood spaces, the **venous sinuses.** From these it returns by veins or a series of sinuses to the auricle by way either of the kidney and ctenidium, of the kidney alone, or of the ctenidium alone.

DIGESTIVE AND EXCRETORY ORGANS

The mouth of the gastropod lies at the end of the proboscis or of the snout, if either is present, or else on the lower part of the head proper, and it opens into the **pharynx** or **buccal cavity** (Fig. 59). Thickenings around the aperture form **lips.** Within the pharynx are characteristic structures formed of horny material, for the rasping and trituration of food. These are the jaw or jaws (absent in carnivorous genera, in many opisthobranchs, and in the heteropods), and the radula. Most land pulmonates, such as *Helix,* have a single jaw, often arched, placed in the roof of the mouth. Most prosobranchs except carnivorous ones have two jaws, placed dorsolaterally just within the mouth, and these may have an elaborate sculpture of small ridges resembling the teeth of a file. Just beyond the jaws, its front part working against them, is the **radula,** a ribbon-like band, bearing transverse rows of minute teeth, which is borne longutudinally by a bulging, tonguelike object (the **odontophore or buccal mass**) that projects into the buccal cavity from its posterior end, is composed partly of cartilage and partly of muscle, and is covered by a layer of cuticular material. The radula is produced continuously in the **radular sac** at its rear end, and works forward as its frontal part, on the projecting surface of the odontophore, is worn away. Its relative length and breadth vary in different genera. In *Littorina* it is several times the length of the animal, in *Buccinum* about 30 mm. long, and in other genera relatively much shorter. The struc-

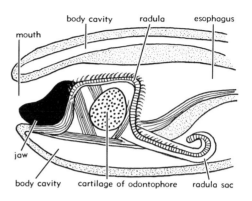

Fig. 59. *Charonia opis* (Röding), diagrammatic longitudinal (but not quite median) vertical section of buccal cavity, the buccal mass or odontophore forming the median elevation supporting the radula, much enlarged (129).

ture of the radula differs considerably in various groups of the Gastropoda and is an important aid in classification, unfortunately not available to the paleontologist. The different types of radula are described subsequently. **Salivary ducts** also open into the pharynx near the radular sac. In some carnivorous genera their secretion is acid, and this may help the radula in piercing the shell of their prey.

From the pharynx the masticated food passes in to the **esophagus** (Fig. 60), a tube which in many genera is the longest section of the alimentary canal. The salivary ducts, already mentioned, originate in one or two pairs of **salivary glands** lying to the side of the pharynx or of the esophagus, and in the latter case the ducts run for part of the way along the sides of the esophagus. In many pulmonates and opisthobranchs and a few prosobranchs there is a widened part of the esophagus termed the **crop,** in which food can be stored temporarily before it is passed on to the stomach for digestion. In carnivorous forms, such as *Buccinum,* various glands, such as the one known as "Leiblein's gland," open into the esophagus and give rise to secretions aiding digestion. In many Archaeogastropoda the middle part of the esophagus bears lateral glandular pouches in which digestive enzymes are secreted. In many tectibranchs (but not *Acteon*) the esophagus has two dilated portions (anterior and posterior crops), separated by a **triturating gizzard** in which are

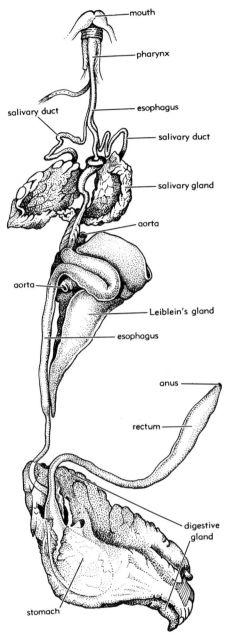

mouth
pharynx
salivary duct
esophagus
salivary duct
salivary gland
aorta
aorta
Leiblein's gland
esophagus
anus
rectum
digestive gland
stomach

Fig. 60. *Concholepas peruviana* Lamarck, with dissected alimentary canal and associated organs (119).

three calcareous plates. By the action of these the food is thoroughly triturated and masticated before passing to the stomach.

The **stomach,** which may be merely a dilation of the alimentary canal, but more frequently is a well-marked bag, lies at the posterior end of the esophagus. Its position is more or less at the base of the visceral hump, and it abuts against or is even more or less surrounded by the brownish **digestive gland,** forming most of the coiled hump in spiral gastropods. Ducts (hepatic), usually two in number, open into the stomach from the digestive gland. The latter consists essentially of repeated ramifications of the ducts, ending ultimately in blind caeca. It is primarily an organ of intercellular digestion, but in many carnivorous forms it produces an enzyme-bearing fluid that aids digestion of food in the stomach. In tectibranchs the digestive gland is also an organ of excretion, performing a function similar to that of the kidney in taking up waste matter from the blood. This matter is compacted and leaves the body with the feces.

The two main openings of the stomach are those of the intestine and esophagus. As a result of torsion the former is anterior and the latter posterior in the more primitively organized gastropods (such as *Diodora* and *Scutum*). In more advanced forms, the position of the esophageal opening becomes nearer to that of the intestine, until in the pulmonates and tectibranch opisthobranchs the two are in close proximity. At the posterior end of the stomach, except in more advanced gastropods (in a few of which it is vestigial) is the **style sac.** In Archaeogastropoda this is a gradually contracted part of the stomach leading directly to the intestine. In such forms it contains a rod of loosely compacted feces (the protostyle of Morton), which, by rotation, stirs up the contents of the stomach to assist their complete digestion. This rod is continuous, on the one hand, with fecal matter in the intestine, and, on the other hand, with the string of food from the esophagus. In some Caenogastropoda, belonging mainly to the superfamilies Rissoacea, Cerithiacea, Calyptraeacea, and Strombacea, and in one group of pteropods, the protostyle is replaced by the **crystalline style,** a cylindrical hyaline rod, which, besides functioning mechanically in the manner described, contains an enzyme which further aids digestion. Gastropods in which a crystalline style is present are all microphagous herbivores, which feed in such a manner that there is an al-

most continuous stream of food along the alimentary canal. The structure is thus absent in carnivorous forms and in herbivores that feed only at intervals. In some gastropods, including those with a crystalline style, the wall of the stomach bears a cuticular structure (**gastric shield**) against which the style rotates. A further appendage to the stomach, situated at the opposite end to the style sac, is the **posterior caecum**, developed in most Archaeogastropoda (but not in Fissurellidae) and in a few opisthobranchs and pulmonates, but not in higher prosobranchs. It is commonly more or less coiled and its function is to assist in the sorting of the contents of the stomach by means of the cilia with which it is lined.

From the stomach the intestine takes an anterodorsal course, passing under the kidney and enlarging to some extent to form the **rectum**, which runs along the right side of the roof of the mantle cavity, to terminate, usually not far from the mantle's edge, in the **anus**. In the Archaeogastropoda, apart from the Patellina and the Helicinidae, the rectum passes through the ventricle of the heart. In some prosobranch and tectibranch genera **anal glands** open into the rectum close to the anus, and are concerned with preparation of the feces. An interesting exception to the general absence of remains or traces of the soft parts in fossil gastropods is Dr. R. Casey's (13) discovery of the mold of the intestine preserved in a Lower Cretaceous specimen.

The **kidneys** (alternatively termed **renal organs** or **nephridia**) are the main organs for excretion of the waste products of metabolism. Two are present in gastropods in which the heart has two auricles, except those belonging to the Neritacea, that is, in all Archaeogastropoda except the Patellina and the Neritacea. Otherwise, only one is present. When two are present, the left one is much reduced in size and only the right one functions. When a single one is present, however, it appears to be the homologue of the left one in forms in which there are two. The kidney, reddish or dark brown in color, lies just behind the mantle cavity and adjoins both the digestive gland and the pericardial cavity. It communicates with the latter by a narrow ciliated passage (**renopericardial canal**) and with the mantle cavity either through simple apertures or by a

duct (**ureter**). It is a sac with a spongy internal structure, due to the presence of numerous intricate folds of the epithelium of its outer wall, which are covered by cells containing uric acid. The venous blood flows through the organ past these structures, which serve to extract waste products from it before it passes to the ctenidia. The excreta from the kidney pass into the mantle cavity. In the Archaeogastropoda (except the Neritacea) the right kidney also serves as a duct for the passage of genital products to the mantle cavity (Fig. 8).

REPRODUCTIVE ORGANS *88941*

In most prosobranch gastropods the sexes are distinct, but there are a few exceptions. Except in most Archaeogastropoda and certain genera of other groups, a male organ (**penis**) or, as the case may be, the series of female genital organs described below, is present, and sexual union precedes fertilization. In both sexes the gonad is embedded in or lies upon the digestive gland. Spermatozoa from the male gonad, or **testis**, collect in the greatly coiled proximal part of the genital duct, which thus acts as a **vesicula seminalis**. They then pass through a shorter, ciliated, part of the genital duct, the **vas deferens**, to the **prostate gland**, which runs along the floor of the mantle cavity on the right-hand side, parallel with the rectum. From the prostate a narrow duct runs along the right side of the neck to the penis, the proximal end of which lies on the head or neck behind the right tentacle; the penis may be an organ of considerable size.

The female genital organs are more complicated in the higher prosobranchs. The duct serving to conduct the ova from the female gonad (**ovary**) is termed the **oviduct**. Its proximal part, in which the ova collect, leads to two successive glandular regions, the **albumen gland** (which produces the albuminous fluid by which the eggs are surrounded) and either a **jelly gland** or a **capsule gland** (producing either the jelly in which masses of eggs are deposited or the material of their capsules). Between the albumen and capsule glands lies the **spermatheca** or **receptaculum seminis**, a lateral pouch in which incoming sperm can be stored until required. From the capsule gland the ova pass through the **vestibule** and **vagina** to the female aperture, which

lies close to the anus just within the mantle cavity. Adjoining the distal end of the capsule gland is the **bursa copulatrix** or **uterus**, which receives the male organ during sexual union. Fertilization of the ova takes place at the anterior end of the albumen gland.

In all Archaeogastropoda except the Neritacea, however, the genital products are discharged by both sexes, by way of the kidney, ureter, mantle cavity, and exhalant current, into the sea. Fertilization of the ova, which are usually shed singly, depends on their being encountered by spermatozoa. In such forms the prostate and penis are absent in the male, as are all genital organs that normally lie anterior to the proximal part of the oviduct in the female. In the males of certain other prosobranch genera, such as *Vermetus* and *Magilus,* in which the animal is sessile and sexual union impossible, and in *Turritella,* in which a screen of pinnate tentacles virtually closes the mantle cavity, a penis is also absent and the spermatozoa are discharged into the sea. In these groups they enter the female with the inhalant current and the ova are fertilized internally.

All the Opisthobranchia and Pulmonata, and a few prosobranchs, including *Crepidula, Capulus,* some *Acmaea, Valvata,* and *Trichotropis,* Scalidae and Janthinidae, are hermaphrodite, each individual having both male and female sexual organs and being capable of producing both ova and spermatozoa. Most hermaphrodite gastropods are **protandrous,** that is, in any individual a period of male maturity, during which spermatozoa are produced, precedes one of female maturity. Copulation is usual, free shedding of genital products, as in the Archaeogastropoda, being unknown. Hermaphrodite gastropods may be divided into two groups (not corresponding with accepted taxonomic groups), namely, "Digonopora," in which the male and female orifices are separate, and "Monogonopora," in which they are united. In the first group sexual union may be unilateral (each individual functioning only as a male or as a female in one mating episode), or reciprocal but not simultaneous (each individual acting first as one sex and then as the other in such an episode). In the second group reciprocal sexual union is simultaneous. The spermatozoa may remain

stored after union for a period, before fertilization occurs. Parthenogenesis (reproduction without fertilization) occurs in the prosobranchs *Hydrobia jenkinsi* and *Campeloma rufini,* in which species males are unknown. Self-fertilization has been recorded under experimental conditions in a number of pulmonates, both land and aquatic, but whether it takes place in nature to any extent is difficult to determine.

In hermaphrodite forms both ova and spermatozoa are produced in one gonad, termed the **hermaphrodite gland,** which lies embedded in the spiral digestive gland. From the gonad they pass at first along the same duct (**little hermaphrodite duct**), which is much convoluted, but towards its distal end they have begun to follow two distinct channels. This duct opens into, or close to the mouth of, the albumen gland or glands, and fertilization of the ova by incoming spermatozoa following sexual union takes place not far from this point, in some forms in a distinct **fertilization chamber.** A small receptaculum seminis adjoins the place of fertilization. From here the ova and outgoing sperms enter the **great hermaphrodite duct,** in which their paths become separated by longitudinal folds or by a partition. The female portion of this duct (oviduct) is dilated and puckered, its major, posterior, part constituting a mucous gland or a capsule gland, or both in succession. The ventral, male, portion of the great hermaphrodite duct (vas deferens) is relatively narrow and not puckered.

The details of the anterior part of the genital system in hermaphrodite gastropods differ considerably in different groups. In forms in which the male and female genital openings are distinct, the vas deferens diverges completely from the oviduct, usually becomes dilated to form a prostate gland, and then becomes narrow and tubelike until it leads into the penis sac behind the male genital opening. The penis, which is retractile, lies within this sac. In some forms (e.g., *Aplysia*) in which there is a common genital aperture the oviduct and vas deferens remain contiguous for the whole of their course. In *Helix* the male and female ducts diverge completely and then converge again, so that the penis sac and vagina continuing the oviduct meet behind the common genital aperture, an additional mucous

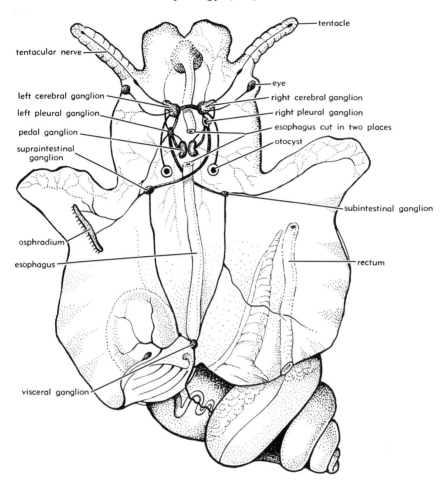

FIG. 61. Nervous system a caenogastropod, *Pomatias elegans* (MÜLLER) (58).

gland opening into the vagina not far from the aperture. A bursa copulatrix or sac homologous to it opens out of the vagina in most forms, but is absent in some. A remarkable sac which opens into the vagina near the genital aperture in many Helicidae is the **dart sac.** The dart, which is produced in this, is a small, sharply pointed, dagger-like, calcareous structure which is extruded and becomes embedded in the flesh of the partner just before sexual union. The genital openings usually lie just behind the right tentacle. When they are separate the male opening lies in a slightly more anterior position.

NERVOUS SYSTEM

The nervous system in the Gastropoda consists of a number of nerve centers or **ganglia,** which are joined by nerve cords (**commissures** or **connectives**), and communicate by means of threadlike nerves with various parts of the animal. The most important ganglia, which are paired but not quite symmetrically disposed, are the **cerebral** (receiving nerves from the eyes and tentacles, and also from the otocysts or hearing organs, in forms where these exist), the **pleural** (innervating the walls of the body cavity, the siphon, etc.), and the **pedal** (from which arise the nerves of the foot). The

cerebral and pleural ganglia are always in fairly close proximity, arranged around the esophagus in the animal's cephalic region. The pedal ganglia are close to the pleural ganglia in many gastropods, but in some are more removed. Several other ganglia usually occur, their identity and positions varying according to the particular group.

In the less advanced Caenogastropoda (Fig. 61) a visceral (or abdominal) **ganglion** is situated a considerable distance posterior to these three pairs of ganglia, in the region between the rear of the pallial cavity and the visceral mass. Some forms have two such ganglia. Between the visceral ganglion and the three anteriorly situated pairs are two other ganglia, the **subintestinal ganglion** on the right side of the animal and the **supraintestinal** one on the left. From these originate the pallial nerves, which divide up to form a network around the mantle edge. The supraintestinal ganglion also innervates the ctenidium and osphradium, while smaller nerves from the subintestinal ganglion innervate the columellar muscle and walls of the body cavity. Posteriorly, each of these two ganglia is joined by a nerve cord to the visceral ganglion or ganglia, and anteriorly each is joined to one of the pleural ganglia. The supraintestinal ganglion, however, although it lies on the left side, is joined to the right pleural ganglion and the subintestinal ganglion to the left, the respective nerve commissures crossing so that the one from the right pleural ganglion passes over that from the left. The so-called **visceral loop,** formed by the circuit of nerve cords joining the pleural ganglia to the visceral ganglion and passing through the intermediate ganglia mentioned, thus forms a figure 8. This condition is described as "streptoneurous" and is clearly the result of the "torsion" undergone by the animal in early ontogeny. In the more advanced prosobranchs there is a marked tendency to concentration of the ganglia (apart from the visceral ones) in the anterior region; in *Buccinum,* for example, the subintestinal and supraintestinal ganglia are situated in the collar of ganglia surrounding the esophagus. In such a case the nerve cords of the visceral loop cross close to these two ganglia on their posterior side.

In the Archaeogastropoda (Fig. 62*A*), the most primitive order of prosobranchs, there

is a marked absence of concentration of nerve centers, the ganglia being elongated or the commissures including a series of ganglion cells. The pleural and pedal ganglia are fused into a single mass. The foot is innervated by a conspicuous pair of almost parallel, elongated, ganglionated nerve cords joined by numerous cross-connectives to form a structure recalling a rope-ladder. This last condition is also found in some less advanced Caenogastropoda (e.g., Pomatiasidae). In some gastropods the anterior series of ganglia includes, in addition to those already mentioned, a pair of **buccal ganglia** which are connected by a short loop with the cerebral ganglia and innervate the buccal mass.

In most Opisthobranchia (Fig. 62*B*) and Pulmonata the nerve cords of the visceral loop do not cross in the manner described above, and these subclasses have, therefore, been grouped together under the name Euthyneura. Exceptions are members of the family Acteonidae, which are streptoneurous, although classified as opisthobranchs; *Chilina* is streptoneurous, although a pulmonate. In some opisthobranchs the visceral loop is well extended, with the visceral ganglion or ganglia remote from the pleural ganglia; subintestinal and supraintestinal ganglia are not developed. In other opisthobranchs the visceral loop is much shortened or altogether absent, all the ganglia being in close proximity and united by short commissures to form a ring at the posterior end of the esophagus. A similar concentration is found in the pulmonates, the visceral loop being close to the main group of ganglia and formed by two visceral ganglia separated by an abdominal one, all joined by very short commissures. The osphradial nerve, when present, communicates with the supraintestinal ganglion. A small **osphradial ganglion** may be present near the osphradium.

RADULA

A few notes on the radula (Fig. 63), already referred to, may appropriately follow the foregoing account of the soft parts, since it also is not found fossil. It is a rasplike structure consisting of numerous similar, symmetrical, transverse rows of **teeth,** or **unci,** borne on a supporting band. The horny material of which it is formed is

usually alluded to as chitin, a term originally applied to the material forming the integument of arthropods. Its composition is complex and variable; basically protein, it also contains sodium, iron, phosphorus and several other elements (93). The teeth vary greatly in number in different genera, tending to be largest and fewest in carnivorous forms. They also vary considerably in shape, some being broad and comblike, with a number of cutting points (**cusps** or **cones**), and others narrow and pointed. The total number of teeth in a gastropod radula ranges from one to about 750,000, the latter being the number present in *Umbrella*. The number of rows present may be very few or as many as several hundred. The structure

of the radula is constant in any one species and all the transverse rows of teeth are alike, or almost so. The radula is added to continuously in the radula sac at its rear end, and at the same time the worn teeth in front are discarded. In the opisthobranch group, Sacoglossa, there is a small pouch for their reception.

The term **median, central,** or **rachidian tooth** is applied to a single tooth present at the middle of each row in the majority of radulae. On either side of this, in the most fully developed radulae, other teeth, termed **marginals** or **uncini,** are present in most herbivorous prosobranchs. When there are two or perhaps several very similar teeth at the middle of each row, all are sometimes

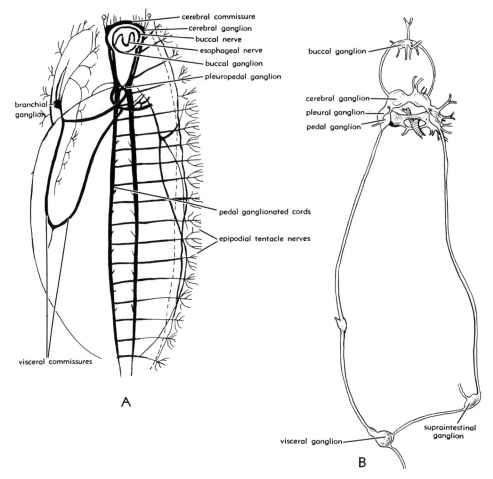

Fɪɢ. 62. Nervous system of *(A)* an archaeogastropod, *Haliotis tuberculata* Lɪɴɴé (121) and *(B)* an opisthobranch, *Akera bullata* Müʟʟᴇʀ (80).

regarded as medians; if the number is even, no tooth lies absolutely in the middle. The part of the radula which includes the median and admedian teeth is termed the **rachis** and the parts with the marginal teeth are the **pleurae.** Special terms may be used for individual teeth in various types of radula. Teeth of any of the series mentioned may be absent. The radula formula is a series of numbers (usually 5) referring to the teeth of each series present in the appropriate place in every row, a 0 being included if those of any series are absent, and the "infinity" symbol (∞) if they are too numerous to count, as is sometimes the case with the marginals. Thus, 1:1:1:1:1 denotes the presence of one median tooth, with one admedian on each side of it and one marginal at each end of the row, but 1:0:1:0:1 denotes the presence of a median and marginals only, with admedians absent. There may be several admedians on each side, but the number is never very large. If marginals are absent, the "0" on each side may be omitted from the formula, which is thus reduced to three numbers. The average number of rows of teeth present in the radula of any species may be added at the end of the formula, preceded by a multiplication sign, for example 1:1:1:1:1 ($\times 42$).

The prosobranchs have been divided by GRAY, TROSCHEL, and others into a number of groups which take their names from the prevalent type of radula, a classification based on the radula separating to a considerable extent the same groups as one based on the general characters of the soft parts and shell; in most groups, however, there are species in which the radula shows abnormalities. The most important of these groups are as follows.

RHIPIDOGLOSSA

The formula is ∞ :ca.5:1:ca.5: ∞. The very numerous marginals are long, narrow, hooked and arranged in a somewhat fanlike manner. The admedians, of which there are several (most frequently about 5) on each side, are not always very different from the median one. In the Neritidae the outermost admedian on each side, termed a **capituliform tooth,** is broad and flat-topped. All the Archaeogastropoda except the limpets have a rhipidoglossan radula.

DOCOGLOSSA

The number of teeth, which are lancelike or clawlike in shape, is small, and two or more teeth may be regarded as medians. Marginals or admedians, or uncommonly both sets, may be absent. There is thus no constant formula. That of *Patella* is 3:1:(2+0+2):1:3, the medians (indicated in parentheses) numbering 4, grouped as indicated. The limpets (Acmaeidae, Patellidae, Lepetidae) constitute this group.

TAENIOGLOSSA

The usual formula is 2:1:1:1:2, but there are variations. The median tooth most frequently has a number of cusps, with the middle one the largest. The admedians are broad and commonly cuspidate. The two marginals on each side are narrow and hooklike or cuspidate. Many of the less advanced Caenogastropoda have a radula of this type.

PTENOGLOSSA

The radula has an indefinite number of long, hooked teeth, of which the outermost are the largest. Two families of Caenogastropoda, Scalidae and Janthinidae, have this type of radula, but in the former the teeth are small and in the latter they are large and there is a smooth band along the middle of the radula.

RACHIGLOSSA

The radula formula is 1:1:1 or 0:1:0. The median tooth has one to about 14 sharp cusps and the admedians, if present, are usually broad and rakelike, with numerous cusps, but in some genera they have only two large cusps. In some of the advanced Caenogastropoda that have been classed as Rachiglossa, however, the typical rachiglossate radula has degenerated. Thus, some species, belonging to different families, have lost the admedians, and in the genus *Harpa* the radula has completely atrophied in the adult.

TOXOGLOSSA

In most genera of the three families (Conidae, Turridae, Cancellariidae) classified under this heading, the radula consists only of long teeth, which there is evidence for regarding as marginals. The formula is thus 1:0:0:0:1, or 1:0:1, as usually given.

In *Conus* the teeth are very large and a poison gland is associated with them.

STENOGLOSSA

The Rachiglossa and Toxoglossa have been combined under the name Stenoglossa, this name referring to the relative narrowness of the radula, although there is little resemblance between the two constituent groups in other respects.

GYMNOGLOSSA

This name is applied to the Eulimidae and Pyramidellidae, and denotes the absence of a radula, which is not needed owing to a parasitic mode of life.

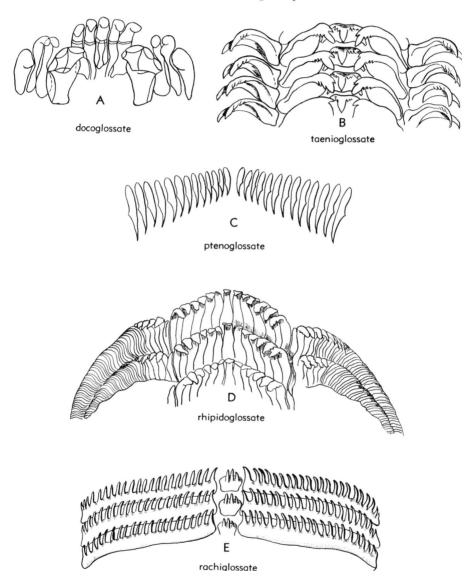

FIG. 63. Gastropod radulae. Docoglossate, *Patella (Ancistromesus) pica* REEVE (97); taenioglossate, *Vermetus grandis* GRAY (20); ptenoglossate, *Janthina fragilis* LAMARCK (67); rhipidoglossate, *Margarita umbilicalis* BRODERIP & SOWERBY (20); rachiglossate, *Fasciolaria trapezium* LAMARCK (20).

In the Pulmonata and Opisthobranchia there is also great diversity in the structure of the radula, but in these groups it has not been used in classification. An extensive literature exists on the radulae in both subclasses.

MORPHOLOGY OF HARD PARTS

OCCURRENCE OF SHELL IN GASTROPODA

A shell is present in the great majority of the gastropods and in most forms is completely external when the head-foot mass is withdrawn. This is the case even in some families, such as the Cypraeidae, Marginellidae, Olividae, and Hydatinidae, in which the shell is almost enveloped by the mantle or the foot is much enlarged when these organs are protruded. In some genera, such as *Sinum, Harpa,* and many opisthobranchs, however, the soft parts cannot be entirely withdrawn into the shell. The latter may even be completely internal, as in some opisthobranchs and in the slugs. In such cases it has frequently suffered degradation, being reduced to a small calcareous plate in the case of the slugs. It is absent in a few groups.

Among the prosobranchs the shell-less condition is associated with a parasitic life in the case of genera such as *Paedophoropus, Entoconcha, Pseudosacculus, Asterophila,* and *Ctenoscalum,* and with a pelagic life in the case of *Pterotrachea,* but the marine, sluglike *Titiscania* leads a crawling existence. The opisthobranchs include the shell-less nudibranchs, which are widely distributed in present-day seas.

GENERAL FEATURES OF SHELL

The gastropod shell is essentially a protective structure that permanently covers the visceral mass and provides a retreat for the head-foot mass, which is extruded from it when active. Typically, it may be regarded as a conelike tube (showing much diversity, however, in cross-sectional shape), which is closed at its apical end, formed first during growth, and open at the other end, where growth increments are added, while at the same time there is usually a progressive increase in diameter. It is convenient to allude

to this tube as the **helicocone,** the opening at its extremity being termed the **aperture** (Fig. 64). In most gastropods the shell assumes a spiral form as the helicocone, during growth, coils repeatedly about an imaginary **axis** passing through its apex. If the direction of growth of the helicocone is constantly perpendicular to the axis as coiling takes place, the outermost point on the edge of the apertural margin will trace a plane spiral and the resulting shell may be described as **planispiral,** or as **isostrophic** when the cross-section of the helicocone is such that there is symmetry about a median plane (e.g., Bellerophontidae, Fig. 65*J*). With most gastropod shells, however, the direction of growth of the helicocone has a component parallel with the axis and, except when this component is relatively small, the spiral body formed will have a protruding apex, and may even be considerably drawn out like a corkscrew. Spiral shells with a distinctly protruding apex are described as **conispiral.**

Each complete coil of the helicocone is termed a **whorl.** In most shells each coil conceals part of the preceding one, and then the term whorl commonly refers only to the visible part of each coil. Each coil embraces the preceding one up to a line of contact known as the **suture,** which itself forms a spiral when the shell is considered as a whole. As only one side of the shell can be viewed at a time, it is customary to regard any whorl as bounded by two sutures, notwithstanding their essential continuity. They are best referred to as the **adapical** and **abapical** sutures of the whorl in question, according to whether they are nearer to or farther from the apex.

The helicocone may be coiled so broadly with respect to the axis that a conical cavity, known as an **umbilicus,** remains surrounding the axis. In this case, in addition to the usual suture on the outer surface of the shell, a second suture (**umbilical suture**) may be visible within the umbilicus. If the shell has no protruding apex, but a depressed adapical surface, this surface will constitute a second umbilicus, known as the **adapical umbilicus.** A shell with an adapical umbilicus is described as **involute** (Fig. 65*I*), and one in which the last whorl completely envelops and obscures the preceding ones as **convolute** (Fig. 65*A*). Planispiral

and isostrophic shells may be either involute or convolute.

The **columella** of a shell is the pillar, surrounding the axis, formed by the **adaxial** wall of the coiled helicocone. A solid columella is produced by the complete fusion of successive parts of this wall as the shell grows. The term **spire** denotes, collectively, the adapical visible part of all the whorls except the last. The **periphery** of the shell (or of any particular whorl) is the part farthest from the axis, while the **base** of the shell is the abapically facing part of the surface, delimited in most shells by the periphery, but in certain genera, when so defined, by a spiral carina or angulation serving as an obvious boundary.

In some gastropod shells, such as the limpets, the helicocone is not coiled in a spiral, but has the form of a simple depressed cone. The terminology relevant to such shells is correspondingly simple.

The direction of coiling of an adult gastropod in relation to the head-foot mass is described as **endogastric.** This means that, when the shell rests on the crawling head-foot mass, it is so coiled that the body of the shell extends backwards, away from the head. The result is that the head withdraws into the shell before the foot, the operculum on the latter (if present) closing the aperture. The opposite condition, in which the body of the shell tends to extend forward over the head, and the foot withdraws into the shell before the head, is termed **exogastric,** and is found in gastropods only in a very early developmental stage, prior to torsion. It is the normal condition in the cephalopod *Nautilus*.

VARIETY IN SHELL FORM

The general form of a coiled gastropod shell depends on a number of interrelated factors, chief among which are the cross-sectional shape of the helicocone, the degree of overlap of successive coils, and the openness of coiling of the whole spiral with respect to the axis. Not in every genus, moreover, are the mode of coiling and the rate of increase in the cross-sectional area of the helicocone constant during growth.

In some shells the helicocone is so loosely coiled that the whorls remain **disjunct,** not touching one another. In other forms the earlier whorls form a close coil, but the

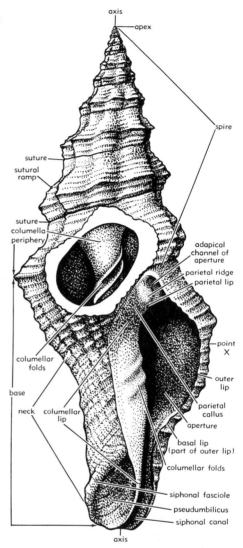

Fig. 64. Typical gastropod shell, *Latirus lynchi* (BASTEROT), Mio., Fr., showing terminology of its various parts. The columella is seen through a "window" in the last whorl (115n).

later ones, or perhaps only part of the last whorl, become disjunct (Fig. 65D). In some species of the land prosobranch genus *Opisthostoma* and also in the Paleozoic marine genera *Scoliostoma* and *Brilonella* the terminal part of the last whorl bends up towards the apex. In the family Vermetidae, while the helicocone is at first spirally coiled in some species, in later growth stages it becomes very irregularly contorted and often

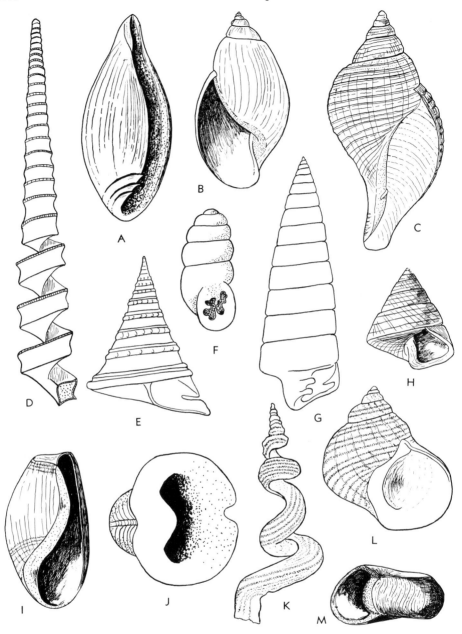

FIG. 65. Variety in gastropod shell form.——*A.* Convolute, *Acteonella gigantea* D'ORBIGNY, Cret., Fr., ×0.7 (78).——*B.* Sinistral, *Physa meigsi* DALL, Plio., Fla., ×1.2 (116).——*C.* Fusiform, *Fasciolaria tulipa* (LINNÉ), Plio., Fla., ×3 (116).——*D.* Turriculate (with later whorls disjunct), *Nerinella libanotica* DELPEY, L.Cret., Syria, ×1.3 (117).——*E.* Coeloconoid, *Pyrgotrochus luciensis* (D'ORBIGNY), M.Jur., Fr., ×0.5 (127).——*F.* Pupiform, *Gastrocopta baudoni* (MICHAUD), Plio., Fr., ×16 (130).——*G.* Cyrtoconoid, *Nerinea requieniana* D'ORBIGNY, U.Cret., Fr., ×0.67 (78).——*H.* Trochiform, *Calliostoma erosum* DALL, Plio., N.Car., ×2.7 (116).——*I.* Involute, *Bulla striata* BRUGUIÈRE, Plio., Fla., ×1.7 (116).——*J.* Isostrophic, *Bellerophon vasulites* MONTFORT, M.Dev., Ger., ×1 (115n).——*K.* Irregularly coiled, *Vermetus spiratus* PHILIPPI, Rec., Carib., ×1 (135).——*L.* Turbiniform, *Turbo militaris* REEVE, Rec., IndoPac., ×0.7 (135).——*M.* Discoidal and sinistral, *Helisoma disstoni* (DALL), Plio., Fla., ×1.3 (116).

disjunct (Fig. 65*K*). The irregular form is correlated with the fact that the shell becomes partly cemented to the substratum. In the Caecidae the initial coiled stage is often lost and the shell then consists of a small, hornlike tube. Irregularity in coiling may arise as a pathological condition. Shells in which the whorls are slightly disjunct owing to this cause are described as **scalari-form**. There has been confusion in the past between irregularly coiled gastropods and the tests of coiled serpulid worms, but study of the shell structure enables the two groups to be distinguished.

The genus *Xenophora* is able to cement extraneous objects, such as small pebbles, shells of Foraminifera, and other shells, to its test. The Paleozoic euomphalids *Lytospira* and *Straparollus (Philoxene)* had the same habit.

Terms used commonly to describe the general form of a gastropod shell are defined in the Glossary. Some need little explanation in view of their etymology, whereas others (e.g., bucciniform, naticiform, patelliform) are derived from the names of common genera having the form that they denote. If the whole shell (or only its spire) approaches a cone in shape but has convex sides, it (or the spire) may be described as **cyrtoconoid** (Fig. 65*G*), and, if its sides are concave, as **coeloconoid** (Fig. 65*E*). MOSELEY (229) long ago showed that, when a coiled gastropod shell retains the same shape and proportions at all stages of growth, any particular point on the growing edge of the helicocone traces a logarithmic spiral. Certain mathematical properties result from this fact; for example, the heights of successive whorls measured along any plane passing through the axis form a geometrical progression. The whole subject is admirably discussed by THOMPSON (99). MOSELEY himself showed how the surface area and volume of a shell ideally regular in form can be calculated mathematically. In practice, however, there is seldom more than an approximation to this ideal condition.[1]

DIRECTIONAL TERMINOLOGY OF GASTROPOD SHELL

There are two conventional methods of posing a gastropod shell for illustration. Most authors place it with the axis vertical and apex uppermost, but in France and a few other countries the shell is placed with its apex lowermost. The second method has the advantage that the aperture is more clearly illuminated when (as is conventional in illustration) the specimen is lighted from the top left-hand side. Exponents of either method are apt to use such terms as "upper" and "lower" according to the way in which they are accustomed to view specimens, and French authors use the term *"plafond"* for the part of the marginal region of the aperture farthest from the apex. To avoid confusion it is thus advisable not to use terms suggested by conventional orientation of the shell, although "apex" and "base" are too firmly established to be discarded.

D'ORBIGNY (78), who made a great advance in gastropod descriptive terminology, referred already to these differing practices and decided to establish two directional terms "anterior" and "posterior." "Je désignerai toujours comme *antérieure* la partie de la coquille d'où sort l'animal, et *postérieure* le côté de la spire où l'extrémité du pied se montre dans les coquilles allongées." Thus originated the practice, adopted by many subsequent authors, of describing the direction from the apex to the base parallel with the axis as "anterior" and the opposite direction as "posterior." If, now, we consider how coiled gastropods carry their shell when crawling (Figs. 51, 67, 68), it is evident that D'ORBIGNY's anterior direction (in the shell) approximates to the true anterior direction (as defined by the direction in which the animal normally progresses when active) when the shell has a high spire (as mentioned by him), or when (as in the Cypraeidae and Conidae) the aperture is narrow and elongate. When, however, the aperture is relatively broad, it may be said that, the lower the spire of the shell, the more does the true anterior direction differ from that defined by D'ORBIGNY, until in planispiral shells it is outward (toward the outer lip) from the axis and not parallel with it. The terms "anterior" and "posterior," defined by reference to the living animal, cannot, therefore, be applied consistently to coiled shells regarded as

---

[1] A recent mathematical treatment of the form of the gastropod shell is that of CINTRA & DE SOUZA LOPES (14), who disagree with THOMPSON's conclusions.

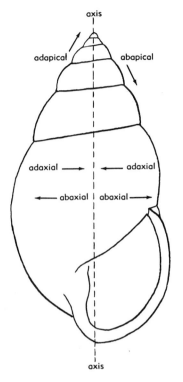

FIG. 66. Directional terminology for a gastropod shell (115n). For high-spired but not all other shells, abapical=anterior, adapical=posterior, and the left and right sides are as viewed in the figure.

geometrical structures. Their replacement by "abapical" and "adapical" (Fig. 66) is advocated. Since, moreover, the directions to be described as "left" and "right" depend on those which are regarded as "anterior" and "posterior" (to which they are perpendicular), it follows that these terms also can be applied satisfactorily to coiled gastropod shells only when the apex points straight to the rear when the animal is crawling. The left side of the shell in such a case is the side on the observers' left when the shell is viewed with its apex uppermost and its aperture facing him. The side of the shell on which the aperture lies may be called the "apertural" side and the opposite side the "abapertural" side. Application of the terms "ventral" and "dorsal" to gastropod shells is not recommended.

In the case of patelliform shells like the limpets, symmetrically poised on the soft parts of the animal and having little play in relation to them, the terms "anterior" and "posterior," defined from the soft parts, are applicable accurately to the shell.

DEXTRAL, SINISTRAL, AND HYPERSTROPHIC SHELLS

In the apertural view of most coiled gastropod shells the aperture lies on the observer's right when the apex is uppermost; in other words, the shell, viewed from above the apex, coils in a clockwise direction as it grows. Such shells, provided that (as is most commonly the condition) the genitalia of the animal lie on the right-hand side of the head-foot mass or of the pallial cavity, are termed **dextral**. A sinistral gastropod is one that is the mirror image of a dextral form in every respect. The aperture appears on the observer's left when viewed as described first above (Fig. 65*B*), and the genitalia are on the left-hand side of the head-foot mass or pallial cavity. Sinistrality may be a family character (Triphoridae), a character only of certain genera of families in which most genera are dextral, or a specific character in genera in which most species are dextral, for example, the well-known English Pleistocene (Red Crag) species *Neptunea contraria* (LINNÉ). Very rarely it may arise as an individual abnormality.

A further case, however, is when an apparently sinistral shell belongs to a dextrally organized animal (i.e., one with its genitalia on the right-hand side) or *vice versa*. Such a shell may be regarded as a dextral one in which the spire side is deeply umbilicate and the basal side less deeply umbilicate or even protruding. Gastropods in which such conditions obtain are described as **hyperstrophic (ultradextral** and **ultrasinistral** are also used in this connection). Planispiral shells constitute an intermediate type between such shells and those with a normal protruding spire. Thus in the family Ampullariidae (Fig. 67), *Pila, Ampullaria,* and *Ampullarius* are normal dextral genera; *Marisa* and *Pseudoceratodes* are involute and almost planispiral; and *Lanistes,* apparently sinistral, in fact is hyperstrophic. The Planorbidae (Fig. 65*M*) are sinistral and hyperstrophic-discoidal. It should be noted that, following the convention of most authors who have dealt with them, dextral and sinistral hyperstrophic shells of Paleozoic age are illustrated in this work with the aperture to the right or left respectively.

Usually, hyperstrophy can be detected only when the soft parts are available for anatomical study. The Macluritacea, an important group of Lower Paleozoic gastropods, are, however, known to have been hyperstrophic because of the direction of coiling of the operculum. Figure 68 shows a restoration of a representative of this family, indicating how the hyperstrophic shell was probably carried by the crawling gastropod. The term **orthostrophic** may be used as the converse of hyperstrophic, denoting normality in coiling.

APICAL WHORLS

The majority of gastropod shells that have escaped abrasion or corrosion preserve in their successive whorls a record of their development from the time when the primitive shell-gland began to secrete a calcareous test. Exceptions are those genera, such as *Patella,* in which the earliest-formed shell is cast off when the shell begins to acquire its adult shape. In some families, moreover, notably the Thiaridae, the apical whorls are discarded following the withdrawal of the tip of the visceral spiral from them and the secretion of a septum above it; this process is known as **"decollation."** The earliest formed test is horny in some genera, such as *Scaphella,* and is soon lost; in such cases its former presence may be indicated by a scar on the apex of the calcareous shell, culminating in a point.

In land and fresh-water gastropods and many marine species the earliest whorls are succeeded by the later ones with no evidence of any discontinuity, the mode of coiling being constant and the ornament of the adult shell appearing gradually. In others, however, certain whorls at the apex are clearly demarcated from those that follow (Fig. 69). The demarcation may consist only of a small swelling (or **varix**) parallel to the axis, or it may be indicated by a sudden incoming of ornament or change in ornament, or by a change in shell texture. At times, however, the axis of the early whorls forms a distinct angle, in some species even exceeding 90 degrees, with that

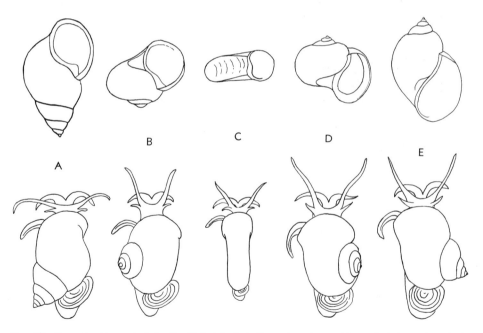

FIG. 67. Hyperstrophic conispiral, discoidal (planispiral), and orthostrophic conispiral species of the family Ampullariidae. In each case the animal is dextrally organized, as shown by the positions of the siphon (always on the left) and operculum. The species represented are *(A) Lanistes (Meladomus) pyramidalis* Bourguignat, W.Afr.; *(B) Lanistes carinatus* (Olivier), Egypt; *(C) Marisa cornuarietis* (Linné), S.Am.; *(D) Ampullarius gevesensis* (Deshayes), S.Am.; *(E) Pila ovata* (Olivier), E.Afr.; all reduced (124, 126).

operculum

A

B   C

FIG. 68. Restoration of *Palleseria longwelli* (KIRK), Ord., N.Am., an early hyperstrophic marine gastropod (55). *A-C.* Left lateral, oblique front, and right lateral views; note in *A* counter-clockwise coiling of the operculum; ×0.93.

of the later ones, or the early whorls may appear to be coiled in the direction opposite to those succeeding them. The number of such early whorls is usually about two or three, but is as many as eight in some species.

The term **protoconch** is applied to the initial whorls, particularly when these are delimited from the later ones, although it is frequently used when there is no sharp separation; in the latter case the initial whorls so designated are taken to end where the first elements of the ornament of the adult shell appear. The part of the shell formed subsequent to the protoconch may be termed the **teleoconch.**

It is still doubtful if discontinuity between the protoconch and teleoconch always coincides with a definite episode in the life-history of the gastropod. LEMCHE has noted that in all opisthobranchs studied by him the early, apparently sinistrally coiled, whorls are those of the pelagic larva, the change to a normal mode of coiling taking place when the animal settles and begins to undergo metamorphosis. The significance of the varix or change in shell texture, which may mark the termination of the

protoconch, needs further investigation. The discontinuity may occur in forms (e.g., Volutidae) that pass through the veliger stage and undergo metamorphosis while still within the egg, hatching out as creepers. Moreover, the work of MARIE LEBOUR, THORSON, and others suggests that there are many cases where a shell bears no record of the transition from a pelagic to a benthonic mode of life. The first traces of adult ornament may appear while the animal is still a pelagic larva.

The size of the protoconch in proportion to that of the full-grown shell varies greatly. Genera in which it is remarkably large include some members of the Volutidae, such as *Cymbium* and *Scaphella,* in which it forms a smooth, domelike structure, attaining a diameter of 23 mm. in one species. Its size may vary considerably even in the

FIG. 69. Various gastropod protoconchs.——*A.* Conical, *Scala dentiscalpium* (WATSON), Rec., ×30 (136). ——*B.* Conical multispiral, *Cymatium vespaceum* (LAMARCK), Rec.; ×8 (123).——*C.* Mammillated, *Cerithiopsis ridicula* WATSON, Rec., ×45 (136).——*D.* Mammillated, *Clavilithes rugosus* (LAMARCK), Eoc., Fr., ×5.5 (41).——*E.* Obtusely conical, *Nassarius babylonicus* (WATSON), Rec., ×13 (136).——*F.* Domelike, paucispiral, with reticulate ornament, *Melatoma tholoides* (WATSON), Rec., ×17 (136).——*G.* With papillose ornament, *Murex acanthodes* WATSON, Rec., ×18 (136).——*H.* With decussate ornament, *Daphnella compsa* (WATSON), Rec., ×18 (136).——*I.* Disjunct, with erect tip, *Charonia (Austrotriton) woodsi* (TATE), Mio., Austral., ×14.5 (123).——*J.* Deviated paucispiral, *Columbarium acanthostephes* (TATE), Mio., Austral., ×11 (120).——*K.* Deviated paucispiral, *Pterospira hannafordi* (McCoy), Mio., Austral., ×2 (120).——*L.* Heterostrophic and submerged, *Partulida spiralis* (MONTAGU), Rec., ×55 (101). ——*M.* Heterostrophic, *Turbonilla lactea* (LINNÉ), Rec., ×52 (101).——*N.* Heterostrophic, *Odostomia albella* (LOVÉN), Rec., ×48 (101).——*O.* Heterostrophic, *Odostomia dipsycha* WATSON, Rec., ×42 (136). ——*P.* Heterostrophic, *Eulimella nitidissima* (MONTAGU), Rec., ×48 (101).

FIG. 70. Submerged heterostrophic protoconchs of Recent European opisthobranch shells, revealed by breaking away shell wall (66). *(A) Acteon tornatilis* (LINNÉ); *(B) Retusa ovata* (JEFFREYS); *(C) Cylichna cylindracea* (PENNANT); all ×18.

offspring of a single individual, the differences being attributed largely to the relative success of embryos in devouring the "nurse eggs," incapable of development, associated with them within the common egg space (102), or in the exercise of cannibal proclivities among individuals newly hatched from an egg cluster. The size of the adult shell does not depend on that of the protoconch.

The remarkable type of protoconch formed of whorls apparently coiled in the direction opposite to those of the teleoconch is described as **heterostrophic** (Fig. 69L-P), and is particularly characteristic of, although not confined to, the Opisthobranchia, in which the family Pyramidellidae is now included. In involute opisthobranch genera, such as *Bulla,* the protoconch is commonly hidden, but it may be revealed by breaking away part of the wall of the last whorl (Fig. 70). In the prosobranch family Architectonicidae there is a heterostrophic protoconch, the tip of which points down into the umbilicus of the teleoconch. Where the anatomy of the larval animal has been investigated it has been found that heterostrophic protoconchs are hyperstrophic; thus, although the protoconch of the dextral shell *Odostomia eulimoides* HANLEY appears to be sinistral, the larval animal which secreted it was dextrally organized like the adult animal. This, of course, would be expected. The term **homeostrophic** is used as the converse of heterostrophic, to describe a protoconch obviously coiled in the same

manner as the teleoconch. A protoconch is described as **deviated** when its axis forms a well-marked angle with that of the teleoconch; most heterostrophic protoconchs are deviated. According to the number of its whorls, a protoconch (like the whole shell) may be described as **paucispiral** or **multispiral**. Its general form may be described by such self-explanatory adjectives as globular, bulbous, mammillated, subcylindrical, conical, etc. Most protoconchs are smooth, except, perhaps, for the incoming of elements of ornament on their last whorl. In some genera, however, the protoconch whorls have a very distinctive ornament. Thus in *Alvania* they bear spiral lines or rows of puncta, while in some Turridae, such as *Daphnella* (Fig. 69H) and *Philbertia* (Fig. 86A), they have a very distinctive oblique, reticulate ornament. The ornament of the protoconch of the Paleozoic Pseudozygopleuridae is very constant within the family but that of adult stages is variable and gives a basis for distinguishing the numerous genera and species.

SPIRE WHORLS AND SUTURES

Each spire whorl (Fig. 64) consists of the part of the surface of the helicocone that is not covered by the succeeding coil, so that its height (i.e., width from suture to suture) depends on the steepness of the coiling, that is, on the slope of the sutures. In many shells this remains almost constant during growth, but in some it becomes more gentle or even reversed in later growth

stages, while in others it becomes steeper near the aperture. In many shells with strong ribs or varices the suture undulates where it crosses them, and in some genera of the Cymatiidae the undulations are so marked that the spire has a distorted appearance. In outline a spire whorl may be wholly or partly convex, flat or concave. It may present one or more obtuse angulations, often accentuated to form a **keel** or **carina,** which may be sharp or rounded. A well-marked angulation (**shoulder**) is often present near the adapical suture, from which it is separated by a more or less flat zone known as a **sutural shelf** (if almost perpendicular to the axis) or as a **sutural ramp** (if inclined). The character of the suture obviously depends mainly on two factors, the outline of the outer face of the helicocone and the extent to which each whorl overlaps the preceding one. In many gastropods

the suture tends to follow an angulation of the helicocone that forms the boundary of the base of the last whorl. If, as in some species of *Turritella,* the suture drops below this angulation, the whorls are said to **imbricate.** Descriptive terms applied to the suture are mainly self-explanatory. It will be **flush** when the whorl side is flat and the suture follows the angulation just mentioned (Fig. 71*G*); almost flush when the whorl surfaces that meet at it are **adpressed,** that is, very gradually convergent (Fig. 71*A*), as shown by the fact that the aperture (unless there is an infilling of callus) is narrowly angular adapically. A suture is said to be **impressed** when the whorl surfaces are both inturned toward the axis where they meet along it (Fig. 71*F*), or **grooved** (**channeled** of some authors) when only a narrow band of each is inturned (Fig. 71*D*). When (as is more frequently the

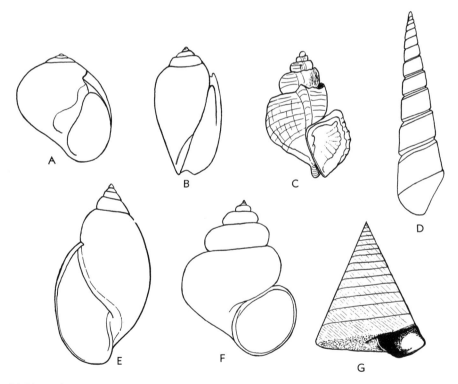

FIG. 71. Types of gastropod shell sutures.——*A*. With whorls adpressed, *Natica floridana* DALL, Mio., Fla., ✕4 (116).——*B*. Canaliculate (for mantle appendage), *Olivella lata* DALL, Mio., Fla., ✕3.6 (116).——*C*. Canaliculate, *Trigonostoma sericea* (DALL), Plio., Fla., ✕2.2 (116).——*D*. Grooved, *Pseudomelania bicarinata* HUDLESTON, M.Jur., Eng., ✕1 (121).——*E*. With abutting whorls, *Physa meigsi* DALL, Plio., Fla., ✕1.2 (116).——*F*. Impressed, *Viviparus viviparus* (LINNÉ), Rec., Eu., ✕1 (105).——*G*. Flush, *Epulotrochus epulus* (D'ORBIGNY), L.Jur.(Lias.), Fr., ✕2.5 (128).

case) the surface of the lower whorl only is inturned, it may be said merely to abut against the preceding one when they meet at an angle at the suture (Fig. 71*E*). The suture is **canaliculate** when it lies in a troughlike depression resulting from the fact that the whorl shoulder rises above it (Fig. 71*C*). In *Oliva* and related genera there is a narrow sutural canal (Fig. 71*B*) which is occupied by a cordlike posterior appendage of the mantle when this is not protruded. In some species of the Turridae and other families, the sutures are difficult to see owing to the prominence of spiral ornament. In genera in which the mantle extends widely over the surface of the shell, all or some of the sutures are obscured by the inductura (see below), termed **enamel** when highly polished.

LAST WHORL AND APERTURE

The last whorl, which begins at the growth line meeting the adapical end of the aperture, is the only whorl of which the entire outer surface remains visible. The outline of its base in most species is convex for some distance from the periphery, but often has a reversal of curvature at the origin of a relatively narrow abapical part of the whorl sometimes known as the **neck.** This usually includes the siphonal canal, referred to below. In *Tibia* the abapical end of the whorl forms a pointed projection or rostrum.

The margin of the aperture is termed the **peristome.** Its abaxial part, extending from the suture to the foot of the columella and forming the termination of the outer side of the helicocone, is termed the **outer lip** or **labrum.** It should be noted that an imaginary extension of the suture in a spiral direction around the last whorl would meet the outer lip at a point X (Fig. 64). The part of the lip on the abapical side of this point may be alluded to as the **basal lip.** The remaining, adaxial, part of the peristome is termed the **inner lip** (less commonly, **labium**) and consists of two parts, the **columellar lip,** formed by the columella, and the **parietal lip,** extending from the columella to the suture. The parietal lip may be formed by the actual surface of the helicocone, in which case the peristome is said to be discontinuous, or else by a coating of smooth shelly matter extending out

of the aperture and constituting, in fact, the inner wall of the last coil of the helicocone. This shelly coating, which is secreted by the entire surface of the mantle, has long been known as **callus,** a rather unsatisfactory term which some authors, following KNIGHT, prefer to replace by **inductura.** The inductura may have a distinct margin extending across the inner lip, as in *Viviparus,* so that the whole apertural margin is continuous, and in some shells the terminal part of the helicocone may become slightly detached.

At the abapical end of the aperture the margins of the inner and outer lips may meet in an uninterrupted curve, in which case the shell is described as **holostomatous** (Fig. 72*A*). In many shells, however, the presence of an inhalant siphon gives rise to a discontinuity of the apertural margin at this point, and the shell is termed **siphonostomatous** (Fig. 72*B,C*). The outlet of the canal is marked by a sinus of the margin (**siphonal notch**) often lying in a plane more or less perpendicular to the axis; and this outlet in some groups lies at the extremity of a narrow prolongation of the aperture known as the **siphonal canal.** The latter may be straight, bent, or curved, and is a slender, fragile structure in some species of *Fusinus, Murex,* and other genera. The slender rostrum present in such genera as *Aporrhais* and *Tibia* is not to be mistaken for a siphonal canal. In *Aporrhais* the siphon draws in its current of water through a broad sinus between the rostrum and the outer lip. A small notch of the apertural margin between the columella and outer lip does not necessarily indicate the presence of a siphon. Such a notch is present in some species of the pulmonate genus *Achatina,* in which, of course, there is no siphon.

In some shells the outer and parietal lips meet at the end of the suture in an acute angle to which a distinct groove may lead. A short ridge (**parietal ridge**) situated on the parietal lip a short distance from the suture in some species of the Cerithiidae and other families delimits a small recess in this corner of the aperture. The function of the ridge is unknown. The term "posterior canal" has been applied to this corner of the aperture when narrow and produced, and the mantle fold occupying it, although not a definite siphon, presumably serves (at

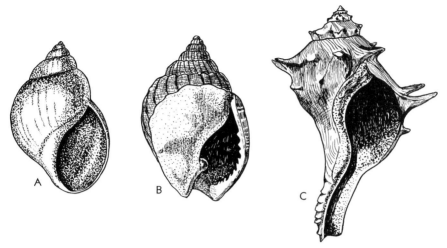

FIG. 72. Holostomatous and siphonostomatous shells.——*A. Ampullella bulimoides* (D'ORBIGNY), L.Cret., Fr., ×0.7 (78).——*B. Nassarius johnsoni* (DALL), Mio., Fla., ×2 (116).——*C. Busycon (Echinofulgur) echinatum* (DALL), Plio., Fla., ×0.8 (116).

least in some species) as an exhalant channel. In some genera of the Strombacea (e.g., *Rimella*) the aperture is continued adapically by a narrow, parallel-sided channel, which may ascend high up the spire and, in some species, ultimately descend again on another side. This channel is not formed until the shell is full-grown. Some authors have assumed that it has an exhalant function, but this has still to be confirmed by observations on the living gastropod. It seems to be equivalent to one of the labral digitations that occur in this superfamily and are mentioned below. In a group of land operculates belonging to the family Cyclophoridae, a narrow tube projects or extends along the suture from where the latter terminates at the margin of the aperture. It is regarded as a device for breathing when the aperture is closed by the operculum.

In some families the outer lip has a parallel-sided slit or a deep sinus. A slit occupies a peripheral position in the Bellerophontacea, and in the Pleurotomariacea it is most commonly either peripheral or on the adapical side of the periphery, but exceptionally (as in the Luciellidae and Portlockiellidae and in *Cataschisma*) it may be on the abapical side of the periphery. In the Nerineidae and Conidae such a slit adjoins the suture. The presence of the slit enables feces and excrement to be discharged where

they are not likely to foul the inhalant current. In the Turridae a sinus of varying depth at the shoulder of the whorl or on the ramp between it and the suture fulfills a similar function. In *Haliotis* and a few other genera, a row of orifices (**tremata**), and in the Mesozoic genus *Trochotoma,* a single elongated orifice, also serve or served this purpose.

In some species the thickness of the outer wall of the last whorl remains constant as far as the apertural margin, or this margin may even be somewhat sharpened. Often, however, the outer lip becomes thickened (**varicose**) when spiral growth of the shell is complete, and it may be thickened at intervals before this stage, during growth halts. The thickening may be on the inner or outer sides, or partly on both. In some forms the shell wall is turned outward and backward (**reflected** or **everted**) at the apertural margin, or else inward (**inflected**), as in the Cypraeidae. In *Cassis* it is both thickened on the inner side and has a thin marginal reflection. The outer lip in many forms bears crenulations, ridges, denticles or spines at its edge, while just within the aperture the outer wall may bear threads or thicker ridges, often termed **lirae.** These correspond to depressions on the exterior of the shell. In some genera of the Strombacea the outer lip is greatly expanded at full growth, sometimes forming a **wing,** one side

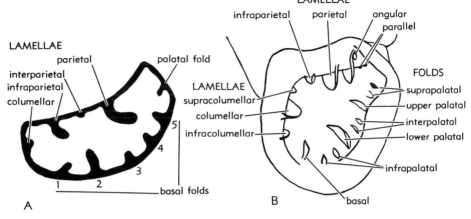

Fig. 73. Apertural lamellae and folds; terminology in *(A)* Strobilopsidae and *(B)* Pupillidae (131).

of which may adhere to the spire. Finger-like processes (**digitations**) project from the wing. The habits of the living species *Aporrhais pespelicani* (LINNÉ) do not change when the wing develops and its function, if any, is unknown.

The inductura may extend over the columella, as well as over the parietal region, and its margin may become very distinct abapically and detached in many genera, forming a thin wall. This is conspicuously developed in *Cassidaria,* for example. When there is a well-defined siphonal notch in the apertural margin, lamellae marking its successive growth stages frequently form a rounded or angular ridge (**siphonal fasciole**) (Fig. 64), which disappears beneath the margin of the inductura. The siphonal fasciole may sweep around in so broad a curve that it surrounds a well-marked cavity (**false umbilicus**).

In some groups the whole inner lip is modified considerably by additional shelly matter. In *Nassarius* and *Phalium* the inductura becomes detached even adapically, forming a broad, flattened expansion of the lip. In the Cypraeidae a thick coating extends over the whole surface of the apertural side of the last whorl, which it more or less flattens. An adapical extension of this coating forms the margin of a canal-like outlet at that end of the aperture, while further shelly matter greatly broadens the abapical part of the inner lip, leaving in many forms a median depression or **fossula.**

In the Neritidae a wide, flattened plate of shelly matter, sometimes termed a sep-

tum, projects from the last whorl so that its oblique, often denticulate edge forms the inner lip, the columella and most of the internal walls of the shell having disappeared by resorption. It is proposed to employ the term **labial area** for the surface of this plate or any similar more or less flattened surface, the margin of which is formed by the inner lip. In some species of the Phymatopleuridae the parietal surface is commonly resorbed and smoothed. The labial area frequently bears folds, ridges, denticles, and other protuberances not connected with the whorl ornament. Strong transverse ridges occur on it in the Cypraeidae, Cassididae, and other families, and in some Neritidae it bears groups of pustules or weak oblique ridges. Strong folds of the inner lip which pass spirally up the interior of the shell are discussed in the section on internal shell features.

Teeth, folds, and lamellae protruding from various parts of the peristome and constricting the aperture are found in many genera of land pulmonates. Lamellae are particularly numerous in the Clausiliidae. Figure 73 indicates the terms applied to them in the families Pupillidae and Strobilopsidae. The adjective **palatal,** applied to structures located on the outer lip, is to be noted.

UMBILICUS

The old terms "perforate" and "imperforate," applied to a shell in order to denote the presence or absence of an umbilicus, are inappropriate and best abandoned. The alternative adjectives **umbilicate** or **omphalous**

may be used in the first connection, and **nonumbilicate** or **anomphalous** in the second. If the umbilicus is completely open at its entrance, the shell is described as **phaneromphalous,** if partly plugged there by shelly matter, as **hemiomphalous,** and if a plug completely obscures its presence, as **cryptomphalous.** The European Eocene species, *Cepatia cepacea* (LAMARCK), in which the umbilicus is hidden by a convex wad marking the termination of the inductura, is a good example of a shell of the last type.

Being enclosed by the adaxial part of the helicocone wall, the umbilicus in most shells is a spiral cavity with the wall of each coil bulging inwards towards the axis. In some shells the boundary of the umbilicus at its opening in the base of the shell is marked by a well-defined angulation, or perhaps a beaded cord, but its margin is often indefinite, particularly when the shell is smooth. In *Globularia* and some related genera an angulation, termed a "rim" by WRIGLEY and a *"limbe"* by French authors, continues or branches off from the sharp margin of the outer lip, encircling the umbilical opening and ascending spirally into the umbilicus. Between it and the margin of the inner lip is a smooth, rather flattened band termed a "sheath" by WRIGLEY. A rather similar ridge, originating somewhat higher on the inner lip, is present in some species of *Angaria* and *Turbo,* and marks the limit to which the shell ornament extends. In many Naticidae a thick cord of shelly matter, semicircular in cross-section, ascends spirally into the umbilicus from near the middle of the inner lip and is termed the **funicle.** In some umbilicate Nerineacea, folds of the adaxial wall of the whorls project into the umbilicus, as well as into the shell interior. In families such as the Architectonicidae, in which there is a broad umbilicus, this surface of the whorls frequently has its own system of ornament, differing from that on the spire.

GROWTH LINES AND ORNAMENT

Successive stages of growth at the aperture remain marked on the surface of the shell by growth lines, which may or may not stand out in relief. Long growth halts are sometimes indicated by more conspicuous markings (**growth rugae**) or, in some

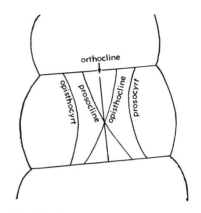

FIG. 74. Directional terminology for growth lines in dextral shell (115n).

genera, by prominent ribs (**varices**). From a study of the growth lines it is possible to reconstruct the shape of the outer lip even when the aperture of the shell is damaged. A growth line, or part of one, leaning in the direction of growth of the helicocone (i.e., to the left in a dextral shell as usually viewed) is described as **prosocline;** if leaning away from this direction, as **opisthocline;** and if crossing the whorl in a direction perpendicular to the suture, as **orthocline** (Fig. 74). Growth lines frequently have a simple or sigmoidal curve. If arched forward they may be termed **prosocyrt,** if backward, **opisthocyrt** (Fig. 74). In shells in which a sinus or slit is present in the outer lip, its track, as clearly indicated by the growth lines, forms a band, termed an **anal fasciole,** on the surface of the shell. Its position and characters may serve as a basis of classification, as in the family Turridae. If, as in most Pleurotomariacea, the outer lip has a parallel-sided slit or a narrow notch, this generates on the surface of the whorls a narrow, well-defined band on which the growth lines form a series of crescents or **lunulae,** because the end of the slit or notch is usually more or less semicircular. This type of anal fasciole is termed a **selenizone** (slit band in older literature).

The relief pattern present on many gastropod shells is variously termed **ornament,** ornamentation, or sculpture; the first term is here preferred. Gastropod ornament has two components. **Collabral ornament** results from rhythmic or periodic fluctuations in the shell-secreting activity of the whole

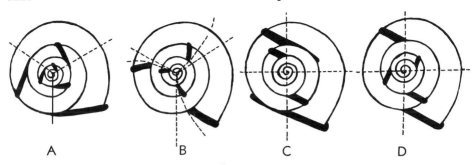

FIG. 75. Arrangement of varices in Cassididae (108); *(A) Cassis flammea* (LINNÉ); *(B) Phalium strigatum* (GMELIN); *(C) Phalium plicaria* (LAMARCK); *(D) Phalium glaucum* (LINNÉ). The shells are viewed in plan from above the apex; all reduced.

mantle edge, producing elevations and depressions parallel with the outer lip (labrum) and growth lines. **Spiral ornament,** passing continuously round the whorls parallel with the suture, is the result of differential secretory activity of various parts of the mantle edge. Elements of ornament that are markedly oblique both to the direction of growth and to the growth lines occur much more rarely in the gastropods than in the pelecypods. Among forms in which such ornament is present are the Paleozoic Luciellidae and *Planozonides.* The protoconch of the living genus *Philbertia* (Fig. 86*A,C*) has oblique reticulate ornament. The term **axial** has been much used for elements of ornament which are more or less parallel with the axis, but is clearly inappropriate for depressed shells. The term **transverse** is applicable to any element crossing a whorl in a direction which would intersect both sutures. In certain Turridae ribs passing transversely across the whorls are not exactly collabral.

There is such great variety in the elements of gastropod ornament that it is difficult to devise a precise descriptive terminology for them. Collabral elements are described as threads, riblets, costae (or ribs) and varices according to their width and prominence; while spiral elements include striae and grooves, if depressions, and threads, cords, ribbons, bands, carinae, astragals, etc., if elevations.

The elements of spiral ornament may override the collabral elevations or be confined to their intervals. Various patterns are formed by a combination of the two types of ornament. When narrow elements of both types intersect, the resulting pattern is described as **cancellate.** Rounded protuberances termed **tubercles** if large, **pustules** if somewhat smaller, or **granules** if small, or pointed ones termed **spines,** often occur where spiral and collabral elements intersect, or they may be present on the costae even in the absence of spiral ornament. In the Muricidae vaulted scales protrude from the varices and costae where these are crossed by the spiral elements. Spiral grooves or striae present on some shells may have a series of minute depressions (**puncta**) and are then said to be **punctate.** When both transverse and spiral elements are broad and low, the spiral depressions may consist of rows of rounded pits.

Costae may extend right across a whorl from suture to suture or only across part of the whorl. In some shells they are in exact alignment across successive whorls, in others they are in partial alignment, and in still others they have no tendency to alignment. When varices are interspersed with costae of normal prominence, their distribution is often related to the coiling of the whorls. In some Muricidae varices, three to every whorl, are aligned down the sides of the shell. In the Cymatiidae and Bursidae they are also in alignment, but are present only on alternate whorls. WRIGLEY (108) has shown that when some Cassididae (Fig. 75) are viewed in plan from above the apex, the angular intervals between successive varices (reckoning backwards from the aperture) are 225°, 225°, 270°, 225°, 225°, 270°, etc. Each cycle of three varices thus occupies a total angle of coiling of 720°, that is, two complete whorls. Nevertheless, there are shells in which the distribution of varices follows no regular plan.

INTERNAL CHARACTERS OF SHELL

As fossil gastropods frequently occur in the form of internal molds (termed "steinkerns" by some workers), the internal characters of the shell are of interest to paleontologists. Internal molds of thick-shelled species often differ considerably in appearance from the original shell, as in some Cypraeidae, where the mold shows spiral coiling which is obscured by enamel on the exterior of the shell. In thin-shelled forms, such as some Tonnidae, the main features of the external ornament are impressed on the interior of the shell, but in thick-shelled forms there are traces only of the more prominent carinae and tubercles. When, as in many Muricidae, Cymatiidae, Bursidae, and Cassididae, a thickened outer lip with internal denticles and lirae is formed periodically during growth halts, denticulate ribs often remain on the interior of the shell, producing pitted grooves on the internal molds. There is an elaborate pattern of circular pits on internal molds of some species of *Campanile*.

Folds present on the columellar lip in genera of certain families, such as the Volutidae, Mitridae, Cancellariidae, and Vasidae, remain coiled spirally around the columella almost to the apex; they are termed **columellar folds** (Fig. 64). When the aperture has a siphonal notch or canal, this may be represented by a distinct fold (**siphonal fold**) on the abapical part of the columella of each whorl. Most genera of Nerineidae and Itieriidae have internal folds of varying prominence and complexity, and these are alluded to as **columellar, parietal, palatal,** and **basal folds** according to their respective situation on the columella, the adapical wall of the whorl, the outer wall, or the basal or abapical wall (part overlapped by a succeeding whorl and backing on to its adapical wall). In certain genera of these families the internal folds are so elaborate that the space left for the soft parts to occupy was very restricted and tortuous (Fig. 76). The same condition existed in some of the Soleniscinae.

In some shells the tip of the visceral spiral becomes withdrawn from the earlier whorls during growth, and these are completely filled with shelly matter (as in *Terebra*) or else sealed off at intervals by irregularly spaced septa. In some genera the internal walls of the shell are removed by resorption. The process is only partial in the Cypraeidae and Conidae, in which the walls are reduced to considerable tenuity. Their complete removal takes place in the Neritidae and Ellobiidae and in the genus *Olivella,* among other groups.

In coiled shells the head-foot mass is attached to the columella by a broad, partly coiled columellar muscle (Fig. 53). The attachment area, which is situated within

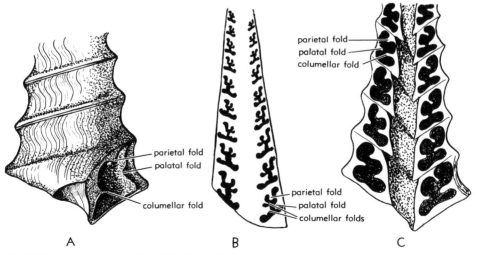

A   B   C

FIG. 76. Internal characters of the shell in Nerineidae; *(A,C) Cossmannea dilatata* (D'ORBIGNY), U.Jur., Fr., internal folds as seen in axial section and at aperture, ×1 (128); *(B) Bactroptyxis brevivoluta* (HUDLESTON), M.Jur., Eng., axial section, ×2 (121).

the last whorl some distance back from the aperture, advances progressively as the shell grows, but rarely leaves an easily visible scar. In *Bellerophon* and *Sinuites* there are two symmetrically arranged muscle scars on the adaxial wall of the last whorl half a coil back from the aperture. Patelliform shells often retain distinct muscle attachment scars. Usually the scar has the form of a horseshoe and is open on the anterior side.

In some genera of the Capulidae and Calyptraeidae, which have a depressed, cap-like shell, there is a thin internal process projecting from part of the wall of the shell. It ranges from a cap-shaped structure projecting from near the middle of the shell (as in *Crucibulum*) to a thin, flat plate attached around part of the margin (as in *Crepidula*). Its function appears to be to help the animal to remain secure to its shell.

STRUCTURE OF SHELL

In living gastropods the calcareous shell, at least at some period during growth, has a coating of horny material (**conchiolin**) known as the **periostracum** or **epidermis**. This protects the shell against the chemical or solvent action of the moist medium in which the mollusk lives. It varies greatly in thickness and its surface, although plain in many species, in others is covered with hairs or bristles. It soon disappears when the animal dies and it is not preserved. The same is true of other conchiolin parts such as most operculae.

The solid shell is an aggregate of crystals of calcium carbonate, with traces of other chemical substances, penetrated by a fine membranaceous network of organic material. Analyses of gastropod shells belonging to 20 different living marine species, published by CLARKE & WHEELER (15), show that organic matter and combined water together account for from 1.14 to 9.06 per cent of the total weight, the most common amount being about 2 per cent. Calcium carbonate forms at least 96.6 per cent and usually about 98 per cent of the total amount of inorganic constituents. Small quantities of silica, alumina and oxide of iron occur in most shells, and in some there is a small amount of magnesium carbonate. The shells of land gastropods often contain calcium phosphate. A later work of ref-

erence in this connection is that of VINO-GRADOV (104).

The calcium carbonate of gastropod shells occurs mainly as aragonite, but calcite is present in some species.. BØGGILD (6) refers to a *Bellerophon* shell which proved to consist entirely of calcite, but secondary change is to be suspected, although he considered it to be "without doubt the original structure." X-ray analysis of some Pennsylvanian bellerophontids preserved in a bituminous matrix, according to KNIGHT, shows two shell layers, the outer one calcitic and the inner one aragonitic but lacking the lamellar structure that characterizes the nacreous layers of pleurotomariids, trochids or turbinids (KNIGHT, *in litt.*). The same author recognizes several distinct types of shell structure, as determined by the mode of crystal aggregation, and two or more of them are present as distinct layers in most shells.

Nacreous structure (always originally of aragonite) is formed by thin leaves of equal thickness (less than 0.001 mm.), which are parallel with the shell surface or almost so, and are separated by equally thin leaves of an organic substance, so that they flake away very easily. Nacre has a characteristic pearly luster, and forms the inner layer of the shell in a great many Archaeogastropoda, although not in all. Unpublished X-ray investigations indicate that the nacreous layer of molluscan shells may be altered in fossilization to calcite without losing its characteristic luster and probably laminar structure. Conditions rather than time seem to have been the controlling factor. Thus in some Ordovician gastropods and Upper Cretaceous ammonites with excellent luster, X-ray diffraction methods have shown that the nacre consists of calcite, whereas in certain Upper Carboniferous ammonites and nautiloids it remains as aragonite (information from J. B. KNIGHT).

Crossed-lamellar structure (aragonite except in a few rare instances) is the most frequent structure of the layers of gastropod shells. It consists of more or less rectangular, parallel lamellae which are perpendicular to the surface of the shell, with their long side parallel to it (Fig. 77). Their thickness is of the order 0.02 to 0.04 mm., and each (when the structure is most regular) is as wide as the thickness of the shell layer to

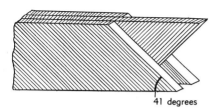

41 degrees

FIG. 77. Crossed-lamellar structure (6). Parts of three lamellae of the first order are seen, each composed of thin lamellae of the second order inclined in alternate directions; the top (narrow) face of the primary lamellae is usually parallel with the surface of the shell; much enlarged.

which it belongs and up to several mm. in length, thinning out as a wedge between other lamellae at each end. These primary lamellae are built up of parallel lamellae of a second order, which are less than 0.001 mm. thick and lie transverse to the primary lamellae; they are inclined to the longer side of the latter at an angle of 41 degrees, the direction in which they slope alternating in adjacent primary lamellae.

The prismatic structure is confined to calcite layers in the great majority of gastropod shells, but *Buccinum undatum* has an outer layer of prismatic aragonite. The regularity of the structure varies considerably in different species. The prismatic layer is most commonly the outer one, and the prisms are usually perpendicular to the surface, but in some shells (e.g., Neritidae) they are oblique or parallel to the surface. Among species examined by Bøggild, an outer calcitic prismatic layer was found to be present in all Scalidae, Janthinidae, and Neritidae, and in some Patellidae, Fissurellidae, Littorinidae, Muricidae, Thaididae, and Fusinidae, among other families. In some *Haliotis* shells a layer of prismatic calcite was found to lie between aragonitic layers.

Structure of the type termed homogeneous by Bøggild is found in the heteropods and pteropods, the mineral being aragonite in these groups. The calcium carbonate appears structureless in ordinary transmitted light, but under crossed nicols whole areas extinguish in one direction. The **foliated structure** described by the same worker is confined to calcite, and consists, like the aragonite nacreous structure, of parallel flakes of the mineral. He mentions its presence in species of *Bellerophon* and *Patella*. KNIGHT is doubtful of the described structure in

Bellerophon.

Grained structure, confined to calcite, consists of a mass of grains irregular in shape and in optical orientation. There are transitions between it and prismatic structure, and it is stated to occur in *Janthina* and in some species of *Scala.*

The **complex structure** studied by Bøggild, confined to aragonite, is a highly irregular modification of crossed-lamellar structure. It forms the inner shell layer of some species of *Nerita.*

It will thus be seen that the structure of gastropod shells is highly varied. The great majority of such shells, including all opisthobranchs and pulmonates, are formed of three, four, or in some of more than four distinct layers, all with crossed-lamellar structure, the direction of the primary lamellae differing in the various layers. In the majority of higher prosobranchs the number of layers is three, the primary lamellae of the middle layer being perpendicular to those of the innermost and outermost layers.

In the course of fossilization aragonitic shells are usually the first to disappear by solution. Hence, in many formations gastropod shells are represented only by molds, with the exception of those belonging to such genera as *Scala,* in which the shell is partly calcitic. Replacement of original aragonite by calcite is also very common.

COLOR PATTERN

Many living gastropods have a color pattern, simple or elaborate, which is a great aid in specific recognition. Like the relief ornament or sculpture, this may be resolved into two components, a spiral one marking a tendency of particular parts of the mantle edge to secrete pigment continuously, and a transverse component, marking a rhythm in secretory activity. The transverse component, however, shows more tendency to be oblique to the growth lines than in the case of the relief ornament, and in some species it consists of zigzagging lines or of loops. The lighter and darker spiral color bands respectively coincide with or else represent raised sculptural bands and depressions (109).

The biochemistry of shell pigments has been the subject of recent work. It is thought that the secretion of pigment is primarily a means of disposal of waste

products of metabolism, although color patterns may play their part in natural selection. Thus the color of some marine gastropods harmonizes well with that of the seaweed on which they live and some species of *Ovula* are either yellow or red, depending on the color of the *Gorgonia* with which they are associated. The color pattern of some land snails may serve to render them less conspicuous in their surroundings.

That color patterns are not necessarily

protective is shown by the fact that many marine shells in which they are particularly elaborate are, in actual life, coated with a thick periostracum. A distinction can be drawn between pigments (indigoids, pyrroles) which can be extracted from a crushed shell by solution in acid, and a group (melanins) which is intimately associated with the conchiolin of the shell and insoluble in acid. Pigments of the first group occur mainly in the Archaeogastropoda and

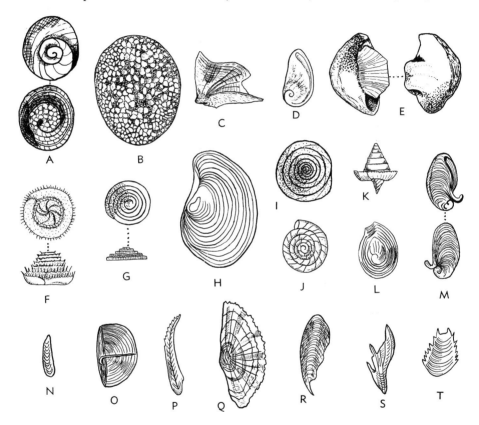

FIG. 78. Gastropod opercula: top row, calcareous; middle rows, horny, closing aperture; bottom row, horny, not closing aperture (outer surface illustrated except where otherwise stated).——*A. Turbo (Callopoma) saxosus* WOOD, Rec., W.C.Am., inner surface above, ×1 (20).——*B. Turbo sarmaticus* LINNÉ, Rec., S.Afr., ×1 (115n).——*C. Septaria janelli* (LEGUILLOU), Rec., E.Indies, ×1 (115n).——*D. Natica multipunctata* WOOD, Plio., Eng., ×1 (137).——*E. Neritopsis radula* (LINNÉ), Rec., IndoPac., inner surface on left, ×2 (115n).——*F. Tenagodus bernardi* MÖRCH, Rec., Austral., side view below, ×3 (35).——*G. Palaeocyclotus exaratus* (SANDBERGER), U.Eoc., Italy, side view below, ×6 (133).——*H. Pila reflexa* (SWAINSON), Rec., W.Indies, ×1 (20).——*I. Cittarium pica* (LINNÉ), Rec., W.Indies, ×0.7 (115n).——*J. Aulopoma grande* (PFEIFFER), Rec., Ceylon, ×1.3 (115n).——*K. Torinia variegata* (GMELIN), Rec., IndoPac., ×2 (35).——*L. Gabbia australis* TRYON, Rec., Austral., (89). ×6——*M. Rissoina inca* D'ORBIGNY, Rec., Peru, inner surface above, much enlarged (35).——*N. Conus* sp., Rec., ×2 (20).——*O. Rissoella globularis* (FORBES & HANLEY), Rec., Eng., much enlarged (35).——*P. Strombus pugilis* LINNÉ, Rec., W. Indies, ×1 (20).——*Q. Cassis tuberosa* (LINNÉ), Rec., Brazil, ×1 (35).——*R. Struthiolaria scutulata* (MARTYN), Rec., N.Z., ×2 (115n).——*S. Terebellum terebellum* (LINNÉ), Rec., IndoPac., ×4 (115n).——*T. Alectrion (Xeuxis) dispar* (ADAMS), Rec., IndoPac., ×2 (35).

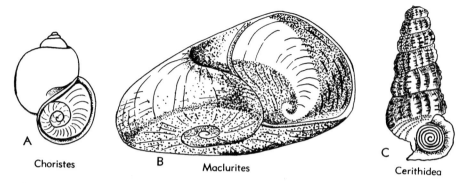

A Choristes B Maclurites C Cerithidea

Fig. 79. Spiral opercula of dextral gastropods (the middle one hyperstrophic), showing counter-clockwise coiling of outer side.——*A. Choristes elegans* Carpenter, Rec., N.Am., ×5 (32).——*B. Maclurites logani* Salter, Ord., N.Am., ×0.75 (115n).——*C. Cerithidea obtusa* (Lamarck), Rec., IndoPac., ×1.1 (114).

the tectibranch opisthobranchs, while the second group is found in the higher prosobranchs and in the pulmonates (16-18).

Gastropods retaining traces of color pattern are known from Ordovician beds onward. It is particularly persistent in the Neritacea, being preserved in some specimens of *Naticopsis* from the Devonian and Carboniferous, and commonly in *Neritoma* from the Jurassic and in *Theodoxus* and related genera from later formations. Its preservation is moderately common in *Pseudomelania* from the Jurassic but much less so in other genera, such as *Mourlonia* of the Carboniferous. It is noteworthy that the color pattern may persist in silicified shells (for example, in many specimens from the Upper Carboniferous and Permian of North America) even when they have been etched out with hydrochloric acid.

SOLID STRUCTURES ASSOCIATED WITH SHELL

The **operculum** is usually the only solid accessory to the shell (Fig. 78). It is present in the majority of prosobranch genera, although absent in many Cancellariidae, Conidae, Harpidae, Marginellidae, Volutidae, Mitridae, Cypraeidae, and Tonnidae. It is absent in all adult opisthobranchs, except the Acteonidae and Pyramidellidae, and in all pulmonates, except *Amphibola*. The primary function of the operculum, which is secreted and borne by the rear part of the dorsal side of the foot, is to close the aperture when the head-foot mass has retreated into the shell, but in many forms in which it is present, it is much reduced and does not

serve this purpose. It may sometimes have a secondary use. Thus, some species of *Lambis* and *Strombus,* in which the operculum is long and sharp, make use of it for progression, digging it into the sand and then extending the foot by a sudden movement. The Xenophoridae also make use of the operculum in locomotion.

Most opercula are light structures of horny material, but some, including the massive bodies found in certain Turbinidae, are calcareous. Most calcareous opercula (but not that of *Septaria*) conform with the shape of the aperture of the shell. Some 20 main types of operculum have been distinguished (95), and these have been divided into three main classes according to whether their structure is spiral, concentric, or lamellar. Most opercula are flat and plate-like, but conical and cylindrically spiral types occur. The circular, spiral form with numerous volutions seems to be most primitive. In dextral gastropods the operculum, if spiral, always grows in a direction that is counter-clockwise when its outer surface is viewed (Fig. 79), while in sinistral forms the direction is opposite. This provides a means of distinguishing between a truly sinistral and a hyperstrophic dextral shell when a spiral operculum is preserved with it. In this way we know that the Ordovician gastropod *Maclurites* was hyperstrophic. Wrigley (110) has described the complicated internal structure of the calcareous operculum of *Natica*.

Only calcareous gastropod opercula have been described in the fossil record, and they are rare except in certain formations. In the

family Oriostomatidae (Silurian-Devonian) the operculum is multispiral and domed, with the thickness exceeding the diameter in some species. Fossil *Neritopsis* opercula have been mistaken for cephalopod jaws and allotted the generic names *Peltarion* EUDES-DESLONGCHAMPS (Liassic, France), *Cyclidia* ROLLE (Tertiary, Rumania), *Scaphanidia* ROLLE (Liassic, England, and Cretaceous, Germany) and *Rhynchidia* LAUBE (Triassic, Tyrol). A Cretaceous fresh-water gastropod, *"Ampullaria?" powelli* WALCOTT, originally thought to be Carboniferous in age, has a flat, oval, calcareous operculum of the "concentric" type. Opercula very similar to that of this species and resembling those of *Viviparus,* except for their calcareous composition, abound in a thin layer of non-marine origin in the Pliocene Etchegoin Formation in the San Joaquin Valley of California, and were described by HANNA & GAYLORD as *Scalez petrolia.*

Mention must also be made of the **epiphragm** secreted by some pulmonate gastropods to function as a temporary operculum, sealing the aperture during winter hibernation or dry-weather estivation. Merely a thin membrane in some genera, in certain species of Helicidae it is a strong disc of calcium carbonate formed by the hardening of a white sticky fluid secreted by the mantle. When the animal again becomes active the epiphragm is pushed aside and discarded. There is no reason why these bodies should not be found in deposits containing fossil land shells.

A further type of accessory to a gastropod shell is the calcareous support constructed and cemented to the substratum by certain Hipponicidae, in which the animal is sessile. This support, secreted by the foot, is held by a strong muscle, and when the shell rests upon it, its opening is tightly sealed. In *Rothpletzia* the support is a conical or cylindrical structure which is much deeper than the actual shell.

A unique type of calcareous structure within the shell is the **clausilium** found in the land pulmonate genus *Clausilia.* It is a narrow, thin, curved plate with a stalklike process at one end which curves around the columella; it lies within the last whorl well back from the aperture. It functions as an operculum by sliding into position to close

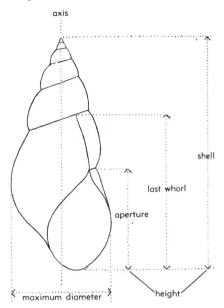

FIG. 80. Standard measurements of a conispiral gastropod shell (115n).

the shell when the head-foot mass is well withdrawn into it.

MEASUREMENT OF GASTROPOD SHELLS

Certain standard measurements are usually given when gastropod shells are described. Other measurements, chosen according to the type of shell under consideration, have been used in various statistical studies and cannot here be discussed. The standard measurements are made in directions either parallel with or perpendicular to the axis of the shell.

The **height** of a shell or of its spire, last whorl, or aperture, is for most genera defined as the perpendicular distance between two planes perpendicular to the axis and touching both extremities of the shell or of the part measured (Fig. 80). It should be noted that the heights of the spire and of the aperture are together equal to that of the whole shell, and that the measurement usually given as the height of the last whorl is the sum of the height of the aperture (i.e., of the ultimate height of the helicocone) and of the distance (parallel with the axis) advanced by the adapical side of the helicocone when describing the last coil. The measurement usually cited as the height of

any preceding whorl, however, is the projection on to the axis of the distance between the two sutures of the whorl at some selected position; it is the distance there advanced by the adapical side of the helicocone when describing a complete coil. With depressed shells it is preferable to record the breadth of any whorl, that is, the actual distance from suture to suture.

The maximum (or major) and minimum (or minor) **diameters** of the shell are, respectively, the maximum and minimum distances between two planes parallel with the axis and touching the shell on exactly opposite sides. In most shells the maximum diameter lies between the outer lip and the opposite side, and the minimum diameter is perpendicular to this.

The main difficulty likely to arise when these measurements are made is that of determining the exact direction of the axis. Slight differences in the tilt of the shell do not greatly affect the measurements of height, but often appreciably affect those of diameter. For this reason, BOYCOTT (10) preferred to define the diameter of the shell as "the greatest dimension that can be found starting with the edge of the lip to a point on the opposite side of the shell on the last whorl." The direction of this measurement may be very oblique to the axis.

It must be added that in certain groups, such as the Bellerophontacea and Cypraeacea, the custom has arisen of taking as the "height" of the shell a measurement not determined in the way stated above. The height of a patelliform shell is that of a perpendicular from the apex to the plane of the aperture, the length is the anteroposterior diameter of the aperture, and the breadth is the diameter of the aperture from left to right.

The angular measurements of a shell most frequently recorded relate to the spire and to the slope of the sutures (Fig. 81). If the whorls increase in diameter at a regular rate, straight lines can be drawn from the apex or from just above it (since the apex is not a mathematical point) so as to touch all the whorls. The **spire angle** (or spiral angle) is the angle between two such lines passing down opposite sides of the shell. The angle between straight lines touching any two adjacent whorls on opposite sides of the shell may be termed the **incremental**

angle of that part of the shell. When the whorls in question are near the apex, the incremental angle is known as the **apical angle.** In a coeloconoid shell the incremental angle increases steadily during growth, and in a cyrtoconoid shell it decreases steadily. It is sometimes useful with shells of these types to cite the **mean spire angle,** measured by the angle between straight lines joining the apex to the periphery of the last whorl on opposite sides of the shell.

The steepness of coiling of any particular part of a shell is best measured by the angle between the suture, viewed normally to the axis so as to appear as a straight line, and

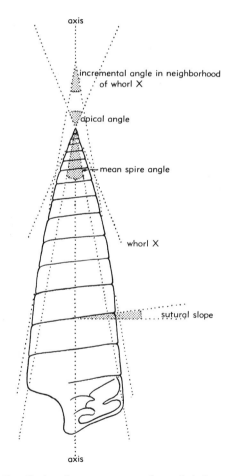

FIG. 81. Angular measurements of a conispiral gastropod shell. When the whorl diameter increases at a constant rate the apical angle, incremental angle, and mean spire angle are identical, and may be termed the spire angle (115n).

a plane perpendicular to the axis. This may be termed the **sutural slope.** This measurement is termed the "sutural angle" by many writers, but, as originally defined by D'ORBIGNY (the pioneer of conchological measurement or conchometry), the sutural angle is the angle between the suture, viewed as stated, and a line down the side of the shell touching the whorls (78).

SHELL GROWTH IN RELATION TO LIFE HISTORY

So far as is known, the coiling of a gastropod shell has no periodicity. Regularity in the distribution of varices on the whorls of a shell in some forms shows that growth halts and coiling may be interrelated, but it is unknown if they are influenced by external factors. In some species growth of the spiral shell continues throughout life. This is the case with *Trochus niloticus* LINNÉ, specimens of which attain an age of ten years in the Andaman Islands, their growth slowing down towards the end but never ceasing. In the Zonitidae, a terrestrial group, many species are stated to add to their whorls almost indefinitely, the rate of growth varying with the season and food supply. In many species, however, growth of the shell ceases long before the death of the animal, and at full growth definite structures of the aperture, such as the wing-like outer lip of *Aporrhais,* are in some forms developed for the first time. In full-grown specimens of *Campanile* from the English Eocene, the heavy shell is much worn down on the same side as the aperture, suggesting that it lived long enough after growth had ceased for such abrasion to occur by continual dragging of the shell along the sea floor. In some gastropods the last whorl of the full-grown shell is more irregular in shape or more loosely coiled than the preceding ones.

In many shells secretion of calcium carbonate continues when growth has finished. It usually takes place from the entire surface of the mantle, thickening the shell walls from the interior, especially near the apex.

SEXUAL DIMORPHISM IN PROSOBRANCH SHELLS

The sexes are separate in most prosobranchs (*Valvata* being the most important exception), while the pulmonates and opisthobranchs are hermaphrodite. Sexual dimorphism, if present in the first group, affects both size and proportions of the shell, the females, when full-grown, tending to have larger and broader shells than the males (Fig. 82). Extreme cases are those of *Lacuna pellucida* DA COSTA and *Crepidula plana* SAY, female shells of which at certain stations were found respectively to average 10 and 15 times the weight of the males. In many species, however, differences between the shells of the two sexes are inappreciable.

CALCAREOUS EGGS

In the higher prosobranchs the eggs are usually enclosed in parchment-like capsules of various shapes, which are frequently washed up on sea beaches. The volutid genus *Alcithoe* produces calcareous egg capsules, which are attached isolated to stones or shells. The writer knows of no record of a fossil egg capsule. At the time of deposition of the famous Solnhofen beds (Jurassic) of Germany, in which such remains could conceivably have been preserved, it is possible that few capsule-producing gastropods had evolved.

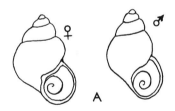

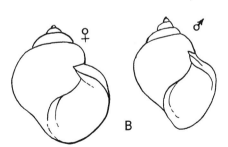

FIG. 82. Sexual dimorphism in gastropods.——*A. Pomatias elegans* (MÜLLER), female with the more tumid whorls, ×1.25 (136).——*B. Littorina rudis* (MATON), female, ×4, with larger shell, more tumid whorls, and less angular aperture than male, ×5 (130).

Land pulmonates produce comparatively few eggs, which may be laid in hollows on the ground and perhaps slightly covered by earth. Some forms, such as large tropical shells of the family Achatinidae, produce eggs of considerable size with a calcareous shell, a recorded length, possibly a maximum, being 45 mm. Large oval bodies up to 30 mm. in length, believed to be fossil eggs of *Filholia elliptica* (J.SOWERBY), are found in the Oligocene of England, and similar bodies, probably eggs of *Limicolaria,* occur in the Miocene deposits of Koru, Uganda.

MORPHOLOGICAL TERMS APPLIED TO GASTROPOD SHELLS

Terms considered most important are in capitals (as **APERTURE**); less important terms are printed in uncapitalized letters (as **advolute**); use is not recommended of those in italics (as *altitude*).

ABAPERTURAL. Away from shell aperture.

ABAPICAL. Away from shell apex toward base along axis or slightly oblique to it.

ABAXIAL. Away from shell axis outward.

aciculate. Slender, tapering to sharp point.

ADAPERTURAL. Toward shell aperture.

ADAPICAL. Toward shell apex along axis or slightly oblique to it.

ADAXIAL. Toward shell axis inward.

adpressed. Condition of whorls that overlap in such manner that their outer surfaces converge very gradually.

advolute. Condition of whorls that barely touch one another, not distinctly overlapping.

alate. Expanded like a wing; refers commonly to outer lip.

altitude. See height.

anal fasciole. Band on whorls generated by indentation of outer lip (either a sinus, notch, or slit) situated close to the adapical suture and anal opening (*see* selenizone, slit band).

anastrophic. Heterostrophic, with protoconch coiled about same axis as teleoconch and nucleus directed toward base of shell, as in *Architectonica.*

ancyloid. Shaped like the genus *Ancylus* (i.e., patelliform), with apex strongly directed anteriorly.

ANGULATION. Edge along which two surfaces meet at an angle.

ANOMPHALOUS. Lacking umbilicus.

antecurrent. See prosocline.

ANTERIOR. Direction in which head tends to point when animal is active; in a crawling gastropod, the head is closest to part of the apertural margin lying farthest from the shell apex and in high-spired conispiral gastropod shells and some other types "anterior" is equivalent to "abapical."

anterior canal. See siphonal canal.

APERTURAL. Pertaining to aperture or on same side as aperture.

APERTURE. Opening at last-formed margin of shell, providing outlet for the head-foot mass.

APEX. First-formed end of shell, generally pointed.

apical angle. In plane through axis, angle subtended between two straight lines that touch adjacent whorls on opposite sides near apex; identical with spire angle if whorls increase at regular rate.

appressed. See adpressed.

astragal. Steep-sided, round-topped elevation of major strength extended spirally around whorls.

auriform. Ear-shaped.

AXIAL. Parallel or subparallel with shell axis.

AXIS. (1) Imaginary line through shell apex about which whorls of conispiral and discoid shells are coiled; (2) in isostrophic shells (such as bellerophonts), imaginary line through initial point of helicocone directed normal to plane of symmetry.

basal fasciole. See siphonal fasciole.

basal lip. Margin of aperture extending from foot of columella to position of imaginary continuation of suture; usually regarded as part of outer lip, but usefully distinguished at times.

BASE. (1) In conispiral shells, part of surface lying on abapical side of periphery of last whorl or (when so defined, in certain genera) of a carina or angulation that forms an obvious lower boundary on side of whorl; (2) in patelliform shells, the abapically located apertural side. [This term is not applicable to isostrophic shells like *Bellerophon,* and its use for the flattened apertural side of cypraeid shells is inconsistent with normal usage.]

beak. Short spout constituting a rudimentary siphonal canal, formed by protrusion of apertural margin near foot of columella.

biconical. Having form resembling that of two cones placed base to base.

body whorl. See last whorl.

boss. Rounded elevation somewhat larger than shell prominence termed "tubercle."

bucciniform. Having approximate shape of a *Buccinum* shell.

callosity. Local thickened part of inductura.

CALLOUS. Coated with thickened inductura.

CALLUS. Thickened inductura on parietal region or extending from inner lip over base or into umbilicus; shelly substance composing thickened inductura.

CANAL. Narrow, semitubular extension of aperture (*see* siphonal canal).

cancellate. Having ornament of intersecting spiral and transverse threads or cords.

capuliform. Having shape of a simple depressed cone with eccentric apex and near-apical part of shell slightly coiled, as in *Capulus.*

CARINA. Prominent spiral ridge or keel.

CARINATE. Bearing a keel (carina).

cingulate. Spirally ornamented.

clathrate. Having ornament of spiral and transverse components that intersect to form a broad lattice.

clausilium. Small plate that functions as an operculum in Clausiliidae, being received into a groove in columella.

clausium. See clausilium.

clavate. Club-shaped.

COELOCONOID. Approaching conical but with concave sides.

coinductura. Rather thick, obliquely layered shelly coating, extending in some bellerophont gastropods over inner lip from within aperture, covering part of inductura proper.

COLLABRAL. Conforming to shape of outer lip, as shown by growth lines.

COLUMELLA. Solid or hollow pillar surrounding axis of a coiled shell, formed by adaxial walls of whorls.

COLUMELLAR FOLD. Spirally wound ridge on columella that projects into shell interior.

COLUMELLAR LIP. Adaxial part of inner lip comprising visible terminal part of columella.

concrescent. See collabral.

conical. Cone-shaped, with tip of cone formed by shell apex; best restricted to conispiral shells.

CONISPIRAL. With spire projecting as cone or conoid.

conoidal. Approaching a cone in shape; restriction of this term to shells with convex sides, according to usage of some authors, is unjustified (*see* cyrtoconoid, coeloconoid).

CONVOLUTE. With last whorl completely embracing and concealing earlier ones; like involute but lacking umbilici; (definition in this way is accepted generally, although common earlier usage does not discriminate convolute from involute). [LINNÉ termed *Conus* a concolute shell.]

CORD. Round-topped moderately coarse spiral or transverse linear elevation on shell surface.

coronate. Bearing tubercles or nodes at shoulder of whorls.

COSTA. Round-topped elevation of moderate width and prominence (greater than cord) disposed collabrally on shell surface.

costate. Having costae.

costella. Like costa but smaller.

costellate. Having costellae.

crenate. With outer lip notched serially or scalloped or bearing minute rounded teeth.

crispate. With crinkled margin.

cryptomphalous. With opening of umbilicus completely plugged.

CYRTOCONOID. Approaching a cone in shape but with convex sides.

decollation. Discarding of apical whorls.

decussate. Having ornament consisting of two sets of obliquely disposed linear ridges that cross to form a series of X's; this term, often misapplied to mean cancellate, correctly refers to the ornament of protoconchs of some Turridae.

depressed. Low in proportion to diameter.

deviated. Condition of protoconch in which its axis forms distinct angle with axis of teleoconch.

DEXTRAL. Right-handed; term originally applied to any shell with aperture on observer's right when shell apex is directed upward, or with apparent clockwise coiling when viewed from above apex, but in fact definition depends on features of soft anatomy. A dextral gastropod has genitalia on the right side of the head-foot mass or pallial cavity and the shell of such an animal commonly has the aperture on right when viewed with the apex uppermost; in hyperstrophic dextral species, however, the apex is directed downward when aperture is on right.

DIAMETER. Distance, conventionally only in conispiral shells, between two planes parallel with each other and with shell axis which touch opposite sides of shell; diameter generally designated as maximum or minimum.

digitation. Finger-like outward projection from outer lip.

DISCOIDAL. Approaching a disc in form; convolute or involute and more or less flattened.

disjunct. Condition of whorls when out of contact.

effuse. Condition of aperture when margin is interrupted by short spout for siphonal outlet.

elevated. High in proportion to diameter.

emarginate. With margin of outer lip notched or variously excavated.

embryonic shell. Part of shell formed before hatching.

enamel. Glossy inductura.

endogastric. Coiled so as to extend backward from aperture over extruded head-foot mass, as is normal in most adult gastropods (*see* exogastric).

entire. Condition of aperture when margin is uninterrupted by siphonal canal or other emargination.

everted. With edge of outer lip turned outward.

evolute. Coiled with whorls out of contact; this term is used commonly to signify "with broad umbilicus" when applied to ammonites but not so referring to gastropods.

excurvate. Bent outward.

exhalant channel (or canal). Channel at junction of outer and parietal lips, or canal between extensions of these lips, occupied by mantle fold by which exhalant current leaves mantle cavity (*gouttière postérieure* of French authors). [The channeled posterior digitation of such genera as *Rimella* should not be mistaken for an exhalant channel.]

exogastric. Coiled so as to extend forward from the aperture over front of extruded head-foot mass, as in earliest gastropod ontogeny before torsion.

explanate. With outer lip spreading outward and becoming flattened.

extraconic. Nearly conical but with concave sides (*see* coeloconoid).

false umbilicus. Depression at base of shell affecting

only last whorl, usually bordered by siphonal fasciole, sometimes termed pseudumbilicus.

fasciculate. Arranged in clusters.

fasciole. Band generated by narrow sinus or notch in, or lamellose projection of, successive growth lines.

fimbriated. Regularly puckered at the margin.

flaring. Widening outward toward opening.

fold. Spirally wound ridge on interior of shell wall (*see* columellar fold, parietal fold).

fossula. Shallow linear depression of inner lip in some cypraeids.

funicle. Spirally wound narrow ridge extending upward from inner lip into umbilicus, as in Naticidae.

fusiform. Slender spindle-shaped, tapering almost equally toward both ends, as in genus formerly called *Fusus*.

gibbose, gibbous. Very convex or tumid.

globose. More or less spherical.

gradate. Rising in steps owing to presence of whorl shoulders.

granulated. Covered with grains or small tubercles.

GROWTH LINES. Collabrally disposed surface markings of shell, generally not prominent as to relief, that denote former positions of outer lip.

GROWTH RUGAE. Irregular ridges or undulations of shell surface determined by former positions of outer lip.

HEIGHT. Distance between two planes perpendicular to shell axis and touching adapical and abapical extremities of shell or part being measured; this definition does not apply to Bellerophontacea or Cypraeacea, in which established practice differs (*see* remarks concerning whorl).

heliciform. Shaped more or less like shell of *Helix*.

HELICOCONE. Distally expanding coiled tube that forms most gastropod shells.

helicoid. See heliciform; use of this term in a geometrical sense is unsuitable for gastropod shells.

hemiomphalous. With umbilicus partly plugged at its opening.

HETEROSTROPHIC. Condition of protoconch when whorls appear to be coiled in opposite direction to those of teleoconch.

HOLOSTOMATOUS. With apertural margin uninterrupted by siphonal canal, notch, or by other extension.

homeostrophic. Having whorls of protoconch clearly coiled in same direction as those of teleoconch.

HYPERSTROPHIC. Dextral anatomically, with genitalia on right, but shell falsely sinistral, being actually ultradextral; or *vice versa*.

immersed. Condition of initial whorls when sunk within later ones and concealed by them.

imperforate. See anomphalous and remarks concerning "perforate."

impressed. Condition of suture having both adjoined whorl surfaces turned inward adaxially.

incremental angle. In plane through entire axis, angle between two straight lines that touch contiguous whorls on opposite sides at part of shell in question.

INDUCTURA. Smooth shelly layer secreted by general surface of mantle, commonly extending from inner side of aperture over parietal region, columellar lip, and (in some genera) part or all of shell exterior.

inflated. Swollen.

inflected. With edge of outer lip turned inward.

INNER LIP. Adaxial margin of aperture extending from foot of columella to suture and consisting of columellar and parietal lips.

INVOLUTE. With last whorl enveloping earlier ones so that height (or "width" in shells like bellerophonts) of aperture corresponds to that of shell; early whorls more or less visible in umbilici (*see* convolute).

ISOSTROPHIC. With two faces of shell symmetrical with respect to a median plane perpendicular to axis.

keel. Prominent spiral ridge (*see* carina).

labial area. Flattened or callus-coated surface extending from inner lip.

labium. See inner lip.

labral. Pertaining to outer lip.

labrum. Outer lip.

lamella. Thin plate.

lanceolate. Shaped like a lance-head (i.e., sharply pointed at one end), broader at other.

larval shell. Hard parts of pelagic larva before it settles down and undergoes metamorphosis.

LAST WHORL. In coiled shells, last-formed complete volution of helicocone.

left. Side of shell closest to left side of head-foot mass when this is extruded and active; side on left when shell is oriented with aperture facing observer and apex upward, except in depressed and discoidal shells.

lenticular. Having form of a biconvex lens.

lira. Fine linear elevation on shell surface or within outer lip.

lirate. Bearing lirae.

longitudinal. Diversely used by different authors; best avoided in describing gastropod shells.

lower. According to conventional orientation (except generally in France, Italy, Sweden), lower refers to abapical part of shell.

lunula. Crescentic linear ridge on selenizone, concave toward aperture.

mammillated. (1) With dome-shaped protuberance forming protoconch; (2) with dome-shaped protuberances forming shell ornament.

marginate. Condition of outer lip with strengthened margin.

mean spire angle. In plane through shell axis, angle between two straight lines that touch a whorl near apex and last whorl on opposite sides.

multispiral. With numerous whorls.

muricate. Spiny.

naticiform. With globose last whorl and small spire, like shell of *Natica*.

neck. Distal part of base of siphonostomatous shell, beginning where outline of left side changes from convex to concave.

nodose. With small knotlike protuberances.

nucleus. Earliest-formed part of shell or operculum; this term preferably should not be used for juvenile shell designated as "protoconch."

obconical. Approximately cone-shaped but with cone inverted.

obovate. Egg-shaped with narrower end downward.

oligogyral. See paucispiral.

omphalous. With an umbilicus.

operculate. With an operculum.

OPERCULUM. Corneous or calcareous structure borne by foot and serving for closure of aperture, wholly or partly.

OPISTHOCLINE. Leaning (i.e., inclined adapically) backward with respect to growth direction of helicocone, referring commonly to growth lines.

opisthocyrt. Arched backward with respect to growth direction of helicocone, referring to growth lines.

ORNAMENT. Relief pattern on surface of many shells (*see* sculpture).

ornamentation. See ornament.

ORTHOCLINE. At right angles to growth direction of helicocone, referring commonly to growth lines.

ORTHOSTROPHIC. Coiled in normal manner, not hyperstrophic.

outer face (of whorl). Surface between shoulder and abapical suture or margin of base; same as side of whorl.

OUTER LIP. Abaxial margin of aperture extending from suture to foot of columella.

ovate. Egg-shaped.

palatal. Belonging to outer lip, referring commonly to folds and lamellae.

parasigmoidal. Curved like reversed "S."

PARIETAL FOLD. Spirally wound ridge on parietal region that projects into shell interior.

parietal lip. Part of inner lip situated on parietal region.

PARIETAL REGION. Basal surface of helicocone just within and just without aperture; the redundant expression "parietal wall" should not be used, for "parietal" signifies pertaining to wall.

parietal ridge. Protuberance from parietal lip near adapical corner of aperture.

patelliform. Forming a simple depressed cone; limpet-shaped.

patulous. Condition of aperture marked by somewhat strong expansion.

paucispiral. With relatively few whorls.

penultimate. Next to last-formed, commonly referring to whorl preceding last.

perforate. With umbilicus; although much used in literature in sense indicated, it is highly inappropriate, for an umbilicus is not a perforation.

perinductura. Continuous outer shell layer in some

gastropods formed by edge of mantle reflected back over outer lip.

PERIOSTRACUM. Coat of horny material (conchiolin) covering calcareous shell at least during some part of growth.

PERIPHERY. Part of shell or any particular whorl farthest from axis.

peristome. Margin of aperture.

peritreme. See peristome.

PHANEROMPHALOUS. With completely open umbilicus; may be wide, narrow, or very minute.

pillar. See columella.

planispiral. Coiled in a single plane, ideally with symmetrical sides, as in *Bellerophon* (*see* isostrophic); loosely used for discoidal shells with asymmetrical sides.

pleural angle. In plane through entire shell axis, angle between two straight lines lying tangential to last two whorls on opposite sides.

plication. Spirally wound ridge on interior of shell wall (*see* fold).

polygyral. See multispiral.

POSTERIOR. Direction opposite to that in which head tends to point when animal is active; this term is used often to mean adapical, but such practice is undesirable except in high-spired shells.

primary. Describing element of spiral ornament appearing early in ontogeny.

PROSOCLINE. Leaning (i.e., inclined adapically) forward with respect to growth direction of helicocone, referring commonly to growth lines.

prosocyrt. Arched forward with respect to growth direction of helicocone.

PROTOCONCH. Apical whorls of shell, especially where clearly demarcated from later ones.

protractive. See prosocline.

pseudoselenizone. Band on shell surface resembling a selenizone but not identifiable as trace of an apertural sinus or slit.

pseudumbilicus. Depression or cavity in shell base affecting only last whorl, and therefore not a true umbilicus; sometimes termed false umbilicus.

punctate. Minutely pitted.

punctum. Minute pit on shell surface but not a tubule penetrating shell substance as in some brachiopods. [Plural, "puncta," not "punctae."]

pupiform. Cylindrical, with rounded ends, like an insect pupa or shell of the genus formerly called *Pupa.*

pustule. Small rounded surface elevation, according to convention more diminutive than "tubercle."

pyramidal. Having form of a pyramid (i.e., with lateral surface divided into several similar and more or less flattened parts).

pyriform. Pear-shaped.

RAMP. Abapically inclined flattened band on shell surface, which in some shells forms the adapical part of whorls, limited abaxially by a ridge or angulation.

recurved. With distal end (e.g., of siphonal canal)

bent away from observer when shell is viewed from apertural side.

reflected. Turned outward and backward at margin, referring to outer and columellar lips.

resorption. Removal of once-formed shell by action of the living gastropod.

reticulate. Forming a network of obliquely intersecting linear ridges.

retractive. See opisthocline.

retrocurrent. See opisthocline.

revolving. Passing spirally around whorls.

rib. See costa.

ribbon. Flat spiral surface elevation.

riblet. See costella.

ridge. Extended, somewhat angular linear elevation on shell surface.

right. Compare remarks under "left."

rimate. Consisting of a very narrow cavity, referring commonly to umbilicus.

rostrum. Attenuated extremity of last whorl other than siphonal canal, as in *Tibia*.

rotelliform. Almost lenticular but with low obtuse spire, like shell of genus formerly called *Rotella* (*see* umboniform).

scalariform. With whorls disjunct or tending to become so, referring commonly to a pathological condition.

SCULPTURE. Relief pattern on shell surface; virtually identical to "ornament" and about equally used.

secondary. Describing element of spiral ornament appearing later than the earliest ones in ontogeny.

SELENIZONE. Spiral band of crescentic growth lines or threads (lunulae) generated by a narrow notch or slit and characteristic of dibranchiate gastropods; corresponds to "anal fasciole" of some other groups.

septum. Transverse plate secreted within early-formed whorls of some shells (as Euomphalidae) for closing them off.

SHOULDER. Angulation of whorl forming abaxial edge of sutural ramp or shelf.

shoulder angle. Shoulder, as defined above.

side (of whorl). Surface between shoulder, if present, and abapical suture or margin of base.

sigmoidal. S-shaped.

SINISTRAL. With genitalia on left side of head-foot mass or pallial cavity, soft parts and shell arranged as in mirror image of dextral (*see* dextral).

SINUS. Curved re-entrant of apertural margin or of growth lines.

SIPHONAL CANAL. Tubular or troughlike extension of anterior (abapical) part of apertural margin for inclosure of inhalant siphon.

SIPHONAL FASCIOLE. Distinctive band of abruptly curved growth lines near foot of columella marking successive positions of siphonal notch.

siphonal fold. Ridge corresponding to siphonal notch wound spirally around columella.

SIPHONAL NOTCH. Narrow sinus of apertural margin near foot of columella serving for protrusion of inhalant siphon.

SIPHONOSTOMATOUS. With apertural margin interrupted by canal, spout, or notch for protrusion of siphon.

SLIT. Parallel-sided re-entrant of outer lip ranging from shallow incision to deep fissure as much as half a whorl in extent.

slit band. Trace of slit around whorls (*see* selenizone).

spine. Thornlike protuberance.

SPIRAL (adj.). As applied to elements of ornament, passing continuously around whorls, almost parallel with suture.

spiral (noun). Curved line or surface starting from point of origin and extending outward with continuously increasing radius of curvature.

SPIRE. Adapical visible part of all whorls except last.

spire angle. In plane through entire shell axis, angle between two straight lines which touch all whorls on opposite sides; such lines can be drawn only if rate of whorl increase is constant.

spout. Rudimentary siphonal canal.

squamose. With scales.

squat. Broad in proportion to height (in a family or genus in which most species are slender).

stria. Very narrowly incised shallow groove.

strombiform. Roughly biconical but with expanded outer lip, as in shell of *Strombus*.

styliform. Parallel-sided except at sharp-pointed apex.

subulate. Slender and tapering to point, sides convex, awl-shaped.

sutural shelf. Horizontal flattened band, which in some shells adjoins adapical suture of whorls.

sutural slope. Angle between suture and plane perpendicular to axis; equivalent to "sutural angle" of many authors but not as first defined by D'ORBIGNY (1842).

SUTURE. Continuous line on shell surface where whorls adjoin.

TELEOCONCH. Entire shell exclusive of protoconch.

THREAD. Fine linear surface elevation.

transcurrent. Passing continuously around whorls across growth lines (*see* spiral).

TRANSVERSE. Crossing direction of helicocone growth (*see* collabral).

TREMA. Orifice in outer wall of some shells for excretory function; occurs singly or in series (plural, tremata).

trochiform. With flat-sided conical, not highly acute spire and rather flat base, like shell of *Trochus*.

tubercle. Moderately prominent small rounded elevation on shell surface.

turbinate. *See* turbiniform.

turbiniform. With broadly conical spire and convex base, as in shell of *Turbo*.

turreted. Used with different meanings, by most authors in the same sense as turriculate (q.v.).

turriculate. With acutely conical spire composed of numerous rather flat whorls; term derived from Latin *turricula* (little tower), much used by French authors *(turriculé).*

turrited. See turriculate.

ultradextral. With shell seemingly sinistral but soft parts organized dextrally (*see* hyperstrophic).

ultrasinistral. With shell seemingly dextral but soft parts organized sinistrally (*see* hyperstrophic).

umbilical suture. Continuous line separating successive whorls as seen in umbilicus of phaneromphalous shells.

umbilicate. With an umbilicus.

UMBILICUS. Cavity or depression formed around shell axis between faces of adaxial walls of whorls where these do not coalesce to form a solid columella; in conispiral shells (except hyperstrophic ones) its opening is at base of shell but involute shells may have two umbilici (upper or adapical and lower or abapical in asymmetrical forms, left and right in isostrophic forms).

umboniiform. Almost lenticular, but with low obtuse spire, like shell of genus *Umbonium* (formerly *Rotella*).

varicose. Bearing a varix or varices.

VARIX. Transverse elevation more prominent than costa and generally spaced more widely; it is evidence of growth halt during which a thickened outer lip developed (plural, varices).

volution. Any complete coil of helicocone (*see* whorl).

wall. Any part of framework of shell.

WHORL. (1) Any complete coil of helicocone; (2) exposed surface of any complete coil of helicocone. Distinctions here indicated are important, for in defining height of last whorl the complete coil is considered, whereas height of spire whorls takes account only of the exposed surface of a coil between successive sutures.

wing. More or less flattened expansion of outer lip.

CLASSIFIED MORPHOLOGICAL TERMS

A grouping of morphological terms that relate to characters of gastropod shells for the purpose of classification in various categories is considered to be useful. In the lists that follow, terms rated as most important are printed in boldface type (as **spire**) and others in lightface type (as pupiform); italicized terms given in the foregoing glossary are here omitted because use of them is not recommended.

Terms relating to main parts of shell. **Aperture, apex, axis, base, helicocone, last whorl,** neck, operculate, **operculum, protoconch, spire, suture, teleoconch, umbilicus, wall, whorl.**

Directional and dimensional terms. **Abapertural, abapical, abaxial, adapertural, adapical, adaxial,** anterior, **axial, diameter, height, left, lower,** opisthocline, opisthocyrt, **orthocline, posterior, prosocline,** prosocyrt, **right, spiral, transverse.**

Form terms. Aciculate, alate, ancyloid, auriform, biconical, bucciniform, capuliform, **carinate,** clavate, **coeloconoid,** conical, **conispiral,** conoidal, **convolute, cyrtoconoid,** depressed, deviated, **dextral, discoidal,** disjunct, elevated, evolute, excurvate, fusiform, gibbose, gibbous, globose, heliciform, **heterostrophic, hyperstrophic,** immersed, inflated, **involute, isostrophic,** lanceolate, lenticular, marginate, multispiral, naticiform, obconical, obovate, ovate, patelliform, paucispiral, planispiral, pupiform, pyramidal, pyriform, recurved, rotelliform, scalariform, **sinistral,** squat, strombiform, styliform, subulate, trochiform, turbinate, turbiniform, turriculate, ultradextral, ultrasinistral, umboniiform.

Terms relating to sutures and coiling. Adpressed, advolute, anastrophic, **convolute, dextral,** disjunct, endogastric, exogastric, **heterostrophic,** homeostrophic, **hyperstrophic,** impressed, **involute, isostrophic, last whorl,** multispiral, **orthostrophic,** paucispiral, **penultinate whorl,** planispiral, **sinistral, suture,** umbilical suture, volution, **whorl.**

Terms relating to umbilicus. **Anomphalous,** cryptomphalous, false umbilicus, funicle, hemiomphalous, omphalous, **phaneromphalous,** pseudumbilicus, rimate, umbilical suture, umbilicate, **umbilicus.**

Terms relating to axis. **Abaxial, adaxial, axial, axis, columella, columellar fold, columellar lip,** fold, plication, siphonal fold.

Terms relating to spire and protoconch. **Abapical, adapical,** anastrophic, **apex,** apical angle, channeled suture, decollation, deviated, gradate, **heterostrophic,** homeostrophic, **hyperstrophic,** immersed, incremental angle, mammillated, mean spire angle, multispiral, nucleus, **orthostrophic,** outer face (of whorl), paucispiral, penultimate whorl, **periphery,** pleural angle, **protoconch, ramp,** rostrum, **shoulder,** side (whorl), **spire,** spire angle, sutural shelf, sutural slope, **suture, whorl.**

Terms relating to aperture. **Abapertural, adapertural, alate, apertural, aperture,** basal lip, beak, **callus, canal, columellar lip,** crenate, crispate, digitation, effuse, emarginate, entire, everted, excurvate, exhalant channel, explanate, flaring, fossula, funicle, holostomatous, inflected, inhalant channel, **inner lip,** labial area, labral, labrum, marginate, **outer lip,** palatal, **parietal fold,** parietal lip, **parietal region,** parietal ridge, patulous, peristome, profile, recurved, reflected, **sinus, siphonal canal, siphonal notch,** siphonostomatous, **slit,** spout, **varix,** wing.

Terms relating to surface features. Anal fasciole, **angulation,** astregal, boss, callosity, **callous, callus,** cancellate, **carina, carinate,** cingulate, clathrate, coinductura, **collabral, cord,** coronate, **costa,** costate, costella, costellate, decussate, enamel, fasciculate, fasciole, fimbriated, granulated, **growth lines, growth rugae,** inductura, keel, lira, lirate, lunula, mammillated, muricate, nodose, **opisthocline,** opisthocyrt, **ornament, orthocline,** parasigmoidal, perin-

ductura, **periostracum,** primary, **prosocline,** proso-cyrt, pseudoselenizone, punctate, punctum, pustule, reticulate, revolving, ribbon, ridge, **sculpture,** sec-

ondary, **selenizone,** sigmoidal, **sinus, siphonal fasciole,** slit band, spine, **spiral,** squamose, stria, **thread, trema,** tubercle, varicose, **varix.**

FOSSIL TRACES OF GASTROPODA

Some geological formations may yield indirect evidence of the presence of gastropods on the sea floor where they accumulated as sediment. Tracks and burrows will be considered first.

Gastropoda crawl by means of a series of waves of contraction of the muscles of the sole of the foot. According to movement of these waves, they may be divided into two groups, in the first of which the waves pass from rear to front, and, in the second, in the opposite direction. Both groups include **monotaxic forms,** in which the whole sole is affected by a single series of waves, and **ditaxic forms,** in which a median band divides the sole longitudinally into two halves, each with its own series of waves. The first group also includes some **tetrataxic forms,** in which each half of the foot is itself divided longitudinally into two areas affected by distinct series of waves, so that there are four systems of waves in all. It will thus be seen that a gastropod crawling, for example, over a sand flat exposed at low tide, will leave a track the nature of which will depend partly upon the system of muscle waves of the foot. The nature of the track will also be affected when, for example, the foot has a propodium that ploughs aside the sediment as the animal crawls; and when progression is irregular, owing to mechanical difficulties in carrying the shell. In the case of some species with a tall spire, the shell is lifted and trailed alternately and leaves an interrupted groove, usually within the main track. The amount of detail preserved in the track will, of course, depend upon the nature and moisture content of the sediment in which it is formed.

Among tracks formed by living gastropods of the ditaxic groups are those of *Nucella lapillus* (Linné) (Fig. 83), long ago figured by Nicholson & Etheridge (77), *Littorina littorea* (Linné), and *Monodonta lineata* (DaCosta). Such tracks are divided by a median groove into two parts, each with transverse ridges, often slightly arched. In *Monodonta lineata* these

ridges are relatively wide-spaced and oblique. Abel (1, p. 207-219) has made detailed observations on the fast-crawling South African species, *Bullia rhodostoma* Gray, the track of which appears tripartite owing to the presence of two longitudinal grooves formed by posterior projections of the foot.

Among the fossil tracks preserved in certain shallow-water formations are some which have been attributed to gastropods, in some cases very tentatively, by workers who described and assigned generic names to them. Thus *Archaeonassa* Fenton & Fenton was founded upon parallel-sided furrows, bounded by lateral ridges and crossed by arched transverse ridges, found in the Lower Cambrian of British Columbia; *Palaeobullia* Götzinger & Becker upon tracks with a median furrow and obliquely ridged lateral bands, from the Eocene Greifenstein sandstone of Austria; and *Subphyllochorda* of the last two authors on tracks of a different type from the same formation. The introduction of generic names suggesting affinity with certain Recent genera seems injudicious. Abel (1, p. 241) gave a list of generic names assigned to "problematica" which, in his view, are gastropod tracks.

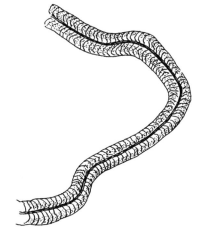

Fig. 83. Track of *Nucella lapillus* (Linné) on firm sand, ×0.4 (77).

They are *Nereites, Nemertites, Myrianites, Nereograpsus, Nemapodia, Gyrochorda, Phyllochorda,* and *Phyllodocites.* The same worker thought that the Upper Cambrian track *Climactichnites* LOGAN was formed by a shell-less opisthobranch. Structures from the Pennsylvanian of Texas described under the generic names *Aulichnites* and *Olivellites* by FENTON & FENTON were regarded as possibly burrows rather than surface tracks of gastropoda. Although it is probable that some of these tracks and burrows were formed by gastropods, it is doubtful if there are any reliable criteria by which those due to animals of this group can be distinguished from those of some other invertebrates.

Some carnivorous gastropods, notably *Natica,* bore into the shells of other mollusks by means of their proboscis and radula (probably assisted chemically in the case of *Natica*) and extract the soft parts for food, leaving a circular perforation in the shell of their prey as evidence of its fate. Fossil shells bored in this manner occur commonly in many Tertiary formations, but only rarely in older deposits. The oldest known examples are brachiopods from the Ordovician of North America. Several such specimens have also been described from the Devonian of that continent and from the Permian of Russia.

It is now known that fecal pellets of invertebrates, including gastropods, are an important constituent of many marine and estuarine muds, and also that each species excretes its own characteristic type of pellet. While the pellets in ancient sediments will in most cases have become obliterated in the course of diagenesis, it is possible that they are preserved in some formations, and the subject deserves investigation.

ONTOGENY

EMBRYONIC AND LARVAL LIFE

In most archaeogastropods the ova are shed into the sea and there fertilized; in the higher groups of gastropods fertilization takes place internally, and in most case the eggs are laid or shed before the young animal hatches out, but some forms are viviparous, and emergence from the ovum takes place within the parent, most commonly in the terminal part of the oviduct. In many marine gastropods the young animal hatches out as a larva, which is very different in appearance from the adult animal and leads a free-swimming existence in the plankton for a period. In fresh-water and land gastropods and in some marine forms there is no free larval stage and the animal emerges from the egg in its final creeping (plantigrade) stage, with the main morphological features of the adult animal already developed. It is not unusual to find that, of two congeneric species sharing the same habitate, one has a pelagic larva, while in the other the young hatch out in the crawling stage. Respective examples in the British fauna are the intertidal forms *Littorina littorea* (LINNÉ) and *L. littoralis* (LINNÉ). A third member of the genus, *L. neritoides* (LINNÉ), lives well above high-water mark, but yet has a pelagic larva. In some marine forms temperature conditions may control whether the animal hatches out in time to pass through a free larval stage or whether (in a colder sea) it undergoes the corresponding changes within the egg. Embryonic life is shortest in some Archaeogastropoda, as in such forms the larva emerges from the egg at an earlier stage of development than in any other gastropod group.[1] Under experimental conditions it was found that in *Haliotis tuberculata* LINNÉ larvae had emerged within 8 to 13 hours after fertilization, and in *Patella vulgata* LINNÉ within 24 hours. The period between fertilization and hatching out is naturally much longer when development to the plantigrade stage is completed within the egg and a free larval stage omitted. In the marine prosobranch *Littorina littoralis* (LINNÉ) it was found to be three weeks, and in the land prosobranch *Pomatias elegans* (MÜLLER) as long as three months.

The size and, to some extent, the form of the protoconch are known to depend within any given genus upon the duration of embryonic life in the particular species. In species in which the gastropod emerges from the egg in the crawling stage the

[1] By no means all Archaeogastropoda hatch out as a trochophore larva. Of 17 British species listed by M. LEBOUR (65), nine do so and eight, including *Diodora apertura* (MONTAGU) and *Calliostoma zizyphinum* (LINNÉ), hatch out in the creeping stage.

protoconch tends to be much larger and more domelike than in congeneric species that pass through a pelagic larval stage. Moreover, the percentage of gastropod species in which this stage is passed through increases from nil in Arctic and Antarctic seas to 85 per cent or more in tropical seas. This fact suggests that when widespread genera, such as *Natica,* are well represented in a given fossil fauna, the dominant type of protoconch may throw some light on contemporary temperature conditions (102).

EARLY ONTOGENY OF PROSOBRANCHIA

The early stages of development following fertilization of the ovum, those of cleavage and gastrulation, have been studied in a number of gastropod species, and follow much the same course as in other invertebrate groups, as described in standard works on embryology. The earliest stage of development to which reference need now be made is that of the **trochophore** or **trochosphere,** the form in which the larva emerges early from the egg in certain Archaeogastropoda. The appearance of the trochophore larva of *Patella* is familiar from reproductions of the illustrations of PATTEN & F. G. W. SMITH (Fig. 84). Its diameter is about 0.18 mm. and its shape may be described as that of a cup with a domelike lid. It swims in the plankton by means of cilia that surround the periphery and cover its anterior end. Near its posterior end, on one side, there remains at first the primitive opening of the gastrula stage, the blastopore. This then closes temporarily and opens again to form the stomodaeum, an invagination located where the mouth later opens. A shallow dorsal depression marks the beginning of the shell gland.

The trochophore develops within a few hours into the **veliger larva** (Fig. 85), the stage at which a great number of marine gastropods hatch out from the egg. Its chief feature is the swimming organ known as the velum. In its simplest form (found in *Patella* and *Haliotis,* for example) this consists of an anterior girdle of large ciliated cells which have developed from the cells encircling the periphery of the trochophore. In some genera, however, the velum consists of two, four or six large, radiating, paddle-shaped lobes (Fig. 86). Movements of the

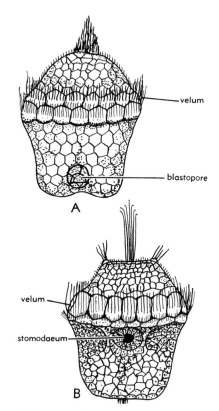

FIG. 84. Two stages in development of trochophore larva of *Patella vulgata* LINNÉ, *(A) ca.* 30 hours, *(B) ca.* 44 hours after fertilization, ×270 (92).

powerful cilia borne by the velum cells or lobes cause the larva to spin around in a counterclockwise direction and to move upward in the water. When their motion ceases, it sinks again. At about the same time as the velum forms, the shell gland begins to secrete a shell, at first horny and then calcareous. This is at first bowl-shaped, but soon deepens, beginning to assume a coiled nautiloid form as the visceral hump within it grows. At the same time the mantle flap has begun to develop on the ventral side of the animal, its margin adjoining that of the shell aperture. Within the mantle flap is a rudimentary mantle cavity, and between the edge of the mantle flap and the velum a bulge represents the foot.

While still a veliger, the young prosobranch gastropod undergoes a fundamental change in the orientation of its organs, which may be regarded as a combination of

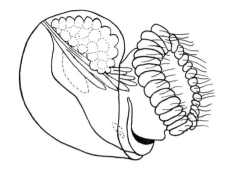

F<small>IG</small>. 85. Pretorsional veliger larva of *Haliotis tuberculata* L<small>INNÉ</small>, 27 hours after fertilization, ×190
(25)

two movements.[1] As the result of the first, known as the "anopedal flexure," the alimentary canal, instead of being aligned from front to rear, becomes bent so that the rectum points to the front and the anus discharges into the mantle cavity. The second change, described as the process of **torsion,** involves a rotation of the mantle and juvenile shell, with its enclosed viscera, through an angle of 180 degress in relation to the velum (from which the head later develops) and the foot.[2] As a result the mantle cavity comes to occupy an anterodorsal position, while the coiling of the shell assumes the endogastric direction typical of the adult gastropod. Effects of this torsion on the cells from which various organs of the adult animal later arise are far-reaching. Thus, when they develop, the nerve cords connecting the cerebral and pleural to the visceral ganglia are found to be crossed (most obviously in the Archaeogastropoda and less advanced Caenogastropoda) rather like a figure 8, instead of being parallel. The gut has been twisted into a loop. It is, moreover, obvious that the positions of the left and right ctenidia, osphradia, hypobranchial glands, heart auricles, and kidneys of the ancestral untorqued form become transposed as the result of torsion, so that when, as in most prosobranchs, only one of each of these organs remains, this, although now on the left-hand side, represents the original right-hand organ.

Torsion appears to be a steady process in some gastropods, as, for example, in *Pomatias elegans* (M<small>ÜLLER</small>), in which it occurs within the egg, not beginning until 3.5 weeks after the first cleavage, and continu-

ing for 10 days. In other gastropods, however, it takes place in two stages, each involving a rotation of 90 degrees or thereabouts. In *Calliostoma zizyphinum* (L<small>INNÉ</small>), *Patella vulgata* L<small>INNÉ</small>, and *Haliotis tuberculata* L<small>INNÉ</small>, torsion starts respectively about 60, 60, and 30 hours after fertilization, its first stage occupies 4, 10 to 15, and 3 to 6 hours, and the second stage 32, 30, and 200 hours. Recent work by C<small>ROFTS</small> (26) has shown that torsion originates through the action of a single asymmetrically placed larval retractor muscle attached to the shell interior on the right side of the apex.

The period of larval life (clearly an important factor in dispersal) and the stage in development when the larva settles on the sea floor vary greatly. In most Archaeogastropoda pelagic life is of relatively short duration. In *Haliotis tuberculata* it lasts only 40 hours, and the slow second phase of torsion takes place largely when the animal is benthonic and in process of losing the velum with its cilia. Feeding starts as soon as swimming ceases. Complete metamorphosis is a gradual process, about two months elapsing before the organs of the adult animal are fully developed. Many Caenogastropoda, on the other hand, have a long life as a veliger larva even after torsion, and during this period a spiral shell of several whorls (8 being the largest number recorded) may grow, on which elements of the adult ornament may already have begun to appear (Fig. 86). Ultimately the larva sinks to the bottom where, if the sea floor is suitable, it begins to crawl and undergoes metamorphosis to the adult condition. Large numbers of larvae must fail to find suitable conditions on sinking and they perish.

Certain generic names were assigned to gastropod larvae before their identity was realized. Among such names were *Sinusigera* D'O<small>RBIGNY</small> and *Macgillivraya* F<small>ORBES</small>. K<small>ROHN</small> gave the generic name *Echinospira* to a type of larva in which the true shell is surrounded by a secondary thin, transparent, membranaceous noncalcareous shell, which acts as a float. This type of larva occurs most commonly in the cypraeid families Eratoi-

---

[1] As evidence of the distinctness of the processes of flexure and torsion, P<small>ELSENEER</small> (83, p. 120), refers to some abnormal embryos which exhibit the effects of the former but not of the latter, and which have a shell not coiled in a spiral.

[2] Figure 9 illustrates the process of torsion in the veliger larva of *Patella vulgata.*

Fig. 86. Late veliger larvae, showing larval shells (mostly hidden in *(D)* by the foot and lobes of velum).
——*A. Philbertia linearis* (MONTAGU), ×70 (127).——*B. Cerithiopsis tubercularis* (MONTAGU), ×80
(65).——*C. Philbertia gracilis* (MONTAGU), ×16 (65).——*D. Aporrhais pespelicani* (LINNÉ), ×32 (65).

dae and Lamellariidae but is also found in the species *Capulus ungaricus* (LINNÉ).

EARLY ONTOGENY IN OPISTHO-BRANCHIA AND PULMONATA

Owing partly to practical difficulties in rearing larvae of opisthobranch gastropods in the laboratory—less easily overcome than in the case of the Archaeogastropoda, in which the ova are fertilized externally—less is known of the embryology and early post-embryonic ontogeny of the opisthobranchs. *Aplysia punctata* CUVIER, *Philene aperta*

(LINNÉ) and *Adalaria proxima* (ALDER & HANCOCK) are among the opisthobranchs of which the development has been studied. The early ontogeny is much accelerated in comparison with that of an archaeogastropod. Torsion and anopedal flexure take place at an early stage, well before hatching. THOMPSON (100) has described how, in *Adalaria proxima,* torsion is brought about during the later stages of cleavage and is not recognizable as a mechanical process. The shell, which is endogastric from the beginning, and the velum are formed before

hatching. The animal emerges from the egg as a veliger larva, and this begins to undergo metamorphosis before settling.

The larval shells of most opisthobranchs are hyperstrophic, that is, they appear to be coiled sinistrally although the animal is dextral. When the larva settles on the sea floor the coiling begins to become orthostrophic, so that in the adult gastropod the protoconch, which was the larval shell, is heterostrophic. It has, however, been shown that when (as may happen in a few opisthobranch species) the pelagic larval stage is omitted and the animal hatches out in the plantigrade stage, the initial whorls of the shell are not heterostrophic. In many adult opisthobranch shells the protoconch is completely hidden by the later whorls, but it can be revealed by carefully cutting part of these away (Fig. 70). In some cases the larval shell varies considerably in specimens of the same species. Thus at some localities that of *Diaphana minuta* (BROWN) alternates between two types, one with half a whorl only, and the other with one and a half whorls.

In its postveliger ontogeny the opisthobranch undergoes a series of changes, commonly referred to as "detorsion," by which the effects of an original torsion through an angle of 180 degrees are to a varying extent reversed. Thus, the opening of the pallial cavity, which is anterior and dorsal in the veliger, is displaced to the right or even somewhat to the rear. The anus, anterior in the veliger, is similarly displaced to the rear to a varying extent, as are also the ctenidium and osphradium. The auricle, which lies to the right of the ventricle in the early postveliger, moves to a position behind it. The process in the species *Onchidella celtica* (FORBES & HANLEY) has been described step by step by FRETTER (37, p. 709) and in *Adalaria proxima* (ALDER & HANCOCK) by THOMPSON (100); the first species, previously regarded by some authorities as a pulmonate, has no free larval stage and hatches out as a crawler. The effects of opisthobranch "detorsion" are also seen in the euthyneurous condition of most genera, but it should be made clear that uncrossing of the visceral loop is not a process that can be followed step by step in ontogeny. The more elevated position of the supra-intestinal ganglion in relation to that of the infra-intestinal ganglion in the adult opistho-

branch is the chief evidence of ancestral streptoneury displayed by the nervous system.

The development of the embryo has been studied in a number of species of the Pulmonata, in which group, of course, there is no free larval stage. Early ontogeny is condensed, and stages corresponding to the trochophore and veliger larvae are not recognizable. Torsion does not constitute so distinct an episode as in the case of the lower prosobranchs, but the adult animal reveals its effects and those of anopedal flexure in the usual way—by the endogastric shell, the dorsal, anteriorly directed pulmonary chamber, and the more or less anteriorly directed anus, and its situation on the right. While some authorities have considered that the effects of "detorsion" are observable in the adult pulmonate, just as in the opisthobranch, others are not of this opinion, pointing out that the heart occupies the same position as in the prosobranchs. Other theories have been advanced, therefore, to account for the euthyneurous condition of the pulmonates. According to the "zygosis theory" of KRULL (57), the nervous system of pulmonates has arisen from that of the prosobranchs by a series of events involving the loss of the left-hand half of the visceral loop and the acquisition of new ganglia and a connective on the right side (53). This, however, is pure speculation, not confirmed by any sequence of events in ontogeny.

ONTOGENY OF SHELL

Reference has already been made to the gastropod protoconch and the frequent discontinuity between it and the later whorls, a discontinuity that is not, apparently, necessarily associated with the transition from a planktonic to plantigrade condition, except in the case of the opisthobranchs. In ornamented shells the first elements of ornament may or may not appear on the protoconch; in rather rare instances (e.g., *Daphnella*, Fig. 69H), the protoconch has well-marked ornament differing from that of the succeeding whorls. During the period when paleontological research was much influenced by the work of HYATT and others, who sought to demonstrate that the MÜLLER-HAECKEL Law of Recapitulation was applicable to the hard parts of the developing invertebrate, detailed studies were carried out on the

changes in ornament and whorl outline that take place during the growth of the gastropod shell. Thus among the Eocene Fusinidae of Europe, studied by GRABAU (41), there are species in which an even convexity of the whorl outline and ornament of collabral costae crossed by spiral threads continue throughout growth, whereas in other forms these characters are confined to the earlier whorls, the later ones losing their ornament, becoming flattened laterally, and developing a distinct shoulder. These facts were held to prove that shells of the latter type were descended from shells of the former. Shells in which elements of the adult ornament had already begun to appear on the protoconch were regarded as instances of "accelerated" development, while shells in which ornament was lost on the later

whorls were described as "phylogerontic." The inferences drawn from such studies are now largely discredited. In some gastropod shells (e.g., certain Cerithiidae and Strombidae) there are very pronounced changes in whorl ornament during growth, but their significance is unknown, and it seems improbable that they throw any light on phylogeny. Allusion may, finally, be made to certain features of the shell which do not appear in some gastropod genera until sexual maturity is reached. Such features are the winged outer lip found in many Strombacea; the toothed inner and outer lips, and the projections of both enclosing anterior and posterior canals in many Cypraeacea; and the expanded inner lip of some Cassididae.

EVOLUTION OF GASTROPODA

An extensive literature contains discussions of the origin and significance of torsion, gastropod asymmetry, and the evolution of the various groups of gastropods now living. It is very generally accepted that the class arose originally from mollusks that did not undergo torsion and had complete bilateral symmetry. WENZ and KNIGHT considered that this ancestral form may well have been a representative of the Monoplacophora, a group of mollusks with simple univalve shells, represented in the earliest Cambrian rocks, but they wrote before the recent discoveries of living species assigned to this group, and if the Paleozoic forms were all organized like the Recent ones, it is evident that they could not have included the immediate ancestor of the gastropods. In the present work YONGE discusses the various theories accounting for torsion, and favors GARSTANG's hypothesis that it originated as a sudden mutation in the larva, which proved to have great survival value. The new developments of anopedal flexure and torsion, with the resulting anterior anus and endogastrically curved shell, may have afforded the possibility for the latter to develop into a spiral structure into which the head-foot mass could retreat for protection, and which it could carry when actively crawling; it was, perhaps, owing to this protection that the gastropod was able to explore life in other marine environments.

Asymmetry of the adult shell was not a necessary consequence of torsion, for, as KNIGHT has shown, there is good evidence that the bellerophontids were torqued. Embryological work has shown that in modern gastropods asymmetry precedes torsion, but this cannot be accepted as evidence that such was the case in phylogeny. Asymmetry may have been determined by mechanical causes arising from a changed poise of the coiled shell, itself due to some change in habits. The originally isostrophic shell would thus have been modified into an anisostrophic and ultimately conispiral structure, and the organs on the right side of the animal, occupying in orthostrophic dextral forms the inner side of the coil, would have undergone progressive reduction because of the more restricted space available for them, eventually to become atrophied in many lines of descent. This does not explain why dextrality of organization and coiling became the rule except in relatively rare instances, but this may have been determined by the original direction of torsion.

The earliest forms considered to be true gastropods belong to the family Coreospiridae and appear in the Lower Cambrian. They are bilaterally symmetrical, completely or partially coiled forms referred to the Bellerophontacea, but differ from other members of that superfamily in the absence

of an anal emargination. It is unknown if these or, indeed, any of the Bellerophontacea, had an operculum, although the protective efficiency of the shell, endogastric as a consequence of torsion, would have been imperfect unless the aperture was sealed by this structure, borne by the foot as the last organ to retreat into it. The Upper Cambrian marked the incoming of the first asymmetrical gastropod shells, belonging to the Pleurotomariacea and the Macluritacea. The former superfamily is of great interest as its representatives have survived to the present day, so that their anatomy can be studied. Their primitive character is shown by the fact that the organs of the pallial complex are paired, and those on the right-hand side are only slightly smaller than those on the left in the Pleurotomariidae themselves. The operculum is corneous in those modern representatives of the family in which it is known. Presumably it was of similar composition in extinct forms, as there is no record of the preservation of fossil opercula attributable to any pleurotomariacean. The Macluritacea are a highly interesting group which did not survive the Devonian Period. The shell (Fig. *79B*) is apparently sinistral, but was provided (at least in *Maclurites*) with a heavy calcareous operculum, from the direction of coiling of which we know that it was, in fact, hyperstrophic. Thus, the hyperstrophic condition, met with rarely in the adult stage of later gastropods, was early and apparently unsuccessfully explored in one whole superfamily. The Ordovician saw the incoming of several other gastropod superfamilies referred to the Archaeogastropoda but now extinct. Of the chief superfamilies of this order which are still living, the Patellacea (if represented by the Metoptomatidae) first appeared in the Middle Silurian, the Neritacea in the Middle Devonian, and the Trochacea in the Triassic.

Study of the respiratory processes in some modern representatives of the Pleurotomariina *(Haliotis, Emarginula, Diodora)* indicates the relationship of the labral emargination in the first two genera, and of the apertural orifice in the last, to the inhalant currents and the positions of the ctenidia. In modern Pleurotomariina we know that the two ctenidia lie on either side of the line of the labral emargination, row

of tremata, or apical orifice, as the case may be, and that in *Emarginula, Haliotis,* and *Diodora* (and presumably in genera of the Pleurotomariidae, although they have not yet been studied living) the inhalant currents enter the mantle cavity from the front symmetrically about this line, the exhalant current leaving by way of the emargination, tremata, or apical orifice. The presence of a labral emargination well removed from the suture in extinct forms is thus evidence of the existence of two ctenidia, one possibly reduced. The complete loss of the right ctenidium, a condition found in the Trochacea and probably already acquired in early Paleozoic times by such groups as the Microdomatacea, meant the introduction of a new mode of circulation of the respiratory currents, by which the inhalant current enters the mantle cavity to the left of the head, and the exhalant current is discharged over the right "shoulder." This system of circulation has persisted in higher prosobranchs, the marginal part of the mantle at the entry of the inhalant current being eventually extended to form a siphon in many forms.

The primitive Archaeogastropoda — in fact, all superfamilies of this order, except the Neritacea—also differ from more advanced gastropods in their method of reproduction. The ova and spermatozoa are shed by way of the right kidney and exhalant current into the sea, where fertilization occurs. Not until the mechanism for internal fertilization was acquired, by development of the pallial genital ducts and their associated organs, was there a possibility of migration to fluviatile and terrestrial habitats.

The remaining gastropods differ from the Archaeogastropoda (except the Patellacea and Helicinidae) in having only one auricle, a condition originally associated with the loss of the right-hand ctenidium. They comprise, first, the higher prosobranchs (Caenogastropoda), the obvious direct descendants of the archaeogastropods, which mostly retain the mantle cavity and left ctenidium, with the auricle lying in front of the ventricle, the sexes being distinct in most species, and the visceral nerve cords crossing, least obviously in the more advanced forms owing to anterior concentration of the nerve ganglia. They also include the opisthobranchs and pulmonates, in which the ani-

mal is hermaphrodite, the visceral commissures do not cross, the nerve ganglia are much concentrated anteriorly, and an operculum is mostly lacking. Subordinate living groups are the pelagic heteropods and pteropods, now considered to belong respectively to the prosobranch order Caenogastropoda and to the Opisthobranchia.

The assignation of extinct families and genera to higher taxa must necessarily be based on the somewhat uncertain evidence of shell characters. In WENZ's work (105) marine Caenogastropoda are considered to have appeared first in the Triassic with genera assigned to the superfamilies Littorinacea, Cerithiacea, and Naticacea. Certain Paleozoic nonmarine genera, however, are tentatively assigned to superfamilies of this order, *Dendropupa* to the Cyclophoracea and *Bernicia* to the Rissoacea, from which the reader might be tempted to conclude that nonmarine caenogastropods were probably the earliest to appear. Contributors to the present *Treatise* consider, however, that certain extinct groups which WENZ included in the Archaeogastropoda were more advanced evolutionarily. The first of these groups is the Subulitacea, which appeared in the Ordovician. Among its members are shells which are bucciniform, fusiform and mitriform in shape, and have apertures that are notched or even slightly produced and contracted abapically. The inference is that the Subulitacea had an inhalant canal, and since in living gastropods this feature is confined to certain Caenogastropoda and since also (in contrast to the Murchisoniacea, referred to below) the Paleozoic group had no counterbalancing archaeogastropod shell features, the presence of the canal is thought to be an adequate reason for including the group in the more advanced order. The resemblance of the Subulitacea to modern Buccinidae and Mitridae may, however, be due to convergence, for among Mesozoic gastropods are no genera linking them with these families, nor is there any convincing evidence for associating them with the Strombidae, near which FISCHER and STOLICZKA placed them.

The Loxonematacea, which appeared first in the Middle Ordovician, were also thought by WENZ to be Archaeogastropoda. They are, however, turriculate, many-whorled forms much resembling certain families,

particularly the Turritellidae, included in the caenogastropod superfamily Cerithiacea, to which a number of workers, including contributors to the present *Treatise,* have thought them ancestral. The presence of a deep mid-labral sinus in earlier members of the Loxonematacea certainly suggests that they were dibranchiate. In later members, however, the sinus became shallower and located nearer the suture, from which it is probably to be inferred that in any case such forms had lost the right ctenidium. A broad labral sinus is present in many living Cerithiacea (some Turritellidae, *Potamides,* and others), although these are monobranchiate, and its functional significance is unknown, for it now has no connection with the exhalant current; it may be a vestigial feature. The view is taken by contributors to the present *Treatise* that, whether or not the earliest Loxonematacea were dibranchiate, caenogastropod characters were predominant in at least the great majority of members of the superfamily; the group has, therefore, been removed from the Archaeogastropoda. As first suggested by KNIGHT in 1944 (56) certain genera, such as *Acanthonema* of the Lower Devonian, placed by WENZ in the Loxonematacea, are here included in the Turritellidae.

Evidence as to the evolutionary advancement of another early group, the Murchisoniacea, is ambiguous. In this group, which makes its appearance in the Upper Cambrian or Lower Ordovician, there is an emargination near the middle of the labrum, usually generating a selenizone, and it is to be inferred from its presence that the ctenidia were paired and the respiratory currents directed as in the Pleurotomariacea. Some Murchisoniacea, however, have a distinct incipient canal at the abapical end of the aperture, strongly suggesting that the animal had a short inhalant siphon. We are, therefore, faced with the problem of reconciling the presence of this structure (now found only in gastropods belonging to the Caenogastropoda) with that of paired ctenidia, and we must accept the possibility that in the Murchisoniacea the typical zygobranch respiratory system had been modified by at least partial localization of the inhalant currents. Moreover, this was the earliest gastropod superfamily to include relatively high-spired forms, the general morphology

of the shell being very similar to that of the much later Cerithiidae. In the present state of our knowledge it is impossible to decide if archaeogastropod or caenogastropod characters predominated in the Murchisoniacea, and the group has been retained in the more primitive order, but with its position queried.

Apart from the groups just considered, the earliest known caenogastropods are the nonmarine forms already mentioned. They comprise certain pupoidal genera of Carboniferous age, once thought to be pulmonates but all included in the Cyclophoracea in the *Treatise,* together with the small naticiform shell *Bernicia,* originally assigned to the Hydrobiidae, but transferred to the Viviparidae by KNIGHT, BATTEN & YOCHELSON herein. The Permian Karroo beds of Rhodesia have yielded small fresh-water gastropods indistinguishable from *Hydrobia.* Of important modern caenogastropod superfamilies other than those already mentioned, the Scalacea and Strombacea first appeared in the Jurassic, and the Calyptraeacea, Cypraeacea, and Tonnacea in the Cretaceous. It was not until the Tertiary that the most advanced prosobranch groups, particularly those with long siphonal canals, reached the acme of their development.

There is little evidence as to the precise ancestry of most of these caenogastropod groups. The most convincing line of descent, evidence for which has been accepted both by COSSMANN and by contributors to the present *Treatise,* is one leading from the Pleurotomariacea by way of the Murchisoniacea to the Loxonematacea and ultimately to the Cerithiacea. There is little doubt that other caenogastropods sprang from archaeogastropods belonging to groups entirely distinct from the Murchisoniacea, although there are objections to some alleged lineages reconstructed by COSSMANN and others. There is every reason to believe that the Caenogastropoda arose polyphyletically.

The remaining two subclasses now recognized in the Gastropoda are the Opisthobranchia and the Pulmonata. Although at an earlier period some zoologists considered the opisthobranchs to be more primitive than the prosobranchs, there is now general agreement that the prosobranchs were the source from which both of the subclasses

in question were derived. It might be thought highly probable that different groups classed as opisthobranchs or as pulmonates would prove to be derived independently from different prosobranch groups, in the case of the pulmonates by adaptation along parallel lines to a terrestrial life. In all discussions of their origin by competent authorities, however, the view has been taken that both groups were monophyletic, and most authors have considered them to be closely related phylogenetically. Their hermaphrodite organization and euthyneurous condition led to their association by various authorities from SPENGEL onward in a major taxon, the Euthyneura. GRAHAM (74), from his work on the molluscan stomach, has concluded that both pulmonates and opisthobranchs were evolved from one of the higher groups of monotocardian prosobranchs (i.e., caenogastropods). MORTON (14) has considered that the two groups "did not come off remotely from each other, but arose quite close together, possibly at a single point," and has thought this point of origin to be some advanced archaeogastropod which (like modern Trochacea) had lost the right-hand pallial organs, and which in addition had acquired pallial genital organs. His reason for not accepting a more advanced prosobranch as the ancestral form lies mainly in the relatively primitive radula in both groups. One remarkable feature of opisthobranchs that have retained a spiral shell is the heterostrophic protoconch, resulting from hyperstrophic coiling of the larval shell, and this feature is also present in some primitive pulmonates, although it has been lost in most members of this order, possibly because there is no free larval stage. No satisfactory theory has been advanced attributing any functional significance to the heterostrophic protoconch, nor does it seem likely that it is an instance of recapitulated ancestry. It may, like torsion, have originated as a mutation affecting the larval stage.

Two families now classified as opisthobranchs, the Pyramidellidae and Acteonidae, are less removed from prosobranchs than other families of their order, and so appear to have undergone less evolutionary change since its original divergence. Both groups are operculate and have shells into which

the entire head-foot mass can retreat, and in both the auricle is anterior to the ventricle; the Acteonidae, furthermore, are conspicuously streptoneurous and have the penis uninvaginable—both prosobranch characters. Opisthobranch characters possessed by both groups are a heterostrophic protoconch, a hermaphrodite organization, and certain features of the alimentary canal; the Pyramidellidae, it should be noted, are euthyneurous, with a marked concentration of ganglia, and they lack a ctenidium.

The Pyramidellacea were probably the first opisthobranch superfamily to make its appearance. The earliest forms included in this taxon by contributors to the *Treatise* belong to the family Streptacididae, of which the genus *Donaldina* is found possibly in the Devonian and certainly in the Lower Carboniferous. The protoconch is heterostrophic in some genera (*Streptacis* and *Donaldina*) of the family, although in *Platyconcha* it is discoidal and undeviated. According to the views of KNIGHT, the Pyramidellacea arose from the Loxonematacea, and since the latter group, as already seen, may well have been transitional from archaeogastropod to caenogastropod in evolutionary advancement, such an origin would be in keeping with MORTON's views. The Acteonidae appeared first in the Lower Carboniferous with the genus *Acteonina*, in which the protoconch, apparently consisting of a single whorl, is reported to be deviated and partly immersed. If the hypothesis of a monophyletic origin of the opisthobranchs is correct, derivation of the Acteonidae from the Pyramidellacea should presumably be assumed, but must have been accompanied by a considerable modification in shell characters. The tectibranch, or, at least, tectibranch-like opisthobranchs became moderately abundant in the Mesozoic, *Acteonina* and *Cylindrobullina* occurring in the Triassic, to be joined by *Bulla*-like forms (*Palaeohydatina*) in the Jurassic. The most notable genus of fossil opisthobranchs, *Acteonella*, consisting of mostly large, ovate, thick-shelled forms with prominent columellar folds, is particularly characteristic of the Cretaceous.

The affinities and origin of the Nerineacea, an important group of Jurassic and Cretaceous shells, mostly with complicated internal folds (in this respect resembling *Acteonella*) are problematic. In some genera belonging to this group, particularly those constituting the families Ceritellidae and Itieriidae, the shell has a distinctly opisthobranch facies, and the protoconch is known to be heterostrophic in at least two genera, *Pseudonerinea*, belonging to the former family, and, according to COSSMANN (21, v. 12, p. 209), *Itruvia*, belonging to the latter. COSSMANN, therefore, erected a new opisthobranch suborder, Entomotaeniata, for the superfamily. The group, however, has certain features not found in typical opisthobranchs—a short siphonal canal and a narrow anal emargination of the outer lip, situated, as in the Conidae, next to the suture and giving rise to an anal fasciole. YOCHELSON has suggested derivation of the nerineids from the Permian genus *Labridens*, which has comparable internal folds and is referred by him to the Subulitidae. On the other hand, if columellar folds could have been developed in one group they could also have appeared in another, and the nerineids could have had their origin in the Pyramidellacea. Their systematic position and the part they played in gastropod evolution must for the present remain undecided.

Malacologists, relying on the evidence of soft anatomy, have differed to some extent in their views as to the precise source of origin and interrelationships of the pulmonates. PELSENEER (80) thought it probable that they were derived from a primitive opisthobranch, such as *Acteon*, and further regarded the Ellobiidae as their most primitive family, ancestral both to the remaining Basommatophora and to the Stylommatophora. BOETTGER (5) has accepted the view that the pulmonates sprang from the Acteonidae, but has considered their most primitive family to be the Siphonariidae rather than the Ellobiidae, which he places near the middle of the tree of descent of the Basommatophora and from which he considers the Stylommotophora to have been derived. HUBENDICK (53), basing his argument on the more primitive type of radula found in the pulmonates and on the nervous system, has disagreed with the theory of their opisthobranch origin, and has thought that they arose directly from Archaeogastropoda. Reference has already been made to the views of GRAHAM (44)

and MORTON (74). The latter worker, from a study of living Ellobiidae, has no doubt that this family was the basal stock of the pulmonates, constituting "one of the most ideally primitive living groups."

Turning, now, to the fossil record, we find that the earliest gastropods which have been regarded as pulmonates occur in the Lower Carboniferous and belong to the genus *Maturipupa*, in which the shell aperture has a prominent parietal tooth. This genus continues into the Upper Carboniferous where we also find *Anthracopupa*, with both columellar and parietal teeth, and *Dendropupa*, the apertural details of which are uncertain. The authors who originally described these genera noted their resemblance to modern land gastropods of the family Pupillidae, to which they accordingly referred them. WENZ (105), however, referred *Anthracopupa* and *Maturipupa* to the pulmonate family Ellobiidae and *Dendropupa* to the prosobranch family Cyclophoridae. In this *Treatise* KNIGHT, BATTEN and YOCHELSON propose to include all these genera in the Cyclophoridae. Among modern representatives of this family are several genera quite similar in external appearance to those Paleozoic forms and with toothed apertures. On the other hand, there can be no doubt as to the close resemblance of the fossil forms to some Ellobiidae. Modern Cyclophoridae are land shells; most modern Ellobiidae are aquatic, some living in the sea between tide marks and some in fresh water, but a few have a terrestrial habitat. The Paleozoic forms occur in nonmarine formations, but it is not possible to say definitely if they lived on land or in fresh water. The reasons for considering them to be Cyclophoridae rather than pulmonates are not very strong. Discoidal shells found in Permian nonmarine formations have been referred by some authors to the pulmonate genus *Planorbis* and a genus *Palaeorbis* is available for them. They are almost certainly worms.

Records of pulmonates from early Mesozoic formations, for example, of supposed species of *Helix, Planorbis,* and *Vertigo* from the English Lower Lias published in 1867 by MOORE (71), were with little doubt based on misidentifications. Unquestionable Basommatophora, represented by such genera as *Lymnaea, Physa, Planorbis,* and *Ellobium,* make their appearance in abundance in late Jurassic fresh-water formations. These also contain the earliest gastropods (apart from those from the Upper Paleozoic already mentioned) which have been regarded as land prosobranchs. The first reliable records of land pulmonates (Stylommatophora) are from the Upper Cretaceous. Deposits of this age in southern France have yielded some particularly interesting species of this group.

An interesting theory of the origin of the pteropods (or at least of the family Spiratellidae) is that of LEMCHE (66), that they originated as opisthobranch larvae which failed to sink to the bottom and undergo metamorphosis, but continued to lead a pelagic life until maturity was reached. Pteropods are first known definitely from the lowest beds of the Eocene, a few records from the Cretaceous being unreliable. The opinion of earlier workers that certain Lower Paleozoic organisms, such as *Conularia* and *Hyolithes,* were pteropods has now been abandoned. Were the forms in question to be accepted as such, the views expressed above as to the origin of the opisthobranchs could scarcely be maintained. The heteropods, pelagic prosobranchs, first appeared in the Albian stage of the Middle Cretaceous, if the genus *Bellerophina* D'ORBIGNY is correctly referred to this group. Little is ever likely to be known of the geological history of the shell-less gastropod groups, some of which are opisthobranchs and others pulmonates, and for discussions as to their relationships reference must be made to the neontological literature.

GASTROPOD CLASSIFICATION

HISTORY

In a brief review of the history of classification of the Gastropoda it is unnecessary to go back beyond CUVIER, who first recognized the group as a distinct taxon of the mollusks, and whose earliest classification, of 1797 and 1800 (27, 28), was based on obvious external characters. Major groups were defined by the presence or absence of a visible shell, and groups of the second rank

by the nature of the shell (multivalve, as in *Chiton,* and "conivalve" or "spirivalve"); spirivalve shells were classified according to the characters of the aperture, whether entire, notched, or canaliculate. CUVIER did not name his taxa or define their status.

A classification proposed in 1801 by LA-MARCK was based on much the same external criteria, but he included both gastropods and cephalopods (as now understood) in his order *mollusques céphalés,* shell-bearing cephalopods being separated from other univalves only in his secondary "taxis" (arrangement of members of any given taxon in taxa of next subordinate rank). Even in 1812 (60) and 1819 LAMARCK failed to recognize the essential unity of the gastropods, as now understood. His *mollusques céphalés* were divided into five taxa (given the rank of orders in 1819), four of which are now included in the gastropods. He restricted the term *gastéropodes* to one of these, consisting of forms without an external shell, while forms with simple external spiral shells constituted the second, for which the name *trachélipodes* was proposed. The other two were CUVIER's (1804) *ptéropodes* and a newly recognized group, *hétéropodes.* The distinctions between LA-MARCK's five orders were based on external morphology, particularly the nature of the foot and of the shell. The *trachélipodes* were subdivided according to the presence or absence of an inhalant siphon. RAFINESQUE (87) followed LAMARCK, but renamed the *trachélipodes* as Spironotia. No subsequent worker accepted LAMARCK's restricted definition of a gastropod.

Meanwhile, other workers had begun to pay attention to the respiratory system as a possible basis of classification. DUMÉRIL in 1806 (32) adopted CUVIER's conception of the Gastropoda, dividing this group into three taxa: Dermobranchiata, with external gills; Tubispirantia, with internal gills and an inhalant siphon; and Adelobranchiata, with internal gills but no siphon. This classification was based on imperfect knowledge, and only the second of these taxa consisted of forms placed in one subclass at the present day. DUMÉRIL followed CUVIER in regarding the Pteropoda as a distinct molluscan order. In DEBLAINVILLE's earliest scheme, first outlined in 1814 with knowledge of unpublished work by CUVIER, the

name gastropods was not assigned to any taxon, the *mollusques céphalés* being divided into no fewer than ten newly named orders based primarily on the respiratory organs. In seven of these, which included the *cryptodibranches (céphalopodes* of CUVIER) and the *ptérobranches (ptéropodes* of CUVIER) these organs and the shell (if present) are symmetrical, and in three, which included the *pulmobranches* (air-breathing forms) and the *pectinibranches,* asymmetrical. CUVIER's considered classification of the gastropods, regarded as a molluscan class, appeared in 1817 (30), and was based mainly upon their respiratory organs and sexual organization, although reference was also made to the presence or absence of an operculum. Seven orders were recognized: *nudibranches,* no shell, gills on back; *inférobranches,* no shell, gills below mantle edge; *tectibranches,* shell present but covered by mantle, gills on back or side, hermaphrodite; *pulmonés,* air-breathing with pulmonary cavity, hermaphrodite; *pectinibranches,* with spiral shell, sexes separate, gills pectinate, in mantle cavity; *scutibranches,* gills as in *pectinibranches,* but animal supposed to be self-fertilizing; and *cyclobranches,* shell not spiral, numerous gills arranged in a circlet. *Chiton* was associated with *Patella* in the last group.

The classification proposed by GOLDFUSS in 1820 (40) was largely based on that of CUVIER, but the chitons were separated as a distinct order, Crepidopoda, and the Pectinibranchia were reduced by the separation of siphonate forms as a taxon of correlative rank, Siphonobranchia. In his treatment of the chitons he was not followed by other authors until long after. In the same year SCHWEIGGER (88) adopted CUVIER's classification, assigning new names to some of his orders, among them Aspidobranchiata for the *scutibranches.*

In 1821 GRAY (46) announced his "natural arrangement of Mollusca according to their internal structure." The heteropods and pteropods (under new names) figured as classes ranking equally with the Gasteropodophora, as he termed the remaining gastropods. This last class was divided into two subclasses, the first consisting of air-breathing forms and the second of forms breathing by means of branchia under the mantle. This second subclass was divided into no

fewer than 11 orders, the diagnoses of which refer to the nature of the branchia, reproductive processes, presence or absence of an operculum, shell characters, and (in some cases) the retractor muscle.

DeBlainville, in a classification published in 1824 (4), adopted a new basis for his primary taxis of the Paracephalophora (as he renamed the Gastropoda), dividing the class into three subclasses, the first dioecious, the second monoecious, and the third supposedly self-fertilizing. The respiratory system was in each the basis of the secondary taxis. The pteropods were reduced in rank so as to constitute merely a family of the order Nucleobranchiata of the monoecious subclass. We may note deBlainville's transference of *Dentalium* from the phylum Vermes, in which it had been included by Cuvier and Lamarck, to the self-fertilizing subclass of his Paracephalophora, of which it constituted an order named Cirrhobranchiata. It continued to form a low-ranking gastropod taxon until 1862, when Bronn (11) recognized and named the Scaphopoda as a distinct class.

Latreille (1825) (64), like deBlainville, made the genital system his primary "taxobasis" (character upon which a taxonomic subdivision or taxis is based), dividing a restricted class Gastropoda into two so-called "sections" (i.e., subclasses), Hermaphrodita and Dioecia, and removing the Scutibranchia and Cyclobranchia to an entirely different branch of the Mollusca characterized by the absence of a penis.

In 1840 Gray (47) departed considerably from his earlier system, and recognized two main subdivisions of the Gastropoda, Ctenobranchiata and Heterobranchiata, which corresponded, respectively, to the Streptoneura and Euthyneura of later systems, although the respiratory organs formed his taxobasis. We may note the division of the Ctenobranchiata into two taxa, Zoophaga and Phytophaga, according to the supposed method of feeding. This classification was extended by Gray in 1850 (48), the Ctenobranchiata being then divided into orders Pectinibranchiata (a restriction of the original use of this term) and Scutibranchiata, the latter including the foreign elements Dentaliidae and Chitonidae. In 1853, however, Gray (49) redistributed the majority of ctenobranch families among two sub-

orders, Proboscidifera and Rostrifera, according to the presence or absence of a retractile proboscis.

Milne Edwards (70) introduced in 1848 a new idea and terminology into the classification of the gastropods. He divided the class into two subclasses, *gastéropodes ordinaires* and *gastéropodes nageurs (hétéropodes)*, appending the chitons as a "group satellite." The *gastéropodes ordinaires* were divided into two "sections," *gastéropodes pulmonés* and *gastéropodes branchifères*, and this last group into the two orders *opisthobranches* and *prosobranches*, according to relative positions of the heart and branchia. The Opisthobranchiata and Prosobranchiata were soon widely accepted as gastropod taxa of major rank, although they were ignored by Gray.

S. P. Woodward (1851), in his well-known *Manual* (107), recognized as orders the three main gastropod subdivisions (termed by him Prosobranchiata, Pulmonifera, and Opisthobranchiata) of the present day, with the heteropods, for which he adopted deBlainville's name Nucleobranchiata, forming a fourth order. He divided the prosobranchs into the Siphonostomata and Holostomata according to apertural characters. His last arrangement, being based on shell characters, was long favored by paleontologists, but corresponds to no grouping based on soft anatomy. Among Woodward's Holostomata were included such foreign elements as the Dentaliidae and Chitonidae.

In the classification of Adams & Adams (2) the Prosobranchiata, Opisthobranchiata, and Pulmonifera are recognized as subclasses of the Gastropoda, although the Heteropoda are accepted as a fourth subclass and the Pteropoda regarded as a distinct class. The arrangement adopted by these two workers was largely based on that of Gray, but under the prosobranch order Pectinibranchiata we find a new suborder, Toxifera, added to the Proboscidifera and Rostrifera.

Lovén, in 1848 (67), was responsible for fundamental studies of the gastropod radula and the suggestion that this organ might be a useful taxobasis. Gray (49) adopted the idea and divided each of his ctenobranch suborders, Prosocidifera and Rostrifera, into taxa based on the radula and bearing such names as Toxoglossa, Taenioglossa, Gym-

noglossa, and Rachiglossa, although it should be noted that the first three names were assigned to groups in both suborders. This scheme was adopted in GRAY's elaborate but uncompleted classification of the gastropods published in 1857 (50). One innovation introduced by GRAY was the reduction of the Heteropoda from the rank of subclass to that of a mere section of the order Pectinibranchiata.

It remained for TROSCHEL & THIELE (103) to study the radula throughout the Gastropoda and to emend GRAY's classification. The groups into which TROSCHEL divided the "Gastropoda dioecia" (i.e., Prosobranchia) on the basis of the radula are the Taenioglossa, Toxoglossa, Rhachiglossa, Pteroglossa, Rhipidoglossa, and Docoglossa. In the voluminous treatise of BRONN and KEFERSTEIN (11) we find the Pteropoda at last reunited with the Gastropoda, forming one of five orders, of which the four others are the Opisthobranchia, Heteropoda, Prosobranchia, and Pulmonata, all designated by their modern names. The Chitonidae appear as the first of five suborders of the Prosobranchia, the others being the Cyclobranchia, Aspidobranchia, Ctenobranchia, and Neurobranchia (the last comprising the Cyclostomatidae, Helicinidae, and Aciculidae). The primary subdivisions of the Ctenobranchia are the Siphonostomata and Holostomata. KEFERSTEIN was the first to designate both major subdivisions of the Pulmonata by the names (Stylommatophora, Basommatophora) that they still retain, although A. SCHMIDT had proposed the former some years previously. LACAZE-DUTHIERS had already shown that the Dentaliidae could not be included among the gastropods, but had considered them to form an order of the Acephala [Pelecypoda]. BRONN first raised them to a distinct class of the Mollusca, which he termed the Scaphopoda or Prosopocephala.

Yet another primary taxobasis for the gastropods was proposed by MÖRCH in 1865 (72). His Monotocardia included forms in which the heart has a single auricle and reproduction is by copulation, and the Diotocardia comprised forms in which there are two auricles and in which the genital products are discharged for external fertilization. The Monotocardia were then subdivided into a hermaphrodite group (consisting of the Pulmonata and Opisthobranchia) and a dioecious group, termed the Exophallia. The taxon Prosobranchia was thus abandoned, its constituents being divided between the Diotocardia (Aspidobranchia of older classifications) and the Monotocardia Exophallia.

VON IHERING (54) based far-reaching conclusions on his researches on the molluscan nervous system. He claimed to have found evidence for a diphyletic origin of forms previously classed as Gastropoda. The Prosobranchia, which he renamed Arthrocochlides and considered to rank as a phylum, were derived from segmented worms, whereas the pulmonates and opisthobranchs, grouped together as a class called Ichnopoda and included with the pteropods and cephalopods in a further phylum, Platycochlides, were derived from flatworms. The chitons, renamed Placophora, together with his Aplacophora (chaetoderms and *Neomenia*), belonged to yet another phylum, which he named the Amphineura. VON IHERING then subdivided his Arthrocochlides into the classes Chiastoneura and Orthoneusa, according to whether there was obvious crossing of the visceral nerve cords or not.

SPENGEL in 1881 (94) strongly criticized these conclusions, particularly the idea that the gastropods were diphyletic. He also showed that the distinction between orthoneurous and chiastoneurous prosobranchs was unimportant, the nerve cords actually crossing in both groups. SPENGEL was the first to demonstrate that structure of the nervous system and distribution of respiratory and other organs in the prosobranchs are to be regarded as the result of torsion, of which he found no evidence in the opisthobranchs and pulmonates. Accepting VON IHERING's conclusion that the Amphineura comprise a distinct taxon, he divided the gastropods into an order Streptoneura, coinciding with the prosobranchs (with suborders Zygobranchia and Azygobranchia defined by the presence of two ctenidia or one) and an order Euthyneura, composed of the "tribes" Ichnopoda (restricted to Opisthobranchia), Pulmonata, and Pteropoda.

A paper by MACDONALD (68) is of interest as proposing a formal scheme of gastropod classification in which the reproductive system, radula, and respiratory organs are

adopted as taxobases at successive declining levels, with suggestion that the otocysts (previously studied by LACAZE-DUTHIERS) are of taxonomic use.

FISCHER (35), in his well-known *Manuel,* reverted to older ideas. The Pteropoda were regarded as a molluscan class distinct from a broadly conceived class Gastropoda, and the latter was considered to include six orders: Pulmonata, Opisthobranchiata, Nucleobranchiata (heteropods), Prosobranchiata, Polyplacophora, and Aplacophora.

LANKESTER in 1883 (63) introduced the concept of the archimollusk and developed the ideas of SPENGEL on torsion and asymmetry. His conception of the Gastropoda was the same as that of FISCHER, the group being divided into a subclass Isopleura (identical with VON IHERING's Amphineura) and a subclass Anisopleura (virtually identical with the Gastropoda as now restricted) with two branches, Streptoneura and Euthyneura. The heteropods, which many authors had interpreted as a distinct order or subclass, had already been included by GRAY (50) in his suborder Rostrifera of the Pectinibranchiata; LANKESTER also regarded them as a group of subordinate rank, forming a taxon (Natantia) of the azygobranch Streptoneura. He included the pteropods, however, among the Cephalopoda.

BOUVIER (9) produced in 1887 a revised classification of the Prosobranchia in the light of work on the nervous system and was responsible for uniting the most advanced monotocardian prosobranchs (Rachiglossa and Toxoglossa) as a single group, the *sténoglosses.* This group, destined to become the order Neogastropoda, consisted of the Zoophaga of GRAY with exception of certain families, notably the Strombidae and Cypraeidae.

In a scheme of classification published in 1888 (59) LACAZE-DUTHIERS adopted the nervous system as his taxobasis, and introduced a series of new names for the taxa of the highest two gastropod categories. In their contents, however, these taxa coincided with or differed very little from those already recognized, and his nomenclature has been ignored by later writers.

PERRIER (86) proposed in 1889 to subdivide the Diotocardia and the stenoglossate Monotocardia according to the characters of the nephridium.

The main contribution of PELSENEER (79) to gastropod taxonomy was the complete merging of the Pteropoda with the tectibranch Opisthobranchia. In his 1906 *Treatise* (82) we find the Thecosomata included in one tribe of this order and the Gymnosomata in another. PELSENEER regarded the Amphineura as a distinct class of the Mollusca.

The latest neontological classification of the Gastropoda is that of THIELE, first published in 1925 (97) and extended in the first volume of his *Handbuch der systematischen Weichtierkunde* (98). The class Gastropoda, from which the chitons, designated by SCHUMACHER's name Loricata, are excluded, is divided into three subclasses, the Prosobranchia, Opisthobranchia, and Pulmonata. The Prosobranchia are divided into three orders, two of which are renamed. The order Archaeogastropoda is co-extensive with the Diotocardia of MÖRCH and BOUVIER. The five "Sippen" or "stirpes" (groups that would rank as subclasses or superfamilies in the present standard hierarchy) into which it is divided include the Zeugobranchia and Docoglossa. The order Mesogastropoda consists mainly of the Taenioglossa and includes the Heteropoda as one of 15 "stirpes." The name Stenoglossa, for the most advanced prosobranch order, which includes four "stirpes," is adopted from BOUVIER and PELSENEER; WENZ (105) has since replaced it by the name Neogastropoda. The Opisthobranchia are divided into four orders, Pleurocoela (Tectibranchia of earlier authors), Pteropoda, Sacoglossa, and Acoela (composed of the suborders Notaspidea and Nudibranchia). The Pulmonata are divided, as by many previous authors, into the orders Basommatophora and Stylommatophora.

It is noteworthy that, although so many different features of soft anatomy have been used as bases of classification, a considerable measure of agreement obtains as to the main groups into which living gastropods fall. There have naturally been differences in assessment of the relative taxonomic ranks of different groups, resulting, for example, in disagreement as to whether two subclasses, Prosobranchia (=Streptoneura) and Euthyneura, or three, namely, Prosobranchia, Opisthobranchia, and Pulmonata, should be recognized. Moreover, problems

have been encountered in deciding where to place certain (but remarkably few) border-line families, such as the Acteonidae, Pyramidellidae, and Siphonariidae, while the taxonomic rank and position of highly aberrant groups, notably the pteropods and heteropods, has been a source of uncertainty. There have been no widely discrepant systems of neontological classification, however.

Paleontologists, although able to view the whole succession of gastropod faunas from Cambrian times to the present day, have made few contributions to gastropod taxonomy except at family and lower levels, but have accepted the taxa based on living forms, attempting to fit extinct groups of gastropods into them. Unlike students of the pelecypods, they have mostly hesitated to propose schemes of classification based solely on shell features. An exception is the suggestion of GENEVIÈVE TERMIER (31) that all marine gastropods, fossil and living, may be separated by their growth lines into three groups, each corresponding to a main line of descent. In Group I the growth lines are prosocline or prosocyrt, in Group II they are opisthocyrt, and in Group III opisthocline. Groups I and II do not coincide with any groups defined by soft anatomy. All the shell-bearing opisthobranchs, together with the Stenoglossa and the Nerineacea, fall, however, into Group III.

There has been no other serious attempt to reconstruct a tree of gastropod descent from the succession of fossil forms and to found a scheme of classification in which subclasses and orders correspond to its main branches. Authors such as LANKESTER (63) have, indeed, presented a scheme of classification based on the comparative morphology of living forms as an alleged tree of descent, and NAEF (76) published a hypothetical phylogenetic tree with the six gastropod orders recognized by him coming off as branches at various levels. It is clear that only intensive study of fossil shells and the discovery of many new faunas will enable us to unravel gastropod phylogeny. At the present time we are not in a position to abandon the neontological classification, although it may well cut across true lines of descent.

As can readily be understood, authorities have differed in their views regarding the positions to assign to some extinct gastropod groups in neontological classification. The bellerophontids have usually been regarded as aspidobranch prosobranchs, but some workers have considered them to be heteropods, and SIMROTH (90) thought that they were a distinct class of Mollusca intermediate between the Cephalopoda and the Gastropoda. WENZ (106) accepted them as gastropods, but thought that they should constitute a subclass ranking equally with the prosobranchs, while they formed one of NAEF's (76) six gastropod orders. Reference has already been made to differences in opinion as to the systematic position of the Nerineacea, and of the Murchisoniacea and Loxonematacea. There are several early Mesozoic families, such as the Pseudomelaniidae, regarded by WENZ (105) as archaeogastropods on evidence not accepted by contributors to the present *Treatise*.

In the numerous classifications of the Gastropoda that have been proposed, a great number of names have been assigned to groups of higher rank than families. Some of these names soon dropped into oblivion, but some have been in frequent use, although the groups that they designate have constantly changed their taxonomic rank. For convenience of reference, a list of the most important of such names follows.

MOST IMPORTANT NAMES APPLIED TO HIGHER TAXONOMIC CATEGORIES OF GASTROPODA

Acoela THIELE, 1926 (97, p. 110). Order of the subclass Opisthobranchia; consists of the Nudibranchia, together with the Notaspidea.

Archaeogastropoda THIELE, 1925 (97, p. 74). Order of the subclass Prosobranchia; consists of the group formerly known as Scutibranchia or Aspidobranchia, together with the Docoglossa.

Aspidobranchia SCHWEIGGER, 1820, as "Aspidobranchiata" (88, p. 616, 720). Proposed for the group termed "scutibranches" by CUVIER and extended by later authors (KEFERSTEIN, BERNARD) so as to remain equivalent to the Scutibranchia, as also subsequently extended, in which sense the group includes all Archaeogastropoda except the Docoglossa and is identical with the Rhipidoglossa (PELSENEER included the Docoglossa also).

Azygobranchia SPENGEL, 1881 (94, p. 373). Proposed for a suborder of the order (later subclass) Streptoneura (=Prosobranchia), in which only one ctenidium is present, and used by LANKESTER as an ordinal name in this sense; restricted by BOUVIER and others, however, to Diotocardia (now

Archaeogastropoda) with only one ctenidium, and thus restricted, its chief families are the Trochidae, Turbinidae, Neritidae, and Helicinidae.

Basommatophora KEFERSTEIN, 1864 (BRONN's *Klassen und Ordnungen des Thier-Reichs*, v. 3, p. 1246); often attributed to A. SCHMIDT. Order of the subclass Pulmonata consisting essentially of the aquatic forms.

Caenogastropoda COX, 1959 (23). Proposed for the order of Prosobranchia formerly known by the name Pectinibranchia, as restricted by GRAY in 1850. It combines the Mesogastropoda and the Stenoglossa or Neogastropoda.

Cephalaspidea FISCHER, 1883 (35, p. 550). Division of the Opisthobranchia characterized by a cephalic disc and including the benthonic forms with spiral shells; regarded by THIELE as a suborder of the opisthobranch order Pleurocoela and by BOETTGER as an order of a subclass Euthyneura.

Ctenobranchia SCHWEIGGER, 1820, as "Ctenobranchiata" (88, p. 616, 723). Proposed for the group termed "pectinibranches" by CUVIER; adopted by GRAY (1840, 1853) for a major subdivision of the Gastropoda almost identical with the present subclass Prosobranchia.

Cyclobranchia CUVIER, 1817, as "cyclobranches" (30, p. 451), latinized as "Cyclobranchiata" by SCHWEIGGER, 1820 (88). Group originally consisting of the Patellidae and the chitons, in which a circlet of gill lamellae is present; restricted by later authors by elimination of chitons and in this sense it corresponds to the Docoglossa.

Diotocardia MÖRCH, 1865 (72, p. 399). Gastropoda in which (typically) the heart has two auricles, although the Docoglossa were included; identical with the order Archaeogastropoda of the Prosobranchia.

Docoglossa TROSCHEL, 1866 (103, p. 10). Subdivision of the Gastropoda defined by radular characters and identical with the superfamily Patellacea of the Archaeogastropoda (synonym, Cyclobranchia of authors).

Entomotaeniata COSSMANN, 1896 (21, p. 5). Proposed as a suborder of the Opisthobranchia to include the Nerineidae and related families.

Euthyneura SPENGEL, 1881 (94, p. 373). Gastropoda in which the visceral nerve cords do not cross; a major subdivision consisting of the subclasses Opisthobranchia and Pulmonata.

Gymnoglossa GRAY, 1853 (49, p. 129). Group of Gastropoda lacking a radula and consisting mainly of the Eulimidae and Pyramidellidae, usually referred to the Prosobranchia; THIELE terms this group the Aglossa, but FISCHER introduced that name for several taxonomically distinct groups with no radula.

Gymnosomata DEBLAINVILLE, 1824 (4, p. 273). One of two subdivisions (now suborders) of the Pteropoda, including forms in which the mantle and shell are absent in the adult.

Heteropoda LAMARCK, 1812, as "hétéropodes," (60, p. 124), latinized as "Heteropoda" by CHILDREN (1823). Group of pelagic gastropods considered by some early authors to form a distinct order, but considered by THIELE to form a "stirps" (suborder) of the order Mesogastropoda; the chief genera are *Atlanta, Carinaria,* and *Pterotrachea.*

Holostomata FLEMING, 1828 (*History of British Animals,* p. 297). Proposed as subdivision of the Pectinibranchia of undefined status and adopted by S. P. WOODWARD, ZITTEL, and other authors, mainly paleontologists.

Mesogastropoda THIELE, 1925 (97, p. 74). Order of the subclass Prosobranchia consisting of the Pectinibranchia (Ctenobranchia of earlier authors), except for families now included in the Stenoglossa or Neogastropoda; almost co-extensive with the Taenioglossa.

Monotocardia MÖRCH, 1865 (72, p. 398). Name originally assigned to all Gastropoda having a heart with single auricle; some authors who have adopted the name (e.g., COOKE, 1895) have restricted it to Prosobranchia in which there is only one auricle, and in this sense it is an alternative name to Pectinibranchia as restricted by GRAY.

Neogastropoda WENZ, 1938 (105, p. 71). Proposed as new name for the Stenoglossa, the most advanced of the three orders of the subclass Prosobranchia.

Neurobranchia KEFERSTEIN, 1864 (in BRONN's *Klassen und Ordnungen des Thier-Reichs*, v. 3, p. 1023, 1061). Proposed as a suborder of the Prosobranchia for the three land operculate families Cyclostomatidae, Helicinidae, and Aciculidae; not now considered to form a taxonomic unit.

Nucleobranchia DEBLAINVILLE, 1824, as "Nucleobranchiata" (4, p. 282). Originally proposed as an order for all pelagic gastropods, i.e., the Heteropoda (=Nectopoda of DEBLAINVILLE) and the Pteropoda, but restricted by FISCHER to the latter, regarded as an order.

Nudibranchia DEBLAINVILLE, 1814, as "nudibranches" (*Bull. Soc. philomat. Paris,* p. 188, *ex* CUVIER, MS), latinized as "Nudibranchiata" by H.R.SCHINZ (1822). Order or suborder of the Opisthobranchia in which a shell is absent in the adult and a normal ctenidium is absent or replaced by secondary gills.

Opisthobranchia MILNE EDWARDS, 1848, as "opisthobranches" (70, p. 107), latinized as "Opisthobranchiata" by S. P. WOODWARD (1851) and MORRIS & LYCETT (1951). Subclass (originally order) of the Gastropoda, in most genera with auricle is posterior to the ventricle.

Pectinibranchia DEBLAINVILLE, 1814, as "pectinibranches" (*Bull. Soc. philomat. Paris,* p. 178, *ex* CUVIER, MS.), latinized as "Pectinibranchia" by GOLDFUSS (1820). Instituted by CUVIER as an order for gastropods with comblike ctenidia, the group originally being almost equivalent to the Proso-

branchia; restricted by GRAY (1850) by omission of the Scutibranchia, and used in this sense by later authors.

Platypoda GRAY, 1857 (50, p. 64). Group of Prosobranchia included by GRAY in his suborder "Rostrifera" and now included in the Taenioglossa; characterized by a more or less flattened foot adapted for creeping.

Pleurocoela THIELE, 1926 (97, p. 105). Order of the subclass Opisthobranchia consisting of Tectibranchia of earlier authors except Notaspidea.

Prosobranchia MILNE EDWARDS, 1848, as "prosobranches" (70, p. 107), latinized as "Prosobranchiata" by S.P.WOODWARD (1851) and MORRIS & LYCETT (1851). Subclass (originally order) of the Gastropoda in which the auricle is anterior to the ventricle and the visceral loop forms a figure 8.

Ptenoglossa GRAY, 1853 (49, p. 129). Suborder of the Prosobranchia in which the radula has a large number of hooked teeth; as now restricted, the Ptenoglossa contain only two families (Scalidae, Janthinidae).

Pteropoda CUVIER, 1804, as "ptéropodes" (29, p. 232), latinized as Pteropoda by DUMÉRIL (1806). Group of pelagic Mollusca long considered to constitute a class ranking equally with the Gastropoda but now regarded as an order of the Opisthobranchia.

Pulmonata CUVIER, 1817, as "pulmonés" (30, p. 401), latinized as "Pulmonifera" by FLEMING (1822) and as "Pulmonata" by WIEGMANN & RUTHE (1832). Subclass of the class Gastropoda characterized by modification of the mantle cavity for air-breathing.

Rachiglossa GRAY, 1853 (49, p. 127). Group of prosobranch Gastropoda defined by characters of the radula; originally confined to the Volutidae, but as extended by TROSCHEL, consists of the superfamilies Muricacea, Buccinacea, and Volutacea.

Rhipidoglossa MÖRCH, 1865, as "Rhipidoglossata" (72, p. 399), published in the form Rhipidoglossa by TROSCHEL (1866). Group of Gastropoda characterized by features of the radula, and identical with the Aspidobranchia or Scutibranchia; the Rhipidoglossa, together with the Docoglossa, constitute the order Archaeogastropoda.

Sacoglossa VONIHERING, 1876 (54, p. 146). Order of the Opisthobranchia in which the radula has a single series of strong teeth, preserved in a special sac when worn out; the shell is much reduced or absent.

Scutibranchia CUVIER, 1817, as "scutibranches" (30, p. 445), latinized as Scutibranchia by GOLDFUSS (1820). Name originally applied to *Haliotis, Fissurella,* and *Emarginula* (i.e., the Zygobranchia), together with some extraneous elements, but has been extended by some authorities to include all Archaeogastropoda except the Docoglossa, being thus equivalent to the Rhipidoglossa.

Siphonostomata DEBLAINVILLE, 1824 (4, p. 195).

Proposed as a "family" of DEBLAINVILLE's order Siphonobranchiata; the name was applied by S.P. WOODWARD to a "section" of the order Prosobranchia and has been adopted by ZITTEL and other paleontologists for one of two groups of the Taenioglossa.

Stenoglossa BOUVIER, 1887, as "sténoglosses" (9, p. 471), latinized as Stenoglossa by PELSENEER (1906). Order of the subclass Prosobranchia combining the Toxoglossa and Rachiglossa; renamed Neogastropoda by WENZ (1938).

Streptoneura SPENGEL, 1881 (94, p. 373). One of two major subdivisions of the Gastropoda consisting of forms in which the visceral nerve cords cross, the visceral loop forming a figure 8; virtually equivalent to the subclass Prosobranchia.

Stylommatophora A.SCHMIDT, 1856 (*Abhandl. naturwiss. Ver. Sachsen u. Thüringen,* v. 1, p. 8). One of two major subdivisions of the Pulmonata, now considered to rank as an order, comprising the terrestrial forms.

Taenioglossa F.H.TROSCHEL, 1848, as "Taenioglossata" (in WIEGMANN's *Handb. der Zoologie,* ed. 3). Group of gastropods characterized by features of the radula and including most families now classified in the prosobranch order Mesogastropoda.

Tectibranchia CUVIER, 1817, as "tectibranches" (30, p. 395), latinized as Tectibranchia by GOLDFUSS (1820). Group now considered as an order of the subclass Opisthobranchia; a ctenidium is present on the right side, and there is usually an external or internal shell.

Thalassophila GRAY, 1850 (48, p. 119). Originally proposed for the pulmonate families Amphibolidae and Siphonariidae and accepted by FISCHER as a suborder; these families are now included in the order Basommatophora.

Thecosomata DEBLAINVILLE, 1824 (4, p. 271). One of two subdivisions (now suborders) of the Pteropoda, including forms in which a shell is present.

Toxoglossa TROSCHEL, 1848, as "Toxoglossata" (in WIEGMANN's *Handb. der Zoologie,* ed. 3). Group of gastropods characterized typically by features of the radula (although obsolete in some forms) and comprising part of the prosobranch order Neogastropoda (families Conidae, Turridae, and Terebridae); name refers to the poison gland associated with the radula of *Conus.*

Zeugobranchia VONIHERING, 1876 (54, p. 139). Group of the Archaeogastropoda in which two ctenidia are present; contains families Pleurotomariidae, Haliotidae, and Fissurellidae.

Zygobranchia SPENGEL, 1881 (94, p. 372). Same as Zeugobranchia.

CLASSIFICATION ADOPTED IN THIS TREATISE

In accordance with the most general practice, the gastropods are here divided into three subclasses, Prosobranchia, Opistho-

branchia, and Pulmonata. The accompanying diagrams (Figs. 87, 88) show the distinctive anatomical features of these groups, a primitive and a more advanced prosobranch being both illustrated. In Thiele's classification, currently adopted by most neontologists, the subclass Prosobranchia is divided into three orders, Archaeogastropoda, Mesogastropoda, and Stenoglossa. Only the first of these is dealt with in the

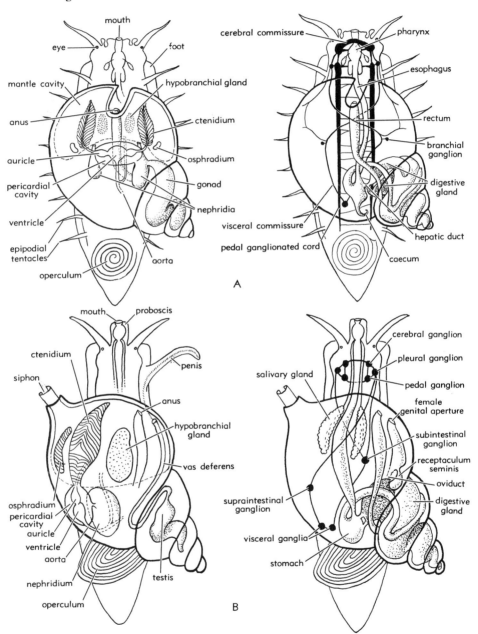

Fig. 87. Schematic representation of *(A)* a zygobranch archaeogastropod and *(B)* a siphonostomatous caenogastropod (122).

present part of the *Treatise* (except for the Supplement). The name Archaeogastropoda is here adopted as being preferable to any of the earlier names (Scutibranchia, Aspidobranchia and Diotocardia) which it replaced, as there has been some inconsistency in their use and it does not in itself imply the existence of any particular anatomical condition in the groups, many extinct, to which it is applied. This taxon is

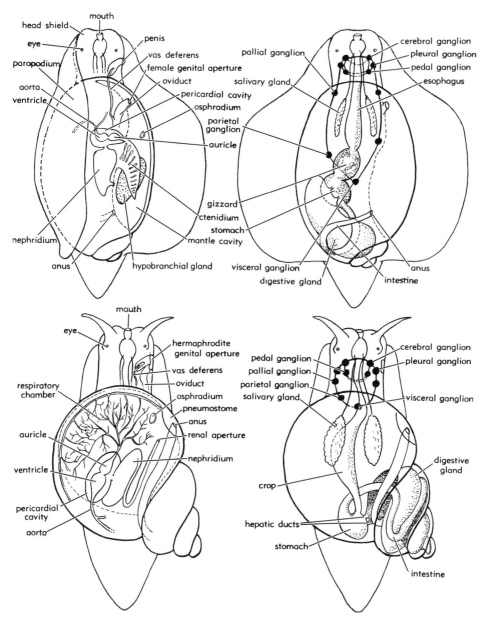

FIG. 88. Schematic representation of *(A)* a tectibranch opisthobranch with parapodia folded back on one side in left-hand diagram and on both sides in right-hand diagram, and *(B)* a fresh-water (basommotophoran) pulmonate (122).

a diverse assemblage, comprising gastropods in which the primitive features attributed to the hypothetical newly torqued ancestral form are retained to a varying extent. It has been subdivided in several ways by past authorities; by GRAY (1850) into Podophthalma and Edriophthalma; by TROSCHEL (1857) into Rhipidoglossa and Docoglossa; by BOUVIER (1887) into *zygobranches* and *azygobranches* (although SPENGEL's Azygobranchia had included monotocardian prosobranchs also); by PERRIER (1889) into *diotocardes (s.s.)* and *hétérocardes* (=Docoglossa). NAEF (1911) recognized four distinct orders, Belleromorpha, Zygobranchia, Trochomorpha and Docoglossa, among the forms now termed Archaeogastropoda. While there is no strong objection to some such arrangement, it has been decided here to recognize only a single order, and to divide this into suborders.

The first of these, the Bellerophontina, constitutes the most primitive group, in which the shell has complete bilateral symmetry and bears clear evidence that the ctenidia were paired and equal. Had we full knowledge of the soft anatomy of this group we might find good grounds for its recognition as a distinct order, but the available evidence does not justify this procedure.

Much might be said for the union of all asymmetrical gastropods in which there is clear evidence of the retention of two ctenidia in a second suborder. As already explained, however, there are reasons for thinking that the Murchisoniacea, although dibranchiate, were much more advanced in other characters than the Pleurotomariacea. The group has, therefore, been elevated to the rank of a suborder, reference of which to the Archaeogastropoda is queried. The Pleurotomariacea and a newly erected superfamily Fissurellacea, both of which have modern representatives clearly retaining many primitive features, form the essential constituents of another suborder, the Pleurotomariina (Zygobranchia of some neontological classifications). With them it has been decided to associate provisionally the long extinct superfamily Trochonematacea.

A further suborder Macluritina has been erected for the inclusion of the Macluritacea, a peculiar Lower Paleozoic group characterized by a hyperstrophically coiled shell, together with the apparently derivative superfamily, the Euomphalacea. In these groups the shell has a spiral ridge representing an anal channel, but its position suggests that the right ctenidium had been lost.

The next suborder, the Trochina, is constituted by the numerous monobranchiate archaeogastropods with ordinary orthostrophic, mainly conispiral shells and simple outer lips. Its many modern representatives belong to the superfamily Trochacea, but it also includes the extinct Platyceratacea, Microdomatacea, Anomphalacea, and Oriostomatacea.

C. M. YONGE (112) has expressed the opinion that the Neritacea should constitute a distinct order on account of their peculiar combination of anatomical characters; in particular, they have a very complex pallial genital system, although in many features they have not advanced beyond the archaeogastropod stage of evolution. They are here recognized as a distinct suborder, the Neritopsina.

The last archaeogastropod suborder here recognized is the Patellina (formerly the Docoglossa), which most previous workers have recognized as a well-characterized group on account of the peculiar radula of the Recent representatives and of the simple patelliform shell.

The remaining prosobranchs have been considerd by many authorities to constitute a single major taxon, to which the name Pectinibranchiata was restricted by GRAY in 1850. This group, which it is proposed to regard as an order, has been renamed Caenogastropoda, for consistency with the decision to adopt THIELE's name Archaeogastropoda for the more primitive order. It has been subdivided in different ways by different workers: into Zoophaga and Phytophaga by GRAY (1850); Proboscidifera and Rostrifera by GRAY (1853); Proboscidifera, Toxifera and Rostrifera by ADAMS & ADAMS (1853-4); Holostomata and Siphonostomata by a number of authorities; Taenioglossata, Rhachiglossata and Toxoglossata by MÖRCH (1865); and *ténioglosses* and *sténoglosses* by BOUVIER (1887). These last two subdivisions have been latterly assigned the rank of orders with the names

Mesogastropoda and Neogastropoda, but the division of caenogastropod taxa among them has to some extent been decided in a very arbitrary manner. It is not here proposed to make a taxonomic division of the Caenogastropoda which will be binding on contributors who will be dealing with this order in Part J of the present *Treatise*. Classification of the opisthobranchs and pulmonates will also be discussed in that Part.

Summary of Classification[1]

As in previously published *Treatise* volumes, it is thought to be desirable to furnish in tabular form an outline of classification down to subfamily level as formulated by the authors contributing to this section on Gastropoda. The numbers of genera and subgenera assigned to each family and higher-rank taxa are given in parentheses following the name of the taxon, a single number signifying genera and two numbers signifying genera and subgenera. For example, "Coreospiridae (3)" indicates that 3 genera are included in this family, none divided into subgenera; "Sinuitinae (4;1)" indicates that this subfamily contains 4 genera and 1 subgenus (additional to a nominotypical subgenus not counted), or in other words, the subfamily contains 5 differently named taxa of generic-subgeneric rank. This method of making a census differs from that previously employed in *Treatise* tabulations (as p. L7-L10 and p. O160-O167) wherein nominotypical subgenera were included, thus enlarging in somewhat spurious manner the reported numbers of generic taxa.

The stratigraphic occurrence of each cited suprafamilial and familial taxon is given and the authorship of systematic descriptions belonging to it is indicated by code letters enclosed in parentheses. With reference to this statement of authorship, explanation needs to be given that whereas indicated authorship of any unit invariably covers preparation of the diagnosis of that unit, it does not necessarily include authorship of all constituent taxonomic divisions. For example, the diagnosis and general discussion of the suborder Pleurotomariina was prepared by Cox and KNIGHT, therefore being recorded by code letters as "(CX, KN)." Family-group divisions of this suborder, however, were organized in diverse manner,

some by KNIGHT, BATTEN, and YOCHELSON, some of these authors with collaboration of Cox, some by Cox alone, and some by KEEN. The summary of classification affords a convenient means of explicit statement of the authorship of systematic descriptions; for this purpose, adopted code letters for the names of authors are as follows.

Authorship of Systematic Descriptions

BATTEN, R. L. ....BA
Cox, L. R. CX
KEEN, A.M. ....KE
KNIGHT, J. B. ....KN
ROBERTSON, ROBERT ....RO
YOCHELSON, E. L..................................YO

The sequence of taxa recorded in the following tabulation, according to preference of most authors, is determined mainly by order of appearance in the geologic record, proceeding from oldest to youngest. Stratigraphic and geographic distribution are shown graphically in Figures 88A to 88E, inclusive.

Main Divisions of Gastropoda Described in Treatise Part I

Gastropoda *(class)* (794;414).[2] *L.Cam.-Rec.* (CX)

Prosobranchia *(subclass)* (789;414).[2] *L.Cam.-Rec.* (CX)

Archaeogastropoda *(order)* (732;407). *L.Cam.-Rec.* (CX)

Bellerophontina *(suborder)* (54;6). *L.Cam.-L.Trias.* (CX-KN)

Helcionellacea *(superfamily)* (4). *L.Cam.-U.Cam.* (KN-BA-YO)

Helcionellidae (1). *L.Cam.-U.Cam.* (KN-BA-YO)

Coreospiridae (3). *L.Cam.-U.Cam.* (KN-BA-YO)

Bellerophontacea *(superfamily)* (50;6). *U.Cam.-L.Trias.* (KN-BA-YO)

Cyrtolitidae (6). *U.Cam.-L.Sil.* (KN-BA-YO)

Sinuitidae (12;2). *U.Cam.-M.Perm.* (KN-BA-YO)

Sinuitinae (4;1). *U.Cam.-M.Dev.* (KN-BA-YO)

Bucanellinae (5;1). *U.Cam.-M.Perm.* (KN-BA-YO)

Euphemitinae (3). *?Dev., L.Carb.(Miss.)-Perm.* (KN-BA-YO)

Bellerophontidae (29;4). *U.Cam.-L.Trias.* (KN-BA-YO)

---

[1] This section, with accompanying diagrams designed to show graphically the recorded stratigraphic and geographic distribution of gastropod family-group taxa, has been prepared by R. C. MOORE.

[2] Contains additional generic-rank taxa not described in this volume.

Tropidodiscinae (4). *U.Cam.-Dev.* (KN-BA-YO)

Bucaniinae (8). *L.Ord.-Dev.* (KN-BA-YO)

?Carinaropsinae (5). *?L.Ord., M.Ord.-Dev.* (KN-BA-YO)

Pterothecinae (4). *M.Ord.-M.Dev.* (KN-BA-YO)

Bellerophontinae (6;2). *M.Ord.-L.Trias.* (KN-BA-YO)

Knightitinae (2;2). *Dev.-M.Perm.* (KN-BA-YO)

Family Uncertain (3). *U.Ord.-U.Carb.(U. Penn.).* (KN-BA-YO)

Macluritina *(suborder)* (50;9). *U.Cam.-Trias., ?U.Cret.* (CX-KN)

Macluritacea *(superfamily)* (15;2). *U.Cam.-Dev.* (KN-BA-YO)

Onychochilidae (10). *U.Cam.-L.Dev.* (KN-BA-YO)

Onychochilinae (5). *U.Cam.-L.Dev.* (KN-BA-YO)

Scaevogyrinae (5). *U.Cam.-M.Ord.* (KN-BA-YO)

Macluritidae (5;2). *L.Ord.-Dev.* (KN-BA-YO)

Euomphalacea *(superfamily)* (35;7). *L.Ord.-Trias., ?U.Cret.* (KN-BA-YO-CX)

Helicotomidae (8). *L.Ord.-M.Jur.* (KN-BA-YO-CX)

Euomphalidae (22;7). *L.Ord.-Trias., ?U.Cret.* (KN-BA-YO-CX)

Omphalotrochidae (5). *Dev.-M.Perm., ?U. Trias.* (KN-BA-YO-CX)

Pleurotomariina *(suborder)* (168;51). *U.Cam.-Rec.* (CX-KN)

Pleurotomariacea *(superfamily)* (136;20). *U. Cam.-Rec.* (KN-BA-YO-CX)

Sinuopeidae (13). *U.Cam.-M.Perm.* (KN-BA-YO)

Sinuopeinae (3). *U.Cam.-U.Sil.* (KN-BA-YO)

Platyschismatinae (5). *L.Ord.-M.Perm.* (KN-BA-YO)

Turbonellininae (5). *U.Sil.-L.Perm.* (KN-BA-YO)

Raphistomatidae (19;2). *U.Cam.-M.Perm.* (KN-BA-YO)

Ophiletinae (5;1). *U.Cam.-L.Ord.* (KN-BA-YO)

Raphistomatinae (6). *M.Ord.-U.Dev., ?L. Carb.(Miss.).* (KN-BA-YO)

Liospirinae (3;1). *?L.Ord., M.Ord.-M.Perm.* (KN-BA-YO)

Omospirinae (5). *M.Ord.-L.Jur.* (KN-BA-YO-CX)

Eotomariidae (25;1). *U.Cam.-L.Jur.* (KN-BA-YO-CX)

Eotomariinae (17;1). *U.Cam.-L.Jur.* (KN-BA-YO-CX)

Agnesiinae (3). *L.Dev.-U.Trias.* (KN-BA-YO-CX)

Neilsoniinae (5). *L.Carb.(Miss.)-U.Trias.* (KN-BA-YO-CX)

Lophospiridae (5;2). *Ord.-M.Trias.* (KN-BA-YO-CX)

Lophospirinae (3;2). *Ord.-Sil.* (KN-BA-YO)

Ruedemanniinae (2). *M.Ord.-M.Trias.* (KN-BA-YO-CX)

Luciellidae (5). *Ord.-U.Carb.(Penn.).* (KN-BA-YO)

Phanerotrematidae (3). *M.Ord.-L.Dev.* (KN-BA-YO)

Gosseletinidae (14). *M.Ord.-Trias.* (KN-BA-YO-CX)

Gosseletininae (7). *M.Ord.-Trias.* (KN-BA-YO-CX)

Coelozoninae (7). *M.Ord.-L.Dev.* (KN-BA-YO)

Euomphalopteridae (2;1). *M.Sil.-U.Sil.* (KN-BA-YO)

Portlockiellidae (4). *Dev.-M.Perm.* (KN-BA-YO)

Catantostomatidae (1). *M.Dev.* (KN-BA-YO)

Porcelliidae (3). *Dev.-M.Jur.* (KN-BA-YO-CX)

Rhaphischismatidae (1). *L.Carb.(Miss.)* (KN-BA-YO)

Phymatopleuridae (9;1). *L. Carb.(Miss.)-Trias.* (KN-BA-YO-CX)

Polytremariidae (2). *L.Carb.(Miss.)-M.Perm.* (KN-BA-YO)

Laubellidae (1). *M.Trias.* (CX)

Schizogoniidae (2). *M.Trias.-U.Trias.* (CX)

Zygitidae (1). *M.Trias.* (CX)

Kittlidiscidae (1). *M.Trias.* (CX)

Temnotropidae (1). *M.Trias.-U.Trias.* (CX)

Pleurotomariidae (11). *Trias.-Rec.* (CX)

Trochotomidae (2;1). *U.Trias.-U.Jur.* (CX)

Scissurellidae (3;2). *U.Cret.-Rec.* (KE)

Haliotidae (1;10). *?U.Cret., Mio.-Rec.* (CX)

Family Uncertain (7). *L.Ord.-U.Trias.* (KN-BA-YO-CX)

Trochonematacea *(superfamily)* (5;2). *M. Ord.-M.Perm.* (KN-BA-YO)

Trochonematidae (5;2). *M.Ord.-M.Perm.* (KN-BA-YO)

Fissurellacea *(superfamily)* (27;29). *Trias.-Rec.* (CX)

Fissurellidae (27;29). *Trias.-Rec.* (CX-KE)

Emarginulinae (14;20). *?Trias., Jur.-Rec.* (CX-KE)

Diodorinae (4;2). *Jur.-Rec.* (CX-KE)

Fissurellinae (9;7). *Eoc.-Rec.* (KE)

Patellina *(suborder)* (32;37). *?M.Sil., M.Trias.-Rec.* (CX-KN)

Patellacea *(superfamily)* (23;32). *?M.Sil., M. Trias.-Rec.* (CX-KN)

Metoptomatidae (3). *M.Sil.-M.Perm.* (KN-BA-YO)

Symmetrocapulidae (2). *Trias.-Jur.,* *?Cret.*
(CX)
Acmaeidae (10;19). *M.Trias.-Rec.* (CX-KE)
Patellidae (4;12). *?Jur., Eoc.-Rec.* (KE-CX)
Patellinae (2;11). *?Jur., Rec.* (KE-CX)
Nacellinae (2;1). *Eoc.-Rec.* (KE)
Lepetidae (4;1). *Mio.-Rec.* (KE)
Cocculinacea *(superfamily)* (5;5). *Mio.-Rec.*
(KE)
Cocculinidae (1;3). *Mio.-Rec.* (KE)
Lepetellidae (4;2). *Rec.* (KE)
Superfamily and family Uncertain (4). *L.Jur.-*
U.Cret. (CX)

Trochina *(suborder)* (232;214). *L.Ord.-Rec.*
(CX-KN)

Platyceratacea *(superfamily)* (19;7). *L.Ord.-*
M.Perm. (KN-BA-YO)
Holopeidae (13). *L.Ord.-M.Perm.* (KN-BA-
YO)
Holopeinae (6). *L.Ord.-U.Dev.* (KN-BA-
YO)
Gyronematinae (7). *M.Ord.-M.Perm.* (KN-
BA-YO)
Platyceratidae (6;7). *M.Ord.-M.Perm.* (KN-
BA-YO)
Microdomatacea *(superfamily)* (10). *M.Ord.-*
M.Perm. (KN-BA-YO)
Microdomatidae (5). *M.Ord.-M.Perm.* (KN-
BA-YO)
Elasmonematidae (5). *U.Sil.-U.Carb.(Penn.).*
(KN-BA-YO)
Anomphalacea *(superfamily)* (9). *Sil.-M.Perm.*
(KN-BA-YO)
Anomphalidae (9). *Sil.-M.Perm.* (KN-BA-
YO)
Oriostomatacea *(superfamily)* (8;1). *U.Sil.-L.*
Dev., ?Trias. (KN-BA-YO)
Oriostomatidae (3). *U.Sil.-L.Dev.* (KN-BA-
YO)
Tubinidae (5;1). *L.Dev., ?Trias.* (KN-BA-
YO-CX)
Trochacea *(superfamily)* (192;207). *Trias.-*
Rec. (KE)
Trochidae (96;136). *Trias.-Rec.* (KE-CX)
Proconulinae (12). *Trias.-U.Cret.* (CX)
Chilodontinae (5;1). *M.Trias.-U.Cret.* (CX)
Margaritinae (20;14). *Trias.-Rec.* (KE-CX)
Angariinae (5;1). *Trias.-Rec.* (KE-CX)
Monodontinae (17;31). *?Trias., M.Jur.-Rec.*
(KE-CX)
Gibbulinae (11;18). *U.Jur.-Rec.* (KE-CX)
Calliostomatinae (9;27). *L.Cret.-Rec.* (KE-
CX)
Trochinae (3;19). *U.Cret.-Rec.* (KE-CX)
Umboniinae (16;6). *U.Cret.-Rec.* (KE-CX)
Solariellinae (5;9). *U.Cret.-Rec.* (KE)
Halistylinae (1). *Pleist.-Rec.* (KE)
Subfamily Uncertain (2). *M.Trias.-U.Cret.*
(CX)
Ataphridae (5;2). *Trias.-U.Cret.* (CX)

Stomatellidae (8;4). *Trias.-Rec.* (KE-CX)
Turbinidae (39;51). *M.Trias.-Rec.* (KE-CX)
Astraeinae (4;15). *Trias.-Rec.* (KE-CX)
Liotiinae (10;5). *Trias.-Rec.* (KE-CX)
Helicocryptinae (1). *M.Jur.-L.Cret.* (CX)
Petropomatinae (1). *L.Cret.* (CX)
Turbininae (3;17). *L.Cret.-Rec.* (KE-CX)
Colloniinae (7;4). *U.Cret.-Plio.* (KE)
Homalopomatinae (10;10). *Paleoc.-Rec.*
(KE)
Subfamily Uncertain (3). *L.Jur.-U.Cret.*
(CX)
Cyclostrematidae (37;9). *U.Jur.-Rec.* (KE-
CX)
Skeneinae (27;6). *U.Jur.-Rec.* (KE-CX)
Cyclostrematinae (9;3). *U.Cret.-Rec.* (KE)
Phasianellidae (4;5). *Paleoc.-Rec.* (KE-RO)
Velainellidae (1). *Eoc.* (KE)
Orbitestellidae (2). *Rec.* (KE)

Neritopsina *(suborder)* (83;82). *M.Dev.-Rec.*
(CX-KN)

Neritacea *(superfamily)* (83;82). *M.Dev.-Rec.*
(CX-KN)
Plagiothyridae (3). *M.Dev.-L.Carb.(Miss.).*
(KN-BA-YO)
Neritopsidae (14;3). *M.Dev.-Rec.* (KN-BA-
YO-CX)
Naticopsinae (8;2). *M.Dev.-U.Cret.* (KN-
BA-YO-CX)
Dawsonellidae (1). *U.Carb.(Penn.).* (KN-
BA-YO)
Neritidae (26;41). *Trias.-Rec.* (KE-CX)
Neritinae (21;39). *M.Trias.-Rec.* (KE-CX)
Neritiliinae (2). *Rec.* (KE)
Smaragdiinae (3;2). *Mio.-Rec.* (KE)
Helicinidae (28;32). *U.Cret.-Rec.* (KE)
Dimorphoptychiinae (1). *U.Cret.-Paleoc.*
(KE)
Helicininae (10;14). *?Paleoc., Mio.-Rec.*
(KE)
Hendersoniinae (3). *?Paleoc., Pleist.-Rec.*
(KE)
Proserpininae (1;1). *?Oligo., Rec.* (KE)
Stoastomatinae (7;11). *Pleist.-Rec.* (KE)
Ceratodiscinae (3;5). *Rec.* (KE).
Proserpinellinae (3;1). *Pleist.-Rec.* (KE)
Deianiridae (1). *U.Cret.* (CX)
Phenacolepadidae (2;3). *Eoc.-Rec.* (KE)
Hydrocenidae (1;3). *Pleist.-Rec.* (KE)
Titiscaniidae (1). *Rec.* (KE)
Family Uncertain (6). *L.Carb.(Miss.)-Perm.*
(KN-BA-YO)

Murchisoniina *(suborder)* (49;6). *?U.Cam., L.*
Ord.-U.Trias. (CX-KN)

Murchisoniacea *(superfamily)* (29;6). *?U.*
Cam., L.Ord.-U.Trias. (KN-BA-YO)
Murchisoniidae (21;6). *?U.Cam., L.Ord.-U.*
Trias. (KN-BA-YO-CX)
Plethospiridae (8). *L.Ord.-U.Trias.* (KN-BA-
YO)

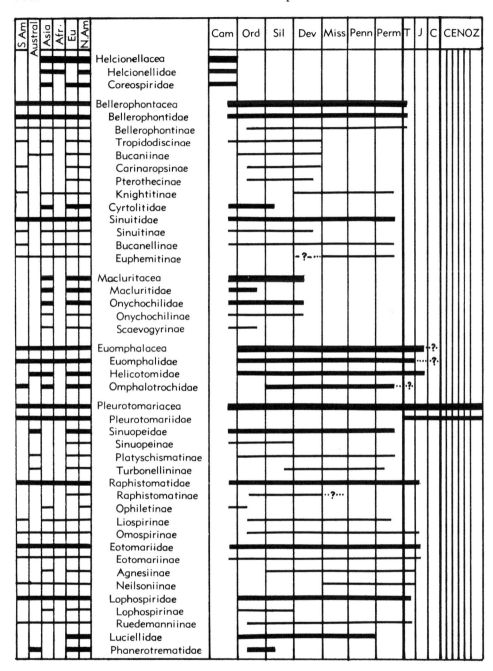

FIG. 88A. Stratigraphic and geographic distribution of gastropod family-group taxa described in *Treatise* Part I (MOORE, n).

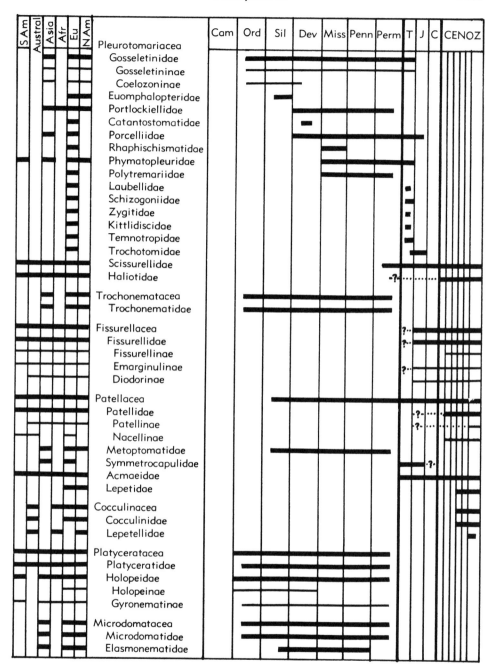

F<small>IG</small>. 88B. Stratigraphic and geographic distribution of gastropod family-group taxa, continued from Fig. 88A, (M<small>OORE</small>, n).

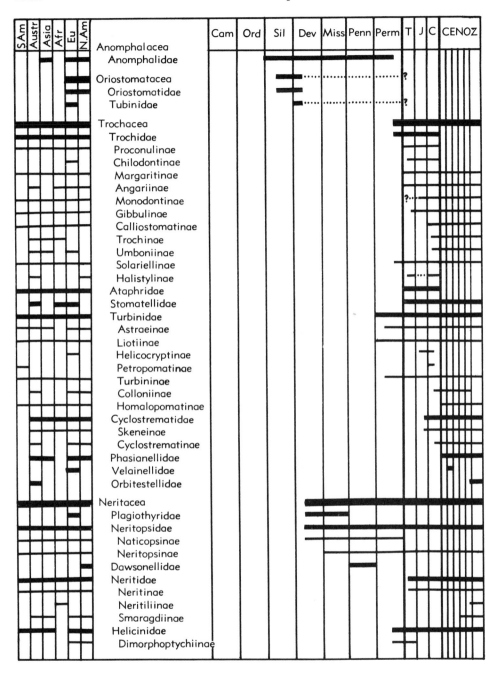

Fɪɢ. 88C. Stratigraphic and geographic distribution of gastropod family-group taxa, continued from Fig. 88B, (Mᴏᴏʀᴇ, n).

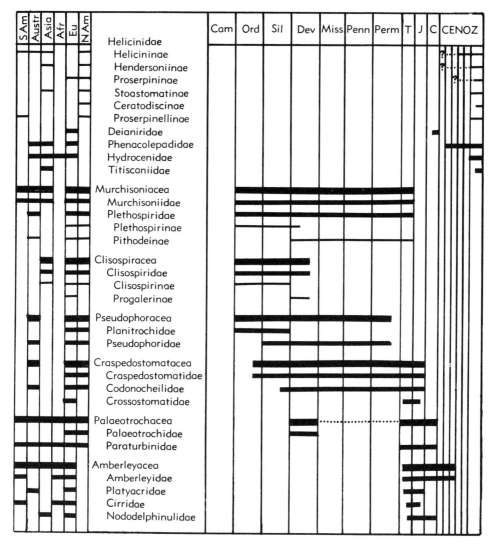

Fig. 88D. Stratigraphic and geographic distribution of gastropod family-group taxa, continued from Fig. 88C,(Moore, n).

Plethospirinae (3). *L.Ord.-L.Dev.* (KN-BA-YO)

Pithodeinae (5). *Dev.-U.Trias.* (KN-BA-YO-CX)

Suborder Uncertain (84;2). *?L.Cam., L.Ord.-Oligo.* (KN-BA-YO-CX)

Clisospiracea *(superfamily)* (5). *L.Ord.-M.Dev.* (KN-BA-YO)

Clisospiridae (5). *L.Ord.-M.Dev.* (KN-BA-YO)

Clisospirinae (2). *L.Ord.-Sil.* (KN-BA-YO)

Progalerinae (3). *L.Dev.-M.Dev.* (KN-BA-YO)

Pseudophoracea *(superfamily)* (15). *L.Ord.-L. Carb.(Miss.).* (KN-BA-YO)

Planitrochidae (6). *L.Ord.-U.Sil.* (KN-BA-YO)

Pseudophoridae (9). *Sil.-M.Perm.* (KN-BA-YO)

Craspedostomatacea *(superfamily)* (16). *U. Ord.-Jur.* (KN-BA-YO-CX)

Craspedostomatidae (8). *U.Ord.-Jur.* (KN-YO-CX)

Codonocheilidae (6). *U.Sil.-M.Jur.* (KN-BA-YO-CX)

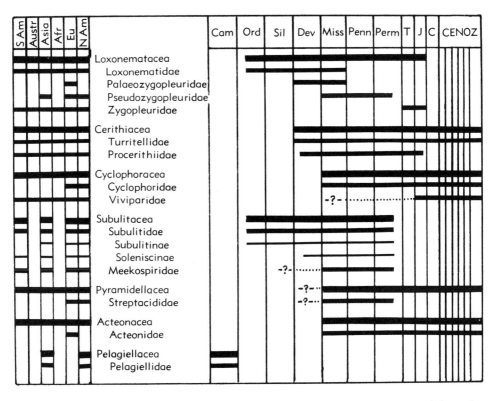

FIG. 88E. Stratigraphic and geographic distribution of gastropod family-group taxa, continued from Fig. 88D, (MOORE, n).

Crossostomatidae (2). *M.Trias.-M.Jur.* (CX)
Palaeotrochacea *(superfamily)* (7). *L.Dev.-U. Cret.* (KN-BA-YO)
  Palaeotrochidae (4). *L.Dev.-U.Dev.* (KN-BA-YO)
  Paraturbinidae (3). *Trias.-U.Cret.* (CX)
Amberleyacea *(superfamily)* (26;2). *M.Trias.-Oligo.* (CX)
  Platyacridae (5). *M.Trias.-U.Jur.* (CX)
  Cirridae (7;1). *U.Trias.-M.Jur.* (CX)
  Amberleyidae (9;1). *M.Trias.-Oligo.* (CX)
  Nododelphinulidae (5). *U.Trias.-U.Cret.* (CX)
Superfamily and family Uncertain (15). *?L. Cam., L.Ord.-U.Trias.* (KN-BA-YO-CX)
Caenogastropoda *(order)* (57;7).[3] *Ord.-Rec.* (CX)
Loxonematacea *(superfamily)* (31;5). *M.Ord.-U.Jur.* (KN-BA-YO-CX)
  Loxonematidae (7). *M.Ord.-L.Carb.(Miss.).* (KN-BA-YO)
  Palaeozygopleuridae (2). *Dev.-L.Carb.(Miss.).* (KN-BA-YO)
  Pseudozygopleuridae (9;5). *L.Carb.(Miss.)-M. Perm.* (KN-BA-YO)

Zygopleuridae (12). *Trias.-U.Jur.* (CX)
Family Uncertain (1). *Perm.* (KN-BA-YO)
Cerithiacea *(superfamily)* (7).[3] *L.Dev.-Rec.* (KN-BA-YO-CX)
  Turritellidae (4).[3] *L.Dev.-Rec.* (KN-BA-YO-CX)
  Procerithiidae (3).[3] *M.Dev.-U.Jur.* (KN-BA-YO-CX)
Cyclophoracea *(superfamily)* (6).[3] *L.Carb. (Miss.)-Rec.* (KN-BA-YO-CX)
  Cyclophoridae (4).[3] *L.Carb.(Miss.)-Rec.* (KN-BA-YO-CX)
  Dendropupinae (4). *L.Carb.(Miss.)-L.Perm.* (KN-BA-YO)
  Viviparidae (2).[3] *?L.Carb.(Miss.), Jur.-Rec.* (KN-BA-YO-CX)
Rissoacea *(superfamily)* (1). *Perm.-Rec.* (CX)
  Hydrobiidae (1).[3] *Perm.-Rec.* (CX)
Subulitacea *(superfamily)* (13;2). *M.Ord.-M. Perm.* (KN-BA-YO)
  Subulitidae (10;2). *M.Ord.-M.Perm.* (KN-BA-YO)
  Subulitinae (5;2). *M.Ord.-M.Perm.* (KN-BA-YO)

Soleniscinae (5). *M.Dev.-M.Perm.* (KN-BA-YO)

Meekospiridae (3). *?U.Sil., L.Carb.(Miss.)-M.Perm.* (KN-BA-YO)

Opisthobranchia *(subclass)* (4).[3] *?Dev., L.Carb.(Miss.)-Rec.* (KN-BA-YO)

Order Uncertain (3).[3] *?Dev., L.Carb.(Miss.)-Rec.* (KN-BA-YO)

Pyramidellacea *(superfamily)* (3).[3] *?Dev., L.Carb.(Miss.)-Rec.* (KN-BA-YO)

Streptacididae (3). *?Dev., L.Carb.(Miss.)-Perm.* (KN-BA-YO)

Pleurocoela *(order)* (1).[3] *L.Carb.(Miss.)-Rec.* (KN-BA-YO)

Acteonacea *(superfamily)* (1).[3] *L.Carb.(Miss.)-Rec.* (KN-BA-YO)

Acteonidae (1).[3] *L.Carb.(Miss.)-Rec.* (KN-BA-YO)

?Gastropoda Incertae Sedis (1). *Cam.* (KN-BA-YO)

Pelagiellacea *(superfamily)* (1). *Cam.* (KN-BA-YO)

Pelagiellidae (1). *Cam.* (KN-BA-YO)

---

[3] Contains additional generic-rank taxa not described in this volume.

REFERENCES

Abel, Othenio
(1) 1935, *Vorzeitliche Lebensspuren:* xv+644 p. (Jena).

Adams, Henry, & Adams, Arthur
(2) 1853-58, *The genera of recent Mollusca arranged according to their organization:* v. 1, 1853-54; v. 2, 1854-58; v. 3, 1858 (London).

Bernard, F.
(3) 1890, *Recherches sur les organes palléaux des gastéropodes prosobranches:* Ann. Sci. nat., Zool., v. 9, p. 89-404, pl. 1-15 (Paris).

Blainville, Henri de
(4) 1824, *Mollusques:* Dict. Sci. nat., v. 32, p. 1-392 (Strasbourg, Paris).

Boettger, C. R.
(5) 1955, *Die Systematik der euthyneuren Schnecken:* Deutsch. zool. Gesell., Verhandl. for 1954, p. 253-280 (Leipzig).

Bøggild, O. B.
(6) 1930, *The shell structure of the mollusks:* Acad. Roy. Sci. Lettres Danemark, Mém., ser. 9, v. 2, p. 230-326, pl. 1-15 (København).

Boutan, Louis
(7) 1885, *Recherches sur l'anatomie et le développement de la Fissurelle:* Arch. Zool. expériment. et générale, ser. 2, v. 13 *bis,* 173 p., pl. 31-44 (Paris).
(8) 1899, *La cause principale de l'asymétrie des mollusques gastéropodes:* Same, ser. 3, v. 7, p. 203-342.

Bouvier, E. L.
(9) 1887, *Système nerveux, morphologie générale et classification de gastéropodes prosobranches:* Ann. Sci. nat., Zool., v. 3, 510 p., 19 pl. (Paris).

Boycott, A. E.
(10) 1928, *Conchometry:* Malac. Soc. London, Proc., v. 18, p. 8-31.

Bronn, H. G. & Keferstein, Wilhelm
(11) 1862-66, *Weichthiere (Malacozoa):* in BRONN, H. G., Klassen und Ordnungen des Thier-Reichs, v. 3, pt. 2, p. 523-1500, pl. 45-136 (Leipzig, Heidelberg).

Bütschli, O.
(12) 1887, *Bemerkungen über die wahrscheinliche Herleitung der Asymmetrie der Gastropoden, spec. der Asymmetrie im Nervensystem der Prosobranchiaten:* Morphol. Jahrb., ed. GEGENBAUR, v. 12, p. 202-222, pl. 11, 12 (Leipzig).

Casey, Raymond
(13) 1959, *A Lower Cretaceous gastropod with fossilized intestines:* Palaeontology, v. 2 (in press) (London).

Cintra, H. & Souza Lopes, H. de
(14) 1952, *Sur la forme et quelques caractéristiques mathématiques des coquilles des gastéropodes (Mollusca):* Revista brasileira de Biol., v. 12, p. 185-200 (Rio de Janeiro).

Clarke, F. W. & Wheeler, W. C.
(15) 1917, *The inorganic constituents of marine invertebrates:* U. S. Geol. Survey Prof. Paper 102, 56 p. (Washington).

Comfort, Alexander
(16) 1950, *Biochemistry of molluscan shell pigments:* Malac. Soc. London, Proc., v. 28, p. 79-85.
(17) 1951, *Observations on the shell pigments of land pulmonates:* Same, v. 29, p. 35-43.
(18) 1951a, *The pigmentation of molluscan shells:* Biol. Reviews, v. 26, p. 285-301 (Cambridge).
(19) 1957, *The duration of life in molluscs:* Malac. Soc. London, Proc., v. 32, p. 219-241.

Cooke, A. H.
(20) 1895, *Molluscs:* Cambridge Natural History, ed. HARMER, S. F., & SHIPLEY, A. E., v. 3, p. i-xi, 1-459 (London).

Cossmann, Maurice
(21) 1895-1925, *Essais de paléoconchologie comparée:* livr. 1, 1895; 2, 1896; 3, 1899; 4, 1901; 5, 1903; 6, 1904; 7, 1906; 8, 1909; 9, 1912; 10, 1916; 11, 1918; 12, 1921; 13, 1925 (Paris).

Cox, L. R.
(22) 1955, *Observations on gastropod descriptive terminology:* Malac. Soc. London, Proc., v. 31, p. 190-202.
(23) 1959, *Thoughts on the classification of the Gastropoda:* Same, v. 33 (in press).

————, & **Knight, J. B.**
(24) 1959, *Suborders of Archaeogastropoda:* Same, v. 33 (in press).

Crofts, D. R.
(25) 1937, *The development of Haliotis tuberculata, with special reference to organogenesis during torsion:* Roy. Soc., Philos. Trans., ser. B, v. 228, p. 219-268, pl. 21-27 (London).
(26) 1955, *Muscle morphogenesis in primitive gastropods and its relation to torsion:* Zool. Soc. London, Proc., v. 125, p. 711-750.

Cuvier, Georges
(27) 1797 (not 1798, as frequently given), *Tableau élémentaire de l'histoire naturelle des animaux:* xvi+710 p., 14 pl. (Paris).
(28) 1800, *Leçons d'anatomie comparée:* v. 1 (contenant les organs du mouvement), xxxi+521 p., 9 pl. (Paris).
(29) 1804 *Concernant l'animal de l'Hyale, un nouveau genre de mollusques nus intermédiaire entre l'Hyale et le Clio et l'établissement d'un nouvel ordre dans la classe des mollusques:* Mus. Natl. Hist. nat., Ann., v. 4, p. 223-234, pl. 59 (Paris).
(30) 1817, *Le règne animal, distribué d'après son organisation:* v. 2, xviii+532 p. (Paris).

Delpey, Geneviève (later Termier, Geneviève)
(31) 1941, *Gastéropodes marins. Paléontologie — Stratigraphie:* Soc. géol. France, Mém., no. 43, 114 p., 28 pl. (Paris).

Duméril, A. M. C.
(32) 1806, *Zoologie analytique, ou méthode naturelle de classification des animaux:* xxxii+344 p. (Paris).

Eales, N. B.
(33) 1950, *Torsion in Gastropoda:* Malac. Soc. London, Proc., v. 28, p. 53-61, pl. 4-5.
(34) 1950a, *Secondary symmetry in gastropods:* Same, v. 28, p. 185-196.

Fischer, Paul
(35) 1880-87, *Manuel de conchyliologie:* xxiv+1369 p., 23 pl. (Paris).

Fretter, Vera
(36) 1941, *The genital ducts of some British stenoglossan prosobranchs:* Marine Biol. Assoc., Jour., v. 25, p. 173-211 (Cambridge).
(37) 1943, *Studies in the functional morphology and embryology of Onchidella celtica (Forbes & Hanley) and their bearing on its relationships:* Same, v. 25, p. 685-720.
(38) 1946, *The genital ducts of Theodoxus, Lamellaria and Trivia, and a discussion on their evolution in the prosobranchs:* Same, v. 26, p. 312-351.

Garstang, Walter
(39) 1929, *The origin and evolution of larval forms:* Rept. Brit. Assoc. Advance. Sci. (Glasgow, 1928), p. 77-98 (London).

Goldfuss, G. A.
(40) 1820, *Handbuch der Zoologie:* Handbuch der Naturgeschichte, ed. SCHUBERT, G. H., Theil 3, Abt. 1, xliv+696 p. (Nürnberg).

Grabau, A. W.
(41) 1904, *Phylogeny of Fusus and its allies:* Smithson. Misc. Coll., v. 44, no. 1417, 157 p., 18 pl. (Washington).

Graham, Alastair
(42) 1938, *On a ciliary process of food-collecting in the gastropod Turritella communis Risso:* Zool. Soc. London, Proc., ser. A, v. 108, p. 453-463.
(43) 1939, *On the structure of the alimentary canal of style-bearing prosobranchs:* Same, ser. B, v. 109, p. 75-109.
(44) 1949, *The molluscan stomach:* Roy. Soc. Edinburgh, Trans., v. 61, p. 737-778.
(45) 1955, *Molluscan diets:* Malac. Soc. London, Proc., v. 31, p. 144-159.

Gray, J. E.
(46) 1821, *A natural arrangement of Mollusca, according to their internal structure:* London Medical Repository, v. 15, p. 229-239.
(47) 1840, *Synopsis of the contents of the British Museum:* ed. 42, iv+248 p. (London).
(48) 1850, *Systematic arrangement of the figures:* in GRAY, M. E., Figures of molluscous animals, v. 4, p. 63-206 (London).
(49) 1853, *On the division of ctenobranchous gasteropodous Mollusca into larger groups and families:* Ann. & Mag. Nat. History, ser. 2, v. 11, p. 124-133 (London).
(50) 1857, *Guide to the systematic distribution of Mollusca in the British Museum:* pt. 1, xii+230 p. (London).

Guiart, Jules
(51) 1901, *Contribution à l'étude des gastéropodes opisthobranches et en particulier des céphalaspides:* Soc. zool. France, Mém., v. 14, p. 5-219 (Paris).

Hoffmann, Heinrich
(52) 1932-9, *Opisthobranchia:* in BRONN, H. G., Klassen und Ordnungen des Tier-Reichs,

v. 3, pt. 2, book 3, xi+1247 p., 1 pl. (Leipzig).

Hubendick, Bengt
(53) 1947, *Phylogenie und Tiergeographie der Siphonariidae. Zur Kenntnis der Phylogenie in der Ordnung Basommatophora und des Ursprungs der Pulmonatengruppe:* Zool. Bidrag, v. 24, p. 1-216 (Uppsala).

Ihering, Herman von
(54) 1876, *Versuch eines natürlichen Systemes der Mollusken:* Deutsch. malak. Gesell., Jahrb., 1876, p. 97-148 (Frankfurt a.M.).

Knight, J. B.
(55) 1952, *Primitive fossil gastropods and their bearing on gastropod classification:* Smithson. Misc. Coll. v. 117, no. 13, 56 p., 2 pl. (Washington).

————, **Bridge, Josiah, Shimer, H. W. & Shrock, R. R.**
(56) 1944, *Paleozoic Gastropoda:* in SHIMER, H. W., & SHROCK, R. R., Index fossils of North America, p. 437-479 (New York, London).

Krull, Herbert
(57) 1935, *Anatomische Untersuchungen an einheimischen Prosobranchiern und Beiträge zur Phylogenie der Gastropoden:* Zool. Jahrb., Abt. Anat., v. 60, p. 399-464 (Jena).

Lacaze-Duthiers, Henri
(58) 1872, *Du système nerveux des mollusques gastéropodes pulmonés aquatiques et d'un nouvel organe d'innervation:* Arch. Zool. expériment. et générale, v. 1, p. 437-500, pl. 1-4 (Paris).
(59) 1888, *La classification des gastéropodes, basée sur les dispositions du système nerveux:* Acad. Sci. Paris, Comptes Rendus, v. 106, p. 716-724.

Lamarck, J. B. de
(60) 1812, *Extrait du cours de zoologie du Muséum d'Histoire Naturelle:* 127 p. (Paris).

Lamy, Edouard
(61) 1937, *Sur le dimorphisme sexuel des coquilles:* Jour. Conchyl., v. 81, p. 283-301 (Paris).

Lang, Arnold
(62) 1891, *Versuch einer Erklärung der Asymmetrie der Gasteropoden:* Vierteljahrsschrift. naturforsch. Gesell. Zurich, Jahrg. 36, p. 339-371.

Lankester, E. R.
(63) 1883, *Mollusca:* Encyclopaedia Britannica, ed. 9, v. 16, p. 632-695 (London).

Latreille, P. A.
(64) 1825, *Familles naturelles du Règne Animal:* 570 p. (Paris).

Lebour, M. V.
(65) 1937, *The eggs and larvae of the British prosobranchs, with special reference to those living in the plankton:* Marine Biol. Assoc., Jour., v. 22, p. 106-166 (Cambridge).

Lemche, Henning
(66) 1948, *Northern and Arctic tectibranch gasteropods. I. The larval shells. II. A revision of the cephalaspid species:* K. dansk. vidensk. selsk. biol. Skr., v. 5, no. 3, 136 p. (København).

Lovén, S. L.
(67) 1848, *Malacozoologi:* Öfversigt kgl. Vetenskaps-Akad. Förhandl., for 1847, p. 175-199, pl. 3-6 (Stockholm).

Macdonald, J. D.
(68) 1880-81, *On the natural classification of Gasteropoda:* Linn. Soc. London (Zool.), Jour., v. 15, p. 161-167, 241-244.

Menke, C. T.
(69) 1830, *Synopsis methodica Molluscorum, generum omnium et specierum earum, quae in Museo Menkeano adservantur:* xvi+168 p. (Pyrmonti).

Milne Edwards, Henri
(70) 1848, *Note sur la classification naturelle des mollusques gastéropodes:* Ann. Sci. nat., Zool., ser. 3, v. 9, p. 102-112 (Paris).

Moore, Charles
(71) 1867, *On abnormal conditions of secondary deposits when connected with the Somersetshire and South Wales coal-basin and on the age of the Sutton and Southerndown series:* Geol. Soc. London, Quart. Jour., v. 23, p. 449-568, pl. 14-17.

Mörch, O. A. L.
(72) 1865, *Sur la classification moderne des mollusques:* Jour. Conchyl., v. 13, p. 396-401 (Paris).

Morton, J. E.
(73) 1955, *The functional morphology of the British Ellobiidae (Gastropoda pulmonata) with special reference to the digestive and reproductive systems:* Roy. Soc., Philos. Trans., ser. B, v. 239, p. 89-160 (London).
(74) 1955a, *The evolution of the Ellobiidae, with a discussion on the origin of pulmonates:* Zool. Soc. London, Proc., v. 125, p. 127-168.

Moseley, Henry
(75) 1838, *On the geometrical forms of turbinated and discoid shells:* Roy. Soc., Philos. Trans., v. 128, p. 351-370, pl. 9 (London).

Naef, Adolf
(76) 1911, *Studien zur generellen Morphologie der Mollusken. 1 Teil: Über Torsion und Asymmetrie der Gastropoden:* Ergebnisse

u. Fortschr. Zool., ed. SPENGEL, v. 3, p. 73-164 (Jena).

Nicholson, H. A. & Etheridge, Robert
(77) 1880, *A monograph of the Silurian fossils of the Girvan district in Ayrshire:* ix+341 p., 24 pl (Edinburgh, London).

Orbigny, Alcide d'
(78) 1842-3, *Paléontologie française. Terrains crétacés:* v. 2, 456 p., atlas, pl. 149-236 *bis* (Paris).

Pelseneer, Paul
(79) 1893, *La classification générale des mollusques:* Bull sci. France Belgique, v. 24, p. 347-371 (Lille).
(80) 1894, *Recherches sur divers opisthobranches:* Acad. Roy. Belgique, Mém. cour., v. 53, no. 8, 157 p., 25 pl. (Bruxelles).
(81) 1899, *Recherches morphologiques et phylogénétiques sur les mollusques archaiques:* Same, v. 57, 113 p., 24 pl.
(82) 1906, *Mollusca:* Treatise on Zoology, ed. E. R. LANKESTER, pt. 5, 355 p. (London).
(83) 1911, *Recherches sur l'embryologie des gastropodes:* Acad. Roy. Belgique, Mém., ser. 2, v. 3, fasc. 6, 167 p., 22 pl. (Bruxelles).
(84) 1934, *La durée de la vie et l'âge de la maturité sexuelle chez certains mollusques:* Soc. Roy. zool. Belgique, Ann., v. 64, p. 93-104 (Bruxelles).
(85) 1935, *Essai d'éthologie zoologique d'après l'étude des mollusques:* Acad. Roy. Belgique, Publ. Fondation A. De Potter, no. 1, 662 p. (Bruxelles).

Perrier, Rémy
(86) 1889, *Recherches sur l'anatomie et l'histologie du rein des gastéropodes prosobranches:* Ann. Sci. nat. Zool., ser. 7, v. 8, p. 61-315, pl. 5-13 (Paris).

Rafinesque, C. S.
(87) 1815, *Analyse de la Nature, ou Tableau de l'univers et des corps organisés:* 224 p. (Palermo).

Schweigger, A. F.
(88) 1820, *Handbuch der Naturgeschichte der skelettlosen ungegliederten Thiere:* xvi+ 776 p. (Leipzig).

Simroth, Heinrich
(89) 1896-1907, *Gastropoda prosobranchia:* in BRONN, H. G., Klassen und Ordnungen des Tier-Reichs, v. 3, pt. 2, book 1, vii+1056 p. 63 pl. (Leipzig).
(90) 1906, *Versuch einer neuen Deutung der Bellerophontiden:* Sitzungsber. naturforsch. Gesell. Leipzig, Jahrg. 32, p. 3-8.

———, **& Hoffmann, Heinrich**
(91) 1908-28, *Pulmonata:* in BRONN, H. G., Klassen und Ordnungen des Tier-Reichs, v. 3, pt. 2, book 2, xvi+1354 p., 44 pl. (Leipzig).

Smith, F. G. W.
(92) 1935, *The development of Patella vulgata:* Roy. Soc., Philos. Trans., ser. B, v. 225, p. 95-125 (London).

Spek, Josef
(93) 1919, *Beiträge zur Kenntnis der chemischen Zusammensetzung und Entwicklung der Radula der Gastropoden:* Zeitschr. wissensch. Zool., v. 118, p. 313-363, pl. v, vi (Leipzig).

Spengel, J. W.
(94) 1881, *Die Geruchsorgane und das Nervensystem der Mollusken:* Zeitschr. wiss. Zool., v. 35, p. 333-383, pl. 17-19 (Leipzig).

Taki, Iwao
(95) 1950, *Morphological observations on the gastropod operculum:* Venus, v. 16, p. 32-48 (Tokyo).

Termier, Geneviève, & Termier, Henri
(96) 1952, *Classe des gastéropodes:* Traité de Paléontologie, ed. J. PIVETEAU, v. 2, p. 365-460, Masson (Paris).

Thiele, Johannes
(97) 1925-1956, *Mollusca = Weichtiere:* Handbuch der Zoologie, gegründet W. KÜKENTHAL, v. 5, p. 15-258 (last 2 p. only in 1956, with Nachtrag by S. JAEKEL, p. 259-275) (Berlin, Leipzig).
(98) 1929-31, *Handbuch der systematischen Weichtierkunde:* v. 1 (Loricata & Gastropoda), vi+778 p. (Jena).

Thompson, D'A. W.
(99) 1917, *On growth and form:* xv+793 p. (Cambridge).

Thompson, T. E.
(100) 1958, *The natural history, embryology, larval biology and post-larval development of Adalaria proxima (Alder and Hancock)* (Gastropoda Opisthobranchia): Roy. Soc., Phil. Trans., ser. B, v. 242, p. 1-58 (London).

Thorson, Gunnar
(101) 1946, *Reproduction and larval development of Danish marine bottom invertebrates:* Meddel. Komm. Danmarks Fiskeri- og Havunders., Plankton, v. 4, 523 p. (København).
(102) 1950, *Reproduction and larval ecology of marine bottom invertebrates:* Biol. Reviews Cambridge Philos. Soc., v. 25, p. 1-45.

Troschel, F. H.
(103) 1856-93, *Das Gebiss der Schnecken, zur Begründung einer natürlichen Classification:* v. 1, 252 p., 1856-61; v. 2, 409 p., 1866-93 (p. 247-409 by J. THIELE) (Berlin).

Vinogradov, A. P.
(104) 1953, *The elementary chemical composition of marine organisms:* Sears Foundation Ma-

rine Research, Mem., no. 2, xiv+647 p. (New Haven).

Wenz, W.
(105) 1938-44, *Gastropoda. Allgemeiner Teil und Prosobranchia:* Handbuch der Paläozoologie, ed. O. H. SCHINDEWOLF, v. 6, pts 1-7, 1639 p.; Teil 1, 1938; 2, 1938; 3, 1939; 4, 1940; 5, 1941; 6, 1943; 7, 1944 (Berlin).
(106) 1940, *Ursprung und frühe Stammesgeschichte der Gastropoden:* Archiv f. Molluskenkunde, v. 72, p. 1-10 (Frankfurt a. M.).

Woodward, S. P.
(107) 1851-56, *A manual of the Mollusca:* pt. 1, viii+158 p., pl. 1-12, 1851; pt. 2, xii+330 p., pl. 13-24, 1854; pt. 3, xvi+486 p., 1856 (London).

Wrigley, Arthur
(108) 1934, *English Eocene and Oligocene Cassididae, with notes on the nomenclature and morphology of the family:* Malac. Soc. London, Proc., v. 21, p. 108-130, pl. 15-17.
(109) 1948, *The colour patterns and sculpture of molluscan shells:* Same, v. 27, p. 206-217.
(110) 1949, *The Structure of the calcareous operculum of Natica:* Same, v. 28, p. 23-26.

Yonge, C. M.
(111) 1938, *Evolution of ciliary feeding in the Prosobranchia, with an account of feeding in Capulus ungaricus:* Marine Biol. Assoc., v. 22, p. 453-468 (Cambridge).
(112) 1947, *The pallial organs in the aspidobranch Gastropoda and their evolution throughout the Mollusca:* Philos. Trans. Roy. Soc., ser. B, v. 232, p. 443-518 (London).

Zittel, K. A. von
(113) 1881-85, *Mollusca und Arthropoda:* Handbuch der Palaeontologie, pt. 1 (Palaeozoologie), v. 2, 893 p. (München, Leipzig).

SOURCES OF ILLUSTRATIONS

(114) Adams, Arthur, & Reeve, L.
(115) Cox, L. R.
(116) Dall, W. H.
(117) Delpey, Geneviève
(118) Edwards, F. E.
(119) Haller, Béla
(120) Harris, G. F.
(121) Hudleston, W. H.

(122) Ivanov, A. B.
(123) Kesteven, H. L.
(124) Kobelt, Wilhelm
(125) Lacaze-Duthiers, Henri
(126) Lang, Arnold
(127) Lebour, M. V.
(128) Orbigny, Alcide d'
(129) Parker, T. J., & Haswell, W. A.

(130) Pelseneer, Paul
(131) Pilsbry, H. A.
(132) Quoy, J. R. C., & Gaimard, J. P.
(133) Sandberger, C. L. F.
(134) Taylor, J. W.
(135) Tryon, G. W.
(136) Watson, R. B.
(137) Wood, S. V.

SYSTEMATIC DESCRIPTIONS

By J. BROOKES KNIGHT[1], L. R. COX[2], A. MYRA KEEN[3], R. L. BATTEN[4], E. L. YOCHELSON[5], and ROBERT ROBERTSON[6]

CONTENTS

[1] Honorary Research Associate, Smithsonian Institution, Washington, D.C.; Longboat Key, Fla.
[2] British Museum (Natural History), London, England.
[3] School of Mineral Sciences, Stanford University, Stanford, Calif.
[4] Department of Geology, University of Wisconsin, Madison, Wis.
[5] United States Geological Survey, Washington, D.C.
[6] Museum of Comparative Zoology, Harvard University, Cambridge, Mass.

INTRODUCTION

The authorship of this section, mainly concerned with the Archaeogastropoda, is as follows: All genera with Paleozoic type species by J. B. KNIGHT, R. L. BATTEN & E. L. YOCHELSON; all genera with Mesozoic type species by L. R. Cox; Cenozoic Pleurotomariidae, Haliotidae, and Neritopsidae by L. R. Cox; Cenozoic Fissurellidae and Scissurellidae by MYRA KEEN aided in part by GRACE JOHNSON; Phasianellidae by ROBERT ROBERTSON; all other genera with Cenozoic type species by MYRA KEEN. Contributions have been integrated by L. R. Cox.

Acknowledgments for advice on various matters relating to Recent gastropods are made to Prof. ALASTAIR GRAHAM, Dr. D. R. CROFTS, Dr. VERA FRETTER, Dr. J. E. MORTON, and Dr. H. BURRINGTON BAKER. Also, appreciation is expressed to Mrs. Nancy Lou Patterson, who prepared most of the drawings on Paleozoic gastropods in systematic portions of the text and to Miss M. F. PRIOR, Miss L. RIPLEY, Mrs. SALLY KAICHER, and the late Mr. G. L. WILKINS for work on other illustrations. Prof. JEAN ROGER of Paris kindly loaned specimens of *Michaletia semigranulata* and *Cochleochilus cottaldinus*. Dr. N. D. NEWELL supplied photographs of type specimens of *Paraeuryalox, Hesperocirrus,* and *Sororcula.*

Class GASTROPODA Cuvier, 1797

[*nom. correct.* DUMÉRIL, 1806, *pro* 'gastéropodes' CUVIER, 1797, invalid vernacular name, *nom. auct. conserv.* proposed Cox, 1958 (ICZN pend.)] [*=Gasteropodia+Spironotia* RAFINESQUE, 1815; Gasteropoda SCHWEIGGER, 1820 (also GOLDFUSS, 1820); Gasteropodophora GRAY, 1821; Paracephalophora DE BLAINVILLE, 1824; Gastraeopoda₂ BECK, 1837; Pselaphocephala BRONN, 1862; Gasterozoa THIELE, 1926]

Definition of the class has been given in a foregoing section (p. *186*). *L.Cam.-Rec.*

Subclass PROSOBRANCHIA Milne Edwards, 1848

[*nom. emend.* KEFERSTEIN, 1863 (*pro* Prosobranchiata *nom. correct.* S. P. WOODWARD, 1851, also MORRIS and LYCETT, 1851, *pro* 'prosobranches' MILNE EDWARDS, 1848, invalid vernacular name), *nom. auct. conserv.* proposed Cox, 1958 (ICZN pend.)] [*=*Ctenobranchiata SCHWEIGGER, 1820, *extent.* GRAY, 1840; Streptoneura SPENGEL, 1881]

Gastropoda displaying full effects of larval torsion in that auricle (or auricles), together with ctenidium (or ctenidia) when present, lie anterior to ventricle; visceral nerve cords cross, one from right pleural ganglion to left side passing above and one from left pleural ganglion to right side passing below alimentary canal; mantle cavity open to front, containing, on right side, anteriorly directed rectum and anus. Except in a few forms, mantle cavity also contains either one ctenidium and osphradium, lying on left side, or paired but rarely equal ctenidia and osphradia. Head with single pair of tentacles. Sexes distinct except in a few genera. Operculum commonly but not invariably present. Shell of many shapes, absent only rarely. Habitat marine, fresh-water, or terrestrial. *L.Cam.-Rec.*

Order ARCHAEOGASTROPODA Thiele, 1925

[*=*Scutibranches CUVIER, 1817 (*partim*); Scutibranchia GOLDFUSS, 1820, restricted FISCHER, 1885; Aspidobranchiata SCHWEIGGER, 1820, *extent.* PELSENEER, 1893; Diotocardia MÖRCH, 1865]

Prosobranchia in which ctenidia (present in all but a few genera) are "aspidobranch" (i.e., bipectinate, with filaments alternating on two sides of axis) and free at front end; ctenidia and osphradia paired in more primitive families, otherwise single. No siphon or proboscis. Heart with two auricles, except in Patellacea and Helicinidae. Kidneys two, except in Patellacea and Neritacea, the right large, the left reduced. Gonoduct, except in Neritacea, opening in both sexes into right kidney, genital products being thence discharged by way of ureter and mantle cavity into the sea; male thus without prostate and penis. Nervous system not concentrated, pedal cords ladder-like. Inner layers of shell nacreous in many but not all genera. Habitat marine (except some Neritacea). *L.Cam.-Rec.*

Suborder BELLEROPHONTINA Ulrich & Scofield, 1897

[*nom. correct.* Cox & KNIGHT (*ex* Bellerophontacea ULRICH & SCOFIELD, 1897, subordinal name)] [*=*Prorhipidoglossa, Amphigastropoda SIMROTH, 1906; Planspiralia, Belleromorpha NAEF, 1911]

Shell most commonly isostrophic, rarely slightly asymmetrical; mostly closely coiled, but in some genera cyrtiform; predominantly with median labral sinus or slit, or tremata, probably exhalant in function and usually generating a selenizone; shell wall of variable thickness, no evidence of nacre; operculum unknown; presence of paired and equal ctenidia and osphradia, also of single pair of retractor muscles, inferred (latter from muscle scars); nothing known of other soft parts. *L.Cam.-L.Trias.*

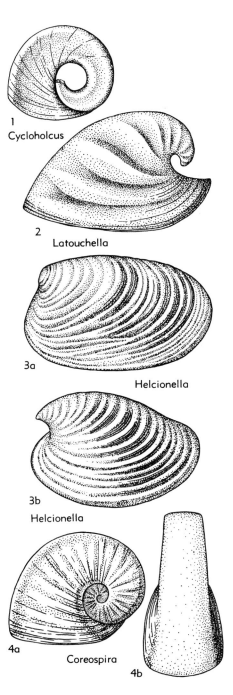

FIG. 89. Helcionellacea (Helcionellidae, Coreospiridae) (p. *1172*).

Superfamily HELCIONELLACEA Wenz, 1938

[*nom. transl.* KNIGHT, BATTEN & YOCHELSON, herein (*ex* Helcionellinae WENZ, 1938)]

Cap-shaped to coiled bellerophontiform shells; commonly with strong rugae clearly defined on both interior and exterior; with septum or septa partitioning off the apex. *L.Cam.-U.Cam.*

Family HELCIONELLIDAE Wenz, 1938

[*nom. transl.* KNIGHT, BATTEN & YOCHELSON herein (*ex* Helcionellinae WENZ, 1938)]

Elongate cap-shaped shells lacking a train; apex not central, presumably posterior. *L.Cam.-U.Cam.*

Helcionella GRABAU & SHIMER, 1909 [*Metoptoma? rugosa* HALL, 1847 =*Helcion subrugosa* D'ORBIGNY, 1850, *pro H. rugosa* (HALL) D'ORBIGNY, 1850, *non H. rugosa* J.SOWERBY, 1817)] [?=*Quilcanella* RUSCONI, 1952 (125, p. 86); ?*Pichynella* RUSCONI, 1954 (125, p. 2)]. Shell moderately low to high cap-shaped, with very strong concentric rugae; muscle scars unknown. *Cam.*, N.Am.-N.Afr.-NE.Asia.——FIG. 89,*3*. **H. subrugosa* (D'ORBIGNY), *L.Cam.*, N.Y.; *3a,b*, individuals showing extremes in variation, ×3.3.

Family COREOSPIRIDAE Knight, 1947

Shell with complete or incomplete coiling; no anal emargination; flattened, with nearly rectangular cross section; with posterior trainlike extension of shell margin. *L.Cam.-U.Cam.*

Latouchella COBBOLD, 1921 [**L. costata*] [=*Oelandia* WESTERGÅRD, 1936]. Cap-shaped, with apex curved backward; surface with strong collabral rugae; much resembles *Helcionella* except for its posterior train and inferred orientation (16, p. 366). *Cam.*, N.Am.-Eu.-NE.Asia.——FIG. 89,*2*. *L. pauciplicata* (WESTERGÅRD), *M.Cam.*, Swed.; left side; ×4.

Coreospira SAITO, 1936 [**C. rugosa*]. Tightly coiled, loosely coiled, or whorls barely in contact; disclike, outer whorl face flattened and with protruding margin; surface with collabral rugae or growth lines. *L.Cam.-M.Cam.*, N.Am.-NE.Asia. —— FIG. 89,*4*. **C. rugosa*, *L.Cam.*, Korea; *4a,b*, left side, anterior, both ×10.

Cycloholcus KNIGHT, 1947 [**C. nummus*]. Disclike, possibly with pierced umbilici; sides with a rounded groove (73, p. 5). *U.Cam.*, N.Am.—— FIG. 89,*1*. **C. nummus*, Tenn.; ×2.7.

Superfamily
BELLEROPHONTACEA
M'Coy, 1851

[*nom. transl.* WENZ, 1938 (*ex* Bellerophontidae M'COY, 1851)]

Characters as defined for suborder, but invariably with median emargination or tremata. *U.Cam.-L.Trias.*

Although the soft parts of bellerophont gastropods have never been observed, their shells are very similar in many respects to those of the pleurotomarians and show significant homologies with them. As with pleurotomarians, the bellerophont shell typically consists of a long narrow tube (the helicocone) which expands from a point and is coiled loosely on itself. In both groups an anal emargination occurs close to the middle of the labrum. In view of this fact, it is difficult to avoid the conclusion that the internal anatomy of the bellerophonts was very much like that of the pleurotomarians. The groups differ in that the coiling of the bellerophont shell is isostrophic, whereas the pleurotomarian shell is conispiral. The living pleurotomarians retain vestiges of primitive symmetry, for both members of bilaterally paired internal organs, such as ctenidia, are in general developed, although not equally. In this respect they differ from all other living gastropods. Because the bellerophonts appear earlier in the fossil record the vestigial symmetry was probably expressed more fully in them, a view supported by the bilaterally symmetrical shell. Indeed, it seems probable that the degree of bilateral symmetry was as high as could be consistent with torsion in early ontogeny (Fig. 57, *Knightites*).

The bilateral symmetry of the shell has led some workers to infer that torsion did

FIG. 90. Bellerophontacea (Cyrtolitidae) (p. *1174-1175*).

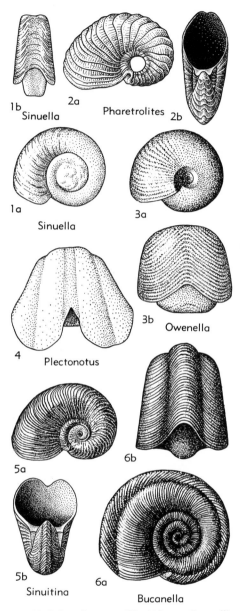

FIG. 91. Bellerophontacea (Sinuitidae——Bucanellinae). (p. *1175*).

not take place in the bellerophonts as it does in Pleurotomariacea and all other Anisopleura (SIMROTH, 1906; WENZ, 1940; MOORE, in MOORE, LALICKER & FISCHER, 1952; BOETTGER, 1955). If this were true, the shell would have been carried by bellerophont gastropods with the outer lip and

anal emargination behind, an orientation quite opposite to that of the pleurotomarians, which resemble the bellerophonts so closely in other respects. The massive coil, which is commonly accompanied by an even more massive parietal inductura, would then have been poised above the head, in the position termed "exogastric" by some authors. This would have presented mechanical difficulties of no small magnitude for an animal moving about with its shell, and it is hard to see how the head and foot could have been withdrawn into the shell.

Apparently these authors were misled by the belief that torsion originally took place after development of adult musculature. CROFTS (1955) has shown that the larval left-hand muscle, the right-hand (columellar) muscle of the adult, had not begun to develop until after torsion had reached 90 degrees, so that torsion was not the cause of asymmetrical coiling.

For these reasons the Bellerophontacea are thought to have undergone torsion although they had a symmetrically coiled shell (76). They are here classed in the Prosobranchia and interpreted as the earliest and most primitive Archaeogastropoda. Because of their apparent affinities with the pleurotomarians, it is suggested that they were not only aspidobranch, but also rhipidoglossate, feeding chiefly on vegetable matter.

Family CYRTOLITIDAE S. A. Miller, 1889

[?=Procarinariidae WENZ, 1938]

Anal emargination a shallow sinus, commonly angular but without slit or selenizone; coiling generally open, especially in adult whorls. *U.Cam.-L.Sil.*

Strepsodiscus KNIGHT, 1948 [*S. major*]. Anal emargination a deep angular sinus; coiling slightly asymmetrical, with closely coiled early whorls protruding toward left, last whorl disjunct, all whorls sharply crested; has posterior train; growth lines are only surface features known (75, p. 3). *U.Cam.*, N.Am.——FIG. 90,6. *S. major*, Colo.; 6a-c, left side, apertural, anterior views, ×1.3.

Cloudia KNIGHT, 1947 [*C. buttsi*]. Anterior lip with gently curved sinus; coiling close, with wide, steep umbilici; whorl section lozenge-shaped, with sharply rounded lateral angles; ornament unknown (73, p. 5). *U.Cam.*, N.Am.——FIG. 90,1. *C. buttsi*, Ala.; 1a,b, apertural and left sides of steinkern, ×1.

Trigyra RAYMOND, 1908 [*T. ulrichi*]. Anterior

emargination shallow, V-shaped; coiling disjunct; 5 strong spiral costae on outer whorl surface, comprising a single median one, 2 on outer angles, and 2 about midway between the others; surface marked by 2 sets of fine obscure threads that cross one another. *M.Ord.*, N.Am.——Fig. 90,2. *T. ulrichi*, Vt.; *2a,b*, anterior and left side, ×2.

Cyrtolites Conrad, 1838 [*C. ornatus*] [=*Microceras*, Hall, 1845]. Anterior lip with somewhat shallow, angular sinus, aperture quadrate, whorls barely in contact or possibly disjunct in some species; with sharp median carina and pair of lateral ridges; umbilici widely open; ornament wide collabral undulations and fine cancellating threads. *M.Ord.-L.Sil.*, N.Am.-Eu.——Fig. 90,4. *C. ornatus*, U.Ord., N.Y.; *4a,b*, left side and apertural views, ×2.

Cyrtodiscus Perner, 1903 [*Oxydiscus (Cyrtodiscus) procer*; SD Knight, 1937]. Anterior lip with shallow V-shaped sinus; coiling discoidal with whorls seemingly in contact; ornament spiral threads or wanting. *M.Ord.-U.Ord.*, N.Am.-Eu.-Asia.——Fig. 90,3. *C. procer* (Perner), Ord., Czech.; *3a,b*, left side and adapertural views, ×2.

?Procarinaria Perner, 1911 [*Carinaria bohemica* Perner, 1903]. Anterior lip sharply angular but without sinus; whorls enlarging very rapidly, angular above, with high, thin carina; ornament collabral undulations. *U.Sil.*, Eu.——Fig. 90,5. *P. bohemica* (Perner), Czech.; left side, ×2.

Family SINUITIDAE Dall in Zittel-Eastman, 1913

[=Protowarthiidae Ulrich & Scofield, 1897 (ICZN pend.)]

Anal emargination mostly an open U-shaped sinus but narrowing to a broad slit in some advanced Euphemitinae. *U.Cam.-M.Perm.*

Subfamily BUCANELLINAE Koken, 1925

[*nom. transl.* Knight, Batten & Yochelson, herein (*ex* Bucaniellidae Koken, 1925)]

Sinus relatively small; phaneromphalous; surface marked by fine, sharp collabral or spiral threads. *U.Cam.-M.Perm.*

Owenella Ulrich & Scofield, 1897 [*Bellerophon antiquatus* Whitfield, 1878]. Rounded, as wide as long, umbilici narrow. *U.Cam.*, N.Am.——Fig. 91,3. *O. antiquata* (Whitfield), Wis.; *3a,b*, left and anterior side, ×3.3.

Sinuella Knight, 1947 [*S. minuta*]. Small, narrow, with shallow peripheral groove; umbilici wide (73, p. 8). *U.Cam.*, N.Am.——Fig. 91,1. *S. minuta*, Tex.; *1a,b*, left and anterior sides, ×20.

Bucanella Meek, 1871 [*B. nana*]. With 3 spiral lobes, the central more prominent than the lateral ones. *Ord.-Dev.*, N.Am.-S.Am.-Eu.-N.Afr.

B. (Bucanella) [=*Bucaniella* Koken, 1896 (obj.); *Tritonophon* Öpik, 1953]. Spiral lobes clearly marked, umbilici wide. Ornament transverse in earlier species, spiral in later ones. *L.Ord.-Dev.*,

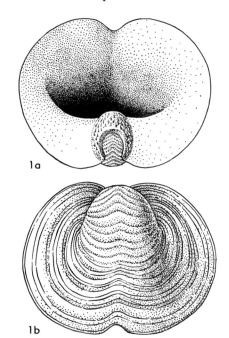

Ptomatis

Fig. 92. Bellerophontacea (Sinuitidae——Sinuitinae) (p. *1177*).

N.Am.-Eu.——Fig. 91,6. *B. (B.) nana*, L.Ord., Colo.; *6a,b*, left and anterior sides, ×5.3.

B. (Plectonotus) Clarke, 1899 [*P. derbyi*; SD Clarke, 1913]. Sinus relatively narrow, pointed; pseudoselenizone bordered by faint threads; central lobe broad, indistinct; umbilici narrow; ornament unknown. *Dev.*, N.Am.-S.Am.-Eu.-N.Afr. ——Fig. 91,4. *B. (P.) derbyi* (Clarke), Brazil; anterior side of steinkern, ×1.

Pharetrolites Wenz, 1943 [*Cyrtolites pharetra* Lindström, 1884]. Anterior lip with shallow angular sinus; discoidal coil with few whorls and wide, pierced umbilici; ornament collabral imbricating lamellae (147, p. 1941). *M.Sil.*, Eu.—— Fig. 91,2. *P. pharetra* (Lindström), Gotl.; *2a,b*, left and apertural sides, ×2 (90).

Sinuitina Knight, 1945 [*Tropidocyclus cordiformis* Newell, 1935]. Moderately narrow; central lobe narrow, not sharply delimited; a small channel within a narrow ridge surrounding the narrow open umbilici (71, p. 333). *Sil.-M.Perm.*, N.Am.-Eu.——Fig. 91,5. *S. cordiformis* (Newell), U. Penn., Kan.; *5a,b*, left and apertural sides, ×2.

Subfamily SINUITINAE Dall in Zittel-Eastman, 1913

[*nom. transl.* Knight, Batten & Yochelson, herein (*ex* Sinuitidae Dall, 1913)]

Sinus relatively wide. *U.Cam.-M.Dev.*

Anconochilus Knight, 1947 [*A. barnesi*]. Lateral

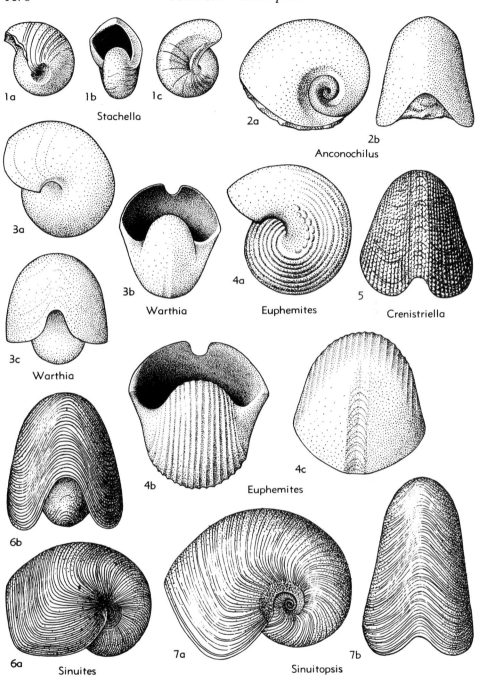

1a 1b 1c
Stachella

2a
2b
Anconochilus

3a

3b
Warthia

4a
Euphemites

5
Crenistriella

3c
Warthia

4b
Euphemites

4c

6b

6a
Sinuites

7a

7b
Sinuitopsis

FIG. 93. Bellerophontacea . Sinuitidae——Sinuitinae, Euphemitinae) (p. 1175-1179).

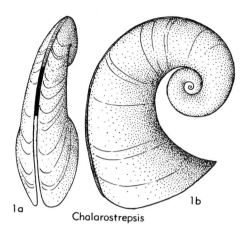

1a

1b

Chalarostrepsis

FIG. 94. Bellerophontacea (Bellerophontidae——
Tropidiscinae) (p. *1179*).

lips merging into a posterior train; surface features
unknown (73, p. 7). *U.Cam.*, N.Am.——FIG. 93,
2. **A. barnesi*, Tex.; *2a,b*, left and anterior sides,
×1.

Sinuites KOKEN, 1896 [**Bellerophon bilobatus*
SOWERBY, 1839; SD BASSLER, 1915]. Lateral lips
lobelike, close to sides; bases of columellar lips
surrounded by a delicate inductura. *Ord.*, N.Am.-
Eu.-N.Afr.-NE.Asia.

S. (Sinuites) [=*Protowarthia* ULRICH & SCOFIELD,
1897; *Discolites* EMMONS, 1855 (*non* MONTFORT,
1808)]. Relatively wide, anomphalous. *Ord.*, N.
Am.-Eu.-N.Afr.——FIG. 93,6. **S. (S.) bilobatus*
(SOWERBY), M.Ord., Eng.; *6a,b*, left and anterior
sides, ×1.5.

S. (Sinuitopsis) PERNER, 1903 [**S. neglecta;* SD
COSSMANN, 1904]. Rather narrow, with shallow
open umbilici. *U.Ord.*, Eu.-NE.Asia.——FIG. 93,
7. **S. (S.) neglecta*, Czech.; *7a,b*, left and anterior sides, ×2.

Ptomatis CLARKE, 1899 [**Bellerophon patulus*
HALL, 1843; SD PERNER, 1903] [=*Fuchsella*
SPRIESTERSBACH, 1942 (133, p. 156)]. Anterior
sinus shallow, wide; apertural margins widely explanate; parietal inductura (in type species) moderately thick, bearing longitudinal pustules, lacking behind, as though abraded; collabral ornament of growth lines and undulations, *M.Dev.*,
N.Am.-S.Am.-S.Afr.——FIG. 92,*1*. **P. patulus*
(HALL), N.Y.; *1a,b*, apertural and abapertural
sides, ×1.3.

Crenistriella KNIGHT, 1945 [**Bellerophon crenistria*
HALL, 1879]. Lateral lips gently convex in side
view; shallow peripheral depression; ornament
many spiral rows of fine pustules (71, p. 344).
M.Dev., N.Am.——FIG. 93,*5*. **C. crenistria*
(HALL), N.Y.; anterior side, ×3.

Subfamily EUPHEMITINAE Knight, 1956

Sinus relatively narrow, almost a slit in
more advanced species; anterior lip thin,
joining at sharp angle the thickened lateral
lips, which are close to the sides; shell exterior entirely covered by inductural layers
which comprise the periunductura (102),
secreted by an anterior flap of the mantle,
and the inductura proper, parietal in position and secreted by a posterior lobe of the
mantle that extends over the periunductura
for a considerable distance beyond the aperture; in some species, a third layer (coinductura, 102) forms a parietal thickening over

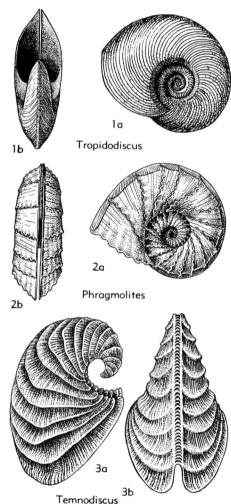

1a

1b   Tropidodiscus

2a

2b   Phragmolites

3a

3b

Temnodiscus

FIG. 95. Bellerophontacea (Bellerophontidae——
Tropidiscinae) (p. *1179*).

the inductura proper within the aperture; a more or less broad selenizone occurs but is generally obscured by the perinductura. *?Dev., Miss.-Perm.*

Euphemites WARTHIN, 1930 [*pro Euphemus* M'COY, 1844 (*non* LAPORTE-CASTELNAU, 1836)] [*Bellerophon urii* FLEMING, 1828; SD WAAGEN, 1880]. Numerous (approximately 10) more or less strong sharp spiral cords on parietal inductura, reaching far within whorls and commonly continuing with

inductura over exterior rather more than a half volution; similar cords on coinductura where this layer is present; perinductural pustules occur in some species. *?Dev., L.Carb.(Miss.)-Perm.*, Eu.-N.Am.-S.Am.-N.Afr.-Asia.——FIG. 93,4. *E. urii* (FLEMING), L.Carb., Scot.; *4a-c,* left, apertural, abapertural sides, ×2.7.

Warthia WAAGEN, 1880 [*W. brevisinuata;* SD DE KONINCK, 1882]. Closely resembles *Euphemites* but lacks ornament. *U.Carb.(Penn.)-M.Perm.*, Asia-Austral.-N.Am. —— FIG. 93,3. *W. polita*

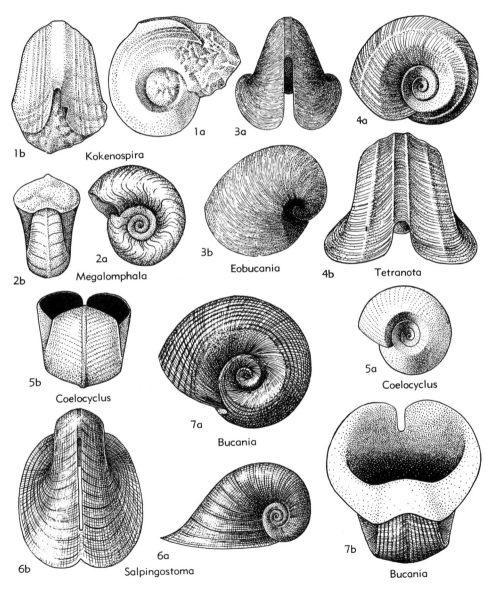

FIG. 96. Bellerophontacea (Bellerophontidae——Bucaniinae) (p. *1179-1180*).

WAAGEN, Perm., India; *3a-c,* left, apertural, anterior sides, ×4.

?**Stachella** WAAGEN, 1880 [**Bellerophon pseudohelix* STACHE, 1877; SD deKONINCK, 1883]. Slightly asymmetrical; no ornament except growth lines; organization of shell layers unknown. *L. Perm.-M.Perm.,* Eu.-SE.Asia.——FIG. 93,*1.* **S. pseudohelix* (STACHE), *M.Perm.,* Ger.; *1a-c,* left, apertural, right sides, ×1 (134).

Family BELLEROPHONTIDAE M'Coy, 1851

Anal emargination generally consisting of a slit. *U.Cam.-L.Trias.*

Subfamily TROPIDODISCINAE Knight, 1956

Coil narrow, with wide umbilici; slit deep; commonly with a definite posterior train. *U.Cam.-Dev.*

Chalarostrepsis KNIGHT, 1948 [**C. praecursor*]. Last half whorl disjunct; slit deep; no ornament except growth lines (76, p. 5). *U.Cam.,* N.Am.——FIG. 94,*1.* **C. praecursor,* Can.(Que.); *1a,b,* oblique anterior, left side, ×2.7.

Tropidodiscus MEEK & WORTHEN, 1866 [*pro Tropidiscus* MEEK, 1866 (*non* STEIN, 1855)] [**Bellerophon curvilineatus* CONRAD, 1842] [=*Tropidocyclus* deKONINCK, 1882 (obj.); *Oxydiscus* KOKEN, 1889 (obj.); *Zonidiscus* SPITZ, 1907; *Joleaudella* PATTE, 1929]. Lenticular, with acuminate periphery; slit deep, narrow, selenizone narrow; ornament collabral lines or imbricating lamellae. *L. Ord.-Dev.,* N.Am.-S.Am.-Eu.-Asia.——FIG. 95,*1.* **T. curvilineatus* (CONRAD), L.Dev., N.Y.; *1a,b,* left and apertural sides, ×1.3.

Phragmolites CONRAD, 1838 [**P. compressus*] [=*Conradella* ULRICH & SCOFIELD, 1897]. Whorls more or less rounded; apertural margins flaring periodically to form narrow, strongly scalloped varices; deep, narrow slit between low, sharp keels which are joined at top by the selenizone; ornament obscure spiral threads. *M.Ord.-U.Ord.,* N. Am.-Eu.——FIG. 95,*2. P. obliqua* (ULRICH & SCOFIELD), M.Ord., Minn.; *2a,b,* left and anterior sides, ×2.7.

Temnodiscus KOKEN, 1896 [**Cyrtolites lamellifer* LINDSTRÖM, 1884; SD REED, 1920] [=*Cyrtolitina* ULRICH in ULRICH & SCOFIELD, 1897 (obj.)]. Whorls disjunct; slit moderately deep; varices formed by rather strong foliaceous periodic expansions of lateral lips; ornament numerous spiral cords. *M.Ord.-Sil.,* N.Am.-Eu.——FIG. 95,*3.* **T. lamellifer* (LINDSTRÖM), M.Sil., Gotl.; *3a,b,* left and anterior sides, ×2.7.

Subfamily BUCANIINAE Ulrich & Scofield, 1897

[*nom. transl.* KNIGHT, BATTEN & YOCHELSON, herein (*ex* Bucaniidae ULRICH & SCOFIELD, 1897)] [=Salpingostominae KOKEN, 1925]

Apertural margins tending to flare; umbilici open; mostly with slit and selenizone,

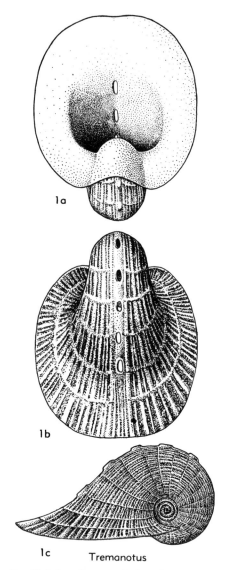

1a

1b

1c   Tremanotus

FIG. 97. Bellerophontacea (Bellerophontidae—Bucaniinae) (p. *1180*).

but some with slit not continuing into the apertural expansion and others with a series of tremata. *L.Ord.-Dev.*

Tribe BUCANIIDES Ulrich & Scofield, 1897

[*nom. transl.* KNIGHT, BATTEN & YOCHELSON, herein (*ex* Bucaniidae ULRICH & SCOFIELD, 1897)]

Exhalant emargination a short slit. *M. Ord.-Dev.*

Eobucania KOBAYASHI, 1955 [**E. pulchra*]. With few rapidly expanding whorls, apertural margin

with moderately deep slit, slightly concave seleni-zone between pair of threads on slight dorsal elevation; ill-defined angulation marking off lateral from posterior slopes; aperture flaring slightly at angulation (78, p. 404). L.Ord., N.Am.——Fig. 96,3. *E. pulchra,* Can.(B.C.); *3a,b,* anterior and left sides, ×4 (Kobayashi).

Bucania HALL, 1847 [*Bellerophon sulcatinus* EMMONS, 1842; SD WAAGEN, 1880] [=?*Tubogyra* PERNER, 1903; *Loxobucania* KNIGHT, 1942 (70, p. 487)]. Aperture but little, if at all, expanded, wider than long, especially at rear; ornament spiral threads, or threads normal to anterior margin and converging forward, or both types of threads crossing to form a pitted surface. *M.Ord.-Sil.,* N.Am.-Eu.-NE.Asia.——Fig. 96,7. *B. sulcatina* (EMMONS), M.Ord., N.Y.; *7a,b,* left and apertural sides, ×1.3.

Tetranota ULRICH & SCOFIELD, 1897 [*Bucania bidorsata* HALL, 1847]. Resembles *Bucania* in form but selenizone lies on low crest between pair of spiral cords; some species with additional spiral cords on slopes between crest and circumumbilical angle; ornament collabral threads. *M.Ord.-U.Ord.,* N.Am.-Eu.——Fig. 96,4. *T. bidorsata* (HALL), M.Ord., N.Y.; *4a,b,* left and anterior sides, ×2.7.

Kokenospira BASSLER, 1915 [pro *Kokenia* ULRICH & SCOFIELD, 1897 (non HOLZAPFEL, 1895)] [*Bucaniella esthona* KOKEN, 1889]. Resembles *Tetranota* but has higher whorls and narrower umbilici; spiral cords more numerous and smaller. *M.Ord.-U.Ord.,* N.Am.-Eu.——Fig. 96,1. *K. esthona* (KOKEN), Ord. (float), Ger., *1a,b,* right side and anterior view of steinkern, ×1.3.

?Megalomphala ULRICH & SCOFIELD, 1897 [*Bellerophon contortus* EICHWALD, 1860]. Like *Bucania* but lacks spiral sculpture. *M.Ord.-Dev.,* N.Am.-Eu.——Fig. 96,2. *M. contorta* (EICHWALD), M.Ord., Est.; *2a,b,* left and apertural sides, ×1 (37).

Coelocyclus PERNER, 1903 [*Bellerophon (Coelocyclus) rarissimus*]. Like *Bucania* but with umbilical slopes conforming to uniform conical slope and without spiral ornament. *M.Sil.-M.Dev.,* N.Am.-Eu.——Fig. 96,5. *C. perplexus* (WALCOTT), M. Dev., Nev.; *5a,b,* left and apertural sides, ×0.7.

Tribe SALPINGOSTOMATIDES Koken, 1925

[*nom. transl.* KNIGHT, BATTEN & YOCHELSON, herein (*ex* Salpingostominae KOKEN, 1925)]

Exhalant orifice consisting of one or more tremata. *M.Ord.-Sil.*

Salpingostoma C. F. ROEMER, 1876 [*Bellerophon megalostoma* EICHWALD, 1840]. Aperture expanded widely; slit a trema confined to whorl side, not extending onto lip, generating a selenizone; ornament growth lines. *M.Ord.-Sil.,* N.Am.-Eu.——Fig. 96,6. *S. boulli* (WHITFIELD), M.Ord., Minn.; *6a,b,* left and apertural sides, ×0.7.

Tremanotus HALL, 1865 [*T. alpheus*] [=*Trematonotus* FISCHER, 1883 (obj.); *Gyrotrema* LIND-

STRÖM, 1884 (obj.); *Tremagyrus* PERNER, 1903]. Aperture rather widely expanded at final growth stage; slit represented by a row of tremata, all but last few closed, not extending onto expanded lip; ornament spiral cords of several sizes or growth lines alone. *M.Ord.-M.Sil.,* N.Am.-Eu.-Austral.——Fig. 97,1. *T. alpheus,* M.Sil., N.Y.; *1a-c,* apertural, adapertural, left sides, ×0.7.

Subfamily CARINAROPSINAE Ulrich & Scofield, 1897

[*nom. transl.* KNIGHT, BATTEN & YOCHELSON, herein (*ex* Carinaropsidae, ULRICH & SCOFIELD, 1897)]

Shell with tendency toward rapid expansion of whorls, reduction of coiling, and generally development of parietal lip into a platelike extension; inner floor of whorls bearing a longitudinal keel; selenizone on a moderately developed dorsal crest. *?L.Ord., M.Ord.-Dev.*

Bucanopsis ULRICH, in ULRICH & SCOFIELD, 1897 [*B. carinifera*] [=*Bucaniopsis* REED, 1921 (obj.)]. Longitudinal keel on floor of whorls well developed but with coiling moderately reduced and parietal extension slight; ornament fine spiral threads. *M.Ord.-Sil.,* N.Am.-Eu.——Fig. 98,1. *B. carinifera,* M.Ord., Ky.; *1a-c,* apertural, abapertural, left sides, ×2.7.

Sphenosphaera KNIGHT, 1945 [*Bellerophon clausus* ULRICH in ULRICH & SCOFIELD, 1897]. Coil reduced only slightly; parietal extension moderate; longitudinal keel on floor of whorl well developed but rounded; ornament only growth lines (71, p. 334). *M.Ord.-M.Sil.,* N.Am.-Eu.——Fig. 98,2. *S. clausa* (ULRICH), M.Ord., Tenn.; *2a-c,* apertural, abapertural, left sides, ×1.3.

Carinaropsis HALL, 1847 [*Carinariopsis carinata* (HALL) FISCHER, 1885; (=*Cyrtolites subcarinatus* D'ORBIGNY, 1850, pro *Cyrtolites carinatus* (HALL) ORB., 1850, *non Cyrtolites carinatus* SOWERBY, 1839); SD FISCHER, 1885] [=*Carinariopsis* FISCHER, 1885 (obj.); *Phragmostoma* HALL, 1861]. Coil greatly reduced, parietal extension platelike; longitudinal keel on floor of whorl well developed; ornament growth lines. *M.Ord.-U.Ord.,* N.Am.-Eu.——Fig. 98,3. *C. cymbula* (HALL), M.Ord., Ky.; *3a-c,* apertural, abapertural (with window), left sides, ×1.3.

Phragmosphaera KNIGHT, 1945 [*P. miranda*]. Coil somewhat reduced, parietal extension platelike; no longitudinal keel on floor of whorl; ornament fine spiral threads (71, p. 338). *Dev.,* N.Am.——Fig. 98,5. *P. miranda,* M.Dev., N.Y.; *5a,b,* abapertural and apertural sides, ×1.

Gyrospira BOUCOT, 1956 [*G. tourteloti*]. Disjunct after first 2 whorls with aperture flaring on sides and back; slit about 0.3 whorl in depth, a gently arched selenizone on crest of whorl; surface with obscure collabral undulations (7, p. 46). *?Dev.,* S.Am.——Fig. 98,4. *G. tourteloti,* Bolivia; *4a,b,* right and apertural sides, ×1.3.

Subfamily PTEROTHECINAE Wenz, 1938

[*nom. transl.* KNIGHT, BATTEN & YOCHELSON, herein (*ex* Pterothecidae WENZ, 1938]

Helicocone expanding very rapidly, coil vestigial; well-developed plate within aperture suggesting that of *Crepidula* and forming a chamber that protects the visceral mass in the otherwise shallow, open shell; aperture widely explanate; selenizone on dorsal crest; ornament growth lines. *M.Ord.-M. Dev.*

Trends initiated in the Carinaropsinae seem to be perfected in this subfamily, possibly as a result of adaptation to creeping

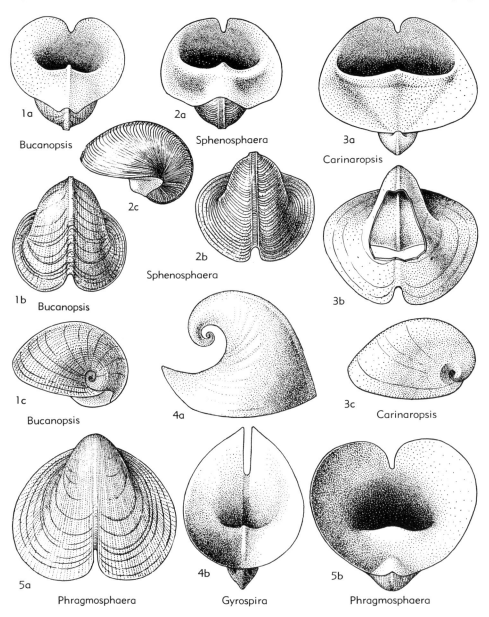

FIG. 98. Bellerophontacea (Bellerophontidae——Carinaropsinae) (p. *I*180).

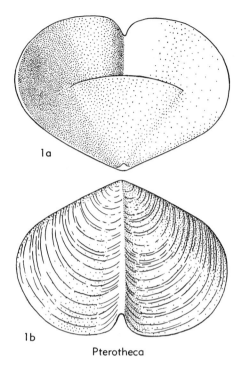

1a

1b

Pterotheca

FIG. 99. Bellerophontacea (Bellerophontidae——
Pterothecinae) (p. *I*182).

about on the soft surface of very fine sediments; many fossil specimens occur in rock composed of such fine sediment.

Pterotheca SALTER, 1853 [*Atrypa transversa* PORTLOCK, 1843; SD S.A.MILLER, 1889] [=*Clioderma* HALL, 1861; *Aulacomerella* VON HUENE, 1900 (60, p. 210)]. Shell elliptical in outline; visceral chamber triangular, with a pair of short diverging septa near apex on inner surface of the apertural plate. *M.Ord.-U.Ord.,* N.Am.-Eu.——FIG. 99,*1.* *P. transversa* (PORTLOCK), Ire.; *1a,b,* apertural and abapertural sides, ×1.3.

Cyclotheca TEICHERT, 1935 [*Pterotheca bohemica* BARRANDE, 1867]. Shell roughly diamond-shaped in outline; inner surface of visceral plate with many regular, fine, transverse striae. *U.Sil.,* Eu. ——FIG. 100,*3.* *C. bohemica* (BARRANDE), Czech.; *3a,b,* abapertural and apertural sides, ×3.3.

Aspidotheca TEICHERT, 1935 [*A. schrieli*]. Shell subcircular in outline; visceral plate longitudinally quadripartite. *L.Dev.,* Eu.——FIG. 100,*1.* *A. schrieli,* Ger.; *1a,b,* apertural and abapertural sides, ×0.7.

Pedasiola SPRIESTERSBACH, 1919 [*P. rhenana;* SD KNIGHT, 1937]. Shell elliptical in outline, with raised hooklike apex; apertural plate short, stout, with median ridge and 2 lateral wings; externally

with median fold bordered by a groove on each side; anal emargination and surface features not well known. *M.Dev.,* Eu.——FIG. 100,*2.* *P. rhenana,* Ger.; *2a,b,* apertural and abapertural sides, ×0.7.

Subfamily BELLEROPHONTINAE M'Coy, 1851

[*nom. transl.* KNIGHT, BATTEN & YOCHELSON, herein (*ex* Bellerophontidae M'COY, 1851)]

Superficially resembling *Nautilus;* whorls commonly broadly rounded; umbilici narrow or absent; ornament growth lines. *M. Ord.-L.Trias.*

Cymbularia KOKEN, 1896 [*C. galeata;* SD PERNER, 1903]. Early whorls rounded but last one strongly angulated and somewhat asymmetrical in adult stage, with narrow deep slit; umbilici closed on one or both sides. *M.Ord.-M.Sil.,* N.Am.-Eu.—— FIG. 102,*1.* *C. galeata,* Ord., Est.; *1a-c,* left, apertural and anterior sides, ×1.3.

Liljevallospira KNIGHT, 1945 [*Bellerophon tubulosus* LINDSTRÖM, 1884]. Like *Bellerophon* but with backward projections from each lateral lip curving into the umbilici and nearly closing them, the projections forming on each side hollow spiral tubes that open behind the aperture (71, p. 334). *M.Sil.;* Eu.——FIG. 102,*2.* *L. tubulosus* (LINDSTRÖM), Gotl.; *2a-c,* left and apertural sides, section, ×1.5 (90).

Prosoptychus PERNER, 1903 [*Bellerophon (Prosoptychus) plebeius;* SD KNIGHT, 1937]. Like *Bellerophon* but final lateral lips somewhat explanate and columellar margins of lip thickened; parietal inductura moderately thick. *U.Sil.,* Eu.——FIG. 101,*1.* *P. plebeius* (PERNER), Czech.; *1a,b,* left and abapertural sides, ×2.

Bellerophon MONTFORT, 1808 [*B. vasulites*]. Whorls commonly broadly rounded but some may have a subdued crest. *Sil.-L.Trias.,* cosmop.

B. (Bellerophon) [=*Bellerophus* DEBLAINVILLE, 1825 (obj.); *Mogulia* WAAGEN, 1880; *Waagenia* DEKONINCK, 1882 (*non* NEUMAYR, 1878, *nec* BAYLE, 1879); *Waagenella* DEKONINCK, 1883 (*pro Waagenia* DEKONINCK, 1882); *Sphaerocyclus* PERNER, 1903]. Inductura thin, in some species laterally extended over axial region; ornament commonly growth lines. *Sil.-L.Trias.,* cosmop.—— FIG. 102,*4.* *B. (B.) vasulites,* M.Dev., Ger.; *4a-c,* apertural, anterior, left sides, ×2.

B. (Aglaoglypta) KNIGHT, 1942 [*Bellerophon koeneni* CLARKE, 1904]. Like *B. (Bellerophon)* but ornamented with quincuncially arranged pustules (70, p. 487). *M.Dev.-U.Dev.,* cosmop.—— FIG. 102,*6.* *B. (A.) koeneni* (CLARKE), M.Dev., N.Y., ×2.

B. (Pharkidonotus) GIRTY, 1912 [*Bellerophon percarinatus* CONRAD, 1842]. Like *B. (Bellerophon)* but with a strongly thickened inductura that may be padlike in shape; ornament generally collabral undulations; selenizone on crest of low dorsal ridge; no umbilici. *L.Carb.(Miss.)-Perm.,*

N.Am.-Eu.——Fig. 102,5. *B. (P.) percarinatus* (Conrad), M.Penn., Mo.; *5a-c,* apertural, left, abapertural sides, ×2.

Ptychosphaera Perner, 1903 [*P. constricta]. Whorl with several asymmetrical constrictions at early growth stage and with slight asymmetry of coil at adult stage; a deep, angular sinus culminates seemingly in a short slit. *U.Sil.,* Eu.——Fig. 102,7. *P. constricta,* Czech.; apertural side, ×2.

?Ptychobellerophon Delpey, 1941 [*P. gubleri]. Columellar fold on each side borders depression resembling siphonal channel; seemingly no anal emargination (28, p. 36). (Possibly the lateral channels functioned as inhalant canals, but it is improbable that currents passed from one side to the other as postulated by Delpey; the path of the exhalant currents is unknown.) *L.Perm.,* SE. Asia.——Fig. 102,3. *P. gubleri,* IndoChina; apertural side, ×2 (28).

Subfamily KNIGHTITINAE Knight, 1956

Strong spiral ornament; selenizone somewhat depressed, bordered by generally obscure ridges; umbilici narrow. *Dev.-M. Perm.*

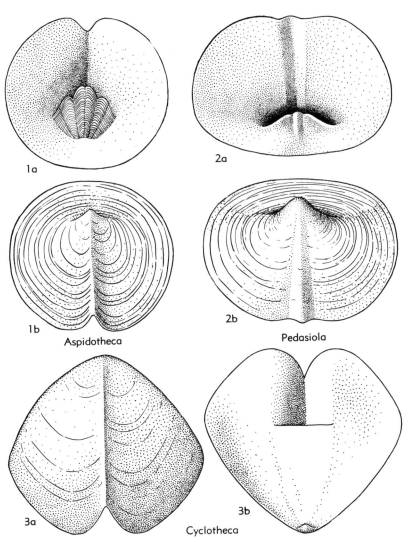

1a

1b
Aspidotheca

2a

2b
Pedasiola

3a

3b
Cyclotheca

Fig. 100. Bellerophontacea (Bellerophontidae——Pterothecinae) (p. *I*182).

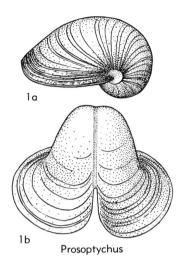

1a

1b
Prosoptychus

FIG. 101. Bellerophontacea (Bellerophontidae——
Bellerophontinae) (p. *1182*).

The spiral ridges are the loci of a pair of shallow mantle folds within the shell that seem to have carried ciliary currents of clean oxygenated water into the inhalant chamber of the mantle cavity. From here the current passed through the ctenidia to the exhalant chamber where it picked up waste and foreign matter and passed by way of the excurrent opening (the slit) to the outside (Fig. 57).

Knightites MOORE, 1941 [**K. multicornutus*]. Spiral ornament generally conspicuous, commonly crossed by well-developed collabral elements (102, p. 149). *Dev.-M.Perm.,* N.Am.-S.Am.-Eu.-N.Afr.-Asia.

K. (Retispira) KNIGHT, 1945 [**R. bellireticulata*]. Lateral lips of aperture expanded only moderately or not at all; incurrent channels inconspicuous; parietal inductura commonly thin; collabral ornament ranging from fine growth lines to cords and undulations (71, p. 335). *Dev.-M.Perm.,* N. Am.-S. Am.-Eu.-N. Afr.-Asia.——FIG. 103,*5.* **K. (R.) bellireticulata* (KNIGHT), M.Perm., Tex.; *5a,b,* left and anterior sides, ×5.

K. (Cymatospira) KNIGHT, 1942 [**Bellerophon montfortianus* NORWOOD & PRATTEN, 1855]. Lateral lips of aperture strongly expanded at final growth stage; collabral undulations prominent at intermediate growth stage, especially on ridges over inhalant canals along selenizone; parietal inductura with toothlike extension into aperture (70, p. 487). *U.Miss.-Penn.,* N.Am.——FIG. 103, *1.* **K. (C.) montfortianus* (NORWOOD & PRATTEN), U.Penn., Tex.; *1a,b,* apertural and abapertural sides, ×1.3.

K. (Knightites). Collabral elements tending periodically to form projecting tubes on inhalant ridges; lateral lips without marked final expansion. *U.Penn.-M.Perm.,* N.Am.——FIG. 103,*2.* **K. (K.) multicornutus,* U.Penn., Kan.; *2a-c,* abapertural side of large specimen, left and apertural sides of smaller mature specimen, ×1.5.

Patellilabia KNIGHT, 1945 [**P. tentoriolum*]. Apertural margins progressively expanding backward and at sides; parietal inductura with forward projecting tooth; ornament numerous spiral threads (71, p. 336). *Miss. (L.Carb.)-L.Perm.,* N.Am.-S. Am.——FIG. 103,*3.* **P. tentoriolum,* U.Penn., Mo.; *3a,b,* apertural and abapertural sides, ×0.7.

?BELLEROPHONTACEA, INCERTAE SEDIS

Isospira KOKEN, 1897 [**I. bucanioides*]. Isostrophic coiling but without trace of sinus or slit; ornament cancellate, of spiral and collabral cords; parietal lip unknown. *U.Ord.,* Eu.——FIG. 103,*4.* **I. bucanioides,* Est.; anterior side, ×2.7 (80).

BELLEROPHONTACEA, GENERA INQUIRENDA

Patellostium WAAGEN, 1880 [**Bellerophon macrostoma* C.F.ROEMER, 1844; SD ULRICH & SCOFIELD, 1897]. Wide expansion of apertural margins is only character surely determinable. *M.Dev.,* Eu.

Euphemitella TASCH, 1953 [**E. emrichi*]. Based on steinkerns representing unrecognizable genus or genera (137, p. 397). *U.Penn.,* Kan.

Suborder MACLURITINA Cox & Knight, 1960

Shell hyperstrophic to depressed-orthostrophic, commonly with angulation on outer part of upper whorl surface coinciding with or forming outer border of channel thought to have been exhalant; shell wall thick, outer layer calcitic, inner layers thick, aragonitic but not nacreous; operculum heavy, calcareous, paucispiral in *Maclurites* with attachments for 2 retractor muscles, unknown in other genera; right ctenidium inferred to have been reduced and in some forms possibly absent; nature of reproductive system and other soft parts uncertain [The outer layer may show preserved color pattern.] *U.Cam.-Trias., ?U. Cret.*

Superfamily MACLURITACEA Fischer, 1885

[*nom. transl.* KNIGHT, BATTEN & YOCHELSON herein (*ex* Macluritidae FISCHER, 1885)]

Hyperstrophic (except genuinely sinistral *Omphalocirrus*), with or without umbilicus

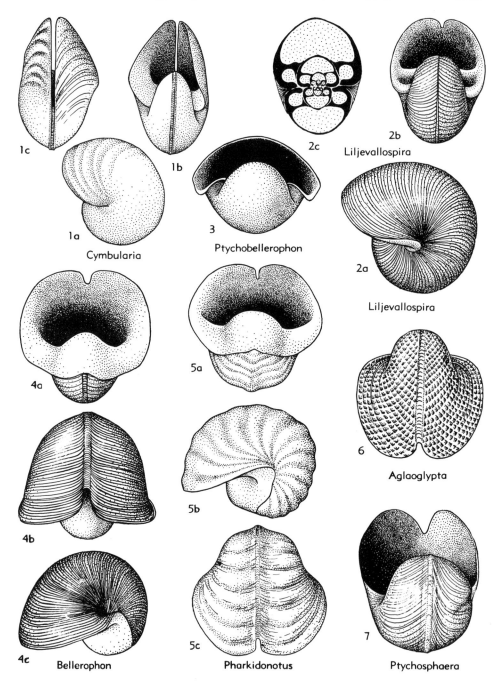

1c 1b 2c
1a Cymbularia 3 Ptychobellerophon 2b Liljevallospira
4a 5a 2a Liljevallospira
4b 5b 6 Aglaoglypta
4c Bellerophon 5c Pharkidonotus 7 Ptychosphaera

FIG. 102. Bellerophontacea (Bellerophontidae——Bellerophontinae) (p. *1182-1183*).

on upper side, lower side (base) flat or more or less protruding; with conspicuous channel, presumably exhalant in function, surrounding upper side within a ridge, and marked by a sinus in some forms; abandoned tip of helicocone not closed off by septa. *U.Cam.-Dev.*

These gastropods are inferred to be hyperstrophic, notwithstanding their apparently sinistral coiling, from the position of the channel (presumed to be exhalant) occupying a ridge or keel around what may be assumed to be the upper side. This inference is supported strongly by the operculum of *Maclurites,* which corresponds to that of a dextral gastropod (76) with a pair of retractor muscles. Members of this superfamily probably possessed paired ctenidia

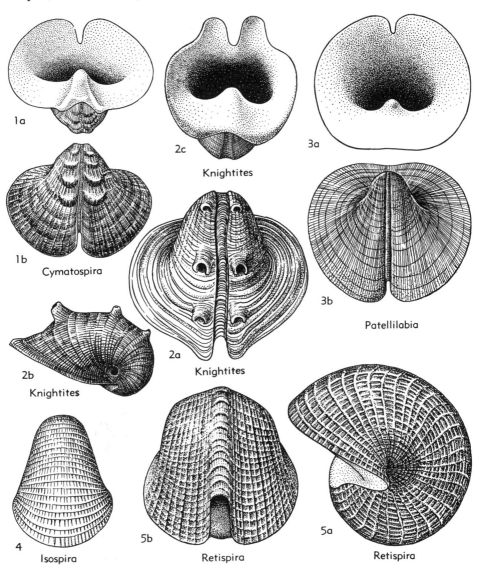

FIG. 103. Bellerophontacea (Bellerophontidae——Knightitinae; incertae sedis) (p. *1184*).

and other organs, like surviving Pleurotomariacea. The Macluritacea are thought, however, to have arisen from the Bellerophontacea as an independent group, distinct from the Pleurotomariacea.

Family ONYCHOCHILIDAE Koken, 1925

Relatively small, with base more or less protruding, like the spire of an orthostrophic gastropod. *U.Cam.-L.Dev.*

Subfamily ONYCHOCHILINAE Koken, 1925

[*nom. transl.* KNIGHT, BATTEN & YOCHELSON, herein (*ex* Onychochilidae KOKEN, 1925)]

Basal "spire" high. *U.Cam.-L.Dev.*

Matherella WALCOTT, 1912 [*pro Billingsia* S.A.MILLER, 1889 (*non* DEKONINCK, 1876, *nec* FOORD, 1886)] [**Billingsia saratogensis* S.A.MILLER, 1889]. Shell trochiform, anomphalous; outer lip opisthocline; surface with growth lines. *U.Cam.,* N.Am.-NE.Asia.——FIG. 104,3. **M. saratogensis* (MILLER), N.Y.; ×4.

Matherellina KOBAYASHI, 1937 [**Matherella walcotti* KOBAYASHI, 1933; SD KNIGHT, 1937]. Like *Matherella* but with sinus on outer lip close to basal angle. *L.Ord.,* NE.Asia.——FIG. 104,5. **M. walcotti* (KOBAYASHI), China; ×4.

Laeogyra PERNER, 1903 [**L. bohemica*]. Like *Matherella* but with deeper sutures and transverse cords; not well known. *M.Ord.,* Eu.

Onychochilus LINDSTRÖM, 1884 [**O. physa;* SD COSSMANN, 1915] [=*Palaeopupa* FOERSTE, 1893; *Onycochilus* COSSMANN, 1915 (obj.)]. Subtrochiform to pupiform; outer lip opisthocline; deeply phaneromphalous; with or without ornament. *M.Sil.,* N.Am.-Eu.——FIG. 104,4. **O. physa,* Gotl.; ×10.

Sinistracirsa COSSMANN, 1908 [*pro Donaldia* PERNER, 1903 (*non* ALLAUD, 1898)] [**Donaldia altera* PERNER, 1903] [=*Boycottia* TOMLIN, 1931 (obj.)]. Basal "spire" rather high; seemingly anomphalous; outer lip gently opisthocline, with sinus in upper margin; ornament numerous very fine spiral threads. *L.Dev.,* Eu.——FIG. 104,2. **S. altera* (PERNER), Czech.; ×1.3.

Subfamily SCAEVOGYRINAE Wenz, 1938

[*nom. transl.* KNIGHT, BATTEN & YOCHELSON, herein (*ex* Scaevogyridae WENZ, 1938)]

Basal "spire" low. *U.Cam.-M.Ord.*

Scaevogyra WHITFIELD, 1878 [**S. swezeyi;* SD MILLER, 1889]. Hyperstrophic naticiform; umbilicus large and deep, with steep sides surrounded by sharp angulation that carries the exhalant channel; basal "spire" small. [Because the steinkern of this thick-shelled form was not recognized as such, a flaring aperture was attributed to the type species and the original error was exaggerated by WENZ,

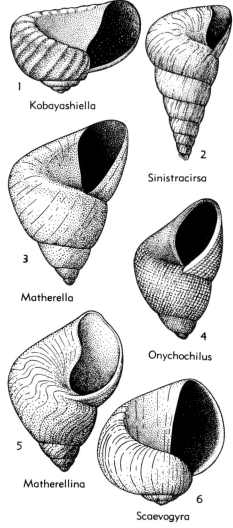

FIG. 104. Macluritacea (Onychochilidae——Onychochilinae, Scaevogyrinae) (p. *1187*).

7.] *U.Cam.,* N.Am.-NE.Asia.——FIG. 104,6. **S. swezeyi,* Wis.; ×1.3.

Kobayashiella ENDO, 1937 [**Straparollina circe* WALCOTT, 1905]. Much like *Scaevogyra* but with opisthocline collabral cords on base and whorl face and with blunter circumumbilical ridge. *U. Cam.,* NE.Asia.——FIG. 104,1. **K. circe* (WALCOTT), China; ×10.

Antispira PERNER, 1903 [**A. praecox*]. Seemingly like *Scaevogyra* but with cancellate ornament; poorly known. *M.Ord.,* Eu.

Versispira PERNER, 1903 [**V. contraria*]. Seemingly like *Scaevogyra* but steinkern of type species shows bore of final whorl blocked by a septum about 0.5

volution back from aperture; poorly known. *M. Ord.,* Eu.

?Helicotis KOKEN, 1925 [**Temnodiscus rugifer* KOKEN, 1897]. Periphery subangular; lip strongly opisthocline on outer surface, less so within umbilicus; ornament collabral cords; poorly known. *M.Ord.,* Eu.

Family MACLURITIDAE Fischer, 1885

[=Maclureidae CARPENTER, 1858 (*nom. correct.* KOKEN, 1925, *pro* Maclureadae and "Maclureade" CARPENTER, 1858); Macluriidae PILSBRY, 1888, ICZN pend.]

Relatively large; base flat or gently protruding. *L.Ord.-Dev.*

Lecanospira BUTTS, 1926 [**Ophileta compacta* SAL-

TER, 1859; SD ULRICH & BRIDGE, 1931]. Discoidal, with flat base and wide umbilicus above; whorls with sharp crest; lip with deep angular sinus culminating at crest; ornament strongly opisthocline growth lines on upper part of outer and umbilical walls. *L.Ord.,* N.Am.

L. (Lecanospira). Upper sutures within deep angular grooves; umbilical slope of whorls flat or slightly concave; growth lines prosocyrt on base of whorls.——FIG. 105,3. **L. (L.) compacta* (SALTER), Que.; ×1.3.

L. (Barnesella) BRIDGE & CLOUD, 1947 [**B. lecanospiroides*]. Differs from *L. (Lecanospira)* in having shallower upper sutures, growth lines less prosocyrt on base, and umbilical slope of whorl

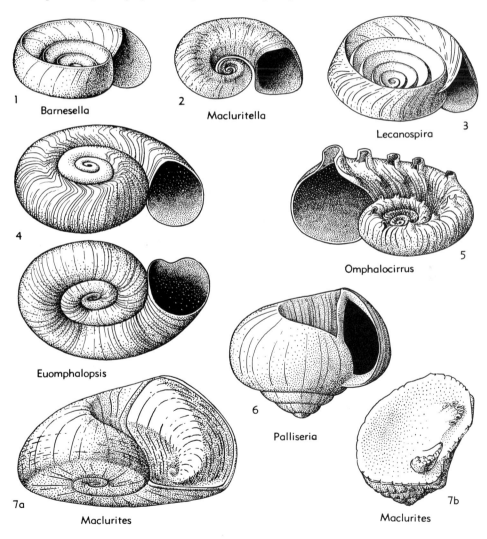

1   Barnesella

2   Macluritella

3   Lecanospira

4   Euomphalopsis

5   Omphalocirrus

6   Palliseria

7a   Maclurites

7b   Maclurites

FIG. 105. Macluritacea (Macluritidae) (p. *1188-1189*).

sigmoid (9, p. 545).——Fig. 105,*1.* **L. (B.) lecanospiroides* (Bridge & Cloud), Tex.; ×1.3.

Macluritella Kirk, 1927 [**M. stantoni*]. Planispiral, with obscure angulation on upper whorl surface and shallow sinus at angulation. *L.Ord.,* N.Am.

M. (Macluritella). Whorls slightly disjunct, base flat.——Fig. 105,*2.* **M. (M.) stantoni,* Colo.; ×2.7.

M. (Euomphalopsis) Ulrich & Bridge, 1931 [**E. involuta*]. Whorls in contact, base slightly concave.——Fig. 105,*4.* **M. (E.) involuta,* Mo.; *4a,b,* oblique views from above and below, ×3.

Maclurites Lesueur, 1818 [**M. magna;* SD de Koninck, 1881] [=*Maclurita* deBlainville, 1823 (obj.); *Maclurea* Emmons, 1842 (obj.); *Maclureia* Bronn, 1848 (obj.); *Maclurina* Ulrich & Scofield, 1897]. Shell large, heavy, with flat base; upper surface strongly convex, with deep, steep-walled umbilicus; whorls with subangular crest, locus of a slight sinus; ornament growth lines and in some species spiral cords; operculum calcareous, paucispiral from nucleus, which lies near base toward parietal lip, nuclear part in some species protruding like a horn; inner surface with large projecting roughened apophysis for attachment of left retractor muscle and smaller roughened area above for right retractor muscle. *Ord.,* N.Am.-Eu.-NE.Asia.——Fig. 105,*7. M. logani* (Salter), M.Ord., Can.(Que.); *7a,* apertural view, operculum in place, ×0.7; *7b,* inner surface of operculum showing 2 muscle scars (right, below; left, above), ×0.7.

Palliseria Wilson, 1924 [**P. robusta*] [=*Mitrospira* Kirk, 1930]. Much like *Maclurites* but base protruding as domelike "spire"; operculum unknown. *M.Ord.,* N.Am.——Fig. 105,*6.* **P. robusta.* Low.M.Ord., Nev.; ×0.7.

Omphalocirrus Ryckholt, 1860 [**Euomphalus goldfussi* d'Archiac & deVerneuil, 1842; SD Cossmann, 1915] [=*Coelocentrus* Zittel, 1882 (obj.); *Polyenaulus* Etheridge, 1917 (obj.); *Arctomphalus* Tolmachov, 1926]. Like *Maclurites* in size and shape but genuinely sinistral, with shallower umbilicus and row of short spoutlike protrusions developed periodically along whorl crest. *Dev.,* N.Am.-Eu.——Fig. 105,*5.* **O. goldfussi* (d'Archiac & deVerneuil), M.Dev., Ger.; ×0.5.

Superfamily EUOMPHALACEA deKoninck, 1881

[*nom. transl.* Wenz, 1938 (*ex* Euomphalidae deKoninck, 1881)]

Shell mostly discoidal; orthostrophic or hyperstrophic; commonly with channel presumed to be exhalant occupying angulation on outer part of upper whorl surface; mostly widely phaneromphalous; shell wall relatively thick, with external prismatic layer of calcite which may be pigmented and in-

ternal layer of aragonite which is lamellar but not nacreous. *L.Ord.-U.Cret.*

Because the angulation on the outer part of the upper whorl surface carries a presumably exhalant channel, and in some genera even a short slit and selenizone with ample space on its inner side, it is reasonable to suppose that the ctenidia and other organs of euomphalaceans were paired, as in other primitive Prosobranchia. The superfamily seems to have been derived from the Macluritacea.

Family HELICOTOMIDAE Wenz, 1938

Spire slightly elevated; umbilicus relatively narrow; shoulder angulation generally a carina, with notch or short slit and selenizone in some forms; seemingly without septa. Operculum calcareous, wedge-shaped in some genera, unknown but probably corneous in others. *L.Ord., ?M.Jur. (Baj.)*

Orospira Butts, 1926 [**O. bigranosa*]. Spire a low cone; whorls narrow, numerous (about 10), with elevated carina at outer edge of upper whorl surface; short slit and arched selenizone at crest of carina, slit at culmination of deep angular sinus; outer whorl face rounded but sloping inward below; ornament elaborate (for early Paleozoic), with spiral cords on upper whorl surface and umbilicus, and transverse threads or cords forming tubercles where they cross spirals. [Small wedge-shaped calcareous opercula associated with some specimens probably belong to genus.]. *L. Ord.,* N.Am.——Fig. 106,*3.* **O. bigranosa,* Mo.; ×2.

Polhemia Cullison, 1944 [**P. taneyensis*]. Differs from *Orospira* in shape of whorls and nearly complete lack of collabral ornament; whorls with deep groove at upper suture adjoined by 2 carinae separated by concave zone, outer carina at upper-outer angulation, with shallow slit and convex selenizone; outer whorl face concave between upper-outer carina and sharp lower-outer angulation; base narrowly phaneromphalous, with low circumumbilical ridge; ornamented with growth lamellae above base, and on base with lamellae crossed by spiral threads. Operculum as in *Orospira* (25, p. 54). *L.Ord.,* N.Am.——Fig. 106,*2.* **P. taneyensis,* Mo.; ×2.

?Lophonema Ulrich in Purdue & Miser, 1916 [**Helicotoma peccatonica* Sardeson, 1896]. Much like *Polhemia* but angulations and carina seemingly rounded; poorly known. [When better known may prove to be senior synonym of *Polhemia.*] *L.Ord.,* N.Am.

Helicotoma Salter, 1859 [**H. planulata*]. [=*Palaeomphalus,* Koken, 1925]. Spire low,

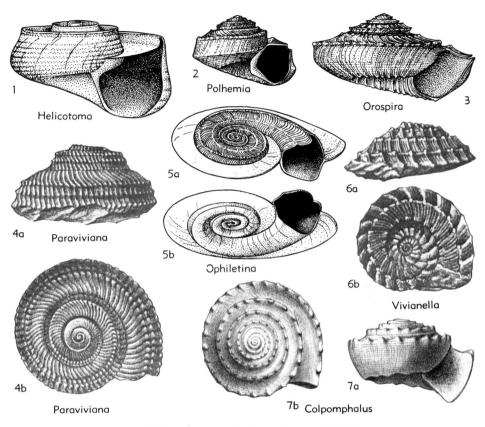

1 Helicotoma

2 Polhemia

Orospira 3

4a Paraviviana

5a

5b Ophiletina

6a

6b Vivianella

4b Paraviviana

7a

7b Colpomphalus

FIG. 106. Euomphalacea (Helicotomidae) (p. *1189-1190*).

gradate, with nearly horizontal ramp bordered at upper-outer angulation by a carina carrying a short slit that generates a convex selenizone; growth lines on sides strongly opisthocline above and prosocyrt. Operculum unknown. *L.Ord.-M.Ord.,* N.Am.-Eu.-NE.Asia-Austral.——FIG. 106, 1. **H. planulata,* M.Ord., Can.(Que.); ×2.

Ophiletina ULRICH & SCOFIELD, 1897 [**O. sublaxa*]. Coiled approximately in a plane, last half whorl in contact only with flange of previous whorl; low carina at upper-outer angulation, with short slit and selenizone; last whorl bearing wide flange near middle of outer whorl face; ornament low sharp transverse lamellae. Operculum unknown. *M.Ord.,* N.Am.-Eu.——FIG. 106,5. *O. angularis* (ULRICH & SCOFIELD), Minn.; *5a,b,* oblique views from above and below showing peripheral flange, ×2.7.

?**Vivianella** Cox, 1958 [*pro Viviana* KOKEN, 1896, *non* BIGOT, 1888] [**Viviana ornata* KOKEN, 1896]. Shell small, forming very depressed cone broadly truncated at apex owing to planispiral coiling of early whorls; upper surface of later whorls with prosocline collabral ridges and jagged me-

dian·and peripheral carinae; base feebly convex, with broad umbilicus bordered by similar carina; aperture imperfectly known. *U.Trias.(Nor.)-M.Jur.(Baj.),* Eu.——FIG. 106,6. **V. ornata* (KOKEN), U.Trias., Aus.; *6a,b,* ×7 (79).

?**Paraviviana** KUTASSY, 1940 [**Solarium gradatum* KOKEN, 1897]. Shell forming depressed cone broadly truncated at apex owing to planispiral coiling of early whorls; upper surface of later whorls with angulation delimiting broad, gently sloping ramp, second angulation at periphery; base and aperture imperfectly known; ornament of close, regular collabral ridges prosocline on ramp. *U.Trias.(Nor.),* Aus.——FIG. 106,4. **P. gradata* (KOKEN); *4a,b,* ×4 (79).

?**Colpomphalus** COSSMANN, 1916 [**Straparollus altus* D'ORBIGNY, 1853]. Spire low; upper whorl surface concave or flat, extending to tuberculate periphery; outer whorl face more or less convex, inclined inward abapically to tuberculate angulation forming umbilical border; aperture subquadrangular, peristome continuous, angular at junction of columellar and basal lips. *L.Jur.(Lias.)-M.Jur.(Bathon.),* Eu., N.Afr.——FIG. 106,7. *C. exsertus* (HUDLESTON), Baj., Eng.; *7a,b,* ×1.7 (59).

Family EUOMPHALIDAE de Koninck, 1881

[=Schizostomidae EICHWALD, 1871 (ICZN pend.); Polytropidae KOKEN, 1925; Poleumitidae, Ecculiomphalinae WENZ, 1938]

Shell mostly discoidal with wide umbilicus, but varying in form through wide range; abandoned early part of whorls closed off by septa; presumed exhalant channel generally present within outer-upper angulation, rarely with short slit or selenizone; outer calcitic shell layer may be pigmented and in several genera foreign materials such as other shells may be cemented to outer surface. *L.Ord.-Trias., ?U.Cret.*

Lytospira KOKEN, 1896 [*Euomphalus angelini* LINDSTRÖM, 1884; SD PERNER, 1907]. Openly coiled, some species hyperstrophic; broadly angular sinus in outer lip culminating at low bluntly

FIG. 107. Euomphalacea (Euomphalidae) (p. *I191-I192*).

angular spiral ridge near mid-line of upper surface; some species cement shells or other foreign substances to outer surface. *L.Ord.-M.Sil.*, N.Am.-Eu.——Fɪɢ. 107,6. **L. angelini* (Lɪɴᴅsᴛʀöᴍ), M. Ord., Swed.; *6a*, apertural view, ×1.3; *6b*, from above with window showing septa, ×1.3.

Ecculiomphalus Pᴏʀᴛʟᴏᴄᴋ, 1843 [**E. bucklandi;* SD S.A.Mɪʟʟᴇʀ, 1889] [=*Eccyliomphalus* Aɢᴀssɪᴢ, 1846 (obj.); *Eccyliopterus* Rᴇᴍᴇʟé, 1888]. Much like *Lytospira* but with high frill-like crest at upper-outer edge; surface with sharp collabral threads. [Commonly confused with *Lytospira*, especially when preserved as steinkerns.] *L.Ord.-Sil.*, N.Am.-Eu.-NE.Asia.——Fɪɢ. 107,5. *E. alatus* C.F.Rᴏᴇᴍᴇʀ, M.Ord., Ire.; *5a*, oblique apertural view, ×1; *5b*, oblique from below, ×1.

Lesueurilla Kᴏᴋᴇɴ, 1898 [**Maclurea infundibulum* Kᴏᴋᴇɴ, 1896; SD Pᴇʀɴᴇʀ, 1903] [=*Lesuerella* Pᴇʀɴᴇʀ, 1903 (obj.); *Pachystrophia* Pᴇʀɴᴇʀ, 1903]. Hyperstrophic, with rounded base and shallow open umbilicus; early whorls tightly coiled but last whorl free; whorls high and sharply angular above, with narrow pseudoselenizone on crest of angulation, and rounded below. *Ord.*, N. Am.-Eu.——Fɪɢ. 107,1. **L. infundibulum* (Kᴏᴋᴇɴ), M.Ord., Swed.; *1a,b*, oblique from above and below, ×1.3.

Poleumita Cʟᴀʀᴋᴇ & Rᴜᴇᴅᴇᴍᴀɴɴ, 1903 [*pro Polytropis* ᴅᴇKᴏɴɪɴᴄᴋ, 1881 (*non* Sᴀɴᴅʙᴇʀɢᴇʀ, 1874)] [**Euomphalus discors* J.Sᴏᴡᴇʀʙʏ, 1814] [=*Polytropina* Dᴏɴᴀʟᴅ, 1905 (obj.)]. Shape like *Straparollus (Euomphalus)*, but upper whorl surface bearing numerous collabral lamellae of 2 orders and faint revolving cords; upper-outer angulation with channel and small sinus over it; operculum unknown, probably corneous. [Differs from *Oriostoma*, with which it has been long confused, in closure of abandoned whorls by septa, in lacking a nacreous inner layer, and in having no calcareous operculum.] *L.Sil.*, N.Am.-Eu.——Fɪɢ. 107,3. **P. discors* (Sᴏᴡᴇʀʙʏ), Gotl.; *3a,b*, oblique from below and above, ×0.7.

Centrifugus Bʀᴏɴɴ, 1834 [**C. planorbis*] [=*Inachus* Hɪsɪɴɢᴇʀ, 1837 (*non* Fᴀʙʀɪᴄɪᴜs, 1798) (obj.); *Hisingeria* Uʟʀɪᴄʜ & Sᴄᴏғɪᴇʟᴅ, 1897 (*pro Inachus* Hɪsɪɴɢᴇʀ, 1837) (obj.)]. Shell with nearly flat spire, widest at carina around base, with short narrow slit and selenizone not far from upper suture; 5 strong spiral cords above peripheral carina with weaker cord between each pair, spiral ornament on base faint. [Slit on upper whorl surface probably is exhalant opening.] *U.Sil.*, Eu.——Fɪɢ. 107,2. **C. planorbis*, Gotl.; *2a,b*, oblique from above and below, ×0.7.

Sinutropis Pᴇʀɴᴇʀ, 1903 [**S. esthetica*; SD Pᴇʀɴᴇʀ, 1907]. Shape like *Straparollus (Euomphalus)*, but with rounder whorls and no upper-outer angulation; moderately deep rounded sinus culminates at position of angulation; ornamented with numerous fine spiral and collabral threads. *U.Sil.*,

Eu.——Fɪɢ. 107,4. **S. esthetica*, Czech.; oblique from above, ×1.3.

Straparollus ᴅᴇMᴏɴᴛғᴏʀᴛ, 1810 [**S. dionysii*]. Shape variable, with almost complete range from moderately high conispiral to discoidally hyperstrophic; channel (probably exhalant) or slight sinus on outer-upper angulation. [Restudy of original description shows that spelling *Straparolus* was a printing error subject to automatic correction.] *Sil.-M.Perm.*, cosmop.

S. (Euomphalus) J.Sᴏᴡᴇʀʙʏ, 1814 [**E. pentangulatus*; SD Mᴇᴇᴋ & Wᴏʀᴛʜᴇɴ, 1866] [=*Schizostoma* Bʀᴏɴɴ, 1834; *Phymatifer* ᴅᴇKᴏɴɪɴᴄᴋ, 1881; *Liomphalus* Cʜᴀᴘᴍᴀɴ, 1916; *Amphelissa* Eᴛʜᴇʀɪᴅɢᴇ, 1921; *Paromphalus* Gʀᴀʙᴀᴜ, 1936]. Subdiscoidal, with depressed to slightly elevated spire, whorls with channel-bearing angulation at outer-upper edge; sutures generally deep; base widely phaneromphalous; lower surface of whorls rounded to angular; commonly ornamented with fine collabral growth lines and faint spiral threads, some species with row of nodes on lower angulation or on both lower and upper. *Sil.-M.Perm.*, cosmop.——Fɪɢ. 108,1. **S. (E.) pentangulatus* Sᴏᴡᴇʀʙʏ, L.Carb., Eng.; *1a,b*, oblique from above and below, ×1.

S. (Philoxene) Kᴀʏsᴇʀ, 1889 [**Euomphalus laevis* ᴅ'Aʀᴄʜɪᴀᴄ & ᴅᴇVᴇʀɴᴇᴜɪʟ, 1842]. Trochiform to discoidal, with wide umbilicus; whorls rounded; surface commonly with scars of attached shell fragments. *Dev.*, Eu.——Fɪɢ. 108,2. **S. (P.) laevis* (Aʀᴄʜɪᴀᴄ & Vᴇʀɴᴇᴜɪʟ), M.Dev., Ger.; *2a,b*, oblique from above and below, ×1.7.

S. (Serpulospira) Cᴏssᴍᴀɴɴ, 1916 [*pro Serpularia* F.A.Rᴏᴇᴍᴇʀ, 1843 (*non* Fʀɪᴇs, 1829, *nec* Müɴsᴛᴇʀ, 1840)] [**Serpularia centrifuga* F.A.Rᴏᴇᴍᴇʀ, 1843]. Whorls rounded, last half whorl disjunct. *Dev.-U.Carb.*, Eu.——Fɪɢ. 108,3. **S. (S.) centrifugus* (F.A.Rᴏᴇᴍᴇʀ), Dev., Ger.; ×1.3.

S. (Straparollus). Shell trochiform to discoidal, with deep, moderately wide umbilicus; whorls rounded but with slight shoulder that is locus of very shallow sinus. *Carb.(Miss.-Penn.)*, N. Am.-Eu.-Austral.——Fɪɢ. 108,4. **S. (S.) dionysii*, L.Carb., Belg.; *4a,b*, oblique from below and above, ×1.

S. (Amphiscapha) Kɴɪɢʜᴛ, 1942 [**Straparolus (Euomphalus) reedsi* Kɴɪɢʜᴛ, 1934]. Hyperstrophic discoidal, base flat, with spiral rib projecting very slightly beyond side, which is flat or slightly concave, to outer-upper margin where smooth or rugose ridge carried internal exhalant channel; upper whorl surface sloping inward (70, p. 488). *Penn.(U.Carb.)-L.Perm.*, N.Am.-S.Am.——Fɪɢ. 108,10. **S. (A.) reedsi* (Kɴɪɢʜᴛ), M.Penn., Mo.; *10a,b*, oblique from above and below, ×1.3.

S. (Leptomphalus) Yᴏᴄʜᴇʟsᴏɴ, 1956 [**S. (Leptomphalus) micidus*]. Much like *S. (Euomphalus)*, but with coil almost symmetrically discoidal and usual angulations of both upper and lower

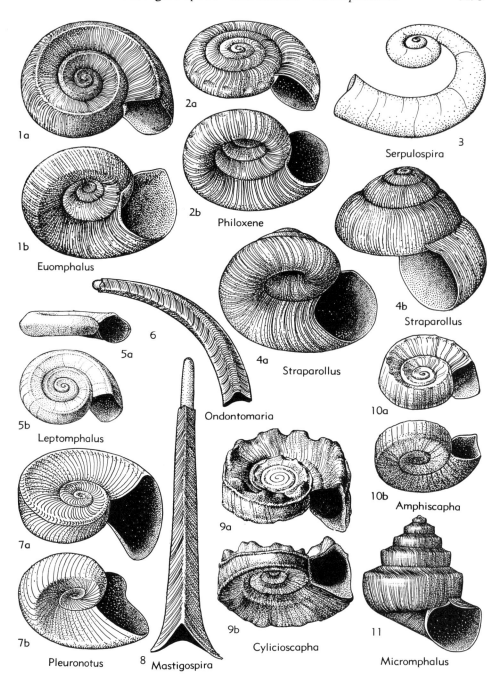

1a
2a
3
Serpulospira
1b
Euomphalus
2b
Philoxene
4b
Straparollus
6
5a
4a
Straparollus
5b
Leptomphalus
Ondontomaria
10a
7a
10b
Amphiscapha
9a
7b
Pleuronotus
8 Mastigospira
9b
Cylicioscapha
11
Micromphalus

FIG. 108. Euomphalacea (Euomphalidae) (p. I192-I195).

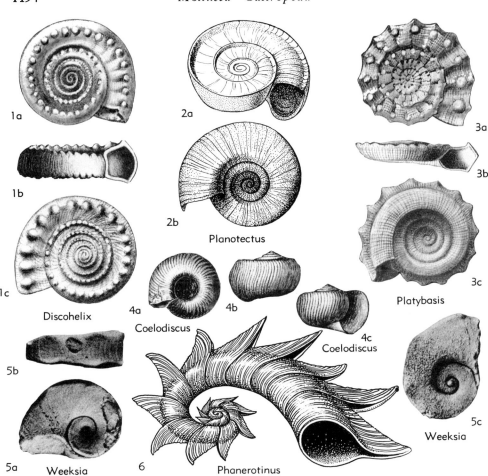

1a 2a 3a 3b 1b 2b Planotectus 3c 1c Discohelix 4a Coelodiscus 4b Platybasis 4c Coelodiscus 5b 5c Weeksia 5a Weeksia 6 Phanerotinus

Fig. 109. Euomphalacea (Euomphalidae) (p. *1194-1196*).

whorl surfaces much subdued (154, p. 197). *M. Perm.*, N.Am.-Eu.-E.Asia.——Fig. 108,5. **S. (L.) micidus*, Tex.; 5*a,b*, apertural view and oblique from above, ✕1.3.

Pleuronotus HALL, 1879 [**Euomphalus decewi* BILLINGS, 1861]. Like *Straparollus (Euomphalus)* in shape, but whorls deeper and with strong angular sinus culminating at outer-upper angulation in shallow slit that generates selenizone. *Dev.*, N.Am.-Eu.-Austral.——Fig. 108,7. **P. decewi* (BILLINGS), M.Dev., Can.(Ont.); 7*a,b*, oblique from above and below, ✕0.7.

Mastigospira LaRocque, 1949 [**Hyolithes alatus* WHITEAVES, 1892]. Shell straight or gently curved, without coiling, roughly triangular in cross section; abandoned tip shut off by septa; upper surface with angulation which is culmination of a deep V-shaped sinus, a broader rounded sinus below; each side of aperture extended in a point

(87, p. 114). *M.Dev.*, N.Am.——Fig. 108,8. **M. alatus* (WHITEAVES) Can.(Man.); from above, ✕0.7 (87).

?Odontomaria C.F.ROEMER, 1876 [**O. elephantina*]. Not well known but possibly senior synonym of *Mastigospira*. *M.Dev.*, Eu.——Fig. 108, 6. **O. elephantina*, Ger.; oblique from above, ✕1 (123).

Micromphalus KNIGHT, 1945 [**M. turris*]. Trochiform, relatively high, gradate; narrowly phaneromphalous; growth lines prosocline on upper shoulder, orthocline below; with slight sinus on blunt angulation (72, p. 585). *M.Dev.-Miss.*, N. Am.——Fig. 108,11. **M. turris*, M.Miss., Ky.; ✕2.

Phanerotinus J.deC.SOWERBY, 1844 [**Euomphalus cristatus* PHILLIPS, 1836; SD deKONINCK, 1881] [=*Phanerotina* PAETEL, 1875 (obj.)]. All but early whorls openly coiled; channel on anterior

face of large periodic leaflike extensions that protrude horizontally from upper part of outer whorl face. [Late Paleozoic open-coiled euomphalids lacking leaflife expansions, although commonly referred to this genus, are more properly assigned to *Straparollus (Serpulospira)*.] *L.Carb.*, Eu.——Fig. 109,6. *P. cristatus* (PHILLIPS), Eng.; oblique from above, ×0.5.

Cylicioscapha YOCHELSON, 1956 [*Amphiscapha (Cylicioscapha) texana*]. Somewhat like *S. (Amphiscapha)* but with deeper umbilicus and with exhalant channel in supplemental, commonly noded angulation rising in adult above outer whorl as a spiral cord; with protruding basal cord as in *S. (Amphiscapha)*; labrum projecting forward at primitive upper angulation and with sinus and channel at supplemental angulation (154, p. 199). *M.Penn.-M.Perm.*, N.Am.——Fig. 108,9. *C. texana* (YOCHELSON), U.Penn., Tex.; *9a,b*, oblique from above and below, ×1.3.

Planotectus YOCHELSON, 1956 [*P. cymbellatus*]. Upper whorl surface very gently arched within sharp carina; outer whorl face sloping inward to rounded basal surface; umbilical walls steep; labrum projecting forward at carina, with channel within (154, p. 200). *M.Perm.*, N.Am.——Fig. 109,2. *P. cymbellatus*, Tex.; *2a,b*, oblique from above and basal view, ×1.5.

Discohelix DUNKER, 1848 [*D. calculiformis*]. Discoidal, either upper or lower face (assuming dextrality) the more impressed; protoconch deviated but not heterostrophic; whorls subquadrate in cross section, barely overlapping; ornament collabral and in some shells spiral threads, tubercles

at both angulations in most species. *M.Trias.-U. Cret.(Senon.)*, cosmop.
D. (Discohelix). Growth lines gently opisthocyrt on outer whorl face. *M.Trias.-U.Cret.(Senon.)*, cosmop. —— Fig. 109,1. *D. (D.) sinistra* (D'ORBIGNY), M.Lias., Fr.; *1a-c*, ×1 (110).
D. (Amphitomaria) KOKEN, 1897 [*Euomphalus cassianus* KOKEN, 1889]. Shell small; no ornament except growth lines, which are strongly prosocyrt on slightly concave outer whorl face and have small notches where they cross its 2 well-defined bordering carinae. *M.Trias.(Ladin.)*, Eu.——Fig. 110,6. *D. (A.) cassiana* (KOKEN), S. Tyrol; *6a,b*, ×2 (196).

Anisostoma KOKEN, 1889 [*pro Platystoma* HÖRNES, 1855 (*non* MEIGEN, 1803)] [*Platystoma suessi* HÖRNES, 1855]. Shell and whorls as in *Discohelix* except that last whorl bends down through right angle just before circular aperture, labrum of which has broad, flat, kidney-shaped expansion almost as wide as base of shell, in plane of which it lies. *M.Trias.-U.Trias.*, Eu.——Fig. 110,3. *A. suessi*, U.Trias.(Nor.), Aus.; *3a-c*, ×2, ×3, ×2 (79).

Woehrmannia J.BÖHM, 1895 [*W. böhmi* KITTL, 1899 (ICZN pend.)]. Shell small, discoidal; spire flat or protruding very slightly; upper surface of whorls bordered by smooth or denticulate carina, below which, on steep outer face of last whorl, are 1 or 2 further carinae; no other ornament except growth lines; umbilicus without bordering carina. *M.Trias.-U.Trias.*, Eu.——Fig. 110,2. *W. lineata* (KLIPSTEIN), U.Trias.(Carn.), S.Tyrol; *2a-c*, ×3 (89).

Nummocalcar COSSMANN, 1896 [*Solarium poly-*

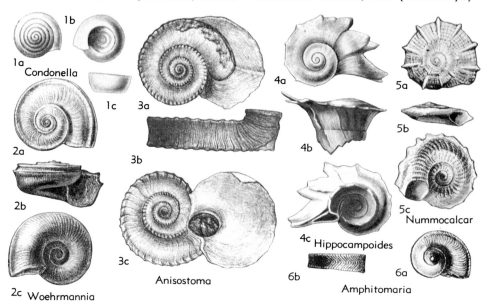

FIG. 110. Euomphalacea (Euomphalidae) (p. 1195-1196).

gonium D'ARCHIAC, 1843]. Shell discoidal or with very slightly protruding spire; upper surface with regular transverse ribs ending at carinate periphery in angular projections or spines; these remain exposed by and produce undulations of suture on earlier whorls; intervals with fine cancellate ornament; umbilical border not carinate; aperture broader than high. *M.Jur.(Baj.)-U.Cret.(Senon.)*, Eu., N.Afr.

N. (Nummocalcar). Shell rather small; spire protruding slightly; whorl diameter increasing relatively rapidly; outer whorl face not delimited from base; umbilicus only about 0.3 of shell diameter, with crenulations at its border. *M.Jur.(Baj.)-U.Cret.(Senon.)*, Eu., N.Afr.——FIG. 110, 5. *N. (N.) polygonium* (ARCHIAC), Bathon., Fr.; *5a-c*, ×2, ×2, ×1 (17).

N. (Platybasis) COSSMANN, 1916 [*Straparollus pulchellus* D'ORBIGNY, 1850]. Medium-sized, discoidal, whorl diameter increasing relatively slowly; ribs tuberculate; angulation separating outer whorl face from base, which appears flattened; umbilicus wide, without crenulations at border. *M.Jur.(Baj.)*, Eu.——FIG. 109,3. *N. (P.) pulchellus* (D'ORBIGNY), Baj., Fr.; *3a-c*, ×2.5 (111).

Hippocampoides WADE, 1916 [*H. serratum*]. Shell subcylindrical, whorl height proportionately large for family, whorl diameter increasing rapidly; spire protruding only slightly, whorls flat, with collabral rugae that may produce jagged projections on sharply carinate periphery; unornamented or with spiral striations; outer whorl face concave, sloping inward slightly abapically toward 2nd carina forming border of umbilicus. *U.Cret. (Campan.)*, Tenn.——FIG. 110,4. *H. serratus; 4a-c*, ×1.3 (226).

?Coelodiscus BRÖSAMLEN, 1909 [*Euomphalus minutus* ZIETEN, 1832]. Shell small, involute or with slightly protruding, obtuse spire; whorls evenly rounded, overlapping slightly, smooth or with parasigmoidal collabral threads; aperture ovate, higher than broad. *L.Jur.(L.Lias.)-M.Jur.(Baj.)*, Eu.——FIG. 109,4. *C. aratus* (TATE), L.Lias., Ger.; *4a-c*, ×7 (11).

?Condonella McCLELLAN, 1927 [*C. suciensis*]. Rather small, discoidal; spire flat, of slowly increasing whorls; outer whorl face convex, sloping inward abapically, limited above by peripheral and below by circumumbilical angulation; no ornament except collabral threads; aperture imperfectly known. *U.Cret.*, N.Am.——FIG. 110,1. *C. suciensis*, San Juan I.; *1a-c*, ×1 (147).

?Weeksia STEPHENSON, 1941 [*Pseudomalaxis amplificata* WADE, 1926]. Shell discoidal; whorls increasing rapidly in diameter, subrectangular in cross section, smooth; upper and circumbasal angulations obscurely nodose, outer face of shell between them almost flat; upper and umbilical surfaces shallowly concave; protoconch a smooth button projecting above level of succeeding whorls.

U.Cret., N.Am.——FIG. 109,5. *W. lubbocki* STEPHENSON, Tex.; *5a-c*, ×2 (220).

Family OMPHALOTROCHIDAE Knight, 1945

[*nom. transl.* KNIGHT, BATTEN & YOCHELSON, herein (*ex* Omphalotrochacea KNIGHT, 1945)]

Shell trochiform, with broad sinus in upper part of outer lip and forward protrusion below; narrowly to widely phaneromphalous. *Dev.-M.Perm., ?U.Trias.*

This family is thought to have been derived from earlier euomphalids, possibly from close allies of *Centrifugus*. If this was so, the sinus high on the outer lip may be the morphological and functional homologue of the exhalant slit in that genus. Both *Centrifugus* and omphalotrochids have a protruding section of the lip low on the whorl face; commonly this is thickened and bears within it a more or less well-marked channel. This combination of features suggests that the Omphalotrochidae may have been in the process of losing the right ctenidium and adopting an independent left-to-right flow of ciliary currents in the mantle cavity. If this was so, the channel in the forward extension may have been inhalant.

Orecopia KNIGHT, 1945 [*Platyschisma? mccoyi* WALCOTT, 1884]. Base nearly flat, minutely phaneromphalous, surrounded by thick funicle; outer lip with broad rounded sinus above and forward projection at periphery; shell much thickened by secondary deposits within (72, p. 586). *Dev.*, N.Am.-Eu.——FIG. 111,1. *O. mccoyi* (WALCOTT), U.Dev., Nev.; ×1.6.

Omphalotrochus MEEK, 1864 [*Euomphalus (Omphalotrochus) whitneyi*]. Shell gradate, trochiform, with moderately wide umbilicus; lip with broad rounded sinus above and forward projection below, commonly showing internal channel. *Penn.(U.Carb.)-M.Perm.*, N.Am.-S.Am.-Eu.-Asia. ——FIG. 111,4. *O. whitneyi* (MEEK), L.Perm., Calif.; ×1.3.

Discotropis YOCHELSON, 1956 [*D. publicus*]. Discoidal, with flat or gently rounded, phaneromphalous base and pair of prominent spiral ridges or carinae; shallow labral sinus above lower or peripheral carina, which forms salient (154, p. 203). *U.Penn.-M.Perm., ?U.Trias.* N.Am.-Eu.—— FIG. 111,2. *D. publica*, M.Perm., Tex.; *2a,b*, apertural view and oblique from above, ×2.

Babylonites YOCHELSON, 1956 [*B. carinatus*]. Conical, with flat phaneromphalous base; sutures shallow; outer whorl face approximately conformable to sides of cone, gently concave for its upper 0.7 with concave or convex band above periphery; shallow labral sinus above forward-projecting

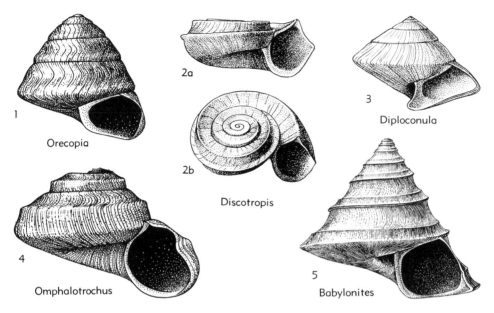

FIG. 111. Euomphalacea (Omphalotrochidae) (p. *1196-1197*).

periphery (154, p. 202). *M.Perm.*, N.Am.——Fig. 111,5. *B. carinatus, Tex.; ×1.

Diploconula YOCHELSON, 1956 [**D. biconvexa*]. Spire and base conical, narrowly phaneromphalous; shell heavy; periphery subangular; labral sinus very shallow; angular umbilical funicle (154, p. 203). *M.Perm.*, N.Am.——Fig. 111,3. *D. biconvexa, Tex.; ×1.3.

Suborder PLEUROTOMARIINA Cox & Knight, 1960

[=Fissibranchiata STOLICZKA, 1868; Zeugobranchia VON IHERING, 1876; Zygobranchia SPENGEL, 1881]

Shell commonly conispiral, more rarely discoidal, auriform, patelliform, or other shapes; mostly with exhalant notch, slit, trema, or series of tremata, generating a selenizone (except in patelliform genera with apical trema); outer shell layer calcitic, inner layers aragonitic and nacreous except in patelliform genera; operculum corneous and multispiral in conispiral, absent in patelliform, genera; ctenidia paired, right ctenidium (except in Fissurellacea) reduced to varying extent; epipodium present; pallial genital organs wanting; heart with 2 auricles, ventricle traversed by rectum; radula rhipidoglossate. *U.Cam.-Rec.*

In this group the inhalant current is drawn into the mantle cavity near the middle and the exhalant current is discharged through a labral emargination, which exists in most forms, or else through a trema or series of tremata in the shell wall.

Superfamily PLEUROTOMARIACEA Swainson, 1840

[*nom. transl.* WENZ, 1938 (*ex* Pleurotomariidae KING, 1850, *nom. correct. et transl. ex* Pleurotomariae SWAINSON, 1840)]

Shells mostly conispiral, but rarely discoidal or auriform; inner shell layer aragonitic, nacreous. Operculum, in living representatives, corneous, multispiral. *U.Cam.-Rec.*

This ancient line first appears in late Upper Cambrian strata and is preceded in the fossil record of the Gastropoda only by the Helcionellacea, the Bellerophontacea, and the questionable Pelagiellacea. The group has much in common with bellerophontaceans, for example, in nature of the exhalant emargination, and in three of the four surviving families the presence of actual or potential paired retractor muscles. Pleurotomariaceans in which the shell is conispiral differ from bellerophontaceans in having an asymmetrically coiled shell with its inner layers nacreous. The superfamily is thought

to be derived from the Bellerophontacea, retaining as primitive characters paired ctenidia and other organs. The Pleurotomariacea attained the acme of their development in Paleozoic time. They are thought to have given rise directly to a number of other superfamilies belonging to the Archaeogastropoda, several of which seem to have lost the right ctenidium independently; ultimately this group seems to have been the source of other orders.

Family SINUOPEIDAE Wenz, 1938

[*nom. transl.* KNIGHT, BATTEN & YOCHELSON, herein (*ex* Sinuopeinae WENZ, 1938)]

Shell trochiform, turbiniform, rotelliform, or naticiform; exhalant emargination in form of a U-shaped sinus. *U.Cam.-M.Perm.*

Subfamily SINUOPEINAE Wenz, 1938

Turbiniform or rotelliform; sinus wide, approximately at mid-height of labrum. *U. Cam.-U.Sil.*

Sinuopea ULRICH, 1911 [**Holopea sweeti* WHITFIELD, 1880]. Turbiniform, anomphalous, sutures deep; sinus relatively narrow, low on labrum. *U. Cam.-L.Ord.,* N.Am.——FIG. 112,5. **S. sweeti* (WHITFIELD), U.Cam., Wis.; ×1.3.

Horiostomella PERNER, 1903 [**H. otiosa*]. Like *Sellinema* but with lower spire, larger last whorl, and wider umbilicus. *U.Sil.,* Eu.——FIG. 112,6. **H. otiosa,* Czech.; ×2.7.

Sellinema PERNER, 1903 [**S. dive;* SD PERNER, 1907]. Turbiniform, narrowly phaneromphalous, with deep sutures; sinus very broad. *U.Sil.,* Eu. ——FIG. 112,3. **S. dive,* Czech.; ×4.

Subfamily PLATYSCHISMATINAE Knight, 1956

Rotelliform or naticiform; sinus at or above middle of labrum. *L.Ord.-M.Perm.*

Chepultapecia ULRICH in WELLER & ST. CLAIR, 1928 [**Raphistoma leiosomella* SARDESON, 1896]. Umboniform, sutures shallow; narrowly phaneromphalous; sinus culminating at middle of labrum. *L.Ord.,* N.Am.——FIG. 112,1. **C. leiosomella* (SARDESON), Minn.; *1a,b,* apertural view and oblique from above, ×4.

Umbospira PERNER, 1903 [**U. nigricans;* SD PERNER, 1907]. Low rotelliform, probably phaneromphalous; with faintly arched pseudoselenizone; surface glossy. *U.Sil.,* Eu.——FIG. 112,8. **U. nigricans,* Czech.; oblique from above, ×4.

Pycnotrochus PERNER, 1903 [**P. viator;* SD PERNER, 1907]. Trochiform, gradate, moderately large, with a narrow ramp; outer lip with sinus culminating at angulation of ramp; columellar lip thickened; broad concave callus filling umbilicus.

[The only known specimens, the types, are too imperfect to form a basis for restoration.] *U.Sil.,* Eu.

Platyschisma M'COY, 1844 [**Ampullaria helicoides* J.DEC.SOWERBY, 1826; SD DEKONINCK, 1881]. Naticiform, narrowly phaneromphalous; sinus and faint pseudoselenizone slightly above mid-height of whorl face; columellar lip thin, slightly sinuous. *L.Carb.(Miss.),* Eu.-N.Am.-Austral.——FIG. 112, 2. **P. helicoides* (SOWERBY), Belg., ×0.7.

Colpites KNIGHT, 1936 [**Naticopsis monilifera* WHITE, 1880]. Naticiform, anomphalous; sinus above mid-height of whorl face; columellar and parietal lips thickened; surface glossy, with row of nodes just below upper suture. *Penn.(U.Carb.)-M.Perm.,* N.Am.-Eu.——FIG. 112,7. **C. monilifer* (WHITE), Penn., Mo.; ×2.7.

Subfamily TURBONELLININAE Knight, 1956

Shell turbiniform; sinus small, mostly low on labrum. *U.Sil.-L.Perm.*

Turbomaria PERNER, 1907 [**Pleurotomaria sepulta* PERNER, 1903]. Exhalant sinus small, low on labrum, columellar lip sinuous; fine spiral and collabral threads. *U.Sil.,* Eu.——FIG. 112,9. **T. sepulta* (PERNER), Czech.; ×2.7.

Leptozone PERNER, 1907 [**Pleurotomaria (Leptozone) esthetica*]. Like *Turbomaria* but sinus higher on labrum and with wash of shell material within funnel-shaped umbilicus. *L.Dev.,* Eu.——FIG. 112, 10. **L. esthetica* (PERNER), Czech.; ×2.7.

Rhineoderma DEKONINCK, 1883 [**Pleurotomaria radula* DEKONINCK, 1843]. Trochiform, with broadly subangular periphery; with shallow labral notch generating broad ornamented selenizone between pair of threads on periphery; umbilicus narrow, funnel-shaped and smooth; spiral threads of several orders bearing small nodes where crossed by transverse threads. *L.Carb.(Miss.),* Eu.-N.Am.—— FIG. 112,11. **L. radula* (DEKONINCK), Belg., ×2.

Turbonellina DEKONINCK, 1881 [**Trochus lepidus* DEKONINCK, 1843; SD KNIGHT, 1937]. Broadly beehive-shaped; sinus quite low on labrum, partly on base; spiral and collabral threads. *L.Carb.,* Eu. ——FIG. 112,4. **T. lepida* (DEKONINCK), Belg.; *4a,b,* oblique from above and below, showing aperture and sinus, ×2.

?Keeneia ETHERIDGE, 1902 [**K. platyschismoides*]. Large, rounded above, with rather flat base; sinus low, at peripheral angle; transverse threads. *L. Perm.,* Austral.——FIG. 112,12. **K. platyschismoides,* ×0.5.

Family RAPHISTOMATIDAE Koken, 1896

[*nom. correct.* KNIGHT, BATTEN & YOCHELSON, herein (*pro* Raphistomidae KOKEN, 1896)]

Shell lenticular, turbiniform, or gradate, with angular labral sinus culminating gen-

erally at periphery in a short slit, sinus, or notch that generates a selenizone. *U.Cam.-M.Perm.*

Subfamily OPHILETINAE Knight, 1956

Generally low-spired with wide umbilicus; labral sinus V-shaped, culminating at

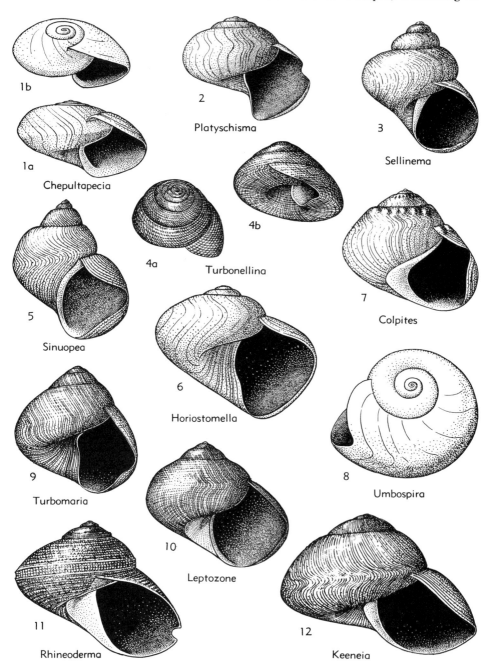

FIG. 112. Pleurotomariacea (Sinuopeidae——Sinuopeinae, Platyschismatinae, Turbonellininae) (p. *I*198).

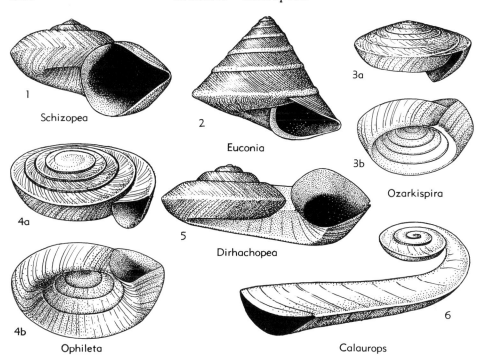

1 Schizopea
2 Euconia
3a
3b Ozarkispira
4a
5 Dirhachopea
4b Ophileta
6 Calaurops

FIG. 113. Pleurotomariacea (Raphistomatidae——Ophiletinae) (p. *1200*).

periphery in short notch that generates an obscure selenizone. *U.Cam.-L.Ord.*

Schizopea BUTTS, 1926 [**S. washburnei*] [=*Roubidouxia* BUTTS, 1926; *Rhachopea* ULRICH & BRIDGE, 1931]. Spire low, widely phaneromphalous, sutures deep; sinus culminating at blunt angulation that forms periphery. *U.Cam.-L.Ord.*, N.Am.——FIG. 113,*1*. *S. typica* (ULRICH & BRIDGE), L.Ord., Mo.; ×1.

Dirhachopea ULRICH & BRIDGE, 1931 [**D. normalis*]. Spire low, widely phaneromphalous, last whorl disjunct; labral sinus culminating at blunt seemingly double-edged angulation that forms periphery, probably with short notch. *U.Cam.-L.Ord.*, N.Am.——FIG. 113,*5*. **D. normalis*, U.Cam., Mo.; ×2.

Euconia ULRICH in ULRICH & SCOFIELD, 1897 [**Pleurotomaria etna* BILLINGS, 1865; SD PERNER, 1907] [=?*Jarlopsis* HELLER, 1954 [1956] (55, p. 32)]. Trochiform, sutures shallow; sinus culminating at angular periphery just above upper suture, probably in short notch. *L.Ord.*, N.Am.——FIG. 113,*2*. **E. etna* (BILLINGS), Newf.; ×1.3.

Ophileta VANUXEM, 1842 [**O. complanata*; SD S.A.MILLER, 1889]. With angular labral sinus culminating at periphery in notch that generates selenizone on upper side of peripheral angle. *L.Ord.*, N.Am.-NE.Asia.

O. (Ophileta) [=*Polygyrata* WELLER, 1903]. Whorls approximately as high as wide, umbilical sutures relatively deep. *L.Ord.*, N.Am.-NE.Asia. ——FIG. 113,*4*. **O. (O.) complanata*, Tex.; *4a,b*, aperture oblique from above and below, ×1.3.

O. (Ozarkispira) WALCOTT, 1924 [**O. leo*]. Whorls about twice as high as wide, umbilical slopes continuous. *L.Ord.*, N.Am.——FIG. 113,*3*. **O. (O.) leo* (WALCOTT), Can.(Alba.); *3a,b*, aperture oblique from above and below, ×2.7.

Calaurops WHITFIELD, 1886 [**C. lituiformis*] [=*Orthostoma* CONRAD, 1838 (*non* AUDINET-SERVILLE, 1834)]. First 3 or 4 whorls discoidal, with wide umbilicus and angular deep sinus culminating at periphery, seemingly generating a selenizone; last whorl disjunct, rodlike, with angular periphery bearing deep sinus continued into the extension; coiled whorls abandoned and filled solidly with secondary deposits that leave cast of interior of later part of shell with tapering pointed apex. *L.Ord.*, N.Am.——FIG. 113,*6*. **C. lituiformis*, Vt.; ×0.7.

Subfamily RAPHISTOMATINAE Koken, 1896

[*nom. correct. et transl.* KNIGHT, BATTEN & YOCHELSON, herein (*ex* Raphistomidae KOKEN, 1896)]

Base commonly narrow, anomphalous or narrowly phaneromphalous, upper surface more or less flattened; with deep V-shaped

labral sinus in most species, culminating in a shallow notch that generates a selenizone at periphery. *M.Ord.-U.Dev., ?L.Carb.*

Scalites EMMONS, 1842 [**S. angulatus*]. Resembles *Acteonina* in shape but much larger and wider, with broad ramp around low gradate spire terminating in sharp peripheral angulation; base extended, subconical; labrum with angular sinus above, culminating at periphery, where it may generate a selenizone. *M.Ord.*, N.Am.——FIG. 114. **S. angulatus*, Vt.; ×1.

Raphistoma HALL, 1847 [*non* RAFINESQUE, 1815, ICZN Op. 225] [**Maclurea striatus* EMMONS, 1842; SD DEKONINCK, 1881]. Upper surface nearly flat, base anomphalous or narrowly phaneromphalous; sinus culminating in notch that generates an angular selenizone forming periphery; upper lip sigmoid; ornamented by collabral cords. *M. Ord.-Sil.*, N.Am.-Eu.——FIG. 115,2. **R. striatum* (EMMONS), M.Ord., Vt.; *2a,b*, apertural view and from above, showing characteristic bends in growth lines, ×1.5.

Pararaphistoma VOSTAKOVA, 1955 [**Helicites qualteriatus* SCHLOTHEIM, 1820] [=*Pararaphistoma (Climacoraphistoma)* VOSTAKOVA, 1955 (144, p. 83)]. Shell lenticular to low-spired with "stair step" profile; widely phaneromphalous; growth lines sweeping back smoothly from suture, without a sigmoidal bend (144, p. 83). Ord., Eu.-N. Am.

Buechelia C. SCHLÜTER, 1894 [**B. goldfussi*]. Shape like *Raphistoma* but with narrowing at base that suggests a canal. *M.Dev.*, Eu.-N.Am.——FIG. 115, *1*. **B. goldfussi*, Ger.; ×1.

Arizonella STOYANOW, 1948 [**A. allecta*]. Like *Buechelia* but without canal-like narrowing at base; spire slightly gradate (135, p. 789). *U.Dev.*, N. Am.——FIG. 115,3. **A. allecta*, Ariz.; ×1.3 (135).

?Scalitina SPRIESTERSBACH, 1919 [**S. montana*] [=*Ampulloscalites* WENZ, 1938 (147, p. 167)]. Turbiniform except for wide ramp above, terminating at sharp angle with shallow groove just below on side; columellar lip widely arcuate; sinus probably present on labrum but unknown. *Dev.-L.Carb.*, Eu.——FIG. 115,4. **S. montana*. M.Dev., Ger.; ×0.7.

Subfamily LIOSPIRINAE Knight, 1956

Shell lenticular, with moderately deep V-shaped sinus culminating in short slit that generates a convex selenizone mostly or entirely on its upper side. *?L.Ord., M.Ord.-M.Perm.*

Liospira ULRICH & SCOFIELD, 1897 [**Pleurotomaria micula* HALL, 1862; SD McLEARN, 1942] [=*Eocryptaenia* KOKEN, 1925]. Surface glossy, without ornament; selenizone convex, forming periphery but largely on upper side; cryptom-

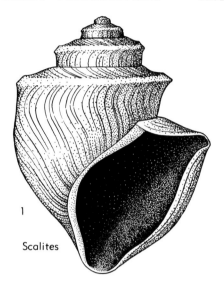

FIG. 114. Pleurotomariacea (Raphistomatidae——Raphistomatinae) (p. I201).

phalous. *?L.Ord., M.Ord.-Sil.*, N.Am.-Eu.-NE. Asia.——FIG. 116,2. **L. micula* (HALL), U.Ord., Ky.; ×4.

?Arastra STOYANOW, 1948 [*A. torquata*]. Shell thick, minutely phaneromphalous; base extending slightly above lower margin of selenizone, extension rhythmically bent downward to produce frilled periphery; surface undulating (135, p. 790). *U.Dev.*, N.Am.——FIG. 116,*1*. **A. torquata* Ariz.; ×2.

Trepospira ULRICH & SCOFIELD, 1897 [**Pleurotomaria sphaerulata* CONRAD, 1842]. Shell like *Liospira* except for row of nodes just below upper suture and variation in details; selenizone wholly on upper side of periphery. *Dev.-M.Perm.*, N.Am.-S.Am.-Eu.-N.Afr.

T. (Trepospira) [=*Kansana* TASCH, 1953 (137, Am.-S.Am.-Eu.-N.Afr.——FIG. 116,4. **T. (T.) sphaerulata* (CONRAD), U.Penn., Ill., ×2. p. 397)]. Subsutural nodes rounded, base cryptomphalous or anomphalous. *Dev.-M.Perm.*, N.

T. (Angyomphalus) COSSMANN, 1916 [**Euomphalus radians* DEKONINCK, 1843]. Subsutural nodes lengthened radially; umbilicus partly open, surrounded by narrow circumumbilical funicle. *L.Carb.*, Eu.——FIG. 116,3. **T. (A.) radians* (DEKONINCK), Belg.; ×2.

Subfamily OMOSPIRINAE Wenz, 1938

Shell gradate, with ramp; labral slit or sinus relatively wide, shallow, generating selenizone just within outer margin of ramp. *M.Ord.-L.Jur.(Lias.).*

Omospira ULRICH in ULRICH & SCOFIELD, 1897 [**O.*

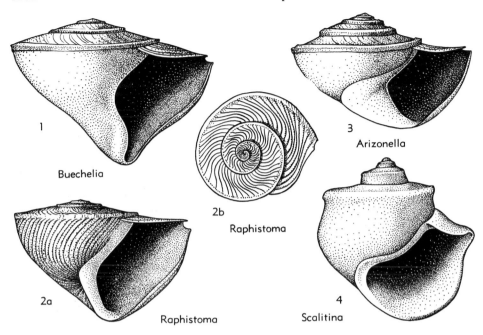

1 Buechelia

2b Raphistoma

3 Arizonella

2a Raphistoma

4 Scalitina

Fig. 115. Pleurotomariacea (Raphistomatidae——Raphistomatinae) (p. *1201*).

laticincta]. Relatively high-spired, anomphalous; selenizone about half width of ramp, without bordering threads, sloping downward and outward; sides below selenizone rounded. *M.Ord.-Sil.*, N.Am.-Eu.——Fig. 116,9. *O. laticincta*, M. Ord., Tenn.; ✕1.

Baylea deKoninck, 1883 [*Trochus yvanii* Léveillé, 1835] [=*Yvania* Fischer, 1885 (obj.)]. Turbiniform; short labral slit on outer edge of sloping ramp, bordered by strong threads; ornamented primarily with spiral threads but with collabral threads and nodes in some species. *L. Carb.(Miss.)-M. Perm.*, N. Am.-Eu.-SE. Asia.—— Fig. 116,7. *B. yvanii* (Léveillé), L.Carb., Belg.; ✕1.3.

Hypselentoma Weller, 1929 [*Pleurotomaria perhumerosa* Meek, 1872]. Like *Omospira* but with shallow groove below periphery and spiral threads on sides. *U.Penn.*, N.Am.——Fig. 116,8. *H. perhumerosa* (Meek), Neb.; ✕2.25.

Callistadia Knight, 1945 [*C. bella*]. Relatively low-spired, narrowly phaneromphalous; selenizone bordered by cords; ornamented with revolving cords (72, p. 577). *Penn.-M.Perm.*, N.Am.-SE. Asia.——Fig. 116,5. *C. bella*, M.Perm., Tex.; ✕2.7.

Sisenna Koken, 1896 [*Pleurotomaria turbinata* Hörnes, 1855; SD Cossmann, 1897]. Relatively low-spired, anomphalous or narrowly phaneromphalous, with spiral ridges, one delimiting broad, sloping ramp; collabral ornament almost confined

to growth lines which are prosocyrt below ramp angle at which selenizone lies. *L.Trias.-L.Jur. (Lias.)*, cosmop.——Fig. 116,6. *S. turbinata*, U. Trias.(Carn.), Aus.; ✕2 (79).

Family EOTOMARIIDAE Wenz, 1938

[*nom. transl.* Knight, Batten & Yochelson, herein (*ex* Eotomariinae Wenz, 1938)]

Shell turbiniform to trochiform; labral slit invariably present, generating concave selenizone bordered by threads at approximately mid-height of whorl. *U.Cam.-L.Jur.(Lias.)*.

Subfamily EOTOMARIINAE Wenz, 1938

[=Ptychomphalinae, Ptychomphalininae Wenz, 1938]

Slit moderate to deep, umbilicus narrow or absent; ornament collabral and spiral elements, collabral dominant. *U.Cam.-L.Jur. (Lias.)*.

Tribe PTYCHOMPHALIDES Wenz, 1938

[*nom. transl.* Knight, Batten & Yochelson, herein (*ex* Ptychomphalinae Wenz, 1938)] [=Ptychomphalininae Wenz, 1938]

Labral slit deep, selenizone flat or concave, commonly bordered by extended cords or flanges. *U.Cam.-L.Jur.(Lias.)*.

Taeniospira Ulrich & Bridge, 1931 [*T. eminencensis*]. Turbiniform; labral sinus V-shaped, culminating in moderately deep slit that generates concave selenizone bordered by low threads; narrowly phaneromphalous; ornamented with col-

labral threads that are strongly prosocline above selenizone and opisthocline below it. *U.Cam.*, N. Am.——FIG. 118,2. **T. eminencensis*, Mo.; ×1.

Mourlonia DEKONINCK, 1883 [**Helix carinatus* J. SOWERBY, 1812] [=*Ptychomphalina* FISCHER, 1885; *Cryptaulus* FOERSTE, 1923; *Promourlonia* LONGSTAFF, 1924; *Foersteria* TOMLIN, 1929 (*pro Cryptaulus* FOERSTE, 1923, *non* BAVAY, 1903); *Eocryptaulina* FOERSTE, 1936 (*pro Foersteria* TOMLIN, 1929, *non* SZÉPLIGETI, 1896); *Spiroraphella* GRABAU, 1936]. Turbiniform; labral sinus relatively shallow but culminating in rather deep slit; ornament dominantly collabral but also spiral; growth lines strongly prosocline above selenizone and below it except for short distance at top; color pattern of wide transverse spots above selenizone may be preserved. *M.Ord.-L.Perm.*, N.Am.-Eu.-Asia-Austral.——FIG. 117,1. **M. carinata* (SOWERBY), L.Carb., Eng.; ×0.7.

Oehlertia PERNER, 1907 [**Pleurotomaria (Oehlertia) senilis*] [=?*Bembexia (Pleurotobembex)* SOLLE, 1956]. Trochiform, with moderately wide umbilicus; labral sinus shallow, culminating in fairly deep slit that generates a selenizone between pair of carinae; ornament as in *Mourlonia*. *L. Dev.*, Eu.——FIG. 117,2. **O. senilis* (PERNER), Czech.; ×2.

Tropidostropha LONGSTAFF, 1912 [**Pleurotomaria griffithii* M'COY, 1844]. Shell large, with angular periphery carrying flat or convex selenizone between pair of lamellae; slit deep; growth lines gently prosocline above selenizone and, except next to it, almost vertical below; umbilicus narrow, funnel-shaped; an obscure spiral thread around lower surface; vertical lacunae in outer shell layers. *L.Carb.*, Eu.——FIG. 118,4. **T. griffithii* (M'COY), Ire.; ×0.5.

Euconospira ULRICH in ULRICH & SCOFIELD, 1897 [**Pleurotomaria turbiniformis* MEEK & WORTHEN, 1861; SD KNIGHT, 1937] [=*Trechmannia* LONG-

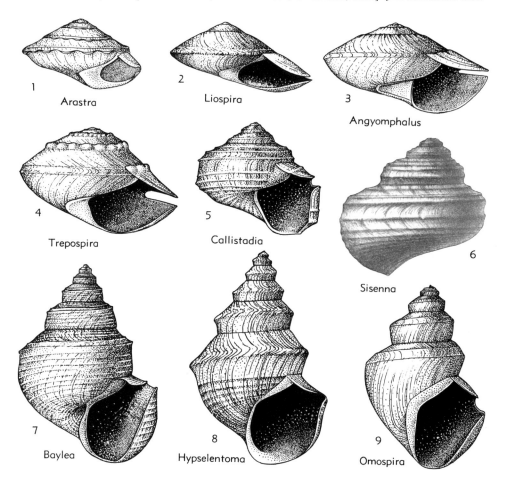

1 Arastra
2 Liospira
3 Angyomphalus
4 Trepospira
5 Callistadia
6 Sisenna
7 Baylea
8 Hypselentoma
9 Omospira

FIG. 116. Pleurotomariacea (Raphistomatidae——Liospirinae, Omospirinae) (p. *I201-I202*).

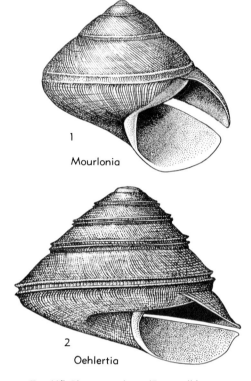

1
Mourlonia

2
Oehlertia

Fig. 117. Pleurotomariacea (Eotomariidae——
Eotomariinae) (p. *I203*).

staff, 1912; *Pernotrochus* H.Chronic, 1952 (14, p. 120)]. Trochiform, base moderately convex to slightly concave, anomphalous or with pseudumbilicus; labral sinus shallow, culminating in deep slit that generates a selenizone between pair of carinae; ornament and color pattern as in *Mourlonia. Miss.(L.Carb.)-M.Perm.*, N.Am.-Eu.-NC.Asia.——Fig. 118,*10*. **E. turbiniformis* (Meek & Worthen), U.Penn., Ill.; ×2.7.

Spiroscala Knight, 1945 [**S. pagoda*]. Trochiform, with sharply conical spire; selenizone bordered by conspicuous protruding cords; base nearly flat, narrowly phaneromphalous; ornament spiral and transverse; latter dominant (72, p. 574). *Miss.(L.Carb.)-M.Perm.*, N.Am.-Eu.-Austral.——Fig. 118, *3*. **S. pagoda*, U.Penn., Tex.; ×4.

Shwedagonia Batten, 1956 [**S. elegans*]. Turbiniform, with spire slightly to strongly coeloconoid; phaneromphalous; slit very narrow and deep, about 0.8 of final whorl in depth; selenizone narrow, deeply embedded, both slit and selenizone bordered below by broad smooth flat area with fine opisthocline growth lines, followed by a thread, thus simulating lower part of selenizone; ornament collabral growth lines or sharp threads

and faint spiral threads (5, p. 43). *L.Perm.-M. Perm.*, cosmop.——Fig. 118,*1*. **S. elegans*, M. Perm., Tex.; ×5.3.

Rhaphistomella Kittl, 1891 [**Pleurotomaria radians* Wissmann in Münster, 1841] [=*Raphistomella* Diener, 1926 (obj.)]. Small, sublenticular, with obtuse spire, phaneromphalous, protruding periphery carrying selenizone; slit short; growth lines strongly prosocline above selenizone, prosocyrt below. *M.Trias.(Ladin.)-U.Trias.(Rhaetic)*, Eu.——Fig. 119,*1*. **R. radians* (Wissmann), U. Trias.(Carn.), S.Tyrol; *1a,b*, ×3 (64).

Euzone Koken, 1896 [**E. alauna;* SD Cossmann, 1897] [=*Polyelasma* Cossmann, 1897 (obj.)]. Small-medium, globose-turbiniform, phaneromphalous, angulation bordering umbilicus; whorls few, convex; selenizone at periphery, slightly overlapped on earlier whorls, wide, raised, bordered by cords and with prominent wide-spaced lunulae; ornament strong collabral threads prosocline above selenizone, orthocline below. *M.Trias.(Anis.)-U. Trias.(Carn.)*, Eu.——Fig. 119,*2*. **E. alauna*, M. Trias.(Anis.), Aus.; *2a*, abapertural side, ×1; *2b*, growth lines, ×1.5 (79).

Luciellina Kittl, 1900 [**L. contracta;* SD Diener, 1926]. Lenticular or biconical, anomphalous or cryptomphalous, with prominent carina forming periphery at mid-height; base strongly convex; ornament spiral cords; selenizone including peripheral carina and a band below it, hence hidden on spire. *M. Trias. (Ladin.)-U. Trias. (Carn.)*, Eu. (Hung.-Aus.).——Fig. 123,*1*. **L. contracta*, M. Trias.(Ladin.), Hung.;×3 (Kittl).

Ptychomphalus Agassiz, 1839 [**Helicina compressa* J.Sowerby, 1813] [=*Cochlicarina* Brown, 1843 (obj.); *Cryptaenia* Eudes-Deslongchamps, 1864]. Sublenticular, cryptomphalous, umbilicus obscured by groove-encircled callous coating; spire low, obtuse, base strongly and evenly convex; surface smooth except for faint spiral threads and small nodes adjoining adapical suture in some species; selenizone peripheral, more or less overlapped on spire whorls; slit short. *L.Jur.*, Eu.——Fig. 119,*3*. **P. expansus* (Sowerby), L.Lias., Fr.; *3a,b*, apertural and basal views, ×1 (111).

Tribe EOTOMARIIDES Wenz, 1938

[*nom. transl.* Knight, Batten & Yochelson, herein (*ex* Eotomariinae Wenz, 1938)]

Labral slit only moderately deep, selenizone concave between a pair of threads, commonly with its lower border forming shell periphery. *M.Ord.-M.Perm.*

Eotomaria Ulrich & Scofield, 1897 [**E. canalifera* Ulrich in Ulrich & Scofield, 1897] [=*Spiroraphe* Perner, 1907]. Sublenticular, coeloconoidal, minutely phaneromphalous; deep sinus culminating in short slit that generates a selenizone just above periphery. *M.Ord.-Sil.*, N. Am.-Eu.-NE.Asia.——Fig. 118,*7*. **E. canalifera* Ulrich, M.Ord., Tenn.; ×1.

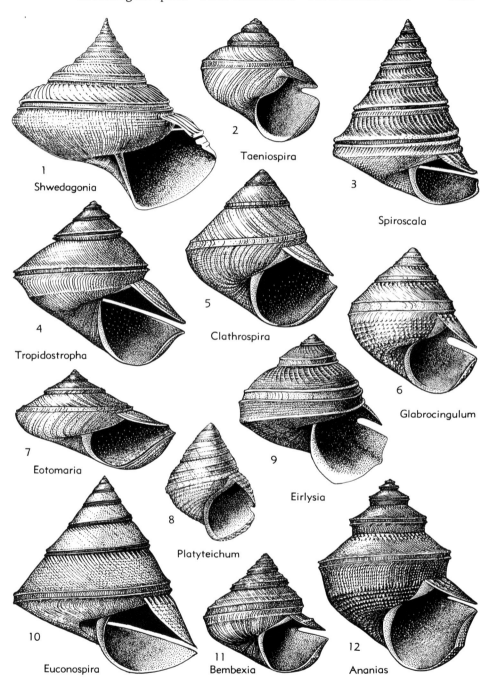

FIG. 118. Pleurotomariacea (Eotomariidae——Eotomariinae) (*1202-1206*).

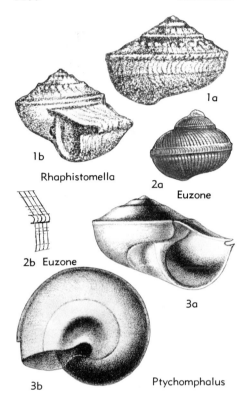

1a

1b

Rhaphistomella

2a

Euzone

2b Euzone

3a

3b

Ptychomphalus

FIG. 119. Pleurotomariacea (Eotomariidae——
Eotomariinae) (p. *1204*).

Clathrospira ULRICH & SCOFIELD, 1897 [*Pleurotomaria subconica* HALL, 1847] [=*Palaeoschisma*
DONALD, 1902]. Turbiniform, with conical spire
and shallow sutures, narrowly phaneromphalous;
growth lines strongly prosocline above selenizone
and strongly opisthocline below it, but rounding
to gently prosocline on base, outlining a moderately deep labral sinus that culminates in a short
slit; selenizone bordered by fine threads; growth
lines and lunulae periodically strengthened, very
fine spiral threads numerous. *M.Ord.-Sil.,* N.Am.-
Eu.——FIG. 118,5. *C. subconica* (HALL), M.Ord.,
N.Y.; ×2.

Bembexia OEHLERT, 1888 [*Pleurotomaria larteti*
MUNIER-CHALMAS, 1876]. Turbiniform, slightly
gradate, with moderately deep sutures, narrowly
phaneromphalous to anomphalous; labral sinus
moderately deep, selenizone concave between moderately strong threads; collabral lines or lirae and
a spiral thread on upper whorl surface. *L.Dev.-
L.Carb.(Miss.),* Eu.-N.Am.——FIG. 118,11. *B.
larteti* (MUNIER-CHALMAS), L.Dev., Fr.; ×1.

Glabrocingulum THOMAS, 1940 [*G. beggi*]. Turbiniform, spire varying from gradate to conical; conspicuous transverse and spiral threads with nodes

at their intersections, ornament most prominent
near upper suture and at base (140, p. 38). *L.
Carb.(Miss.)-M.Perm.,* Eu.-E.Asia-N.Am.-S.Am.

G. (Glabrocingulum). Spire low conical, slightly
gradate; many specimens with funicle in umbilicus.
L.Carb.(U.Miss.)-M.Perm., Eu.-E.Asia-N.Am.-S.
Am.——FIG. 118,6. *G. (G.) beggi,* L.Carb.,
Scot.; ×2.

G. (Ananias) KNIGHT, 1945 [*Phanerotrema?
welleri* NEWELL, 1935]. Gradate, some species
closely resembling *Worthenia* and others *Glabrocingulum* s.s.; umbilicus without funicle (72, p.
573). *Miss.(L.Carb.)-Penn.(U.Carb.),* N.Am.-
Eu.-SE.Asia.——FIG. 118,12. *G. (A.) welleri*
(NEWELL), U.Penn., Kan.; ×1.3.

Platyteichum CAMPBELL, 1953 [*P. costatum*].
Turbiniform, anomphalous or minutely phaneromphalous; ornamented with spiral threads and cords
(12, p. 23). *L.Perm.,* Austral.——FIG. 118,8. *P.
costatum;* ×1.

Eirlysia BATTEN, 1956 [*E. exquisita*]. Variably
turbiniform, with rounded angulation surrounding flattish phaneromphalous base and gently concave selenizone between 2 threads slightly above
mid-whorl; labral slit about 0.15 whorl deep;
collabral and spiral ornament variously developed,
the former commonly dominant (5, p. 44). *M.
Perm.,* N.Am.——FIG. 118,9. *E. exquisita,* TEX.;
×2.7.

Subfamily AGNESIINAE Knight, 1956

Coiling sinistral or hyperstrophic. *L.Dev.-
U.Trias.*

The protoconch in some species of
Agnesia seems to be sinistral, like the teleoconch. The peculiar selenizone of this genus
is known only in the type species. In *Hesperiella,* the inturned heterostrophic protoconch suggests hyperstrophy. Assuming that
these genera are related, they are oriented
for description as sinistral.

Hesperiella HOLZAPFEL, 1889 [*Pleurotomaria contraria* DEKONINCK, 1843; SD KNIGHT, 1937].
Pupiform, with protoconch coiling inward;
selenizone low on whorls, gently arched; ornament collabral threads and cords. *L.Dev.-U.Carb.,*
Eu.——FIG. 120,1. *H. contraria* (DEKONINCK),
L.Carb., Belg.; *1a,b,* posterior and oblique view of
apex, ×5.

Agnesia DEKONINCK, 1883 [*Pleurotomaria acuta*
PHILLIPS, 1836]. Trochiform, with convex base;
selenizone showing V-shaped lunulae with notch-
within-slit pattern; ornament collabral and spiral
threads. Protoconch of type species unknown. *L.
Dev.-M.Perm.,* N.Am.-Eu.-SE.Asia.——FIG. 120,2.
A. acuta (PHILLIPS), L.Carb., Eng.; ×2.

Enantiostoma KOKEN, 1896 [*Pleurotomaria perversa* HÖRNES, 1856]. Small, sinistral, turbiniform,
broadly phaneromphalous; selenizone narrow,

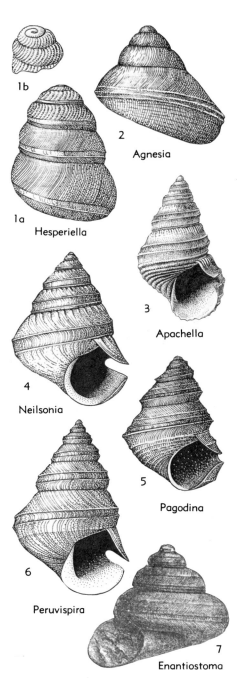

FIG. 120. Pleurotomariacea (Eotomariidae—
Agnesiinae) (p. I206-I207).

peripheral; ornament weak collabral and spiral threads, the former prosocline (having regard to sinistrality) above selenizone, opisthocline below it. *U.Trias.(Nor.)*, Eu.——FIG. 120,7. **E. perversum*, Aus.; ×2.7 (79).

Subfamily NEILSONIINAE Knight, 1956

Shell relatively high-spired. *L.Carb. (Miss.)-U.Trias.*

Neilsonia THOMAS, 1940 [**N. roscobiensis*]. Selenizone relatively broad, located low on final whorl and just above sutures on spire; ornament collabral with tendency toward noding at upper end (140, p. 46). *L.Carb.(Miss.)-M.Perm.*, N.Am.-Eu.-SE. Asia.——FIG. 120,4. **N. roscobiensis*, L.Carb., Scot.; ×3.3.

Peruvispira, J.CHRONIC, 1949 [**P. delicata*]. Very small; selenizone on protruding carina; ornament growth lines (13, p. 146). *L.Perm.-M.Perm.*, S. Am.-N.Am.——FIG. 120,6. **P. delicata*, L.Perm., Peru; ×10.

Pagodina WANNER, 1942 [**P. typus*]. Somewhat gradate; selenizone just above angular periphery; ornament spiral (146, p. 166). *Perm.*, SE.Asia.——FIG. 120,5. **P. typus*, E. Indies; ×3 (146).

Apachella WINTERS, 1956 [**A. translirata*]. Much like *Neilsonia* but with selenizone above middle of last whorl and well above suture on spire; ornament absent or various combinations of spiral and collabral; some species with a parietal tooth close to outer lip (151, p. 44). *L.Perm.-M.Perm.*, cosmop.——FIG. 120,3. **A. translirata*, M.Perm., Ariz.; ×4.

Pareuryalox HAAS, 1953 [**P. perornata*]. Littoriniform, narrowly phaneromphalous; whorls convex, not carinate; ornament minutely beaded spiral cords; selenizone wide, occupying almost all lower half of each spire whorl, with median beaded keel and another forming its upper border; inner lip reflected, almost hiding umbilicus. *U.Trias*, Peru. ——FIG. 202A,2. **P. perornata; 2a-d*, apertural, abapertural, apical, basal sides, ×3 (50).

Family LOPHOSPIRIDAE Wenz, 1938

[*nom. transl.* KNIGHT, BATTEN & YOCHELSON, herein (*ex* Lophospirinae WENZ, 1938)]

Shell with median labral sinus that generally culminates in a median angulation, and commonly with angulations both above and below; selenizone or pseudoselenizone convex; form of shell variable, whorls may be disjunct in late growth stages or throughout. *Ord.-M.Trias.*

Subfamily LOPHOSPIRINAE Wenz, 1938

Labral exhalant emargination generally a sharp V-shaped sinus, with or without a short notch. *Ord.-Sil.*

Many early Lophospirinae have homeo-

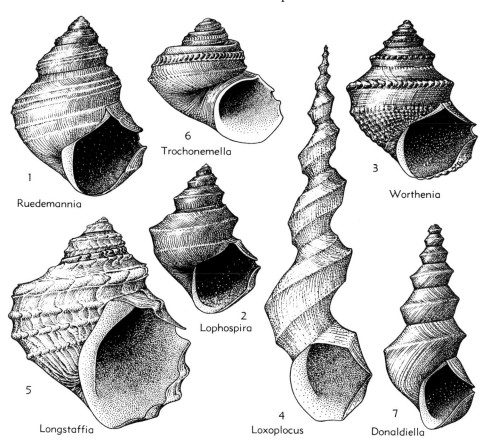

FIG. 121. Pleurotomariacea (Lophospiridae——Lophospirinae, Ruedemanniinae) (p. *1208-1209*).

morphic counterparts in the Trochonematidae. So close is the similarity that it is difficult to decide whether or not some should be separated in different families or superfamilies.

Loxoplocus FISCHER, 1885 [*Murchisonia tropidophora* WHITEAVES, 1884 (=*M. soluta* WHITEAVES, 1884)]. Sinus deep, angular; selenizone or pseudoselenizone convex. *Ord.-Sil.*, N.Am.-Eu.-NE.Asia.

L. (Lophospira) WHITFIELD, 1886 [*Murchisonia bicincta* HALL, 1847 (=*M. milleri* S.A.MILLER, 1877, pro *M. bicincta* HALL, non M'COY, 1844); SD OEHLERT, 1888] [=*Schizolopha* ULRICH in ULRICH & SCOFIELD, 1897; *Ptychonema* PERNER, 1903]. Turbinate, gradate; whorls mostly contiguous. *Ord.-Sil.*, N.Am.-Eu.-NE.Asia.——FIG. 121,2. *L. (L.) milleri* (MILLER), M.Ord., N.Y.; ×1.3.

L. (Loxoplocus). At least later whorls disjunct. *M.Ord.-Sil.*, N.Am.-NE.Asia.——FIG. 121,4. *L. (L.) solutus* (WHITEAVES), M.Sil., Ont.; ×0.7.

L. (Donaldiella) COSSMANN, 1903 [pro *Goniospira* DONALD, 1902 (non COSSMANN, 1895)] [*Goniospira filosa* DONALD, 1902] [=*Pagodispira* GRABAU, 1922]. Spire high, whorls mostly in contact. *M.Ord.-Sil.*, N.Am.-Eu.-NE.Asia.——FIG. 121,7. *L. (D.) filosa* (DONALD), U.Ord., Scot.; ×2.7.

Trochonemella OKULITCH, 1935 [*Lophospira(?) notabilis* ULRICH & ULRICH & SCOFIELD, 1897]. Shape like *Trochonema (s.s.)*, narrowly phaneromphalous; sinus relatively shallow, culminating in wide notch that gives rise to a selenizone. *M. Ord.*, N.Am.——FIG. 121,6. *T. notabilis* (ULRICH), Tenn.; ×1.3.

Longstaffia COSSMANN, 1908 [pro *Tubulosa* COSSMANN, 1908 (non SCHWEIGGER, 1820)] [*Pleurotomaria tubulosa* LINDSTRÖM, 1884]. Turbiniform; convex selenizone generated by deep notch (or shallow slit) on a carina somewhat above middle of labrum; several other spiral carinae or cords with shallow labral reentrants marked by transverse lamellae. *M.Sil.*, Eu.——FIG. 121,5. *L. tubulosa* (LINDSTRÖM), Gotl.; ×2.

Subfamily RUEDEMANNIINAE Knight, 1956

Exhalant emargination of labrum a true slit that generates a selenizone. *M.Ord.-M.Trias.*

In tracing *Ruedemannia* into the Devonian, a succession of species is found to approach *Worthenia* more and more closely. The latter genus, which appears in the Mississippian, converges in various characters with Carboniferous genera of the Eotomariidae (such as *Glabrocingulum*); indeed, some species of *G. (Ananias)* are distinguishable from *Worthenia* only by the absence of a convex crenulated selenizone.

Ruedemannia FOERSTE, 1914 [*Lophospira (?Seelya) lirata* ULRICH in ULRICH & SCOFIELD, 1897] [=*Coronilla* PERNER, 1907 (*non* BENEDEN, 1871)]. Turbiniform; slit short, selenizone wide, with median thread; spiral thread on slope above selenizone and 2 below. *M.Ord.-Dev.*, N.Am.-Eu.——FIG. 121,*1.* *R. lirata* (ULRICH), U.Ord., Ky.; ×2.7.

Worthenia DEKONINCK, 1883 [*Turbo tabulatus* CONRAD, 1835] [=*Platyworthenia* H.CHRONIC, 1952 (14, p. 121)]. Shape like *Loxoplocus (Lophospira)* but highly ornamented with spiral and collabral threads; convex selenizone strongly crenulated; anomphalous or minutely phaneromphalous. *L.Carb.(Miss.)-M.Trias.,* cosmop.——FIG. 121,*3.* *W. tabulata* (CONRAD), U.Penn., Pa.; ×1.3.

Family LUCIELLIDAE Knight, 1956

More or less trochiform, with marginal frill and broad shallow labral notch just below frill generating a broad selenizone; ornament on upper whorl surface generally includes oblique strongly opisthocline threads or cords normal to prosocline growth lines. *Ord.-U.Carb.*

Rhombella BRIDGE & CLOUD, 1947 [*Roubidouxia umbilicata* ULRICH & BRIDGE in DAKE & BRIDGE, 1932]. Spire low conical, base nearly flat, with moderately wide umbilicus; labral sinus culminating at periphery in shallow notch that generates a selenizone; whorl section rhomboidal (9, p. 550). *L.Ord.,* N.Am.——FIG. 122,*2.* *R. umbilicata* (ULRICH & BRIDGE), Mo.; ×0.7.

Prosolarium PERNER, 1903 [*P. procerum*]. Oblique threads very fine; umbilicus with smooth concave callus; frill small, not fluted. *U.Sil.,* Eu.——FIG. 123,*3.* *P. procerum,* Czech.; ×1.3.

Epiptychia PERNER, 1907 [*Clisospira potens* PERNER, 1903]. Relatively high-spired, anomphalous; frill short, scalloped; ornament of prosocline, slightly imbricating growth lamellae with fine oblique threads between and normal to them.

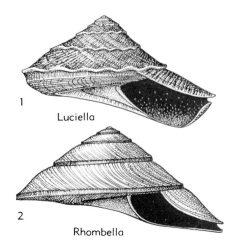

FIG. 122. Pleurotomariacea (Luciellidae) (p. I209).

L.Dev., Eu.——FIG. 123,*2.* *E. potens* (PERNER), Czech.; ×1.3.

Luciella DEKONINCK, 1883 [*Pleurotomaria eliana* DEKONINCK, 1843]. Frill fluted, spiral cords numerous on base between umbilical callus and selenizone, oblique threads on upper surface moderately coarse. *M.Dev.-U.Carb.(Penn.),* Eu.-N.Am.——FIG. 122,*1.* *L. eliana* (DEKONINCK), L.Carb., Belg., ×1.3.

Echinocirrus RYCKHOLT, 1860 [*Cirrus armatus* DE KONINCK, 1843] [=*Cirridius* DEKONINCK, 1881 (obj.)]. Like *Luciella,* but threads normal to growth lines are replaced by 3 series of coarse cords terminating at periphery in 3 rows of tubular openings. *L.Carb.,* Eu.——FIG. 123,*4.* *E. armatus* (DEKONINCK), Belg.; *4a,b,* from above and below, ×1.3.

Family PHANEROTREMATIDAE Knight, 1956

Well-marked selenizone bordered by sharp threads high on whorl; labral slit short; anomphalous. *M.Ord.-L.Dev.*

Brachytomaria KOKEN, 1925 [*Pleurotomaria baltica* DEVERNEUIL, 1845]. Turbiniform, gradate, with tapering anomphalous base and thickened columellar lip; ornament (in type species) comprising sharp lamellar collabral threads. *M.Ord.,* Eu.——FIG. 124,*1.* *B. baltica* (DEVERNEUIL), Est.; ×1.3.

Ulrichospira DONALD, 1905 [*U. similis*]. Like *Brachytomaria* but with higher, more attenuated spire. *L.Sil.,* Eu.——FIG. 124,*3.* *U. similis,* Eng.; ×3 (119).

Phanerotrema FISCHER, 1885 [*Pleurotomaria labrosa* HALL, 1860]. Shape and position of selenizone much as in *Brachytomaria* but with shallower sutures and larger last whorl; collabral

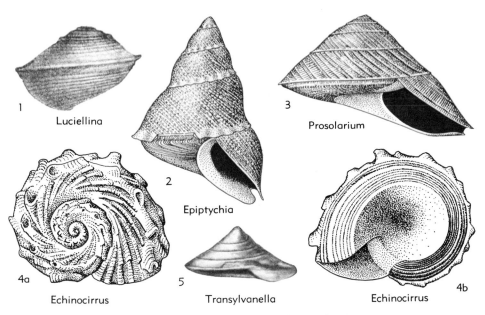

FIG. 123. Pleurotomariacea (Luciellidae, Eotomariilae, Family Uncertain) (p. *1204, 1209, 1223*).

lamellae or spiral cords, or both. *L.Sil.-L.Dev.,* N.Am.-Eu.-Austral.——FIG. 124,2. **P. labrosum* (HALL), L.Dev., N.Y.; ×0.7.

Family GOSSELETINIDAE Wenz, 1938

[*nom. transl.* KNIGHT, BATTEN & YOCHELSON, herein (*ex* Gosseletininae WENZ, 1938)]

Labral slit short, selenizone flat and generally without bordering threads. *M.Ord.-Trias.*

Subfamily GOSSELETININAE Wenz, 1938

Slit and selenizone narrow, above mid-whorl. *M.Ord.-Trias.*

Pseudocryptaenia KOKEN, 1925 [**Pleurotomaria lahuseni* KOKEN, 1897]. Rotelliform, small, phaneromphalous; outer lip with short notchlike sinus or slit, selenizone narrow and slightly raised at outer margin of upper whorl surface; ornament growth lines. *M.Ord.,* Eu.——FIG. 125,1. **P. lahuseni* (KOKEN), Est.; ×4 (80).

Stenoloron OEHLERT, 1888 [**Pleurotomaria (Stenoloron) viennayi*]. Turbiniform, phaneromphalous; narrow selenizone high on whorl face. *M.Sil.-L.Dev.,* Eu.——FIG. 125,4. **S. viennayi* (OEHLERT), L.Dev., Fr.; ×1 (108).

Platyloron OEHLERT, 1888 [**Pleurotomaria bishofi* GOLDFUSS, 1844]. Rotelliform, small, anomphalous; broad convex selenizone on upper whorl face. *M. Sil.-M.Dev.,* Eu.——FIG. 125,3. **P. bishofi* (GOLDFUSS), M.Dev., Ger.; ×4.

Umbotropis PERNER, 1903 [**U. albicans*]. Umboni-

form, with narrow umbilicus; slit and selenizone above mid-whorl; surface smooth, glossy. *L.Dev.,* Eu.——FIG. 125,2. **U. albicans,* Czech.; ×4.

?**Triangularia** FRECH, 1894 [**T. paradoxa*]. Conical triangular, with many narrow whorls and wide umbilicus; flat selenizone on upper whorl face. *L.Dev.,* Eu.——FIG. 125,6. **T. paradoxa,* Ger.; *6a,b,* apical and apertural views, ×2 (44).

Gosseletina FISCHER, 1885 [*pro Gosseletia* DE KONINCK, 1883 (*non* BARROIS, 1882)] [**Pleurotomaria callosa* DEKONINCK, 1843]. Turbiniform, anomphalous, with much thickened inner lip; slit short; narrow flat selenizone high on whorl face; surface of type species glossy but other species referred to genus have spiral and collabral ornament and are narrowly phaneromphalous. *?Dev., L.Carb.(Miss.)-Perm., ?Trias.,* Eu.-NC.Asia-N.Am. ——FIG. 125,5. **G. callosa* (DEKONINCK), L.Carb., Belg.; ×1.3.

Rufilla KOKEN, 1896 [**R. densecincta;* SD COSSMANN, 1897]. Small, globular, narrowly phaneromphalous; whorls evenly convex, smooth or with spiral ornament; selenizone rather broad, high on whorl side, with median spiral cord and bordered by two others; growth lines gently prosocyrt above selenizone, more strongly so below. *U.Trias. (Carn.),* Eu.——FIG. 125,7. **R. densecincta,* Aus.; ×5 (79).

Subfamily COELOZONINAE Knight, 1956

Slit broad and short. *M.Ord.-L.Dev.*

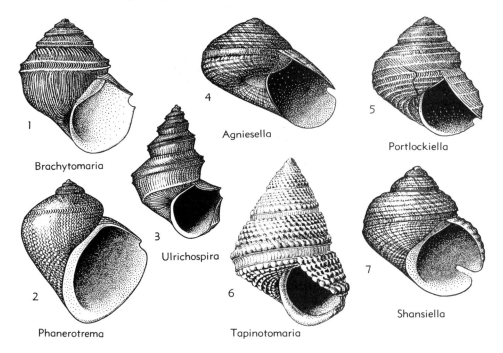

1, Brachytomaria; 2, Phanerotrema; 3, Ulrichospira; 4, Agniesella; 5, Portlockiella; 6, Tapinotomaria; 7, Shansiella

FIG. 124. Pleurotomariacea (Phanerotrematidae, Portlockiellidae) (p. I209, I212).

Tribe COELOZONIDES Knight, 1956

Selenizone broad, depressed. *M.Ord.-M. Dev.*

Latitaenia KOKEN, 1925 [*Pleurotomaria rotelloidea* KOKEN, 1896]. Rotelliform; slit and selenizone moderately high on whorl face; base rounded, narrowly phaneromphalous; ornament growth lines. *M.Ord.-U.Ord.*, Eu.——FIG. 126,1. *L. rotelloidea* (KOKEN), M.Ord., Norway; ×2.

Euryzone KOKEN, 1896 [*Helicites delphinuloides* SCHLOTHEIM, 1820; SD PERNER, 1907]. Widely trochiform with moderately wide umbilicus and deep sutures; slit and selenizone moderately high on whorl face; ornament faint spiral and transverse threads. *U.Ord.-M.Dev.*, Eu.-SE.Asia-N.Am. ——FIG. 126,3. *E. delphinuloides* (SCHLOTHEIM), M.Dev., Ger.; ×0.75.

Conotoma PERNER, 1907 [*Pleurotomaria (Clathrospira [Conotoma]) eximia*]. Trochiform, narrowly phaneromphalous; broad selenizone on low peripheral angle; ornament collabral and spiral threads, lunulae strong and widely spaced. *U.Sil.*, Eu.——FIG. 126,7. *C. eximia* (PERNER), Czech.; ×1.

Coelozone PERNER, 1907 [*Pleurotomaria (Coelozone) verna*]. Low trochiform, with somewhat flattened anomphalous base; selenizone just above periphery. *U.Sil.*, Eu.——FIG. 126,6. *C. verna* (PERNER), Czech.; ×1.3.

Tribe PLANOZONIDES Knight, 1956

Selenizone flush with surface or slightly raised; ornament fine obliquely spiral threads normal to growth lines. *M.Ord.-L. Dev.*

Cataschisma E.B.BRANSON, 1909 [*C. typa*] [=*Globispira* KOKEN, 1925]. Shell rounded; short broad slit and faint selenizone low on whorl face; narrowly phaneromphalous. *M.Ord.-M.Sil.* N.Am.-Eu.——FIG. 126,4. *C. exquisita* (LINDSTRÖM), M. Sil., Gotl.; ×5.3.

Pleurorima PERNER, 1907 [*Pleurotomaria (Pleurorima) migrans* (=*Pleurotomaria pragensis* KOKEN, 1889); SD COSSMANN, 1908]. Shell thin, turbiniform; selenizone on crest of broad ridge; ornament as for tribe but with spiral threads on selenizone; ?anomphalous. *U.Sil.*, Eu.——FIG. 126,2. *P. pragensis* (KOKEN), Czech.; ×0.7.

Planozone PERNER, 1907 [*P. ramificans*]. Turbiniform, anomphalous; selenizone wide, nearly flat, slightly elevated above surface and located above mid-whorl. *L.Dev.*, Eu.——FIG. 126,5. *P. ramificans*, Czech.; ×10.

Family EUOMPHALOPTERIDAE Koken, 1896

Lenticular to trochiform, phaneromphalous, with exhalant channel developed

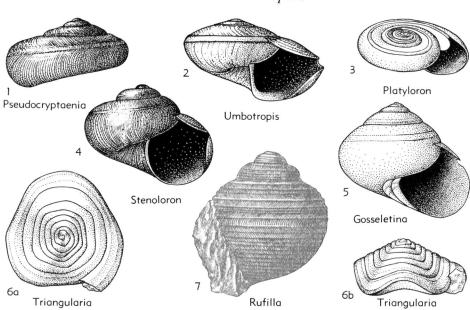

1 Pseudocryptaenia
2 Umbotropis
3 Platyloron
4 Stenoloron
5 Gosseletina
6a Triangularia
7 Rufilla
6b Triangularia

Fɪɢ. 125. Pleurotomariacea (Gosseletinidae——Gosseletininae) (p. *1210*).

within anterior edge of a more or less extensive frill or carina. *M.Sil.-U.Sil.*

Euomphalopterus C.F.Roemer, 1876 [**Turbinites alatus* Wahlenberg, 1821]. With channel-bearing frill; homologue of usual pleurotomarian lunulae appearing as series of narrow plates within frill and concave anterior face of last one forming exhalant channel; ornament numerous lamellar transverse threads. *M.Sil.-U.Sil.*, Eu.-N.Am.

E. **(Euomphalopterus)** [= *Evomphalopterus* Fischer, 1885 (obj.); *Bathmopterus* Kirk, 1928]. Frill wide, pendent. *M.Sil.*, Eu.-N.Am.——Fɪɢ. 127,2. **E. alatus* (Wahlenberg), Gotl.; ×0.7.

E. **(Pleuromphalus)** Perner, 1903 [**P. seductor;* SD Perner, 1907]. Frill a relatively narrow horizontal carina, undulating in some species. *U.Sil.*, Eu.——Fɪɢ. 127,3. **E. (P.) seductor* (Perner), Czech.; ×1.3.

Crenilunula Knight, 1945 [**Pleurotomaria limata* Lindström, 1884]. Frill short, with exhalant channel replaced by median notch on distal end of lamellar lunulae (72, p. 582). *M.Sil.-U.Sil.*, Eu. ——Fɪɢ. 127,1. **C. limata* (Lindström), M. Sil., Gotl.; ×1 (90).

Family PORTLOCKIELLIDAE Batten, 1956

Turbiniform to trochiform, with notch or short labral slit giving rise to depressed selenizone low on whorl; spiral cords dominant, collabral threads also present. *Dev.-M.Perm.*

Agniesella Cossmann, 1909 [*pro Pleuroderma* Perner, 1907 (*non* Tschudi, 1837)] [**Pleurotomaria (Pleuroderma) aratula* Perner, 1907]. Turbiniform with rounded whorls and gently arched selenizone; umbilicus moderately wide; growth lines gently prosocline above and below selenizone; ornament flat revolving cords. *L.Dev.*, Eu.—— Fɪɢ. 124,4. **A. aratula* (Perner), Czech.; ×1.3.

Portlockiella Knight, 1945 [**P. kentuckyensis*] [=*Portlockia* deKoninck, 1881 (subj.) (*non* M'Coy, 1846)]. Selenizone below line of suture; ornament spiral cords with wide concave interspaces and collabral threads (72, p. 579). *Miss. (L.Carb.)*, N.Am.-Eu.——Fɪɢ. 124,5. **P. kentuckyensis*, M.Miss., Ky.; ×2.7.

Shansiella Yin, 1932 [**S. altispiralis*] [=*Latischisma* Thomas, 1940 (140, p. 59)]. Turbiniform, anomphalous, whorls rounded; slit short, selenizone above line of suture but below mid-whorl; ornament dominantly spiral cords or threads. *L. Carb.(Miss.)-L. Perm.*, E. Asia-N. Am.-Eu.-N. Afr. ——Fɪɢ. 124,7. *S. carbonaria* (Norwood & Pratten), M. Penn., Mo.; ×0.7.

Tapinotomaria Batten, 1956 [**T. rugosa*]. Turbiniform; slit a mere notch, selenizone low on whorl, concave, depressed; ornament dominantly spiral, finer collabral threads commonly forming nodes and even spines where crossing spiral elements, the latter commonly large and fasciculate (5). *L.Perm.-M.Perm.*, N.Am.——Fɪɢ. 124,6. **T. rugosa*, M.Perm., Tex.; ×5.3.

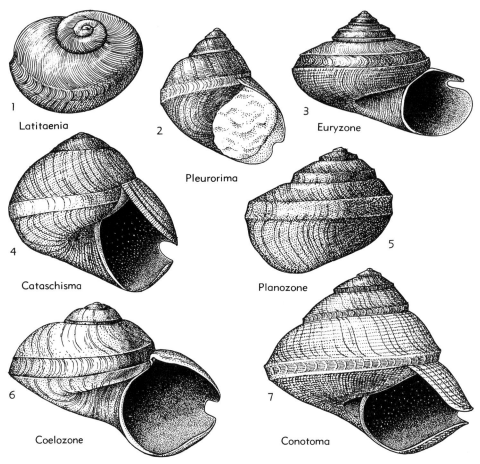

1 Latitaenia
2 Pleurorima
3 Euryzone
4 Cataschisma
5 Planozone
6 Coelozone
7 Conotoma

FIG. 126. Pleurotomariacea (Gosseletinidae——Coelozoninae) (p. *1210-1211*).

Family CATANTOSTOMATIDAE Wenz, 1938

[*nom. transl.* KNIGHT, BATTEN & YOCHELSON, herein (*ex* Catantostomatinae WENZ, 1938)]

Last whorl distorted and with highly specialized inhalant and exhalant openings. *M.Dev.*

Catantostoma SANDBERGER, 1842 [**C. clathratum*]. Ornament spiral and transverse cords; selenizone bordered by cords, concave, terminating at trema (?exhalant) that suggests a short slit; last 0.3 of whorl between trema and aperture without slit or selenizone, growing obliquely downward and backward around a circular inhalant opening with marked constriction of the aperture proper. [Unusual characters of last whorl may denote adaptation to stationary mode of life.] *M.Dev.*, Eu.——FIG. 128,*1*. **C. clathratum*, Ger.; *1a*, side, showing both trema and inhalant orifice below; *1b*, side, showing ?exhalant trema; ×4.

Family PORCELLIIDAE Broili (*ex* Koken MS.), 1924

Coiling pseudo-isostrophic or euomphaloid but protoconch invariably dextral orthostrophic; with deep slit and narrow selenizone at or near mid-whorl; umbilici above and below about equal in some species; shell thin, ornamented with nodes and spiral and collabral threads. *Dev.-M.Jur.(Baj.).*

Porcellia LÉVEILLÉ, 1835 [**P. puzo*; SD DEKONINCK, 1883] [=*Tomoceras* WHITE & ST. JOHN, 1867; *Leveillia* NEWTON, 1891 (obj.); *Brittsoceras* MILLER, DOWNS, & YOUNGQUIST, 1949 (101, p. 603)]. With characters of family. [Pseudo-isostrophic species superficially resemble ammonites but are distinguished readily by their lack of septa, deep slit, and orthostrophic protoconch. The genus may represent an adaptation for free swimming.] *Dev.-U.Carb.(Penn.),* ?*Perm.,* Eu.-SE.

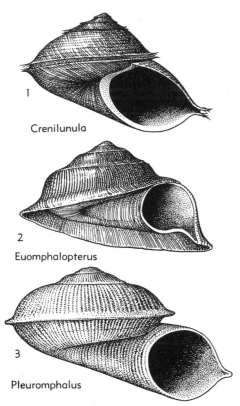

1
Crenilunula

2
Euomphalopterus

3
Pleuromphalus

FIG. 127. Pleurotomariacea (Euomphalopteridae)
(p. I212).

Asia-N.Am.——FIG. 129,1. *P. puzo, L.Carb.,
Belg.; 1a-c, from above, from below, and apertural, ×1.3.
Kokenella KITTL, 1891 [*Porcellia fischeri HÖRNES,
1855] [=Kokeniella KOKEN, 1896 (obj.)]. Discoidal; ornament sigmoidal transverse riblets nodose at outer end and fine spiral threads; selenizone at mid-whorl. M.Trias.(Anis.)-U.Trias.
(Nor.), Eu.-Timor.——FIG. 129,2. *K. fischeri
(HÖRNES), U.Trias.(Nor.), Aus.; 2a,b, apical and
apertural views, ×0.7 (79).
Talantodiscus P.FISCHER, 1885 [*Pleurotomaria
mirabilis J.A.EUDES-DESLONGCHAMPS, 1849]. Discoidal with initial whorls protruding slightly;
ornament tubercles on upper surface near periphery, sigmoidal transverse ribs on base, and sinuous
spiral threads; selenizone above mid-whorl. L.Jur.
(M.Lias.)-M.Jur.(Baj.), Eu.——FIG. 129,3. *T.
mirabilis (EUDES-DESLONGCHAMPS), M.Lias., Fr.;
3a,b, apical and side views, ×0.8 (111).

Family RHAPHISCHISMATIDAE
Knight, 1956

Shell rotelliform, with deep narrow slit
close to upper suture. L.Carb.

Rhaphischisma KNIGHT, 1936 [pro Rotellina DE
KONINCK, 1881 (non AGASSIZ, 1846)] [*Rotellina
planorbiformis DEKONINCK, 1881]. Spire depressed,
with lower lip reaching far inward and forming
heavy callus that fills umbilicus. L.Carb., Eu.——
FIG. 129,4. *R. planorbiformis (DEKONINCK),
Belg.; 4a,b, oblique from above and below, ×2.

Family PHYMATOPLEURIDAE
Batten, 1956

Shell highly ornamented; moderately deep
slit and selenizone somewhat below mid-
whorl, selenizone slightly depressed below
surface; parietal ornament partly or wholly
resorbed within aperture in many species.
L.Carb.(Miss.)-Trias.

Glyptotomaria KNIGHT, 1945 [*G. apiarium]. Shape
highly variable, turbiniform or high trochiform
beehive-shaped to discoidal, base commonly flattened; sutures deep to linear; umbilicus wanting,
or narrow to widely conical; constant ornament
of sharp collabral and spiral lirae, former prosocline just above selenizone but orthocline below
it and with broad sinus on base; selenizone depressed, bordered by cords, and bearing sharp
regularly spaced lunulae; shallow sinus at upper

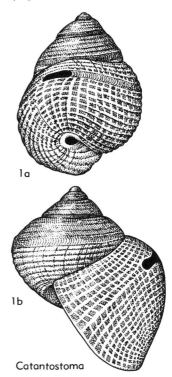

1a

1b

Catantostoma

FIG. 128. Pleurotomariacea (Catantostomatidae)
(p. I213).

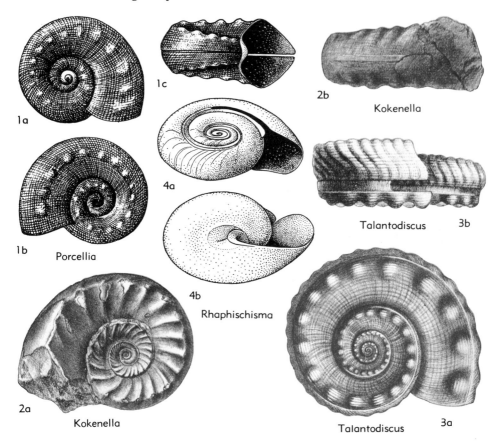

FIG. 129. Pleurotomariacea (Porcellidae, Rhaphischismatidae) (p. I213-I214).

end of columellar lip (72, p. 577). *Miss.-M.Perm.*, N.Am.

G. (Glyptotomaria). Trochiform to beehive-shaped or discoidal with flat base surrounded by rope-like fasciculation of spiral threads. *Penn.-M.Perm.*, N.Am.——FIG. 130,10. *G. (G.) apiarium*, U. Penn., Tex.; ×3.

G. (Dictyotomaria) KNIGHT, 1945 [*Pleurotomaria scitula* MEEK & WORTHEN, 1861]. Turbiniform, with moderately deep sutures and somewhat flat base (72, p. 576). *Miss.-Penn.*, N.Am.——FIG. 130,8. *G. (D.) scitula* (MEEK & WORTHEN), M. Penn., Mo.; ×4.

Borestus THOMAS, 1940 [*B. wrighti*] [=*Platy-pleurotomaria* WANNER, 1942 (146, p. 157)]. Gradate turbiniform, superficially resembling *Worthenia* but with depressed selenizone near mid-whorl and with shoulder on basal angulation sharp; ornament sharp spiral and transverse threads (140, p. 53). *L.Carb.(Miss.)-M.Perm.*, Eu.-SE. Asia-N.Am.-S.Am.——FIG. 130,1. *B. wrighti*, L.Carb., Scot., ×2.7.

Paragoniozona NELSON, 1947 [*P. nodolirata*]. Trochiform; selenizone depressed, low on whorl; sutures shallow; ornament of pustules that cover much of shell, including selenizone (105, p. 460). *Penn.(U.Carb.)*, N.Am.-SE.Asia.——FIG. 130,2. *P. nodolirata*. M.Penn., Tex.; ×4.

Phymatopleura GIRTY, 1939 [*pro Orestes* GIRTY, 1912 (*non* BLACKINSTONE & FRYER, 1880, *nec* REDTENBACHER, 1906)] [*Orestes nodosus* GIRTY, 1912]. Turbiniform or trochiform, with depressed selenizone above basal angulation; ornament sharp spiral and collabral threads with one or more spiral rows of nodes high on whorl face. *Penn.*, N.Am.——FIG. 130,6. *P. nodosus* (GIRTY), M. Penn., Okla.; ×5.

Callitomaria BATTEN, 1956 [*C. stanislavi*]. Turbiniform, gradate, minutely phaneromphalous, relatively wide vertical whorl face below wide ramp; flat selenizone occupying middle of whorl face and about half its width; ornament 2 spiral cords on ramp (at its lower edge and close to suture respectively) and about 6 sharp spiral cords on

base; sharp collabral threads on ramp and base in some species (5, p. 43). *M.Perm.,* N.Am.——Fig. 130,9. **C. stanislavi,* Tex.; ×2.7.

Discotomaria BATTEN, 1956 [**D. basisulcata*]. Shell rather flat with low gradate spire; whorls rising in steps; upper surface of whorl a concave shoulder or ramp; outer face vertical with projecting flange separating it from base; base beneath flange first sloping gently inward and then flattening abruptly to narrow umbilicus; slit about 0.25 whorl deep, selenizone occupying upper half of

smooth band at middle of outer whorl-face; base with shallow sinus below flange; highly ornamented with spiral and collabral elements (5, p. 43). *U.Penn.-M.Perm.,* N.Am.——Fig. 130,5. **D. basisulcata,* M.Perm., Tex.; 5a,b, apertural and umbilical views, ×4.

Eymarella COSSMANN, 1897 [*pro Echetus* KOKEN, 1896 (*non* KRØYER, 1864)] [**Pleurotomaria subscalariformis* HÖRNES]. Small, trochiform, with blunt apex due to discoidal coiling of early whorls, broadly phaneromphalous; ornament cancellating

FIG. 130. Pleurotomariacea (Phymatopleuridae) (p. *1215-1217*).

collabral and spiral threads; selenizone impressed, at slightly flattened periphery, not overlapped on spire whorls. *M.Trias.(Ladin.)-U.Trias.(Nor.)*, Eu.——Fig. 130,*3*. **E. subscalariformis*, U.Trias. (Nor.), Aus.; *3a,b,* ×2.5; ×6 (79).

Euryalox Cossmann, 1897 [*pro Sagana* Koken, 1896 (*non* Walker, 1855)] [**Pleurotomaria juvavica* Koken, 1896]. Turbiniform, phaneromphalous, whorls evenly convex; ornament narrow cancellating spiral cords and collabral threads; selenizone peripheral, impressed, rather wide, bordered by spiral cords, and not overlapped on spire whorls; umbilical margin an angulation. *M.Trias.(Anis.)-U.Trias.(Nor.)*, Eu.-E.Indies(Timor).——Fig. 130, 7. *E. geometrica* (Koken), U.Trias.(Carn.), Aus.; ×1.3 (79).

Codinella Kittl, 1899 [**Trochus generelli* Stoppani, 1858]. Small, elevated, cyrtoconoid, anomphalous; base short; whorls flat or feebly convex, with weak spiral ornament; selenizone at midwhorl, growth lines prosocyrt below it, prosocline above; aperture small, much broader than high. *M.Trias.(Ladin.)*, Eu.——Fig. 130,*4*. **C. generelli* (Kittl), S.Tyrol; ×4, ×4, ×6 (66).

Family POLYTREMARIIDAE Wenz, 1938

[*nom. transl.* Knight, Batten & Yochelson, herein (*ex* Polytremariinae Wenz, 1938)]

Exhalant emargination a labral slit or row of tremata; heavily thickened extension of columellar lip separated by a deep fissure from parietal lip, ornament spiral cords or threads. *L.Carb.-M.Perm.*

Polytremaria d'Orbigny, 1850 [**Pleurotomaria catenata* deKoninck, 1843]. With series of exhalant tremata; grooved extension of columellar lip curving around umbilicus. *L.Carb.*, Eu.——Fig. 131,*2*. **P. catenata* (deKoninck), Belg.; showing tremata and curved pulley-like inner lip; ×2.7.

Plocostoma Gemmellaro, 1889 [**Pleurotomaria (Plocostoma) neumayri;* SD Knight, 1937]. With narrow, probably short exhalant slit; selenizone narrow, borne by step high on outer whorl face; extension of parietal lip seemingly toothlike. *M. Perm.*, Eu.——Fig. 131,*6*. **P. neumayri* (Gemmellaro), Sicily; protrusion on columellar lip broken; ×2.7.

Family LAUBELLIDAE Cox, n. fam.

Small, ovate-conical, elevated, narrowly phaneromphalous; with angular sinus high on labrum culminating in short slit that generates raised selenizone close to adapical suture; helicocone contracted and commonly bent upward near aperture. *M.Trias.*

Laubella Kittl, 1891 [**Pleurotomaria delicata*

Laube, 1868; SD Diener, 1926]. With characters of family; ornament spiral threads sometimes cancellated by collabrals. *M.Trias.(Ladin.)*, Eu.——Fig. 133,*1*. **L. delicata*, S.Tyrol; *1a,b,* ×6 (64).

Family SCHIZOGONIIDAE Cox, n. fam.

Small, turbiniform to almost discoidal; last whorl with flattened outer face bordered by carinae or angulations, one or both nodose; spire gradate; labral emargination shallow, at upper angulation. *M.Trias.-U. Trias.*

Schizogonium Koken, 1889 [**Pleurotomaria scalaris* Münster, 1841; SD Diener, 1926]. Anomphalous to broadly phaneromphalous; both carinae well defined. *M.Trias.(Ladin.)*, Eu.——Fig. 132,*1*. **S. scalare*, S.Tyrol; ×4 (89).

Pseudoschizogonium Kutassy, 1937 [**P. turriculatum*]. Depressed-turbiniform, phaneromphalous; selenizone nodose, with nodes continued by prosocline collabral ridges on horizontal upper whorl face. *U.Trias.(Carn.)*, Eu.——Fig. 133,*3*. **P. turriculatum*, Hung.; *3a-c*, ×1.5, ×1.5, ×5 (84).

Family ZYGITIDAE Cox, n. fam.

Small, depressed - turbiniform, broadly phaneromphalous, with domelike spire; selenizone broad, depressed, at periphery on last whorl and not overlapped on spire; nodose angulation at margin of umbilicus; aperture subquadrate, with straight columellar lip leaning toward axis; labral slit rather deep (about 0.12 of last whorl). *M.Trias.*

Zygites Kittl, 1891 [**Pleurotomaria delphinula* Laube, 1868 (*pro Delphinula cancellata* Klipstein, 1845, *non* Kiener, 1838-9)]. General surface and selenizone with ornament of cancelling spiral and collabral threads; also strong collabral folds on upper whorl face. *M.Trias.(Ladin.)*, Eu.——Fig. 133,*4*. **Z. delphinula* (Laube), S.Tyrol; *4a,b*, ×2 (64).

Family KITTLIDISCIDAE Cox, n. fam.

Small, depressed-turbiniform to lenticular, broadly phaneromphalous; relatively broad selenizone occupying whole of outer face, which is bordered by 2 prominent carinae. *M.Trias.*

Kittlidiscus Haas, 1953 [*pro Schizodiscus* Kittl, 1891 (*non* Hall & Clarke, 1888)] [**Pleurotomaria bronni* Klipstein, 1845 (=*P. plana* Klipstein, 1845, *non* Münster, 1844)]. Whorls with narrow shoulder; ornament collabral threads and spiral grooves on spire, spiral cords on base and umbilicus. *M.Trias.(Ladin.)*, Eu.——Fig. 133,*2*. **K. bronni* (Klipstein), S.Tyrol; *2a,b*, ×3 (64).

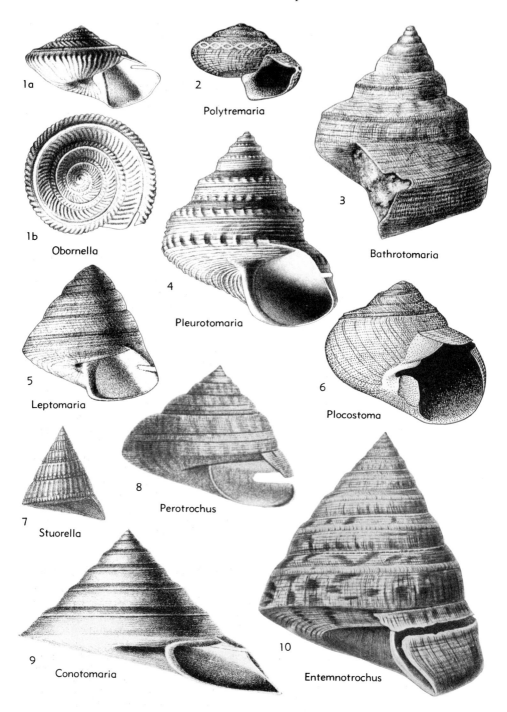

FIG. 131. Pleurotomariacea (Polytremariidae, Pleurotomariidae) (p. *1217-1220*).

FIG. 132. Pleurotomariacea (Schizogoniidae)
(p. *1217*).

Family TEMNOTROPIDAE Cox, n. fam.

Small, depressed turbiniform, some shells approaching auriform or neritiform, of few whorls increasing rapidly in diameter; labrum with slit generating selenizone occupying carina rather high on whorls, at angle of broad, gently sloping ramp; aperture very broad and oblique. *M.Trias.-U.Trias.*

Temnotropis LAUBE, 1870 [**Sigaretus carinatus* MÜNSTER, 1841]. Anomphalous or narrowly phaneromphalous; ornament spiral cords predominating over collabral threads; in some species further carinae below' the one carrying selenizone. *M.Trias.(Ladin.)-U.Trias.(Carn.),* Eu. —— FIG. 133,5. *T. carinata* (MÜNSTER), M.Trias.(Ladin.), S.Tyrol; *5a,b,* ×2 (89).

Family PLEUROTOMARIIDAE Swainson, 1840

[*nom. correct.* KING, 1850 (ex Pleurotomariae SWAINSON, 1840)]

Mostly medium-sized to large, trochiform; exhalant emargination a slit that generates selenizone on whorl face, in most genera at or near mid-whorl. *Trias.-Rec.*

Pleurotomaria DEFRANCE, 1826 [validation, ICZN pend.] [**Trochus anglicus* J.SOWERBY, 1818; SD S.P.WOODWARD, 1851] [=*Pleurotomarium* DE BLAINVILLE, 1825 (suppression, ICZN pend.)] Trochiform, moderately high to depressed, anomphalous to broadly phaneromphalous, gradate, with outer whorl face flattened, at least in earlier growth stages; selenizone moderately broad, near mid-whorl; ornament sinuous spiral cords with tubercles at shoulder and in some species at margin of base. *L.Jur.-L.Cret.(Apt.),* cosmop.——FIG. 131,4. **P. anglica* (SOWERBY), L.Lias., Fr.; ×0.7 (111).

Bathrotomaria Cox, 1956 [**Trochus reticulatus* J. SOWERBY, 1821]. Trochiform, elevated to depressed, anomphalous to broadly phaneromphalous; whorls (at least in earlier growth stages) angulate, with usually broad ramp; second carina or angula-

tion, just overlapped on spire, delimiting base; selenizone at ramp angle; ornament spiral threads commonly cancellated by collabral threads. *L.Jur.-U.Cret.(Senon.),* cosmop.——FIG. 131,3. *B. reticulata* (J.SOWERBY), U.Jur.(Kim.), Eng.; ×0.8 (232).

Leptomaria E. EUDES-DESLONGCHAMPS, 1864 [**Pleurotomaria amoena* J. A. EUDES-DESLONGCHAMPS, 1849]. Conical or cyrtoconoid, anomphalous to broadly phaneromphalous; whorls weakly to strongly convex, not angular, last one rounded at periphery of convex base; selenizone at mid-whorl; ornament spiral threads that may be cancellated by collabral threads. *M.Jur.(Baj.)-U.Cret.(Dan.),* cosmop.——FIG. 131,5. **L. amoena* (J.A.EUDES-DESLONGCHAMPS), M.Jur.(Baj.), Fr.; ×1.3 (111).

Stuorella KITTL, 1891 [**Trochus subconcavus* MÜNSTER, 1841]. Rather small, conical, anomphalous or narrowly phaneromphalous; whorls flat, last one with angular periphery and flattened base; selenizone narrow, just above periphery, between 2 spiral cords; ornament axial costellae ending in nodes above selenizone and crossed obliquely by prosocline growth threads. *M.Trias.(Ladin.)-U. Trias.(Carn.),* Eu.——FIG. 131,7. **S. subconcava* (MÜNSTER), M.Trias.(Ladin.), S.Tyrol; ×3 (89).

Pyrgotrochus P.FISCHER, 1885 [**Pleurotomaria bitorquata* J.A.EUDES-DESLONGCHAMPS, 1849]. Conical or coeloconoid, anomphalous or narrowly phaneromphalous; whorls flat or concave, last one with swollen band, commonly tuberculate or puckered, at periphery of flattened base; band visible on spire whorls, which also bear spiral threads; selenizone broad, below mid-whorl. *L.Jur.-M.Cret.(Cenom.),* cosmop.——FIG. 134,2. **P. bitorquatus* (J.A.EUDES-DESLONGCHAMPS, M. Lias, Fr.; ×1 (111).

Conotomaria Cox, 1959 [**Pleurotomaria mailleana* D'ORBIGNY, 1843]. Conical, anomphalous to broadly phaneromphalous; whorls flat or slightly sigmoidal in outline, periphery angular, may be bulging; selenizone at or above mid-whorl, quite close to suture in some species, not coinciding with an angulation; predominant ornament spiral cords. *M.Jur.(Baj.)-U.Cret.(Senon.),* cosmop.—— FIG. 131,9. **C. mailleana* ('D'ORBIGNY), M.Cret. (Cenom.), Fr.; ×1 (110).

Obornella Cox, 1959 [**Pleurotomaria plicopunctata* J.A.EUDES-DESLONGCHAMPS, 1849]. Low-turbiniform to sublenticular, phaneromphalous; base strongly convex; ornament close-spaced collabral costellae and spiral threads, former usually dominant; periphery commonly crenate; selenizone narrow, smooth, projecting, on upper whorl face near periphery; labral slit short. *L.Jur.(U.Lias.)-U.Jur. (Oxford.),* Eu.——FIG. 131,1. **O. plicopunctata* (J.A.EUDES-DESLONGCHAMPS), M.Jur.(Baj.), Fr.; *1a,b,* ×1 (111).

Chelotia BAYLE in P. FISCHER, 1885 [**Pleurotomaria concava* DESHAYES, 1832]. Cyrtoconoid, rather

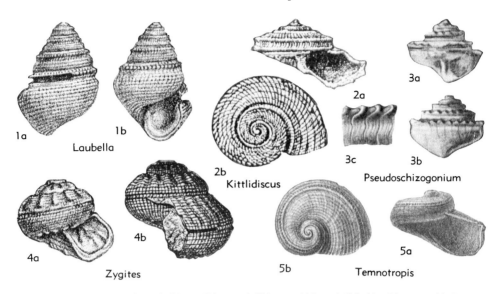

FIG. 133. Pleurotomariacea (Schizogoniidae, Laubellidae, Zygitidae, Kittlidiscidae, Temnotropidae) (p. *1217-1219*).

broadly phaneromphalous; whorls feebly convex, last one rounded at periphery of base; selenizone narrow, between 2 narrow spiral cords rather high on whorl, not easily seen between coarse, nodose spiral cords that constitute the ornament; labral slit narrow and very long, said to extend back for more than a whorl from aperture. *Eoc.,* Eu.

Perotrochus P.FISCHER, 1885 [*Pleurotomaria quoyana* FISCHER & BERNARDI, 1856]. Turbiniform, anomphalous, broader than high; whorls moderately convex, last one subangular at periphery of base; selenizone at or just below mid-whorl, moderately broad, flush, bearing obscure spiral threads; ornament fine cancellating spiral and collabral threads; labral slit extending around 0.1 of last whorl. *Oligo.-Plio.,* Eu.-Japan; *Rec.,* Japan-S.Afr.——FIG. 131,*8.* *P. quoyana* (FISCHER & BERNARDI), Rec., Carib.; ×1 (147).

Mikadotrochus LINDHOLM, 1927 [*Pleurotomaria beyrichi* HILGER, 1877]. Trochiform, narrowly phaneromphalous, whorls feebly convex, last one rounded or subangular at periphery of base; selenizone broad, flush, spirally grooved, below mid-whorl; ornament obscurely nodose spiral cords; labral slit broad, extending around 0.12 of last whorl or less, its upper margin produced beyond lower margin and merging into strongly prosocline, convex labrum. *Plio.-Rec.,* Japan.—— FIG. 134,*1.* *M. beyrichi* (HILGER), Rec.; ×0.7 (173).

Entemnotrochus P.FISCHER, 1885 [*Pleurotomaria adansoniana* CROSSE & FISCHER, 1861]. Trochiform, rather broadly phaneromphalous; whorls feebly convex or obtusely angular, last one angular at

periphery of rather flattened base; selenizone moderately broad, above mid-whorl, with well-marked lunulae; ornament obscure spiral cords with collabral threads near suture; labral slit long, extending around 0.5 of last whorl or more. *Eoc.-Mio.,* Eu.-N.Am.; *Rec.,* Carib.-W.Pac. —— FIG. 131,*10.* *E. adansoniana* (CROSSE & FISCHER), Rec., Carib.; ×0.8 (147).

Family TROCHOTOMIDAE Cox, n. fam.

[=Ditremariinae WENZ, 1938]

Turbiniform; exhalant outlet an elongate elliptical trema, some shells with median constriction, generating selenizone on upper face of whorls; base with funnel-like depression affecting last whorl only; peristome discontinuous. *U.Trias.(Rhaet.)-U.Jur.*

Trochotoma J.A.EUDES-DESLONGCHAMPS, 1843 [*T. conuloides;* SD S.P.WOODWARD, 1851] [=*Ditremaria* D'ORBIGNY, 1843; *Rimulus* D'ORBIGNY, 1842 (*nom. nud.*)]. Columellar lip emerging from basal depression, strongly inclined, without denticulations; outer lip strongly prosocline. *U.Trias. (Rhaet.)-U.Jur.(Portland.),* Eu.

T. (Trochotoma). Spire moderately elevated, conical or gradate; selenizone above mid-whorl, at ramp angle when this is present; peripheral carina frequent, delimiting base; ornament spiral cords. *U.Trias.(Rhaet.)-U.Jur.(Portland),* Eu. —— FIG. 135,*1.* *T. bicarinata* (D'ORBIGNY), M.Lias., Fr.; *1a,b,* ×1 (111).

T. (Discotoma) HABER, 1934 [*Ditremaria amata* D'ORBIGNY, 1850]. Very depressed, whorls in-

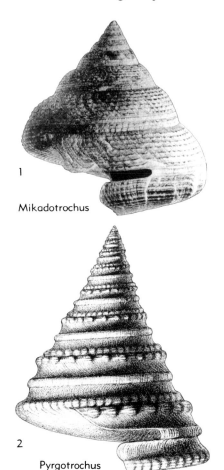

1
Mikadotrochus

2
Pyrgotrochus

Fig. 134. Pleurotomariacea (Pleurotomariidae)
(p. *1219-1220*).

creasing rapidly in diameter; ornament of upper face transverse folds crossed by spiral cords. *M.Jur. (Bathon.)-U.Jur.(Portland.),* Eu.——Fig. 135,*2. *T. (Discotoma) amata* (D'ORBIGNY), *M.Jur. (Callov.),* Fr.; *2a,b,* ×1 (111).

Valfinia Cox, 1958 [*pro Didymodon* P.FISCHER, 1885 (*non* BLAKE, 1863)] [*Trochus quinquecinctus* ZIETEN, 1832]. Like *Trochotoma (s.s.),* but with 1 or 2 blunt denticles on columellar lip; spiral cords beaded. *Jur.,* Eu.——Fig. 135,*3. *V. thurmanni* (DELORIOL), *U.Jur.(Kimm.),* Fr.; *3a,b,* ×1.3 (111).

Family SCISSURELLIDAE Gray, 1847

[*nom. transl.* GRAY, 1857 (*ex* Scissurellina GRAY, 1847)]
[Help in preliminary organization of data was given by Miss GRACE JOHNSON and is here acknowledged.]

Shell small, porcelaneous except for thin nacreous layer within; few-whorled, tur-

binate to depressed; outer lip with slit or hole; operculum round, multispiral, with central nucleus (138, 147). *U.Cret.-Rec.*

Scissurella D'ORBIGNY, 1824 [**S. laevigata;* SD GRAY, 1847] [=*Schismope* JEFFREYS, 1856; *Woodwardia* CROSSE & FISCHER, 1861]. With open anal slit extending back from aperture, generating a selenizone.

S. (Scissurella). Spire flattened, selenizone on upper half of whorl. *U.Cret.-Rec.,* cosmop.—— Fig. 136,*1. *S. laevigata,* Rec., Medit.; *1a,b,* ×15 (213).

S. (Anatoma) WOODWARD, 1859 [**S. crispata* FLEMING, 1828] [=*Schizotrochus* MONTEROSATO, 1877 (obj.)]. Spire somewhat elevated; slit on middle portion of whorl, selenizone weak. *Plio.-Rec.,* cosmop.——Fig. 136,*4. *S. (A.) crispata,* Rec., North Sea, ×10 (147).

Incisura HEDLEY, 1904 [**Scissurella lyttletonensis* SMITH, 1894]. Auriform, last whorl large; slit in outer lip short. *Rec.,* Australasia.

I. (Incisura). Whorls smooth. *Rec.,* N.Z.——Fig. 136,*3. *I. (I.) lyttletonensis* (SMITH), Rec., N.Z., ×15 (147).

I. (Scissurona) IREDALE, 1924 [**Scissurella rosea* HEDLEY, 1904]. Early whorls with fine collabral riblets. *Rec.,* Australasia.

Sinezona FINLAY, 1927 [**Scissurella brevis* HEDLEY, 1904] [=*Schismope* AUCTT. (*non* JEFFREYS); =*Woodwardia* AUCTT. (*non* CROSSE & FISCHER)]. Slit closed at lip margin, leaving a foramen in outer lip. *Plio.-Rec.,* Eu.-N.Am.-Australasia.—— Fig. 136,*2. *S. brevis* (HEDLEY), Rec., N.Z.; ×15 (147).

Family HALIOTIDAE Rafinesque, 1815

[*nom. transl. et correct.* FLEMING, 1822 (*ex* Haliotidia RAFINESQUE, 1815, subfamily name)] [=Schismatobranchia GRAY, 1821]

Shell auriform, depressed, with spire more or less strongly excentric and protruding only slightly or not at all; aperture broad, occupying most of underside; to left of aperture a broad, smooth labial area, beyond which narrow base of shell is just exposed in some species; shell wall with spiral row of small tremata, commonly on tubular projections, which become infilled progressively during growth, the last few (5 to 9) remaining open and serving as exhalant outlets; interior nacreous; no operculum. *?Cret., Mio.-Rec.*

Records of *Haliotis* from the Cretaceous need confirmation. *H. antiqua* BINKHORST, 1861, from Maastricht, was thought by KAUNHOWEN (1898) to be a trochid. The type of *H. cretacea* LUNDGREN, 1894, from Sweden, needs re-investigation. *H. lomaen-*

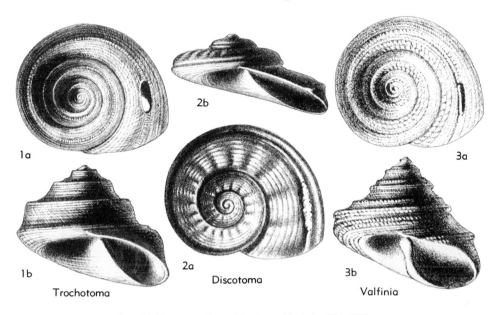

1a

2b

3a

1b

2a

3b

Trochotoma   Discotoma   Valfinia

FIG. 135. Pleurotomariacea (Trochotomidae) (p. *1220-1221*).

sis ANDERSON, 1902, Chico Group of California, was rejected as a haliotid by WOODRING (1931) but accepted by VOKES (1935).

The researches of CROFTS (1929, 1937, 1955) on the anatomy and larval ontogeny of this family, and of YONGE (1947) on respiratory processes, are of great importance for the understanding of the Pleurotomariina. Only one genus, divided into several more or less intergrading subgenera, is here recognized, although generic rank has recently been claimed for *Exohaliotis,* on anatomical as well as conchological grounds.

Haliotis LINNÉ, 1758 [**H. asinina;* SD MONTFORT, 1810] [=*Teinotis* ADAMS & ADAMS, 1854 (obj.); *Haleotis* BINKHORST, 1861 (obj.); *Tinotis* FISCHER, 1885 (obj.)]. *?Cret., Mio.-Rec.,* cosmop.

H. (Haliotis). Shell elongate and narrow, with apex very eccentric, almost marginal; ornament of spiral cords, almost obsolete on latter half of last whorl except on abapical side of tremata. *Rec.,* IndoPac.——FIG. 137,4. **H. (H.) asinina,* Philippines; ×0.7 (213).

H. (Euhaliotis) WENZ, 1938 [**H. midae* LINNÉ, 1758]. Labial area in adult shell forming projecting flange, outer edge of which forms shell periphery; ornament of prominent wavy transverse lamellae. *Rec.,* S.Am., S.Afr.

H. (Exohaliotis) COTTON & GODFREY, 1933 [**H. cyclobates* PÉRON & LESUEUR, 1816]. Almost circular; spire more elevated than in other sub-

genera; ornament numerous nodose spiral cords and collabral rugae. *Rec.,* Austral.

H. (Marinauris) IREDALE, 1927 [**M. melculus;* SD WENZ, 1938]. Rather small for genus, apex not strongly excentric; no angulation at row of tremata; tremata large; ornament spiral cords on abapical side of tremata or on entire surface. *Rec.,* Austral.

H. (Notohaliotis) COTTON & GODFREY, 1933 [**H. naevosa* MARTYN, 1784 (not binominal) =*H. rubra* LEACH, 1814]. Tremata on tubular projections situated on angulation separating upper whorl surface from flat or concave outer face; ornament spiral cords and threads crossed by irregular transverse ribs oblique to collabral lines. *Mio.-Rec.,* Austral.——FIG. 137,3. **H. (N.) rubra* LEACH, Rec.; ×0.7 (213).

H. (Ovinotis) COTTON, 1943 [**H. ovina* GMELIN, 1791]. Tremata on tubular projections situated on angulation less pronounced than in *N. (Notohaliotis);* ornament knobby, transverse ribs oblique to collabral lines, and obscure spiral threads. *Mio.-Rec.,* IndoPac.-Austral.

H. (Padollus) MONTFORT, 1810 [**P. rubicundus* MONTFORT (non *Haliotis rubicunda* RÖDING, 1798) ?=*H. scalaris* LEACH, 1814, or perhaps *H. parva* LINNÉ, 1758] [=*Neohaliotis* COTTON & GODFREY, 1933]. With broad spiral rib on adapical side of tremata, corresponding groove on interior of shell, and prominent thin collabral lamellae on adapical side of rib; tremata on tubular projections on second rib, and commonly a row of frilly projections near periphery. *Rec.,*

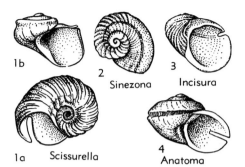

1b

2
Sinezona

3
Incisura

1a Scissurella

4
Anatoma

FIG. 136. Pleurotomariacea (Scissurellidae)
(p. 1221).

Austral.-IndoPac.-S.Afr.——FIG. 137,2. *H. (P.) scalaris* LEACH, Austral.; ×0.5 (168).

H. (Paua) FLEMING, 1952 [**H. iris* MARTYN, 1784 (specific name validated ICZN)]. Of few whorls, cap-shaped, last whorl rising above level of submarginal apex; even convexity of surface modified by only slight angulation at row of tremata; labral area broad, its margin forming shell periphery; ornament collabral and oblique undulations, and spiral cords. *Mio.-Rec., N.Z.-Japan.*

H. (Sanhaliotis) IREDALE, 1929 [**H. varia* LINNÉ, 1758]. Even convexity of surface interrupted by only slight angulation at row of tremata; ornament spiral cords, commonly nodose. *Mio.-Rec., IndoPac.-Calif.-Austral.-W.Afr.*

H. (Schismotis) GRAY, 1856 [**S. excisa*=*Haliotis albicans* QUOY & GAIMARD, 1834, ?=*H. laevigata* DONOVAN, 1808]. Large; whorls evenly convex, smooth except for almost obsolete spiral striae; tremata small, flush. *Rec., Austral.*

H. (Sulculus) ADAMS & ADAMS, 1854 [**H. incisa* REEVE, 1846; SD COSSMANN, 1918]. Small to medium-sized; tremata on angulation separating upper whorl surface from concave outer face; ornament spiral striae or cords and (in some specimens) irregular transverse ridges or nodes. *Mio.-Rec.,* Medit.E.Atl.-Japan-N.Z.——FIG. 137,1. *H. (S.) tuberculata* LINNÉ, Rec., Guernsey; *1a,b,* abapertural and apertural sides, ×1 (213).

PLEUROTOMARIACEA
Family UNCERTAIN

?**Ceratopea** ULRICH, 1911 [**C. keithi*]. Genus known from its relatively large heavy horn-shaped operculum with inner end pitted for muscle attachment, in some showing evidence of a pair of retractor muscles; outer side with blunt angulation that probably corresponds to a peripheral angulation of shell, upper surface set off from parietal surface by a rounded ridge and sharp change of direction of growth lines; inner surface sharply rounded and lower surface gently arched,

with growth lines broadly concave toward shell. [Small wedge-shaped calcareous opercula that differ in form from the type species of *Ceratopea* have been referred to this genus but they seem more likely to belong to *Orospira* or undescribed relatives of it.] *L.Ord.,* N.Am.-Eu.——FIG. 138,1. **C. keithi,* Va.; *1c,d,* views of operculum from below and above; *1b,* view showing peripheral carina; *1a,* oblique view into attachment pit; all ×1.

Spirotomaria KOKEN, 1925 [**Pleurotomaria rudissima* KOKEN, 1897]. Turbiniform; narrowly phaneromphalous; labrum gently prosocline and convex above selenizone and also below except close to selenizone; numerous spiral threads. *M. Ord.,* Eu.——FIG. 138,6. **S. rudissima* (KOKEN), Est.; ×1 (80).

Ptychozone PERNER, 1907 [**Worthenia aberrans* PERNER, 1903]. Turbiniform, with inconspicuous broad selenizone high on rounded outer whorl face; sharp spiral threads and growth lines. *U.Sil.,* Eu.——FIG. 138,4. **P. aberrans* (PERNER), Czech.; ×2.7.

Platyconus PERNER, 1907 [**Pleurotomaria (Platyconus) incumbens*]. Trochiform, with relatively low spire and rounded anomphalous base; selenizone roundly convex; fairly strong transverse and spiral cords, former prosocline above and below selenizone. *U.Sil.,* Eu.——FIG. 138,5. **P. incumbens* (PERNER), Czech.; ×1.

Gyroma OEHLERT, 1888 [**Pleurotomaria baconnierensis*]. Turbiniform, narrowly phaneromphalous; with broad selenizone and seemingly short slit; spiral and collabral threads. [When better known this genus may prove to be the same as *Ptychozone* PERNER.] *L.Dev.,* Eu.——FIG. 138,3. **P. baconnierensis* (OEHLERT), Fr.; ×3.7 (108).

Trachybembix J.BÖHM, 1895 [**Pleurotomaria junonis* KITTL, 1894; SD DIENER, 1926] [=*Trachybembyx* DIENER, 1926 (obj.)]. Rather small, turbiniform, variably phaneromphalous; base strongly convex; last whorl with 3 carinae, one juxtasutural, one median, 3rd at margin of base and in some shells overlapped on spire; collabral lines or ridges present in some; narrow selenizone between 2 ridges said to be carried by median carina. [The presence of this selenizone is not obvious in published figures and needs verification; if there is no selenizone, the genus should be removed from the Pleurotomariacea.) *M.Trias. (Ladin.),* Eu.——FIG. 138,2. **T. junonis* (KITTL), S.Tyrol.; ×1.5 (65).

Transylvanella KUTASSY, 1937 [**T. acmaeiformis*]. Low trochiform, broadly phaneromphalous, sharply carinate at periphery; spire coeloconoid, its whorls flat, with spiral cords; selenizone just above periphery; aperture low, oblique. *U.Trias.(Carn.),* Eu.——FIG. 123,5. **T. acmaeiformis,* Hung.; ×1.5 (84).

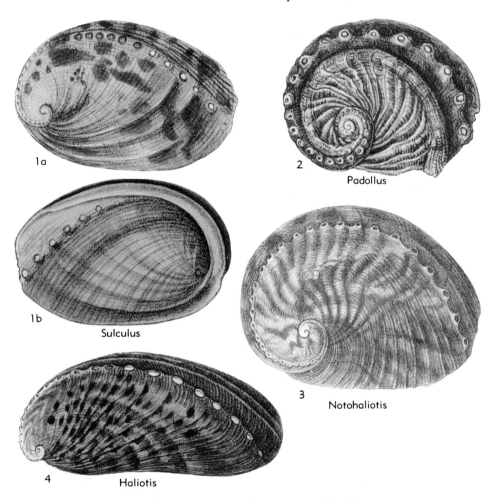

1a

1b
Sulculus

2
Padollus

3
Notohaliotis

4 Haliotis

FIG. 137. Pleurotomariacea (Haliotidae) (p. *1222-1223*).

Superfamily
TROCHONEMATACEA
Zittel, 1895

[*nom. transl.* KNIGHT, BATTEN & YOCHELSON, herein (*ex* Trochonematidae ZITTEL, 1895)]

Turbiniform, with channel at labrum within a spiral angulation about midway between sutures or higher on whorl, or with shallow sinus at about the same position; ornament spiral angulations, threads or cords, or rows of nodes, with collabral threads or growth lines; shell with nacreous lining. *M.Ord.-M.Perm.*

The Trochonematacea and Trochonematidae have usually been made a catchall for several heterogeneous groups of fossil gastropods of the Paleozoic and Mesozoic, but are here greatly reduced. According to either conception, they include only extinct forms. Inferences as to their anatomy and phylogeny can, therefore, be made only from shell features and from apparently related forms that appear more readily understandable.

In Middle and Late Ordovician time, species of trochonematacean genera (some as yet undescribed) resembled in remarkable detail those of the contemporary pleurotomariacean family Lophospiridae. It is, therefore, thought that the Trochonematacea were derived from the latter family. They differ chiefly in that the deep labral sinus or slit of the Lophospiridae is replaced by

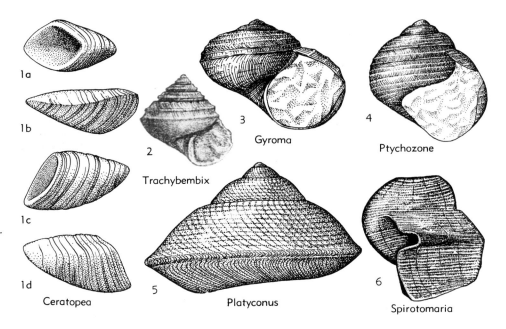

1a

1b

2

Trachybembix

1c

1d

Ceratopea

3

Gyroma

5

Platyconus

4

Ptychozone

6

Spirotomaria

FIG. 138. Pleurotomariacea (Family Uncertain) (p. *1223*).

an internal channel in a homologous position. It seems very possible that the more primitive trochonemataceans retained paired ctenidia, as was almost certainly true of the Lophospiridae, but that the right-hand ctenidium was lost in later genera, the anal tube moving to the right and the channel or sinus in the lip becoming vestigial.

Family TROCHONEMATIDAE Zittel, 1895

With characters of superfamily. *M.Ord.-M.Perm.*

Proturritella KOKEN, 1889 [**P. gracilis*] [*Gonionema* KOKEN, 1896; *Pseudeunema* COSSMANN, 1899 (*pro Gonionema* KOKEN, 1896); *Nematotrochus* KOKEN, 1925]. With subangular labral sinus culminating on median of 3 spiral carinae; narrowly phaneromphalous; ornament cancellate. *M.Ord.*, Eu.——FIG. 139,*6*. **P. gracilis*, Swed.; ×2.7.

Trochonema SALTER, 1859 [**Pleurotomaria umbilicata* HALL, 1847]. Turbiniform to aciculate, with a major spiral angulation having channel within; later whorls disjunct in some forms. *M.Ord.-L.Dev.*, N.Am.-Eu.-NE.Asia.

T. (**Trochonema**). Turbiniform; narrowly phaneromphalous; with 4 spiral angulations; sutures channeled. *M.Ord.-U.Ord.*, N.Am.-Eu.-NE.Asia.

——FIG. 139,*7*. **T. (T.) umbilicatum* (HALL), M.Ord., Can.(Que.); ×2.

T. (**Eunema**) SALTER, 1859 [**Eunema strigillatum*]. Much like *Trochonema (s.s.)* but with high spire. *M.Ord.-U.Sil.*, N.Am.-Eu.——FIG. 139,*1*. **T. (E.) strigillatum* (SALTER), M.Ord., Can.(Que.); ×1.3.

T. (**Trochonemopsis**) MEEK, 1872 [**Trochonema tricarinata*]. Much like *Trochonema (s.s.)* but with 3 spiral angulations; suture not channeled. *L.Dev.*, N.Am.——FIG. 139,*2*. **T. (T.) tricarinatum* (MEEK), L.Dev., Ohio; ×1.3.

Amaurotoma KNIGHT, 1945 [**Pleurotomaria subsinuata* MEEK & WORTHEN, 1861]. Turbiniform, with shallow sinus high on labrum; ornament of spiral cords and collabral threads (*72*, p. 583). *Miss.-Penn.*, N.Am.——FIG. 139,*4*. **A. subsinuata* (MEEK & WORTHEN), M.Penn., Ill.; ×5.

Cyclobathmus KNIGHT, 1940 [**Trepospira haworthi* BEEDE, 1907]. Turbiniform, gradate; broad shallow sinus in lip above shoulder angulation; ornament of spiral cords. (*68*, p. 314). *M.Perm.*, N.Am.-Eu.-NC.Asia.——FIG. 139,*3*. **C. haworthi* (BEEDE), M.Perm., Tex.; ×8.

?**Cyclites** KNIGHT, 1940 [**Pleurotomaria multilineata* GIRTY, 1908, =*Wortheniopsis depressa* BEEDE, 1907]. Low, turbiniform, slightly gradate; channel within shoulder angle; ornament of spiral cords or threads (*68*, p. 310). *M.Perm.*, N.Am.-NC.Asia-SC.Asia-SE.Asia.——FIG. 139,*5*. *C. depressus* (BEEDE), Tex.; ×6.

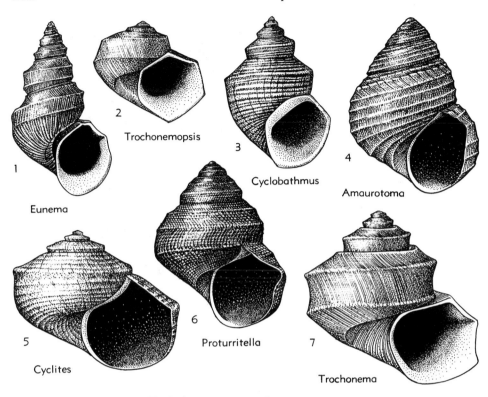

1 Eunema
2 Trochonemopsis
3 Cyclobathmus
4 Amaurotoma
5 Cyclites
6 Proturritella
7 Trochonema

Fig. 139. Trochonematacea (Trochonematidae) (p. *1225*).

Superfamily FISSURELLACEA Fleming, 1822

[*nom. transl.* Cox, 1959 (*ex* Fissurelladae Fleming, 1822)]
[Help in preliminary organization of data, given by Miss Grace Johnson, is here acknowledged]

Shell conical, porcelaneous; protoconch spiral; with perforation, slit, notch, or emargination for passage of exhalant current; muscle scar horseshoe-shaped, open anteriorly (138, 147). *Trias.-Rec.*

Family FISSURELLIDAE Fleming, 1822

[*nom. correct.* d'Orbigny, 1839 (*pro* Fissurelladae Fleming, 1822)]

With characters of superfamily. *Trias.-Rec.*

Subfamily EMARGINULINAE Gray, 1834

[*nom. transl.* Cossmann, 1888 (*ex* Emarginulidae Gray, 1834)]

Apex present in most forms; when wholly removed by perforation, apex replaced by projecting shelf within; slit anterior to apex. *?Trias., Jur.-Rec.*

Emarginula Lamarck, 1801 [**E. conica*] [=*Emarginulus* Montfort, 1810 (obj.); *Imarginula* Gray,

1821 (obj.)]. Slit of varying extent; apex varying in position; no septum within. *?M.Trias., L.Jur.-Rec.*, cosmop.

E. (Emarginula). Slit long and narrow, selenizone depressed between two ribs; shell short-ovate, elevated; ornament radial riblets cancellated by collabral threads. *?M.Trias., Rec.*, Eu.-N.Am.-S.Am.-Australasia.——Fig. 140,1. **E. (E.) conica*, Rec., Eng.; *1a-c*, ×3 (184).

E. (Altomarginula) Haber, 1932 [**E. desnoyersi* J.A.Eudes-Deslongchamps, 1842]. Very elevated, with apex pointing to rear and located above margin; slit deep, selenizone in well-impressed groove; ornament radial threads. *M.Jur.(Bathon.)*, Eu.——Fig. 140,7. **E. (A.) desnoyersi*, Fr.; ×3 (147).

E. (Arginula) Palmer, 1937 [**E. arata* Conrad, 1933]. Larger than *E. (Emarginula)*, slit broader and shorter, selenizone not depressed between two ribs. *M.Eoc.*, SE.USA.

E. (Entomella) Cossmann, 1888 [**E. clypeata* Lamarck, 1803]. Apex near posterior margin, slit short and broad, selenizone not on a rib. *Eoc.*, Eu.——Fig. 140,3. **E. (E.) clypeata*, Eoc., Fr., *3a-c*, ×3 (215).

E. (Semperia) Crosse, 1867 [**S. paivana*; SD Cossmann, 1888]. Juvenile shells as in *E. (Emar-*

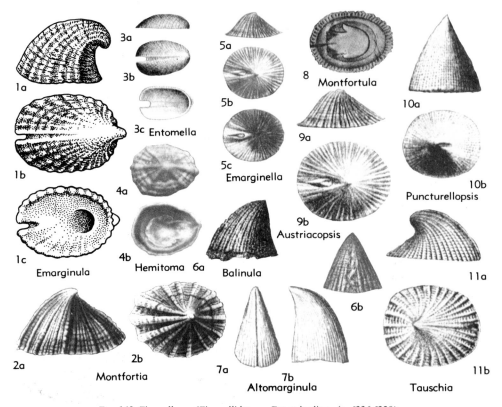

FIG. 140. Fissurellacea (Fissurellidae——Emarginulinae (p. I226-I228).

ginula) but adults with slit closed at margin, forming a perforation on anterior slope. *Eoc.-Rec.*, Eu.

E. (Subzeidora) IREDALE, 1924 [**E. connectens* THIELE, 1924]. Apex posterior, incurved; slit very long. *Rec.*, S.Pac.

E. (Tauschia) HABER, 1932 [**E. orthogonia* TAUSCH, 1890]. Like *Emarginula (s.s.)* but with raised riblike selenizone. *L.Jur.*, Eu.-Afr.——FIG. 140,11. **E. (T.) orthogonia* TAUSCH, L.Lias., S.Tyrol; *11a,b,* ×1.5 (147).

Austriacopsis HABER, 1932 [**Rimula austriaca* HÖRNES, 1853]. Patelliform, apex not far from median; exhalant outlet an elongate trema between apex and middle of anterior margin. *Jur.*

A. (Austriacopsis). Not greatly elevated; trema pyriform, midway between apex and anterior margin, tapering anteriorly to narrow slit; ornament moderately strong radial ribs. *Jur.(Lias.-Portland.)*, Eu.——FIG. 140,9. **A. (A.) austriaca* (HÖRNES), L.Lias., Aus.; 9a,b, ×1.5 (147).

A. (Puncturellopsis) HABER, 1932 [**Fissurella acuta* J.A.EUDES-DESLONGCHAMPS, 1842]. Elevated; trema elliptical, near apex; ornament radial threads. *M.Jur.(Baj.-Bathon.)*, Eu.——FIG. 140,10. **A. (P.) acuta* (J.A.EUDES-DESLONG-

CHAMPS), M.Jur.(Bathon.), Fr.; *10a,b,* ×1.5 (147).

A. (Balinula) DACQUÉ (*ex* HABER, MS.), 1933 [**Emarginula? triontina* GRECO, 1899]. Elevated; trema pyriform, elongate, near anterior margin; ornament cancellate. *M.Jur.(Aalen.-Baj.)*, Eu. ——FIG. 140,6. **A. (B.) triontina* (GRECO), M. Jur.(Aalen.), Italy; 6a,b, ×4.5 (189).

Clypidina GRAY, 1847 [**Patella notata* LINNÉ, 1767]. Conical, surface with fine radiating ribs; apex not recurved; anterior notch short.

C. (Clypidina). Internal groove on anterior slope weak or wanting. *Rec.*, S.Pac.

C. (Montfortula) IREDALE, 1915 [**Emarginula rugosa* QUOY & GAIMARD, 1834] [=*Plagiorhytis* FISCHER, 1885 (*non* CHAUDOIR, 1848)]. Internal groove distinct. *Plio.-Rec.*, Australasia.——FIG. 140,8. **C. (M.) rugosa* (QUOY & GAIMARD), Rec., Austral., ×1 (147).

Emarginella PILSBRY, 1891 [**Emarginula cuvieri* AUDOUIN, 1826]. Shell coarsely latticed; mantle partially enveloping shell. *Rec.*, E.Afr.-E.Indies. ——FIG. 140,5. **E. cuvieri* (AUDOUIN), Rec., Red Sea; ×1 (147).

Emersonia HABER, 1932 [**Cemoria costata* EMERSON, 1870]. Small, cap-shaped, with posteriorly

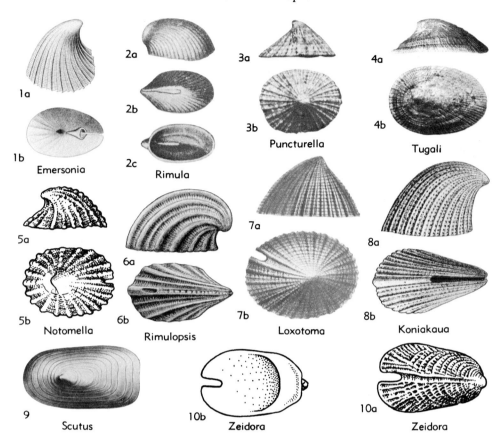

FIG. 141. Fissurellacea (Fissurellidae——Emarginulinae) (p. *1228-1230*).

pointing, hooklike, almost terminal apex; narrow exhalant slit extending halfway to apex from anterior margin and funnel-shaped internal plate towards apex from extremity of slit; ornament radial riblets of 2 orders, collabral threads in intervals. *L.Jur.*, Eu.——FIG. 141,*1*. **E. costata* (EMERSON), M.Lias., Ger.; exterior, interior showing septum, *1a,b,* ×4 (181).

Hemitoma SWAINSON, 1840 [**Patella tricostata* SOWERBY, 1823, *ex* HUMPHREY MS (*non* GMELIN, 1791) =*P. octoradiata* GMELIN, 1791] [=*Subemarginula* GRAY, 1847 (obj.); *Siphonella* ISSEL, 1869 (*non* HAGENOW, 1851)]. Shell low to moderately elevated, but not conical; internal groove distinct, with a short slit or notch anteriorly. *Eoc.-Rec.*, Eu.-N.Am.-S.Am.-S.Pac.

H. (Hemitoma). With several symmetrically arranged heavy ribs; selenizone not forming a stout ridge; posterior slope not concave. *Rec.*, Carib.——FIG. 140,*4*. **H. (H.) octoradiata* (GMELIN), Rec., W.Indies; *4a,b,* ×1 (147).

H. (Montfortia) RÉCLUZ, 1843 [**Emarginula australis* QUOY & GAIMARD, 1834; SD IREDALE,

1915]. Selenizone forming stout ridge; anterior slope convex, posterior concave behind apex. *Eoc.-Rec.*, Eu.-N.Am.-S.Am.-S.Pac.——FIG. 140,*2*. *H. (M.) australis* (QUOY & GAIMARD), Rec., Austral., ×1 (147).

H. (Montfortista) IREDALE, 1929 [**M. excentrica*]. With concentric latticing. *Rec.*, Austral.

Loxotoma FISCHER, 1885 [**Emarginula neocomiensis* D'ORBIGNY, 1843]. Like *Emarginula (s.s.)* but asymmetrical, selenizone and marginal exhalant slit forming an acute angle with mid-line of shell. *U.Jur.(Portland.)-Eoc.*, Eu. —— FIG. 141,*7*. **L. neocomiensis* (D'ORBIGNY), L.Cret.(Neocom.), Fr.; *7a,b,* ×2 (110).

Notomella COTTON, 1957 [**Emarginula candida* A. ADAMS, 1852] [=*Entomella* COTTON, 1945 (*non* COSSMANN, 1888)]. Resembling *Emarginula*, ovate, depressed-conical, apex recurved; anal slit long and narrow. *Tert.-Rec.*, Australasia-IndoPac.—— FIG. 141,*5*. **N. candida* (A.ADAMS), Rec., E.Indies; *5a,b,* ×2 (216).

Puncturella LOWE, 1827 [**Patella noachina* LINNÉ, 1758] [=*Cemoria* LEACH, 1852 (*non* RISSO,

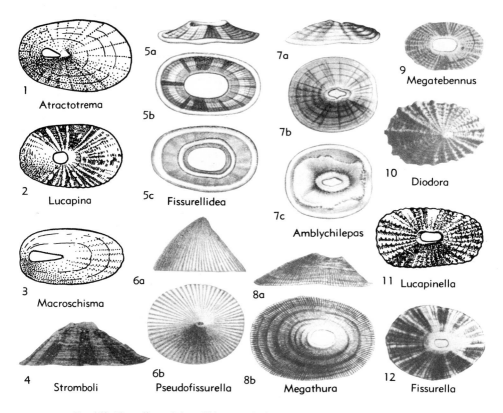

FIG. 142. Fissurellacea (Fissurellidae——Diodorinae, Fissurellinae) (p. *1230-1231*).

1826); *Sipho* BROWN, 1827 (*non* FABRICIUS, 1823); *Vacerra* IREDALE, 1924 (*non* GODMAN, 1900)]. Conical, with perforation on anterior slope or near apex entering conduit or curved shelly plate within; internal groove and selenizone weak or wanting. *Eoc.-Rec.*

P. (**Puncturella**). Perforation near summit, apex recurved, persistent in adult. *Oligo.-Rec., Eu.-N.Pac.*——FIG. 141,*3*. **P. noachina* (LINNÉ), Rec., Norway; *3a,b*, ×2 (147).

P. (**Altrix**) PALMER, 1942 [**Fissurella altior* MEYER & ALDRICH, 1886] [*=Folia* PALMER, 1937 (*non* LOHMAN, 1892)]. Apex truncated by a constricted perforation; internal septum thin. *M.Eoc., SE.USA.*

P. (**Cranopsis**) A.ADAMS, 1860 [**C. pelex*] [*=Rimulanax* IREDALE, 1924]. Perforation at middle of anterior slope; internal groove visible. *Plio.-Rec., Eu.-IndoPac.*

P. (**Fissurisepta**) SEGUENZA, 1863 [**F. papillosa;* SD WOODRING, 1928]. Perforation at apex; internal septum strong; no internal groove; surface sculpture weak. *Mio.-Rec., Eu.-W.Atl.-IndoPac.-Australasia.*

P. (**Rixa**) IREDALE, 1924 [**Glyphis watsoni* BRA-

ZIER, 1894]. Apex truncated, closed posteriorly by internal shelf. *Rec.,* Austral.

Rimula DEFRANCE, 1827 [**R. blainvilli;* SD GRAY, 1847] [*=Rimularia* WALDHEIM, 1834 (obj.)]. Apical whorls present, inclined to right; perforation on anterior slope, long and narrow; no internal septum. *Cret.-Rec., Eu.-N.Am.-S.Am.-IndoPac.*——FIG. 141,*2*. **R. blainvilli,* Eoc., Fr.; *2a-c,* ×5 (147).

Rimulopsis HABER, 1932 [**Emarginula goldfussi* ROEMER, 1836]. Small, cap-shaped, apical region narrow, extending well beyond posterior margin, apex slightly recurved; ornament symmetrical radial ribs and collabral threads. Elliptical trema on anterior slope. *Jur.,* Eu.

R. (**Rimulopsis**). Anterior slope with broad median rib bearing selenizone and small trema placed some distance from anterior margin. *Jur.(Lias.-Portland.),* Eu.——FIG. 141,*6*. *A. deslongchampsi* (COSSMANN), M.Jur.(Bathon.), Eng.; *6a,b,* ×6 (104).

R. (**Koniakaua**) DACQUÉ, 1933 (*ex* HABER MS) [**Rimula multistriata* ZITTEL, 1873]. Trema midway between apex and margin; selenizone in deep groove. *U.Jur.(Tithon.),* Eu.——FIG. 141,*8*.

R. (K.) multistriata (ZITTEL), Czech.; *8a,b,* ×5 (157).

Scutus MONTFORT, 1810 [**S. antipodes*] [=*Parmophorus* DEBLAINVILLE, 1817 (obj.); *Parmophora* DESMAREST, 1859 (obj.); *Parmaphora* BOWDICH, 1822 (obj.); *Scutum* SOWERBY, 1842 (obj.); *Aviscutum* IREDALE, 1940]. Depressed, oblong, apex not absorbed; selenizone wanting; muscle scar near margin. *Eoc.-Rec.,* Eu.-Austral.-IndoPac.

S. (Scutus). Shell large, truncate anteriorly, smooth. *Mio.-Rec.,* Eu.-IndoPac.-Australasia.——FIG. 141,9. **S. (S.) antipodes,* Rec., SE.Austral.; ×0.5 (147).

S. (Nannoscutum) IREDALE, 1937 [**N. forsythi*]. Shell small, stout, with strong concentric linear sculpture. *Rec.,* Australasia.

S. (Proscutum) FISCHER, 1885 [**Parmophorus compressus* DESHAYES, 1861]. Small, thin, narrow, anterior border rounded. *Eoc.,* Eu.

Tugali GRAY in DIEFFENBACH, 1843 [**T. elegans,* =*Emarginula parmophoidea* QUOY & GAIMARD, 1834] [=*Tugalia* GRAY, 1847 (obj.)]. Surface radiate-cancellate; apex entire, posterior, recurved; margin crenulate within, sinuate anteriorly. *Mio.-Rec.,* Australasia-IndoPac.-Antarct.

T. (Tugali). Apex at posterior third. *Mio.-Rec.,* IndoPac.-Australasia.——FIG. 141,4. **T. (T.) parmophoidea* (QUOY & GAIMARD), Rec., N.Z.; *4a,b,* ×0.7 (147).

T. (Parmophoridea) WENZ, 1938 [**Tugalia antarctica* STREBEL, 1907] [=*Parmaphorella* STREBEL, 1907 (*non* MATTHEW, 1886)]. Apex above posterior margin; selenizone short. *Rec.,* Antarct.

Zeidora A.ADAMS, 1860 [**Z. calceolina*] [=*Crepiemarginula* SEGUENZA, 1880; *Legrandia* BEDDOME, 1883 (*non* HANLEY, 1872)]. Apex posterior, recurved; selenizone on anterior slope, with elevated edges and anterior slit; septum within on posterior margin. *Plio.-Rec.,* Eu.-W.Atl.-Pac.-RedSea.

Z. (Zeidora). Internal septum broad. *Plio.-Rec.,* Eu.-W.Atl.-Pac.——FIG. 141,10. **Z. calceolina,* Rec., Japan; *10a,b,* ×4 (191).

Z. (Nesta) H.ADAMS, 1870 [**N. candida*]. Septum weak. *Rec.,* Red Sea.

Subfamily DIODORINAE Wenz, 1938

Shell conical, apex perforate; perforation bounded by callus within that is truncate posteriorly; muscle scar open anteriorly, with hook-shaped terminations (3). *Jur.-Rec.*

Diodora GRAY, 1821 [**Patella apertura* MONTAGU, 1803 = *P. graeca* LINNÉ, 1758] [=*Fissuridea* SWAINSON, 1840; *Glyphis* CARPENTER, 1857 (*non* AGASSIZ, 1843); *Capiluna* GRAY, 1857; *Monodilepas* FINLAY, 1927]. Ornament cancellate; margin in a single plane, crenulate within. *U.Cret.-Rec.,* Afr.-N.Am.-S.Am.-Pac.-Austral.

D. (Diodora). Perforation oval, at apex. *U.Cret.-Rec.,* Afr.-N.Am.-S.Am.-W.Pac.-S.Pac. —— FIG.

142, 10. *D. (D.) graeca* (LINNÉ), Rec., Medit.; ×1 (147).

D. (Austroglyphis) COTTON & GODFREY, 1934 [**D. lincolnensis* COTTON, 1930]. Perforation rectangular. *Rec.,* Austral.

D. (Elegidion) IREDALE, 1924 [**D. audax*] [=*Eligidion* COTTON & GODFREY, 1945 (*errore*)]. Perforation on anterior slope. *Rec.,* Austral.

Megathura PILSBRY, 1890 [**M. californica* = *Fissurella crenulata* G.B.SOWERBY, 1825] [=*Macrochasma* DALL, 1915 (obj.)]. Large, perforation large, oval; muscle scar faint; surface radiately striate; inner margin finely crenulate. *Plio.-Rec.,* Japan-W.N.Am.——FIG. 142,8. **M. crenulata* (SOWERBY), Rec., Calif.; *8a,b,* ×3 (147).

Pseudofissurella HABER, 1932 [**Fissurella corallensis* BUVIGNIER, 1852]. Small, rather high, apex just posterior to median, perforation small, with slight posterior slant; ornament fine rounded radial riblets. *Jur.,* Eu.——FIG. 142,6. **P. corallensis* (BUVIGNIER), U.Jur.(Raurac.), Fr.; *6a,b,* ×7.5 (147).

Stromboli BERRY, 1954 [**Fissurella beebei* HERTLEIN & STRONG, 1951]. Perforation slanting, slightly in front of apex. *Rec.,* C.Am.——FIG. 142,4. **S. beebei* (HERTLEIN & STRONG), Rec., W.Mex., ×0.5 (192).

Subfamily FISSURELLINAE Fleming, 1822

Exhalant perforation at or near apex, bordered within by a rounded callus (2). *Eoc.-Rec.*

Fissurella BRUGUIÈRE, 1789 [**Patella nimbosa* LINNÉ, 1758; SD LAMARCK, 1799] [=*Fissurellus* DEMONTFORT, 1810 (obj.)]. Apex nearly central, inner margin of shell smooth or weakly crenulate. *Oligo.-Rec.,* Eu.-N.Am.-C.Am.-S.Am.

F. (Fissurella). Shell with border dark internally. *Eoc.-Rec.,* Eu.-Atl.-Pac.——FIG. 142,12. **F. nimbosa* (LINNÉ), Rec., W.Indies; ×0.7 (147).

F. (Balboaina) PEREZ-FARFANTE, 1943 [**Patella picta* GMELIN, 1791] [=*Balvoina* CARCELLES, 1951 (*errore*); *Balboina* PEREZ-FARFANTE, 1952 (*errore*)]. Like *F. (Fissurella)* but larger, internal callus broader. *Rec.,* southern S.Am.

F. (Carcellesia) PEREZ-FARFANTE, 1952 [**F. (C.) doellojuradoi*]. Perforation with a small tooth on either side. *Rec.,* S.Am.

F. (Clypidella) SWAINSON, 1840 [**Patella pustula* GMELIN, 1791 (*non* LINNÉ, 1758) = *F. punctata* FISCHER, 1857]. Depressed, saddle-shaped, ends elevated; perforation in front of middle; margin somewhat crenulate. *Rec.,* Atl.-W.Indies.

F. (Cremides) ADAMS & ADAMS, 1854 [**F. alabastrites* REEVE, 1849; SD COSSMANN & PEYROT, 1917]. Perforation central, shell with well-developed radial ribs; inner margin crenulate. *Oligo.-Rec.,* N.Am.-C.Am.

Amblychilepas PILSBRY, 1890 [**Fissurella trapezina* G.B.SOWERBY, 1835 = *F. javanicensis* LAMARCK, 1822] [=*Sophismalepas* IREDALE, 1924]. Saddle-

shaped, shell elevated at ends; hole large; margins of shell thickened, not crenulate. *Rec.,* S.Atl.-S.Pac.——Fig. 142,7. **A. javanicensis* (LAMARCK), Rec., Austral.; *7a-c,* ×1 (147).

Atractotrema COSSMANN, 1888 [**Fissurella grata* DESHAYES, 1861]. Small, perforation in front of apex, obovate; sculpture faint. *Eoc.,* Eu.——Fig. 142,*1.* **A. grata* (DESHAYES), Eoc., Fr.; ×3 (177).

Cosmetalepas IREDALE, 1924 [**Fissurella concatenata* CROSSE & FISCHER, 1864] [=*Profissurellidea* WENZ, 1938]. Thin, depressed, surface with small rounded pits; perforation large, oblong. *Mio.-Rec.,* Austral.

Fissurellidea D'ORBIGNY, 1841 [**F. megatrema* = *Fissurella hiantula* LAMARCK, 1822]. Depressed, margin with a thickened rim, perforation large. *Eoc.-Rec.,* Eu.-Afr.-S.Am.-Austral.

F. (Fissurellidea). With fine radial riblets; perforation central. *Eoc.-Rec.,* Eu.-S.Am.-Austral.——Fig. 142,*5.* **F. (F.) hiantula* (LAMARCK), Rec., Arg.; *5a-c,* ×1 (147).

F. (Pupillaea) G.B.SOWERBY, 1835 [**Fissurella aperta* G.B.SOWERBY, 1825] [=*Pupilia, Papillaea* "GRAY" of authors, spelling errors]. Marginal rim depressed; perforation eccentric. *Plio.-Rec.,* S.Am.-S.Afr.

Lucapina G.B.SOWERBY, 1835, *ex* GRAY MS [**Fissurella cancellata* G.B.SOWERBY, 1835 (*non* GRAY, 1825) = *Foraminella sowerbii* SOWERBY, 1835 *ex* GUILDING MS] [=*Foraminella* SOWERBY, 1835 *ex* GUILDING MS (obj.); *Chlamydoglyphis* PILSBRY, 1890]. Inner margin not thickened, finely crenulate. *Mio.-Rec.,* W.Indies-W.N.Am.——Fig. 142, *2.* **L. sowerbii* (SOWERBY), Rec., Fla.; ×1.5 (2).

Lucapinella PILSBRY, 1890 [**Clypidella callomarginata* DALL, 1872, *ex* CARPENTER MS; SD PILSBRY, 1891]. Apex subcentral, large perforation; crenulate within at each end, posterior margin slightly elevated. *Oligo.-Rec.,* W.Indies-N.Am.-S.Am.——Fig. 142,*11.* Rec., Calif.; ×1.5 (213).

Macroschisma G.B.SOWERBY, 1839, *ex* GRAY MS [**Patella macroschisma* SOLANDER, 1786, *ex* HUMPHREY MS] [=*Macrochisma* GRAY, 1840; *Machrochisma* SWAINSON, 1840 (obj.)]. Shell long and narrow, perforation near posterior margin. *Rec.,* Australasia-SW.Pac.-IndianO.

M. (Macroschisma). Perforation long-triangular, wide end near posterior margin. *Rec.,* IndianO.-SW.Pac.——Fig. 142,*3.* **M. macroschisma* (SOLANDER), Rec., Austral.; ×1.5 (219).

M. (Dolichoschisma) IREDALE, 1940 [**M. producta* A.ADAMS, 1854]. With broad raised ridge from perforation to anterior margin. *Rec.,* Australasia.

M. (Forolepas) IREDALE, 1940 [**M. tasmaniae* G.B.SOWERBY, 1862]. Shell and perforation broader than in *M. (Macroschisma).* *Rec.,* Australasia.

Megatebennus PILSBRY, 1890 [**Fissurellidea bimaculata* DALL, 1872]. More elevated than *Fissurellidea.* *Plio.-Rec.,* W.N.Am.-Austral.——Fig. 142,*9.* **M. bimaculatus* (DALL), Rec., Calif.; ×1 (147).

Suborder PATELLINA von Ihering, 1876

[*nom. transl.* COX & KNIGHT, herein (*ex* Patelloidea VON IHERING, 1876)] [=Cyclobranchia (GOLDFUSS, 1820, *partim*) GRAY, 1821; Docoglossa TROSCHEL, 1866; Onychoglossa SARS, 1878; Phyllidiobranchia LANKESTER, 1883; *hétérocardes* PERRIER, 1889; Heterocardia BERNARD, 1890]

Shell conical or cap-shaped, bilaterally symmetrical, without perforation or marginal notch, without internal septum; muscle attachment scar semicircular or horseshoe-shaped, open on anterior side; outer shell layer calcitic, inner layers aragonitic, iridescent in some but not nacreous; no operculum; living forms with single bipectinate ctenidium or with circlet of small branchiae beneath mantle margin or with neither; pallial genital organs wanting; heart with single auricle, ventricle not traversed by rectum; radula long, docoglossate, **teeth clawlike, number in each row small,** exercising effective rasping stroke during outward protraction of odontophore. [Habitat littoral zone, clinging to rocks.] *?M.Sil.-L.Trias., M.Trias.-Rec.*

Superfamily PATELLACEA Rafinesque, 1815

[*nom. transl.* THIELE, 1925 (*ex* Patellidae, *nom correct.* GRAY, 1834, *pro* Patellaria RAFINESQUE, 1815)]

With characters of suborder. *?M.Sil.-L.Trias., M.Trias.-Rec.*

?Family METOPTOMATIDAE Wenz, 1938

Shell patelliform or helcioniform; muscle scar horseshoe-shaped with anterior opening not closed by pallial line, scar broadest at anterior end; nature of inner shell layers and of possible coiled protoconch imperfectly known. *M.Sil.-M.Perm.*

The Metoptomatidae are seemingly represented by undescribed species and genera occurring as far back as early Middle Ordovician time. Their derivation is uncertain, but it seems probable that they arose from the early pleurotomarian stem or even from the still more primitive bellerophonts. No direct evidence can be cited to indicate that this family was docoglossate but, on the other hand, there is not yet enough evidence to establish it as a superfamily unrelated to but convergent with the Patellacea.

Palaeoscurria PERNER, 1903 [**P. calyptrata;* SD COSSMANN, 1904]. Externally resembling *Lepetopsis* but musculature entirely unknown. [Existence of supposed muscle scars described and figured

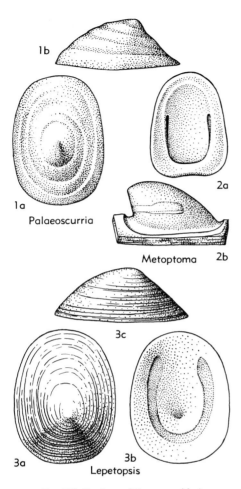

FIG. 143. Patellacea (Metoptomatidae)
(p. *I231-I232*).

by PERNER cannot be verified; possibly congeneric
with *Lepetopsis.*] M.Sil., Eu.——Fig. 143,*1*. *P.
calyptrata,* Czech.; *1a,b,* from above and left side,
×2.7.

Metoptoma PHILLIPS, 1836 [*M. oblonga;* SD S.A.
MILLER, 1889]. Helcioniform, with open horseshoe-shaped muscle scar; apex posterior; anterior
slope convex and posterior approximately vertical.
L. Carb.(Miss.)-Perm., N. Am.-Eu.-SE. Asia. ——
FIG. 143,*2*. *M. oblonga,* L.Carb., Eng.; *2a,* interior, showing muscle scars; *2b,* steinkern, right
side; ×2.

Lepetopsis WHITFIELD, 1882 [*Patella levettei
WHITE, 1882]. Thin patelliform, with open horseshoe-shaped muscle scar; apex slightly in front of
center, posterior slope convex, anterior straight or
concave. Miss.-M.Perm., N.Am.-Eu.-SE.Asia.——
FIG. 143,*3*. *L. levettei* (WHITE), M.Miss., Ind.;

3a, from above; *3b,* interior showing scar (upper
part anterior); *3c,* left side; all ×1.3.

?Family SYMMETROCAPULIDAE
Wenz, 1938

[*nom. transl. et correct.* Cox, herein (*ex* Symetrocapulinae
WENZ, 1938)]

Cap-shaped, longitudinal profile down-
curved from submedian summit to more or
less anteriorly placed and directed beak;
protoconch coiled, of 1.5 to 2 whorls, retained (unless eroded) by adult shell; muscle scar unknown. *Trias.-Jur., ?Cret.*

For lack of definite evidence to the con-
trary, this group is provisionally retained
in the Patellina, following WENZ, although
it may eventually prove to be related to the
caenogastropod family Capulidae.

Symmetrocapulus DACQUÉ, 1933 [*Patella rugosa
J.SOWERBY, 1816 (*non* RÖDING, 1798) = *P. tes-
soni* J.A.EUDES-DESLONGCHAMPS, 1843] [=*Sym-
etrocapulus* HABER, 1932 (*nom. nud.)*]. Rather
large; beak at anterior third to quarter of length;
ornament radial riblets and concentric folds. *Jur.,
?Cret.,* Eu.——FIG. 144,*1*. *S. rugosus* (J.SOWER-
BY), M.Jur.(Bath.), Fr.; *1a,b,* from above and left
side, ×2 (147).

?Phryx BLASCHKE, 1905 [*Capulus (Phryx) bilateralis*]. Rather small, domelike, with submedian
summit and terminal beak; no ornament except
growth striae; protoconch unknown. *M.Trias.-U.
Trias.,* Eu.-Asia.——FIG. 144,*2*. *P. bilateralis,*
M.Trias.(Ladin.), S.Tyrol; right side, ×1 (147).

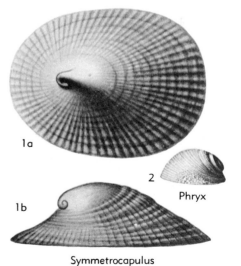

FIG. 144. Patellacea (Symmetrocapulidae)
(p. *I232*).

Family ACMAEIDAE Carpenter, 1857

Shell conical, porcelaneous; respiratory organ a single ctenidium, no branchial cordon. *M.Trias.-Rec.*

Scurriopsis GEMMELLARO, 1879 [*S. neumayri;* SD HABER, 1932]. Shell variably elevated, apex slightly or well anterior to median; ornament collabral threads with radial elements variable. *M.Trias.-U.Jur., ?L.Cret.,* Eu.-Afr.

S. (Scurriopsis). Well-elevated, broadly elliptical, apex only slightly anterior to median; cancellating collabral and radial threads on entire surface; muscle scar (observed in type species) horseshoe-shaped with broad anterior gap. *M.Trias.-U.Jur.,* Eu., N.Afr.——FIG. 145,8. *S. (S.) neumayri,* L.Lias., Sicily; *8a,b,* from above and left side, ×1 (130).

S. (Hennocquia) WENZ, 1938 (*ex* HABER, 1932, *nom. nud.*) [*Patella hennocquii* TERQUEM, 1855]. Only moderately elevated, ovate, with anterior end the narrower; apex well anterior; radial riblets almost confined to posterior end. *L.Jur.(L.Lias.),* Eu.——FIG. 145,6. *S. (H.) hennocquii* (TERQUEM), Fr.; *6a,b,* from above and right side, ×1 (224).

S. (Dietrichiella) WENZ, 1938 (*ex* HABER, 1932, *nom. nud.*) [*Patella kindopensis* DIETRICH, 1914]. Small, moderately elevated, rather narrowly elliptical; apex well anterior; radial riblets very obscure. *U.Jur., ?L.Cret.,* E.Afr.-Eu.—— FIG. 145,3. *S. (D.) kindopensis* (DIETRICH), U. Jur.(Kimm.), E.Afr.; *3a,b,* from above and left side, ×2 (130).

Marbodeia CHELOT, 1887 [*pro Guerangeria* COSS-MANN, 1885 (*non* OEHLERT, 1881)] [*Patella clypeola* J.A.EUDES-DESLONGCHAMPS, 1842]. Small, narrowly elliptical, depressed, convex in profile except for apex, which forms projecting stud limited by a depression; ornament depressed, rounded radial riblets. *M.Jur.(Bathon.),* Eu.——FIG. 145,1. *M. clypeola* (J.A.EUDES-DESLONGCHAMPS), Fr.; *1a,b,* from above and right side, ×1.5 (17).

Conorhytis COSSMANN, 1907 [*Patella squamula* J.A. EUDES-DESLONGCHAMPS, 1863]. Moderately large, well-elevated, broadly elliptical, apex just anterior to median; ornament fine squamae or wrinkles with irregular quincuncial arrangement, and obscure radial threads. *M.Jur.(Baj.-Bathon.),* Eu.——FIG. 145,7. *C. raduloides* (COSSMANN), M.Jur.(Bathon.); *7a,b,* from above and right side, ×1 (170).

Deslongchampsia MORRIS & LYCETT (*ex* M'COY, MS), 1851 [*Patella appendiculata* J.A.EUDES-DESLONGCHAMPS, 1842; SD LAUBE, 1868 (TATE, 1868, Appendix to S.P.WOODWARD, *Manual of Mollusca,* p. 39, designated *D. eugenei* MORRIS & LYCETT as type species in the same year, but LAUBE's designation is here accepted)]. Of small-medium size, cap-shaped, rather depressed, suborbicular, with apex anterior to median and point-

ing anteriorly; broad, smooth sulcus runs from apex to rounded lobelike projection of anterior margin; remainder of surface radially costate. *M. Jur.(Bathon.)-U.Jur.(Oxford.),* Eu.——FIG. 145,2. *D. appendiculata* (J.A.EUDES-DESLONGCHAMPS), M.Jur.(Bathon.), Fr.; *2a-c,* from above, anterior, and left side, ×1 (147).

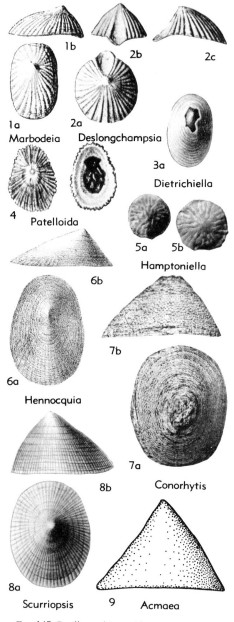

FIG. 145. Patellacea (Acmaeidae——Acmaeinae) (p. I233-I234).

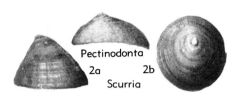

FIG. 146. Patellacea (Acmaeidae——Acmaeinae) (p. *1234*).

Hamptoniella WENZ, 1938 [*pro Hamptonia* HABER, 1932 *(nom. nud.) non* WALCOTT, 1920] [**Um-brella? hamptonensis* MORRIS & LYCETT, 1851]. Small, circular, flat or almost so; apex submedian; surface with straight or undulating low, rounded, subradial ribs, increasing outward by intercalation and forking. *M.Jur.(Bathon.)*, Eu.——FIG. 145,5. *H. hamptonensis* (MORRIS & LYCETT), Eng.; 5*a,b*, specimens from above, ×1.8 (COX, n).

Acmaea ESCHSCHOLTZ, 1833 (ICZN Op. 344, 1955) [**A. mitra;* SD DALL, 1871] [=*Niveotectura* HABE, 1944]. Smooth to radially ribbed, oval, apex mostly subcentral; muscle impressions joined by a thin line anteriorly. *Oligo.-Rec.,* Pac.

A. (Acmaea). Apex central, shell white, nearly smooth. *Pleist.-Rec.,* W.N.Am.——FIG. 145,9. **A. (A.) mitra,* Rec., Washington; left side, ×2 (147).

A. (Actinoleuca) OLIVER, 1926 [**Patella campbelli* FILHOL, 1880]. High, finely ribbed. *Oligo.-Rec.,* Australasia.

A. (Asteracmea) OLIVER, 1926 [**Helcioniscus illibratus* VERCO, 1906]. *Rec.,* Australasia.

A. (Atalacmea) IREDALE, 1915 [*Patella fragilis SOWERBY, 1823]. Small, thin, apex in front of center. *Mio.-Rec.,* N.Z.

A. (Chiazacmea) OLIVER, 1926 [**Patelloida flammea* QUOY & GAIMARD, 1834]. *Rec.,* S.Pac.

A. (Collisella) DALL, 1871 [**A. pelta* ESCH-SCHOLTZ, 1833]. Larger than *A. (Acmaea),* exteriorly dark colored, a colored margin within; sculpture various. *Pleist.-Rec.,* NW.N.Am.-C.Am.

A. (Collisellina) DALL, 1871 [**Patella saccharina* LINNÉ, 1758]. *Rec.,* IndoPac.

A. (Conacmea) OLIVER, 1926 [**A. parviconoidea* SUTER, 1907]. *Rec.,* Australasia.

A. (Conoidacmaea) HABE, 1944 [*Patella heroldi DUNKER, 1861]. *Pleist.-Rec.,* Japan.

A. (Kikukozara) HABE, 1944 [**Collisella (K.) langfordi*]. *Rec.,* Japan.

A. (Naccula) IREDALE, 1924 [*Nacella parva AN-GAS, 1878 = *Patelloida punctata* QUOY & GAIM-ARD, 1834]. *Rec.,* Australasia.

A. (Notoacmea) IREDALE, 1915 [**Patelloida pileopsis* QUOY & GAIMARD, 1834]. *Plio.-Rec.,* Japan-Australasia.

A. (Parvacmea) IREDALE, 1915 [**A. daedala* SUTER, 1907]. Small, thin, beaks well forward, hooked. *Oligo.-Rec.,* N.Z.

A. (Patelloida) QUOY & GAIMARD, 1834 [**P. rugosa;* SD GRAY, 1847]. Radially ribbed; with strong color markings as in *A. (Collisella). Rec.,* IndoPac.——FIG. 145,4. **A. (P.) rugosa* (QUOY & GAIMARD), Rec., E.Indies; 4*a,b,* exterior and interior, anterior toward top, ×1 (147).

A. (Radiacmea) IREDALE, 1915 [**A. cingulata* HUTTON, 1883]. *Rec.,* S.Pac.

A. (Subacmea) OLIVER, 1926 [**Notoacmea scopulina*]. *Rec.,* Australasia.

A. (Tectura) GRAY, 1847 [*Patella parva DACOSTA, 1778 = *P. virginea* MÜLLER, 1776] [=*Erginus* JEFFREYS, 1877]. Apex high, in front of center, ribbing weak, radial and concentric. *Plio.-Rec.,* Eu.

A. (Thalassacmea) OLIVER, 1926 [*Notoacmea badia]. *Rec.,* N.Z.

Lottia GRAY, 1833 [**L. gigantea* G.B.SOWERBY, 1834; SD DALL, 1871] [=*Tecturella* CARPENTER, 1860 *(non* STIMPSON, 1854); *Tecturina* CARPEN-TER, 1861, *Lecania* CARPENTER, 1866 *(non* MAC-QUART, 1839), *pro Tecturella*]. Large, low, apex nearly marginal; muscle impressions joined by a curved line. *Rec.,* W.N.Am.

Pectinodonta DALL, 1882 [**P. arcuata*]. Low, somewhat arched, apex blunt, subcentral; animal blind; in deep water. *Rec.,* Atl.-Japan.——FIG. 146,1. **P. arcuata,* Rec., W.Indies; ×2 (147).

Potamacmaea PEILE, 1922 [**Tectura fluviatilis* BLANFORD, 1868]. Rounded, finely radially ribbed; in brackish to fresh water. *Rec.,* India.

Scurria GRAY, 1847 [*Patella scurra LESSON, 1841]. High, apex subcentral; sculpture more concentric than radial. *Rec.,* W.S.Am.——FIG. 146,2. **S. scurra* (LESSON), Rec., W.S.Am.; ×1 (147).

Family PATELLIDAE Rafinesque, 1815

[*nom. correct.* GRAY, 1834 *(pro Patellaria* RAFINESQUE, 1815)]

Iridescent to porcelaneous within; with a branchial cordon (pallial gill lamellae) but no true ctenidium. *?Jur., Eoc.-Rec.*

Subfamily PATELLINAE Rafinesque, 1815

[*nom. transl.* THIELE, 1929 *(ex* Patellidae, *nom. correct.* GRAY, 1834, *pro* Patellaria RAFINESQUE, 1815)]

Shell strong and solid, interior iridescent; embryonal shell not evident. *?Jur., Rec.*

Patella LINNÉ, 1758 [**P. vulgata;* SD FLEMING, 1818] [=*Patellaria* GMELIN, 1793; *Patellus* MONT-FORT, 1810 (obj.); *Patellopsis* THIELE in TROSCHEL, 1891 *(non* NOBRE, 1896); *Costatopatella* PALLARY, 1912; *Granopatella, Laevipatella* PALLARY, 1920]. Round to elliptical, apex subcentral; rarely smooth. *?U.Cret., Eoc.-Rec.,* Eu.-Afr.-C.Am.-Pac.-IndoPac.-Austral.-E.Asia.

P. (Patella). Oval, with strong radial ribs, apex nearly central. *?U.Cret., Eoc.-Rec.,* Eu.-Afr.——FIG. 147,2. **P. (P.) vulgata,* Rec., Fr.; from above, anterior toward top, ×1 (147).

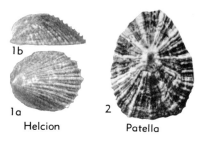

Helcion   Patella

Fig. 147. Patellacea (Patellidae——Patellinae)
(p. *1234-1235*).

P. (Ancistromesus) DALL, 1871 [*P. mexicana* BRODERIP & SOWERBY, 1829]. Adult very large and solid. *Pleist.-Rec.,* W.C.Am.

P. (Cymbula) ADAMS & ADAMS, 1854 [*P. compressa* LINNÉ, 1758]. Large, elongate-ovate, finely ribbed. *Rec.,* IndoPac.

P. (Olana) ADAMS & ADAMS, 1854 [*P. cochlear* BORN, 1778]. Anterior margin prolonged, shell spoon-shaped. *Rec.,* S.Afr.

P. (Patellastra) MONTEROSATO, 1884 [*P. lusitanica* GMELIN, 1791]. Rounded; radial ribs weakly nodose. *Mio.-Rec.,* Eu.

P. (Patellidea) THIELE in TROSCHEL, 1891 [*P. granularis* LINNÉ, 1758]. *Rec.,* S.Afr.

P. (Patellona) THIELE in TROSCHEL, 1891 [*P. granatina* LINNÉ, 1758; SD TOMLIN, 1931]. *Rec.,* S.Afr.-W.Afr.

P. (Penepatella) IREDALE, 1929 [*Penepatella inquisitor*]. *Rec.,* Austral.-Japan.

P. (Scutellastra) ADAMS & ADAMS, 1854 [*P. plicata* BORN, 1778 = *P. barbara* LINNÉ, 1758] [=*Patellanax* IREDALE, 1924]. *?Eoc., Rec.,* Pac.

Helcion DEMONTFORT, 1810 [*Patella pectinata* BORN, 1778]. Rather thin-shelled, cap-shaped, apex submarginal. *?Jur., Plio.-Rec.,* Eu.-Afr.-Pac.

H. (Helcion). Radially ribbed. *?Jur., Rec.,* Eu.-Afr.-Pac.——FIG. 147,*1.* *H. (H.) pectinatus* (BORN), Rec., S.Afr.; *1a,b,* from above and left side, ×1 (147).

H. (Ansates) SOWERBY, 1839 [*Patella pellucida* LINNÉ, 1758] [=*Patina* GRAY, 1847 (obj.)]. Apex higher than in *H. (Helcion). Plio.-Rec.,* N.Atl.

H. (Patinastra) THIELE in TROSCHEL, 1891 [*Patella pruinosus* KRAUSS, 1848]. With weak radial ribs. *Rec.,* S.Afr.

H. (Rhodopetala) DALL, 1921 [*Nacella? rosea* DALL, 1872]. Small, smooth, apex overhanging margin. *Rec.,* N.Pac.

Subfamily NACELLINAE Thiele, 1929

Shell solid in some species, in others thin-shelled to transparent; interior with metallic glaze. *Eoc.-Rec.*

Nacella SCHUMACHER, 1817 [*N. mytiloides (=*Patella mytilina* HELBLING, 1779)]. Cap-shaped, apex hooked. *Eoc.-Rec.,* Eu.-S.Am.-Antarct.

N. (Nacella). Apex submarginal; shell nearly transparent. *Eoc.-Rec.,* Eu.-S.Am.-Antarct.——FIG. 148,*2.* *N. (N.) mytilina* (HELBLING), Rec., Strait of Magellan; right side, ×1 (147).

N. (Patinigera) DALL, 1905 [*Patella magellanica* GMELIN, 1791] [*pro Patinella* DALL, 1871 (*non* GRAY, 1848)]. Apex nearly central, shell sturdier than in *N. (Nacella). Rec.,* Antarct.

Cellana H.ADAMS, 1869 [*Nacella cernica*] [=*Helcioniscus* DALL, 1871]. Shell fairly solid, apex subcentral; radial ribs strong; interior brilliantly glazed. *Mio.-Rec.,* S.Pac.-IndoPac.——FIG. 148, *1.* *C. cernica* (ADAMS), Rec., Mauritius; from above, anterior toward right, ×1 (147).

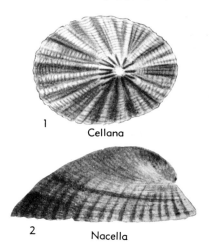

1   Cellana

2   Nacella

FIG. 148. Patellacea (Patellidae——Nacellinae)
(p. *1235*)

Family LEPETIDAE Dall, 1869

Small, colorless shells, conical or cap-shaped, apex in front of center; smooth or with inconspicuous sculpture; muscle scar as in Acmaeidae. Animal without ctenidia or branchial cordon. *Mio.-Rec.*

Lepeta GRAY, 1847 [*Patella caeca* MÜLLER, 1776]. With fine radial ribs. *Plio.-Rec.,* Eu.-Arct.-N.Atl.-N.Pac.

L. (Lepeta). Rather small, exterior beaded; tip of muscle scar in front of apex. *Plio.-Rec.,* Eu.-N. Atl.——FIG. 149,*1.* *L. (L.) caeca* (MÜLLER), Rec., North Sea; *1a,b,* from above and right side, ×1 (147).

L. (Cryptobranchia) MIDDENDORFF, 1851 [*Patella caeca concentrica;* SD DALL, 1869] [=*Cryptoctenidia* DALL, 1918 (obj.)]. Larger, nearly smooth, tip of muscle scars not in front of apex. *Plio.-Rec.,* N.Pac.-Arct.

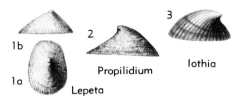

FIG. 149. Patellacea (Lepetidae) (p. *I235-I236*)

Iothia GRAY, 1850 [*non Iothia* FORBES, 1849 *(errore pro Lottia,* ICZN pend.)] [*Patella fulva* MÜLLER, 1776] [=*Pilidium* FORBES & HANLEY, 1849 (*non* MÜLLER, 1846) (obj.)]. Small, apex submarginal; with fine radial ribs. *Plio.-Rec.,* Eu.——FIG. 149, 3. *I. fulva* (MÜLLER), Rec., Scot.; right side, ×2 (147).

Propilidium FORBES, 1849 [*Patella ancyloides* FORBES, 1840] [=*Rostrisepta* SEGUENZA, 1866]. Minute, spiral apex normally present; a small triangular septum inside the beak, as in *Puncturella;* surface finely cancellate. *Mio.-Rec.,* Eu.-Arct.——FIG. 149,2. *P. ancyloides* (FORBES), Rec., North Sea; left side, ×5 (147).

Punctolepeta HABE, 1958 [*P. minuta*]. Minute, with reticulate ornament. *Rec.,* Japan.

Superfamily COCCULINACEA Thiele, 1909

[*nom. correct.* THIELE, 1925 (*pro* Cocculinoidea THIELE, 1909)]

Resembling Patellacea but with apex turned backward. *Mio.-Rec.*

Family COCCULINIDAE Dall, 1882

Shell small, conical to cap-shaped. [Deep water.] *Mio.-Rec.*

Cocculina DALL, 1882 [*C. rathbuni;* SD DALL, 1908]. Shell colorless, with radiating and concentric sculpture; muscle scar as in *Phenacolepas. Mio.-Rec.,* Eu.-Atl.-N.Am.-N.Z.-E.Indies.
  C. (Cocculina). Apex nearly central. *Mio.-Rec.,* Eu.-E.N.Am.-W.N.Am.——FIG. 150,*1. *C. (C.) rathbuni,* Rec., Carib.; *1a,b,* from above and right side, ×2 (147).
  C. (Maoricrater) DELL, 1956 [*Notoacmaea explorata* DELL, 1953]. *Rec.,* N.Z.
  C. (Notocrater) FINLAY, 1927 [*C. craticulata* SUTER, 1908] [=*Coccopygia* DALL, 1889 (*non* REICHENBACH, 1862); *Dallia* JEFFREYS, 1883 (*non* BEAN, 1878)]. Apex hooked, near posterior margin; surface smooth or radially spinose. *Rec.,* Atl.-N.Z.
  C. (Pseudococculina) SCHEPMAN, 1908 [*P. rugosoplicata;* SD WENZ, 1938]. With spiral embryonal whorls persisting. *Rec.,* E.Indies-Atl.

Family LEPETELLIDAE Dall, 1881

[*nom. transl.* THIELE, 1925 (*ex* Lepetellinae DALL, 1881)] [=Addisoniidae DALL, 1882; Bathysciadiidae DAUTZENBERG & FISCHER, 1900]

Small, low to steeply conical, smooth; apex central or behind middle, not spiral; aperture rounded to oval. *Rec.*

Lepetella VERRILL, 1880 [*L. tubicola*]. Apex elevated, nearly central. *Rec.,* N.Atl.-Carib.-N.Z.
  L. (Lepetella). Apex slightly hooked behind; shell margin nearly circular. *Rec.,* N.Atl.-Carib.——FIG. 150,2. *L. (L.) tubicola* Rec., Mass.; right side, ×5 (147).
  L. (?Tecticrater) DELL, 1956 [*Cocculina compressa* SUTER, 1908]. *Rec.,* N.Z.
  L. (Tectisumen) FINLAY, 1927 [*Cocculina clypidellaeformis* SUTER, 1908]. Saddle-shaped, anterior and posterior margins arched upward. *Rec.,* N.Z.

Addisonia DALL, 1882 [*A. paradoxa*]. Apex back of middle, blunt. *Rec.,* Atl.-Medit.——FIG. 150,4. *A. paradoxa,* Rec., NW.Atl.; right side, ×2 (147).

Bathysciadium DAUTZENBERG & FISCHER, 1900 [*B. conicum* (=*Lepeta costellata* LOCARD, 1898)]. Steeply conical, with radial striae. *Rec.,* Atl.-Pac.——FIG. 150,3. *B. costellatum* (LOCARD), Rec., Azores; right side, ×10 (147).

Cocculinella THIELE, 1909 [*Acmaea minutissima* SMITH, 1904]. Low, narrow-oval. *Mio.-Rec.,* Indian O.-Austral.——FIG. 150,5. *C. minutissima* (SMITH), Rec., Andaman I.; *5a,b,* from above and left side, ×7.5 (147).

?PATELLINA, Superfamily and Family UNCERTAIN

The following genera of Mesozoic patelliform gastropods seem closely related. *Brunonia* has been referred to the Siphonariidae and *Rhytidopilus* to the Acroriidae

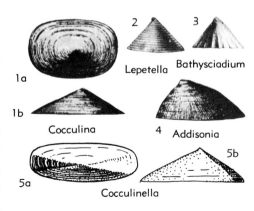

FIG. 150. Cocculinacea (Cocculinidae, Lepetellidae) (p. *I236*)

FIG. 151. ?Patellina (Superfamily and Family Uncertain) (p. *1237*).

COSSMANN, assumed also to belong to the Pulmonata. In no specimen, however, has the muscle scar been observed, and affinities with the pulmonates have yet to be proved. In the following descriptions it is assumed, without proof, that the apex, if not median, is anterior to median.

Berlieria DELORIOL, 1903 [**B. ledonica*]. Founded on broadly elliptical, patelliform internal molds of medium size; surface with concentric undulations and curved oblique furrow running from apex to anterior margin. *U.Jur.(Argov.)*, Jura.Mts.(Fr.-Switz.).

Rhytidopilus COSSMANN, 1895 [**Patella humbertina* BUVIGNIER, 1852]. Thin, patelliform, broadly elliptical, with subcentral apex; surface with concentric undulations; two furrows bordering a slightly elevated sector run from apex to anterior margin. *M.Jur.(Bathon.)-L.Cret.(Alb.)*, Eu.——FIG. 151,2. **R. humbertinus* (BUVIGNIER), U.Jur. (Kimm.), Fr.; *2a,b*, from above and anterior side, ×2.5 (18).

Pseudorhytidopilus COX, n.gen., herein (*pro* HABER, 1932, *nom. nud.*) [**P. lennieri* COX, n.sp., herein (*pro* HABER, 1932, *nom. nud.*) (=*Helcion castellana* LENNIER, 1868[1], *non Patella castellana* THURMANN & ÉTALLON, 1861]. Like *Rhytidopilus*, but lacking anterior elevated sector. *L.Jur.-U.Jur.*, Eu.

Brunonia MÜLLER, 1898 [**B. grandis*]. Large,

patelliform, variably elevated, commonly asymmetrical; apex at or anterior to mid-length; surface with irregular concentric folds and (in some specimens) a narrow anterior elevated sector, as in *Rhytidopilus*. *U.Cret.(L.Senon.)*, Ger.——FIG. 151,1. **B. grandis; 1a,b*, from above and right side, ×1 (206).——FIG. 151,3. *B. irregularis* MÜLLER; *3a,b*, from above and right side, ×1 (206).

Suborder TROCHINA Cox & Knight, 1960

[=azygobranches chiastoneures BOUVIER, 1887; Trochomorpha NAEF, 1911]

Shell mostly conispiral, with spire not greatly elevated, more rarely discoidal; outer lip simple; inner shell layers and in some forms complete shell aragonitic and nacreous; operculum calcareous or corneous and spiral in Trochacea, calcareous and multispiral in Oriostomatacea, otherwise unknown; with single bipectinate ctenidium (left); pallial genital organs wanting; heart with 2 auricles, ventricle traversed by rectum; radula rhipidoglossate. *L.Ord.-Rec.*

---

[1] *Études géol. et pal. sur l'embouchure de la Seine*, p. 80, pl. 8B, figs. 8,8a. Diagnosis: Large *Pseudorhytidopilus* orbicular in outline. The species and genus (as subgenus of *Scurria*) were proposed by HABER with bibliographic references but without diagnoses, thus requiring validation before they can be recognized under the Rules.

Superfamily PLATYCERATACEA
Hall, 1859

[*nom. transl.* KNIGHT, BATTEN & YOCHELSON, herein (*ex*
Platyceridae HALL, 1859)]

Primitively turbiniform with prosocline labrum and nacreous inner shell lining except in more advanced platyceratids; one group adapted to stationary habit on calyx of crinoids and to coprophagous feeding. *L. Ord.-M.Perm.*

There is no evidence of any exhalant sinus or channel other than the channel at the juncture of the parietal and outer lips, and it is assumed that the right ctenidium was lost. It is thought that the Platyceratacea were derived independently from the Pleurotomariacea, but the earliest genera recognized seem to have lost all vestiges of features suggesting a dibranchiate condition.

FIG. 152. Platyceratacea (Holopeidae——Holopeinae, Gyronematinae) (p. *1239*).

Family HOLOPEIDAE Wenz, 1938

Turbiniform, with or without spiral ornament; usually with narrow umbilicus. *L. Ord.-M.Perm.*

Subfamily HOLOPEINAE Wenz, 1938

[*nom. transl.* KNIGHT, BATTEN & YOCHELSON, herein (*ex* Holopeidae WENZ, 1938)]

Without or almost without spiral ornament. *L.Ord.-U.Dev.*

Straparollina BILLINGS, 1865 [*S. pelagica;* SD DE KONINCK, 1881]. Columellar lip with thickened triangular area below, generating a circumumbilical ridge. *L.Ord.,* N.Am.-Eu.——FIG. 152,2. *S. pelagica, L.Ord.,* Can.(Newf.); ×1.3.

Holopea HALL, 1847 [*H. symmetrica;* SD BASSLER, 1915] [=*Litiopsis* SALTER, 1866 (obj.); *Haplospira* KOKEN, 1897; *Cirropsis, Tortilla* PERNER, 1903; *Staurospira* PERNER, 1907 (*non* HAECKEL, 1887); *Anastrophina* KNIGHT, 1937 (*pro Staurospira* PERNER, 1907)]. Whorls rounded, in some species disjunct; sutures deep; final whorl may bear coarse rounded ribs. *M.Ord.-Dev.,* N.Am.-Eu.——FIG. 152,*11. *H. symmetrica,* M.Ord., N.Y.; ×2.7.

Globonema WENZ, 1938 [*Nematotrochus bicarinatus* (WAHLENBERG) KOKEN, 1925 (*non* WAHLENBERG, 1821) = *Trochonema (Globonema) kokeni* WENZ, 1938]. Sutures moderately deep; with low carina at periphery above suture and another encircling the umbilicus; numerous collabral threads (147, p. 228). *U.Ord.,* Eu.——FIG. 152,6. *G. kokeni* (WENZ), Norway; ×3.3 (80).

?Threavia LAMONT, 1946 [*T. gulosa*]. With carina low on whorl (85, p. 642). *U.Ord.,* Eu.——FIG. 152,*1. *T. gulosa,* Scot.; ×2.7 (85).

Raphispira PERNER, 1903 [*R. plena*]. Resembling *Holopea* but with a circumumbilical cord. *U.Sil.,* N.Am.-Eu.——FIG. 152,*10. *R. plena,* Czech.; ×1.3.

?Protospiralis CLARKE, 1904 [*Platyostoma (?) minutissima* CLARKE, 1885]. Minute, naticiform, seemingly anomphalous. [Although very small, probably mature.] *U.Dev.,* N.Am.

Subfamily GYRONEMATINAE Knight, 1956

Spiral ornament dominant. *M.Ord.-M. Perm.*

Gyronema ULRICH in ULRICH & SCOFIELD, 1897 [*Trochonema (Gyronema) pulchellum* ULRICH & SCOFIELD, 1897]. Narrowly phaneromphalous with relatively few, strong spiral cords; outer lip prosocline; reflexed columellar lip. *M.Ord.-Sil.,* N.Am.-Eu.-N.Afr.——FIG. 152,4. *G. pulchellum* (ULRICH & SCOFIELD), M.Ord., Minn.; ×4.

Antitrochus WHIDBORNE, 1891 [*A. arietinus;* SD KNIGHT, 1937]. Sinistral, with numerous spiral and prosocline collabral threads. *M.Dev.,* Eu.——FIG. 152,7. *A. arietinus,* Eng.; ×2.

Yunnania MANSUY, 1912 [*Y. termieri;* SD COSSMANN, 1918]. Shell thick, anomphalous; ornament of spiral cords; growth lines prosocline. *Dev.-M.Perm.,* SE.Asia.-N.Am.-Eu.——FIG. 152,9. *Y. termieri,* L.Perm., China; ×3.3.

Araeonema KNIGHT, 1933 [*A. virgatum*] [=*Turbina* DEKONINCK, 1881 (*non* BROWN in HERRMANNSEN, 1847); *Palaeoturbina* WENZ, 1938 (147, p. 234) (*pro Turbina* DEKONINCK, 1881)]. Very small; narrowly phaneromphalous; ornament of faint spiral threads or wanting. *Miss.(L.Carb.)-Penn.(U.Carb.),* N.Am.-Eu.——FIG. 152,8. *A. virgatum,* M.Penn., Mo.; ×13.3.

Rhabdotocochlis KNIGHT, 1933 [*R. rugata*]. Very small, thick-shelled; narrowly phaneromphalous; with strong spiral cords. *Penn.-M.Perm.,* N.Am. ——FIG. 152,12. *R. rugata,* M.Penn., Mo.; ×40.

Cinclidonema KNIGHT, 1945 [*C. texanum*]. With shoulder below suture; anomphalous; columellar lip slightly reflexed; ornament of numerous spiral cords and collabral threads (72, p. 584). *Penn. (U. Carb.)-M. Perm.,* N. Am.-S. Am.-Eu.-SE. Asia. ——FIG. 152,5. *C. texanum,* U.Penn., Tex.; ×1.7.

?Omphalonema GRABAU, 1936 [*O. multispiralis*]. Seemingly without shoulder but with ornament much like *Cinclidonema;* apertural characters unknown. *L.Perm.,* NE.Asia.——FIG. 152,3. *O. multispirale,* China; ×1 (48).

Family PLATYCERATIDAE Hall, 1859

[*nom. correct.* KNIGHT, 1934 (=Platyceridae HALL, 1859)] [=Platystomidae, Cyclonemidae, S.A.MILLER, 1889]

Coprophagous on crinoids and cystoids (BOWSHER, 1955), the shells showing through their range from mid-Ordovician to late Paleozoic progressively more complete adaptation to a stationary life, principally on crinoid calices; earlier members turbiniform or naticiform, with flat columellar lip but with irregular prosocline growth lines; lip becoming more uneven, conforming to irregularities of the crinoid or cystoid calyx, and the primitively coiled shell uncoiling or developing other peculiarities of growth as crinoids became more elaborate in the course of time; ornament present in more primitive stocks but gradually lost. *M.Ord.-M.Perm.*

So great is the variability induced by the stationary habit that systematics of the group are unusually difficult. One has trouble in deciding if two markedly unlike variations represent different genera or subgenera, or are actually conspecific. In the Platyceratidae the outer shell layers are relatively thick and calcitic, so that specimens

resist solution noticeably better than many gastropods that are more largely aragonitic. The inner shell layers of the primitive genus *Cyclonema* are seemingly nacreous and aragonitic, but this layer appears to be lost in the more advanced *Platyceras*.

Naticonema PERNER, 1903 [*N. similare*] [=*Otospira* PERNER, 1903; *Naticellina* PERNER, 1911]. Naticiform to globular, with flat excavated columellar lip; ornament wanting or consisting of spiral growth lines and collabral irregularly sinuous threads. Specimens known on crinoid calices. *M.Ord.-U.Sil.*, Eu.-N.Am.——FIG. 153,*1*. *N. similare*, U.Sil., Czech.; ×2.7.

Cyclonema HALL, 1852 [*Pleurotomaria bilix* CONRAD, 1842]. Basically turbiniform or trochiform but variously modified by stationary coprophagous habit; always with characteristically sharp spiral and finer collabral threads. *M.Ord.-L.Dev.*, N.Am.-Eu.

C. **(Cyclonema)** HALL, 1852 [=*Cyclonemina* PERNER, 1907]. Turbiniform to trochiform, with wavy surfaces and slightly irregular growth lines; columellar lip slightly excavated or irregular. Specimens known on crinoid calices. [The supposed genus *Cyclonemina* is composed of dwarfed, monstrous, or irregular individuals of several species, normal individuals of which are referred to *Cyclonema*. The irregular growth may have been due to inability to find a suitable station on a crinoid calyx.] *M.Ord.-U.Sil.*, N.Am.-Eu. ——FIG. 153,*11*. *C. (C.) bilix* (CONRAD), U. Ord., Ind.; ×2.

C. **(Dyeria)** ULRICH in ULRICH & SCOFIELD, 1897 [*Cyrtolites costatus* JAMES, 1872]. Earlier 3 or 4 whorls rotelliform; final whorl irregularly disjunct; with or without ornament. *M.Ord.-U.Ord.*, N.Am.——FIG. 153,*3*. *C. (D.) costatum* (JAMES), U.Ord., Ohio; ×1.

C. **(Ploconema)** PERNER, 1903 [*P. protendens;* SD PERNER, 1907]. Very like *Cyclonema* but with final whorl disjunct. *L.Dev.*, Eu.——FIG. 153,*5*. *C. (P.) protendens* (PERNER), L.Dev., Czech.; ×1.3.

Platyceras CONRAD, 1840 [*Pileopsis vetusta* J.DEC. SOWERBY, 1829; SD TATE, 1869]. Subgenera varying from naticiform to completely disjunct, some earlier species with spiral and collabral threads or with collabral lines, some with hollow spines arising as marginal tubes, apertural margin of many shells deeply sinuate, conforming to irregularities of crinoid calyx to which it was attached during life. [Apertural irregularities primarily record characters of the host crinoid, not of the gastropod, the reentrants of some shells resembling pleurotomarian sinuses or slits, but having no homologous function.] *Sil.-M.Perm.*, cosmop.

P. **(Tubomphalus)** PERNER, 1903 [*T. crenistria*]. Earliest 3 or 4 whorls rotelliform, final whorl disjunct; ornament wanting, growth lines irregular. *U.Sil.-L.Dev.*, N.Am.-Eu.——FIG. 153,*2*. *P. (T.) crenistrium* (PERNER), L.Dev., Czech.; ×1.3.

P. **(Platyostoma)** CONRAD, 1842 [*Platyostoma ventricosum;* SD HALL, 1859] [=*Platystoma* LINDSTRÖM, 1884 (*non* MEIGEN, 1803) (obj.); *Diaphorostoma* FISCHER, 1885 (obj.); *Platycerina* S.A.MILLER, 1889 (obj.); *Osterlina* TALLANT & PHILLIP, 1956 (136, p. 59)]. Naticiform with several whorls, of which last may or may not be disjunct; anomphalous to minutely phaneromphalous; irregularities of aperture relatively slight. *Sil.-Dev.*, cosmop.——FIG. 153,*13*. *P. (P.) ventricosum* (CONRAD), L.Dev., N.Y.; ×1.

P. **(Platyceras)** [=*Acroculia* PHILLIPS, 1841 (obj.); *Actita* FAHRENKOHL, 1844; *Acrocylia* AGASSIZ, 1846 (obj.); *Acrocyllis* HERRMANNSEN, 1846 (obj.); *Exogyroceras* MEEK & WORTHEN, 1868]. Irregularly capuliform, with 1 or 2 early whorls (or rarely more) coiled; protoconch vermiform; ornament commonly wanting or consisting of spiral and collabral threads. [This and *P. (Orthonychia)* are the most abundant, ubiquitous, and long-ranging members of the family. They are not infrequently preserved on the calices of fossil crinoids if the conditions of burial were suitable.] *Sil.-Miss.*, cosmop.——FIG. 153,*4*. *P. (P.) vetustum* (J.DEC.SOWERBY), Miss., Ire.; *4a*, oblique apertural view; *4b*, apical view; both ×0.7.

P. **(Visitator)** PERNER, 1911 [*V. extraneus*] [=*Aulopea, Distemnostoma, Saffordella* DUNBAR, 1920; *Cowwarrella* TALENT & PHILLIP, 1956, (136, p. 61)]. Coiling irregularly subtrochiform, with 4 to 6 whorls; sinuses, one high on side near upper suture and another near columellar lip, point to usual station over a pair of salients on crinoid; in some specimens a single sinus; ornament lacking. *U.Sil.-L.Dev.*, N.Am.-Eu.-N. Afr.——FIG. 153,*6*. *P. (V.) tennesseense* (DUNBAR), L.Dev., Tenn.; ×0.7.

P. **(Orthonychia)** HALL, 1843 [*Platyceras (Orthonychia) subrectum* HALL, 1859] [=*Igoceras* HALL, 1860; *Palaeocapulus* GRABAU & SHIMER, 1909; *Geronticeras* GRABAU, 1936]. Very similar to *Platyceras (s.s.)* but without coiling except that the vermiform protoconch in some specimens becomes fused to shell; ornament like that of *Platyceras (s.s.)*, or, more commonly, of strong longitudinal folds produced by sinus over strong salient on crinoid calyx. [Specimens are common on crinoid calices.] *?Sil., L.Dev.-M. Perm.*, cosmop.——FIG. 153,*10*. *P. (O.) subrectum* HALL, M.Dev., N.Y.; steinkern, ×0.7.

P. **(Praenatica)** PERNER, 1903 [*Strophostylus gregarius proeva;* SD KNIGHT, 1941 (69, p. 270)] [=*Prosigaretus* PERNER, 1907]. Naticiform to auriform; ornament of fine lamellar growth lines and crowded, oblique, irregular cords; columellar lip slightly thickened, strongly arcuate. *U. Sil.-L.Dev.*, Eu.-N.Am.——FIG. 153,*8*. *P. (P.)*

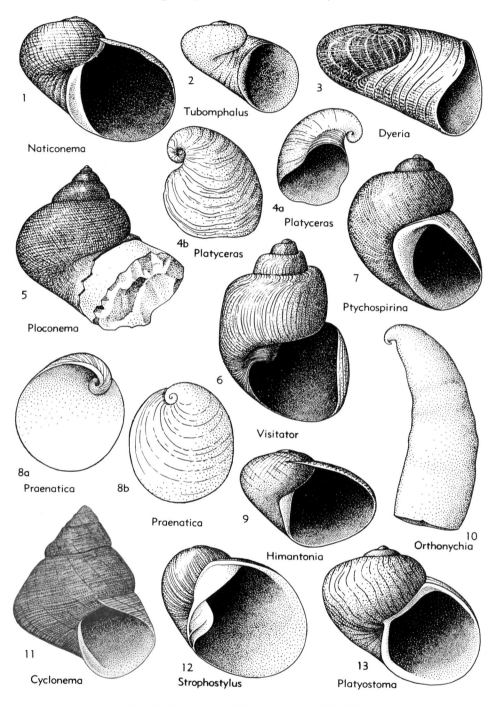

FIG. 153. Platyceratacea (Platyceratidae) (p. I240-I242).

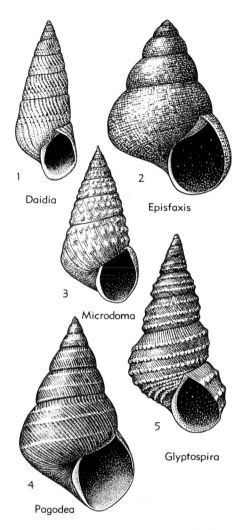

1 Daidia

2 Episfaxis

3

Microdoma

5

Glyptospira

4

Pagodea

FIG. 154. Microdomatacea (Microdomatidae)
(p. *I242-I243*).

N.Am.——FIG. 153,*12*. **S. andrewsi*, L.Dev., Md.;
×1.3.

?Himantonia PERNER, 1911 [*Nerita amoena PER-
NER, 1907]. Naticiform, outer lip strongly prosocline; ornament of strong oblique rounded cords
with narrow interspaces normal to outer lip;
growth lines seemingly without irregularities. *L.
Dev.*, Eu.——FIG. 153,*9*. **H. amoena* (PERNER),
Czech.; ×4.

Superfamily MICRODOMATACEA
Wenz, 1938

[*nom. transl.* KNIGHT, BATTEN & YOCHELSON, herein (*ex*
Microdominae WENZ, 1938)]

Subulate to turbiniform, with simple
rounded aperture, reflexed columellar lip
and nacreous inner shell layer. [Probably
derived from the Pleurotomariacea.] *M.
Ord.-M.Perm.*

Family MICRODOMATIDAE Wenz, 1938

[*nom. transl. et correct.* KNIGHT, BATTEN & YOCHELSON, herein
(*ex* Microdominae WENZ, 1938)]

Umbilicus minute; usually ornamented;
spire relatively high. *M.Ord.-M.Perm.*

Daidia WILSON, 1951 [**Eunema cerithioides* SALTER,
1859]. Turriculate, with slight shoulder at suture
and very slight angulation about midway between
sutures; collabral threads orthocline above and
slightly prosocline below (150, p. 73). *M.Ord.*,
N.Am.——FIG. 154,*1*. **D. cerithioides* (SALTER),
Can.(Que.); ×1 (150).

Episfaxis KNIGHT, 1937 [*pro Cosmina* PERNER, 1903
(*non* ROBINEAU-DESVOIDY, 1830)] [**Cosmina
complacens* PERNER, 1903]. Turbiniform, with
rounded whorls and moderately high spire; ornament a network of fine spiral and orthocline collabral threads. *L.Dev.*, Eu.——FIG. 154,*2*. **E.
complacens* (PERNER), Czech.; ×2.7.

Pagodea PERNER, 1903 [**P. concomitans*]. Turbiniform, with rounded whorls, shallow sutures, and
moderately high spire; labrum orthocline, close
to upper suture, but turning shortly to strongly
prosocline; ornament of 3 low spiral cords and
sharp lamellar collabral threads. *L.Dev.*, N.Am.-
Eu.——FIG. 154,*4*. **P. concomitans*, Czech.; ×2.7.

Microdoma MEEK & WORTHEN, 1867 [**M. conicum*] [=*Tuberculopleura* JAKOWLEW, 1899;
Pleurotrochus SHERZER & GRABAU, 1909; *Microdo-
mus* COSSMANN, 1915 [1916] (obj.)]. Much like
Pagodea but with higher spire and shallower sutures; ornament of protoconch much like that of
Pagodea, broad collabral ribs with fine threads
between them appearing on 4th whorl and 2 spiral
grooves developing gradually on later whorls,
breaking the ribs into 3 rows of pustules. *L.Dev.-
L.Perm.*, N.Am.-Eu.-N.Asia.——FIG. 154,*3*. **M.
conicum*, M.Penn., Ill.; ×6.7.

proevum (PERNER), U.Sil., Czech.; *8a*, view into
aperture; *8b*, apical; both ×0.7.

Ptychospirina PERNER, 1907 [*pro Ptychospira* PER-
NER, 1907 (*non* HALL & CLARKE, 1895)] [**Hol-
opea mima* PERNER, 1903; SD COSSMANN, 1918].
Naticiform, with obliquely oblong aperture and
no true columellar lip; ornament wanting or com-
prising sharp, somewhat irregular collabral threads.
U.Sil.-L.Dev., Eu.-N.Am.——FIG. 153,*7*. **P. mima*
(PERNER), L.Dev., Czech.; ×2.7.

Strophostylus HALL, 1859 [**S. andrewsi* HALL,
1860; SD KEYES, 1890] [=*Helicostylus* KNIGHT,
1934 (obj.)]. Naticiform, with wide aperture;
with spiral columellar plate. *?Sil., L.Dev., ?Penn.*,

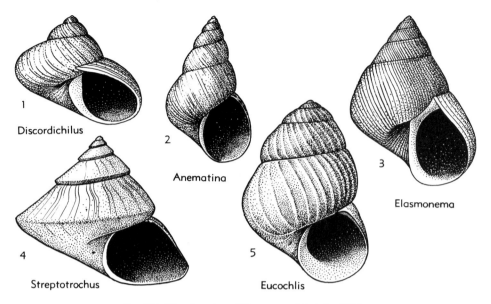

FIG. 155. Microdomatacea (Elasmonematidae) (p. *1243*).

Glyptospira H.CHRONIC, 1952 [**G. cristulata*]. Much like *Microdoma* but with ornament of 2 or 3 strong revolving cords on sides of whorls and 3 to 5 or more weaker cords on base, all crossed by strong lamellar rasplike, prosocline collabral threads (14, p. 127). *L.Perm.-M.Perm.*, N.Am.-Eu.-SE.Asia.——FIG. 154,*5*. **G. cristulata*, M. Perm., Ariz.; ×5.3.

Family ELASMONEMATIDAE Knight, 1956

Umbilicus commonly narrow, rarely minute; ornament wanting or consisting of collabral threads. *U.Sil.-U.Carb.(Penn.)*.

Streptotrochus PERNER, 1907 [**S. rugulosus*]. Trochiform, with angular periphery; labrum with shallow sinus, growth lines orthocline above, then slightly prosocline, next curving gently forward to an opisthocline direction; umbilicus seemingly narrow but not minute. *U.Sil.*, Eu.——FIG. 155,*4*. **S. rugulosus*, Czech.; ×1.3.

Discordichilus COSSMANN, 1918 [**Trochus mollis* LINDSTRÖM, 1884]. Depressed turbiniform, with strongly rounded periphery; labrum strongly prosocline; columellar lip thickened; umbilicus narrow. *M.Sil.*, Eu.——FIG. 155,*1*. **D. mollis* (LINDSTRÖM), Gotl.; ×1.3.

Elasmonema FISCHER, 1885 [*pro Callonema* HALL,

1879 (*non* ÇONRAD, 1875)] [**Loxonema bellatulum* HALL, 1861; SD S.A.MILLER, 1889]. Conoidal, with shallow sutures; narrow funnel-like umbilicus; ornament slightly prosocline cords. *L.Dev.*, N.Am.——FIG. 155,*3*. **E. bellatulum* (HALL), Ohio; ×2.2.

Anematina KNIGHT, 1933 [**Holopea proutana* HALL, 1858]. Somewhat like *Elasmonema* but with higher spire; umbilicus minute; ornament lacking. *Miss.(L.Carb.)-Penn.(U.Carb.)*, N.Am.-Eu.——FIG. 155,*2*. **A. proutana* (HALL), M. Miss., Ind.; ×4.

?Eucochlis KNIGHT, 1933 [**E. perminuta*]. Very small, cyrtoconoid, with narrow umbilicus; ornament of rather widely spaced, prosocline collabral cords. *Penn.*, N.Am.——FIG. 155,*5*. **E. perminuta*, M.Penn., Mo.; ×30.

Superfamily ANOMPHALACEA Wenz, 1938

[*nom. transl.* KNIGHT, BATTEN & YOCHELSON, herein (*ex* Anomphalidae WENZ, 1938)]

Rotelliform to naticiform, with prosocline nonsinuate outer lip; narrowly phaneromphalous, cryptomphalous, or hemiomphalous; columellar lip commonly thickened or callused in various ways; inner shell layers seemingly nacreous. *Sil.-M.Perm.*

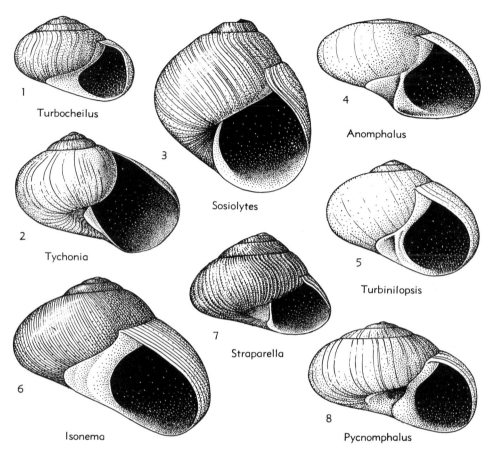

FIG. 156. Anomphalacea (Anomphalidae) (p. *I244-I245*).

Family ANOMPHALIDAE Wenz, 1938

With characters of superfamily. *Sil.-M. Perm.*

?**Turbocheilus** PERNER, 1907 [**Turbo immaturus* PERNER, 1903]. Globular, naticiform; outer lip prosocline above, turning to opisthocline at midwhorl and gently prosocline below; callus-filled umbilicus gently concave externally. *M.Sil.*, Eu.——FIG. 156,*1*. **T. immaturus* (PERNER), Czech.; ×1.3.

Pycnomphalus LINDSTRÖM, 1884 [**P. obesus;* SD PERNER, 1907]. Rotelliform, with numerous whorls and very thick shell; bearing within the umbilicus shelf-like funicle generated by massive thickening at base of columella. *Sil.*, N.Am.-Eu.——FIG. 156,*8*. **P. obesus,* M.Sil., Gotl.; ×2.

Isonema MEEK & WORTHEN, 1866 [**I. depressum* MEEK & WORTHEN, =*Naticopsis linearis* KEYES, 1889, *pro N. depressa* (MEEK & WORTHEN) KEYES, 1889 (*non* WINCHELL, 1864), =*I. humile* MEEK, 1872. Naticiform, labrum strongly prosocline; columellar lip thickened with heavy callus extending over umbilical region; ornament of collabral threads or cords. *L.Dev.,* N.Am.——FIG. 156,*6*. *I. humile* MEEK, Ohio; ×2.

Anomphalus MEEK & WORTHEN, 1867 [**A. rotulus*] [=*Antirotella* COSSMANN, 1918]. Rotelliform, whorls deeply embracing above; outer lip prosocline; adult columellar lip thickened, highly variable from species to species, producing a variety of umbilical characters, so that shell ranges from heavily cryptomphalous to phaneromphalous; exterior polished. *M.Dev.-Penn.(U.Carb.),* N.Am.-Eu.-NE.Asia-SE.Asia.——FIG. 156,*4*. **A. rotulus,* M.Penn., Ill.; ×10.

?**Tychonia** DEKONINCK, 1881 [**Natica omaliana* DE KONINCK, 1843]. Depressed naticiform, with outer lip curving forward from upper suture to about mid-whorl, strongly prosocline below; columellar lip thickened and developing a funicle; surface without ornament. *L.Carb.,* Eu.——FIG. 156,*2*. **T. omaliana* (DEKONINCK), Belg.; ×1.3.

Straparella FISCHER, 1885 [**Straparollus fallax* DE

KONINCK, 1843]. Rotelliform, with broad, gentle labral sinus in outer lip; columellar lip thickened at its base, generating a funicle; ornament of collabral threads. *L.Carb.*, Eu.——FIG. 156,7. **S. fallax* (DEKONINCK), Belg.; ×2.

Turbinilopsis DEKONINCK, 1881 [**T. inconspicua;* SD COSSMANN, 1915 [1916]]. Naticiform, with prosocline outer lip and thickened inner lip with longitudinal groove; narrow umbilicus with callus wash; without ornament. *L.Carb.*, Eu.——FIG. 156,5. **T. inconspicua,* Belg.; ×4.

?Sosiolytes GEMMELLARO, 1889 [**S. schlotheimi*]. Small, naticiform; labrum opisthocline close to suture, turning to roundly and strongly prosocline a short distance below; narrowly phaneromphalous; ornament growth lines alone. *M. Perm.*, Eu.——FIG. 156,3. **S. schlotheimi,* Sicily; ×2.

?Eiselia DIETZ, 1911 [**E. dyadica*]. Small, rotelliform, phaneromphalous, with wide, low collabral cords; labrum seemingly arched forward at about mid-whorl; not well known. *M.Perm.*, Eu.

Superfamily ORIOSTOMATACEA Wenz, 1938

[*nom. transl.* KNIGHT, BATTEN & YOCHELSON, herein (*ex* Oriostomatidae WENZ, 1938)]

Trochiform to discoidal, closely coiled or disjunct; strongly ornamented with spiral cords or spines. *U.Sil.-L.Dev., ?Trias.*

Family ORIOSTOMATIDAE Wenz, 1938

[=Horiostomidae KOKEN, 1897 (ICZN pend.)]

Closely coiled; with heavy multispiral calcareous operculum; shell with nacreous inner layer. *U.Sil.-L.Dev.*

Morphotropis PERNER, 1903 [**M. aliena;* SD PERNER, 1907]. Depressed turbiniform with moderately wide umbilicus; whorls round, sutures deep; ornament of collabral orthocline, fine threads with more widely spaced undulating lamellae. *U.Sil.*, Eu.—— FIG. 157,1. **M. aliena,* Czech.; ×1.3.

Beraunia KNIGHT, 1937 [*pro Eucyclotropis* COSSMANN, 1909 (*non* JORDAN, 1904), *Eucyclotropis* COSSMANN, 1909, *pro Cyclotropis* PERNER, 1903 (*non* TAPPARONE-CANEFRI, 1883)] [**Cyclotropis docens* PERNER, 1903; SD PERNER, 1907] [=*Rhabdospira* PERNER, 1903 (*non* DONALD, 1898)]. Discoidal to depressed turbiniform; whorls rounded, with deep sutures, rarely disjunct; ornament dominantly spiral. *U.Sil.-L.Dev.*, Eu.——FIG. 157,3. **B. docens* (PERNER), U.Sil., Czech.; oblique apertural view with operculum, ×1.3.

Oriostoma MUNIER-CHALMAS, 1876 [**O. barrandei*] [=*Horiostoma* FISCHER, 1885 (obj.)]. Turbiniform; umbilicus moderately wide to narrow; ornament of dominantly spiral carinae, cords or threads with finer collabral elements, in some species producing elaborate crenulations. *U.Sil.-L.Dev.*, N.Am.-Eu.——FIG. 157,2. *O. coronatum*

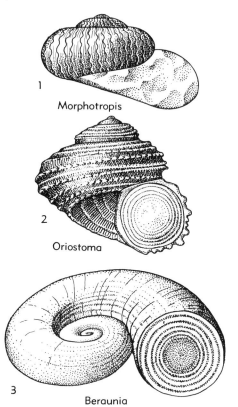

1 Morphotropis

2 Oriostoma

3 Beraunia

FIG. 157. Oriostomatacea (Oriostomatidae) (p. *1245*).

LINDSTRÖM, U.Sil., Gotl.; apertural view showing operculum, ×2 (90).

Family TUBINIDAE Knight, 1956

Mostly disjunct whorls, with more or less expanded aperture; ornament dominantly spiral with pustules or tubular spines aligned on some of spiral cords; operculum unknown, probably wanting in adult; shell structure unknown. [The shape of the shell suggests sedentary habits. The hollow spines or pustules may have been functional when they first appeared on the margins of the aperture.] *L.Dev., ?Trias.*

Semitubina COSSMANN, 1918 [**Tuba spinosa* QUENSTEDT, 1852]. Whorls subturbiniform, disjunct except for earlier ones; aperture slightly expanded; ornament of spiral cords bearing hollow spines at aperture. *L.Dev.*, Eu.——FIG. 158,2. **S. spinosa* (QUENSTEDT), Czech.; apertural view, ×2.

Tubina OWEN, 1859 [**T. armata*]. Coiling nearly discoidal; aperture slightly expanded at final stage;

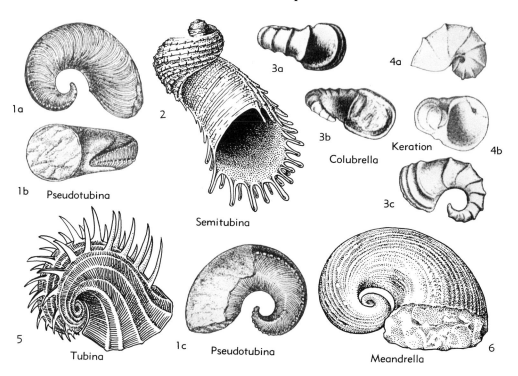

1a
1b Pseudotubina
2
Semitubina
3a
3b
Colubrella
4a
Keration
4b
3c
5
Tubina
1c Pseudotubina
Meandrella
6

FIG. 158. Oriostomatacea (Tubinidae) (p. 1245-1246).

ornament of spiral cords, a few with long hollow spines opening adaperturally, and finer collabral threads. *L.Dev.*, Eu.——FIG. 158,5. **T. armata*, Czech.; oblique, ×1.5.

Meandrella PERNER, 1903 [**M. sculpta*]. Coiling nearly discoidal; aperture slightly expanded; spiral ornament numerous cords, a few of which at early growth stages carried hollow pustules; collabral ornament of fine, sharp, zigzag threads pointing abaperturally on cords and adaperturally between. *L.Dev.*, Eu.——FIG. 158,6. **M. sculpta*, Czech.; oblique, from above, ×1.3.

?**Pseudotubina** KOKEN, 1896 [**P. biserialis*; SD DIENER, 1926]. Hornlike, not quite planispiral, consisting of rather more than a single disjunct whorl; outer face limited above and below, or below only, by carina bearing tubercles or short prickles that disappear near aperture; growth lines parasigmoid on upper face, prosocyrt on lower. *U.Trias.(Carn.)*, Eu.——FIG. 158,1. **P. biserialis*, Aus.; *1a-c*, ×2 (79).

?**Colubrella** KOKEN, 1896 [**C. squamata*]. Mostly hornlike, almost planispiral, consisting of up to two whorls circular or quadrate in cross section and partly or wholly disjunct in most forms; growth lines accentuated at intervals to form col-

labral rings or lamellae, except on inner face of whorls. *M.Trias.(Ladin.)-U.Trias.(Nor.)*, Eu.

C. (Colubrella). Whorls partly or wholly disjunct, last expanded at aperture. *M.Trias. (Ladin.)-U.Trias.(Nor.)*, Eu.——FIG. 158,3. *C. (C.) kokeni* BROILI, U.Trias.(Nor.), S.Tyrol; *3a,b*, ×1.5 (10).

C. (Keration) BROILI, 1907 [**K. nautiliforme*]. Small, nautiliform, whorls in contact, the last only slightly expanded at aperture. *U.Trias. (Carn.)*, Eu.——FIG. 158,4. **C. (K.) nautiliformis*, S.Tyrol; *4a-c*, ×1.5 (10).

Superfamily TROCHACEA Rafinesque, 1815

[*nom. transl.* THIELE, 1925 (*ex* Trochidae GRAY, 1834, *nom. correct.*, *pro* Trochinia RAFINESQUE, 1815)]
[Some help in preliminary organization of data for Tertiary genera was given by Miss GRACE JOHNSON and is here acknowledged.]

Conical, turbiniform or subglobose shells with entire aperture; inner shell layer, and outermost layer in some genera, nacreous; operculum corneous or calcareous, spiral (18, 139, 147). *Trias.-Rec.*

Family TROCHIDAE Rafinesque, 1815

[*nom. correct.* GRAY, 1834 (*pro* Trochinia RAFINESQUE, 1815)]

Peristome discontinuous in most genera, with columellar and outer lips not in same plane. Operculum circular, multispiral, thin, corneous, with central nucleus. *Trias.-Rec.*

Subfamily PROCONULINAE Cox, n. subfam.

Conical, mostly elevated shells with acute apex; nearly all of small or small-medium size; anomphalous or phaneromphalous; base more or less flattened; aperture quadrangular; columellar lip simple or with single plication. *Trias.-U.Cret.*

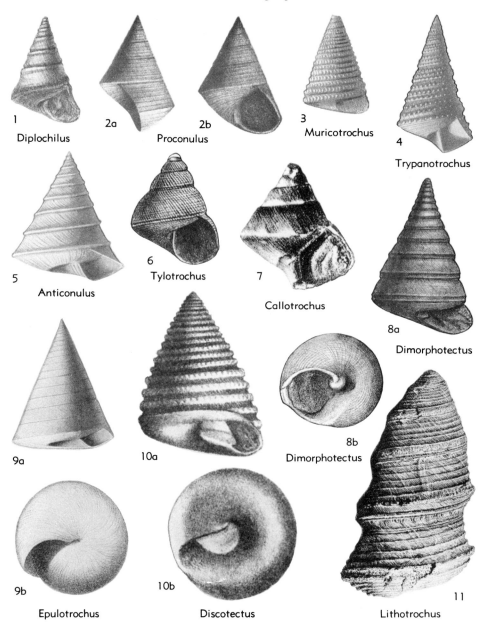

1 Diplochilus
2a 2b Proconulus
3 Muricotrochus
4 Trypanotrochus
5 Anticonulus
6 Tylotrochus
7 Callotrochus
8a Dimorphotectus
9a
10a
8b Dimorphotectus
9b Epulotrochus
10b Discotectus
11 Lithotrochus

FIG. 159. Trochacea (Trochidae——Proconulinae (p. 1248-1249).

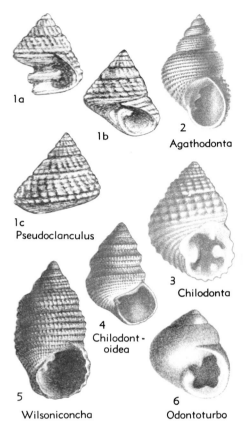

1a

1b
Agathodonta

2

1c
Pseudoclanculus

3
Chilodonta

4
Chilodont-
oidea

5
Wilsoniconcha

6
Odontoturbo

Fig. 160. Trochacea (Trochidae——Chilodontinae)
(p. *1249*).

Diplochilus Wöhrmann, 1894 [*D. gracilis; SD Cossmann, 1916] [=Wöhrmannia Cossmann, 1916 (erroneously cited as 1895) (non J.Böhm, 1895); Raiblia Cossmann, 1916 (both pro Diplochilus Wöhrmann, non Diplochila Brullé, 1835)]. Well-elevated, narrowly phaneromphalous; base flattened; whorls bicarinate near lower suture; sutures deep; apertural characters imperfectly known. Trias., Eu.-Asia.——Fig. 159,1. D. bistriatus (Münster), M.Trias.(Ladin.), S.Tyrol; ×3.5 (89).

Dimorphotectus Cossmann, 1918 [*Tectus hoernesi Koken, 1896 = *Scoliostoma fasciatum Hoernes, 1856]. Coeloconoid, elevated, with very acute apex, anomphalous; whorls numerous, flat or almost so, last carinate or bicarinate at periphery, carinae just exposed on spire whorls; ornament spiral striae commonly obsolete on later whorls; base flattened; columellar lip short, with prominent median fold. M.Trias.(Carn.)-L.Jur., Eu.-N.Z.——Fig. 159,8. *D. fasciatus (Hoernes), U. Trias.(Nor.), Aus.; 8a,b, ×2.5 (79).

?Callotrochus Kutassy in Wenz, 1938 [pro Mesotrochus Kutassy, 1927 (non Wasmann, 1890)] [*Mesotrochus triadicus]. Almost biconical, anomphalous, with spire less elevated and of fewer whorls and with base more extended than in typical genera of subfamily; whorls flat, smooth, except for obscure nodes at abapical suture and on peripheral carina of last; columellar lip straight, simple, thickened. U.Trias.(Nor.), Eu.-S.Am.——Fig. 159,7. *C. triadicus, Hung.; ×1 (200).

Eocalliostoma Haas, 1953 [*Calliostoma interruptum Cox, 1947]. Small, moderately elevated, anomphalous; whorls flat, last subangular at periphery; ornament depressed, irregular transverse ribs that tend to break up on last whorl; base flattened; columellar lip short, with strong fold at lower end. U.Trias.(Nor.), S.Am.——Fig. 180A,3. *E. interruptum (Cox), Peru; ×6 (21).

?Tylotrochus Koken, 1896 [*Trochus konincki Hörnes, 1856]. Moderately elevated, anomphalous, with fewer whorls and more extended base than most genera of subfamily; whorls feebly convex, with delicate ornament of spiral and collabral threads; aperture subquadrate, columellar lip simple. Trias., Eu.-Asia.——Fig. 159,6. *T. konincki (Hörnes), U.Trias.(Carn.), Aus.; ×1.7 (79).

Anticonulus Cossmann, 1918 [*Trochus mariae d'Orbigny, 1853]. Well elevated, phaneromphalous; whorls flat to feebly convex, subimbricate in some species, smooth or spirally grooved, last angular or rounded at periphery; base low, convex; columellar lip simple, of variable inclination. Trias.-L.Jur., Eu.——Fig. 159,5. A. nisus (d'Orbigny), M.Lias., Fr.; ×3 (111).

Proconulus Cossmann, 1918 [*Trochus guillieri Cossmann, 1885]. Well elevated, anomphalous; whorls fairly numerous, flat or almost so, spirally striated or smooth, last with angular or sharply rounded periphery; base feebly convex; columellar lip simple, with moderately broad, callous outer surface having distinct outer margin, commonly an angulation. L.Jur.-U.Cret.(Senon.), cosmop.——Fig. 159,2. P. raulineus (Buvignier), Lias, Fr.; 2a,b, ×1.5 (165).

Epulotrochus Cossmann, 1918 [*Trochus epulus d'Orbigny, 1850]. Well elevated, anomphalous, of very numerous low, smooth, flat whorls, last subangular at periphery; base flattened, slightly excavated mesially; aperture broad, with very oblique, simple, unthickened columellar lip. L. Jur., Eu.——Fig. 159,9. *E. epulus (d'Orbigny), Fr.; 9a,b, ×2.5 (111).

Lithotrochus Conrad, 1855 [*Turritella andii d'Orbigny, 1842 (=Pleurotomaria humboldtii vonBuch, 1839)]. Very large and elevated, slightly cyrtoconoid, anomphalous, with peripherally carinate, imbricate whorls that overlap less in later growth stages; ornament spiral cords, strongest on outer part of base, a very prominent one adjoining peripheral carina; aperture imperfectly

known. *L.Jur.*, S.Am.——Fig. 159,*11*. **L. humboldtii* (vonBuch), Chile; ×0.7 (162).
Trypanotrochus Cossmann, 1918 [**Trochus normanianus* d'Orbigny, 1850]. Well elevated, phaneromphalous; whorls fairly numerous, flat, last
carinate at periphery; ornament nodose spiral
cords; base flattened, umbilical margin carinate;
columellar lip simple, straight or almost so, of
variable inclination. *L.Jur.*, Eu.——Fig. 159,*4*.
*T. normanianus (d'Orbigny), Fr.; ×2 (111).
Muricotrochus Cossmann, 1918 [**M. hudlestoni*].
Well elevated, anomphalous, of numerous low
whorls bearing 2 or more tuberculate spiral cords,
lowest forming periphery; base smooth, flattened;
columellar lip short, simple. *M.Jur.(Baj.)-U.Jur.
(Kimm.)*, Eu.——Fig. 159,*3*. *M. subluciensis*
(Hudleston), *M.Jur.(Baj.)*, Eng.; ×2.5 (59).
Discotectus Favre, 1913 [**Trochus massalongoi*
Gemmellaro; SD Cossmann, 1918]. Cyrtoconoid,
moderately elevated, anomphalous; whorls numerous, last subangular at periphery; base flattened; ornament spiral cords; columellar lip short,
with prominent, median fold produced beyond
aperture as semicircular pad in some species.
M.Jur.(Bathon.)-L.Cret.(Senon.), Eu.——Fig. 159,
10. *D. crassiplicatus* (Etallon), U.Jur.(Kimm.),
Fr.Jura; *10a,b*, ×3.3 (95).

Subfamily CHILODONTINAE Wenz, 1938
[=Polyodontinae Cossmann, 1916]

Turbiniform, conical or pupiform shells
of small or small-medium size; most forms
with margined parietal callus producing
continuous peristome and columellar and
outer lips lying almost in same plane; tooth
or fold present high on columellar lip; other
teeth on one or more lips in some genera.
M.Trias.-U.Cret.

Pseudoclanculus Cossmann, 1918 [**Monodonta cassiana* Wissmann in Münster, 1841]. Small, broadly conical, anomphalous; whorls feebly convex,
with ornament of granose spiral cords; base rather
flattened, bearing in middle arched coating of callus spreading from columellar lip; strong fold
high on columellar lip extending short distance
into aperture; labrum thickened and may be weakly dentate internally. *M.Trias.(Ladin.)-U.Trias.
(Carn.)*, Eu.——Fig. 160,*1*. **P. cassianus* (Wissmann), M.Trias.(Ladin.), S.Tyrol; *1a,b*, ×4;
1c, ×3 (64).
Chilodontoidea Hudleston, 1896 [**C. oolitica*].
Crytoconoid, anomphalous, with high spire of
mesially carinate whorls bearing spiral cords rendered granose by collabral threads; base strongly
convex; small tooth high on columellar lip;
parietal callus in some shells with obtuse swelling
or pair of small denticles; outer lip slightly thickened internally, almost orthocline. *M.Jur.(Baj.)*,
Eu.——Fig. 160,*4*. **C. oolitica*, Eng.; ×2.5 (59).
Wilsoniconcha Wenz, 1939 [*pro Wilsonia* Hudles-

ton, 1896 (*non* Bonaparte, 1838] [**Wilsonia
liassica*]. Pupoidal but with acute apex, anomphalous; ornament spiral cords rendered granose
by collabral threads; aperture obliquely ovate,
extending to left of axis; inner lip with 2 strong
denticles near middle; outer lip slightly thickened,
almost orthocline. *L.Jur.-U.Jur.(Raurac.)*, Eu.——
Fig. 160,*5*. **W. liassica*, Lias., Eng.; ×2.75 (59).
Chilodonta Étallon, 1862 [**C. clathrata;* SD de
Loriol, 1887]. With low conical spire and globose
last whorl; anomphalous; aperture orbicular, with
thickened outer lip and five strong teeth distributed around peristome. *U.Jur.(Oxford.)-U.
Cret.(Maastricht.)*, Eu.
C. (Chilodonta). Spire with cancellating spiral and
collabral threads, base with spiral threads only;
parietal callus thick. *U.Jur.(Oxford.)-U.Cret.
(Maastricht.)*, Eu.——Fig. 160,*3*. **C. (C.)
clathrata*, U.Jur.(Kimm.), Fr.Jura; ×3 (95).
C. (Odontoturbo) deLoriol, 1887 [**O. delicatu-
lus*]. Small, globose, smooth; no parietal callus.
U.Jur.(Kimm.), Eu.——Fig. 160,*6*. **C. (O.)
delicatula*, Fr.Jura; ×6 (95).
Agathodonta Cossmann, 1918 [**Trochus dentigerus
(sic)* d'Orbigny, 1843] [=*Agnathodonta* Wenz,
1938 (obj.).]. High turbiniform, anomphalous,
with strongly convex whorls and base; ornament
granose spiral cords; columellar lip with two
strong, obtuse teeth. *L.Cret.*, Eu.——Fig. 160,*2*.
*A. dentigera (d'Orbigny), L.Cret.(Neocom.), Fr.;
×2 (110).

Subfamily MARGARITINAE Stoliczka, 1868

Small, thin shells, iridescent within; conical, turbiniform, or sublenticular; mostly
phaneromphalous, a few anomphalous; peristome interrupted and columellar and outer
lips unthickened in most but not all genera;
columellar lip only rarely toothed; outer lip
not strongly prosocline. *Trias.-Rec.*

Eosolariella Haas, 1953 [**Margarita turbinea* von
Ammon, 1893]. Depressed turbiniform, rather
broadly phaneromphalous, with whorls and base
strongly convex and smooth; aperture suborbicular; peristome thin, continuous; columellar lip
strongly concave, not reflected, without teeth.
U.Trias., Eu.-S.Am.——Fig. 161,*15*. **E. turbinea*
(vonAmmon), Rhaetic, N.Italy; *15a*, ×1.5; *15b*,
×1.75 (160).
Solarioconulus Cossmann, 1918 [**Trochus nudus*
Münster, 1841] [=*Solariconulus* Wenz, 1938
(obj.).]. Turbiniform, with slightly coeloconoid
spire and sharp apex; narrowly phaneromphalous;
whorls and base convex, smooth or with faint
spiral striae; aperture quadrangular; columellar lip
reflected, without teeth. *M.Trias.(Ladin.)-U.Trias.
(Nor.)*, Eu.-S.Am.——Fig. 161,*16*. **S. nudus*
(Münster), S.Tyrol; ×4 (89).
Atira Stewart, 1926 [**Angaria ornatissima* Gabb,

1864]. Turbiniform, rather broadly phaneromphalous, with last whorl convex or somewhat flattened laterally and angulation forming umbilical margin; ornament faint spiral striae; peristome thin, continuous; columellar lip strongly concave, not reflected, without teeth. *U.Cret.,* N.Am.——Fig. 161,*18.* **A. ornatissima* (GABB), Chico Gr., Calif.; ×3 (221).

Garramites STEPHENSON, 1941 [**G. nitidus*]. Turbiniform, rather broadly phaneromphalous, with strongly convex whorls and base; smooth except for about 4 faint spiral grooves; umbilical margin a crenulated angulation; aperture not known intact. *U.Cret.,* N.Am.——Fig. 161,*13.* **G. nitidus,* Navarro Gr., Tex.; ×5 (220).

Margarites GRAY, 1847 (*ex* LEACH MS.) [**Trochus helicinus* FABRICIUS, 1780 (?=*Turbo helicinus* PHIPPS, 1774)] [=*Margarita* LEACH, 1819 (*non* LEACH, 1814); *Eumargarita* FISCHER, 1885 (obj.); *Valvatella* "GRAY" MELVILL, 1897 (*non* GRAY, 1857)]. Smooth or spirally ribbed, nacre conspicuous. *U.Cret.-Rec.*

M. (**Margarites**). Spire low, whorls nearly smooth, last whorl large. *U.Cret.(Dan.)-Rec.,* Eu.-N.Am.-Arct.——Fig. 161,*4.* **M. (M.) helicinus* (FABRICIUS), Rec., N.Atl.; ×2 (147).

M. (**Bathymophila**) DALL, 1881 [**Margarita? euspira*]. *Rec.,* Carib.

M. (**Cantharidoscops**) GALKIN, 1955 [**M. frigidus* DALL, 1919]. Small, higher than wide, periphery rounded; umbilicus obsolete. *Rec.,* Arct.——Fig. 161,*3.* **M. (C.) frigidus* DALL, Okhotsk Sea; ×3 (185).

M. (**Margaritopsis**) THIELE, 1906 [**Margarita frielei* KRAUSE, 1885]. Spire low, apex blunt. *Rec.,* Arct.

M. (**Periaulax**) COSSMANN, 1888 [**Solarium spiratum* LAMARCK, 1804]. Umbilicus with a beaded margin, spirally ribbed within. *U.Cret.-Plio.,* Eu.-Afr.-N.Am.-E.Indies.——Fig. 161,*5.* **M. (P.) spiratus* (LAMARCK), Eoc., Fr.; *5a,b,* ×3 (147).

M. (**Pupillaria**) DALL, 1909 [*Trochus pupillus GOULD, 1849]. Larger than *M. (Margarites),* with higher spire; with spiral ribs and some axial riblets. *Mio.-Rec.,* N.Atl.-N.Pac.-Arct.

Antimargarita POWELL, 1951 [**Valvatella dulcis* SMITH, 1907]. Thin, elaborately sculptured, low-spired; umbilicus wide, deep. *Rec.,* Antarct.

Basilissa WATSON, 1879 [**B. superba;* SD COSSMANN, 1888]. Thin, carinate, low to high-spired. *U.Cret.-Rec.*

B. (**Basilissa**). Spire low-conical, periphery channeled, base spirally ribbed. *U.Cret.-Rec.,* Eu.-Afr.-Austral.-Pac.——Fig. 161,*1.* **B. (B.) superba,* Rec., Austral.; ×1 (227).

B. (**Ancistrobasis**) DALL, 1889 [**B. costulata* WATSON, 1879]. Spire with interrupted axial ribs. *Rec.,* Carib.

Euchelus PHILIPPI, 1847 [**Trochus quadricarinatus* HOLTEN, 1802 (?=*Trochus asper* GMELIN, 1791); SD HERRMANNSEN, 1847] [=*Aradasia* GRAY, 1850; *Tallorbis* G. & H. NEVILL, 1869; *Huttonia* KIRK, 1882 (*non* PICKARD-CAMBRIDGE, 1880)]. Ovate-conical aperture rounded, outer lip thickened, lirate within; inner lip usually with tooth below. *Plio.-Rec.*

E. (**Euchelus**). Rather small, sturdy; whorls convex; juvenile shells with umbilicus, adult without; operculum few-whorled. *Plio.-Rec.,* IndoPac.——Fig. 161,*14.* **E. (E.) quadricarinatus* (HOLTEN), Rec., India; ×1 (147).

E. (**Antillachelus**) WOODRING, 1928 [**Calliostoma asperrimum* var. *dentiferum* DALL, 1889]. Small, whorls flat-sided, nodosely sculptured; umbilicus wide. *Mio.-Rec.,* W.Indies.——Fig. 161,*6.* **E. (A.) dentiferus* (DALL), Rec., W.Indies; ×3 (147).

E. (**Herpetopoma**) PILSBRY, 1889 [**E. scabriusculus* A.ADAMS & ANGAS, 1867]. Cancellately sculptured; operculum multispiral. *Plio.-Rec.,* Austral.

E. (**Mirachelus**) WOODRING, 1928 [**Calliostoma corbis* DALL, 1889]. Small, without umbilicus; with coarse cancellate sculpture. *Mio.-Rec.,* Carib.

E. (?**Nevillia**) H.ADAMS, 1868 [**N. picta;* SD TOMLIN, 1938]. Small, without umbilicus, otherwise like *E. (Herpetopoma). Rec.,* IndianO.——Fig. 161,*8.* **E. (N.) pictus;* ×5 (159).

E. (**Vaceuchelus**) IREDALE, 1929 [**E. angulatus* PEASE, 1867]. Without basal tooth, otherwise like *E. (Euchelus). Rec.,* S.Pac.

Granata COTTON, 1957. [**Stomatella imbricata* LAMARCK, 1816] [=*Stomatella* AUCTT., *non* LAMARCK]. Ear-shaped, with few whorls; sculpture of numerous spiral ridges. *Rec.,* Austral.

Guttula SCHEPMAN, 1908 [**G. sibogae*]. Like *Margarites* but with angular aperture. *Rec.,* Pac.

Hybochelus PILSBRY, 1889 [**Stomatella cancellata* KRAUSS, 1848] [=*Stomatella* AUCTT., *non* LAMARCK]. Depressed, short-spired, last whorl large; sculpture spiral or cancellate; with or without an umbilicus; no tooth on inner lip. *Rec.,* S. Afr.-Austral.——Fig. 161,*11.* **H. cancellatus* (KRAUSS), S.Afr.; *11a,b,* ×1 (147).

Lischkeia FISCHER in KIENER, 1879 [**Trochus moniliferus* LAMARCK, 1816]. Relatively large, thick-shelled; spire conical, base flattened; sculpture of nodose spiral ribs. *Cret.-Rec.*

L. (**Lischkeia**). Umbilicus partially concealed; columella with weak fold. *U.Cret.(Maastricht.)-Rec.,* Eu.-S.Afr.-Japan.——Fig. 161,*17.* **L. (L.) monilifera* (LAMARCK), Rec., Japan; ×1 (147).

L. (**Calliotropis**) SEGUENZA, 1903 [*Trochus ottoi PHILIPPI, 1844] [=*Solariellopsis* SCHEPMAN, 1908 (*non* DEGREGORIO, 1886)]. Umbilicus wide. *Plio.-Rec.,* W.Atl.-Eu.-S.Pac.——Fig. 161,*9.* **L. (C.) ottoi* (PHILIPPI), Plio.-Pleist., Italy; ×2 (211).

FIG. 161. Trochacea (Trochidae——Margaritinae) (p. 1249-1251).

Margarella THIELE in TROSCHEL, 1893 [**Trochus expansus* SOWERBY, 1838; SD THIELE, 1924] [*pro Margaritella* THIELE in TROSCHEL, 1891 (*non* MEEK & HAYDEN, 1860)]. Small, thin-shelled, globose, nearly smooth. *Mio.-Rec.*

M. (Margarella). With rounded periphery, surface smooth. *Mio.-Rec.,* N.Z.-Antarct.——FIG. 161,*10*.
**M. (M.) expansa* (SOWERBY), Rec., S.Georgia; *10a,b,* ×1.5 (147).

M. (Promargarita) STREBEL, 1908 [**Margarites tropidophoroides*]. With 2 blunt spiral carinae. *Rec.,* Antarct.

M. (Submargarita) STREBEL, 1908 [**Margarites impervia*]. Minute, with fine spiral riblets; nuclear whorls large. *Rec.,* Antarct.

Olivia CANTRAINE, 1835 [**O. otaviana*] [=*Craspedotus* PHILIPPI, 1847 (*non* SCHOENHERR, 1844); *Heliciella* COSTA, 1861; *Danilia* BRUSINA, 1865].

Small, with cancellate sculpture; columella with strong fold, ending in a notch, like *Euchelus. U. Cret.(Dan.)-Rec.,* Eu.-IndoPac.-N.Z.——FIG. 161, *2. *O. otaviana,* Pleist., Italy; ×1 (166).

Seguenzia JEFFREYS, 1876 [**S. formosa;* SD HARRIS, 1897]. With several carinae; aperture with an anal notch above and columellar notch below. *Eoc.-Rec.,* Eu.-W.Atl.-S.Pac.——FIG. 161,*7. *S. formosa,* Rec., off New England; ×5 (147).

Tibatrochus NOMURA, 1940 [**T. husaensis*]. Like *Euchelus* but with smooth aperture. *Rec.,* Japan.

Timisia JEKELIUS, 1944 [**T. pseudopicta*]. *Mio.,* SE.Eu.——FIG. 161,*12. *T. pseudopicta,* Rumania; *12a,b,* ×2 (194).

Tropidomarga POWELL, 1951 [**T. biangulata*]. Shape of *Margarella (Promargarita)* but more strongly sculptured. *Rec.,* Antarct.

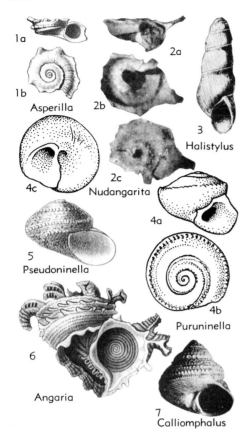

FIG. 162. Trochacea (Trochidae——Angariinae, Halistylinae) (*p. 1252-1262*).

Subfamily ANGARIINAE Thiele, 1924
[=Delphinulinae STOLICZKA, 1868]

Small to moderately large, low-spired or conical; surface with rows of nodes or branching spines; umbilicus wide; aperture nacreous within; operculum horny, thin. *Trias.-Rec.*

Asperilla KOKEN, 1896 [**Delphinula conoserra* QUENSTEDT, 1884; SD KOKEN, 1897 (=**D. longispina* ROLLE, 1860)]. Discoidal or with slightly protruding spire, broadly phaneromphalous, with smooth upper surface spinose at periphery; outer whorl face and base with or without spiral ornament; aperture orbicular or quadrangular, with continuous peristome. *U. Trias.(Nor.) - U. Jur. (Kimm.)*, Eu.——FIG. 162,1. **A. longispina* (ROLLE), U.Jur., Ger.; *1a,b,* ✕1 (11).

Angaria RÖDING, 1798 [**Turbo delphinus* LINNÉ, 1758; SD FISCHER, 1875] [=*Delphinula* LAMARCK, 1804 (obj.); *Delphinulus* MONTFORT, 1810 (obj.); *Praxidice* RAFINESQUE, 1815 *(nom. nud.); Scalator*

GISTEL, 1848 (obj.); *Angarus* GRAY, 1857 *(nom. van.)*]. Spire depressed or flattened.

A. (Angaria). Moderately large, sculpture of strong nodes and recurved to branching spines. *M. Jur.-Rec.,* Eu.-Afr.-IndoPac.-Australasia. —— FIG. 162,6. **A. (A.) delphinus* (LINNÉ), Rec., E. Indies; ✕0.7 (147).

A. (Nudangarita) BEETS, 1942 [**A. (N.) ardjunoi*]. Small, whorls nearly smooth, not noded but with irregular flange or keel below suture. *Neog.,* Borneo.——FIG. 162,2. **A. (N.) ardjunoi,* E.Borneo; *2a-c,* apertural, umbilical, and apical views, ✕5 (163).

Calliomphalus COSSMANN, 1888 [**Turbo squamulosus* LAMARCK, 1804] [=*Callomphalus* COSSMANN, 1918 (spelling error); *Callomphalifer* COSSMANN, 1918 *(nom. van.)*]. Spire conical, sculpture of spiral rows of hollow spines; base with fine cords; an ear-shaped process on inner lip. *U.Cret.(Senon.)-Mio.,* Eu.-N.Am.——FIG. 162,7. **C. squamulosus* (LAMARCK), Eoc., Fr.; ✕0.5 (147).

Pseudoninella SACCO, 1896 [**Delphinula miosolarioides*]. Spire low, rounded; sculpture of irregular spiral rows of nodes; inner lip not recurved. *U. Cret.(Dan.)-Mio.,* Eu.——FIG. 162,5. **P. miosolarioides* (SACCO), M.Mio., Italy; ✕1 (147).

Puruninella BEETS, 1943 [**Delphinula permodesta* MARTIN, 1914]. Smooth, spire rounded; last whorl with shouldered periphery crenulated by a row of nodes. *Eoc.,* E.Indies.——FIG. 162,4. **P. permodesta* (MARTIN), U.Eoc., Java; *4a-c,* apertural, apical, and umbilical views, ✕3 (163).

Subfamily MONODONTINAE Cossmann, 1916

Littoriniform, turbiniform or conical shells of small or medium size, anomphalous with few exceptions; ornament predominantly spiral or smooth; outer lip strongly prosocline in most genera and columellar lip with one or more teeth in many genera. *?Trias., M.Jur.-Rec.*

?Praelittorina KUTASSY, 1937 [**P. triadica;* SD KUTASSY, 1940]. Littoriniform, anomphalous, with subglobose last whorl and low acute spire; ornament spiral threads; aperture imperfectly known. *U.Trias.(Carn.),* Eu.——FIG. 163,9. **P. triadica,* Hung.; ✕1.5 (84).

Ozodochilus COSSMANN, 1918 [**Trochus subfilosus* BUVIGNIER, 1852]. Small, subglobose to littoriniform, with cyrtoconoid spire, anomphalous; whorls flat or feebly convex, base strongly convex; ornament spiral threads, obscurely nodose in some species; peristome lying almost in a single plane and in some shells uninterrupted; columellar lip concave, joining basal lip in even curve and bearing obtuse denticle, scarcely perceptible in some species. *M.Jur.(Baj.)-U.Jur.(Kimm.),* Eu.——FIG. 163,17. **O. subfilosus* (BUVIGNIER), U.Jur. (Raurac.), Fr.; ✕4 (165).

Cochleochilus Cossmann, 1918 [**Trochus cottaldinus* d'Orbigny, 1853]. Biconical, anomphalous, with flat or feebly concave whorls, last one subcarinate at periphery; ornament spiral grooves; base flattened-convex in outline; columellar lip narrowly reflected above, where its outer margin continues that of parietal callosity, abruptly expanded and hollowed out below, where it is bordered on left by a carina that continues the apertural basal margin, describing sharp curve to meet margin of reflected part of lip; tubercle at upper end of hollowed-out part. *M.Jur.(Bathon.)-U.Jur.(Portland.),* Eu.——Fig. 163,16. **C. cottaldinus* (d'Orbigny), U.Jur.(Raurac.), Fr.; ×8 (Cox, n).

Islipia Cox & Arkell, 1950 [**Monodonta lycetti* Lycett, 1863]. Depressed turbiniform, anomphalous whorls and base convex; ornament prominent spiral cords; columellar lip straight, unthickened; to its left, and originating at its lower end, spiral bulge occupies middle of base, limited on outer side by deep groove indenting basal lip. *M.Jur.(Bathon.),* Eu.——Fig. 163,20. *I. lycetti* (Lycett), Eng.; ×2.7 (Cox, n).

Michaletia Cossmann, 1904 [**M. semigranulata*]. Turbiniform, anomphalous but with base excavated mesially; last whorl evenly convex at periphery; ornament granose spiral cords; aperture orbicular, with interrupted peristome; outer lip strongly prosocline; columellar lip very oblique, with callous thickening at top. *Cret.(Barrem.-Maastricht.),* Eu.——Fig. 163,15. **M. semigranulata,* U.Cret.(L.Coniac.), Fr.; ×2.7 (Cox, n).

Monodonta Lamarck, 1799 [**Trochus labio* Linné, 1758] [=*Monodontes* Montfort, 1810 (obj.); *Labio* Oken, 1815 (obj.); *Odontis* Sowerby, 1825 (obj.); *Trochidon* Swainson, 1840; *Pimpellies* Gistel, 1847 (obj.)]. Thick-shelled, spirally sculptured. *U.Cret.(Dan.)-Rec.*

M. (Monodonta). Medium-sized, somewhat globose, columellar teeth wide. *Oligo.-Rec.,* Eu.-IndoPac.-Australasia.——Fig. 163,14. **M. (M.) labio* (Linné), Rec., E.Indies; ×1 (147).

M. (Austrocochlea) Fischer, 1885 [**M. constricta* Lamarck, 1822] [=*Austrochlea* Pilsbry, 1889 (obj.)]. Spiral ribs widely spaced, columellar tooth weak. *Rec.,* Austral.

M. (Incisilabium) Cossmann, 1918 [**M. parisiensis* Deshayes, 1832]. Spiral ribs noded. *Eoc.,* Eu.

M. (Monodontella) Sacco, 1896 [**Turbo quadrulus* Michelotti, 1840]. Small, sculpture clathrate, fine. *Mio.,* Eu.

M. (Osilinus) Philippi, 1847 [**M. punctulata* Lamarck, 1822; SD Bucquoy, Dautzenberg & Dollfus, 1885] [=*Gibbium* Gray, 1847 (non Scopoli, 1777); *Trochius* Gray, 1847; *Neptheusa* Gray, 1852 (=*Nephteusa* Monterosato, 1888); *Trochocochlea* Mörch, 1852; *Caragolus* Monterosato, 1884]. Smooth or with weak spiral ribs;

columellar tooth weak, broad. *U.Cret.(Dan.)-Rec.,* Eu.-Afr.Atl.

Bankivia Krauss, 1848 [**B. varians* (=**Phasianella fasciata* Menke, 1830); SD Fischer, 1875]. Slender, high-spired, nearly smooth; columella with a weak fold. *Mio.-Rec.,* Austral.-S.Pac.

B. (Bankivia). Brilliantly nacreous. *Pleist.-Rec.,* Australasia.——Fig. 163,4. **B. fasciata* (Menke), Rec., Austral.; ×1 (147).

B. (Leiopyrga) Adams & Adams, 1863 [**L. picturata* = *Cantharidus lineolaris* Gould, 1861]. Whorls obtusely carinate, spiral riblets beaded; umbilicus small. *Mio.-Rec.,* S.Pac.

Bathybembix Crosse, 1893 [**Bembix aeola* Watson, 1879] [pro *Bembix* Watson, 1879 (non Fabricius, 1775)]. Thin-shelled, somewhat inflated, spirally nodose to smooth, suture adpressed to channeled; in deep water. *Oligo.-Rec.*

B. (Bathybembix). Smooth or with subdued sculpture on periphery. *Oligo.-Rec.,* Japan-W.N.Am.-E.Atl.——Fig. 163,7. **B. (B.) aeola* (Watson), Rec., Japan; ×0.5 (227).

B. (Ginebis) Otuka, 1942 [**Trochus argenteonitens* Lischke, 1872]. With one row of nodes per whorl. *Oligo.-Rec.,* Japan.

Cantharidus Montfort, 1810 [**Trochus iris* Gmelin, 1791 = *Limax opalus* Martyn, 1784 (ICZN op. 479)] [=*Cantharis* Férussac, 1821 (obj.); *Elenchus* Swainson, 1840 (non Curtis, 1831) (obj.); *Cantharidium* Schaufuss, 1869 (pro *Cantharis*)]. Spire tapering, surface nearly smooth; columellar fold and tooth weak or wanting. *Mio.-Rec.*

C. (Cantharidus). Medium-sized; columella with fold but tooth obscure. *Mio.-Rec.,* Austral.——Fig. 163,19. **C. (C.) iris* (Gmelin), Rec., N.Z.; ×1 (147).

C. (Iwakawatrochus) Kuroda & Habe, 1954 [**Gibbula vittata* Pilsbry, 1903]. Shell as in *Cantharidus,* but radula with cuspate rachidian tooth. *Rec.,* Japan.

C. (Levella) Marwick, 1943 [**L. tersa*]. Minute, smooth, columella without fold. *L.Mio.,* N.Z.——Fig. 163,22. **C. (L.) tersa* (Marwick); ×5 (204).

C. (Micrelenchus) Finlay, 1927 [**Trochus sanguineus* Gray, 1843]. Small, spire relatively low, columellar fold not apparent. *Mio.-Rec.,* N.Z.

C. (Phasianotrochus) Fischer, 1885 [**Trochus badius* Wood, 1828 = *Bulimus eximius* Perry, 1811]. Columellar fold well developed. *Plio.-Rec.,* Austral.

C. (Plumbelenchus) Finlay, 1927 [**Trochus capillaceus* Philippi, 1848 = *T. pruninus* Gould, 1844]. Columellar fold evanescent. *Rec.,* N.Z.

Chrysostoma Swainson, 1840 [**Turbo nicobaricus* "Chemnitz, 1781" (not binominal) = *Helix paradoxa* Born, 1780]. Low-spired, globose, smooth; inner lip with a callus partially concealing false umbilicus. *Cret.-Rec.,* IndoPac.-N.Z.——Fig. 163,

8. *C. paradoxum (Born), Rec., E.Indies; ×1 (147).

Diloma Philippi, 1845 [*Turbo nigerrimus Gmelin, 1791; SD Herrmannsen, 1847] Spire of moderate height to low; aperture oblique; columella weakly dentate. Mio.-Rec.

D. (Diloma). Nearly smooth; columella with a central area of nacre. Rec., W.S.Am.-Pac.——Fig. 163,11. *D. (D.) nigerrima (Gmelin), Rec., Chile; ×1 (147).

D. (Anisodiloma) Finlay, 1927 [*Trochus lugubris Gmelin, 1791]. With nodose spiral ribs. Rec., N.Z.

D. (Cavodiloma) Finlay, 1927 [*Trochocochlea excavata A.Adams & Angas, 1864]. Small, smooth, with blunt peripheral keel. Rec., N.Z.

D. (Chlorodiloma) Pilsbry, 1889 [*Trochus crinitus Philippi, 1849] [=Latona Hutton, 1884 (non Schumacher, 1817)]. Spire higher than in D. (Diloma); shell less nacreous; with an umbilical chink. Rec., Austral.

D. (Fractarmilla) Finlay, 1927 [*Labio corrosa A.Adams, 1853]. Peristome interrupted by last whorl. Rec., N.Z.

D. (Melagraphia) Gray, 1847 [*Turbo aethiops Gmelin, 1791] [=Neodiloma Fischer, 1885 (obj.); Zediloma Finlay, 1927]. Spirally sculptured, with a strong columellar tooth. Mio.-Rec., Eu.-Austral.——Fig. 163,10. *D. (M.) aethiops (Gmelin), Rec., N.Z.; ×1 (147).

D. (Miofractarmilla) Laws, 1948 [*M. bartrumi]. Like D. (Fractarmilla) but with one small elevated tooth in front of columella. L.Plio., N.Z.

D. (Oxystele) Philippi, 1847 [*Trochus merula "Chemnitz" (not binominal) = Trochus sinensis Gmelin, 1791; SD Herrmannsen, 1847] [=Oxytele auctt. (obj.)]. Relatively large; inner lip broad, with a central furrow. Mio.-Rec., Eu.-Afr.-Japan.——Fig. 163,18. *D. (O.) sinensis (Gmelin), Rec., S.Afr.; ×1 (147).

D. (Pictodiloma) Habe, 1946 [*Trochus suavis Philippi, 1850]. Rec., Japan.

Jujubinus Monterosato, 1884 [*Trochus matoni Payraudeau, 1827 = T. exasperatus Pennant, 1777; SD Pilsbry, 1889] [=Manotrochus Fischer, 1885; Mirulinus Monterosato, 1917; Clelandella Winckworth, 1932]. Like Calliostoma in form but more slender and with radula more like that of Monodonta. U.Cret.(Turon.)-Rec.

J. (Jujubinus). With small columellar tooth; peripheral spiral cord nodose. U.Cret.(Turon.)-Rec., Eu.-Atl.-IndoPac.——Fig. 163,2. *J. exasperatus (Pennant), Rec., Medit.; ×2 (147).

J. (Strigosella) Sacco, 1896 [*Trochus strigosus Gmelin, 1791]. No columellar tooth; narrow umbilicus present. Paleoc.-Rec., Eu.

Lesperonia Tournouër, 1874 [*L. princeps]. Like Jujubinus, but smaller and with a strong carina. Oligo., Eu.——Fig. 163,3. *L. princeps, Oligo., Fr.; ×2 (147).

Pachydontella Marwick, 1948 [*P. etiampicta]. Small, turbinate, stout, spirally ribbed; columella with large tooth. Plio., N.Z.——Fig. 163,1. *P. etiampicta; ×2 (204).

Pictiformes Kolesnikov, 1939 [*Monodonta mamilla Andrzejowski, 1830]. With deep suture and faint keel. Mio.(Sarmat.), SW.Asia.

Tegula Lesson, 1835 [*T. elegans (=Trochus pellisserpentis Wood, 1828)]. Of moderate size to large, solid, whorls flat-sided; with or without umbilicus. Mio.-Rec.

T. (Tegula). With nodose spiral ribs; base flattened. Mio.-Rec., N.Am.-S.Am.-Pac.——Fig. 163, 21. *T. (T.) pellisserpentis (Wood), Rec., W.S. Am.; 21a,b, ×1 (147).

T. (Agathistoma) Olsson & Harbison, 1953 [*Trochus viridulus Gmelin, 1791]. Smooth or finely beaded spirally, with a narrow umbilicus. Plio.-Rec., E.C.Am.-W.C.Am.

T. (Chlorostoma) Swainson, 1840 [*Trochus argyrostomus Gmelin, 1791; SD Herrmannsen, 1846]. Smooth or axially ribbed above, base smooth or spirally ribbed. Mio.-Rec., Japan-N. Am.-S.Am.

T. (Omphalius) Philippi, 1847 [*Trochus rusticus Gmelin, 1791; SD Herrmannsen, 1847] [=Neomphalius Fischer, 1885 (obj.)]. Like T. (Chlorostoma) but smooth; most species with umbilicus. Mio.-Rec., Japan-W.N.Am.-?W.Indies.

T. (Promartynia) Dall, 1909 [*Trochus pulligo Gmelin, 1791]. Smooth, with wide umbilicus. Pleist.-Rec., W.N.Am.

Thalotia Gray, 1847 [*Trochus pictus Wood, 1828 (=Monodonta conica Gray, 1827)]. Elevated-conical solid, granular or spirally ribbed. Mio.-Rec.

T. (Thalotia). Periphery rounded, aperture small. U.Tert.-Rec., E.Indies.——Fig. 163,5. *T. conica (Gray), Rec., Austral., ×1 (147).

T. (Alcyna) A.Adams, 1860 [*A. ocellata; SD Pilsbry, 1888]. Aperture relatively large, columella truncate below. Rec., Pac.

T. (Beraua) Beets, 1941 [*Cantharidus (B.) erinaceus]. More conical than in T. (Thalotia) and with sutural nodes stronger. Mio., E.Indies. ——Fig. 163,6. *T. (B.) erinacea (Beets), Mio., Borneo; ×1 (163).

T. (Calthalotia) Iredale, 1929 [*Trochus arruensis Watson, 1880]. Plio.-Rec., Austral.

T. (Odontotrochus) Fischer in Kiener, 1879 [*Trochus chlorostomus Menke, 1843]. Periphery angulate, spire high. Rec., Austral.

T. (Prothalotia) Thiele, 1930 [*Trochus flindersi Fischer, 1878]. Periphery rounded; umbilicus narrow; columella smooth. Rec., Austral.

Turcica A.Adams, 1854 [*T. monilifera] [=Ptychostylis Gabb, 1866]. Spire high, sides flattened; sutures impressed; sculpture nodose. Mio.-Rec.

T. (Turcica). Columella with 1 or 2 large teeth on strong fold. Mio.-Rec., N.Am.-Japan-Austr.

1 Pachydontella
2 Jujubinus
3 Lesperonia
4 Bankivia
5 Thalotia
6 Beruaua
7 Bathybembix
8 Chrysostoma
9 Praelittorina
10 Melagraphia
11 Diloma
12b
12a Turcicula
13 Turcica
14 Monodonta
15 Michaletia
16 Cochleochilus
17 Ozodochilus
18 Oxystele
19 Cantharidus
20 Islipia
21b Tegula 21a
22 Levella

FIG. 163. Trochacea (Trochidae——Monodontinae) (p. *1252-1256*).

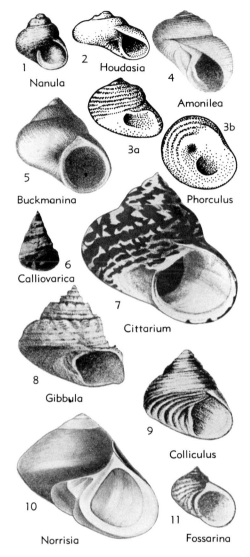

1 Nanula
2 Houdasia
4 Amonilea
3a
3b Phorculus
5 Buckmanina
6 Calliovarica
7 Cittarium
8 Gibbula
9 Colliculus
10 Norrisia
11 Fossarina

Fig. 164. Trochacea (Trochidae——Gibbulinae)
(p. 1256-1257).

——Fig. 163,13. *T. monilifera*, Rec., Austral.; ×1 (147).

T. (Perrinia) ADAMS & ADAMS, 1854 [*Monodonta angulifera* A.ADAMS, 1853; SD PILSBRY, 1889]. Columella with several denticles. *Plio.-Rec.*, E. Indies-Formosa.

Turricula DALL, 1881 [*Margarita imperialis*]. Resembling *Lischkeia*, but with reflected lip and vermiculate sculpture. *Rec.*, Carib.——Fig. 163, 12. *T. imperialis* (DALL), Cuba; *12a,b*, ×1 (217).

Subfamily GIBBULINAE Stoliczka, 1868

Turbiniform shells with considerable size range, mostly phaneromphalous; with predominantly spiral ornament or smooth; peristome interrupted in most genera; outer lip strongly prosocline; columellar lip smooth or (less commonly) with a weak tooth. *U.Jur.-Rec.*

Buckmanina COSSMANN, 1920 [*pro Brasilia* COSSMANN, 1918 (*non* BUCKMAN, 1908)] [*Turbo erinus* D'ORBIGNY, 1853]. Turbiniform, thick-shelled, narrowly phaneromphalous, with strongly convex whorls and base, smooth; aperture orbicular, with thin parietal callus linking columellar and outer lips; columellar lip thickened, not reflected. *U.Jur.(Raurac.)-L.Cret.(Neocom.)*, Eu.-S. Afr.——Fig. 164,5. *B. erinus* (D'ORBIGNY), U.Jur. (Raurac.), Fr.; ×2 (111).

Gibbula RISSO, 1826 [*Trochus magus* LINNÉ, 1758; SD HERRMANNSEN, 1847] [=*Magulus, Puteolus* MONTEROSATO, 1888; *Phorculus* MONTEROSATO, 1888 (*non* COSSMANN, 1888); *Conotrochus* PILSBRY, 1889 (*non* SEGUENZA, 1864); *Phorculellus* SACCO, 1896 (*pro Phorculus*); *Phorculorbis* COSSMANN, 1918; *Forskaliopsis* COEN, 1931 (*non* HAECKEL, 1888)]. Sutures impressed; umbilicus bounded by a ridge. *U.Cret.-Rec.*

G. (Gibbula). Medium-sized, wider than high; last whorl with base set off by an angle. *U.Cret.-Rec.*, Eu.-S.Am.——Fig. 164,8. *G. (G.) magus* (LINNÉ), Rec., Medit.; ×1 (147).

G. (Adriaria) PALLARY, 1917 [*Trochus albidus* GMELIN, 1791]. *Rec.*, Medit.

G. (Amonilea) COSSMANN, 1920 [*Gibbula parnensis* BAYAN, 1870] [*pro Moniliopsis* COSSMANN, 1918 (*non* CONRAD, 1865); *Moniliopsidea* TOMLIN, 1930]. Whorls inflated, sculpture fine, spiral. *Eoc.*, Eu.——Fig. 164,4. *G. (A.) parnensis*, Eoc., Fr.; ×2 (147).

G. (Calliotrochus) FISCHER in KIENER, 1879 [*Turbo phasianellus* DESHAYES, 1863 (not homonym of *T. phasianella* ADAMS, 1850)]. Small, turbiniform, with narrow umbilicus. *Rec.*, Indo-Pac.

G. (Cantharidella) PILSBRY, 1889 [*G. picturata* ADAMS & ANGAS, 1864; SD SUTER, 1913]. Small, polished, umbilicus narrow or wanting. *Rec.*, Australasia.

G. (Colliculus) MONTEROSATO, 1888 [*Trochus adansoni* PAYRAUDEAU, 1827; SD BUCQUOY, DAUTZENBERG & DOLLFUS, 1898] [=*Glomulus* MONTEROSATO, 1888 (=*Glossulus* PALLARY, 1938)]. Small, base with spiral ribs; slight fold on columella. *Eoc.-Rec.*, Eu.-Afr.-Pac.——Fig. 164, 9. *G. (C.) adansoni* (PAYRAUDEAU), Rec., Medit.; ×2 (147).

G. (Enida) A.ADAMS, 1860 [*E. japonica*; SD KOBELT, 1879]. Small, depressed, with wide umbilicus. *Pleist.-Rec.*, Japan-IndoPac.

G. (Eurytrochus) Fischer in Kiener, 1879 [*Clanculus danieli* Crosse, 1862; SD Pilsbry, 1889]. Low-spired, spirally ribbed; periphery bluntly angulate. *Rec.,* S.Pac.

G. (Forskaelena) Iredale, 1918 [*Trochus fanulum* Gmelin, 1791] [pro Forskälia Adams & Adams, 1854 (non Kölliker, 1853)]. Axially ribbed above periphery, spirally below, with a double keel at periphery. *Mio.-Rec.,* Eu.

G. (Hisseyagibbula) Kershaw, 1955 [*Littorina hisseyana* Tenison-Woods, 1876]. *Rec.,* Tasmania.

G. (Notogibbula) Iredale, 1924 [*G. coxi* Angas, 1867 (=*Stomatia bicarinata* Adams, 1854)]. With 2 rounded keels. *Rec.,* Austral.

G. (Phorcus) Risso, 1826 [*P. margaritaceus;* SD Bucquoy, Dautzenberg & Dollfus, 1885]. Apex blunt; spiral sculpture weak. *Oligo.-Rec.,* Eu.-S.Am.-C.Am.

G. (Pseudodiloma) Cossmann, 1888 [*Trochus mirabilis* Deshayes, 1863]. Globose, with thickened lip. *Eoc.,* Eu.-N.Am.

G. (Robur) Kolesnikov, 1939 [*Trochus robur* Davidachvili, 1932]. Turbinate, with 2 low carinae. *Mio.(L.Sarmat.),* SW.Asia.

G. (Rollandiana) Kolesnikov, 1939 [*Trochus rollandianus* d'Orbigny, 1845]. Low-whorled, with broad umbilicus. *Mio.,* SW.Asia.

G. (Steromphala) Gray, 1847 [*Trochus cinerarius* Linné, 1758] [=*Korenia* Friele, 1877 (obj.); *Gibbulastra* Monterosato, 1884; *Gibbuloidella* Sacco, 1896]. Apex and periphery rounded; spirally striate. *Mio.-Rec.,* Eu.

G. (Tumulus) Monterosato, 1888 [*Trochus umbilicaris* Linné, 1758; SD Bucquoy, Dautzenberg & Dollfus, 1898]. Like *G. (Steromphala)* but with higher spire. *Mio.-Rec.,* Eu.

Calliovarica Vokes, 1939 [*C. eocensis*]. Outer lip strongly reflected; with numerous varices crossed by spiral ribs. *Eoc.,* W.N.Am.——Fig. 164,6. *C. eocensis,* Eoc., Calif.; ×1 (225).

Cittarium Philippi, 1847 [*Turbo pica* Linné, 1758] [=*Meleagris* Montfort, 1810 (non Linné, 1758) (obj.); *Livona* Gray, 1847 (obj.)]. Large, turbinate, inner lip with a small callus. *Pleist.-Rec.,* Carib.——Fig. 164,7. *C. pica* (Linné), Rec., W.Indies; ×0.5 (147).

Fossarina A.Adams & Angas, 1864 [*F. patula*] [(=*Minos* Hutton, 1884)]. Small to minute, spiral sculpture very fine. *Rec.*

F. (Fossarina). Aperture entire. *Rec.,* Austral.—— Fig. 164,11. *F. (F.) patula,* S.Austral.; ×3 (147).

F. (Clydonochilus) Fischer, 1890 [*C. mariei*]. Minute, outer lip with a notch below suture. *Rec.,* E.Afr.

F. (Minopa) Iredale, 1924 [*F. legrandi* Petterd, 1879]. Minute, smooth, inner lip interrupted by last whorl. *Rec.,* Austral.

Gaza Watson, 1879 [*G. daedala*]. Turbinate, finely spirally striate; umbilicus partly or entirely concealed by callus. *Rec.*

G. (Gaza). Umbilicus entirely concealed. *Rec.,* Pac.-Carib.

G. (Callogaza) Dall, 1881 [*G. (C.) watsoni*]. Umbilicus partly concealed. *Rec.,* Carib.

Houdasia Cossmann, 1902 [*H. splendens*]. Small, depressed, few-whorled. *Eoc.,* Eu.——Fig. 164,2. *H. splendens,* Eoc., Fr.; ×5 (147).

Nanula Thiele, 1924 [*Gibbula tasmanica* Petterd, 1879]. Small, globose, nearly smooth. *Rec.,* Austral.——Fig. 164,1. *N. tasmanica* (Petterd); ×3 (147).

Norrisia Bayle, 1880 [*Trochiscus norrisi* Sowerby, 1838] [pro Trochiscus Sowerby, 1838 (non Heyden, 1826)]. Large, solid, rounded-conical. *Pleist.-Rec.,* W.N.Am.——Fig. 164,4. *N. norrisi* (Sowerby), Rec., Calif.; ×0.7 (147).

Phorculus Cossmann, 1888 [*Turbo fraterculus* Deshayes, 1863]. Small, depressed, with strong spiral ribs. *Eoc.-Mio.,* Eu.-N.Am.-S.Am.——Fig. 164,3. *P. fraterculus* (Deshayes), Eoc., Fr.; *3a,b,* ×1.5 (147).

Trochinella Iredale, 1937 [*T. perconfusa*]. Thin, pellucid. *Rec.,* Pac.

Subfamily CALLIOSTOMATINAE Thiele, 1924

[=Conulinae Cossmann, 1916 (partim)]

Conical or turbiniform shells mostly of medium to large-medium size, anomphalous or narrowly phaneromphalous, many with flattened base; aperture quadrangular; peristome discontinuous, parietal region without callus in most genera; outer lip strongly prosocline; columellar lip straight, vertical or inclined, meeting parietal lip in abrupt angle, and smooth or with denticle at lower end. *L.Cret.-Rec.*

Calliostoma Swainson, 1840 [*Trochus conulus* Linné, 1758; SD Herrmannsen, 1846] [=*Conulus* Nardo, 1840 (non Leske, 1778); *Ziziphinus* Gray, 1847 (non Gray, 1843); *Montagua* Gray, 1852 (non Fleming, 1828); *Stylotrochus* Seguenza, 1876 (non Haeckel, 1862); *Jacinthinus* Monterosato, 1889 (obj.); *Callistoma, Callistomus, Callisoma* auctt. (obj.)]. Without umbilicus. *L.Cret.(Calliostoma s.lat.)-Rec.* (61).

C. (Calliostoma). Shell thick, with granular spirals on early whorls, later whorls nearly smooth; columellar tubercle distinct. *Mio.-Rec.,* Medit. ——Fig. 165,5. *C. (C.) conulus* (Linné), Rec., Medit.; *5a,b,* ×1 (147).

C. (Alertalex) Dell, 1956 [*A. blacki*]. Thin, iridescent, with smooth, prominent spiral ribs. *Rec.,* N.Z.

C. (Ampullotrochus) Monterosato, 1890 [*Trochus granulatus* Born, 1778]. Entirely granulate. *Rec.,* Medit.-?W.N.Am.

C. (Anceps) Kolesnikov, 1939 [*Trochus anceps*

EICHWALD, 1850]. Thin-walled, with flat base and whorls. *Mio.(Sarmat.)*, SW.Asia.

C. (Benthastelene) IREDALE, 1936 [*B. katherina]. Small, aperture semilunar. *Rec.*, Austral.

C. (Carinator) IKEBE, 1942 [*C. (C.) makiyamai]. Whorls with 2 strong carinae; suture canaliculate. *U.Plio.*, Japan.

C. (Eucasta) DALL, 1889 [*C. (E.) indianum]. With a sulcus near periphery. *Rec.*, Carib.

C. (Fautor) IREDALE, 1924 [*Ziziphinus comptus A.ADAMS, 1855] [=Salsipotens IREDALE, 1924]. Relatively high-spired. *Rec.*, Austral.

C. (Feneoniana) KOLESNIKOV, 1939 [*Trochus feneonianus D'ORBIGNY, 1845]. With sharp basal keel and spiral ribs. *Mio.(Sarmat.)*, SW.Asia.

C. (Laetifautor) IREDALE, 1929 [*C. trepidum HEDLEY, 1907 = C. deceptum SMITH, 1899]. Spiral ribs nodose. *Plio.-Rec.*, Australasia.

C. (Maurea) OLIVER, 1926 [*Trochus tigris GMELIN, 1791 (ICZN, Op. 479)] [=Mauriella OLIVER, 1926; Calliotropis OLIVER, 1926 (non SEGUENZA, 1903); Mucrinops, Venustas FINLAY, 1927 (obj.); Calotropis THIELE, 1929 (pro Calliotropis)]. With pointed spire and rounded periphery. *Mio.-Rec.*, N.Z.

C. (Otukaia) IKEBE, 1942 [*C. kiheiziebisu OTUKA, 1939]. Whorls simply sculptured, with 2 strong spiral keels. *Plio.-Rec.*, Japan.

C. (?Putzeysia) SULLIOTTI, 1889 [*Trochus clathratus ARADAS, 1847] [=Gemmula SEGUENZA, 1876 (non WEINKAUFF, 1875)]. Small, somewhat inflated, with cancellate sculpture. *Mio.-Rec.*, Eu.

C. (Sarmates) KOLESNIKOV, 1939 [*Trochus sarmates EICHWALD, 1850]. With median keel. *Mio. (Sarmat.)*, SW.Asia.

C. (Sinutor) COTTON & GODFREY, 1935 [*Ziziphinus incertus REEVE, 1863]. Sinistral. *Rec.*, Austral.

C. (Spikator) COTTON & GODFREY, 1935 [*C. spinulosum TATE, 1893]. Small, with cancellate sculpture. *Rec.*, Austral.

C. (Tristichotrochus) IKEBE, 1942 [*C. aculeatum SOWERBY, 1912]. With whorls shouldered, primary and secondary spirals mostly granulate. *Oligo.-Rec.*, Japan-W.N.Am.——FIG. 165,7. *C. (T.) aculeatum, Rec., Japan; ×1 (61).

C. (Ziziphinus) GRAY, 1843 [*Z. canaliculatus "MARTYN" HUMPHREY, 1786; SD REHDER, 1937]. Large for genus, spiral ribs smooth. *Oligo.-Rec.*, W.N.Am.

Astele SWAINSON, 1855 [*Trochus subcarinatus SWAINSON, 1855 (non PHILIPPI, 1843) = Calliostoma adamsi PILSBRY, 1890] [=Eutrochus A. ADAMS, 1864 (obj.)]. Like Calliostoma in form but with an umbilicus. *U.Cret.-Rec.*

A. (Astele). Spiral ribs beaded, umbilicus bounded by beaded cord. *U.Cret.-Rec.*, cosmop.——FIG. 165,8. *A. adamsi (PILSBRY), Rec., Tasmania; ×1 (147).

A. (Astelena) IREDALE, 1924 [*Ziziphinus scitulus A.ADAMS, 1855]. Small, aperture semilunar, columella long. *Rec.*, Australasia.

A. (Callistele) COTTON & GODFREY, 1935 [*A. calliston VERCO, 1905]. Umbilicus narrow. *Rec.*, Austral.

A. (Coralastele) IREDALE, 1930 [*C. allanae]. Conical, with pointed spire; umbilical pit deep. *Rec.*, Austral.-Japan.

A. (Dentistyla) DALL, 1889 [*Margarita asperrima DALL, 1881]. Sculpture nodulous; outer lip lirate within. *Mio.-Rec.*, Carib.

A. (Eurastele) COEN, 1946 [*A. (E.) lusitanica]. *Rec.*, Medit.

A. (Leiotrochus) CONRAD, 1862 [*L. distans]. Spire rather low; spiral ribs smooth. *Mio.*, E.N. Am.——FIG. 165,4. *A. (L.) distans (CONRAD), Mio., USA. (Md.); ×1 (203).

A. (Mazastele) IREDALE, 1936 [*Trochus glypta WATSON, 1886]. Sutures sunken; umbilicus very wide. *Rec.*, Austral.

A. (Omphalotukaia) YOSHIDA, 1948 [*Calliostoma hajimeanum]. Like Calliostoma (Otukaia) but umbilicate. *Rec.*, Japan.

A. (Pulchrastele) IREDALE, 1929 [*Calliostoma septenarium MELVILL & STANDEN, 1899]. Small, ribs noded. *Plio.-Rec.*, Austral.

A. (Scrobiculinus) MONTEROSATO, 1889 [*Trochus strigosus GMELIN, 1791]. Umbilicus a mere chink. *Rec.*, N.Afr.

Falsimargarita POWELL, 1951 [*Margarites gemma SMITH, 1915]. Like Calliostoma, but shell thin, iridescent, umbilicate. *Rec.*, Antarct.

?Kishinewia KOLESNIKOV, 1935 [*Phasianella bessarabica D'ORBIGNY, 1844]. High-spired, slightly carinate, aperture rounded. *Mio.(Sarmat.)*, SW. Asia.——FIG. 165,6. *K. bessarabica (D'ORBIGNY), Mio., USSR; ×2 (197).

Metaconulus COSSMANN, 1918 [*Trochus princeps DESHAYES, 1863]. Higher than wide, suture bordered above by nodose keel. *?U.Cret.; Eoc.-Oligo.*, Eu.-N.Afr.——FIG. 165,2. *M. princeps (DESHAYES), Eoc., Fr.; ×1 (147).

Photinastoma POWELL, 1951 [*Trochus taeniatus WOOD, 1828]. Shell resembling Photinula but radula nearer that of Calliostoma. *Rec.*, Antarct.

Photinula ADAMS & ADAMS, 1854 [*Margarita coerulescens KING & BRODERIP, 1831; SD FISCHER, 1875] [pro Photina ADAMS & ADAMS, 1853 (non BURMEISTER, 1838); Kingotrochus VONIHERING, 1902 (obj.)]. Depressed, nearly smooth, umbilicus concealed by callus. *Rec.*, Antarct.-S.Am.

?Sinzowia KOLESNIKOV, 1935 [*Trochus elatior D'ORBIGNY, 1845]. Turriculate, many-whorled, with a peripheral keel. *Mio.(Sarmat.)*, SW.Asia.——FIG. 165,1. *S. elatior (D'ORBIGNY), Mio., USSR.; ×3.3 (197).

Venustatrochus POWELL, 1951 [*V. georgianus]. Shell like other deep-water members of subfamily but radula with numerous lateral teeth. *Rec.*, S.Atl.

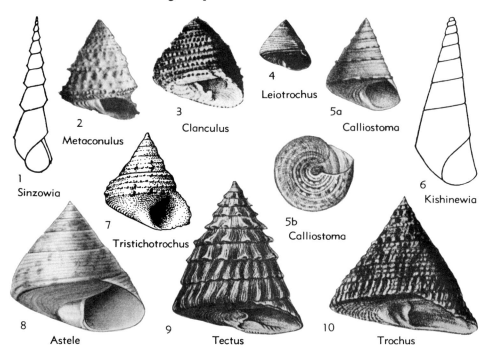

FIG. 165. Trochacea (Trochidae——Calliostomatinae, Trochinae) (p. *1257-1260*).

Subfamily TROCHINAE Rafinesque, 1815

[*nom. correct.* SWAINSON, 1840 (*pro* Trochidia RAFINESQUE, 1815)]

Conical or, less commonly, turbiniform, nodosely ornamented shells with considerable range of size, narrowly phaneromphalous, or anomphalous with base excavated in middle; aperture quadrangular with strongly discordant lips; outer lip sharp, strongly prosocline; columellar lip straight, emerging from umbilicus or basal excavation, smooth, undulating or toothed, commonly forming marked angle with basal margin. *U.Cret.-Rec.*

Trochus LINNÉ, 1758 [**T. maculatus;* SD IREDALE, 1912] [=*Polydonta* SCHUMACHER, 1817 (obj.); *Lamprostoma* SWAINSON, 1840 (obj.)]. Conical, base more or less flattened. *Mio.-Rec.*

T. (Trochus). Medium-sized to large; whorls flat-sided, periphery angular; ornament granose spiral cords; umbilicus or pseudumbilicus with callus coating; columellar lip separated by gap from parietal lip, multidentate to almost smooth, meeting basal lip in well-marked angle. *Mio.-Rec.*, Afr.-IndoPac.-Austral.——FIG. 165,*10.* *T. *(T.) maculatus,* Rec., Philippines; ×1.0 (147).

T. (Belangeria) FISCHER, 1879 [**T. scabrosus* PHILIPPI, 1850]. With a spirally grooved false umbilicus. *Rec.,* IndoPac.

T. (Coelotrochus) FISCHER, 1879 [**T. tiaratus* QUOY & GAIMARD, 1834] [=*Neozelandia* COSSMANN, 1918]. Relatively small, with slightly convex whorls and a deep false umbilicus. *Plio.-Rec.,* N.Z.

T. (Infundibulops) PILSBRY, 1889 [**T. erythraeus* BROCCHI, 1821]. Like *T. (Trochus)* but columella without folds or denticulations. *Pleist.-Rec.,* IndoPac.-Red Sea.

T. (Infundibulum) MONTFORT, 1810 [**T. concavus* GMELIN, 1791] [=*Carinidea* SWAINSON, 1840 (obj.)]. Surface with axial folds, base spirally ribbed; columella with single fold. *Rec.,* IndoPac.

T. (Praecia) GRAY, 1857 [**T. elegantulus* WOOD, 1828]. Relatively small, with wavy axial folds; columella ending in a tooth. *Rec.,* India.

T. (Thorista) IREDALE, 1915 [**Polydonta tuberculata* GRAY, 1843 = *Trochus viridis* GMELIN, 1791] [=*Anthora* GRAY, 1857 (*non* DOUBLEDAY, 1844) (obj.)]. Relatively small; upper surface with spirally arranged nodes; base with smooth spiral ribs. *Pleist.-Rec.,* N.Z.

T. (Thoristella) IREDALE, 1915 [**Polydonta chathamensis* HUTTON, 1873]. Small, smooth, periphery rounded-carinate, columella smooth. *Mio.-Rec.,* N.Z.

Clanculus MONTFORT, 1810 [**Trochus pharaonius* LINNÉ, 1758] [=*Otavia* RISSO, 1826; *Fragella* SWAINSON, 1840 (obj.)]. Rather small, rounded-

conical, surface most commonly beaded; columella with tooth; umbilical pit bordered with crenulate ridge. *U.Cret.-Rec.,* Afr.-IndoPac.-W.C.Am.

C. (Clanculus). With single strong tooth at base of columella. *U.Cret.(Maastricht.)-Rec.,* Eu.-Indo-Pac.-Australasia.——FIG. 165,3. *C. (C.) pharaonius* (LINNÉ), Rec., Red Sea; ×1 (147).

C. (Camitia) ADAMS & ADAMS, 1854 (*ex* GRAY MS) [*Camitia pulcherrima*]. Depressed, smooth. *Rec.,* IndoPac.

C. (Clanculopsis) MONTEROSATO, 1879 [*Trochus cruciatus* LINNÉ, 1758; SD SACCO, 1896] [=*Clanculella* SACCO, 1896]. With more than one denticle at end of columella. *Mio.-Rec.,* Eu.-IndoPac.

C. (Euclanculus) COTTON & GODFREY, 1934 [*C. leucomphalus* VERCO, 1905]. *Rec.,* Austral.

C. (Euriclanculus) COTTON & GODFREY, 1934 [*Trochus flagellatus* PHILIPPI, 1849]. *Plio.-Rec.,* Austral.

C. (Isoclanculus) COTTON & GODFREY, 1934 [*C. yatesi* CROSSE, 1863]. *Rec.,* Austral.

C. (Macroclanculus) COTTON & GODFREY, 1934 [*Monodonta undata* LAMARCK, 1816]. *Rec.,* Austral.

C. (Mesoclanculus) COTTON & GODFREY, 1934 [*Trochus plebejus* PHILIPPI, 1851]. *Rec.,* Austral.

C. (Microclanculus) COTTON & GODFREY, 1934 [*C. euchelioides* TATE, 1893]. *Rec.* Austral.

C. (?Panocochlea) DALL, 1908 [*C. (P.) rubidus*]. Depressed, nearly smooth, a single strong tooth at end of columella. *Rec.,* W.C.Am.

C. (Paraclanculus) FINLAY, 1927 [*P. peccatus*]. *Rec.,* Australasia.

Tectus MONTFORT, 1810 [*Trochus mauritianus* GMELIN, 1791] [=*Pyramis* SCHUMACHER, 1817 (*non* RÖDING, 1798); *Pyramidea* SWAINSON, 1840]. Conical, higher than wide, base nearly smooth; no umbilicus; columella with a strong spiral fold. *U.Cret.-Rec.,* IndoPac.-E.Indies.

T. (Tectus). Medium-sized to large, with axial folds on spire. *U.Cret.-Rec.,* Eu.-Afr.-IndoPac.-Japan.——FIG. 165,9. *T. (T.) mauritianus* (GMELIN), Rec., E.Indies; ×0.7 (147).

T. (Cardinalia) GRAY, 1847 [*Trochus virgatus* GMELIN, 1791]. Upper surface with beaded spiral ribs; columellar fold weak. *Plio.-Rec.,* IndoPac.

T. (Rochia) GRAY, 1857 [*Trochus acutangulus* "CHEMNITZ" (not binominal) = *T. conus* GMELIN, 1791]. Like *T. (Cardinalia)* but with columellar fold ending in tooth. *Plio.-Rec.,* E. Indies.

Subfamily UMBONIINAE Pilsbry, 1886

Medium-sized shells, mostly of lenticular form; umbilicus partly or entirely filled by a callus pad. *U.Cret.-Rec.*

Umbonium LINK, 1807 [*Trochus vestiarius* LINNÉ, 1758; SD PILSBRY, 1889] [=*Globulus* SCHUMACHER, 1817 (obj.); *Rotella* LAMARCK, 1822 (obj.)]. Solid, glossy, smooth or spirally striated. *Mio.-Rec.,* Pac.-E.Indies.

U. (Umbonium). Suture indistinct, callus plug circular, complete. *Plio.-Rec.,* Japan-IndoPac.——FIG. 166,7. *U. (U.) vestiarium* (LINNÉ), Rec., E.Indies; *7a,b,* ×1 (147).

U. (Ethalia) ADAMS & ADAMS, 1854 [*Rotella guamensis* QUOY & GAIMARD, 1834; SD PILSBRY, 1889] [=*Liotrochus* FISCHER in KIENER, 1879]. Callus only partly filling umbilicus. *Mio.-Rec.,* Pac.

U. (Ethaliella) PILSBRY, 1905 [*Ethalia floccata* SOWERBY, 1903]. Callus pad small, not filling umbilicus. *Rec.,* Pac.

U. (Protorotella) MAKIYAMA, 1925 [*P. yuantaniensis*]. Suture abutting, callus broad, filling umbilicus. *Mio.,* Japan.——FIG. 166,10. *U. (P.) yuantaniensis*, Mio., Japan; ×2 (147).

U. (Suchium) MAKIYAMA, 1925 [*U. suchiense* YOKOYAMA, 1923; SD MAKIYAMA, 1927]. Whorls with spiral ribs; callus divided into 2 lobes. *L. Plio.-Rec.,* Japan.——FIG. 166,9. *U. (S.) suchiense,* Plio., Japan; ×0.7 (147).

U. (Zethalia) FINLAY, 1927 [*U. zelandicum* A. ADAMS, 1854] [=*Ethaliopsis* COSSMANN, 1918 (*non* SCHEPMAN, 1908)]. Almost without umbilicus; callus bordered by beaded ridge. *Plio.-Rec.,* N.Z.——FIG. 166,4. *U. (Z.) zelandicum,* Rec., N.Z.; ×1 (147).

Antisolarium FINLAY, 1927 [*Solarium egenum* GOULD, 1849]. Spire conical, with beaded ribs; columellar lip only slightly reflected over umbilicus. *Oligo.-Rec.,* N.Z.-Pac.——FIG. 166,2. *A. egenum* (GOULD), Rec., N.Z.; *2a,b,* ×2 (147).

Callumbonella THIELE, 1924 [*Gibbula gorgonarum* FISCHER, 1883] [=*Umbotrochus* THIELE, 1924 (*non* PERNER, 1908) (obj.)]. Spire conical, periphery angulate, base convex; umbilical callus narrow. *Rec.,* E.Atl.——FIG. 166,11. *C. gorganarum* (FISCHER), Cape Verde; ×2 (147).

Ethminolia IREDALE, 1924 [*E. probabilis*]. Depressed-trochoid, widely umbilicate, small. *Rec.,* Austral.-Japan.

E. (Ethminolia). Whorls shouldered medially. *Rec.,* Austral.

E. (Sericominolia) KURODA & HABE, 1954 [*Minolia stearnsi* PILSBRY, 1895]. Whorls rounded. *Rec.,* Japan.——FIG. 166,8. *E. (S.) stearnsi* (PILSBRY); ×4 (199).

Isanda ADAMS & ADAMS, 1854 [*I. coronata* A.ADAMS, 1854]. Solid, small, polished. *U.Cret.-Rec.,* Indo-Pac.-Austral.-N.Z.

I. (Isanda). Globose, umbilicus bordered by a beaded rib. *Rec.,* IndoPac.——FIG. 166,3. *I. (I.) coronata,* Austral.; ×1 (147).

I. (Archiminolia) IREDALE, 1929 [*Monilea oleacea* HEDLEY & PETTERD, 1905]. *Rec.,* Austral.

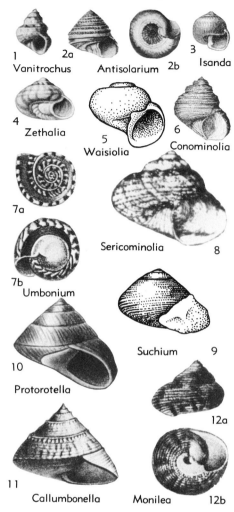

1 Vanitrochus   2a Antisolarium   2b   3 Isanda

4 Zethalia   5 Waisiolia   6 Conominolia

7a

Sericominolia   8

7b Umbonium

Suchium   9

10 Protorotella

12a

11 Callumbonella   Monilea   12b

FIG. 166. Trochacea (Trochidae——Umboniinae)
(p. I260-I261).

I. (Conominolia) FINLAY, 1927 [*Heliacus conicus MARSHALL, 1917]. Spire with three noded ribs; base with numerous spirals; umbilicus wide. U.Cret.(Wangaloan)-Mio., N.Z.——FIG. 166,6. *I. (C.) conica (MARSHALL), U.Cret.(Wangaloan); ×2 (183).

I. (Conotalopia) IREDALE, 1929 (*Minolia henniana MELVILL, 1891]. With 2 spiral keels. Rec., S.Pac.

I. (Parminolia) IREDALE, 1929 [*Minolia agapeta MELVILL & STANDEN, 1896 = Monilea apicina GOULD, 1861]. Rec., S.Pac.

I. (Umbonella) A.ADAMS, 1863 [*Turbo murreus REEVE, 1848]. Whorls smooth; small. Rec., Indo-Pac.

I. (Vanitrochus) IREDALE, 1929 [*Solariella tragema MELVILL & STANDEN, 1869] [=Conotrochus PILSBRY, 1889 (non SCHRÖTER, 1863)]. Small, spire relatively high, with spiral ribs. Oligo.-Rec., E.Indies-Austral.——FIG. 166,1. *I. (V.) tragema (MELVILL & STANDEN), Rec., Loyalty Is.; ×5 (147).

I. (Waisiolia) BEETS, 1942 [*I. (W.) jucanda]. With 2 peripheral angulations; deeply umbilicate. U.Oligo., E.Indies.——FIG. 166,5. *I. (W.) jucanda; ×10 (163).

Monilea SWAINSON, 1840 [*Trochus calliferus LAMARCK, 1822] [=Talopia GRAY, 1842 (nom. nud.)]. Elevated, spirally ribbed. Plio.-Rec., E. Indies-Pac.-India.

M. (Monilea). Medium-sized, inner lip thickened and recurved but not concealing umbilicus. Plio.-Rec., W.Pac.-S.Pac.——FIG. 166,12. *M. (M.) callifera (LAMARCK), Rec., E.Indies; 12a,b, ×1 (147).

M. (Priotrochus) FISCHER in KIENER, 1879 [*Trochus obscurus WOOD, 1828; SD PILSBRY, 1889] [=Aphanotrochus MARTENS, 1880 (obj.)]. Umbilicus closed; inner lip with denticles. Pleist.-Rec., E.Afr.-India.

M. (Rossiteria) BRAZIER, 1895 [*Trochus nucleus PHILIPPI, 1849] [pro Solanderia FISCHER in KIENER, 1879 (non DUCHASSAING & MICHELIN, 1846)]. Small, umbilicus wide, not set off by angle, spirally ribbed within; inner lip widened. Plio.-Rec., E.Indies.

M. (Talopena) IREDALE, 1918 [*M. incerta]. Small, spirally ribbed above, smoother below; umbilicus wide, bounded by smooth rib. Rec., S.Pac.

Subfamily SOLARIELLINAE Powell, 1951

Conical with open umbilicus; aperture more or less circular; radula with an exceptionally small number of marginal teeth (121). U.Cret.-Rec.

Solariella WOOD, 1842 [*S. maculata]. Last whorl rounded or with obsolete keel. Mio.-Rec., Eu.-Atl.-IndoPac.-Arct.-E.Asia-W.Indies.

S. (Solariella). Umbilicus bounded by a beaded spiral rib. U.Cret.-Rec., cosmop.——FIG. 167,8. *S. (S.) maculata, Plio., Eng.; 8a,b, ×2 (231).

S. (Bowdenagaza) WOODRING, 1928 [*Microgaza cossmanni]. Small; aperture relatively large, ovate. Mio., W.Indies.

S. (Ethaliopsis) SCHEPMAN, 1908 [*S. (E.) callomphala]. Umbilicus partly concealed by inner lip. Rec., Atl.-IndoPac.

S. (Machaeroplax) FRIELE, 1877 [*Margarita affinis FRIELE, 1877, ex JEFFREYS MS]. Relatively high-spired, with well-developed spiral ribs and collabral striae. Mio.-Rec., N.Am.-Atl.-Arct.-N.Pac.——FIG. 167,5. *S. (M.) affinis (FRIELE), Rec., N.Atl.; ×5 (213).

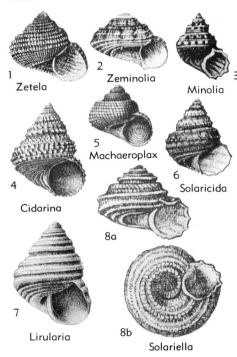

1 Zetela
2 Zeminolia
3 Minolia
5 Machaeroplax
4 Cidarina
6 Solaricida
8a
7 Lirularia
8b Solariella

Fig. 167. Trochacea (Trochidae——Solariellinae)
(p. 1261-1262).

S. (Microgaza) Dall, 1881 [*M. rotella]. Spire low, aperture subquadrate. Rec., Carib.

S. (Micropiliscus) Dall, 1927 [*S. (M.) constricta]. Initial whorls colored, not glassy. Rec., SE.USA.

S. (Solaricida) Dall, 1919 [*S. (S.) hondoensis]. Resembling Cidarina but with wider umbilicus. Rec., Japan.——Fig. 167,6. *S. (S.) hondoensis; ×1 (191).

S. (Spectamen) Iredale, 1924 [*Trochus philippensis Watson, 1880]. Spire moderately high, turriculate. Plio.-Rec., Austral.

S. (Suavotrochus) Dall, 1924 [*S. lubrica Dall, 1881]. Almost or entirely smooth; in deep water. Rec., W.Indies.

S. (Zetela) Finlay, 1927 [*Minolia textilis Murdoch & Suter, 1906]. Small, sculpture sharply cancellate, spiral ribs beaded on last whorl. ?Mio.-Rec., S.Pac.——Fig. 167,1. *S. (Z.) textilis (Murdoch & Suter), Rec., N.Z.; ×5.

Cidarina Dall, 1909 [*Margarita cidaris Carpenter, 1864]. Large, resembling Bathybembix, with channeled suture and nodose sculpture; umbilicus nearly closed by reflected inner lip. Pleist.-Rec., W.N.Am.——Fig. 167,4. *C. cidaris (Carpenter), Rec., Calif.; ×1 (230).

?Lirularia Dall, 1909 [*Margarites lirulata Carpenter, 1864]. Small, with strong spiral and deli-

cate axial sculpture; peristome interrupted by last whorl; umbilicus narrower than in Solariella. Pleist.-Rec., W.N.Am.——Fig. 167,7. L. lirulata (Carpenter), Rec., Washington; ×3 (172).

Minolia A.Adams, 1860 [*M. punctata] [=Minosia Dunker, 1882 (obj.); Minolops Iredale, 1929]. Resembling Solariella but in general larger; periostracum marked with spots and stripes of color. U.Cret.-Rec., W.Pac.-N.Z.——Fig. 167,3. *M. punctata, Rec., Korea; ×1 (147).

?Zeminolia Finlay, 1927 [*Minolia plicatula Murdoch & Suter, 1906]. Small, initial whorls relatively large; umbilicus wide. Mio.-Rec., N.Z.—— Fig. 167,2. *Z. plicatula (Murdoch & Suter), Rec., N.Z.; ×5 (147).

Subfamily HALISTYLINAE Keen, 1958

Small, cylindrical shells, smooth or spirally striate. Radula suggesting some affinity with Umboniinae. Pleist.-Rec.

Halistylus Dall, 1890 [*Cantharidus (H.) columna]. Pleist.-Rec., N.Am.-S.Am.——Fig. 162,3. *H. columna (Dall), Rec., Brazil; ×5 (147).

TROCHIDAE Subfamily UNCERTAIN

Kittlitrochus Cossmann, 1909 [pro Paratrochus Kittl, 1899 (non Pilsbry, 1893)] [*Tectus? margine-nodosus J.Böhm, 1895] [=Paratrochoides Tomlin, 1929 (obj.)]. Small, high cyrtoconoid, with high flat-sided whorls and deep sutures; narrowly phaneromphalous; faint collabral ribs on early whorls; characters of aperture unknown. M.Trias.(Ladin.), S.Tyrol.

Trochodon Seeley, 1861 [*Trochus (Trochodon) cancellatus]. Founded on broken internal molds, showing traces of spiral ribbing, of conical gastropods with internally denticulate outer lip. U. Cret.(Cenom.), Eng.

Family ATAPHRIDAE Cossmann, 1918

Small or small-medium, turbiniform or trochiform, with flat to moderately convex, smooth whorls forming usually cyrtoconoid spire with even outline; shell wall thick; base convex; anomphalous, or possibly cryptomphalous in some forms; aperture orbicular or almost so; columellar lip concave in most forms, meeting parietal lip in uninterrupted curve; callus commonly forming tubercle on columellar lip or semicircular pad partly covering base; operculum and shell structure unknown. Trias.-U.Cret.

Ataphrus Gabb, 1869 [*A. crassus]. Convexity of spire whorls feeble; columellar lip with broad outer face; base without median callus pad. L.Jur.-U.Cret.(Maastricht.), cosmop.

A. (**Ataphrus**). Outer face of columellar lip smooth or with basal denticle, and not limited by a strong carina. *M.Jur.(Baj.) - U.Cret. (Maastricht.)*, cosmop.——Fig. 168,7. *A. (A.) acmon* (D'ORBIGNY), M.Jur.(Baj.), Eng.; ×1.75 (59).

A. (**Endianaulax**) COSSMANN, 1902 [*E. planicallosum*]. Outer face of columellar lip without denticle and limited by strong carina. *L.Jur.(Lias.)-U.Jur.(Portland.)*, Eu.——Fig. 168,5. *A. (E.) richei* COSSMANN, M.Jur.(Baj.), Eng.; ×1.75 (59).

A. (**Plocostylus**) GEMMELLARO, 1878 [*P. typus*]. Columellar lip with conspicuous tubercle facing towards aperture. *L.Jur.(L.Lias.)*, Sicily.——Fig. 168,4. *A. (P.) typus;* ×2.25 (187).

Cirsostylus COSSMANN, 1918 [*Trochus glandulus* LAUBE, 1869]. Columellar lip vertical, with distinct outer margin, and with strong fold at its lower end. *Trias.-L.Jur.(L.Lias.)*, Eu.——Fig. 168,6. *C. glandulus* (LAUBE), M.Trias.(Ladin.), S. Tyrol; ×1.5 (64).

Trochopsidea WENZ, 1938 [*pro Trochopsis* GEMMELLARO, 1879 (*non* EHRENBERG, 1832)] [*Trochopsis moroi;* SD COSSMANN, 1918]. Whorls more convex than in *Ataphrus;* outer face of columellar lip relatively narrow, with narrow furrow parallel to its margin but without tubercle; type species described as having 4 spiral grooves, not reaching margin, in outer wall of aperture. *L.Jur.-M.Jur.(Baj.)*, Eu.——Fig. 168,1. *T. paludinoides* (HUDLESTON), M.Jur.(Baj.), Eng.; ×2.4 (59).

Lewisiella STOLICZKA, 1868 [*Pitonnellus conicus* D'ORBIGNY, 1853]. [=*Aulacotrochus* COSSMANN, 1916]. Moderately elevated, whorls more convex than in *Ataphrus;* inner lip without denticle, but extended above as semicircular callous pad covering middle of base and circumscribed by groove. *L.Jur.*, Eu.——Fig. 168,3. *L. conica* (D'ORBIGNY), U.Lias., Fr.; ×4.5 (111).

?**Parataphrus** CHAVAN, 1954 [*Trochus viadrinus* M. SCHMIDT, 1905]. *Ataphrus*-like, but with spirally striated whorls and very narrow umbilicus; outer lip with outer face widening toward junction with basal lip and with furrow parallel with its margin. *U.Jur.*, Eu.——Fig. 168,2. *P. viadrinus* (SCHMIDT), Ger.; ×4 (167).

Family STOMATELLIDAE Gray, 1840

[=Stomatiidae STOLICZKA, 1868]

Few-whorled, mostly low-spired shells, not umbilicate; operculum wanting in most groups; aperture large, interior of last whorl entirely visible through it from below. *Trias.-Rec.*

Mesogena (KUTASSY, 1940, *nom. nud.*), Cox, n.gen.[1]

[1] Proposed by KUTASSY with citation of type species but without diagnosis and therefore a *nomen nudum*, needing validation.

[*Inoceramus arctus* HOERNES, 1855]. Rather

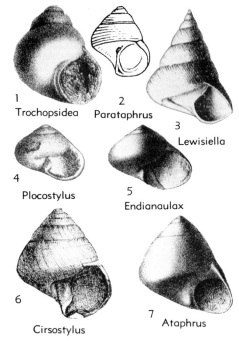

1 Trochopsidea 2 Parataphrus 3 Lewisiella 4 Plocostylus 5 Endianaulax 6 Cirsostylus 7 Ataphrus

FIG. 168. Trochacea (Ataphridae) (p.1263).

small, auriform, with very rapidly expanding whorls and evenly convex surface, without carinae; ornament fine spiral and collabral threads, with collabral undulations in type species. *U.Trias. (Nor.)*, Eu.——Fig. 169,7. *M. arcta* (HÖRNES), Aus.; ×3 (79).

Praestomatia (KUTASSY, 1940, *nom. nud.*), Cox, n. gen.[1] [*Stomatia acutangula* KOKEN, 1897]. Small, with rapidly expanding whorls having flattened upper surface separated by carina from almost vertical, moderately high outer face which may carry 2 spiral angulations; ornament collabral ridges. *U.Trias.(Nor.)-U.Jur.*, Eu.——Fig. 169,1. *P. acutangula* (KOKEN), U.Trias.(Nor.), Aus.; *1a,b*, ×10 (79).

Stomatella LAMARCK, 1816 [*S. auricula;* SD ANTON, 1839] [=*Phymotis* RAFINESQUE, 1815 (*nom. nud.*); *Plocamotis* FISCHER, 1885]. Ear-shaped, without operculum. *Rec.*, E.Indies-IndoPac.

S. (**Stomatella**). Surface smooth. *Plio.-Rec.*, Indo-Pac.——Fig. 169,3. *S. (S.) auricula*, E.Indies; *3a,b*, ×2 (213).

S. (**Gena**) GRAY, 1850 [*Stomatella nigra* QUOY & GAIMARD, 1834; SD THIELE, 1924]. Last whorl finely spirally striate. *Rec.*, IndoPac.

Broderipia GRAY, 1847 [*Scutella rosea* BRODERIP, 1834]. Oval, limpet-shaped. *Rec. Pac.*——Fig. 169,6. *B. rosea* (BRODERIP), S.Pac.; *6a-c*, ×3 (147).

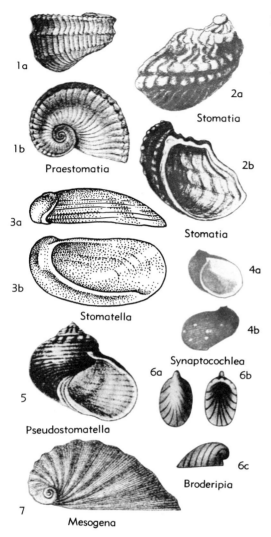

1a

1b
Praestomatia

2a
Stomatia

2b

3a

3b
Stomatella

Stomatia

4a

4b
Synaptocochlea

6a　　6b

5
Pseudostomatella

6c
Broderipia

7
Mesogena

Fig. 169. Trochacea (Stomatellidae) (p. 1263-1264).

Pseudostomatella Thiele, 1924 [*Stomatella papyracea* "Chemnitz," A.Adams (=*Turbo papyraceus* Gmelin, 1791)] [=*Stomatella (partim)* auctt., *non* Lamarck, 1816]. Spire short, conical, not plicate below suture; sculpture of more or less rough spiral ribs; operculum, if present, multispiral. *Rec.,* Austral.-IndoPac.

  P. (Pseudostomatella). Relatively large, spire not flattened, last whorl inflated; sculpture various. *Rec.,* IndoPac.——Fig. 169,5. *P. papyracea* (Gmelin), E.Indies; ×1 (147).

  P. (Stomatolina) Iredale, 1937 [*Stomatella rufescens* Gray, 1847]. Depressed, sculpture spiral or decussate. *Rec.,* Austral.-IndoPac.

Roya Iredale, 1912 [*R. kermadecensis*]. Resembling *Broderipia* but apex not terminal but at about 0.8 of length; muscle impression horseshoe-shaped, in 2 parts. *Oligo-Rec.,* N.Z.-IndoPac.

Stomatia Helbling, 1779 [*S. phymotis*] [=*Stomax* Montfort, 1810 (obj.)]. Whorls plicate below sutures; with several spiral ribs; aperture ovate-triangular; no operculum. *Rec.,* RedSea-Pac.-E.Indies.

  S. (Stomatia). Ear-shaped, oblique, spire small. *Rec.,* IndoPac.——Fig. 169,2. *S. (S.) phymotis*, Red Sea; 2a,b, ×0.7 (147).

  S. (Microtis) Adams & Adams, 1850 [*M. tuberculata* A.Adams, 1850] [*Microtina* A.Adams in Sowerby, 1854 (obj.)]. Low, rather flat, with 2 tuberculate ridges; columellar margin visible within to apex of spire. *Rec.,* Pac.

  S. (?Miraconcha) Bergh in Schepman, 1908 [*M. obscura*]. Shell membranous and iridescent. *Rec.,* E.Indies.

Synaptocochlea Pilsbry, 1890 [*Stomatella montrouzieri* (?=*S. stellata* Souverbie, 1863)]. Spire very short, submarginal; surface spirally striate or decussate; aperture longer than wide; shell somewhat porcelaneous; operculum present. *Rec.,* S. Pac.-Carib.——Fig. 169,4. *S. stellata* (Souverbie), N.Caledonia; 4a,b, ×2 (147).

Family TURBINIDAE Rafinesque, 1815

[*nom. correct. et transl.* Gray, 1824 (*ex* Turbinacea Rafinesque, 1815)]

Strong, solid shells, small to large, few-whorled, globose; rarely smooth but mostly with well-developed sculpture; aperture nacreous within; peristome entire in most genera, rounded, lying in one plane; columella smooth, arched; operculum calcareous, spiral, with central or eccentric nucleus (42). Mainly in warm seas. *M. Trias.-Rec.*

Subfamily ASTRAEINAE Davies, 1933

[=Astraliinae Adams & Adams, 1851]

Conical with more or less carinate periphery; base flattened; operculum most commonly oval. *M.Trias.-Rec.*

Rothpletzella J.Böhm, 1895 [*R. richthofeni* (?=*Coelocentrus infracarinatus* Kittl, 1894)]. Depressed biconical, anomphalous, with carinate periphery; ornament opisthocline ridges crossing orthocline growth lines and ending in hollow thorns at periphery, spiral cords on base. *M.Trias.,* ?*L.Cret.,* Eu. [Most post-Triassic species included by Cossmann in this genus seem unrelated to the type species.]——Fig. 170,1. *R. richthofeni*, M. Trias.(Ladin.), S.Tyrol; ×1 (147).

1 Rothpletzella

2 Astralium

3a Bolma

3b Bolma

4a

5 Ormastralium

6 Pomaulax

4b

7 Astraea

Guildfordia

FIG. 170. Trochacea (Turbinidae——Astraeinae) (p. *1264-1266*).

Coelobolma COSSMANN, 1918 [*C. corbarica*]. Large, depressed conical, anomphalous but with median funnel-like excavation of base; ornament granose spiral cords; aperture very oblique; callosity of inner lip extending rather broadly over base. *U.Cret.(Cenom.-Senon.),* Eu.-Asia.

Astraea RÖDING, 1798 [*Trochus imperialis* GMELIN, 1791; SD SUTER, 1913 = *T. heliotropium* MARTYN, 1784 (ICZN op. 479)] [=*Imperator* MONTFORT, 1810 (obj.); *Canthorbis* SWAINSON, 1840 (obj.); *Macropelmus* GISTEL, 1848 (obj.)]. Periphery variously ornamented with spines. *Eoc.-Rec.,* cosmop.

A. (Astraea). Widely umbilicate. *Mio.-Rec.,* Australasia.——FIG. 170,7. *A. heliotropium* (MARTYN), Rec., N.Z.; ×0.7 (147).

A. (Astralium) LINK, 1807 [*Turbo calcar* LINNÉ, 1758; SD FISCHER, 1873] [=*Calcar* MONTFORT, 1810 (obj.); *Cyclocantha* SWAINSON, 1840; *Stella* HERRMANNSEN, 1849]. Moderately large, resembling *A. (Astraea),* but not umbilicate. *Eoc.-Rec.,* Eu.-E.Indies-W.Indies-?S.Am.——FIG. 170,

2. *A. (A.) calcar* (LINNÉ), Rec., IndianO.; ×1 (213).

A. (Bellastraea) IREDALE, 1924 [*B. kesteveni*]. Stellate, umbilicate, rather small. *Plio.-Rec.,* Austral.

A. (Bolma) RISSO, 1826 [*Turbo rugosus* LINNÉ, 1767] [=*Oobolma* SACCO, 1896]. More turbinate than *A. (Astraea),* not umbilicate, with noded sutures; operculum with spiral ribs. *Mio.-Rec.,* Eu.-W.Afr.-IndoPac.——FIG. 170,3. *A. (B.) rugosa* (LINNÉ), Rec., Medit.; *3a,b,* ×0.7 (147).

A. (Cookia) LESSON, 1832 [*Trochus sulcatus* GMELIN, 1791 (ICZN op. 479)] [=*Tubicanthus* SWAINSON, 1840 (obj.)]. Whorls somewhat inflated, with axial folds above periphery; operculum with 2 ribs. *Rec.,* Australasia.

A. (Distellifer) IREDALE, 1937 [*D. wallisi*]. High-conical, with double row of spinose tubercles at periphery; no umbilicus. *Rec.,* Austral.

A. (Incilaster) FINLAY, 1927 [*Turbo marshalli* THOMPSON, 1907]. Whorls nodose-keeled above suture; not umbilicate. *Eoc.,* Australasia.

A. (Lithopoma) GRAY, 1850 [*Trochus tuber LINNÉ, 1767] [=Pachypoma GRAY, 1850]. Periphery more rounded than in A. (Astraea), sculpture subdued; no umbilicus; operculum with submarginal nucleus, with or without spiral rib, surface coarsely granulose. Mio.-Rec., Carib.

A. (Micrastraea) COTTON, 1939 [*Trochus aureus JONAS, 1844]. Like A. (Astralium) but smaller, more depressed. Rec., Austral.

A. (Opella) FINLAY, 1927 [*A. subfimbriata SUTER, 1917]. Like A. (Bellastraea) but with higher spire. Oligo.-Mio., N.Z.

A. (Ormastralium) SACCO, 1896 [*Trochus fimbriatus BORSON, 1821] [=Tylastralium SACCO, 1896]. Whorls with 2 keels armed with blunt spines; operculum convex, smooth. Mio.-Plio., Eu.——FIG. 170,5. *A. (O.) fimbriata (BORSON), Plio., Italy; ×1 (147).

A. (Pagocalcar) IREDALE, 1937 [*Trochus limbiferus KIENER, 1850]. Periphery a wavy flange; whorls disjunct, adult pagodoid in form. Rec., Austral.

A. (Pomaulax), GRAY, 1850 [*Trochus japonicus DUNKER, 1845; SD FISCHER, 1873] [=Pachypoma AUCTT.; non Pomaulax AUCTT.]. Moderately large, solid, with coarsely granular axial sculpture; operculum ovate, convex, with terminal nucleus. Mio.-Rec., W.N.Am.-Japan.——FIG. 170, 6. *A. (P.) japonicus (DUNKER), Rec., Japan; ×0.7 (179).

A. (Rugastella) IREDALE, 1937 [*Trochus rotularius LAMARCK, 1822]. Like A. (Astralium) but periphery with puckered transverse bars. Rec., Austral.

A. (Uvanilla) GRAY, 1850 [*Trochus unguis WOOD, 1828; SD FISCHER, 1873] [=Pomaulax AUCTT. non GRAY]. Moderate-sized to large, sculptured with granular axial folds; operculum ovate, nucleus nearly terminal, outer face with 2 to 3 strong curved ribs. Mio.-Rec., Eu.-E.Indies-W.N.Am.-C.Am.

Guildfordia GRAY, 1850 [*Astralium triumphans PHILIPPI, 1841; SD FISCHER, 1873]. Depressed, periphery with spines; umbilicus covered in part. Plio.-Rec., IndoPac.-E.Asia.

G. (Guildfordia). Peripheral spines long, recurved, widely spaced; operculum smooth. Plio.-Rec., E.Indies-Japan.——FIG. 170,4. *G. triumphans (PHILIPPI), Rec., Japan; ×0.7 (147).

G. (Pseudastralium) SCHEPMAN, 1908 [*Astralium (P.) abyssorum]. Like G. (Guildfordia) but peripheral spines short and more numerous; operculum granular. Rec., IndoPac.

Subfamily LIOTIINAE Adams & Adams, 1854

Relatively small, with both axial and spiral sculpture; spire low to flattened; operculum chitinous within but with outer

surface calcareous or at least with calcareous granules; aperture nacreous. Trias.-Rec.

Eucycloscala COSSMANN, 1895 [*Trochus binodosus MÜNSTER, 1841; SD COX, herein] [=Trochoscala KOKEN, 1897; Urceolabrum WADE, 1917]. Small, ovate-conical, anomphalous or phaneromphalous, with moderately high spire of convex whorls bearing collabral ribs crossed by few spiral threads; aperture suborbicular, peristome continuous; outer lip varicose. M.Trias.(Ladin.)-U.Cret.(Dan.), Eu.-N.Am.——FIG. 171,10. *E. binodosa (MÜNSTER), M.Trias.(Ladin.), S.Tyrol; ×2.5 (89).

?Microcheilus KITTL, 1894 [*Cochlearia brauni KLIPSTEIN, 1845] [=Microchilus COSSMANN, 1895 (obj.); Pseudocochlearia COSSMANN, 1895 (pro Microcheilus KITTL, non Microchilus BLANCHARD, 1851); Pseudocochlearella WENZ, 1944]. Small, turriculate, with high cyrtoconoid spire of subangular, peripherally costate whorls; coiling of last whorl irregular; aperture orbicular, with much-thickened, continuous peristome. M.Trias. (Ladin.), Eu.——FIG. 171,1. *M. brauni (KLIPSTEIN), S.Tyrol; 1a,b, ×3.75 (64).

Scaevola GEMMELLARO, 1879 [*S. intermedia; SD COSSMANN, 1918]. Sinistral, turbiniform, phaneromphalous; whorls strongly convex, last one somewhat expanded; ornament well separated collabral ribs and spiral threads; aperture orbicular, with continuous thickened peristome. L.Jur., Sicily.——FIG. 171,8. *S. intermedia; ×1 (147).

Pseudoliotina COSSMANN, 1925 [*Liotia sensuyi VIDAL, 1921]. Discoidal, upper face flat; outer face limited by 2 nodose carinae, 3rd carina forming umbilical margin; aperture orbicular, not oblique, with much thickened peristome. U.Cret. (Maastricht.), Eu.——FIG. 171,6. *P. sensuyi; 6a,b, ×2 (18).

Liotia GRAY, 1847 [*Delphinula cancellata GRAY, 1828]. Axial and spiral ribs well developed, forming latticed surface; umbilicus funnel-shaped, bounded by beaded cord; operculum concave, of many narrow whorls. Mio.-Rec., E.Indies-W.Indies-N.Am.-S.Am.——FIG. 171,3. *L. cancellata (GRAY), Rec., Chile; ×3 (213).

Arene ADAMS & ADAMS, 1854 [*Turbo cruentatus MÜHLFELD, 1824; SD WOODRING, 1928]. With several spiral cords or carinae, smooth or with vaulted scales; remainder of surface finely beaded. Mio.-Rec., N.Am.

A. (Arene). With spiral funicular cord in umbilicus and low varix at outer lip; spire moderately elevated. Mio.-Rec., W.Indies-W.N.Am.——FIG. 171,5. *A. cruentata (MÜHLFELD), Rec., W. Indies; ×2 (147).

A. (Marevalvata) OLSSON & HARBISON, 1953 [*Architectonica tricarinata STEARNS, 1872]. Lacking spiral funicular cord; peristome not thickened, spire low. Plio.-Rec., Fla.-W.Indies.

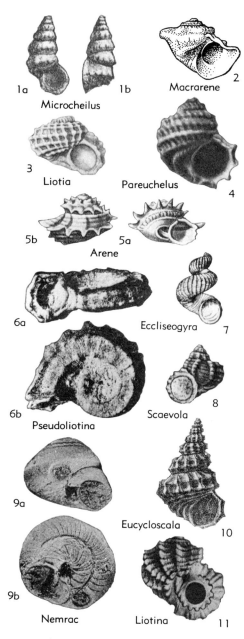

la 1b
Microcheilus
Macrarene 2

3
Liotia
Pareuchelus 4

5b 5a
Arene

6a
Eccliseogyra 7

6b
Pseudoliotina
Scaevola 8

9a
Eucycloscala 10

9b

Nemrac
Liotina 11

Fig. 171. Trochacea (Turbinidae——Liotiinae)
(p. 1266-1267).

Eccliseogyra DALL, 1892 [*Delphinula nitida* VER-RILL, 1885]. Small, iridescent, whorls disjunct, with both axial and spiral riblets. *Rec.*, E.N.Am.——FIG. 171,7. *E. nitida* (VERRILL), Rec., off Md.; ×5 (172).

Ilaira ADAMS & ADAMS, 1854 [*Delphinula evoluta* REEVE, 1843] [=*Liotiaxis* IREDALE, 1936]. Depressed, openly umbilicate, with 4 tuberculate carinae. *Rec.*, E.Indies-Austral.-?Atl.

Liotina FISCHER, 1885 [*Delphinula gervillei* DE-FRANCE, 1818; SD COSSMANN, 1888]. Relatively large, with well-developed lip varix; umbilicus bordered by rib, pitted outside, spiral ridge within; operculum with calcareous layer, tesselated, edges bristly. *Eoc.-Rec.*, Eu.-Afr.-IndoPac.-Austral.

L. (Liotina). Axial sculpture present throughout, inner lip rounded. *Eoc.-Rec.*, Eu.-N.Afr.-E.Afr.-IndoPac.-Australasia.——FIG. 171,11. *L. gervillei* (DEFRANCE), M.Eoc., Fr.; ×2 (147).

L. (Austroliotia) COTTON, 1948 [*Liotia botanica* HEDLEY, 1915]. Low, sculpture latticed as in *Liotia;* umbilicus wide; operculum with faint calcareous granules. *Rec.*, Australasia.

L. (Dentarene) IREDALE, 1929 [*D. sarcina; pro Delphinula crenata* KIENER, 1839 (*non* SOWERBY, 1833)]. Axial sculpture partly obsolete or interrupted; umbilical ridge running into a twisted appendage of inner lip. *Rec.*, E.Indies-Austral.

L. (Globarene) IREDALE, 1929 [*Delphinula cidaris* REEVE, 1843]. Umbilicus small. *Rec.*, E. Indies.

L. (Liotinaria) HABE, 1955 [*Liotia solidula* GOULD, 1859]. Umbilicus narrow and deep, with pitted surface. *Rec.*, Japan.

Macrarene HERTLEIN & STRONG, 1951 [*Liotia californica* DALL, 1908]. Large for family, depressed-turbinate, periphery rounded-stellate. *Rec.*, W.N.Am.——FIG. 171,2. *M. californica* (DALL), Rec., W.Mex.; ×1 (223).

?Nemrac CLARK & DURHAM, 1946 [*N. carmenensis*]. Smooth except for beaded sutural band and axial grooves on base; with wide umbilical ridge crossed by grooves. *Eoc.*, S.Am.——FIG. 171,9. *N. carmenensis*, Eoc., Colombia; ×5 (169).

Pareuchelus BOETTGER, 1907 [*Euchelus (P.) excellens*]. With several spiral ribs latticed by axial sculpture; basal margin of aperture forming angle above last spiral keel. *Eoc.-Plio.*, Eu.-E.Indies.——FIG. 171,4. *P. excellens* (BOETTGER), M.Mio., Hung.; ×10 (147).

Subfamily HELICOCRYPTINAE Cox, n. subfam.

Small, smooth, lenticular, involute shells with narrow apical and very narrow basal umbilici; corner of aperture filled with callus, rendering peristome continuous and almost orbicular. Operculum unknown. *M. Jur.(Bathon.)-L.Cret.(Alb.).*

Helicocryptus D'ORBIGNY, 1850 [*Helix pusilla* ROEMER, 1836 (*non* VALLOT, 1801) (=*Rotella dubia* BUVIGNIER, 1852); SD COSSMANN, 1918] [=*Heliocryptus* WENZ, 1938 (erroneously attributed to D'ORBIGNY, 1850) (obj.)]. Characters of subfamily. Eu.——FIG. 172,1. *H. dubius* (BUVIGNIER), U.Jur.(Raurac.), Switz.; 1a,b, ×4 (96).

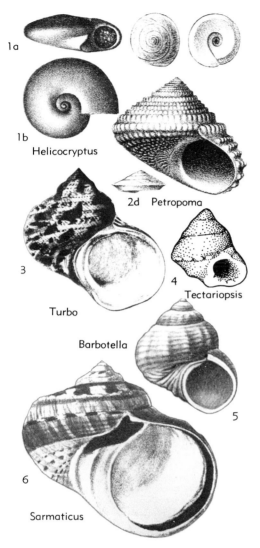

1a

1b
Helicocryptus

2d Petropoma

3
Turbo

4
Tectariopsis

Barbotella

5

6

Sarmaticus

FIG. 172. Trochacea (Turbinidae——Helicocryptinae, Petropominae, Turbininae) (p. 1167-1269).

Subfamily PETROPOMINAE Cox, n. subfam.

Low turbiniform, anomphalous; peristome discontinuous, parietal lip passing under strongly prosocline outer lip; operculum
with low, conical, visibly spiral outer face
and narrowly umbilicate inner face. *L.Cret.*
(Alb.).

The calcareous operculum shows that this
subfamily should be included in the Turbinidae, although the interrupted peristome

is more suggestive of the Trochidae. The
operculum itself is of a unique type.

Petropoma GABB, 1877 [*P. peruanum*]. With low
coeloconoid spire of flattened whorls bearing granose spiral cords, present also on base; callosity of
inner lip extending for moderate distance over
base and with distinct margin. Eu., S.Am.——
FIG. 172,2. *P. peruanum*, Peru; 2a-d, aperture
and 3 views of operculum, all ×4 (188).

Subfamily TURBININAE Rafinesque, 1815
[*nom. correct.* ADAMS & ADAMS, 1851 (*pro* Turbinacea
RAFINESQUE, 1815)]

Generally large shells, whorls rounded,
base convex; aperture round; operculum
thick and heavy, nearly circular, convex outward. *U.Cret.-Rec.*

Turbo LINNÉ, 1758 [*T. petholatus;* SD MONTFORT,
1810] [=*Laeviturbo* COSSMANN, 1918 (obj.);
Bothropoma THIELE, 1924; *Amphiboliturbo*
MAGNE, 1940; *Neocollonia* KURODA & HABE,
1954]. Smooth to strongly sculptured; inner lip
mostly widened or callused. *U.Cret.-Rec.,* Eu.-E.
Asia-IndoPac.-N.Am.-C.Am.-Austral.-Afr.

T. (Turbo). Smooth, rounded, last whorl large;
inner face of operculum flat. *Oligo.-Rec.,* Eu.-
IndoPac.——FIG. 172,3. *T. petholatus*, Rec.,
Philippines; ×0.7 (147).

T. .Barbotella) COSSMANN, 1918 [*T. hoernesi*
BARBOT, 1869]. With irregular radial ribs. *Mio.,*
Eu.——FIG. 172,5. *T. (B.) hoernesi*, Sarmatian,
Caucasus; ×1 (147).

T. (Batillus) SCHUMACHER, 1817 [*T. cornutus*
GMELIN, 1791] [=*Angarina* BAYLE, 1878 (obj.)
(*pro Delphinulopsis* WRIGHT, 1878, *non* LAUBE,
1870)]. Last whorl most commonly with 2 series
of hollow spines; spiral marginal rib on operculum. *Rec.* Japan.

T. (Callopoma) GRAY, 1850 [*T. fluctuosus* WOOD,
1828]. Moderately large, with strong often noded
spiral ribs; operculum with heavy spiral rib at
center bordered by 2 or more weaker ribs. *Mio.-*
Rec., E.Indies-N.Am.-C.Am.

T. (Carswellena) IREDALE, 1931 [*T. exquisitus*
ANGAS, 1877]. Small, with a few noded spiral
ribs, operculum spirally bordered. *Rec.,* Austral.

T. (Dentallopoma) BEETS, 1942 [*T. (D.) denti-*
columellaris]. With deep furrow on columella.
Neogene, E.Indies.

T. (Dinassovica) IREDALE, 1937 [*D. verconis*].
Shell smooth, very large, globose; operculum
oval, inner side elevated. *Rec.,* S.Austral.

T. (Euninella) COTTON, 1939 [*T. gruneri* PHILIPPI,
1846]. Spirally striate, anomphalous, operculum
smooth. *Mio.-Rec.,* Austral.

T. (Halopsephus) REHDER, 1943 [*H. pulcher*
(*non Turbo pulcher* DILLWYN, 1817) = *T. (H.)*
haraldi ROBERTSON, 1958]. Small, smooth, operculum convex, sculptured with axial riblets. *Rec.,*
Carib.

T. (Lunatica) Röding, 1798 [*T. olearius* Linné, 1758 (=*T. marmoratus* Linné, 1758); SD Herrmannsen, 1847] [=*Olearia* Herrmannsen, 1847, *ex* Klein, 1753]. Very large, heavy, spiral ribs few; umbilicate; pillar with a basal expansion; operculum semi-granular. *Plio.-Rec.,* E. Indies-Japan.

T. (Lunella) Röding, 1798 [*T. versicolor* Gmelin, 1791 (=*T. cinereus* Born, 1778); SD Fischer, 1873] [=*Ocana* H.Adams, 1861 (obj.)]. Whorls rounded to slightly carinate; pillar with basal lobe; operculum slightly granular. *Mio.-Rec.,* circumtropic.

T. (Marmarostoma) Swainson, 1829 [*T. chrysostomus* Linné, 1758] [=*Marmorostoma* Gray, 1850 (spelling error); *Senectus* Swainson, 1840]. With spiral ribs; operculum smooth to granular. *Mio.-Rec.,* Eu.-IndoPac.

T. (Modelia) Gray, 1850 [*T. granosus* Martyn, 1784 (ICZN op. 479)]. Medium-sized, sculptured with granular spiral ribs; operculum granular with smooth border. *Mio.-Rec.,* N.Z.

T. (Ninella) Gray, 1850 [*T. torquatus* Gmelin, 1791; SD Fischer, 1873]. Depressed, whorls lirate, rounded to carinate; operculum oval, nucleus eccentric, outer surface concave in center with 2 strong spiral ribs, outer margin thin, granulate. *Eoc.-Rec.,* Eu.-C.Am.-IndoPac.-Austral.

T. (Sarmaticus) Gray, 1847 [*T. sarmaticus* Linné, 1758] [=*Cidaris* Swainson, 1840 (*non* Leske, 1778)]. Large, smooth, depressed; operculum tuberculate. *U.Cret.(Campan.)-Rec.,* Eu.-N.Afr.-S.Afr.——Fig. 172,6. *T. (S.) sarmaticus,* Rec., S.Afr.; ×0.7 (147).

T. (Sarmaturbo) Powell, 1938 [*T. superbus* Zittel, 1864]. Near *T. (Sarmaticus)* but with operculum spirally sculptured on inner face. *U. Oligo.,* N.Z.

T. (Subninella) Thiele, 1929 [*T. undulatus* "Martyn, 1784" (non binominal) = *T. undulatus* Gmelin, 1791]. Moderately large, globose, with fine spiral ribs; umbilicate; operculum strongly convex in middle, with thin outer margin set off by ledge. *Rec.,* Australasia.

T. (Taeniaturbo) Woodring, 1928 [*T. canaliculatus* Hermann, 1781]. Moderately large, whorls rounded to subangular, sculptured with closely spaced spiral cords more or less beaded; not umbilicate; operculum irregularly thickened, weakly granular. *Mio.-Rec.,* W.Indies.

?Prisogaster Mörch, 1850 [*Turbo niger* Wood, 1828; SD Fischer, 1873] [=*Amyxa* Troschel, 1852 (obj.)]. Of medium size, low-spired; smooth or with spiral ribs; aperture rounded, nacreous within; inner lip wide; operculum with a marginal furrow, nucleus eccentric. *Rec.,* Pac.——Fig. 178,6. *P. niger* (Wood), Rec., Chile; ×1 (147).

?Tectariopsis Cossmann, 1888 [*Turbo henrici* Caillat, 1835]. Small, with noded and angulate periphery; aperture with lobed anterior expansion, bordered by several small nodes; umbilicus partly concealed by inner lip. *Eoc.,* Eu.——Fig. 172,4. *T. henrici* (Caillat), Eoc., Fr.; ×1.5 (147).

Subfamily COLLONIINAE Cossmann, 1916

[*nom. transl.* Keen, herein (*ex* Colloniidae Cossmann, 1916)]

Small, not nacreous; turbinate to lenticular; operculum normally paucispiral. *U. Cret.-Plio.*

Collonia Gray, 1850 [*Delphinula marginata* Lamarck, 1804; SD Cossmann, 1888]. Sturdy, nearly smooth, inflated, umbilicate; outer lip thickened, peristome mostly entire; operculum with a central pit. *U.Cret.-Plio.,* Eu.-N.Am.

C. (Collonia). Umbilicus bounded by granular spiral cord. *Paleoc.-Plio.,* Eu.-N.Am.-Austral.——Fig. 173,5. *C. (C.) marginata* (Lamarck), Eoc., Fr.; *5a,b,* ×2 (147).

C. (Bonnetella) Cossmann, 1908 [*Bonnetia planispira* Cossmann, 1907] [=*Bonnetia* Cossmann, 1907 (*non* Robineau-Desvoidy, 1830)]. Minute, lenticular, few-whorled. *Eoc.-Oligo.,* Eu.

C. (Circulopsis) Cossmann, 1902 [*C. (C.) megalomphalus*]. Depressed, base rounded into umbilicus. *U.Cret.(Dan.)-Mio.,* Eu.

C. (Heniastoma) Cossmann, 1918 [*C. (H.) flammulata* Cossmann, 1888]. Spire moderately high; umbilicus bounded by a sharp ridge. *Paleoc.-Mio.,* Eu.

C. (Parvirota) Cossmann, 1902 [*Turbo rotatorius* Deshayes, 1863]. Spire flattened; umbilicus set off by a ridge; sculpture axial. *Paleoc.-Plio.,* Eu.-N.Am.——Fig. 173,7. *C. (P.) rotatoria* (Deshayes), U.Eoc., Fr.; *7a,b,* ×5 (147).

Coanollonia Woodring, 1928 [*C. ambla*]. Depressed, sculpture both axial and radial; peristome incomplete. *Mio.,* W.Indies.——Fig. 173,8. *C. ambla,* Mio., Jamaica; ×5 (147).

Cyniscella Cossmann, 1888 [*Cyclostoma cornupastoris* Lamarck, 1804]. Minute; with spiral grooves; umbilicus bounded by nodose ridge. *Paleoc.-Oligo.,* Eu.——Fig. 173,3. *C. cornupastoris* (Lamarck), Eoc., Fr.; *3a,b,* ×10 (147).

Gelasinostoma Gardner, 1947 [*Collonia elegantula* Dall, 1892]. Depressed, few-whorled; umbilical pit minute, bordered by a rib. *?Eoc., Mio.-Plio.,* E.N.Am.——Fig. 173,1. *G. elegantulum* (Dall), Mio., Fla.; × (186).

Otollonia Woodring, 1928 [*Liotia siderea* Guppy, 1896]. Sculpture of fine, beaded spiral ribs. *Mio.,* W.Indies.——Fig. 173,6. *O. siderea* (Guppy), Mio., Jamaica; *6a,b,* ×5 (147).

Otomphalus Cossmann, 1902 [*O. dumasi*]. With 2 spiral carinae above and at periphery; umbilicus bordered by another carina. *Eoc.,* Eu.——Fig. 173, 4. *O. dumasi,* Eoc., Fr.; *4a,b,* ×3 (147).

Pseudonina Sacco, 1896 [*Delphinula bellardii* Michelotti, 1847]. Resembling *Otomphalus* but more conical, with carinae at and below periphery.

1
Gelasinostoma

2
Pseudonina

3a

3b

4a
Otomphalus

4b

Cyniscella

5a

5b
Collonia

6a

7a
Parvirota
7b

6b
Otollonia

8
Coanollonia

FIG. 173. Trochacea (Turbinidae——Colloniinae)
(p. *1269*).

Mio.-Plio., Eu.——FIG. 173,2. *P. bellardii*
(MICHELOTTI), Mio., Italy; ×3 (147).

Subfamily HOMALOPOMATINAE Keen, n. subfam.

Small shells; axial sculpture reduced or absent, spiral sculpture well developed. *Paleoc.-Rec.*

Homalopoma CARPENTER, 1864 [*Turbo sanguineus* LINNÉ, 1758] [=Leptonyx CARPENTER, 1864 (*non* SWAINSON, 1833)]. Umbilicus wanting or small; operculum with horny and shelly layers, multispiral. *Paleoc.-Rec.*, cosmop.

H. (Homalopoma). With strong spiral grooves; height equal to diameter. *Paleoc.-Rec.*, Eu.-N. Afr.-N.Am.-S.Am.——FIG. 174,9. *H. sanguineum* (LINNÉ), Rec., Medit.; *9a,b*, ×1.5 (147).

H. (Argalista) IREDALE, 1915 [*Cyclostrema fluctuatum* HUTTON, 1883]. Minute, depressed-globose, spirally striate, deeply umbilicate; peritreme interrupted. *Oligo.-Rec.*, Australasia.

H. (Boutillieria) COSSMANN, 1888 [*Turbo eugeni* DESHAYES, 1863] [=Otaulax COSSMANN, 1888]. With a small umbilicus; aperture expanded anteriorly. *L.Cret.(Apt.)-Oligo.*, Eu.-N.Afr.——FIG. 174,3. *H. (B.) eugeni* (DESHAYES), EOC., Fr.; ×3 (147).

H. (Cantrainea) JEFFREYS, 1883 [*Turbo peloritanus* CANTRAINE, 1835] [=Cantraineia, FISCHER, 1885 (obj.)]. Relatively high-spired; umbilicus covered by columellar callus. *Mio.-Rec.*, Eu.

H. (Collonista) IREDALE, 1918 [*Collonia picta* PEASE, 1868]. Slightly umbilicate, outer lip thin, inner with small callus. *Rec.*, Pac.

H. (Eutinochilus) COSSMANN, 1918 [*Collonia miliaris* COSSMANN, 1892] [*pro Homalochilus* COSSMANN, 1892 (*non* FISCHER, 1856)]. Minute, without umbilicus; suture channeled. *Eoc.*, Eu.-N.Am.

H. (Leptothyropsis) WOODRING, 1928 [*Leptothyra philipiana* DALL, 1889]. Low-spired, umbilicus wide; peristome interrupted. *Mio.-Rec.*, W.Indies.

H. (Phanerolepida) DALL, 1907 [*Turbo transenna* WATSON, 1879]. Surface granulate, granules arranged in oblique rows. *Mio.-Rec.*, Japan.

Anadema ADAMS & ADAMS, 1854 [*Omphalius caelata* A.ADAMS, 1854]. Ovate-conical, with nodose spiral ribs and deep narrow umbilicus. *Rec.*, N.W. Afr.

Charisma HEDLEY, 1915 [*C. compacta*]. Minute, broadly conical, base rounded; umbilicus deep and wide; sculpture finely striate. *Rec.*, Austral.

C. (Charisma). Umbilicus set off by angle. *Rec.*, Austral.

C. (Cavostella) LASERON, 1954 [*C. radians*]. Umbilicus bounded by serrate ridge. *Rec.*, Austral.

C. (Cavotera) LASERON, 1954 [*C. simplex*]. Depressed, umbilical ridge weak. *Rec.*, Austral.

Cirsochilus COSSMANN, 1888 [*Delphinula striata* LAMARCK, 1804]. Spirally carinate, base with fine spiral cords; umbilicus deep, set off by ridge. *M. Jur.-Plio., ?Rec.*, Eu.-N.Am.-S.Am.

C. (Cirsochilus). Apical angle uniform; aperture ovate, varix behind outer lip. *M.Jur.(Baj.)-Plio., ?Rec.*, Eu.-E.Indies-W.Indies-S.Am.——FIG. 174, 5. *C. striatum* (LAMARCK), Eoc., Fr.; *5a,b*, ×3 (147).

C. (Claibornia) PALMER, 1937 [*Turbo lineata* LEA, 1933]. Spire more acute in juvenile shells; aperture rounded, without varix behind lip. *Eoc.*, SE.USA.——FIG. 174,2. *C. (C.) lineatum* (LEA), Eoc., Ala., ×4 (209).

Leptocollonia POWELL, 1951 [*L. thielei*] [=?Cynisca ADAMS & ADAMS, 1854 (*non* GRAY, 1844)]. Like *Homalopoma* but umbilicate, thin, colorless, operculum concave and spirally channeled. *Rec.*, S.Atl.-?S.Afr.——FIG. 174,8. *L. thielei*, Rec., S. Georgia I.; ×5 (121).

Leptothyra PEASE, 1869 [*L. costata*]. Whorls angulate, axially ribbed, spirally striate; with a narrow umbilicus. *Rec.*, Hawaii.

Moelleria JEFFREYS, 1865 [*Margarita costulata MÖL-LER, 1842]. Depressed, widely umbilicate; spiral cords fine, stronger below. *Plio.-Rec.*, Eu.-N.Am.——FIG. 174,4. *M. costulata* (MÖLLER), Rec., Norway; 4a,b, ×10 (147).

?Rangimata MARWICK, 1928 [*R. pervia]. Minute, depressed; umbilicus semilunar, notching inner lip. *Mio.*, S.Pac.——FIG. 174,7. *R. pervia, Mio.*, Chatham I.; ×10 (147).

?Tipua MARWICK, 1943 [*Submargarita tricincta MARSHALL, 1919]. Low-spired, with 3 weak carinae on body whorl. *M.Eoc.(Bortonian)*, N.Z.——FIG. 174,6. *T. tricincta* (MARSHALL), Eoc., N.Z.; ×3 (204).

Vexinia COSSMANN, 1918 [*Delphinula crassa BAU-DON, 1853]. Globose, with small umbilicus; inner lip expanded anteriorly. *Eoc.*, Eu.——FIG. 174,1. *V. crassa* (BAUDON), Eoc., Fr.; ×3 (147).

Subfamily UNCERTAIN

Pleuratella MOORE, 1867 [*P. prima]. Rather small, rotelliform, phaneromphalous, smooth; spire depressed; columellar lip with outer face expanded to left and concave below, where it appears to extend to margin of a false umbilicus. [Aperture unknown intact in type species, but preserved in *P. brachyura* GEMMELLARO from Sicily. Not referable to Ataphridae.] *L.Jur.(L.Lias.)*, Eng.-Sicily.

Pterocheilos MOORE, 1867 [*P. primus] [=Tino-chilus FISCHER, 1885 (obj.); Mooria COSSMANN, 1899 (obj.)]. Small, biconical, anomphalous, smooth, with almost flattened spire whorls and carinate periphery; base extended, with obscure angulation around median part; aperture circular, reduced by expanded inner lip, which is also extended below as prominent angular projection. *L.Jur.(L.Lias.)*, Eng.——FIG. 175,1. *P. primus; 1a,b,* ×5 (205).

Turboidea SEELEY, 1861 [*T. nodosa]. Founded on ill-preserved specimen of medium size, turbiniform in shape and phaneromphalous, with large tubercles on last whorl. *U.Cret.(Cenom.)*, Eng.

Family CYCLOSTREMATIDAE Fischer, 1885

Small to minute, turbinate to lenticular, mostly widely umbilicate, smooth to strongly sculptured, porcelaneous. *U.Jur.-Rec.*

Subfamily SKENEINAE Thiele, 1929

[=Delphinoideinae THIELE, 1924]

Small, sculpture weak or wanting; radula with 4-5 marginal teeth. *U.Jur.-Rec.*

Teinostomopsis CHAVAN, 1954 [*T. saharae]. Rotelliform, smooth, anomphalous; inner lip strongly concave, with obtuse denticle at lower end and broad outer face limited by a carina. *U.Jur. (Raurac.)*, Eu.——FIG. 176,15. *T. saharae*, Fr.; ×4 (167).

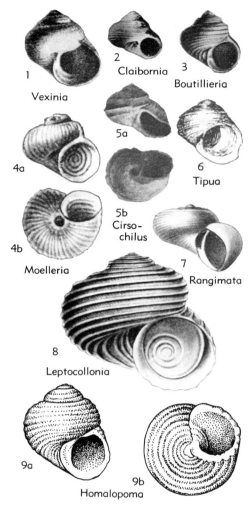

FIG. 174. Trochacea (Turbinidae——Homalopomatinae) (p. 1270-1271).

Cenomanella COSSMANN, 1918 [*Rotella archiaciana D'ORBIGNY, 1843]. Low turbiniform, anomphalous, of evenly convex, spirally striated whorls with deeply canaliculate suture; base callus-coated in middle. *U.Cret.(Cenom.-L.Senon.)*, Eu.——FIG. 176,11. *C. archiaciana* (D'ORBIGNY), U.Cret. (Cenom.), Fr.; ×4 (110).

Skenea FLEMING, 1825 [*Helix serpuloides MON-TAGU, 1808; SD GRAY, 1847] [=Delphinoidea BROWN, 1827 (obj.); Delphionoidea BROWN, 1844 (obj.)]. Depressed, whorls smooth to spirally striate. *Pleist.-Rec.*, Eu.-N.Am.-Japan.——FIG. 176,7. *S. serpuloides* (MONTAGU), Rec., Eng.; ×10 (147).

Cirsonella ANGAS, 1877 [*C. australis]. Spire somewhat elevated. *Mio.-Rec.*, S.Pac.——FIG. 176,17. *C. australis*, Rec., Austral.; 17a,b, ×10 (147).

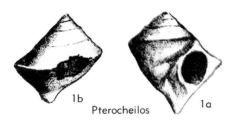

FIG. 175. Trochacea (Turbinidae——Subfamily Uncertain) (p. *1271*).

Conjectura FINLAY, 1927 [*Crossea glabella* MURDOCH, 1905]. Smooth, depressed-turbinate, with basal keel or fold, like *Crossea*. Rec., N.Z.

Crossea A.ADAMS, 1865 [*C. miranda;* SD SUTER, 1913] [=*Crosseia* FISCHER, 1885 (obj.)]. Spire elevated; anterior margin of aperture with or without a projection. *Plio.-Rec.,* S.Pac.-E.Asia.

   C. (**Crossea**). With several strong varices. *Plio.-Rec.,* S.Pac.-IndoPac.——FIG. 176,9. *C. miranda,* Rec., Japan; ×5 (147).

   C. (**Crosseola**) IREDALE, 1924 [*C. concinna* ANGAS, 1868]. Sculpture cancellate, no varices. *Rec.,* S.Pac.

   C. (**Dolicrossea**) IREDALE, 1924 [*C. labiata* TENISON-WOODS, 1876] [=*Doliocrossea,* WENZ, 1938 (spelling error)]. Outer lip varicose. *Rec.,* S.Pac.

Daronia A.ADAMS, 1861 [*Cyclostrema spirula* A. ADAMS, 1850]. Planorboid, spire sunken. *Rec.,* SW. Pac.

   D. (**Daronia**). Peristome continuous. *Rec.,* Indo-Pac.——FIG. 176,2. *D. spirula* (ADAMS), Philippines; *2a,b,* ×1 (147).

   D. (**Eudardonia**) COTTON, 1945 [*Cyclostrema taffaensis* VERCO, 1909]. Peristome discontinuous, aperture reniform. *Rec.,* S.Austral.

?**Dillwynella** DALL, 1889 [*D. modesta*]. Turbinate, not umbilicate. *Rec.,* W.Indies.——FIG. 176,13. *D. modesta,* St. Lucia; ×5 (147).

?**Ganesa** JEFFREYS, 1883 [*G. pruinosa;* SD COSSMANN, 1918]. Turbinate; smooth or striate. *Plio.-Rec.,* Eu.-N.Am.-SW.Pac.

   G. (**Ganesa**). Aperture somewhat ovate. *Rec.,* Atl.——FIG. 176,6. *G. (G.) pruinosa,* N.Atl.; ×3 (193).

   G. (**Granigyra**) DALL, 1889 [*Cyclostrema limatum*]. Surface finely granulate. *Rec.,* W.Indies-Eu.

   G. (**Lissospira**) BUSH, 1897 [*Cyclostrema proximum* TRYON, 1888]. Aperture round. *Plio.-Rec.,* N.Z.-E.N.Am.——FIG. 176,4. *G. (L.) proxima* (TRYON), Rec., New England; ×5 (147).

?**Haplocochlias** CARPENTER, 1864 [*H. cyclophoreus*]. Somewhat conical, spirally striate, outer lip thickened. *Rec.,* W.C.Am.

Kaawatina BARTRUM & POWELL, 1928 [*K. turneri*]. Pyriform, 3-whorled, with axial ribs and an um-

bilical chink. *Plio.,* N.Z.——FIG. 176,16. *K. turneri; 16a,b,* ×10 (147).

Leptogyra BUSH, 1897 [*L. verrilli*]. Lenticular, deeply umbilicate, with spiral striae. *Rec.,* E.N. Am.-W.N.Am.——FIG. 176,5. *L. verrilli,* Delaware Bay; *5a,b,* ×10 (147).

Leucorhynchia CROSSE, 1867 [*L. caledonica*]. Smooth, glossy, sublenticular, umbilicus deep but partly concealed by a columellar basal fold. *U. Cret.-Rec.,* Eu.-IndoPac.——FIG. 176,8. *L. caledonica,* Rec., New Caledonia; *8a,b,* ×5 (147).

Lissotesta IREDALE, 1915 [*Cyclostrema micra* TENISON-WOODS, 1877]. Turbinate, smooth to spirally ribbed, without varices. *Rec.,* S.Pac.

Lissotestella POWELL, 1946 [*Lissotesta tenuilirata* POWELL, 1931]. Like *Lissotesta* in shape but more solid; peristome continuous, varicose. *Rec.,* N.Z.

Lodderena IREDALE, 1924 [*Liotia minima* TENISON-WOODS, 1878]. Nearly discoidal, with heavily variced aperture, peripheral keels and crenulate suture present but no axial sculpture. *Rec.,* Australasia.

Lodderia TATE, 1899 [*Liotia lodderae* PETTERD, 1884] [=*Cyclostremella* TATE, 1898 (*non* BUSH, 1897)]. Lenticular, with several spiral keels and fine axial sculpture. *Rec.,* Australasia.——FIG. 176, 14. *L. lodderae* (PETTERD), Austral.; ×10 (147).

Lophocochlias PILSBRY, 1921 [*Haplocochlias minutissimus*]. Minute, with 6 spiral keels and 2 spirals in umbilicus. *Rec.,* Hawaii.

Munditiella KURODA & HABE, 1954 [*Cyclostrema ammonoceras* A.ADAMS, 1863]. Minute, with regular annular varices on periphery. *Rec.,* Japan.——FIG. 176,12. *M. ammonoceras* (ADAMS); ×20 (198).

Norrisella COSSMANN, 1888 [*Turbo pygmaea* DESHAYES, 1863]. Minute, umbilicate, inner lip flaring. *Eoc.-Mio.,* Eu.-E.Indies.——FIG. 176,3. *N. pygmaea* (DESHAYES), Eoc., Fr.; ×5 (147).

?**Pakistania** EAMES, 1952 [*P. antirotata*]. Sinistral, flattened above, convex below, smooth, periphery carinate; aperture kite-shaped. *Eoc.,* Asia.——FIG. 176,18. *P. antirotata,* Pakistan; ×20 (180).

Philorene OLIVER, 1915 [*P. texturata*]. With fine spiral striae and nodes, umbilicus spirally lirate within. *Rec.,* Pac.

Pondorbis BARTSCH, 1915 [*P. alfredensis*]. Planorboid, with sinuous axial varices. *Rec.,* S.Afr.

Pygmaerota HABE, 1958 [*Cyclostrema duplicatum* LISCHKE, 1872]. Near *Lodderia* but without axial striae. *Rec.,* Japan.

Rhodinoliotia TOMLIN & SHACKLEFORD, 1915 [*Cyclostrema roseotinctum* SMITH, 1871]. Turbinate, with strong spiral ridges. *Rec.,* W.Afr.

Teinostoma, classified here by some workers, is to be included in Vitrinellidae, in *Treatise* Part J.]

Tharsiella BUSH, 1897 [*pro Tharsis* JEFFREYS, 1883 (*non* GIEBEL, 1847)] [*Oxystele romettensis* GRANATA, 1877 (*ex* SEGUENZA, MS)] | =*Porcupinia* COSSMANN, 1900 (*non* HAECKEL, 1887) (*pro Tharsis*); *Porcupina* COSSMANN, 1925 (spelling error)].

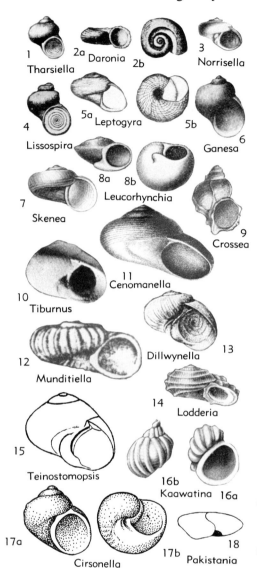

1 Tharsiella
2a Daronia 2b
3 Norrisella
4 Lissospira
5a Leptogyra 5b
6 Ganesa
7 Skenea
8a 8b Leucorhynchia
9 Crossea
10 Tiburnus
11 Cenomanella
12 Munditiella
13 Dillwynella
14 Lodderia
15 Teinostomopsis
16b 16a Kaawatina
17a 17b Cirsonella
18 Pakistania

FIG. 176. Trochacea (Cyclostrematidae——Skeneinae) (p. I271-I273).

Turbinate, smooth, umbilicus partly concealed by columellar lip. *Plio.-Rec.,* Eu.-W.Atl.——FIG. 176, *1. *T. romettensis* (GRANATA), Rec., E.Atl.; ✕5 (147).

?Tiburnus DEGREGORIO, 1890 [**Turbo naticoides* LEA, 1833 (Dec.) = *Natica eborea* CONRAD, 1833 (Nov.)] [=*Platychilus* COSSMANN, 1888 (*non* JAKOLEV, 1874); *Simochilus* HARRIS & BURROWS, 1891 (*pro Platychilus*)]. Low-turbinate, smooth, nacreous within. *Paleoc.-Plio.,* Eu.-Afr.-N.Am.-

Austral.——FIG. 176,*10. *T. eborea* (CONRAD), Eoc., Ala.; ✕4 (209).

Tubiola A.ADAMS, 1863 [**Turbo niveus* GMELIN, 1791; SD STOLICZKA, 1868 (as of CHEMNITZ, 1784, nonbinominal)]. Like *Skenea,* but with a funnel-shaped umbilicus. *Plio.-Rec.,* Atl.-Pac.-Austral.

T. (Tubiola). Low-conical, whorls with growth striae only. *Rec.,* Atl.-Pac.

T. (Partubiola) IREDALE, 1936 [**P. blancha*]. Disc-shaped; whorls with fine spiral striae, growth striae in interspaces. *Plio.-Rec.,* Austral.

Subfamily CYCLOSTREMATINAE Fischer, 1885
[*nom. transl.* COSSMANN, 1917 (*ex* Cyclostrematidae FISCHER, 1885)]

Radula with single strong marginal tooth in each row and several delicate laterals; shell mostly strongly sculptured. *U.Cret.-Rec.*

Cyclostrema MARRYAT, 1818 [**C. cancellatum;* SD GRAY, 1847] [=*Pseudoliotina* COSSMANN, 1925]. Lenticular, with axial varices. *U.Cret.-Rec.,* circumtropic.——FIG. 177,9. **C. cancellatum,* Rec., W.Indies; ✕4 (158).

Brookula IREDALE, 1912 [**B. stibarochila*] [=*Vetulonia* DALL, 1913]. Minute, inflated, glassy. *Mio.-Rec.,* C.Pac.-S.Pac.

B. (Brookula). Spire blunt, interspaces between ribs with spiral sculpture. *Mio.-Rec.,* S.Pac.—— FIG. 177,3. **B. (B.) stibarochila,* Rec., Kermadec I.; ✕10 (147).

B. (Aequispirella) FINLAY, 1923 [**Scalaria corulum* HUTTON, 1884]. Spire pointed, interspaces of ribs spirally sculptured. *Mio.,* Australasia.

B. (Liocarinia) LASERON, 1954 [**Liotia disjuncta* HEDLEY, 1903]. Whorls strongly keeled. *Rec.,* E.Austral.-S.Austral.

B. (Liotella) IREDALE, 1915 [**Liotia polypleura* HEDLEY, 1904]. Spire low, interspaces between ribs smooth. *Rec.,* N.Z.

Chunula THIELE, 1925 [**C. typica*] [=*Chunula* THIELE, 1924 (*nom. nud.)*]. Minute, inflated, few-whorled. *Rec.,* E.Indies.——FIG. 177,5. **C. typica,* Sumatra; ✕10 (147).

Circulus JEFFREYS, 1865 [**Delphinula duminyi* REQUIEN, 1842 = *Solarium philippii* CANTRAINE, 1842]. Minute; smooth or with spiral riblets. *Mio.-Rec.,* Medit.-W.Indies-W.C.Am. —— FIG. 177,2. **C. philippii* (CANTRAINE), Rec., Medit.; *2a-c,* ✕5 (147).

Coronadoa BARTSCH, 1946 [**C. simonsae*]. Minute, depressed, with scalariform ridges. *Rec.,* W.N.Am. ——FIG. 177,8. **C. simonsae,* Rec., Calif.; ✕40 (161).

Munditia FINLAY, 1927 [**Liotina tryphenensis* POWELL, 1926]. Depressed, outer lip varicate; spiral beaded cord in umbilicus. *Plio.-Rec.,* Australasia. ——FIG. 177,4. **M. tryphenensis* (POWELL), Rec., N.Z.; *4a,b,* ✕5 (147).

Parviturbo PILSBRY & McGINTY, 1945 [**P. rehderi*]. Minute, turbinate, spiral ribs few, heavy. *Rec.,* SE.

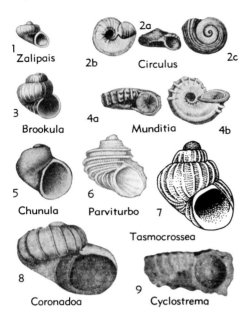

FIG. 177. Trochacea (Cyclostrematidae——Cyclostrematinae) (p. 1273-1274).

USA.——FIG. 177,6. *P. rehderi, Fla.; ×10 (214).
Tasmocrossea DELL, 1952 [*T. benthicola]. Like
Brookula but with a basal fold. Rec., Australasia.
——FIG. 177,7. *T. benthicola; ×25 (175).
Zalipais IREDALE, 1915 [*Cyclostrema lissa SUTER,
1908]. Minute, with fine axial striae. Rec. Austral-
asia.——FIG. 177,1. *Z. lissa (SUTER), Rec., N.Z.;
×10 (147).

Family PHASIANELLIDAE Swainson, 1840

[nom. transl. COSSMANN, 1918 (ex Phasianellinae SWAINSON,
1840)] [=Eutropiinae ADAMS & ADAMS, 1854] [Preparation
of descriptions and selection of illustrations for this family
are the work of MYRA KEEN and ROBERT ROBERTSON.—Ed.]

Ovate to rounded, few-whorled, without
periostracum; smooth or finely spirally
sculptured, rarely spirally ribbed; shell entirely porcelaneous; small species may be
umbilicate; peristome not continuous; operculum calcareous, with eccentric nucleus,
either externally convex or flat and spirally
ridged. Paleoc.-Rec.

Phasianella LAMARCK, 1804 [*Buccinum australe
GMELIN, 1791 (ICZN pend.)] [=Phasianus DE
MONTFORT, 1810 (obj.) (non LINNÉ, 1758); Bolina
RAFINESQUE, 1815 (obj.); Eutropia SWAINSON, 1840
(obj.); Orthopnoea GISTEL, 1847 (obj.); Orthome-
sus PILSBRY, 1888; Mimelenchus IREDALE, 1924].
Medium-sized to large, smooth, long-ovate; non-
umbilicate. Mio.-Rec., Java-Austral.-IndoPac.——

FIG. 178,5. *P. australis, Rec., Austral.; ×0.7
(147).
Gabrielona IREDALE, 1917 [*Phasianella nepeanensis
GATLIFF & GABRIEL, 1908]. Small, globose, smooth
or with fine spiral grooves, umbilicate; operculum
flat and spirally ridged. Mio.-Rec., W.Indies-
Austral.
Tricolia RISSO, 1826 [*Turbo pullus LINNÉ, 1758;
SD GRAY, 1847] [=Eudora GRAY, 1852 (non
PÉRON & LESUEUR, 1810) (obj.); Chromotis ADAMS
& ADAMS, 1863; Eucosmia CARPENTER, 1864 (non
STEPHENS, 1831); Tricoliella MONTEROSATO, 1884
(obj.); Steganomphalus HARRIS & BURROWS, 1891
(obj.); Eulithidium PILSBRY, 1898; Usatricolia
HABE, 1956]. Small, globose or ovate, smooth or
spirally ribbed; smaller species perforate, columel-
lar margin arched; operculum externally convex.
Paleoc.-Rec., world-wide, tropics and warm tem-
perate regions.
T. (Tricolia). Shell fairly thick; suture slightly
impressed. Paleoc.-Rec., Eu.-Carib.-N.Am.——
FIG. 178,1. *T. (T.) pulle (LINNÉ), Rec., Eng.,
×2 (147).——FIG. 178,2. T. (T.) variegata
(CARPENTER), Rec., W.Mex.; type species of
Eulithidium, ×8 (223).
T. (Aizyella) COSSMANN, 1889 [*"Phasianella
herouvalensis DESHAYES," lapsus for P. suessoni-
ensis DESHAYES, 1863]. Spirally ribbed. Eoc., Eu.
T. (Eotricolia) KURODA & HABE, 1954 [*Phasian-
ella megastoma PILSBRY, 1895]. Similar to T.
(Hiloa) but radula differs slightly. Rec., Japan.
T. (Hiloa) PILSBRY, 1917 [*Phasianella thaanumi].
Shell thin, suture impressed; outer lip commonly
reflexed. Rec., Hawaii.
T. (Pellax) FINLAY, 1926 [*Phasianella huttoni
PILSBRY, 1888]. Apex acute. Plio.-Rec., N.Z.-
Austral.
T. (Phasianochilus) COSSMANN, 1918 [*Phasianella
turbinoides LAMARCK, 1804]. Long-ovate, spire
pointed, aperture ovate; umbilical chink present.
Eoc.-Oligo., Eu.——FIG. 178,3. T. (*P.) tur-
binoides, Eoc., Fr.; ×1 (171).
?Pseudophasianus COSSMANN, 1918 [*Turbo elatus
FUCHS, 1870]. Cylindrical, last whorl relatively
small; with small umbilicus. Eoc., Eu.——FIG. 178,
4. *P. elatus (FUCHS), Eoc., Italy; ×1 (147).

Family VELAINELLIDAE Vasseur, 1880

Last whorl twisted into a slender spiral,
simulating a multispiral shell but without
the normal spiral septum. Eoc.

Velainella VASSEUR, 1880 [*V. columnaris] [=Vel-
ainiella COSSMANN, 1918 (spelling error)]. Slender,
aciculate, moderately large, smooth. Eoc., Eu.——
FIG. 179,1. *V. columnaris, Eoc., Fr.; 1a,b, ×1,
×2 (147).

Family ORBITESTELLIDAE Iredale, 1917

Shell thin, pellucid, minute, discoidal,
few-whorled; widely umbilicate, columella

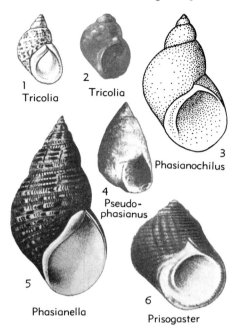

FIG. 178. Trochacea (Turbinidae——Turbininae, Phasianellidae) (p. *1269, 1274*).

vertical; aperture irregular in shape, edges thin. *Rec.*

Orbitestella IREDALE, 1917 [*Cyclostrema bastowi GATLIFF, 1906]. Sculpture of one or more keels crossed by axial ribs. *Rec.*, Austral.——FIG. 179,2. *O. bastowi (GATLIFF); 2a-c, ×25 (147).
?Helisalia LASERON, 1954 [*H. liliputia]. Sculpture of growth lines only. *Rec.*, S.Austral.

Suborder NERITOPSINA Cox & Knight, 1960

[=azygobranches orthoneuroides BOUVIER, 1887; mononéphridés PERRIER, 1889]

Shell commonly coiled and ovoid or globular, more rarely capuliform or patelliform; whorls few; spire, if protruding at all, relatively low; outer shell layers calcitic, unusually stable in fossils, commonly preserving color pattern; inner layers thick, aragonitic, lamellar but not nacreous; operculum (not developed in a few genera) commonly calcareous, in many post-Paleozoic genera with processes projecting from inner face and gripping inner lip; living forms with left kidney only; single, bipectinate ctenidium present on left except in terrestrial forms, attached at its base only; single hypobranchial gland, thought

to be homologue of right one of other Archaeogastropoda, also present; heart with 2 auricles, right one in some reduced or with single auricle; pallial genital organs developed and complex, fertilization internal; retractor muscles paired; radula rhipidoglossate, with outermost admedians large, capituliform. *M.Dev.-Rec.*

Superfamily NERITACEA Rafinesque, 1815

[*nom. transl.* THIELE, 1929 (*ex* Neritacea RAFINESQUE, 1815)]
[Proposed as subfamily name]

Characters as defined for suborder. The superfamily includes marine, fresh-water and terrestrial forms. *M.Dev.-Rec.*

?Family PLAGIOTHYRIDAE Knight, 1956

Turbiniform, with thick shell, dominantly spiral ornament and one or more columellar teeth. *M.Dev.-L.Carb.(Miss.)*

Dirachis WHIDBORNE, 1891 [*D. atavus]. With moderately high spire; two teeth on inner lip; outer lip convex, prosocline; ornament of spiral cords. *M.Dev.*, Eu.——FIG. 180,2. *D. atavus*, Eng.; ×4.
Plagiothyra WHIDBORNE, 1892 [*Monodonta purpurea D'ARCHIAC & DEVERNEUIL, 1842; SD COSSMANN, 1916]. With single tooth on inner lip;

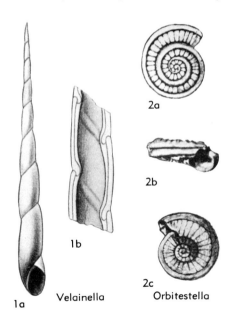

FIG. 179. Trochacea (Velainellidae, Orbitestellidae) (p. *1274-1275*).

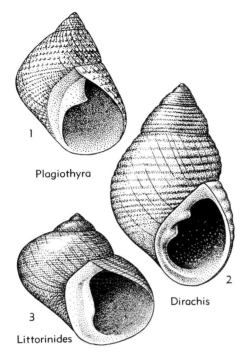

FIG. 180. Neritacea (Plagiothyridae) (p. *1275-1276*).

labrum convex, prosocline; ornament of fine papillae in spiral rows. *M.Dev.*, Eu.——FIG. 180, *1*. *P. purpurea* (d'ARCHIAC & deVERNEUIL), Ger.; ×2.

Littorinides KNIGHT, 1937 [*pro Rhabdopleura* DE KONINCK, 1881 (*non* ALLMAN, 1869)] [*Littorina solida* deKONINCK, 1843]. Low; elongate plate on inner lip culminating below in low tooth; ornament of numerous spiral threads. *L.Carb.*, Eu.—— FIG. 180,*3*. *L. solida* (deKONINCK), Belg.; ×2.

Family NERITOPSIDAE Gray, 1847

Shell globular, spire protruding but slightly or not at all, last whorl large; inner lip broad and smooth, formed by continuous inductura, or by inductura on parietal region merging into excavation of columellar lip on its outer face; inner walls of whorls not resorbed; operculum not spiral. *M.Dev.-Rec.*

Subfamily NATICOPSINAE S.A.Miller, 1889

[*nom. transl.* KNIGHT, BATTEN & YOCHELSON, herein (*ex* Naticopsidae S.A.MILLER, 1889)] [=Hologyridae KITTL, 1899)]

Without ornament except for subsutural collabral threads or cords in some species; outer lip strongly prosocline; parietal lip commonly thickened by inductura, ex-

tended in some species in plane of aperture over part of side of last whorl, and simple or rarely bearing single protuberance; columellar lip strongly arcuate, excavated on its outer face; operculum concentric, asymmetrical; color pattern collabral stripes, spiral bands, spots, and especially zigzag lines. *M.Dev.-U.Cret.*

Naticopsis M'COY, 1844 [**N. phillipsii;* SD MEEK & WORTHEN, 1866]. With moderately high-spired to low, very broad shell; divisible into intergrading subgenera. *M.Dev.-Trias.,* cosmop.

N. (Naticopsis) [=*Naticodon* RYCKHOLT, 1847; *Fedaiella* KITTL, 1894]. Commonly large; globular, but with slightly protruding spire; aperture expanded in direction oblique to axis; parietal and columellar lips moderately thickened or each with toothlike protuberance. *M.Dev.-Trias,* cosmop.——FIG. 181,*7*. **N. (N.) phillipsii*, L.Carb., Ire.; with operculum, ×0.7.——FIG. 181,*8*. **N. (N.) cuccensis*, M.Trias.(Ladin.), S.Tyrol; *8a,b*, ×1 (65).

N. (Jedria) YOCHELSON, 1952 [**Naticopsis meeki* KNIGHT, 1933]. More or less ovoid; heavy subsutural swelling generally bearing collabral cords; parietal lip in adults markedly thickened (155, p. 65)]. *M.Dev.-Perm., ?Trias.,* N.Am.-Eu.—— FIG. 181,*1*. **N. (J.) meeki* (KNIGHT), M.Penn. (U.Carb.), Mo.; ×2.

N. (Marmolatella) KITTL, 1894 [**N. (M.) applanata* KITTL, 1894; SD B.B.WOODWARD, 1895]. Spire more or less flattened; aperture expanded in direction perpendicular to axis; parietal and columellar lips thickened, each commonly with toothlike protuberance. *L.Carb.(Miss.)-U.Trias.,* N.Am.-Eu.——FIG. 180A,*1*. **N. (Marmolatella) applanata*, M.Trias.(Ladin.), S.Tyrol; *1a,b*, ×1 (65).

Dicosmos CANAVARI, 1890 [**D. pulcher*] [=*Hologyra* KOKEN, 1892]. Naticiform; whole of inner lip with thick, bulging inductura; columellar lip less extended than in *Naticopsis*. *M.Trias.(Ladin.)-U.Trias.(Carn.),* Eu.-Indonesia.——FIG. 181,*4*. **D. alpinus* (KOKEN) (=type species of *Hologyra*), U. Trias.(Carn.), S.Tyrol; *4a,b*, ×1 (10).

Planospirina KITTL, 1899 [**Nerita esinensis* STOPPANI, 1858]. Spire low in early stages, but suture descending penultimate whorl before aperture; aperture ovate, broader than high; columellar lip concave, not at all extended as in *Naticopsis*; parietal lip much thickened, columellar lip rather less so. *U.Carb.(M.Penn.)-Trias.,* Eu.-N.Am.—— FIG. 181,*10*. **P. esinensis*, M.Trias.(Ladin.), S. Tyrol; *10a-c*, apertural, abapertural, and apical views, ×1.

?Vernelia J.BÖHM, 1895 [*Natica fastigiata* STOPPANI, 1858 (=*N. excelsa* HAUER, 1851); SD B. B. WOODWARD, 1896]. Medium-sized, littoriniform, with well-elevated spire of convex whorls; aperture

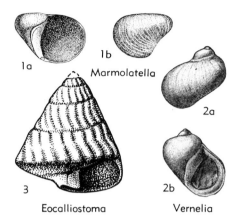

FIG. 180A. *Marmolatella, Vernelia,* and *Eocalliostoma* (p. *1248, 1276*).

ovate, higher than broad, angular and with slight adapical channel; labrum thick, but bevelled off to margin; parietal lip much thickened above. *U. Carb.(Penn.)-Trias.,* Eu.-N.Am.——FIGS. 180A,*2*, 181,*3*. *V. excelsa* (HAUER), M.Trias.(Ladin.), S. Tyrol; 180A,*2a,b*, ×1 (195); 181,*3a,b*, ×1 (specimen in U.S. Natl. Mus.)

?**Pachyomphalus** J.BÖHM, 1895 [*P. concinnus;* SD COSSMANN, 1925]. Small, littoriform, with well-elevated spire of convex whorls; aperture ovate, higher than broad, relatively smaller than in *Vernelia,* angular adapically, labrum thin; inductura narrow on parietal region, more widely spread over base. *M.Trias.(Ladin.),* Eu.——FIG. 181,*2*. *P. concinnus,* S.Tyrol; *2a,b*, ×2 (6).

?**Frombachia** BLASCHKE, 1905 [*F. uhligi*]. Rather small, turbiniform, with fairly broad umbilicus; whorls with 2 spiral angulations; inductura of inner lip spread over base but not obscuring umbilicus. *M.Trias.(Carn.),* Eu.——FIG. 181,*5*. *F. uhligi;* S.Tyrol; *5a,b*, ×1.5 (10).

Haliotimorpha BLASCHKE, 1905 [*H. dieneri*]. Involute, auriform, of few very rapidly enlarging whorls, last one developing peripheral carina, on which are large hollow spines; aperture subrectangular, much broader than high; inner lip flattened, of moderate breadth, with sharp subparallel outer and inner margins, latter concave and without teeth. *M.Trias.(Ladin.)-U.Trias. (Carn.),* Eu.——FIG. 181,*9*. *H. dieneri,* U.Trias. (Carn.), S.Tyrol; *9a,b*, ×1 (10).

Damesia HOLZAPFEL, 1888 [*Crepidula cretacea* MÜLLER, 1851; SD WENZ, 1938]. Globose, with rapidly enlarging whorls and very eccentric, flattened spire almost level with top of aperture; ornament depressed spiral cords; aperture subrectangular, broader than high; inner lip flattened, of moderate breadth, with sharp subparallel outer and inner margins, and largely covering quite

broad umbilicus; inner margin of inner lip concave and without teeth. *U.Cret.(Senon.),* Eu.—— FIG. 181,*6*. *D. cretacea,* Ger.; *6a,b*, ×2 (56).

Subfamily NERITOPSINAE Gray, 1847

[*nom. transl.* KNIGHT, BATTEN & YOCHELSON, herein (*ex* Neritopsidae GRAY, 1847)]

Much like the Naticopsinae except that spire protrudes more than in most genera of that subfamily and shell is ornamented with pustules, which in many species open adaperturally; no umbilicus; operculum, where known, massive, trapeziform, symmetrical. *L.Carb.(Miss.)-Rec.*

Turbonitella DEKONINCK, 1881 [*Turbo biserialis* PHILLIPS, 1836; SD COSSMANN, 1916]. Turbiniform, with slightly flattened base; collar-like adpressed zone between suture and uppermost pustules; 2 rows of collabrally lengthened pustules, one at upper angulation of whorl face and other at lower angulation; columellar lip strongly excavated. *L. Carb.,* Eu.——FIG. 182,*1*. *T. biserialis* (PHILLIPS), Eng.; ×2.

Trachydomia MEEK & WORTHEN, 1866 [*Naticopsis nodosa* MEEK & WORTHEN, 1861] [*=Trachydomus* COSSMANN, 1918 (obj.); *Trachydoma* KNIGHT, 1933 (obj.)] Globular, with adpressed zone; surface covered with pustules that are not segregated sharply into different kinds. *Penn.(U. Carb.)-M.Perm.,* N.Am.-Eu.-NE.Asia-SE.Asia.—— FIG. 182,*5*. *T. nodosa* (MEEK & WORTHEN), M. Penn., Ill.; ×1.3.

Trachyspira GEMMELLARO, 1889 [*T. delphinuloides;* SD COSSMANN, 1916] [*=Platycheilus* GEMMELLARO, 1889; *Sosiospira* GRECO, 1937]. Much like *Trachydomia* but without sutural adpressed zone and with pustules segregated into 2 different categories: numerous small pustules arranged in oblique opisthocline or spiral rows and few large ones arranged in spiral rows. *M.Perm.,* N.Am.-Eu.-NE.Asia.——FIG. 182,*6*. *T. delphinuloides,* Sicily; ×1.

Hungariella KUTASSY, 1933 [*Neritopsis pappi* KUTASSY, 1927]. Medium-sized to large, with well-protruding, acute spire; aperture ovate, higher than broad; inner lip moderately broad, smooth, with sharp protuberance on parietal region, in some shells with other blunter ones below; ornament spiral bands, some tuberculate. *U.Trias. (Nor.),* Eu.——FIG. 182,*4*. *H. stredae* KUTASSY, Hung.; *4a,b*, ×1 (200).

Seisia KUTASSY, 1934 [*S. blaschkei*]. Of medium size, with slightly protruding, very eccentric spire and rapidly increasing whorls; last whorl with 3 or 4 nodose carinae, one delimiting its flat or concave upper surface and lowest forming border of broad false umbilicus; aperture suborbicular; inner lip broad, smooth, with margin almost detached from base. *M.Trias.(Ladin.)-M.U.Trias.(Nor.),* Eu.

——FIG. 182,2. *S. spinosa* KUTASSY, U.Trias. (Carn.), Hung.; *2a,b,* ×3 (84).

Neritopsis GRATELOUP, 1832 [**N. moniliformis*] [=*Radula* GRAY, 1842; also following (based on opercula), *Peltarion* DESLONGCHAMPS & DESLONGCHAMPS, 1858; *Cyclidia, Scaphanidia* ROLLE, 1862; *Rhynchidia* LAUBE, 1868]. Of medium size, with moderately protruding, obtuse spire; last whorl

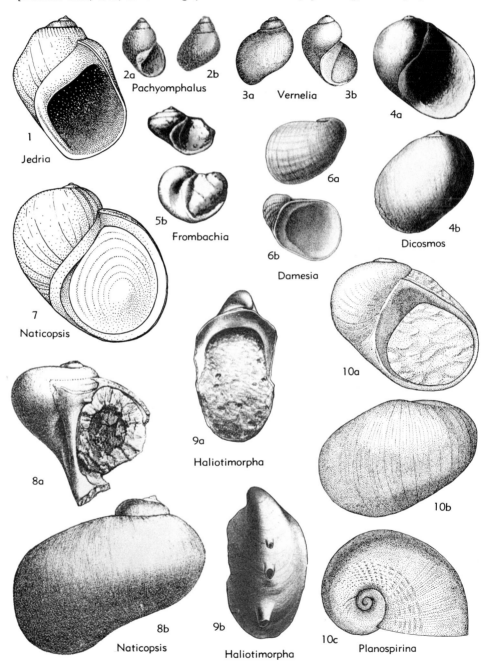

2a   2b
Pachyomphalus

3a   Vernelia   3b

4a

1
Jedria

5b
Frombachia

6a

4b
Dicosmos

6b
Damesia

7
Naticopsis

10a

8a

9a
Haliotimorpha

10b

8b
Naticopsis

9b
Haliotimorpha

10c   Planospirina

FIG. 181. Neritacea (Neritopsidae——Naticopsinae) (p. *1276-1277*).

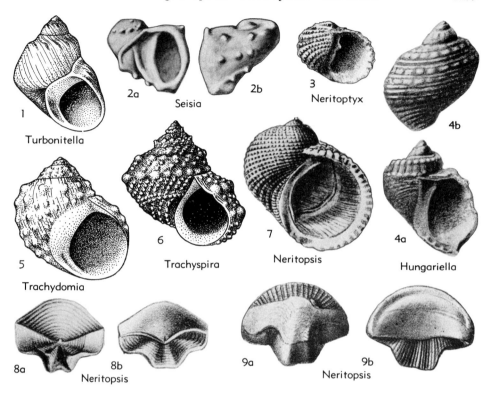

FIG. 182. Neritacea (Neritopsidae——Neritopsinae) (p. *1278*).

globose, evenly convex; ornament spiral cords and in some species collabral ribs; aperture orbicular, inner lip moderately thickened, strongly concave; operculum very solid, trapeziform. *Trias.-Rec.,* cosmop.

N. (Neritopsis). Inner lip without tubercle. *Trias.-Rec.,* cosmop.——FIG. 182,7. N. (N.) *radula* (LINNÉ), Rec., IndoPac.; ✕1 (147).——FIG. 182, 9. N. (N.) sp., Mio., C.Eu.; operculum (*"Cyclidia valida"* ROLLE), 9a,b, ✕5 (201).——FIG. 182,8. N. (N.) sp., L.Jur.(M.Lias.), Fr.; operculum (*"Peltarion bilobatum"* DESLONGCHAMPS), 8a,b, ✕2.3 (182).

N. (Neritoptyx) OPPENHEIM, 1892 [*Nerita gold-fussii KEFERSTEIN* in GOLDFUSS, 1844]. With prominent parietal tubercle. *U.Cret.,* Eu.——FIG. 182,3. *N. (Neritoptyx) goldfussii;* Aus.; ✕2.5 (208).

Family DAWSONELLIDAE Wenz, 1938

Small, heliciform, with a platelike extension of inner lip. *Penn.*

Dawsonella BRADLEY, 1874 [*Anomphalus meeki BRADLEY, 1872*] [=*Dawsoniella* FISCHER, 1887 (obj.)]. Aperture slightly expanded at final stage; with platelike extension of inner lip seemingly lying over lip of larger aperture. *M.Penn.* N.Am.

[Found with *Maturipupa vermillionensis* (BRADLEY) in fresh-water limestone in a Coal Measures sequence; it may have lived in fresh water or more likely was terrestrial.]——FIG. 189,3. *D. meeki* (BRADLEY), Ill.; ✕10.

Family NERITIDAE Rafinesque, 1815

[*nom. transl. et correct.* GRAY, 1834 (*ex* subfamily Neritacea RAFINESQUE, 1815; Neritadae FLEMING, 1822)] [=Protoneridae KITTL, 1899]

Shell globose, turbiniform, capuliform or patelliform; mostly thick-walled; no umbilicus; inner walls of whorls resorbed; inner lip more or less thickened by callus or protruding as septum that narrows aperture, commonly with dentate margin (3). *Trias.-Rec.*

Subfamily NERITINAE Rafinesque, 1815

[*nom. transl.* SWAINSON, 1840 (*ex* Neritidae RAFINESQUE, 1815, *nom. correct.* GRAY, 1834)]

Operculum, where known, with rib on inner side and an apophysis. *M.Trias.-Rec.*

Neritaria KOKEN, 1892 [*N. similis* (=*Natica plicatilis* KLIPSTEIN, 1845)] [=*Protonerita* KITTL, 1894]. Naticiform, smooth, with slightly protruding spire; aperture with slight adapical channel; inner lip not extended as septum or very

little so, not dentate at margin, commonly with protuberance where its columellar and parietal parts meet; callus narrowly spread over base. *M. Trias.-U.Trias.,* cosmop.——Fig. 183,*1.* *N. candida* (KITTL), M.Trias.(Ladin.), S.Tyrol; ×1 (65).

Cryptonerita KITTL, 1894 [*C. elliptica*] [=*Cryptonatica* COSSMANN, 1925 (obj., *errore pro Cryptonerita*)]. Turbiniform, broader than high, smooth, of evenly convex whorls; aperture suborbicular; inner lip concave, not extended as septum or dentate at margin, callus extending very little over base. *M.Trias.(Ladin.)-U.Trias.(Carn.),* Eu.——Fig. 183,*2.* *C. elliptica,* M.Trias.(Ladin.), S.Tyrol; *2a,b,* ×1.5 (65).

Oncochilus ZITTEL, 1882 [*Natica globulosa* KLIPSTEIN, 1845; SD COSSMANN, 1925] [=*Sphaerochilus* COSSMANN, 1898 (obj.)]. Globular; inner lip with smooth, bulging pad of callus bearing 2 broad, prominent folds. ?*U. Carb.(Penn.), Trias.-Cret.,* cosmop.——Fig. 213,*5.* *O. globulosus* (KLIPSTEIN), M.Trias.(Ladin.), S.Tyrol; apertural, ×4 (KNIGHT, n). [J.B.KNIGHT, R.L.BATTEN & E.L. YOCHELSON would place this genus near *Cylindritopsis* in the Subulitacea.]

Neritoma MORRIS, 1849 [*Nerita sinuosa* J.SOWERBY, 1818; SD COSSMANN, 1925] [=*Neritoma* FISCHER, 1885 (obj.)]. Globose, smooth, with slightly protruding spire; inner lip much thickened, diminishing aperture. *L.Jur.-U.Cret.,* cosmop.

N. (Neritoma). Outer lip with narrow median sinus; margin of inner lip oblique, slightly concave, not dentate. *U.Jur.(Oxford.-Portland.),* Eu.——Fig. 183,*9.* *N. (Neritoma) sinuosa* (J. SOWERBY), U.Jur.(Portland.), Fr.; ×1 (201).

N. (Neridomus) MORRIS & LYCETT, 1851 [*Nerita hemisphaerica* MORRIS & LYCETT, 1851 (*non* ROEMER, 1836) = *Neridomus anglica* COX & ARKELL, 1950; SD COSSMANN, 1925 (ICZN pend.)] [=*Neritodomus* FISCHER, 1885 (obj.)]. Outer lip without sinus; margin of inner lip bulging along parietal region, not dentate. *L.Jur.-U.Cret.(Senon.),* cosmop.——Fig. 183,*11.* *N. (Neridomus) anglica* (COX & ARKELL), M.Jur. (Bathon.), Eng.; *11a,b,* ×1 (104).

N. (Staffinia) ANDERSON & COX, 1948 [*Neritina staffinensis* FORBES, 1851]. Outer lip without sinus; inner lip only moderately thickened, but with broad, oblique protrusion near its lower end. *M.Jur.(Bathon.),* Scot.

Trachynerita KITTL, 1894 [*T. fornoensis* (=*Turbo quadrata* STOPPANI, 1858); SD COSSMANN, 1925]. Globose, with low, obtuse spire and obtusely rounded periphery; narrow ramp or row of nodes below suture; aperture with slight adapical channel; inner lip well protruded, with untoothed parasigmoidal margin, and with callus widely spread over base. *M.Trias.(Anis.)-M.Jur.(Bathon.),* cosmop.——Fig. 183,*16.* *T. depressa* (HÖRNES), M.Trias.(Ladin.), S.Tyrol; *16a,b,* ×1 (66).

Platychilina KOKEN, 1892 [*P. wöhrmanni*] [=*Platychelyne* TOMLIN, 1931 (obj.)]. Globose, with low, very eccentric spire; whorls few, rapidly expanding, last one with broad sutural ramp and 2 or more angulations coinciding with rows of tubercles; aperture subquadrangular or polygonal; inner lip moderately protruded, with straight or concave, untoothed margin. *M.Trias.(Ladin.)-U. Trias.(Carn.),* Eu.——Fig. 183,*6.* *P. cainalloi* (STOPPANI), M.Trias.(Ladin.), S.Tyrol; *6a,b,* ×1.3 (66).

Delphinulopsis LAUBE, 1868 [*D. arietina* (=*Pleurotomaria binodosa* MÜNSTER, 1841); SD LAUBE, 1870]. Of few steeply coiled, low-embracing, rapidly enlarging whorls carrying nodose or scaly spiral carinae; inner lip protruded as broad septum with untoothed, oblique margin. *M.Trias. (Ladin.)-U.Trias.(Carn.),* Eu.——Fig. 183,*5.* *D. binodosa* (MÜNSTER), U.Trias.(Carn.), S.Tyrol; *5a,b,* ×1 (64).

Pileolus G.B.SOWERBY, 1823 [*P. plicatus;* SD S.P. WOODWARD, 1851]. Small, patelliform or capuliform, smooth or with radial ribbing; inner lip protruded as broad septum, much reducing aperture. *L.Jur.-Eoc.,* cosmop.

P. (Pileolus). Patelliform, smooth or with radial ribbing; inner lip much protruded as septum with smooth or dentate margin, reducing aperture to lunate slit. *L.Jur.-U.Cret.(Turon.),* cosmop.——Fig. 183,*3.* *P. (P.) plicatus,* M.Jur.(Bathon.), *3a,b,* ×2 (147).

P. (Gargania) GUISCARDI, 1857 [*G. brocchii*]. Capuliform, with raised terminal apex not appreciably incoiled; radially ribbed; inner lip septum well developed, ?not dentate; labrum thick, with broad median depression. *U.Cret.(Cenom.-Turon.),* Eu. —— Fig. 183,*7.* *P. (G.) brocchii* (GUISCARDI), U.Cret., Italy; *7a,b,* ×1, ×2 (190).

P. (Velatella) MEEK, 1873 [*Neritina bellatula* MEEK, 1873; SD COSSMANN, 1925]. Capuliform, with depressed submarginal apex slightly incoiled and curved to one side; smooth or radially ribbed; aperture semioval; outer lip somewhat thickened, smooth or faintly crenate internally; inner lip margin not dentate. *U.Cret.(Maastricht.),* N.Am.——Fig. 183,*8.* *P. (V.) bellatula* (MEEK), Laramie beds, Utah; *8a,b,* ×2.5, ×2 (228).

P. (Tomostoma) DESHAYES, 1824 [*P. neritoides;* SD FISCHER, 1885] [=*Calana* GRAY, 1847]. Capuliform, smooth, apex not terminal; aperture trapezoidal, inner lip with sinus. *Eoc.,* Eu.—— Fig. 183,*4.* *P. (T.) neritoides* (DESHAYES), Eoc., Fr.; *4a-c,* ×2 (147).

Trochonerita COSSMANN, 1907 [*Nerita mammaeformis* D'ORBIGNY, 1850]. Large, trochiform, smooth; whorls feebly convex, last one subangular at periphery of rather flattened base; labrum strongly prosocline; inner lip not dentate at margin, continuous with thin callus widely spread over

base. *L.Cret.,* Eu.——FIG. 183,*15.* *T. mammaeformis* (D'ORBIGNY), L.Cret.(Barrem.), Fr.; ×0.5
(170).

Lissochilus ZITTEL, 1882 [*Nerita sigaretina* Bu-
VIGNIER, 1843; SD COSSMANN, 1925]. Globose,
with slightly protruding spire of shouldered whorls;

FIG. 183. Neritacea (Neritidae——Neritinae) (p. *1279-1280, 1284-1285*).

last whorl with one or more angulations; ornament collabral ridges cancellated in same species by spirals; aperture much reduced by inner lip septum which is not dentate along its convex margin, and is continuous with callus rather widespread over base; outer lip bevelled from thick wall to thin edge; shallow adapical channel present. *M.Jur.(Bathon.) - U.Cret.(Senon.),* cosmop. ——FIG. 183,*13*. **L. sigaretinus* (BUVIGNIER), U.Jur., Fr.; *13a,b,* ×4 (111).

Otostoma D'ARCHIAC, 1859 [**Natica rugosa* ROEMER, 1841 (*non* BOSC, 1801) (=**Natica subrugosa* D'ORBIGNY, 1850); SD COSSMANN, 1925] [=*Desmieria* DOUVILLÉ, 1904 (obj.); *Corsania* VIDAL, 1917; *?Lyosoma* WHITE, 1883]. Globose, with depressed spire and rapidly enlarging whorls; ornament narrow collabral ridges or tuberculate spirals; inner lip septum broad, much reducing aperture, with large teeth along margin; outer lip strongly prosocline. [Original description of *Otostoma,* alleging broad aperture without septum, was based on imperfect specimens; this also was probably the case with *Lyosoma.*] *U.Jur.-Paleoc.,* cosmop.——FIG. 183,*14*. *O. divaricatum* (D'ORBIGNY), U.Cret.(U.Senon.), Hung.; *14a,b,* ×1 (210).

Myagrostoma J.BÖHM, 1900 [**M. plexum*]. Small, much broader than high, with low, obtuse, strongly eccentric spire; whorls with 2 prominent granose carinae, lower one forming periphery; ornament of close-spaced collabrals and spirals; base strongly convex, its outline in apertural view continuous with basal margin of aperture; aperture obliquely extended, constricted by 4 teeth, 2 on inner lip, others respectively on internally thickened basal and outer lips; thin inductura continuous with septum spread rather widely over base. *U.Cret. (Turon.),* SW.Asia.——FIG. 184,*7*. **M. plexum,* Israel; *7a,b,* ×3 (164).

Tournouerella MUNIER-CHALMAS, 1887 [*pro Tournoueria* MUNIER-CHALMAS, 1884 (*non* BRUSINA, 1870)] [**Tournoueria matheroni* MUNIER-CHALMAS, 1884]. Smooth, oviform, higher than broad, most of shell formed by last 1.5 whorls, to which earlier ones form small obtuse apex; last whorl descending and becoming compressed near aperture; aperture ovate, relatively narrow, appearing when viewed directly to project well below evenly rounded base; inner lip septum oblique, moderately broad, with prominent rounded teeth. *L.Cret.-U.Cret.,* Eu.——FIG. 184,*10*. **T. matheroni* (MUNIER-CHALMAS), U.Cret.(Dan.), Fr.; *10a,b,* ×2 (207).

Mesoneritina YEN, 1946 [**Neritella nebrascensis* MEEK & HAYDEN, 1862]. Small, globose, rather thin-shelled, with slightly protruding, obtuse spire; smooth, commonly retaining zigzag color pattern; inner lip somewhat thickened, with straight or concave, untoothed margin, and not appreciably protruded as septum. *L.Cret.,* N.Am.——

FIG. 184,*3*. **M. nebrascensis* (MEEK & HAYDEN), L.Cret., Wyo.; *3a,b,* ×2 (228).

Nerita LINNÉ, 1758 [**N. peloronta;* SD MONTFORT, 1810] [=*Neritarius* DUMÉRIL, 1806 (obj.); *Dontostoma* HERRMANNSEN, 1847; *Tenare* GRAY, 1858 (obj.)]. Sturdy shells, smooth to spirally ribbed; inner lip septum well developed, its surface (labial area) commonly pustulose or irregularly ribbed. [Mainly marine.] *U.Cret.-Rec.,* cosmop.

N. (Nerita). Outer lip thickened, with 2 teeth; labial area flattened, with 2 large teeth at margin. *Paleoc.-Rec.,* Eu.-IndoPac.——FIG. 185,*1*. **N. peloronta,* Rec., W.Indies; ×1 (147).

N. (Amphinerita) MARTENS, 1887 [**N. umlaasiana* KRAUSS, 1848; SD BAKER, 1923] [=*Odontostoma* MÖRCH, 1852 (*non* TURTON, 1829) (obj.); *Melanerita* MARTENS, 1887]. Smooth or finely striate, oblique; labial area smooth, margin weakly dentate. *U.Cret.-Rec.,* Eu.-IndoPac.

N. (Chingua) CLARK & DURHAM, 1946 [**N. (C.) chinguensis*]. Spiral ribs beaded; labial area smooth. *Eoc.,* S.Am.——FIG. 184,*13*. **N. (C.) chinguensis,* Eoc., Colombia; ×2 (169).

N. (Fluvinerita) PILSBRY, 1932 [**N. (F.) alticola* (=*N. tenebricosa* C. B. ADAMS, 1852)]. Smooth, inner lip straight and smooth, labial area narrow; outer lip thin; no opercular stop; operculum with minute granulations. [Fresh-water.]. *Rec.,* W. Indies.

N. (Heminerita) MARTENS, 1887 [**N. pica* GOULD, 1859 (*non* GMELIN, 1791) (=*N. japonica* DUNKER, 1859)]. Finely striate; operculum granular. *Rec.,* Pac.

N. (Puperita) GRAY, 1857 [**N. pupa* LINNÉ, 1758]. Small ovate, smooth. *Mio.-Rec.,* W.Indies.

N. (Ritena) GRAY, 1858 [**N. plicata* LINNÉ, 1758] [=*Pila* MÖRCH, 1852 (*non* RÖDING, 1798); *Cymostyla* MARTENS, 1887]. Spire moderately elevated; outer lip toothed; labial area irregularly costate, with several teeth at margin. *Eoc.-Rec.,* Eu.-Afr.-trop.Am.-IndoPac.

N. (Seminerita) COSSMANN, 1925 [**N. mammaria* LAMARCK, 1804] [=*Seminerita* WENZ, 1938 (obj.)]. Small, with regularly incised growth lines; outer lip thin, inner lip dentate. *U.Cret.(Turon.)-Eoc.,* cosmop.——FIG. 184,*2*. *N. (S.) mammaria,* Eoc., Fr.; *2a,b,* ×3 (147).

N. (Theliostyla) MÖRCH, 1852 [**N. albicilla* LINNÉ, 1758; SD KOBELT, 1879] [=*Natere* GRAY, 1858 (obj.); *Ilynerita* MARTENS, 1887]. Low-spired, outer lip regularly dentate within; labial area granulate, sinuate and finely dentate at margin. *U.Cret.(Senon.)-Rec.,* Eu.-IndoPac.-trop. Am.

Neritina LAMARCK, 1816 [**Nerita pulligera* LINNÉ, 1766 (ICZN Op. 119, 1931)] [=*Laphrostoma* RAFINESQUE, 1815 (obj.); *Lamphrostoma, Lamprostoma* AUCTT. (obj.); *Neritella* GRAY, 1848 (obj.); *Chernites* GISTEL, 1848 (obj.); *Clypeolum* RÉCLUZ, 1850 (*non* RÉCLUZ, 1842); *Labialia, Onychina*

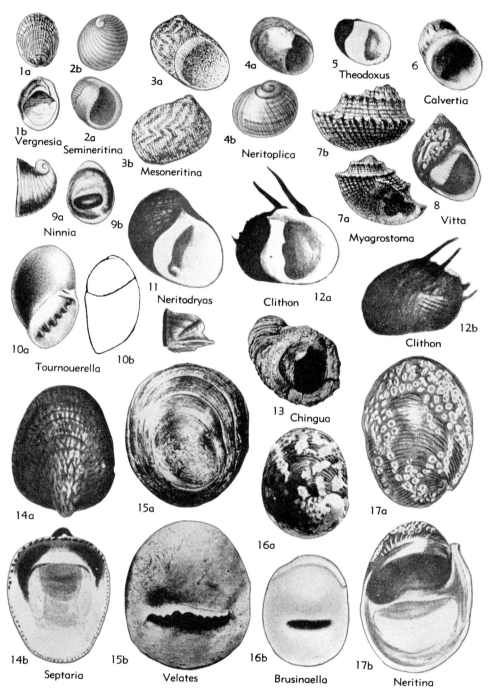

FIG. 184. Neritacea (Neritidae-Neritinae) (p. *1282-1285*).

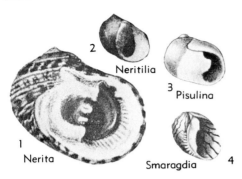

Fig. 185. Neritacea (Neritidae——Neritinae, Neritiliinae, Smaragdiinae) (p. *1282, 1285*).

SCUDDER, 1882 (obj.)]. Smaller and thinner-shelled than *Nerita;* outer lip thin, inner lip smooth or finely dentate. [Marine, brackish, or fresh-water.] *Eoc.-Rec.,* cosmop.

N. (Neritina). Relatively large, low-spired; outer lip overriding last whorl in a projecting point; labial area broad, flat. *Rec.,* IndoPac.——FIG. 184,*17.* *N. (N.) pulligera* (LINNÉ), Rec. E. Indies; *17a,b,* ×1 (147).

N. (Clypeolum) RÉCLUZ, 1842 [*N. latissima* BRODERIP, 1833; SD PILSBRY & BEQUAERT, 1927] [=*Alina* RÉCLUZ, 1842 (*non* RISSO, 1826)]. Aperture flaring, especially posteriorly; height greater than width. *Mio.-Rec.,* C.Am.

N. (Dostia) GRAY, 1847 [*Nerita crepidularia* LAMARCK, 1822 (=*N. violacea* GMELIN, 1791)] [=*Mitrula* RÉCLUZ, 1850 (*non* GRAY, 1821) (obj.)]. Apertural margin entire, labial area shield-shaped, with arcuate and finely toothed edge. *Eoc.-Rec.,* Eu.-IndoPac.——FIG. 183,*10.* *N. (D.) violacea* (GMELIN), *Rec.,* E.Indies; ×1 (147).

N. (Nereina) CRISTOFORI & JAN, 1832 [*Nereina lacustris* (=*Neritina punctulata* LAMARCK, 1816)]. Spire bluntly elevated. *Mio.-Rec.,* W. Indies.

N. (Neripteron) LESSON, 1830 [*N. taitensis;* SD BAKER, 1923] [=*Neritopteron* FISCHER, 1885 (obj.)]. Like *N. (Dostia)* but more elongate and with labial area less symmetrical. *Rec.,* IndoPac.

N. (Neritona) MARTENS, 1869 [*N. labiosa* SOWERBY, 1841]. Larger than *N. (Dostia),* labial area expanded above, aperture narrower; operculum ribbed. *Rec.,* IndoPac.

N. (Provittoida) BAKER, 1923 [*Nerita smithi* WOOD, 1828] [=*Provittoidea* WENZ, 1938 (obj.)]. Spire elevated, pointed. *Rec.,* Indo-Pac.

N. (Pseudonerita) BAKER, 1923 [*Neritina holosericea* GARRETT, 1872]. Small, oblique-ovate, spire elevated; inner lip sinuate, finely dentate. [Brackish water.] *Rec.,* S.Pac.

N. (Vergnesia) DELPEY, 1940 [*V. mopelleti]. Dilated, concentrically striate. *Eoc.,* Fr.——FIG.

184,*1.* *N. (V.) morelleti* (DELPEY), U.Eoc., Fr.

N. (Vitta) MÖRCH, 1852 [*Nerita virginea* LINNÉ, 1758; SD BAKER, 1923] [=*Scapha* MÖRCH, 1852 (*non* RÉCLUZ, 1841) (obj.)]. Spire elevated, pointed; shell smooth, inflated; inner lip toothed. *Mio.-Rec.,* N.Am.-S.Am.-W.Afr.——FIG. 184,*8.* *N. (V.) virginea* (LINNÉ), Rec., W.Indies; ×1 (147).

N. (Vittina) BAKER, 1923 [*N. roissyana* RÉCLUZ, 1841] [=*Paranerita* BOURNE, 1909 (*non* HAMPSON, 1901)]. Resembling *N. (Vitta)* but smaller. *Rec.,* Indo-Pac.

N. (Vittoida) BAKER, 1923 [*N. variegata* LESSON, 1830] [=*Vittoidea* WENZ, 1938 (obj.)]. Shell as in *N. (Vittina),* but radula differing in details. [Brackish water.] *Rec.,* Indo-Pac.

Neritodryas MARTENS, 1869 [*Nerita cornea* LINNÉ, 1758; SD BAKER, 1923]. Moderately large, spire blunt; labial area smooth, a blunt tooth below; operculum ribbed. *Rec.,* IndoPac.——FIG. 184,*11.* *N. cornea* (LINNÉ), Rec., E.Indies; ×1 (147).

Neritoplica OPPENHEIM, 1892 [*"Neritina globulus FÉR."* (*errore pro Nerita globosa* FERUSSAC, 1823) =*Neritina uniplicata* SOWERBY, 1823; SD WENZ, 1938)]. Small, low-spired, smooth; with fold on inner lip. *M.Jur.(Bathon.)-Paleoc.,* Eu.——FIG. 184,*4.* *N. uniplicata* (SOWERBY), Paleoc., Fr.; *4a,b,* ×2 (147).

Septaria FÉRUSSAC, 1807 [*Patella borbonica* BORY deSAINT VINCENT, 1803] [=*Cimber* MONTFORT, 1810 (obj.); *Septarius* GRAY, 1821 (obj.); *Catillus* GRAY, 1847 (*non* BRONGNIART, 1822) (obj.); *Cibota* ADAMS & ADAMS, 1858 (*non* HERRMANNSEN, 1852) (obj.); *Laodia, Paria* GRAY, 1868]. Shell almost isostrophic; last whorl large; aperture expanded; thin labial septum present; subequal muscle scars visible in aperture. *Rec.,* Indo-Pac.

S. (Septaria). Apex projecting beyond left of aperture; labial septum broad. [In swift-flowing streams.] *Rec.,* IndoPac.——FIG. 184,*14.* *S. (S.) borbonica* (BORY deST.VINCENT), Bourbon I.; *14a-c,* ×1 (147).

S. (Navicella) LAMARCK, 1816 [*N. tessellaria;* SD CHILDREN, 1823] [=*Navicellus* GRAY, 1821 (obj.); *Scapha* RÉCLUZ, 1841 (obj.); *Stenopoma* GRAY, 1868]. Apex not projecting beyond left of aperture. *Rec.,* IndoPac.

S. (Paraseptaria) RISBEC, 1942 [*P. parva*]. Patelliform; operculum horny. [Marine.] *Rec.,* New Caledonia.

S. (Sandalium) SCHUMACHER, 1817 [*Sandalium picta;* SD BAKER, 1923 (?=*Patella porcellana* LINNÉ, 1758)] [*non Sandalium* RETZIUS, 1788 (*nom. nud.*); *nec* OKEN, 1815 (*nom. nud.*)] [=*Sandalinum* RÉCLUZ, 1841 (obj.); *Elara* ADAMS & ADAMS, 1856 (obj.); *Elana* GRAY, 1867 (obj.)]. Like *S. (Septaria)* but with narrow labial septum. [Fluviatile, in quiet water.] *Rec.,* Indo-Pac.

Theodoxus MONTFORT, 1810 [*T. lutetianus* (=*Nerita fluviatilis* LINNÉ, 1758; ICZN Op. 335,

1955)] [=*Theodoxis* Montfort, 1810 (obj.); *Elea* Fitzinger, 1833; *Neritoglobus* Kobelt, 1871 (obj.); *Theodoxia* Bourguignat, 1877 (obj.); *Theodora, Theodorus* auctt. (obj.)]. Small, obliquely ovate, spire low or elevated; labial area smooth, with smooth or dentate margin; operculum smooth. [Fluviatile.] *Oligo.-Rec.,* cosmop.

T. (Theodoxus). Inner lip dentate; operculum without apophysis. *Oligo.-Rec.,* Eu.-W.Asia.——Fig. 184,5. *T. (T.) fluviatilis* (Linné), Rec., Ger.; ✕1.5 (147).

T. (Alinoclithon) Baker, 1923 [*Nerita cariosus* Wood, 1828]. Labial area expanded; opercular apophysis weak. [Fluviatile.] *Rec.,* Hawaiian Is.

T. (Brusinaella) Andrussov, 1912 [*Neritina petasata* Seninski, 1905] [=*Brusinaela* Andrussov, 1912 (obj.)]. Aperture a narrow slit between widely expanded labial and labral areas. *Plio.,* SW.Asia.——Fig. 184,16. *T. (B.) petasatus* (Seninski), Plio., Caucasus; *16a,b,* ✕2 (147).

T. (Calvertia) Bourguignat, 1880 [*C. letournouxi* = *Neritina sinjana* Brusina, 1876; SD Wenz, 1929] [=*Burgersteinia, Petrettinia, Saint-Simonia, Tripaloia* Bourguignat, 1880; *Neritodonta* Brusina, 1884]. Obliquely ovate, spire somewhat elevated; blunt tooth or ridge on lower muscle scar; operculum with apophysis. *Mio.-Plio.,* Eu.-SW.Asia.——Fig. 184,6. *T. (C.) sinjanus* (Brusina), U.Plio., Dalmatia; ✕2 (147).

T. (Clithon) deMontfort, 1810 [*Nerita corona* Linné, 1758] [=*Cliton* Lesson, 1830 (obj.); *Corona* Récluz, 1850 (*non* Alber, 1850) (obj.)]. With a subsutural row of spines or nodes. [Fluviatile or brackish.]. *Plio.-Rec.,* IndoPac.-Japan.——Fig. 184,12. *T. (C.) corona* (Linné), Rec., Mauritius; *12a,b,* ✕1 (147).

T. (Meganninia) Davidachvili, 1932 [*T. corrugata* Davidachvili, 1930]. Resembling *Neritina (Neripteron)* in form but with less apparent spire. *Plio.,* SW.Asia.

T. (Neritaea) Roth, 1855 [*Neritina jordani* Sowerby, 1841] [=*Neritoconus* Kobelt, 1871 (obj.)]. Spire somewhat cylindrical, high; inner lip weakly arched and dentate. *Plio.-Rec.,* SW.Asia.-E.Afr.

T. (Neritoclithon) Baker, 1923 [*Neritina neglecta* Pease, 1860]. *Rec.,* Hawaiian Is.

T. (Neritonyx) Andrussov, 1912 [*Neritina unguiculatus* Seninski, 1905]. Resembling *Crepidula;* labial area finely granulate. *Plio.,* SW.Asia.

T. (Ninnia) Westerlund, 1903 [*Neritina schultzi* Grimm, 1877]. Small, labial area wide and deep; aperture contracted. *Plio.-Rec.,* SW.Asia.——Fig. 184,9. *T. (N.) schultzi* (Grimm), Rec., Caspian Sea; *9a,b,* ✕2 (147).

T. (Ninniopsis) Tomlin, 1930 [*Neritaea colchica* Andrussov, 1912]. Resembling *T. (Ninnia)* but larger; labial area flatter. *Plio.,* SW.Asia.

T. (Pictoneritina) Iredale, 1936 [*Neritina oualaniensis* Lesson, 1831]. Like *T. (Vittoclithon)*

but with one large and several small teeth on inner lip. *U.Mio.-Rec.,* IndoPac.

T. (Vittoclithon) Baker, 1923 [*Neritina meleagris* Lamarck, 1822]. Small, smooth; inner lip weakly arched, with one tooth. *Paleoc.-Rec.,* Eu.-trop.Am.-IndoPac.——Fig. 183,12. *T. (V.) meleagris* (Lamarck), Rec., Sumatra; ✕1.5 (147).

Velates deMontfort, 1810 [*V. conoideus* (=*Nerita perversa* Gmelin, 1791)]. Large, spire concealed; resembling *Crepidula;* inner lip serrate. *U.Cret.(Cenom.)-Eoc.,* Eu.-Asia-Afr.-N.Am.——Fig. 184,15. *V. perversus* (Gmelin), Eoc., Fr.; *15a,b,* ✕0.7 (147).

Subfamily NERITILIINAE Baker, 1923

[*nom. correct.* Wenz, 1938 (ex Neritilinae Baker, 1923)]

Small, ovate, smooth, unicolored; inner lip smooth; operculum without ribs or apophyses. [Fresh-water.] *Rec.*

Neritilia Martens, 1879 [*Neritina rubida* Pease, 1867]. Aperture oblique. *Rec.,* tropics.——Fig. 185,2. *N. rubida* (Pease), Rec., Tahiti; ✕3 (147).

?**Septariellina** Bequaert & Clench, 1936 [*S. congolensis*]. Minute; aperture large, ovate-quadrate. *Rec.,* W.Afr.

Subfamily SMARAGDIINAE Baker, 1923

[*nom. correct.* Wenz, 1938 (ex Smaragdinae Baker, 1923)]

Small, obliquely ovate; operculum with ribs and an apophysis. [Marine.] *Mio.-Rec.*

Smaragdia Issel, 1869 [*Nerita viridis* Linné, 1758; SD Kobelt, 1879] [=*Gaillardotia* Bourguignat, 1877 (obj.)]. Spire low, aperture narrow. *Mio.-Rec.,* Carib.-IndoPac.-Medit.

S. (Smaragdia). Aperture nearly the height of the shell. *Mio.-Rec.,* Carib.-IndoPac.——Fig. 185,4. *S. viridis* (Linné), Rec., Medit.; ✕2 (147).

S. (Smaragdella) Baker, 1923 [*Neritina hellvillensis* Crosse, 1881]. *Rec.,* IndoPac.

S. (Smaragdista) Iredale, 1936 [*Smaragdista tragena*]. Aperture 0.75 height of shell. *Rec.,* IndoPac.

?**Magadis** Melvill & Standen, 1899 [*M. eumerintha*]. Spire low, aperture large; sculpture of irregular axial folds. *Rec.,* Austral.

Pisulina Nevill & Nevill, 1869 [*P. adamsiana*]. Smooth, with 1 or 2 large teeth on inner lip. *Rec.,* India.——Fig. 185,3. *P. adamsiana,* Ceylon; ✕3 (147).

Family HELICINIDAE Latreille, 1825

[*nom. correct.* Gray, 1840 (ex Helicinides Latreille, 1825)] [=Helicinadae Guilding, 1828; Helicinaceae Menke, 1828; Oligogyradae Gray, 1847] [Acknowledgment of information and advice generously furnished on the Helicinidae by Dr. H. Burrington Baker is here recorded with appreciation]

Land snails of small to medium size, few-whorled, conical to lenticular; inner walls of whorls resorbed; umbilicus mostly

concealed by columellar lip or filled with a callus pad; operculum semicircular to rhombic, without apophyses, horny, nearly always reinforced exteriorly by a calcareous layer. With pulmonary cavity and no ctenidium. *U.Cret.-Rec.*

?Subfamily DIMORPHOPTYCHIINAE Wenz, 1938

[*nom. correct.* KEEN, herein (*pro* Dimorphoptychinae WENZ, 1938)]

Aperture with three parallel parietal folds and basal fold. *U.Cret.-Paleoc.*

Dimorphoptychia SANDBERGER, 1871 [*Helix arnouldi* MICHAUD, 1837] [=?*Obbinula* STACHE, 1889; *Pseudostrobilus* OPPENHEIM, 1892]. Small, lenticular, umbilicus not evident; periphery with blunt keel. *U.Cret.(Turon.)-Paleoc.,* Eu.——FIG. 187,4. *D. arnouldi* (MICHAUD), Paleoc., Fr.; ×2 (147).

Subfamily HELICININAE Latreille, 1825

[*nom. transl.* SWAINSON, 1840 (*ex* Helicinidae, *nom. correct.* GRAY, 1840, *pro* Helicinides LATREILLE, 1825)]

Distinguished by details of radula; lateral teeth 5, including a comb-lateral and an accessory plate. *?Paleoc., Mio.-Rec.*

Helicina LAMARCK, 1799 (gen. without sp.), 1801 [*Helix neritella* LAMARCK, 1801] [=*Pitonnellus, Pitonnillus* DEMONTFORT, 1810 (obj.); *Colyma* RAFINESQUE, 1815; *Pachytoma* SWAINSON, 1840; *Euneritella* WAGNER, 1905 (obj.); "FKr"[1] *Ampliata* WAGNER, 1907; "FKr" *Festiva* WAGNER, 1910]. Basal callus pad with a furrow. *?Paleoc., Mio.-Rec.,* N.Am.-C.Am.-S.Am.-Pac.Is.

H. (Helicina). Columella thickened below. *?Neog.-Rec.,* C.Am.-S.Am.——FIG. 186,1. *H. neritella* (LAMARCK), Rec., Jamaica; *1a,b,* ×2 (147).

H. (Olygyra) SAY, 1818 [*O. orbiculata*] [=*Oligyra* SAY, 1819 (obj.); "FKr" *Subglobulosa, Succincta* WAGNER, 1905]. Turbinate, basal callus large; surface smooth. *?Paleoc., Mio.-Rec.,* N.Am.-S.Am.——FIG. 186,4. *H. (O.) orbiculata,* Rec., Ala.; *4a-d,* ×2 (147).

H. (Oxyrhombus) FISCHER & CROSSE, 1893 [*H. amoena* PFEIFFER, 1845; SD BAKER, 1922] [="FKr" *Angulata* WAGNER, 1905; "FKr" *Tamsiana* WAGNER, 1907]. *Rec.,* C.Am.

H. (Pseudoligyra) BAKER, 1954 [*H. tenuis* PFEIFFER, 1849]. *Rec.,* Mex.

H. (Tristramia) CROSSE, 1863 [*H. salvini* TRISTRAM, 1861] [=*Caloplisma* FISCHER & CROSSE, 1893; *Retorquata* WAGNER, 1905]. *Rec.,* C.Am.

Alcadia GRAY, 1840 [*Helicina major* GRAY, 1824; SD GRAY, 1847] [=*Isoltia* GUPPY, 1859; *Eualcadia* WAGNER, 1907; "FKr" *Incrustata, Intusplicata, Palliata, Sericea* WAGNER, 1907]. Basal callus large. *Rec.,* C.Am.-W.Indies.

A. (Alcadia). *Rec.,* C.Am.-Carib.

A. (Analcadia) WAGNER, 1907 [*Helicina dysoni* PFEIFFER, 1849; SD BAKER, 1922]. *Rec.,* Antilles.

A. (Emoda) ADAMS & ADAMS, 1856 [*Helicina silacea* MORELET, 1849; SD BAKER, 1922] [=*Glyptemoda* CLENCH & AGUAYO, 1950]. Periostracum with axial folds. *Rec.,* Cuba.

A. (Idesa) ADAMS & ADAMS, 1856 [*Helicina rotunda* D'ORBIGNY in SAGRA, 1842; SD BAKER, 1922] [=*Schrammia* GUPPY, 1895; *Leialcadia* WAGNER, 1907; "FKr" *Mammilla* WAGNER, 1907 (*non* TRYON, 1883); *Hjalmarsona* BAKER, 1940; *Weinlandella* BAKER, 1954]. *Rec.,* Antilles.

A. (Penisoltia) BAKER, 1954 [*Helicina hispida* PFEIFFER, 1839]. *Rec.,* Cuba.

A. (Striatemoda) BAKER, 1940 [*Helicina striata* LAMARCK, 1822 (*non* DEFRANCE, 1821) = *H. subfusca* MENKE, 1828] [=*Diaphana* GUPPY, 1895 (*non* BROWN, 1827)]. Intermediate between *A.* (Emoda) and *A.* (Analcadia). *Rec.,* Puerto Rico.

Bourciera PFEIFFER, 1852 [*B. helicinaeformis*] [=*Pseudhelicina* SYKES, 1907]. With paucispiral operculum. *Rec.,* Ecuador.

Ceratopoma MÖLLENDORFF, 1893 [*Helicina caroli* KOBELT, 1886] [="FKr" *Diversicolor* WAGNER, 1905; *Negopenia* IREDALE, 1941 (*nom. nud.*)]. With a peripheral keel. *Rec.,* Pac. Is.

C. (Ceratopoma). *Rec.,* Pac.Is.

C. (Palaeohelicina) WAGNER, 1905 [*Helicina fischeriana* MONTROUZIER, 1863; SD IREDALE, 1937] [=*Kalokonia, Rhabdokonia* WAGNER, 1905]. *Rec.,* Pac.Is.

Hemipoma WAGNER, 1905 [*Helicina hakodadiensis* HARTMANN, 1890; SD WENZ, 1938]. Differing only slightly from *Ceratopoma. Rec.,* Japan.

Orobophana WAGNER, 1905 [*Helicina uberta* GOULD, 1847; SD BAKER, 1922]. Small, with radial and spiral sculpture; basal callus thick. *Pleist.-Rec.,* Polynesia.——FIG. 186,2. *O. uberta* (GOULD), Rec., Hawaii; ×3 (147).

Pleuropoma MÖLLENDORFF, 1893 [*Helicina dichroa* MÖLLENDORFF, 1890; SD PILSBRY & COOKE, 1934] [="FKr" *Albocincta* WAGNER, 1908]. Small, periphery keeled. *Pleist.-Rec.,* Pac.

P. (Pleuropoma). Keel obtuse, operculum with cross-lamella. *Pleist.-Rec.,* Pac.——FIG. 186,3. *P. dichroa* (MÖLLENDORFF), Rec., Philippines; ×3 (147).

P. (Aphanoconia) WAGNER, 1905 [*Helicina verecunda* GOULD, 1859; SD GUDE, 1914] [="FKr" *Pachystoma, Reticulata, Sculpta* WAGNER, 1905; *Sphaeroconia* WAGNER, 1909 (obj.)]. Keel weak. *Pleist.-Rec.,* Pac.Is.

Schasicheila SHUTTLEWORTH, 1852 [*Helicina alata* PFEIFFER, 1848; SD KOBELT, 1880] [=*Schasichila* FISCHER, 1885 (obj.); *Atoyac* BAKER, 1928 (obj.)]. Operculum semicircular, with strong cal-

---

[1] The abbreviation "FKr" indicates a name proposed by WAGNER for a "Formenkreis," a group of species inferior to a subgenus in taxonomic rank. The status of such names needs clarification, although all of WAGNER's names for "Formenkreise" are here regarded as subjective synonyms.

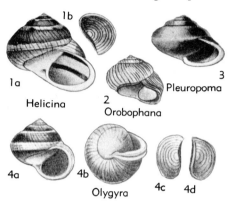

FIG. 186. Neritacea (Helicinidae——Helicininae) (p. I286).

careous layer and pointed extensions on edge by columella. *Rec.*, C.Am.

S. (Schasicheila). *Rec.*, C.Am.

S. (Misantla) BAKER, 1928 [**S. misantlensis* FISCHER & CROSSE, 1893]. *Rec.*, C.Am.

S. (Necaxa) BAKER, 1928 [**Helicina minuscula* PFEIFFER, 1859]. *Rec.*, C.Am.

Sturanya WAGNER, 1905 [**Helicina plicatilis* MOUSSON, 1865; SD KOBELT, 1905] [=*Sturanyella* PILSBRY & COOKE, 1934; *Sturyanella* AUCTT. (obj.)]. Basal callus thick on columella. *Rec.*, Polynesia.

Sulfurina MÖLLENDORFF, 1893 [**Helicina citrina* GRATELOUP, 1840] [=*Hypostrongyla* TOMLIN, 1930; *Pestomena* IREDALE, 1941 (*nom. nud.*)]. Thin-shelled, mostly yellow in color, callus thick. *Rec.*, SW.Pac.

S. (Sulfurina). *Rec.*, E.Indies.

S. (Kosmetopoma) WAGNER, 1905 [**Helicina amaliae* KOBELT, 1886]. *Rec.*, Philippines.

Subfamily HENDERSONIINAE Baker, 1926

Reproductive organs typically more primitive than in Helicininae. *?Paleoc., Pleist.-Rec.*

Hendersonia WAGNER, 1905 [**Helicina occulta* SAY, 1831]. Small, thick-shelled, operculum subspiral, nucleus eccentric. *?Paleoc., Pleist.-Rec.*, N.Am.——FIG. 187,*1.* **H. occulta* (SAY), Rec., Iowa; *1a,b*, apertural view and operculum, ×3 (147).

Miluna WAGNER, 1905 [**M. josephinae*]. Operculum subspiral, with submarginal nucleus; aperture without folds. *Rec.*, China.

Waldemaria WAGNER, 1905 [**Helicina japonica* A. ADAMS, 1861; SD BAKER, 1922]. Globose, with fine radial folds. *Rec.*, Japan.

Subfamily PROSERPININAE Gray, 1847

[*nom. transl.* THIELE, 1929 (*ex* Proserpinidae GRAY, 1847)] [=Despoenidae NEWTON, 1891)]

Lenticular to rounded; without operculum. *?Oligo., Rec.*

Proserpina G.B.SOWERBY, 1839 [**P. nitida* (?=*Helicina linguifera* JONAS, 1839)] [=*Despoena* NEWTON, 1891 (obj.)]. Rounded lenticular, glassy, with one or more parietal folds in aperture. *?Oligo., Rec.*, Eu.-W.Indies.

P. (Proserpina). With 2 parietal and 2 palatal folds. *Rec.*, Jamaica.

P. (Despoenella) BAKER, 1923 [**Odontostoma depressa* D'ORBIGNY in SAGRA, 1842] [=*Odontostoma* D'ORBIGNY, 1841 (*non* TURTON, 1829)]. With parietal folds only. *?Oligo., Rec.*, Eu.-W. Indies.——FIG. 187,*5.* **P. (D.) depressa* (D'ORBIGNY), Rec., Cuba; ×4 (147).

Subfamily STOASTOMATINAE C. B. Adams, 1849

[*nom. correct.* KEEN, herein (*ex* Stoastominae, *nom. transl.* BAKER, 1928, *ex* Stoastomidae C.B.ADAMS, 1849)]

Lateral teeth of radula normally with a mushroom-shaped T-lateral and reduced accessory plate; marginals many, mostly multicuspid. *Pleist.-Rec.*

Stoastoma C.B.ADAMS, 1849 [**S. pisum*] [=*Hemicyclostoma* PFEIFFER, 1865 (obj.)]. Minute, umbilicus only partly concealed. *Rec.*, W.Indies.

Eutrochatella FISCHER, 1885 [**Helicina pulchella* GRAY, 1825] [=*Trochatella* SWAINSON, 1840 (*non* LESSON, 1830); *Krebsia* GUPPY, 1895 (*non* MÖRCH, 1877); "FKr" *Excavata* WAGNER, 1907]. Apex pointed, operculum thick, calcareous layer with folds. *Rec.*, C.Am.-W.Indies.

E. (Eutrochatella). *Rec.*, Cuba.

E. (Cubaviana) BAKER, 1922 [**Helicina politula* POEY, 1852]. *Rec.*, Cuba.

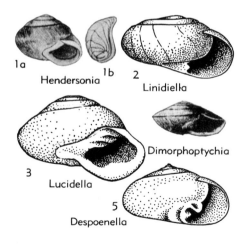

FIG. 187. Neritacea (Helicinidae——Dimorphoptychiinae, Hendersoniinae, Proserpininae, Ceratodiscinae, Proserpinellinae (p. I286-I288).

E. (Microviana) BAKER, 1928 [*Helicina rupestris PFEIFFER, 1839]. Rec., Cuba.

E. (Priotrochatella) FISCHER, 1893 [*Helicina constellata MORELET, 1847]. Rec., Cuba.

E. (Torreviana) AGUAYO, 1943 [*E. (T.) spinopoma]. Rec., Cuba.

E. (Troschelviana) BAKER, 1922 [*Helicina erythraea SOWERBY, 1866]. Rec., C.Am.-W.Ind.

E. (Ustronia) WAGNER, 1908 [*Helicina sloanei d'ORBIGNY, 1845; SD BAKER, 1922]. Rec., Cuba.

Geophorus FISCHER, 1885 [*Helicina agglutinans SOWERBY, 1842] [=Pecoviana IREDALE, 1941 (nom. nud.)]. Operculum triangular to trapezoidal, nucleus eccentric. Rec., Orient.

G. (Geophorus). Rec., E.Indies.

G. (Diplopinax) BARTSCH, 1921 [*G. (D.) tagbilleranus]. Rec., Philippines.

G. (Schistopinax) BARTSCH, 1921 [*G. (S.) siquijorensis]. Rec., Philippines.

Heudeia CROSSE, 1885 [*Helicina sechuanensis HEUDE, 1885]. Relatively high-spired, small. Rec., Orient.

H. (Heudeia). Aperture with twisted outer lip. Rec., China.

H. (Calybium) MORLET, 1891 [*C. massiei]. Lowbiconic, with peripheral keel and apertural folds. Rec., India.

H. (Geotrochatella) FISCHER, 1891 [*Helicina mouhoti PFEIFFER, 1862; SD BAKER, 1922]. Without folds. Rec., IndoChina.

Pyrgodomus FISCHER & CROSSE, 1893 [*Helicina chryseis TRISTRAM, 1861] [=Artecallosa WAGNER, 1908 (obj.)]. Small, high-spired. Rec., trop.Am.

Stoastomops BAKER, 1924 [*S. walkeri]. Minute, conic, aperture small. Rec., W.Indies.

S. (Stoastomops). Rec., W.Indies.

S. (Swiftella) BAKER, 1941 [*S. (S.) boriqueni]. Rec., W.Indies.

Viana ADAMS & ADAMS, 1856 [*Helicina regina MORELET, 1849; SD BAKER, 1922] [=Ampullina deBLAINVILLE, 1824 (non BOWDICH, 1822); Hapata GRAY, 1856 (obj.); Rhynchocheila SHUTTLEWORTH, 1878 (obj.); Fitzia GUPPY, 1895]. Relatively large; outer lip with a sinus above periphery. Rec., Cuba.

Subfamily CERATODISCINAE Pilsbry, 1927

Discoid, few-whorled, mostly spirally sculptured. *Rec.*

Ceratodiscus SIMPSON & HENDERSON, 1901 [*C. solutus]. With fine spiral lines, operculum with calcareous layer. Rec., Antilles.

Fadyenia CHITTY, 1857 [*Stoastoma fadyenianum C.B.ADAMS, 1849; SD BAKER, 1922] [=Lindsleya, Metcalfeia CHITTY, 1857]. Small, spirally sculptured. Rec., W.Indies.

F. (Fadyenia). Depressed to globose-conic. Rec., W.Indies.

F. (Blandia) CHITTY, 1857 [*Stoastoma blandianum C.B.ADAMS, 1849; SD BAKER, 1922]

[=Petitia, Wilkinsonaea CHITTY, 1857]. With periostracal expansions on spiral ribs. Rec., W. Indies.

F. (Lewisia) CHITTY, 1857 [*Stoastoma philippiana C.B.ADAMS, 1850; SD BAKER, 1922]. Rec., W.Indies.

Lucidella SWAINSON, 1840 [*Helix aureola FÉRUSSAC, 1822] [=Prosopis WEINLAND, 1862 (non FABRICIUS, 1804)]. Periostracum sculptured; aperture with internal lamellae; operculum with nearly central nucleus. Mio.-Rec., C.Am.-W.Indies.

L. (Lucidella). With spiral striae. Mio.-Rec., W. Indies.——FIG. 187,3. *L. aureola (FÉRUSSAC), Rec., Jamaica; ×3 (147).

L. (Perenna) GUPPY, 1867 [*Helicina lamellosa (=*H. lirata PFEIFFER, 1849)]. Depressed, with spiral ridges and keel. Rec., W.Indies.

L. (Poenia) ADAMS & ADAMS, 1856 [*Helicina depressa GRAY, 1825; SD PILSBRY, 1912] [=Urichia GUPPY, 1895]. Rec., W.Indies.

L.(Poeniella) BAKER, 1923 [*Helicina christophori PILSBRY, 1897]. With radial and spiral striae. Rec., C.Am.-W.Indies.

Subfamily PROSERPINELLINAE Baker, 1923

Size of shell reduced relative to that of soft parts. *Pleist.-Rec.*

Proserpinella BLAND, 1865 [*P. berendti]. Minute, lenticular, with no apertural folds. Rec., Mex.

Ceres GRAY, 1856 [*Caracolla eolina DUCLOS, 1834; SD KOBELT, 1880]. Spire nearly flat, base rounded; 2 parietal, 2 palatal folds. Rec., Mex.

Linidiella JOUSSEAUME, 1889 [*Proserpina swifti BLAND, 1863] [=Chersodespoena SYKES, 1900]. With columellar fold. Pleist.-Rec., S.Am.

L. (Linidiella). Rec., N.S.Am.——FIG. 187,2. *L. swifti (BLAND), Rec., Venezuela; ×2 (147).

L. (Staffola) DALL, 1905 [*Proserpina derbyi] [=Cyane H.ADAMS, 1870 (non FELDER, 1861)]. Rounded, columellar lamella heavy. Pleist., Brazil.

Family DEIANIRIDAE Wenz, 1938

[nom. correct COX, herein (pro Dejaniridae WENZ, 1938)]

Rather small, rotelliform, anomphalous; inner walls not resorbed; spire depressed, upper face of whorls bordered by carina; base convex; aperture semicircular; outer lip oblique, notched at carina; inner lip straight, oblique, with 2 or 3 plications extending onto labial area, which is continued by callus spread broadly over base; operculum calcareous, with marginal nucleus from which curved groove runs to notch in opposite margin; color pattern commonly preserved. U.Cret.(Campan.-Dan.), Eu.

Deianira STOLICZKA, 1860 [*Rotella bicarinata ZEKELI, 1852; SD COSSMANN, 1909] [=Dejanira LEYMERIE, 1881 (obj.); Leymeria MUNIER-CHAL-

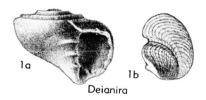

FIG. 188. Neritacea (Deianiridae) (p. I288).

MAS, 1884]. With characters of family.——FIG. 188,*1*. *D. bicarinata* (ZEKELI), U.Cret.(Dan.), Aus.; *1a*, apertural view, ✕1.8 (apparent verticality of inner lip due to foreshortening; *1b*, operculum ✕5 (222).

Family PHENACOLEPADIDAE Thiele, 1929

[=Scutellinidae DALL, 1889]

Conical or cap-shaped shells with apex turned backward and near posterior margin; muscle scar horseshoe-shaped, opening anteriorly. No operculum. *Eoc.-Rec.*

Phenacolepas PILSBRY, 1891 [*Scutella crenulata* BRODERIP, 1834] [*pro Scutella* BRODERIP, 1834 (*non* LAMARCK, 1816); *Scutellina* GRAY, 1847 (*non* AGASSIZ, 1841); *Scutulina* COSSMANN, 1912 (obj.)]. With rugose radial ribs; apertural margin arched, not in one plane. *Rec.*, tropics.-Atl.-Pac.

P. (Phenacolepas).——FIG. 189,*1*. *P. (P.) crenulata* (BRODERIP), Rec., S.Pac.; ✕1 (147).

P. (Amapileus) IREDALE, 1929 [*A. immeritus*]. *Rec.*, Austral.

P. (Cinnalepeta) IREDALE, 1929 [*Patella cinnamomea* GOULD, 1848]. *Rec.*, Pac.

P. (Zacalantica) IREDALE, 1921 [*P. linguaviverrae* MELVILL & STANDEN, 1899]. *Rec.*, Pac.

Plesiothyreus COSSMANN, 1888 [*Capulus parmophoroides* COSSMANN, 1885]. Low, apex overhanging margin. *Eoc.-Rec.*, Eu.-China.——FIG. 189,*2*. *P. parmophoroides* (COSSMANN), Eoc., Fr.; ✕2 (147).

Family HYDROCENIDAE Troschel, 1856

[*nom. correct.* GILL, 1871 (*ex* Hydrocenacea TROSCHEL, 1856)]

Small or minute shells, ovate, slender-spired, inner whorls resorbed; no umbilicus; operculum calcareous, semicircular, with eccentric, terminal nucleus, strong apophysis within. [Air-breathing land forms with pulmonary cavity; mostly living near coast.] *Pleist.-Rec.*

Hydrocena PFEIFFER, 1847 [*Cyclostoma cattaroense* PFEIFFER, 1841]. Smooth or spirally sculptured. *Pleist.-Rec.*, Medit.-Afr.-Pac.-E.Asia.

H. (Hydrocena). Thin, broadly conical, spire of several whorls; smooth. *Pleist.-Rec.*, Medit.-Afr.-

SE.Asia-Pac.——FIG. 189,*4*. *H. cattaroensis* (PFEIFFER), Rec., Dalmatia; *4a*, apertural view, ✕5; *4b,c*, operculum, exterior and side views, ✕10 (147).

H. (Chondrella) PEASE, 1871 [*Cyclostoma parvum* PEASE, 1864]. Operculum ribbed within. *Rec.*, S.Pac.

H. (Georissa) BLANFORD, 1864 [*Hydrocena pyxis* BENSON, 1856] [=*Omphalorissa* IREDALE, 1933 (*nom.nud.*)]. Spirally ribbed. *Rec.*, SE.Asia-Pac.

H. (Georissopsis) PILSBRY & HIRASE, 1908 [*Georissa (Georissopsis) heudei* PILSBRY & HIRASE, 1908]. Operculum large. *Rec.*, China.

Family TITISCANIIDAE Bergh, 1890

[*nom. correct.* PILSBRY, 1892 (*pro* Titiscaniien BERGH, 1890)]

Marine snails without shell or operculum, anatomically related to Neritidae, with pallial cavity and ctenidium. *Rec.*

Titiscania BERGH, 1890 [*T. limacina*]. *Rec.*, Mauritius-Pac.Is.

NERITACEA Family UNCERTAIN

Neritacean fossils are particularly difficult to classify if the systematic descriptions are based on fragmentary or badly preserved material. The following generic names have been proposed for material that is certainly neritacean but quite impossible to assign more closely. Probably all are synonymous with other names and most of them belong to the Neritopsidae.

Hypodema DE KONINCK, 1853 [*Calceola dumontiana* DE KONINCK, 1843; SD KNIGHT, 1937]. Genus based on heavy, thick conical naticopsoid opercula; associated shell unknown. *L. Carb.*, Eu.

Platyostomella ETHERIDGE, JR., 1880 [*Littorina scotoburdigalensis* ETHERIDGE, 1878] [=*Platyostomella* LINDSTRÖM, 1884 (obj.)]. Genus based on

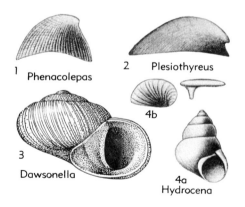

FIG. 189. Neritacea (Dawsonellidae, Phenacolepadidae, Hydrocenidae) (p. I279, I289).

juvenile specimens probably referable to one or more subgenera of *Naticopsis*. L.Carb., Eu.

Catinella STACHE, 1877 [*non* PEASE, 1871] [**C. depressa*]. Name invalid; genus based on unrecognizable steinkerns. *M.Perm.,* Eu.

Neritomopsis WAAGEN, 1880 [**N. minuta*]. Based on a single badly preserved and unrecognizable specimen. *M.Perm.,* SC.Asia.

Catubrina CANEVA, 1906 [**Neritomopsis (Catubrina) solitaria*]. Based on steinkerns, supposedly with resorbed inner whorls, a neritid feature. Even if this is true, the species and genus are unrecognizable. *M.Perm.,* Eu.

Proboscidia MERLA, 1931 [*non* PROBOSKIDIA BORY DE ST.VINCENT, 1827] [**Neritomopsis (Proboscidia) elongata*]. Name invalid; applied to a species represented by steinkerns supposedly with resorbed inner whorls. Species and genus unrecognizable. *M.Perm.,* Eu.

?ARCHAEOGASTROPODA
Suborder MURCHISONIINA
Cox & Knight, 1960

Shell commonly high-spired, with numerous whorls; outer lip with submedian sinus which may culminate in slit or notch and which was presumably exhalant in function; inner shell layers seemingly not nacreous; some genera with incipient abapical apertural canal; paired ctenidia are inferred to have been present by analogy with the Pleurotomariina, but if the abapical canal was inhalant in function, the respiratory system may have undergone evolutionary advances beyond the condition characteristic of that suborder. *?U.Cam., L.Ord.-U.Trias.*

This suborder has been erected for reception of the superfamily Murchisoniacea. It is thought that this was a stock derived from the Archaeogastropoda and still retaining certain features of that order, but showing advances in some characters along lines of evolution that led to Caenogastropoda (= Pectinibranchia). The question of transferring this group from the Archaeogastropoda (in which it has been included previously) to the Caenogastropoda has been considered, but owing to the difficulty of deciding from the available evidence if archaeogastropod or caenogastropod characters predominated, it has been decided to retain the assemblage in the more primitive order, querying such reference in order to emphasize the borderline position that it occupied.

The Murchisoniacea have a labral slit or notch thought to have been exhalant in function. This indentation lies slightly above or below the middle of the labrum in a position which strongly supports the view that a pair of ctenidia inside the mantle cavity were located on opposite sides of the slit, with the anal opening between them, as in the Pleurotomariacea, from which they were probably derived. If, in accordance with past general practice, we consider the presence of the labral emargination to indicate that the Murchisoniacea were essentially pleurotomarian in nature, it would be presumed that they possessed aspidobranch ctenidia and a rhipidoglossate radula; that is, that they agreed with the Archaeogastropoda in a combination of important anatomical characters. This conclusion, however, is not inevitable. Conchologically, the Murchisoniacea show so many points of resemblance to the Cerithiacea that it may be suggested that they were ancestral to that superfamily. As in the Cerithiacea, for instance, murchisoniacean shells seem to lack a nacreous lining; moreover, they are markedly high-spired, many-whorled forms that commonly exhibit a tendency to develop an inhalant canal. Hence there is at least a possibility that in soft anatomy, as well as in shell characters, they were measurably advanced towards a cerithiacean organization; that is, they may well have had ctenidia of pectinibranch type and a taenioglossate radula, or structures transitional thereto.

The Murchisoniacea appear to have been closely related and probably ancestral to the Loxonematacea, and it may well be that the Cerithiacea were more immediately derived from the Loxonematacea, wherein a deep U-shaped labral sinus, present in earlier genera, gradually disappears, suggesting progressive loss of the right-hand ctenidium and consequent adjustments in the pallial complex. If this was the case, transition from a partly archaeogastropod to a caenogastropod organization may have taken place during the evolutionary history of the Loxonematacea. This superfamily here is assigned to the Caenogastropoda.

It must, however, be remembered that the high-spired forms included in the Cerithiacea form only one group of the Caenogastropoda. We do not suggest that

all caenogastropods were descended from Murchisoniacea, whether directly or through the Loxonematacea. The turbiniform and other low-spired caenogastropods were probably derived from such archaeogastropod groups as the Trochonematacea, in which the right-hand ctenidium had, apparently, already disappeared.

Superfamily MURCHISONIACEA Koken, 1896

[*nom. transl.* KNIGHT, BATTEN & YOCHELSON, herein (*ex* Murchisoniidae KOKEN, 1896)]

Labral sinus culminating in a sharp notch or short slit; incipient inhalant canal present in some genera. *?U.Cam., L.Ord.-U.Trias.*

Family MURCHISONIIDAE Koken, 1896

[=Hormotominae WENZ, 1938]

With labral sinus, commonly culminating in short slit or notch that generates a selenizone. *?U.Cam., L.Ord.-U.Trias.*

?**Protospira** RUEDEMANN, 1916 [**P. minuta*]. Small, moderately high-spired, with relatively high whorls; apertural lips unknown. [Genus based on species now represented by a single poorly preserved specimen. It is the only high-spired gastropod known from Cambrian rocks, and this is all that can be said about it. Tentatively placed in the Murchisoniidae, the form could as well be loxonematacean.] *U.Cam.*, N.Am.

?**Gasconadia** ULRICH in WELLER & ST. CLAIR, 1928 [**Murchisonia putilla* SARDESON, 1896]. Small, with spire not quite so high as usual in family; labrum with angular sinus that culminates at bluntly angular periphery without slit or selenizone, gerontic aperture with widely flaring lips; with radially elongate internal tooth on floor of whorl about half-whorl back from aperture (possibly marking attachment for left-hand member of a pair of retractor muscles). *L.Ord.*, N.Am.——FIG. 190,*1*. **G. putilla* (SARDESON), Mo.; *1a*, apertural view, ×2.7; *1b*, base of steinkern with impression of internal tooth, ×4.

Murchisonia D'ARCHIAC & DEVERNEUIL, 1841 [**Turritella bilineata* DECHEN, 1832, *pro Murex turbinatus* (SCHLOTHEIM) DECHEN, 1832 (*non Murex turbinatus* BROCCHI, 1814) =*Muricites turbinatus* SCHLOTHEIM, 1820; SD WOODWARD, 1856]. With labral sinus culminating at about middle of labrum in shallow slit or notch; commonly without ornament other than margins of selenizone and growth lines. [In Middle Devonian close relatives of type species display a burst of forms with elaborate, in part bizarre, shapes and ornament quite incongruous with usual conservatism shown by genus. Recognized subgenera are more or less intergrad-

ing.] *Ord.-Trias.*, N.Am.-Eu.-NE.Asia-SE.Asia-Austral.

M. (**Turritoma**) ULRICH in ULRICH & SCOFIELD, 1897 [**Murchisonia acrea* BILLINGS, 1865] [= *Turritospira* ULRICH in ULRICH & SCOFIELD, 1897 (obj.)]. Slit and selenizone at periphery, relatively low on whorl. *L.Ord.-Sil.*, N.Am.——FIG. 190,*2*. **M. (T.) acrea* (BILLINGS), L.Ord., Can.(Newf.); ×2.

M. (**Hormotoma**) SALTER, 1859 [**Murchisonia gracilis* HALL, 1847; SD DONALD, 1885]. Whorls rounded, with relatively deep sutures, mid-whorl periphery with slit and selenizone. *Ord.Sil.*, N. Am.-Eu.-NE.Asia.——FIG. 190,*3*. **M. (H.) gracilis* (HALL), M.Ord., Can.(Que.); ×2.

M. (**Murchisonia**) [=*Goniostropha* OEHLERT, 1888; *Cyrtostropha* DONALD, 1902; *Mesocoelia* PERNER, 1907]. Selenizone between pair of cords; periphery at mid-whorl, somewhat angular; sutures relatively shallow. [The Middle Devonian burst of bizarre forms occurs in this subgenus.] *L.Sil.-Perm., ?Trias.*, N.Am.-Eu.-SE.Asia-Austral.——FIG. 190,*5*. **M. (M.) bilineata* (DECHEN), M.Dev., Ger.; ×2.7.

M. (**Sinuspira**) PERNER, 1907 [**S. tenera*] [= *Morania* HORNY, 1953 (57, p. 190)]. Sinus culminating in narrow notch with sides not quite parallel and hence not properly defined as slit. *U.Sil.*, Eu.——FIG. 190,*8*. **M. (S.) tenera*, Czech.; ×2.7.

M. (**Hormotomina**) GRABAU & SHIMER, 1909 [**Murchisonia maia* HALL, 1861]. Selenizone with median spiral thread between bordering threads. *M.Dev.*, N.Am.——FIG. 190,*4*. **M. (H.) maia* (HALL), Ohio; ×1.3.

Ectomaria KOKEN, 1896 [**Murchisonia nieszkowskii* F. SCHMIDT, 1858] [=*Solenospira* ULRICH & SCOFIELD, 1897]. With deep angular labral sinus culminating between pair of strong spiral cords, without slit, rounded apex of the sinus generating a pseudoselenizone. *M.Ord.-U.Ord.*, N.Am.-Eu.——FIG. 190,*11*. *E. pagoda* (SALTER), M.Ord., Can.(Que.); ×2.7.

Catazone PERNER, 1907 [**Murchisonia (Catazone) cuneus*]. Differs from *Michelia* in having true slit that generates relatively broad selenizone low on whorls. *U.Sil.*, Eu.——FIG. 190,*6*. **C. cuneus* (PERNER), Czech.; ×1.

Biangularia SPITZ, 1907 [**Pleurotomaria (Biangularia) frechi*]. Spire laterally compressed and twisted in clockwise direction; selenizone arched, bordered by deep striae. *L.Dev.*, Eu.——FIG. 190,*9*. **B. frechi* (SPITZ), Aus.; ×1 (132).

Lodanaria DAHMER, 1925 [**L. munda*]. With widely expanded aperture at gerontic stage; whorls angular; ornament of spiral threads. *L.Dev.*, Eu. ——FIG. 190,*10*. **L. munda*, Ger.; posterior view showing spire and cast of expanded aperture, ×0.5.

Ptychocaulus PERNER, 1907 [**Murchisonia verneuili*

KOKEN, 1889]. Large, very high-spired, narrowly phaneromphalous; whorls wide, flat-sided with flat selenizone bordered by striae; base flat; with flange spiralling up columella within whorls. [Structural details of the columellar flange are not well understood; it may have been partly mem-branous and not simply shelly. Nothing is known of its function.] *L.Dev.,* Eu.——FIG. 190,*12.* *P. *verneuili* (KOKEN), Czech.; posterior view with window showing columellar ridge, ×1.3.

Michelia F.A.ROEMER, 1852 [*M. *cylindrica*; SD KNIGHT, 1937] [=*Coelocaulus* OEHLERT, 1888;

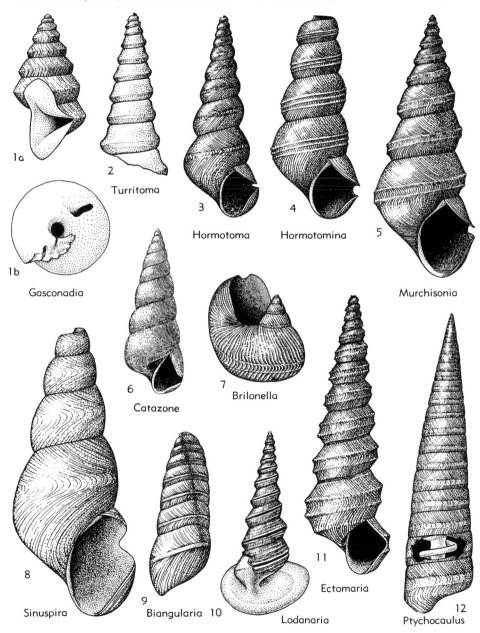

1a

2
Turritoma

3
Hormotoma

4
Hormotomina

5

1b
Gasconadia

6
Catazone

7
Brilonella

Murchisonia

8
Sinuspira

9
Biangularia 10

Lodanaria

11
Ectomaria

12
Ptychocaulus

FIG. 190. Murchisoniacea (Murchisoniidae) (p. *1291-1293*).

Vetotuba ETHERIDGE, JR., 1890; *Coelidium* CLARKE & RUEDEMANN, 1903; *?Melissosoa* CLARKE, 1909]. Narrowly phaneromphalous; with angular sinus culminating in short small notch without parallel sides, resulting pseudoselenizone not sharply limited; sutures shallow. *Ord.-Dev.,* N.Am.-Eu.-Austral.——FIG. 191,*1. M. davidsoni* (OEHLERT), L.Dev., Fr.; ×1.3.

?**Brilonella** KAYSER, 1873 [*Scoliostoma serpens* KAYSER, 1872]. Spire relatively low and whorls few, final one turning upward and backward so that aperture faces backward; slit seemingly shallow, bordered by sharp threads; with collabral ornament of sharp threads. *M.Dev.,* Eu.——FIG. 190,*7.* *B. serpens* (KAYSER), Ger.; posterior view showing twisted final whorl, ×2.7.

Aclisina DEKONINCK, 1881 [*Murchisonia striatula* DEKONINCK, 1843; SD S.A.MILLER, 1889] [= *Aclisoides* DONALD, 1898 (obj.); *Rhabdospira* DONALD, 1898]. Whole whorl, including selenizone, covered by numerous spiral threads; slit short. *L.Carb.(Miss.),* N.Am.-Eu.-NC.Asia.——FIG. 191, *4.* *A. striatula* (DEKONINCK), Belg.; ×2.7.

Micrentoma DONALD, 1898 [*Aclisina nana* DE KONINCK, 1881]. Small, with attenuated apex, anomphalous; sinus shallow, apparently culminating in notch that generates a pseudoselenizone; ornament 5 or 6 spiral cords cut into nodes by collabral striae. *L.Carb.,* Eu.——FIG. 191,*2. *M. nana* (DEKONINCK), Belg.; ×4.

Cerithioides HAUGHTON, 1859 [*C. telescopium*] [=*Glyptobasis* DEKONINCK, 1881 (*non* McLACHLAN, 1871)]. Large, with tapering apex, moderately high whorls and shallow sutures; base nearly flat, anomphalous; ornamented with spiral grooves; shallow slit somewhat below middle of labrum gives rise to flat selenizone not bordered by threads or striae. *L.Carb.,* Eu.——FIG. 191,*10. *C. telescopium,* Ire.; ×0.7.

Glyphodeta DONALD, 1895 [*Murchisonia zonata* DONALD, 1887]. Selenizone arched gently and bordered by striae; with several broad spiral low cords separated by striae below selenizone but without ornament above it. *L.Carb.(Miss.)-M.Perm.,* Eu.-N.Am.——FIG. 191,*7. G. terebriformis* (HALL), M.Miss., Ind.; ×4.7.

Stegocoelia DONALD, 1889 [*Murchisonia (Stegocoelia) compacta*]. With spiral threads or carinae; short slit and selenizone above periphery; shape variable, basis of differentiation of intergrading subgenera. *L.Carb.(Miss.)-M.Perm.,* Eu.-N.Am.-SE.Asia.

S. (Stegocoelia). Spire relatively low, whorls commonly rounded. *L.Carb.(Miss.)-U.Carb.(Penn.),* Eu.-N.Am.-SE.Asia.——FIG. 191,*5. *S (S.) compacta* (DONALD), L.Carb., Scot.; ×12.

S. (Hypergonia) DONALD, 1892 [*Murchisonia quadricarinata* M'COY, 1844]. Spire high, relatively slender. *L.Carb.(Miss.)-U.Carb.(Penn.),*

Eu.-N.Am.-SE.Asia.——FIG. 191,*12. *S. (H.) quadricarinata* (M'COY), L.Carb., Ire.; ×4.

S. (Taosia) GIRTY, 1939 [*Murchisonia copei* WHITE, 1881]. Spire relatively high, with projecting angulation around base and selenizone in flat area above; in some species basal angulation bears row of nodes (47, p. 21). *Penn.(U.Carb.)-M.Perm.,* N.Am.-Eu.-SE.Asia.——FIG. 191,*14. *S. (T.) copei* (WHITE), M.Penn., N.Mex.; ×1.3.

Goniasma TOMLIN, 1930 [*pro Goniospira* GIRTY, 1915 (*non* COSSMANN, 1895; *nec* DONALD, 1902)] [*Murchisonia lasallensis* WORTHEN, 1890]. Whorls with smooth slope above angular periphery; labrum with angular sinus that culminates just below periphery in short slit which generates slightly concave, inwardly sloping selenizone; with pair of spiral threads below selenizone, upper one located at or above lower suture; some species with faint indication of siphonal canal. *Penn.(U.Carb.)-M.Perm.,* N.Am.-S.Am.-Eu.——FIG. 191,*11. *G. lasallense* (WORTHEN), U.Penn., Ill.; ×4.

Cibecuia WINTERS, 1956 [*C. cedarensis*]. Side of whorls flat, conformable to sides of spire; sutures linear; shallow labral sinus culminating in short slit; base anomphalous; convex columellar lip reflexed; ornament faint subsutural nodes and spiral threads on base (151, p.44). *M.Perm.,* N.Am.——FIG. 191,*3. *C. cedarensis,* Ariz.; ×2.7.

Helicospira GIRTY, 1915 [*Murchisonia buttersi* GIRTY, 1912]. Whorls with angular periphery bearing a wavy double-crested selenizone; ornament very fine spiral and widely spaced collabral threads. [Somewhat resembles Triassic *Trypanocochlea* TOMLIN, 1931.] *Perm.* or *Trias.,* N.Am.——FIG. 191,*13. *H. buttersi* (GIRTY), Colo.; ×2.7.

Cheilotomona STRAND, 1928 [*pro Cheilotoma* KOKEN, 1889 (*non* DEJEAN, 1835)] [*Pleurotoma blumi* MÜNSTER, 1841; SD DIENER, 1926]. Small; periphery at mid-whorl and carinate in most forms, carrying or forming lower border of well-marked slit and selenizone, which are also bordered above by spiral cord; ornament spiral cords and collabral threads; aperture with distinct spout as incipient inhalant canal. *M.Trias.(Anis.)-U.Trias.(Carn.),* Eu.——FIG. 191,*6. *C. blumi* (MÜNSTER), M. Trias.(Ladin.), S. Tyrol; 6*a,b,* apertural views, ×2 (64,89).

Trypanocochlea TOMLIN, 1931 [*pro Verania* KOKEN, 1896 (*non* KROHN, 1846)] [*Verania cerithioides* KOKEN, 1896]. Small, anomphalous; whorls angular with periphery at mid-height carrying raised selenizone bearing pointed nodes at intervals and bordered by pair of cords; sutures with spiral cord each side; slit unknown; columella with about 6 weak folds. *U.Trias.(Carn.),* Aus.——FIG. 191,*9. *T. cerithioides;* ×5 (79).

Vistilia KOKEN, 1896 [*V. klipsteini;* SD WOODWARD, 1897]. Narrowly phaneromphalous or cryptomphalous; whorls angular, with sharp periphery at mid-height carrying or forming lower border of

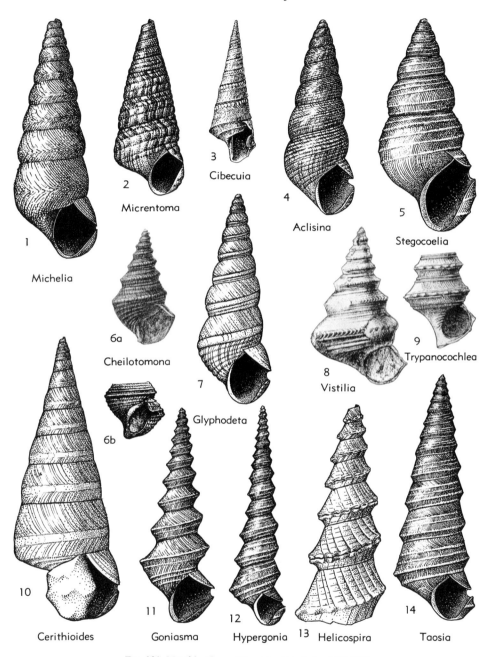

1 Michelia

2 Micrentoma

3 Cibecuia

4 Aclisina

5 Stegocoelia

6a Cheilotomona

6b

7 Glyphodeta

8 Vistilia

9 Trypanocochlea

10 Cerithioides

11 Goniasma

12 Hypergonia

13 Helicospira

14 Taosia

Fig. 191. Murchisoniacea (Murchisoniidae) (p. *1292-1293*).

selenizone with conspicuous lunulae; slit unknown; ornament spiral cords. *M.Trias.(Anis.)-U.Trias.(Nor.)*, Eu.——Fig. 191,8. *V. klipsteini* (KOKEN), U.Trias.(Nor.), Aus.; ×2 (79).

Family PLETHOSPIRIDAE Wenz, 1938

[*nom. transl.* KNIGHT, BATTEN & YOCHELSON, herein (*ex* Plethospirinae WENZ, 1938)]

Spire height variable, mostly not high; with ill-defined siphonal canal. *L.Ord.-U.Trias.*

Subfamily PLETHOSPIRINAE Wenz, 1938

Broadly fusiform, with ill-defined siphonal canal; shallow slit occurring rather high on labrum but with selenizone approximately at mid-whorl between sutures. *L.Ord.-L.Dev.*

Plethospira ULRICH in ULRICH & SCOFIELD, 1897 [*Holopea cassina* WHITFIELD, 1886]. Base narrow, canal relatively broad; ornament wanting except for growth lines. *L.Ord.-M.Sil.*, N.Am.-Eu. ——Fig. 192,1. *P. cassina* (WHITFIELD), L.Ord., USA(Vt.); apertural view showing siphonal canal, ×0.7.

Seelya ULRICH in ULRICH & SCOFIELD, 1897 [*S. ventricosa*]. Rounder than *Plethospira* and with raised selenizone; ornament low spiral cords. *L. Ord.-M.Sil.*, N.Am.-Eu.——Fig. 192,8. *S. ventricosa*, L. Ord., USA(Vt.); ×1.3.

Diplozone PERNER, 1907 [*D. innocens*]. Base relatively broad, canal narrow; ornament sharp collabral threads. *U.Sil.-L.Dev.*, Eu.——Fig. 192,4. *D. innocens*, L.Dev., Czech.; apertural view of juvenile shell showing siphonal canal, ×5.3.

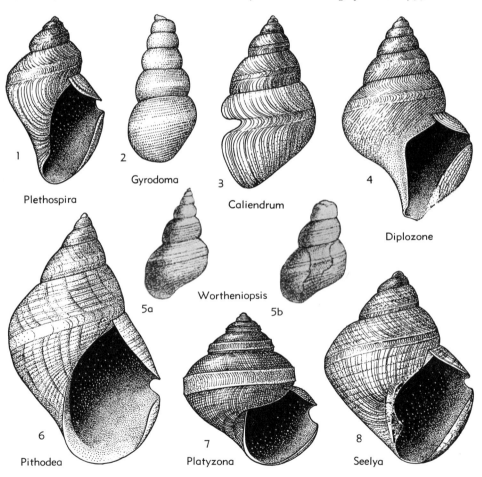

1 Plethospira
2 Gyrodoma
3 Caliendrum
4 Diplozone
5a Wortheniopsis
5b
6 Pithodea
7 Platyzona
8 Seelya

FIG. 192. Murchisoniacea (Plethospiridae——Plethospirinae, Pithodeinae) (p. 1295-1296).

Subfamily PITHODEINAE Wenz, 1938

Base with little or no development of a canal; slit shallow and relatively wide, selenizone wide and flat. *Dev.-U.Trias.*

?Gyrodoma ETHERIDGE, JR., 1898 [*Eunema etheridgei* CRESSWELL, 1893]. Relatively high-spired, with rounded whorls and deep sutures; selenizone broad, flat; ornament numerous spiral threads, except on selenizone. [Little is known of apertural margins.] *Dev.*, Austral.——FIG. 192,2. *G. etheridgei* (CRESSWELL); ×0.7 (69).

Platyzona KNIGHT, 1945 [*Pleurotomaria trilineata* HALL, 1858]. Moderately high-spired to turbiniform, minutely phaneromphalous; ornament dominantly spiral cords which commonly are separated by faint grooves into groups of 3 on base, but also including sparse faint collabral growth lines; suggestion of a canal in some species (72, p.579). *Dev.-M.Perm.*, N.Am.-Eu.——FIG. 192,7. *P. trilineata* (HALL), M.Miss., Ind.; ×3.3.

Pithodea DEKONINCK, 1881 [*P. amplissima*]. Robust, somewhat fusiform, anomphalous; ornament numerous spiral cords. *L.Carb.*, Eu.——FIG. 192,6. *P. amplissima*, Belg.; ×0.5.

Caliendrum BROWN, 1838 [*Buccinum vittatum* PHILLIPS, 1836 [=*Foordella* LONGSTAFF, 1912]. Much like *Pithodea* but with somewhat deeper sutures and lacking spiral ornament. *L.Carb.(Miss.)-U.Carb.(Penn.)*, Eu.-N.Am.——FIG. 192,3. *C. vittatum* (PHILLIPS), L.Carb., Eng.; ×1.

Wortheniopsis J.BÖHM, 1895 [*Pleurotomaria margarethae* KITTL, 1894]. Ovate-conical, acute-spired, anomphalous; whorls evenly convex or with narrow sutural ramp; selenizone narrow, high on whorl side, bordered above by ramp angle when present; ornament spiral threads and growth lines symmetrically recurved to selenizone. *M.Trias.(Ladin.)-U.Trias.(Nor.)*, Eu.——FIG. 192,5. *W. margarethae* (KITTL), M.Trias.(Ladin.), S. Tyrol; 5a,b, abapertural views, ×1.5 (65).

?ARCHAEOGASTROPODA
Superfamilies of Doubtful Subordinal Position

Superfamily CLISOSPIRACEA S. A. Miller, 1889

[*nom. transl.* KNIGHT, BATTEN & YOCHELSON, herein (*ex* Clisospiridae MILLER, 1889)]

Trochiform or patelliform, with base seemingly represented by a narrow but gradually widening lamella that spirals upward inside shell; Shell structure unknown. *L.Ord.-M.Dev.*

These curious gastropods are not well known or understood, and there is not much evidence as to their systematic posi-

tion. Certain resemblances to some of the Calyptraeacea are thought to indicate convergence rather than relationship.

Family CLISOSPIRIDAE S. A. Miller, 1889

With characters of superfamily. *L.Ord.-M.Dev.*

Subfamily CLISOSPIRINAE S. A. Miller, 1889

[*nom. transl.* KNIGHT, BATTEN & YOCHELSON, herein (*ex* Clisospiridae S.A.MILLER, 1889)]

Shell sinistral. *L.Ord.-Sil.*

Mimospira KOKEN, 1925 [*Onychochilus helmhackeri* PERNER, 1900; SD KNIGHT, 1937]. Without (?or with only a very narrow) frill; sutures mod-

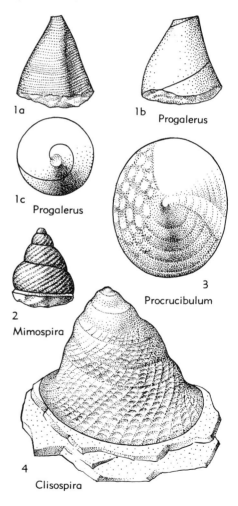

FIG. 193. Clisospiracea (Clisospiridae——Clisospirinae, Progalerinae) (p. 1296-1297).

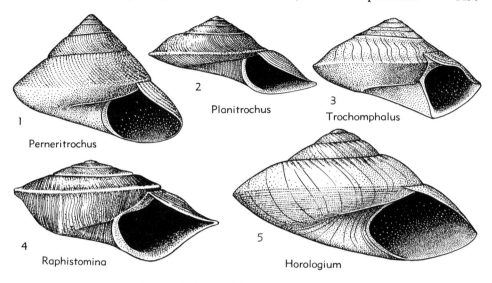

FIG. 194. Pseudophoracea (Planitrochidae) (p. 1297-1298).

erately deep; outer lip and collabral ornament strongly prosocline; base and aperture unknown. *L.Ord.,* Eu.——FIG. 193,2. **M. helmhackeri* (PERNER), Czech.; ×2 (80).

Clisospira BILLINGS, 1865 [**C. curiosa*]. With wide frill; sutures shallow; outer lip prosocline; ornament obliquely cancellate; base and aperture unknown. *L.Ord.-Sil.,* N.Am.-Eu.-NE.Asia.——FIG. 193,4. **C. curiosa,* Can.(Que.); ×2.7.

Subfamily PROGALERINAE Knight, 1956

Shell dextral. *L.Dev.-M.Dev.*

?Procrucibulum PERNER, 1911 [**Calyptraea simplex* PERNER, 1903; SD COSSMANN, 1911]. Patelliform, with slightly twisted apex and low sharp ridge within running in a broad clockwise curve from apex to margin. *L.Dev.,* Eu.——FIG. 193,3. **P. simplex* (PERNER), Czech.; apical view, ×2.

?Paragalerus PERNER, 1903 [**P. holzapfeli*]. Sutures rather deep, outer lip strongly prosocline; ornament fine collabral threads. [Too poorly known to warrant a restoration.] *L. Dev.,* Eu.

Progalerus HOLZAPFEL, 1895 [**P. conoideus*]. High conical, with base represented by a lamella spiralling up inside shell; ornament fine growth lines encircling test. *M.Dev.,* Eu.——FIG. 193,1. **P. conoideus* (HOLZAPFEL), Ger.; *1a,* side view; *1b,c,* steinkern, inside and apical view showing spiral suture, ×1.3.

Superfamily PSEUDOPHORACEA S. A. Miller, 1889

[*nom. transl.* KNIGHT, BATTEN & YOCHELSON, herein (*ex* Pseudophoridae S.A.MILLER, 1889)]

Trochiform, with either gently rounded phaneromphalous base and subangular

periphery or concave base within a more or less extended frill; evidence of nacreous inner shell layers found in some genera referred to each subfamily, but information wholly lacking for others. *L.Ord.-Miss.*

Family PLANITROCHIDAE Knight, 1956

With gently rounded phaneromphalous base and subangular periphery. *L.Ord.-U.Sil.*

Raphistomina ULRICH & SCOFIELD, 1897 [**Raphistoma lapicida* SALTER, 1859] [=*Rotellomphalus* PERNER, 1903]. Lenticular, with sharp carina at periphery, suture falling beneath carina; with channel inside angular periphery and upper surface of peripheral carina flattened. *L.Ord.-Sil.,* N.Am.-Eu. ——FIG. 194,4. **R. lapicida* (SALTER), M.Ord. Can.(Que.); ×2.7.

Trochomphalus KOKEN, 1925 [**Euomphalus dimidiatus* KOKEN, 1896]. Somewhat lenticular, with suture falling above sharp periphery; upper whorl surface with low rounded spiral ridge; umbilicus moderately wide, bordered by sharp angles. *U. Ord.,* Eu.——FIG. 194,3. **T. dimidiatus* (KOKEN), Est.; ×2.5 (80).

?Nematrochus PERNER, 1903 [**N. concurrens*]. High trochiform, with strongly prosocline outer lip and umbilicus plugged with a concave callus. [Too poorly known to warrant reconstruction.] *U.Sil.,* Eu.

Planitrochus PERNER, 1903 [**P. amicus*; SD PERNER, 1907]. Depressed trochiform, with sharp carinate periphery and moderately wide umbilicus; outer lip prosocline above and below periphery; ornament above periphery consisting of collabral

threads, below of growth lines only. *U.Sil.,* Eu.——Fɪɢ. 194,2. **P. amicus,* Czech.; ×1.3.

Horologium Pᴇʀɴᴇʀ, 1907 [**H. kokeni*]. Somewhat like *Planitrochus* but larger and less depressed; ornament above periphery wide radiating undulations or narrow subsutural ramp and below periphery numerous fine spiral threads. *U.Sil.,* Eu.——Fɪɢ. 194,5. **H. kokeni,* Czech.; ×1.

Perneritrochus Cᴏssᴍᴀɴɴ, 1909 [*pro Conotrochus* Pᴇʀɴᴇʀ, 1907 (*non* Pɪʟsʙʀʏ, 1889)] [**Trochus? venalis* Pᴇʀɴᴇʀ, 1903]. Similar to *Plantitrochus* but higher and with more rounded noncarinate periphery and narrower umbilicus; ornament above suture collabral threads, below suture unknown. *U.Sil.,* Eu.——Fɪɢ. 194,1. **P. venalis* (Pᴇʀɴᴇʀ), Czech.; ×2.

Family PSEUDOPHORIDAE S. A. Miller, 1889

[=Palaeonustidae Wᴇɴᴢ, 1938]

Conical, base flat or concave within surrounding frill. *Sil.-M.Perm.*

Siluriphorus Cᴏssᴍᴀɴɴ, 1918 [**Trochus gotlandicus* Lɪɴᴅsᴛʀöᴍ, 1884]. Trochiform, with flat or concave cryptomphalous base; periphery commonly bluntly angular but in some specimens with a blunt, frill-like border; ornament strong, irregular growth lamellae, weaker on base and strongly prosocline. *M.Sil.,* Eu.——Fɪɢ. 195,9. **S. gotlandicus* (Lɪɴᴅsᴛʀöᴍ), Gotl.; ×2.

Hystricoceras Jᴀʜɴ, 1894 [**H. spinosum*]. With concave, anomphalous base surrounded by about 12 semitubular projections on frill-like edge of upper whorl surface. *U.Sil.,* Eu.——Fɪɢ. 195,4. **H. spinosum,* U.Sil., Czech.; ×1.

Pseudophorus Mᴇᴇᴋ, 1873 [**Trochita antiqua* Mᴇᴇᴋ, 1872] [=*Flemingia* ᴅᴇKᴏɴɪɴᴄᴋ, 1881 (*non* Jᴏʜɴsᴛᴏɴ, 1845); *Flemingella* Kɴɪɢʜᴛ, 1936 (*pro Flemingia* ᴅᴇKᴏɴɪɴᴄᴋ, 1881)]. With narrowly phaneromphalous base surrounded by wide frill formed by extension of upper whorl surface; collabral ornament strongly prosocline growth lines above periphery. *Sil.-Miss.(L.Carb.),* N.Am.-Eu.——Fɪɢ. 195,2. *P. profundus* (Lɪɴᴅsᴛʀöᴍ), M.Sil., Gotl.; ×2 (90).

Pseudotectus Pᴇʀɴᴇʀ, 1903 [**P. carinatus*] [=*Palaeonustus* Pᴇʀɴᴇʀ, 1903]. High, with gently convex anomphalous base surrounded by a moderately wide frill. *L.Dev.,* Eu.——Fɪɢ. 195,7. **P. carinatus,* Czech.; ×1.3.

Scalaetrochus Eᴛʜᴇʀɪᴅɢᴇ, Jʀ., 1890 [**Trochus (Scalaetrochus) lindstroemi*]. Trochiform, with rather low whorls and nearly flat cryptomphalous base surrounded by narrow frill; callus deposit beginning in aperture and filling peripheral angle; collabral lines moderately prosocline on upper surfaces. *Dev.,* Austral.——Fɪɢ. 195,1. **S. lindstroemi* (Eᴛʜᴇʀɪᴅɢᴇ, Jʀ.), ×0.7.

Astralites Wʜɪᴛᴇᴀᴠᴇs, 1892 [**A. fimbriatus*]. With nearly flat cryptomphalous base surrounded by digitate and fluted frill; columellar lip with 2 internal grooves passing back about 0.5 whorl and separated by ridge; ornament of upper whorl surface consisting of broadly convex prosocline collabral undulations crossed by discontinuous spiral cords; base with growth lines alone. [The 2 grooves passing inward around the columella strongly suggest by their position and abrupt inward termination that they were loci of a pair of retractor muscles.] *M.Dev.,* N.Am.-Eu.——Fɪɢ. 195,3. **A. fimbriatus,* Can.(Man.); ×1.3.

Protocalyptraea Cʟᴀʀᴋᴇ, 1894 [**P. marshalli*]. Fragile; with very strongly prosocline outer lip; base rather deep within frill but without narrow lamella spiralling up conical shell. [Present interpretation differs somewhat from that of Kɴɪɢʜᴛ (69) and even more markedly from that of Cʟᴀʀᴋᴇ, who interpreted it as having the characters here attributed to *Progalarus*.] *U. Dev.,* N.Am.——Fɪɢ. 195,5. **P. marshalli,* USA(N.Y.); ×10.

Eotrochus Wʜɪᴛғɪᴇʟᴅ, 1882 [**Pleurotomaria concava* Hᴀʟʟ, 1858 =*Pleurotomaria tenuimarginata* S.A.Mɪʟʟᴇʀ, 1877, *pro P. concava* Hᴀʟʟ, 1858 (*non* Dᴇsʜᴀʏᴇs, 1836)]. With flat base within short frill; narrowly phaneromphalous with lamella spiralling up within umbilicus from base of inner lip; ornament spiral threads on base and growth lines above. *M.Miss.,* N.Am.——Fɪɢ. 195,6. **E. tenuimarginatus* (S.A.Mɪʟʟᴇʀ), Ind.; apertural view, with window showing spiral umbilical lamella, ×5.5.

Sallya Yᴏᴄʜᴇʟsᴏɴ, 1956 [**S. linsa*]. With very gently convex narrowly phaneromphalous base within narrow frill; no spiral lamella within umbilicus; labrum strongly prosocline to margin of frill; labium entirely within frill; ornament growth lines alone or spiral lines on base and ripple-like structures or radiating buttress-like ribs on sides (154, p.205). *M.Perm.,* N.Am.——Fɪɢ. 195,8. **S. linsa,* Tex., ×4.

Superfamily CRASPEDOSTOMATACEA Wenz, 1938

[*nom. transl.* Cᴏx & Kɴɪɢʜᴛ, herein (*ex* Craspedostomatidae Wᴇɴᴢ, 1938) ICZN pend.]

Little-known, problematic gastropods mostly with expanded apertures in gerontic stages; shell structure unknown. *U.Ord.-Jur.*

This probably polyphyletic and artificial group is imperfectly known and the taxonomic positions of the various genera are insecure.

Family CRASPEDOSTOMATIDAE Wenz, 1938

[=Brochidiinae, Dichostasiinae Yᴏᴄʜᴇʟsᴏɴ, 1956]

Mostly naticiform, with deep sutures and strong collabral ornament. *U.Ord.-Jur.*

?**Umbonellina** Koken, 1925 [**U. infrasilurica*]. Naticiform, umbilicus plugged with callus; otherwise little known. *U.Ord., Eu.*——Fig. 196,*3.* **U. infrasilurica,* Est.; ?×1 (80).

?**Bucanospira** Ulrich in Ulrich & Scofield, 1897 [**B. expansa*]. Naticiform, with final quarter of last whorl in some specimens disjunct; apertural margins explanate at irregular intervals; ornament of spiral cords and collabral threads. *M.Sil.,* N.Am. ——Fig. 196,*1.* **B. expansa,* Tenn.; ×2.

Craspedostoma Lindström, 1884 [**C. elegantulum*; SD Perner, 1907]. Naticiform; outer lip explanate

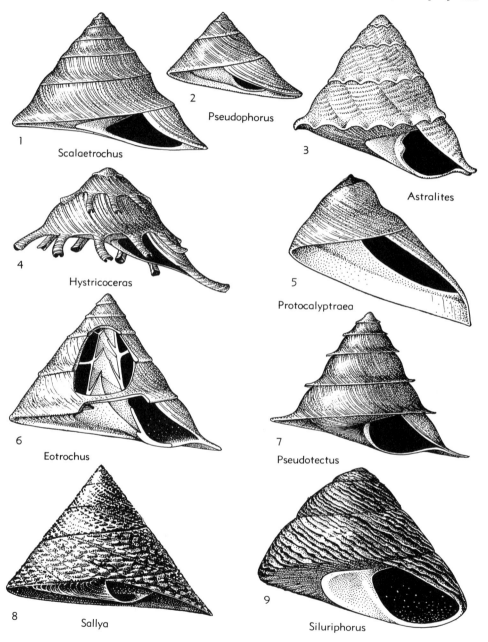

Fig. 195. Pseudophoracea (Pseudophoridae) (p. *1298*).

at late growth stages, with expansion later thickened by numerous lamellae; umbilicus narrow, with sharp funicle; ornament dominantly collabral but with spiral elements in some species. *M.Sil.-U.Sil.*, Eu.——Fig. 196,7. *C. elegantulum*, M.Sil., Gotl.; ×2.7.

Temnospira PERNER, 1903 [*Brochidium (Temnospira) monile*; SD KNIGHT, 1937]. Depressed, with rounded whorls; umbilicus narrow; ornament of collabral lamellar ribs separated by wider interspaces, ribs coalescing to form thickened expansion of aperture at gerontic stages. *M.Sil.*, Eu.—— Fig. 196,6. *T. monilis* (PERNER), Czech.; *6a,b*, apical and umbilical views, ×2.7.

Spirina KAYSER, 1889 [*S. brilonensis*]. Helicocone disjunct, expanding rapidly to explanate aperture; coiling of only slightly more than single whorl, slightly asymmetrical, with umbilicus pierced; ornament of collabral cords. *M.Sil.-M.Dev.*, Eu.

——Fig. 196,8. *S. brilonensis*, M.Dev., Ger.; *8a,b*, abapertural and apical views, ×1.

Natiria DEKONINCK, 1881 [*Natica lirata* PHILLIPS, 1836] [=*Fritschia* PICARD, 1904]. Naticiform, whorls barely in contact; collabral ornament widely spaced thin lamellae with numerous finer threads between, spiral ornament poorly developed or wanting. *L.Carb.-Trias.*, Eu.——Fig. 196,2. *N. lirata* (PHILLIPS), L.Carb., Eng.; ×1.3.

Dichostasia YOCHELSON, 1956 [*D. complex*]. Small, umboniform; narrowly phaneromphalous; with greatly thickened gerontic apertural margins; ornament differing above and below periphery, of various transverse (not strictly collabral) elements above and spiral and collabral below; labrum prosocline, without sinus (154, p. 208). *L.Perm.-M.Perm.*, N.Am.——Fig. 196,4. *D. complex*, M. Perm., Tex.; *4a-c*, abapertural, umbilical, and apical views, ×6.

FIG. 196. Craspedostomatacea (Craspedostomatidae) (p. *I298-I301*).

Brochidium KOKEN, 1889 [**Ceratites? cingulatus* MÜNSTER, 1834; SD COSSMANN, 1916]. Resembling *Temnospira* but more nearly discoidal and with more lamellar collabral ornament and more sharply differentiated aperture thickening. *M.Perm.-Jur.,* Eu.-N.Am.——FIG. 196,5. **B. cingulatum* (MÜNSTER), M.Trias.(Ladin), S.Tyrol; *5a,b,* apertural and apical views, ×2 (64).

Family CODONOCHEILIDAE
S. A. Miller, 1889

[*nom. correct.* KNIGHT, BATTEN & YOCHELSON, herein (*pro* Codonocheilidae S.A.MILLER, 1889]

Turriculate, with shallow sutures. *U.Sil.-M.Jur.*

Codonocheilus WHITEAVES, 1884 [**C. striatum*] [=*Codonochilus* LINDSTRÖM, 1884 (obj.)]. Spire cyrtoconoid; whorls very low, with very shallow sutures; last whorl disjunct; aperture circular and slightly explanate. *U.Sil.,* N.Am.-Eu.——FIG. 197, 3. **C. striatum,* Can.(Ont.); ×6.

?Dihelice W.E.SCHMIDT, 1905 [**D. dathei*]. Pupiform, with notably flat protoconch and cancellate ornament; whorls low; aperture unknown. *M.Dev.,* Eu.——FIG. 197,5. **D. dathei,* Ger.; ×2.7.

Scoliostoma BRAUN, 1838 [**S. dannenbergi*] [= *Mitchellia* DEKONINCK, 1877]. Last whorl twisted upward and on its own axis so that explanate aperture is well above mid-height on spire and facing opposite to usual direction. *M.Dev.-U.Dev.,* Eu.-Austral.——FIG. 197,2. **S. dannenbergi,* M. Dev., Ger.; *2a,* rear view, showing aperture; *2b,* front view, aperture turned away; ×2.

Bathyclides STRAND, 1928 [*pro Bathycles* KOKEN, 1896 (*non* DISTANT, 1893)] [**Bathycles acuminatus* KOKEN, 1896; SD DIENER, 1926] [= *Bathycla* STRAND, 1928 (obj.)]. Small, ovate-conical, broad, phaneromphalous, with sharply pointed apex and smooth, convex whorls; outer lip prosocline, thickened externally and internally when full-grown and at intervals during growth. *U.Trias.(Carn.-Nor.),* Eu.——FIG. 197,1. **B. acuminatus,* U.Trias.(Carn.), Aus.; ×4 (79).

Ventricaria KOKEN, 1896 [**Phasianella acuminata* HÖRNES, 1856; SD DIENER, 1926] Broadly turriculate or phasianelliform, cryptomphalous, with sharply pointed apex and feebly convex, spirally striated whorls; outer lip prosocline, thickened externally. *U.Trias.(Carn.-Nor.),* Eu.——FIG. 197,4. **V. tumida* (HÖRNES), Nor., Aus.; *4a,b,* ×3, ×1 (79).

Pirper DEGREGARIO, 1886 [**Stylifer? (Pirper) caplus*]. Founded on imperfect, low-cyrtoconoid, paucispiral specimen of medium size with smooth, convex whorls and externally thickened outer lip. *M.Jur.(Baj.),* Eu.(Italy).

Family CROSSOSTOMATIDAE Cox, n. fam.

Rotelliform or low-turbiniform, thick-shelled, of smooth, strongly convex whorls; aperture circular, with uninterrupted peristome and outer lip strongly thickened externally. *M.Trias.(Ladin.)-M.Jur.(Baj.),* Eu.

Crossostoma MORRIS & LYCETT, 1851 [**C. pratti*]. Anomphalous; aperture contracted, particularly from inner lip; reflected part of outer lip continued above, where it adheres to penultimate whorl. *L.Jur.-M.Jur.(Baj.),* Eu.——FIG. 198,2. **C. reflexilabrum* (D'ORBIGNY), M. Lias, Fr.; *2a,b,* ap-

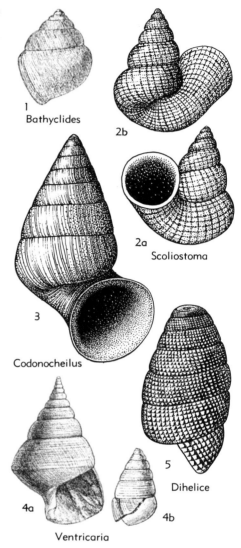

FIG. 197. Craspedostomatacea (Codonocheilidae) (p. 1301).

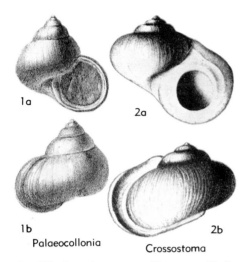

FIG. 198. Craspedostomatacea (Crossostomatidae) (p. *1302*).

Palaeocollonia   Crossostoma

ertural and abapertural views, ×2 (111).

Palaeocollonia KITTL, 1899 [*Delphinula laevigata* MÜNSTER, 1841] [=*Paleocolonia* WENZ, 1938 (obj.)]. Small, turbiniform, broadly phaneromphalous. *M.Trias.(Ladin.),* Eu.——FIG. 198,*1.* *P. laevigata* (MÜNSTER), S.Tyrol.; *1a,b,* apertural and abapertural views, ×3 (89).

Superfamily PALAEOTROCHACEA Knight, 1956

Turbiniform, trochiform, or moderately high-spired; commonly thick-shelled, especially in parts generated by parietal and columellar lips; shell structure and operculum unknown. *L.Dev.-U.Cret.(Senon.).*

Family PALAEOTROCHIDAE Knight, 1956

With characters of superfamily; shell large. *L.Dev.-U.Dev.*

Turbonopsis GRABAU & SHIMER, 1909 [*Turbo shumardi* HALL, 1879]. Turbiniform, with convexly prosocline labrum; ornament comprising strong spiral cord just above suture and heavy opisthocline ridges above cord. *L.Dev.,* N.Am.——FIG. 199,*4.* *T. shumardi* (HALL), USA(Ky.); ×0.7.

Palaeotrochus HALL, 1879 [*Pleurotomaria kearneyi* HALL, 1861]. Trochiform, with sinuous prosocline outer lip; ornament consisting of a strong spiral cord just above suture; growth lines irregular. *L.Dev.,* N.Am.——FIG. 199,*3.* *P. kearneyi* (HALL), USA(N.Y.); ×0.7.

Floyda WEBSTER, 1905 [*F. concentrica*] [= *Floydia* C.L.FENTON, 1918 (obj.); *Scaliconus* WENZ, 1938 (*pro Pileolus* SPRIESTERSBACH, 1919, *non* COOKSON in J.SOWERBY, 1823; *nec* LESSON, 1831; *nec* EHRENBERG, 1843) (147, p.260)]. Trochiform or turbiniform; ornament of broad, low undulations below upper suture. *M.Dev.-U. Dev.,* N.Am.-Eu.——FIG. 199,*2.* *F. concentrica,* U.Dev., USA(Iowa); ×0.5.

?Westerna WEBSTER, 1905 [*Loxonema gigantea* WEBSTER, 1888; SD KNIGHT, 1941 (69, p.385)] [=*Westernia* C.L.FENTON, 1918 (obj.)]. Much like *Floyda* but with higher spire. *U.Dev.,* N.Am. ——FIG. 199,*1.* *W. gigantea* (WEBSTER), USA (Iowa); ×0.5.

Family PARATURBINIDAE Cossmann, 1916

Turbiniform, including large and small forms; anomphalous or narrowly phaneromphalous; aperture suborbicular. *Trias.-U. Cret.*

Paraturbo COSSMANN, 1907 [*Turbo (Paraturbo) heptagoniatus*] [?=*Turboidea* SEELEY, 1861]. Large, thick, anomphalous; whorls with transversely elongated nodes or transverse costae and subordinate spiral cords; base coated with callus, obscuring ornament in some species. *L.Jur.-U. Cret.(Senon.),* cosmop.——FIG. 200,*1.* *P. stephanophorus* (ZITTEL), U.Jur.(Tithon.), Czech.; *1a,b,* ×1 (157).

Chartronella COSSMANN, 1902 [*pro Chartronia* COSSMANN, 1902 (*non* S.S.BUCKMAN, 1898)] [*Chartronia digoniata* COSSMANN, 1902] [=*Chartroniella* COSSMANN, 1916 (obj.)]. Rather small, anomphalous or narrowly phaneromphalous, last whorl bicarinate at periphery; other spiral carinae also present in most species; base smooth, convex. *Trias.-U.Jur.(Portl.),* Eu., S.Am.——FIG. 200,*2.* *C. zetes* (D'ORBIGNY), M.Jur.(Baj.), Eng.; *2a,b,* ×2 (59).

Creniturbo COSSMANN, 1918 [*Trochus dirce* D'ORBIGNY, 1850]. Small, anomphalous; ornament spiral cords cut up by collabral grooves; broad band with two rows of depressed nodes forming flattened periphery; basal ornament not obscured by callus. *U.Jur.(Raurac.),* Fr.——FIG. 200,*3.* *C. dirce* (D'ORBIGNY); ×5 (111).

Superfamily AMBERLEYACEA Wenz, 1938

[*nom. transl.* COX, herein (*ex* Amberleyidae WENZ, 1938)]

Shell dextral or sinistral; commonly littoriniform or turbiniform, more rarely with expanded, discoidal last whorl but protruding apex; aperture orbicular or with margin subangular at foot of columella;

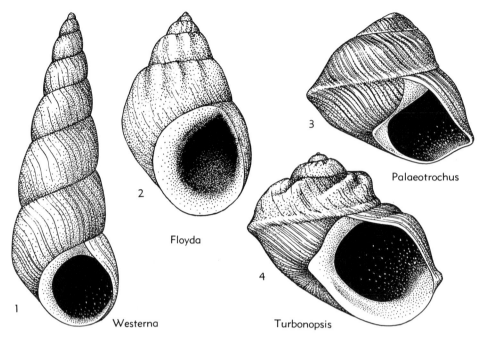

FIG. 199. Palaeotrochacea (Palaeotrochidae) (p. 1302).

spiral element of ornament dominant in most forms, spirals commonly being noded or cancellated by transverse elements; shell structure, where known (in some Amberleyidae), nacreous; operculum unknown. *M.Trias.-Olig.*

While the characters of the genus *Cirrus,* with its usually acute, protruding apex and progressively broadening and more fully embracing whorls, are unique, the similarity to the Amberleyidae of other genera that have been included in the Cirridae is unmistakable. COSSMANN included the Cirridae in the Euomphalacea on account of the subdiscoidal last whorl of *Cirrus,* maintaining that this was an instance in which ontogeny was no guide to affinity. Union of the Cirridae with the Amberleyidae in a single new superfamily serves to bring together a number of genera with obvious similarities, although *Cirrus* itself stands apart from the other included forms. The Platyacridae also seem better included in this superfamily than in the Euomphalacea, where they were placed by WENZ. A tendency for the initial whorls to be planispiral, so well displayed in this family, is

also seen in the South American cirrid genera, *Hesperocirrus* and *Sororcula.* Most Amberleyacea resemble the caenogastropod group Littorinacea in many features of the shell, but the nacreous structure (observable in the Amberleyidae) suggests that they are best included in the Archaeogastropoda.

Family PLATYACRIDAE Wenz, 1938

Shell turbinate, phaneromphalous, with apical truncation due to planispiral coiling of early whorls; either dextral or sinistral; aperture orbicular. *M.Trias.-U.Jur.*

Platyacra ZITTEL, 1882 [*Trochus impressus* SCHAFHÄUTL, 1863]. Sinistral; high-turbinate with early whorls planispiral; later whorls with inframedian carina, forming periphery of base; umbilicus moderately broad, with carinate margin. *U.Trias. (Rhaetic)-L.Jur.,* Eu.——FIG. 201,1. *P. impressa* (SCHAFHÄUTL), U.Trias.(Nor.), Bavaria; ×1.3 (233).

Lepidotrochus KOKEN, 1894 [*L. bittneri;* SD COSSMANN, 1916]. Shell form as in *Platyacra,* but dextral and with narrower umbilicus; ornament of cancellating spiral and collabral threads; *M.Trias.-U.Trias.,* Eu., N.Z.——FIG. 201,4. *Lepidotrochus bittneri,* M.Trias., Aus.; ×1.3 (79).

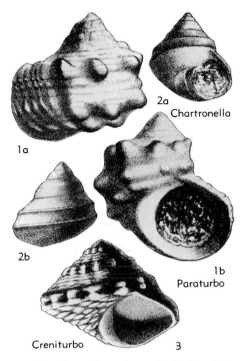

FIG. 200. Palaeotrochacea (Paraturbinidae) (p. *1302*).

Drepanoconcha ZILCH, 1949 [*pro Drepania* DE-GREGORIO, 1930 (*non* HUEBNER, 1816, *nec* LAFONT, 1874] [**Drepania pulchra* DEGREGORIO]. Rather small, sinistral, elevated, but broadly truncated at apex, with early whorls planispiral; later whorls convex, steeply coiled, with narrow collabral riblets. *L.Jur.*, Eu.——FIG. 201,*2*. **D. pulchra* (DE GREGORIO), Sicily; *2a,b*, ×2 (174).

Hyperacanthus KOKEN, 1894 [**Cirrus superbus* HÖRNES, 1855]. High-turbinate with earliest whorls planispiral; later whorls strongly convex, obscurely biangulate, last 2 with nodes or spines at angulations; base convex, with nodose spiral cords; whole surface with dense collabral threads; umbilicus moderately broad; aperture very oblique. *U.Trias.(Nor.)-L.Jur.*, Eu.——FIG. 201,*5*. **H. superbus* (HÖRNES), U.Trias.(Nor.), Aus.; *5a,b*, ×1 (79).

Acrosolarium KOKEN, 1896 [**A. superbum*]. Turbinate with earliest whorls planispiral; later whorls with carina at edge of broad, horizontal sutural shelf; last whorls with 2 further angulations, lower crenate and forming margin of rather narrow umbilicus; aperture unknown. *U.Trias.(Nor.)*, Eu. ——FIG. 201,*3*. **A. superbum*, Aus.; ×1.3 (79).

Family CIRRIDAE Cossmann, 1916

Littoriniform or with expanded, discoidal last whorl, sinistral; aperture suborbicular. *U.Trias.-M.Jur.(Bathon.).*

Cirrus J.SOWERBY, 1815 [**C. nodosus*; SD S.P. WOODWARD, 1851] [*=Cirrhus* FÉRUSSAC, 1821 (obj.)]. Moderately large, broadly phaneromphalous, ranging from high-spired with only slightly expanded last whorl to subdiscoidal; aperture with uninterrupted margin. *U.Trias.-M.Jur. (Bathon.)*, Eu.-S.Am.

C. (**Cirrus**). Apex very acute, but relative whorl diameter and overlap increasing progressively during growth to an extent varying in different species; coiling slightly irregular in some forms; ornament nodose spiral cords or coarse cancellating spiral and collabral ridges. *L.Jur.-M.Jur. (Bathon.)*, Eu.——FIG. 202,*4*. **C. (C.) nodosus*, M.Jur.(Baj.), Eng.; *4a,b*, ×0.8 (59)——FIG. 202, *1*. **C (C.) leachi* J.SOWERBY, M.Jur.(Baj.), Eng.; ×1 (59).

C. (**Discocirrus**) VONAMMON, 1892 [**Porcellia tricarinata* GÜMBEL, 1861]. Discoidal, without protruding apex. *L.Jur.(L.Lias.)*, Eu.

Hamusina GEMELLARO, 1878 [**Turbo bertheloti* D'ORBIGNY, 1850; SD COSSMANN, 1916]. High conical, anomphalous, shell wall thin; whorls, apart from ornament, almost flat, last with sharp peripheral carina continuing line of suture; base

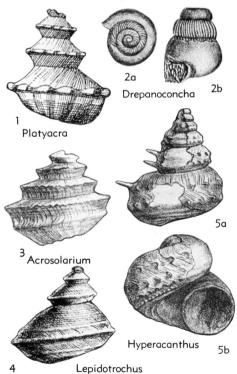

FIG. 201. Amberleyacea (Platyacridae) (p. *1303-1304*).

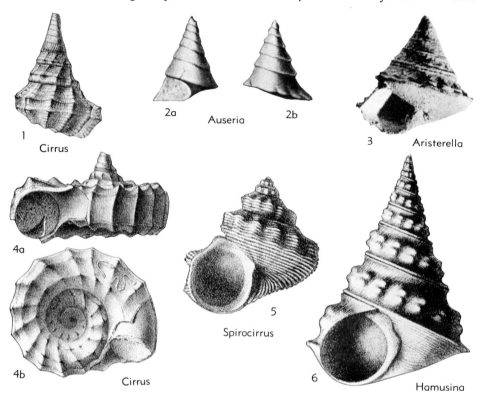

FIG. 202. Amberleyacea (Cirridae) (p. *1304-1305*).

feebly convex; ornament nodes or spiral threads, some nodose. *L.Jur.-M.Jur.(Baj.),* Eu., S.Am.——FIG. 202,6. **H. bertheloti* (D'ORBIGNY), U.Lias., Fr.; ×1 (111).

Spirocirrus COSSMANN, 1916 [**Turbo calisto* D'OR-BIGNY, 1850]. Turbiniform or conical, with moderately broad umbilicus, later whorls not expanded as in *Cirrus;* ornament strong axial ribs crossed by spiral threads, base with spiral threads only; columellar lip slightly reflected. *L.Jur.-M.Jur. (Bathon.),* Eu.——FIG. 202,5. **S. calisto* (D'OR-BIGNY), M.Jur.(Bathon.), Fr.; ×1 (111).

Auseria FUCINI, 1895 [**Trochus (Auseria) pseudonustus;* SD WENZ, 1938]. High conical, anomphalous; whorls smooth, flat-sided, with sharply carinate, crenulated periphery situated just above suture, producing an imbricate spire; base depressed. *L.Jur.(L.Lias.),* Eu.——FIG. 202,2. **A. pseudonustus,* L.Lias., Italy; *2a,b,* ×1 (147).

Hesperocirrus HAAS, 1953 [**H. robusteornatus*]. Littoriniform, small-medium size, phaneromphalous, carinate at periphery of flat or gently convex base; protoconch planispiral; whorls convex, not overlapping; sutures incised; ornament spiral cords bearing nodes where crossed by collabral ribs; aperture orbicular or quadrangular; inner lip more or less reflected over umbilical opening. *U.Trias.,* Peru.——FIG. 202A,*1. *H. robusteornatus; 1a,b,* apertural, abapertural views, ×5; *1c,* abapertural view of another specimen, ×3 (50).

Sororcula HAAS, 1953 [**S. gracilis*]. Small, high conical, narrowly phaneromphalous, carinate at periphery of flattened base; protoconch planispiral; whorls flat or slightly concave, not overlapping; sutures incised; ornament spiral row of tubercles adjoining each suture, tubercles joined in one species by transverse ribs; aperture broader than high, with inner lip reflected over umbilicus. *U. Trias.,* Peru.——FIG. 202A,3. **S. gracilis; 3a-c,* apertural, abapertural, basal views, ×6 (50).

Aristerella DUBAR, 1948 [**Amphitrochilia (Aristerella) undata*]. Medium size, slightly coeloconoid, narrowly phaneromphalous, sharply carinate at periphery of feebly convex base; whorls flat, not overlapping; sutures incised; ornament nodose or undulating spiral cord adjoining each suture and spiral threads on remainder of surface; aperture quadrangular. *L.Jur.(M.Lias.),* N.Afr.——FIG. 202,3. **A. undata,* Morocco; ×1 (36).

Family AMBERLEYIDAE Wenz, 1938

[=Eucyclidae KOKEN, 1896]

Dextral, turbiniform, littoriniform or low turriculate, with convex or imbricat-

1a

1b

2b

3a

2a

2c

3c

1c

2d

3b

Hesperocirrus

Pleuryalox

Sororcula

Fig. 202A. Amberleyacea (Cirridae) (p. 1207, 1305).

ing whorls; apertural margin not continuous across parietal region in most forms; shell structure nacreous. *M.Trias.-Oligo.*

Amberleya Morris & Lycett, 1851 [**A. bathonica* Cox & Arkell, 1950 (=**A. nodosa* Morris & Lycett, *non Terebra nodosa* Buckman, ICZN *pend.*)]. Littoriniform to subturriculate, anomphalous. *Trias.-Oligo.*

A. (**Amberleya**). Ornament nodose; columellar lip concave, its margin joining that of basal lip in even curve. *Trias.-U.Jur.(Raurac.),* Eu.-N.Afr.——Fig. 203,5. **A. (A.) bathonica* Cox & Arkell, M.Jur.(Bathon.), Eng.; ×1 (202).

A. (**Eucyclus**) J.A.Eudes-Deslongchamps, 1860 [**E. obeliscus*]. Ornament spiral carinae; columellar lip more or less straight and vertical, its margin commonly meeting that of basal lip in angle or spoutlike protrusion. *Trias.-Oligo.,* Eu.-S.Am.——Fig. 203,6. **A. (E.) obeliscus* (J.A. Eudes-Deslongchamps), M. Lias., Fr.; ×1 (182).

Eunemopsis Kittl, 1891 [**Turbo epaphus* Laube, 1869; SD Cossmann, 1916]. Small, with moderately acute, conical spire and convex base with small pseudumbilicus; ornament narrow axial costellae ending in nodule near each suture; small denticle at upper end of columellar lip. *M.Trias. (Ladin.)-U.Trias.(Carn.),* Eu.——Fig. 203,7. **E. epaphus* (Laube), M.Trias.(Ladin.), S.Tyrol; ×5 (89).

Paleunema Kittl, 1891 [**Pleurotomaria nodosa* Münster, 1841]. High turbiniform, almost turriculate, anomphalous; whorls imbricate, with prominent peripheral carina just above suture bearing growth lines that form series of back-pointing scales generated by notch in outer lip; base strongly convex, with spiral cords; columellar lip slightly concave. *M.Trias.(Ladin.),* Eu.——Fig. 203,3. **P. nodosa* (Münster), S. Tyrol; ×1.5 (64).

Tectospira Picard, 1904 [**T. chopi*]. Rather small, turbiniform, anomphalous; whorls imbricate, with

FIG. 203. Amberleyacea (Amberleyidae) (p. *1306-1307*).

prominent peripheral carina just above suture and, above it, about 2 weak spiral angulations crossed by collabral threads; base depressed, convex, with spiral cords; aperture oval, broader than high; outer lip notched at peripheral carina; columellar lip strongly concave. *M.Trias.,* Eu.——FIG. 203,*10.* *T. chopi,* Muschelkalk, Ger.; ×3 (212).

Riselloidea COSSMANN, 1909 [*pro Risellopsis* COSSMANN, 1908 (*non* KESTEVEN, 1902)] [*Risellopsis subdisjuncta* COSSMANN, 1908] [=*Risselloidea* COSSMANN, 1909 (? misprint)]. Small, trochiform, anomphalous, with conical spire and flattened base with carinate periphery; whorls with nodose carina adjoining each suture, sutures thus occupying deep channel; ornament axial ridges on whorl side between carinae and spiral cords on base. *Trias.-L.Cret.(Neocom.),* Eu.——FIG. 203,*8.* *R. biarmata* (MÜNSTER), M.Jur., Ger.; ×3 (11).

Eucyclomphalus VONAMMON, 1892 [*Trochus cupido* D'ORBIGNY, 1850; SD COSSMANN, 1916]. Medium-sized, rather broadly phaneromphalous, with high conical spire of whorls with sharp nodose peripheral carina, and convex base bearing spiral cords; columellar lip straight, vertical, not reflected. *L.Jur.,* Eu.——FIG. 203,*4.* *E. cupido* (D'ORBIGNY), M.Lias., Fr.; ×3 (111).

Ooliticia COSSMANN, 1893 [*Turbo phillipsi* MORRIS & LYCETT, 1851]. Medium-sized, stoutly littoriniform, anomphalous, with conical spire slightly exceeding height of aperture, evenly convex periphery, and convex base; ornament broad nodose spiral cords; columellar lip thickened, with blunt fold at its upper end. *L.Jur.-U.Cret.(Maastricht.),* cosmop.——FIG. 203,*2.* *O. phillipsi* (MORRIS & LYCETT), M.Jur.(Baj.), Eng., *2a,b,* ×2 (59).

Onkospira ZITTEL, 1873 [*Turbo ranellatus* QUENSTEDT, 1858 (=*Turbo anchurus* MÜNSTER in GOLDFUSS, 1844)] [=*Oncospira* COSSMANN, 1916 (obj.); *Tritonilla* KOKEN, 1896]. High turbiniform, anomphalous; whorls strongly convex, with spiral cords, collabral riblets, and either 1 or 2 series of varices almost in alignment on successive whorls, last varix situated behind outer lip; inner lip rather broadly reflected. *U.Jur.-L.Cret.,* Eu. ——FIG. 203,*1.* *O. gracilis* ZITTEL, U.Jur. (Tithon.), Czech.; *1a,b,* ×1.2, ×1.5 (157).

Tanaliopsis COSSMANN, 1916 [*Trochus spiniger* J.DEC.SOWERBY, 1833 (cited as *Turbo spiniger* ZEKELI)]. With stoutly conical spire and depressed, feebly convex base; spire with 8 to 10 axial costae aligned on successive whorls and forming nodes at periphery of last; aperture orbicular,

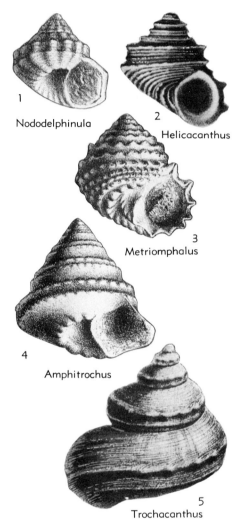

1
Nododelphinula

2
Helicacanthus

3
Metriomphalus

4
Amphitrochus

5
Trochacanthus

Fig. 204. Amberleyacea (Nododelphinulidae)
(p. *1308*).

with continuous peristome. *U.Cret.(Turon.)*, Aus.
——Fig. 203,9. **T. spinigera* (J.deC.Sowerby),
aperture imperfect; ×2 (147).

Family NODODELPHINULIDAE Cox, n. fam.

Small to medium-sized, turbiniform, with
height and breadth almost equal, phaneromphalous; spiral ornament dominant;
aperture orbicular (except in *Amphitrochus*), not very oblique, with continuous
peristome; operculum and shell structure
unknown. *U.Trias.-U.Cret.(Senon.)*.

Nododelphinula Cossmann, 1916 [**Delphinula
buckmani* Morris & Lycett, 1851]. Turbiniform,
broadly phaneromphalous; last whorl with concave, vertical outer face bordered by 2 nodose
spiral carinae, upper of which is exposed on spire
whorls; ornament spiral threads or cords crossed
in some species by collabral threads or ribs; circumumbilical carina with nodes continued by ribs
passing short distance into umbilicus. *M.Jur.(Baj.)-
L.Cret.*, Eu.——Fig. 204,*1*. **N. hudlestoni* Cossmann, M. Jur.(Baj.), Eng.; ×2.5 (59).

Amphitrochus Cossmann, 1907 [**Trochus duplicatus* J.Sowerby, 1817] [=*Amphitrochilia* Cossmann, 1909 (*pro Amphitrochus* Cossmann, 1907,
non Amphitrocha Agassiz, 1862)]. Trochiform,
with conical spire and depressed, concave base;
narrowly phaneromphalous; last whorl with prominent periphery formed by 2 conspicuous nodose
cords, one or both exposed on spire whorls just
above suture which is bordered by further nodose
cord; crenulated or nodose carina at umbilical
margin; aperture quadrate. *U.Trias.(Nor.)-L.Cret.
(Neocom.)*, Eu.——Fig. 204,4. **A. duplicatus*
(J.Sowerby), M.Jur.(Baj.), Eng.; ×2.5 (59).

Helicacanthus Dacqué in Wenz, 1938 [*pro Meta-
canthus* Dacqué, 1936 (*non* Costa, 1847)]
[**Turbo thurmanni* Pictet & Campiche, 1863].
Turbiniform, narrowly phaneromphalous; last
whorl with broad, concave outer face bordered by
two prominent spiral carinae both of which are
exposed on later spire whorls; ornament strong
spiral cords present also on base and within umbilicus. *U.Jur.-L.Cret.*, Eu.——Fig. 204,*2*. **H.
thurmanni* (Pictet & Campiche), L. Cret.(Apt.),
Switz.; ×2 (147).

Trochacanthus Dacqué, 1936 [**Trochus tuberculatocinctus* Münster in Goldfuss, 1844; SD Wenz,
1938]. Turbiniform, rather large; last whorl
strongly convex except peripherally, where it is
flattened between 2 obscurely nodose spiral angulations, both exposed on later spire whorls; ornament fine spiral threads. *M.Cret.-U.Cret.*, Eu.——
Fig. 204,5. **T. tuberculatocinctus* (Münster),
U.Cret.(Senon.), Ger.; ×1 (147).

Metriomphalus Cossmann, 1916 [**Turbo davoustii*
d'Orbigny, 1850]. Small, turbiniform, narrowly
to broadly phaneromphalous, with convex whorls
and base bearing a small number of spiral cords,
one forming margin of umbilicus, carrying nodes
or short prickles, terminal one of each cord forming projection of outer lip. *U.Trias.-U.Cret.
(Senon.)*, Eu.-Asia.——Fig. 204,3. **M. davoustii*
(d'Orbigny), M.Jur.(Baj.), Eng.; ×2.5 (59).

?ARCHAEOGASTROPODA Genera Inquirenda

Atlantobellerophon Trechmann, 1930 [**A. zea-
landicus*]. Large, apparently depressed-conispiral,
with last whorl disjunct (*fide* Marwick); anal
slit deep, peripheral. [Founded on a single imperfect last whorl; apparently pleurotomarian

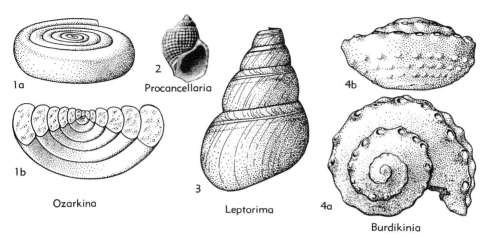

FIG. 205. Archaeogastropoda (Superfamily and Family Uncertain; Genera Inquirenda) (p. *1309*).

rather than bellerophont.] *U.Trias.(Rhaetic, Ota-pirian)*, N.Z.

Burdikinia KNIGHT, 1937 [*pro Polyamma* ETH-ERIDGE, JR., 1917 (*non* KRIECHBAUMER, 1894)] [**Polyamma burdikiensis* ETHERIDGE, JR., 1917]. Large, discoidal, with broad ramp above and narrow base; seemingly with row of hollow spines of unknown length opening adapertually on outer edge of ramp; base turning inward rapidly below ramp, ornamented with about 4 rows of spirally elongated pustules. [There should be no trouble in recognizing this striking genus, but placing it systematically is impossible without more information.] *Dev.*, Austral.——FIG. 205,4. **B. burdikiensis* (ETHERIDGE, JR.); *4a,b,* apical and side views, ×0.7 (69).

Cinctaspira POWELL, 1933 [**C. conica*]. Trochiform, with wide umbilicus and sharp spiral flange at about mid-whorl height. *L.Ord.*, N.Am.

Conchula STEININGER, 1849 [*non* HERRMANNSEN, 1847] [**C. cylindracea*]. Type not figured; unrecognizable; name invalid. *M.Dev.*, Eu.

Cyclora HALL, 1845 [**C. minuta*]. Very minute, naticiform. [Probably based on steinkerns of protoconchs of some other genus, possibly *Cyclonema*; locally very abundant.] *U.Ord.*, N.Am.

Geinitzia DIETZ, 1911 [*non* GEMMELLARO, 1892; *nec* HANDLIRSCH, 1906] [**G. carinata*]. Inadequately described and figured; name invalid. *Perm.*, Eu.

Kebina VOLOGDIN, 1955 [**K. pulchra*]. High-spired, narrowly phaneromphalous, with spiral carinae; very minute. [Known only from section of one specimen (143, p. 355)]. *?L.Cam.*, Russia.

Leptorima PERNER, 1907 [**Murchisonia oehlerti* PERNER, 1903]. Rather high turbiniform; with sharp sinus in outer lip culminating only slightly below suture in deep slit that generates narrow

selenizone which is gently convex outside and more strongly convex within; sutures shallow, covered by adpressed zone; columellar and parietal lips little known; ornament other than growth lines seemingly a slight stria below selenizone. [This remarkable species is so very different from any other known that it defies classification; foundation of a new major category is thought to be unwise in the present state of knowledge.] *U.Sil.*, Eu.——FIG. 205,3. **L. oehlerti* (PERNER), Czech.; ×2.

Ozarkina ULRICH & BRIDGE, 1931 [*pro Ozarkispira* ULRICH & BRIDGE, 1931 (*non* WALCOTT, 1924)] [**Ozarkispira typica* ULRICH & BRIDGE, 1931]. Known from discoidal steinkerns which show numerous narrow, rounded whorls but no surface or apertural features that would permit classification. *L.Ord.*, N.Am.——FIG. 205,1. **O. typica* (ULRICH & BRIDGE), Mo.; *1a,b,* oblique view from above and below, latter showing cross section, ×2.

Ozarkocanus HELLER, 1956 [**O. prearcuatus*]. With high conical, slightly curved, cap-shaped shell; aperture oval; ornament longitudinal costae or threads. [Possibly not a gastropod.] *L.Ord.*, USA.

Pichynella RUSCONI, 1954 [**P. annulata*]. Very minute (1 mm.), possibly a protoconch. [Too little known for systematic assignment.] *L.Ord.*, S.Am.

Pondia ODER, 1932 [**P. powelli*]. Based on 2 fragments, seemingly of a calcareous operculum, possibly of *Maclurites. L.Ord.*, N.Am.

Procancellaria WILCKENS, 1922 [**P. parkiana*]. Ovate, with low spire, anomphalous; whorls convex; ornament cancelling collabral and spiral grooves, the former feebly prosocline; aperture ovate, with uninterrupted peristome, subangular adapically; columellar lip vertical, moderately ex-

panded, without folds. *U.Cret.*, N.Z.——Fig. 205, 2. **P. parkiana;* ×1 (229).

Pythmenema LAMONT & GILBERT, 1945 [**Euomphalus praenantius* PHILLIPS, 1848]. Turbiniform, with strong spiral carinae above periphery and finer ones below. [The original diagnosis of this genus and the description and figures of the type species are quite inadequate for systematic placement more closely than in the Archaeogastropoda.] (86, p. 643.) *U.Sil.*, Eu.

Trochotremaria RYCKHOLT, 1860. No species was ever assigned to this genus.

Umbotrochus PERNER, 1903 [**U. aspersus*] [= *Umbonitrochus* COSSMANN, 1918 (obj.)]. Trochiform, with shallow sutures; roundly angulated periphery; base nearly flat, anomphalous; apertural margins not certainly known. [The single specimen known is not well enough preserved to allow a restoration, nor is it possible to classify the genus. Perhaps it might be referred to the Microdomatacea.] *M.Sil.*, Eu.

SUPPLEMENT
PALEOZOIC AND SOME MESOZOIC CAENOGASTROPODA AND OPISTHOBRANCHIA

By J. BROOKES KNIGHT[1], R. L. BATTEN[2], E. L. YOCHELSON[3], and L. R. COX[4]

INTRODUCTION

When the *Treatise* was first conceived, the senior author, whose field of special study is the gastropods of the Paleozoic, undertook to cover all orders represented in that era, including supposed patelloid gastropods now classified as Monoplacophora. Almost from the beginning R. L. BATTEN and E. L. YOCHELSON were associated with him.

As work on the *Treatise* progressed it became apparent that Part I, covering Scaphopoda, Amphineura, Monoplacophora, and the gastropod order Archaeogastropoda would be ready for publication in a reasonable time. However, manuscript for Part J, planned to include the prosobranch taxa Mesogastropoda and Neogastropoda (here combined as an order named Caenogastropoda), large divisions that are very abundant and varied in post-Paleozoic time, and the subclasses Opisthobranchia and Pulmonata, has been so delayed that it might not appear during the senior author's lifetime.

The authors recognize that no final treatment of the predominantly post-Paleozoic orders can be successful without including consideration of the vast amount of information that will be presented by specialists in these overwhelmingly post-Paleozoic groups. Nevertheless, the authors concerned with Paleozoic groups which include the more primitive members, perhaps ancestral to the better-known ones of later

times, feel that they can contribute important matter too frequently overlooked by students of the younger fossil genera and especially by neontologists.

For this reason and because the student of Paleozoic Gastropoda will profit from having current data on all the orders in his field even though not in final form, consent was obtained to include them in Part I as a Supplement.

With the exceptions to be noted, the three authors already mentioned are responsible for the material here presented, especially the systematics. Dr. L. R. Cox, British Museum (Natural History), who has supervision over sections of the *Treatise* dealing with all gastropods, has examined the manuscript of the Supplement and has been kind enough to add data on authorship and to suggest diagnoses for several taxa that are best known to workers on post-Paleozoic mollusks. Cox has prepared the diagnosis and synonymy for the order Caenogastropoda (replacing Mesogastropoda and Neogastropoda of previously written text) and he is author of the division of the Loxonemataces included in the Family Zygopleuridae; this family, although entirely Mesozoic, has been included here to make the account of the superfamily

[1] Honorary Research Associate, Smithsonian Institution, Washington, D.C.; Longboat Key, Florida.
[2] Department of Geology, University of Wisconsin, Madison.
[3] U. S. Geological Survey, Washington, D. C.
[4] Department of Palaeontology, British Museum (Natural History), London.

complete. The diagnosis of the subclass Opisthobranchia was drafted after a discussion with Prof. ALASTAIR GRAHAM and Dr. VERA FRETTER, leading authorities on this group. For these kindnesses the authors are grateful.

It is planned that when Part J appears the groups covered in this Supplement will be reviewed and integrated systematically with the post-Paleozoic forms by the authors engaged in the task; accordingly, it is not intended that the arrangements here presented will be binding upon them. In the meantime, the arrangement of the suprafamilial taxa is not materially altered from those current in recent years. WENZ (1938) in particular has been followed. However, several large familial categories assigned by that author to the Archaeogastropoda have been placed in the Caenogastropoda and even in the Opisthobranchia. The authors are unable at this time to recognize any compelling reasons for classifying any Paleozoic taxa in the Pulmonata.

Order CAENOGASTROPODA Cox, 1959

[=pectinibranches DEBLAINVILLE, 1814 *(partim)*; Siphonobranchia+Pectinibranchia *(partim)* GOLDFUSS, 1820; Ctenobranchiata SCHWEIGGER, 1820 *(partim)*; Hemipomatostoma+Apomatostoma MENKE, 1830; Pectinibranchiata GRAY, 1850 *(partim)*; Monotocardia Exophallia MÖRCH, 1865; Streptoneura Azygobranchia SPENGEL, 1881 *(partim)*; monotocardes BOUVIER, 1887; Ctenobranchia PELSENEER, 1893; Pectinibranchia PELSENEER, 1906; Mesogastropoda + Stenoglossa THIELE, 1929; Mesogastropoda+Neogastropoda WENZ, 1938]

Shell asymmetrical, of many shapes, porcelaneous; right ctenidium absent, the left monopectinate (but absent in certain families); inhalant siphon present or absent; heart with one auricle; one kidney only; pallial genital organs present in most forms, forming a penis in the male; nervous system moderately to highly concentrated; proboscis present in many forms; radula of several types, mostly with relatively few teeth in a row. Marine, freshwater and terrestrial. *Ord.-Rec.*

Superfamily LOXONEMATACEA Koken, 1889

[*nom. transl.* COSSMANN, 1909 (*ex* Loxonematidae KOKEN, 1889)]

Commonly high-spired, with numerous whorls, mostly anomphalous; deep to obsolescent labral sinus without slit or notch; inner shell layers not nacreous. *M.Ord.-U.Jur.*

Although the sinus in the Loxonematacea does not culminate in a slit or notch, as in the Murchisoniacea, it is thought to have served as an excurrent channel, at least in those genera in which it is deepest. Perhaps the anal tube lay between a pair of ctenidia, as has been postulated for the Murchisoniacea. With passage of time, however, the sinus tends to become shallower and its culmination is found to move toward the suture. This supports the inference that, if the right ctenidium was retained in more primitive forms, it had been lost by Devonian time, and the anus and other pallial organs had been displaced to the positions which they occupy in the Cerithiacea.

The Loxonematacea seem to have been closely related to the Murchisoniacea and probably were derived from them.

Family LOXONEMATIDAE Koken, 1889

[=Holopellidae KOKEN, 1897]

Mostly relatively large; labrum with median sinus, lower segment opisthocline; ornament dominantly collabral; protoconch seemingly of several whorls, unornamented. *M.Ord.-Miss.*

Loxonema PHILLIPS, 1841 [**Terebra? sinuosa* J. DEC.SOWERBY, 1839; SD KING, 1850] [=*Holopella* M'COY, 1851; *Rhabdostropha* DONALD, 1905]. Sinus deep; sutures moderately deep. *M.Ord.-Miss.,* cosmop.——FIG. 206,4. **L. sinuosum* (J.DEC. SOWERBY), M.Sil., Eng.; ×2.

Girvania LONGSTAFF, 1924 [**G. excavata*]. Small, extremely slender, high-spired and many-whorled; with shallow labral sinus; spiral threads and collabral undulations. *U.Ord.,* Eu.——FIG. 206,2. **G. excavata*, Scot.; ×4.

Spiroecus LONGSTAFF, 1924 [**S. girvanensis*]. Whorls rounded except for sloping ramp above low spiral cord occurring somewhat above midwhorl. *U.Ord.,* Eu.——FIG. 206,6. **S. girvanensis*, Scot.; ×4.

Stylonema PERNER, 1907 [**Loxonema (Stylonema) potens*; SD LONGSTAFF, 1909]. Very slender, highspired, many-whorled; with shallow sinus, upper limb extending a little farther beyond aperture than lower; ornament numerous very fine collabral threads. *L.Sil.-L.Dev.,* Eu.——FIG. 206,1. **S. potens* (PERNER), U.Sil., Czech.; ×0.7.

Aulacostrepsis PERNER, 1907 [**A. simplex*]. Much like *Stylonema* but wider, with lower and wider whorls; minutely phaneromphalous, with umbilical opening surrounded by rounded ridge. *L.Dev.,* Eu.——FIG. 206,3. **A. simplex*, Czech.; ×1.3.

Katoptychia PERNER, 1907 [**K. alba;* SD COSSMANN, 1909] [=*Cataptychia* COSSMANN, 1909 (obj.)]. Whorls flat, with shallow sutures; outer lip

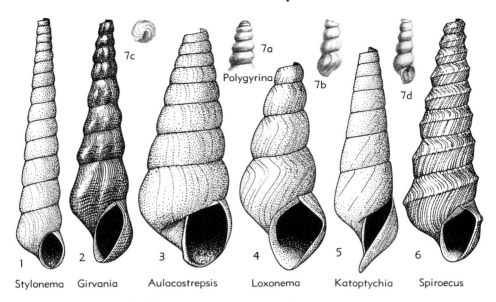

7c

Polygyrina   7a

7b

7d

1	2	3	4	5	6
Stylonema	Girvania	Aulacostrepsis	Loxonema	Katoptychia	Spiroecus

FIG. 206. Loxonematacea (Loxonematidae) (p. *1311-1312*).

strongly opisthocline until close to base, without sinus (unless the subangular juncture of outer and parietal lips may be interpreted as a sinus). *L.Dev.*, Eu.——FIG. 206,5. *K. alba*, Czech.; apertural view, ×2.7.

Polygyrina KOKEN, 1892 [*Turritella lommelii* MÜNSTER, 1841; SD COSSMANN, 1909]. Whorls many, strongly convex; protoconch obtuse, dome-like; growth lines forming broad, symmetrical sinus on spire whorls, their complete curve parasigmoid. *L.Trias.-U.Trias.*, Eu.-Asia.——FIG. 206, 7. *P. lommeli* (MÜNSTER), M.Trias-(Ladin.), S.Tyrol; *7a*, early whorls, ×3; *b-d*, later whorls, ×1 (64).

Family PALAEOZYGOPLEURIDAE Horny, 1955

Relatively small, labral sinus shallow or wanting; protoconch composed of one or (rarely) more smooth whorls; ornament collabral or wanting. *Dev.-L.Carb.*

Palaeozygopleura HORNY, 1955 [*Zygopleura alinae* PERNER, 1907] [=*Bojozyga, Palaeozyga* HORNY, 1955 (58, p.27)]. Small, high-spired, with labral sinus; whorls not shouldered, with shallow sutures or adpressed (58, p.27). *Dev.-L.Carb.*, Eu. ——FIG. 207,1. *P. alinae* (PERNER), L.Dev., Czech.; *1a*, apertural view, ×6; *1b*, early whorls ×14.

Devonozyga HORNY, 1955 [*D. perneri*]. Small, slightly pupiform, with flat-sided, shouldered whorls and no labral sinus (58, p.51). *M.Dev.*, Eu.——FIG. 207,2. *D. perneri*, Czech.; ×14.

Family PSEUDOZYGOPLEURIDAE Knight, 1930

[*nom. transl.* KNIGHT, BATTEN & YOCHELSON, herein (*ex* Pseudozygopleurinae KNIGHT, 1930] [=Palaeostylinae WENZ, 1938]

Gross characters variable but distinguished by nature of ornament and shape of protoconch; first 1 to 1.5 whorls of protoconch smooth, strong collabral ornament appearing on 2nd whorl and continuing to 4th where it gives way very abruptly to adult type of ornament (commonly present but lacking in some species); 1st ornamented whorl commonly slightly swollen, giving protoconch shape suggestive of coronet. *L.Carb.(Miss.)-M.Perm.*

The presence or absence of the pseudozygopleurid type of protoconch can be determined only on specimens in which this part of the shell is exceptionally well preserved, although the shape of the protoconch may be suggestive even if fine details are not discernible. If the protoconch of any genus is unknown its placement here is queried. The distinctive juvenile characters of the Pseudozygopleuridae are shown clearly by many Pennsylvanian and Permian shells but are not yet known in Mississippian genera that it seems impossible to exclude. HORNÝ's stimulating monograph on the Palaeozygopleuridae appeared after

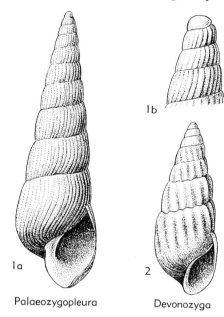

1b

1a 2

Palaeozygopleura Devonozyga

FIG. 207. Loxonematacea (Palaeozygopleuridae)
(p. *1312*).

the section on the Pseudozygopleuridae was completed. There proved to be considerable overlap in respect to genera for which protoconchs are unknown. With these it is impossible to decide definitely between two assignments or possibly others. The authors have concluded to leave their arrangement as it was but are conscious that some at least of the queried genera may prove to belong where HORNÝ placed them. Triassic genera very similar to the Pseudozygopleuridae are referred to the family Zygopleuridae because the protoconchs of well-preserved specimens are smooth.

?**Tmetonema** LONGSTAFF, 1912 [**T. subsulcatum*]. Small, with collabral threads crossing whorls which bear broad, slightly depressed band approximately at mid-height, slight sinus (shown by pattern of threads) occurring above band; threads prosocline close to upper suture but opisthocline crossing band and then gradually prosocline on base; protoconch unknown. [Description derived from LONGSTAFF's photographic illustration; this fails to accord with her diagnosis and line drawings, which do not agree among themselves.] L.Carb., Eu.

?**Knightella** LONGSTAFF, 1933 [*pro Knightia* LONGSTAFF, 1933 (*non* JORDAN, 1907)] [**Knightia irregularis* LONGSTAFF, 1933]. Whorls rounded, sutures moderately deep; outer lip with very shallow sinus; ornament growth lines only. [Shape

of protoconch suggests Pseudozygopleuridae but characteristic larval ornament not demonstrated.] *L.Carb.-U.Carb.*, Eu.——FIG. 208,*6*. **K. irregularis* (LONGSTAFF), L.Carb., Scot.; ✕8.

?**Microptychia** LONGSTAFF, 1912 [**M. wrighti*]. Earlier adult whorls with moderately strong collabral threads outlining shallow sinus; beyond 1st 0.25 of spire threads become obsolete over middle of whorls but are accentuated at shallow sutures; protoconch unknown. *Miss.(L.Carb.)-Penn.(U. Carb.)*, N.Am.-Eu.——FIG. 208,*1*. *M. cerithiformis* (MEEK & WORTHEN), M.Penn., Ill.; ✕2.7.

Helminthozyga KNIGHT, 1930 [**H. vermicula*]. Protoconch characteristic of subfamily, but coiling of later-formed shell quite variable, conical with wide umbilicus or completely disjunct and vermiform; with somewhat lamellar collabral ornament. *Miss.-Penn.*, N.Am.——FIG. 208,*11*. **H. vermicula,* M.Penn., Mo.; ✕20.

?**Eoptychia** LONGSTAFF, 1933 [**Loxonema sulcatum* DEKONINCK, 1881]. Large, with relatively flat whorls and shallow sutures; numerous fine collabral threads; protoconch unknown. *L.Carb.-U. Carb.*, Eu.——FIG. 208,*13*. **E. sulcata* (DE-KONINCK), L.Carb., Belg.; ✕1.

Palaeostylus MANSUY, 1914 [**P. pupoides;* SD COSSMANN, 1918]. With collabral ornament or none. *Miss.-M.Perm.*, N.Am.-SE.Asia.

?**P. (Stephanozyga)** KNIGHT, 1930 [**Zygopleura nodosa* GIRTY, 1915] [*=Nodozyga* HORNÝ, 1955 (58, p. 24)]. Relatively large, with collabral ornament weak or missing on upper part of whorls but strong and nodelike below; with rather deep labral sinus; protoconch unknown. *Miss.-M.Perm.*, N.Am.-SE.Asia.——FIG. 208,*2*. **P. (S.) nodosus* (GIRTY), M.Penn., Mo.; ✕1.3.

P. (Pseudozygopleura) KNIGHT, 1930 [**Loxonema semicostatum* MEEK, KNIGHT, 1930 (=*L. attenuata semicostata* MEEK, 1872)]. Collabral threads or cords on all whorls, or confined to earlier whorls, or absent entirely. ?*Miss., Penn.-M.Perm.*, N.Am.——FIG. 208,*12*. **P. (P.) semicostatus* (MEEK), M.Penn., Mo.; ✕10.

P. (Leptozyga) KNIGHT, 1930 [**Pseudozygopleura (Leptozyga) minuta*]. Very small, cyrtoconoid, with high spire but relatively few whorls. *Penn.,* N.Am.——FIG. 208,*4*. **P. (L.) minutus,* M. Penn., Mo.; ✕20.

P. (Palaeostylus) [=*Pyrgozyga* KNIGHT, 1930]. Very high-spired, with many low broad whorls; collabral ornament orthocline or nearly so. *Penn.-M.Perm.*, N.Am.-SE.Asia.——FIG. 208,*7*. **P. (P.) pupoides,* L.Perm. Cambodia; ✕4.

?**Hemizyga** GIRTY, 1915 [**H. elegans;* SD KNIGHT, 1930]. With both collabral and spiral ornament; labral sinus very shallow or absent. *Miss.-M.Perm.,* N.Am.

?**H. (Hemizyga)** [=*Strianematina* H.CHRONIC, 1952 (14, p.130)]. Collabral ornament of fine to coarse somewhat prosocline threads, spiral ornament mostly on base; protoconch unknown.

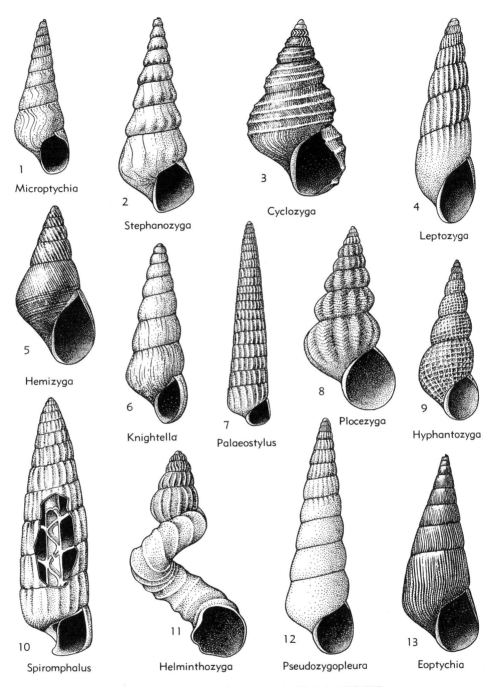

1 Microptychia

2 Stephanozyga

3 Cyclozyga

4 Leptozyga

5 Hemizyga

6 Knightella

7 Palaeostylus

8 Plocezyga

9 Hyphantozyga

10 Spiromphalus

11 Helminthozyga

12 Pseudozygopleura

13 Eoptychia

FIG. 208. Loxonematacea (Pseudozygopleuridae) (p. *1313-1315*).

Miss.-M.Perm., N.Am.——Fig. 208,*5*. **H. (H.) elegans*, M.Penn., Mo.; ×5.3.

H. (Hyphantozyga) KNIGHT, 1930 [**H. (Hyphantozyga) gracilis*]. Spiral and collabral ornament of subequal sharp threads. *Penn.*, N.Am. ——Fig. 208,*9*. **H. (P.) corona*, M.Penn., Mo.; ×10.

H. (Plocezyga) KNIGHT, 1930. [**H. (Plocezyga) corona*]. Collabral ornament of strong cords or ribs, spiral ornament of fine threads or striae. *U.Carb.(Penn.)*, N.Am.——Fig. 208,*8*. **H. (P.) corona*, N.Penn., Mo.; ×10.

Cyclozyga KNIGHT, 1930 [**C. mirabilis*; SD KNIGHT, 1936]. Minute, with protoconch of subfamily, spiral threads on adult shell; shallow sinus low on whorl. *Penn.*, N.Am.——Fig. 208,*3*. **C. mirabilis*, M.Penn., Mo.; ×20.

?Spiromphalus HAYASAKA, 1939 [**S. yabei*]. Much like *Palaeostylus* with deep and (for such a high-spired shell) wide umbilicus, within which is a spiral projecting flange; protoconch unknown (54, p.20). *Perm.*, NE.Asia.——Fig. 208,*10*. **S. yabei*, Japan; apertural view, with window showing spiral flange, ×4.5.

Family ZYGOPLEURIDAE Wenz, 1938

[*nom. transl.* COX, herein (*ex* Zygopleurinae WENZ, 1938)]

Shell slender; protoconch smooth, of up to about 3 regularly increasing whorls; ornament narrow collabral riblets which have parasigmoid curve in most genera; subordinate spiral ornament in some genera. *Trias.-U.Jur.*

Zygopleura KOKEN, 1892 [**Cerithium meyeri* KLIPSTEIN, 1843 (=*Turritella hybrida* MÜNSTER, 1841, *non* DESHAYES, 1832); SD COSSMANN, 1909]. Whorls strongly convex; riblets well defined and with pronounced parasigmoid curve; no spiral ornament. *Trias.-U.Jur.(L.Kimm.)*, cosmop.——Fig. 209,*9*. **Z. meyeri* (KLIPSTEIN), M.Trias.(Ladin.), Italy; ×2.5 (178).

Katosira KOKEN, 1892 [**K. fragilis*]. Whorls flattened-convex; collabral riblets not extending on to base and with parasigmoid curve less pronounced than in *Zygopleura*; weak spiral threads on whorl side, stronger ones on base; apertural margin slightly reflected anteriorly to form ill-defined spout, possibly a rudimentary siphonal outlet. *U.Trias.(Carn.)-M.Jur.(Baj.)*, cosmop.——Fig. 209,*1*. **K. periniana* (D'ORBIGNY), M.Lias., Fr.; ×1 (111).

Kittliconcha BONARELLI, 1927 [**Zygopleura (Kittliconcha) cassiana, pro Loxonema walmstedti* KITTL (*partim*), 1894, *non Turritella walmstedti* KLIPSTEIN, 1843]. Broader and less acute than in most genera of family; whorls strongly convex; collabral riblets strong on spire whorls, where only their opisthocyrt upper part is exposed, obsolete on last whorl except for a varix; no spiral ornament. *M.*

Trias.-(Ladin.), Eu.-S.Am.——Fig. 209,*4*. **K. cassiana*, S.Tyrol.; *4a-c*, ×1 (64).

Anoptychia KOKEN, 1892 [**Melania supraplecta* MÜNSTER, 1841; SD COSSMANN, 1909[1]]. Whorls flat to feebly convex; in some species a carina occupies periphery of last whorl and is just exposed on those of spire; collabral riblets on early whorls only; spiral threads weakly developed on sides, stronger on base. *M.Trias.(Ladin.)-M.Jur.(Baj.)*, cosmop.——Fig. 209,*7*. **A. supraplecta* (MÜNSTER), M.Trias.(Ladin.), S.Tyrol; ×3 (64).

Allocosmia COSSMANN, 1897 [*pro Heterocosmia* KOKEN, 1896, *non* EHRENBERG, 1872] [**Holopella grandis* HÖRNES, 1855]. Large, slightly coeloconoid, very acute at apex; whorls strongly convex, collabral riblets confined to very early ones, spiral threads more persistent; aperture (if appearance is not due to fracture) with spoutlike siphonal outlet. *M.Trias.-L.Jur.*, cosmop.——Fig. 209,*11*. **A. grandis* (HÖRNES), U.Trias.(Nor.), Aus.; *11a,b*, ×1, ×0.5 (79).

Hypsipleura KOKEN, 1892 [**H. cathedralis*]. Slender, with high, almost flat whorls; early whorls with feebly sigmoid riblets, which later fade away progressively, partly or wholly, from their abapical end upward; spiral threads present in some. *M.Trias.(Ladin.)-L.Jur.(M.Lias.)*, Eu.-S.Am.——Fig. 209,*5*. **H. subnodosa* (KLIPSTEIN), M.Trias.(Ladin.), S.Tyrol; *5a-c*, ×1 (64).

Tyrsoecus KITTL, 1892 [**Tyrsoecus cassiani* COX (*nom. nov.*) =**Turritella compressa* MÜNSTER, 1841 (*non* MÜNSTER, 1840); SD COSSMANN, 1909] [=*Stephanocosmia* COSSMANN, 1895 (*pro Coronaria* KOKEN, 1892, *non* LOWE, 1854)]. Whorls low, convex or with median angulation, bearing at mid-height row of blunt tubercles located in some species on axial riblets crossing the strongly parasigmoid growth lines; spiral threads present in some. *M.Trias.(Ladin.)-U.Jur.(Raurac.)*, cosmop.——Fig. 209,*12*. **T. subcompressus* KITTL, M.Trias.(Ladin.), S.Tyrol; *12a,b*, later whorls, ×1 (64).

Goniospira COSSMANN, 1895 [*pro Goniogyra* KITTL, 1894 (*non* AGASSIZ, 1857)] [**Turritella armata* MÜNSTER, 1841]. Small; whorls high, steeply coiled, with sharply angular nodose periphery at mid-height; 2nd angulation, continuing suture, delimiting spirally striated part of base of last; growth lines strongly parasigmoid. *M.Trias.*, Eu.-?Asia.——Fig. 209,*3*. **G. armata* (MÜNSTER), S.Tyrol; *3a,b*, ×1, ×2 (64).

[1] MÜNSTER in 1841 described 2 different species (now included in *Anoptychia*) under the names *Melania supraplecta* and *Turritella supraplecta*. KOKEN, when founding *Anoptychia*, cited *Chemnitzia supraplecta* MÜNSTER as one of its species, and, as at that time only *Melania supraplecta* had been transferred to *Chemnitzia* (by D'ORBIGNY, 1850) it could be argued that this was the species intended. COSSMANN, however, cited *Turritella supraplecta* as type species of *Anoptychia*, although in illustration of it he reproduced KITTL's figure of *Melania supraplecta* in the synonymy of *T. carinata* MÜNSTER (unfortunately a homonym of *T. carinata* LEA). *Melania supraplecta* is here cited as type species of *Anoptychia* (see also HAAS, 1953, p. 122 [no. 50 in following reference list]).

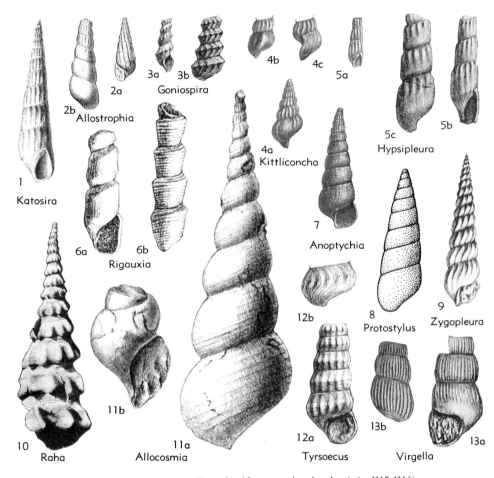

FIG. 209. Loxonematacea (Zygopleuridae, genus inquirendum) (p. *I315-I316*).

?**Raha** MARWICK, 1953 [**Coronaria spectabilis* TRECHMANN, 1918]. Large, coeloconoid; lower part of whorls with strong rounded ribs ending by suture in tubercles; spiral threads present, strongest on unribbed region; collabral lines almost straight. *U.Trias.(Carn.)*, N.Z.——FIG. 209,*10*. **R. spectabilis* (TRECHMANN); ×0.7 (204).

Allostrophia KITTL, 1894 [**Melania perversa* MÜNSTER, 1841]. Sinistral; whorls moderately convex; collabral riblets with strong sigmoid curve, and becoming obsolete on later whorls; no spiral ornament. *M.Trias.(Ladin.)-U.Trias.(Nor.)*, Eu.-S.Am.——FIG. 209,*2*. **A. perversa* (MÜNSTER), M.Trias.(Ladin.), S.Tyrol; *2a,b*, ×1 (10).

?**Virgella** DEGREGORIO, 1930 [**V. jucunda*]. Small, sinistral; early whorls unknown, later ones high, feebly convex, bearing close-spaced narrow collabral riblets parallel with axis, not sigmoid. *L.Jur.*, Sicily.——FIG. 209,*13*. **V. jucunda*; *13a,b*, ×3 (174).

Rigauxia COSSMANN, 1885 [**Chemnitzia canaliculata* RIGAUX & SAUVAGE, 1868; SD COSSMANN,

1909]. Very acute; whorls high, feebly concave to feebly convex, with narrow sutural ramp in some species; presence of narrow parasigmoid collabral riblets, low varices, and spiral threads variable. *L.Jur. - M.Jur.(Callov.)*, Fr.-Sinai.——FIG. 209,*6*. **R. canaliculata* (RIGAUX & SAUVAGE), M.Jur. (Bathon.), Fr.; *6a,b*, ×1, ×1.5 (17).

LOXONEMATACEA Genus inquirendum

Protostylus MANSUY, 1914 [**P. lantenoisi*; SD BATTEN, 1952 (4, p.355)]. Smooth, unornamented, with flat whorls and shallow sutures; labrum and protoconch unknown. *Perm.*, SE.Asia.——FIG. 209,*8*. **P. lantenoisi*, Yunnan; ×1.3.

Superfamily CERITHIACEA Fleming, 1822

[*nom. transl. et correct.* COSSMANN, 1906 (*ex* Cerithiadae FLEMING, 1822)]

Shell mostly high-spired, with many whorls, less commonly of other shapes; operculum spiral; penis absent. *L.Dev.-Rec.*

Family TURRITELLIDAE Woodward, 1851

[Family Turritellidae also erected in the same year independently by W. CLARK; =Acanthonematidae WENZ, 1938]

High-spired, with 8 to 20 or more whorls, spiral ornament commonly conspicuous; shallow labral sinus usually culminating at or above mid-whorl with upper limb extending farther adaperturally than lower; siphonal notch or canal wanting. *L.Dev.-Rec.*

Turritella LAMARCK, 1799 [*Turbo terebra* LINNÉ, 1758]. Moderate to large, slender; whorls convex, neanic primary spirals starting in the order abapical-medial-adapical; outer lip arcuate, lateral sinus shallow, oblique; no basal sinus. *Oligo.-Rec.*, SE.Asia-E.Indies-Japan; *Mio.*, S.Eu.-N.Afr.-trop. & subtrop. Am.

Acanthonema SHERZER & GRABAU, 1908 [*A. holopiforme* (=*Orthonema newberryi* MEEK, 1873); SD GRABAU & SHIMER, 1909]. With spiral row of spirally elongate pustules just below upper suture and in some shells 1 or 2 similar rows just above lower suture; minutely phaneromphalous. *L.Dev.*, N.Am.——FIG. 210,1. *A. newberryi* (MEEK), Ohio; ×2.

Orthonema MEEK & WORTHEN, 1862 [*Eunema? salteri* MEEK & WORTHEN, 1861]. Commonly with very slight subsutural shoulder, principal spiral thread or carina just below it coinciding roughly with culmination of labral sinus, then below this a pair of threads, angulations or carinae; anomphalous. *L.Carb.(Miss.)-M.Perm.*, N.Am.-Eu.——FIG. 210,5. *O. salteri* (MEEK & WORTHEN), M.Penn., Ill.; ×4.

Callispira NELSON, 1947 [*C. quinquecostata*]. Much like *Orthonema* but with 5 or 6 closely spaced spiral cords and labral sinus culminating on 2nd cord (105, p. 464). *Penn.*, N.Am.-NE.Asia.——FIG. 210,4. *C. quinquecostata*, M.Penn., TEX.; ×2.

Family PROCERITHIIDAE Cossmann, 1905

[*nom. correct.* WENZ, 1938 (*pro* Procerithidae COSSMANN, 1905)]

Commonly high-spired; ornament of collabral and spiral elements, former commonly dominant but wanting in some genera; varices rarely present; apertural margin entire or with rudimentary siphonal outlet, at most a small sinus or break.

Procerithium COSSMANN, 1902 [*P. quinquegranosum*]. Small; intersecting collabral and spiral elements producing granulose ornament. *L.Jur. (Lias.)-U.Jur.(Portland)*, cosmop.

Spanionema WHIDBORNE, 1891 [*Loxonema scalaroides* WHIDBORNE, 1889]. Outer lip prosocline, with a few heavy irregularly spaced varices; no

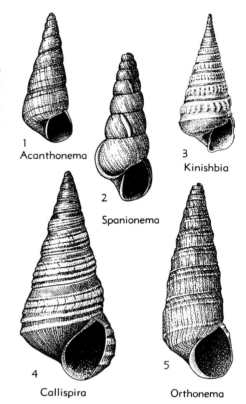

FIG. 210. Cerithiacea (Turritellidae, Procerithiidae) (p. I317).

labral sinus; seemingly anomphalous. *M.Dev.*, Eu.——FIG. 210,2. *S. scalaroides* (WHIDBORNE), Eng.; ×1.3.

Kinishbia WINTERS, 1956 [*K. nodosa*]. High-spired, with many whorls; sides slightly coeloconoidal, base rounded, narrowly phaneromphalous, with short inhalant canal; whorls somewhat inflated but with spiral groove above low peripheral carina; sutures shallow; ornament a row of nodes on shoulder, each composed of 2 or 3 smaller nodes arranged vertically; labrum seemingly orthocline (151, p.44). *M.Perm.*, N.Am.——FIG. 210,3. *K. nodosa*, Ariz.; ×3.3 (151).

Superfamily CYCLOPHORACEA Gray, 1847

[*nom. transl.* KNIGHT, BATTEN & YOCHELSON, herein (*ex* Cyclophoridae GRAY, 1847)]

Prevailing conispiral but varying in shape; pedal ganglia ladder-like; pallial cavity commonly transformed into a lung, without ctenidium; operculum corneous, typically multispiral. Habitat fresh-water and terrestrial. *L.Carb.(Miss.)-Rec.*

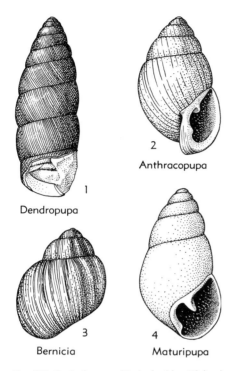

FIG. 211. Cyclophoracea (Cyclophoridae, Viviparidae) (p. *1318-1319*).

Family CYCLOPHORIDAE Gray, 1847

Apertural margins commonly somewhat
thickened or reflexed, with or without
apertural teeth or notches. *L.Carb.(Miss.)-
Rec.*

Subfamily DENDROPUPINAE Wenz, 1938

Small, pupiform, with one or more lamellar teeth in aperture; whorls smooth or
with numerous collabral threads; operculum unknown. *L.Carb.(Miss.)-L.Perm.*

Owing to certain errors in assignment of
geologic age and in understanding of morphological features, genera included in this
subfamily have been placed previously with
pulmonate families, principally the Pupillidae. No compelling reason is now seen to
recognize the occurrence of Pulmonata in
the Paleozoic—indeed, it seems improbable
that representatives of this group appeared
so early. The Dendropupinae may be
classed in the Cyclophoridae close to the
Diplomatinae or actually incorporated in
this subfamily, which contains several pupiform genera with toothed apertures and

ornament consisting of numerous collabral
threads. The occurrence of genera here included in the Dendropupinae indicates that
they are not marine forms but evidence for
assignment of a terrestrial or fresh-water
habitat, or both, is inconclusive.

?Carbonispira YEN, 1949 [**C. scotica*]. Little
known, based on poorly preserved specimen, described characters probably due to crushing and
corrosion (152, p. 238). *L.Carb.,* Eu.

Dendropupa OWEN, 1861 [**Pupa vetusta* DAWSON,
1859] [=*Strophites* DAWSON, 1880 (*non* DE-
SHAYES, 1832); *?Strophella* DAWSON, 1895]. Relatively large, cylindrical pupiform, with numerous
fine collabral threads. [Aperture of type species
poorly known; a specimen with broken whorls
discloses what seem to be lamellar columellar
teeth but their number and position are not clear.
There is little to support DAWSON's drawing of
the aperture.] *Miss.-Penn.,* N.Am.——FIG. 211,*1.*
**D. vetusta* (DAWSON), Penn., Can.(N.Scot.); final
whorl showing broken internal folds, ×6.7.

Maturipupa PILSBRY, 1926 [**Pupa vermilionensis*
BRADLEY, 1872]. Without ornament; aperture with
strong lamellar parietal tooth; columellar lip arcuate and truncate at notched base; labrum not thickened. [Eventually may be shown to represent juvenile stages of *Anthracopupa.*] *L.Carb.(Miss.)-
U.Carb.(Penn.),* N.Am.-Eu.——FIG. 211,*4.* **M.
vermilionensis* (BRADLEY), M.Penn., Ill.; ×13.3.

Anthracopupa WHITFIELD, 1881 [**A. ohioensis*].
Ornament of faint collabral threads; spire and base
both somewhat tapering; aperture with strong
lamellar parietal tooth and columellar tooth, notch
on inner side of upper end of labrum, which, like
columellar lip, is considerably thickened at final
growth stage. *L.Perm.,* N.Am.——FIG. 211,*2.* **A.
ohioensis,* Ohio; ×13.3.

[The remaining subfamilies of the Cyclophoridae
are post-Paleozoic, the majority being confined to
Cenozoic deposits.]

Family VIVIPARIDAE Gray, 1847

Broadly turbiniform; anomphalous or
minutely phaneromphalous; mostly unornamented but spiral cords or rows of
pustules present on some shells. Living
species inhabit fresh water and are viviparous. *?L.Carb., Jur.-Rec.*

Viviparus MONTFORT, 1810 [**V. fluviorum* (=
Helix vivipara LINNÉ, 1758)] [=*Paludina* FÉRUS-
SAC, 1812]. Medium-sized, mostly with smooth,
convex whorls, but some species with carinate or
nodosely carinate whorls. *Jur.-Rec.,* cosmop. [A
record from the Lower Carboniferous of England
was based on an internal mold, perhaps of a marine shell, and needs confirmation before acceptance.]

?**Bernicia** Cox, 1927 [*B. praecursor*]. Small naticiform, but with deep sutures; apertural lips unknown but probably simple. *L.Carb.*, Eu.——FIG. 211,3. *B. praecursor*, Eng.; ×10.

Superfamily RISSOACEA
Adams & Adams, 1854

[*nom. transl.* THIELE, 1929 (*ex* Rissoidae ADAMS & ADAMS, 1854)]

Shell mostly small, commonly turriculate or ovate, more rarely turbiniform to subdiscoidal, smooth or ornamented; mostly holostomatous, aperture circular or ovate. *Perm.-Rec.*

Family HYDROBIIDAE Stimpson, 1865

[*nom. transl.* FISCHER, 1885 (*ex* Hydrobiinae STIMPSON, 1865)]

Shell small or minute, smooth or with collabral threads or riblets, rarely spirally carinate. Operculum horny, spiral. [Mostly in fresh or brackish water.] *Perm.-Rec.*

Hydrobia HARTMANN, 1821 [*Cyclostoma acutum* DRAPARNAUD, 1805; SD GRAY, 1847] [=*Paludestrina* D'ORBIGNY, 1839 (obj.)]. Entire shell, or early whorls only, acute; whorls convex, smooth or with collabral threads; apertural margin uninterrupted, not thickened. *Perm.(Karroo)*, Rhodesia; *U.Jur.(Oxford.)-Rec.*, cosmop.

Superfamily SUBULITACEA
Lindström, 1884

[*nom. transl.* WENZ, 1938 (*ex* Subulitidae LINDSTRÖM, 1884)]

Subulate, acicular to subglobular; commonly with anterior notch and columellar fold, although these are but weakly developed in some, also basically with parietal fold; inner shell layers not sharply differentiated, not nacreous. *M.Ord.-M.Perm.*

Inasmuch as the superfamily is extinct, anatomical features can be inferred only from characters of the shell. The total lack of a sinus or slit in the outer lip argues for advanced anatomical asymmetry. Surely only a single ctenidium, probably of ctenobranch type, was present. Likewise, all other primitively paired pallial organs must have been represented only by the topographically left-hand member. The anterior notch and columellar fold probably were associated with an inhalant siphon and the pallial currents presumably made their exit at the angle where the outer lip joins the preceding whorl. The derivation of the group is uncertain but it probably was close to the Loxonematacea.

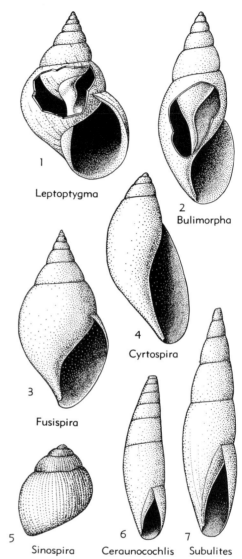

FIG. 212. Subulitacea (Subulitidae—Subulitinae) (p. *1320*).

Family SUBULITIDAE Lindström, 1884

[=Bullimorphidae, Fusispiridae S.A.MILLER, 1889]

Anterior notch present, with at least one columellar fold. *M.Ord.-M.Perm.*

Subfamily SUBULITINAE Lindström, 1884

[*nom. transl.* KNIGHT, BATTEN & YOCHELSON, herein (*ex* Subulitidae LINDSTRÖM, 1884)]

Parietal fold wanting. *M.Ord.-M.Perm.*

Subulites EMMONS, 1842 [*S. elongatus* (=*Macrocheilus subelongatus* D'ORBIGNY, 1850, *pro M.*

elongatus "HALL" =EMMONS, *non M. elongatus* PHILLIPS, 1841)]. Subulate to fusiform, spire high and straight or short and curved; whorls flat or gently arched, with shallow sutures; aperture narrowly elongate, with small but sharp anterior notch; labral inductura present; ornament lacking.

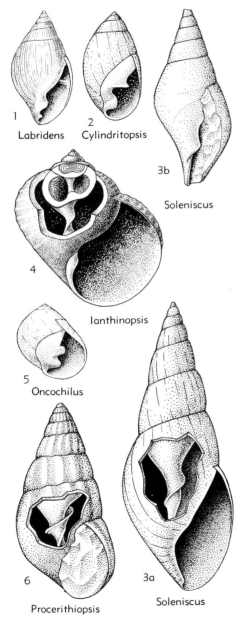

1 Labridens
2 Cylindritopsis
3b
Soleniscus
4
Ianthinopsis
5 Oncochilus
6 Procerithiopsis
3a
Soleniscus

FIG. 213. Subulitacea (Subulitidae——Soleniscinae); Neritacea (*Oncochilus*) (p. 1218, 1320-1321).

[Subgenera are intergrading.] *M.Ord.-L.Dev.,* N. Am.-Eu.-NC.Asia.

S. (Subulites) [=*Polyphemopsis* PORTLOCK, 1843]. Spire straight, whorls high, last one occupying about half of total height; aperture acuminate above, widest below. *M.Ord.-U.Sil.,* N.Am.-Eu.-NC.Asia.——FIG. 212,7. **S. (S.) subelongatus* (D'ORBIGNY), M.Ord., N.Y.; ×1.3.

S. (Cyrtospira) ULRICH in ULRICH & SCOFIELD, 1897 [**C. tortilis;* SD COSSMANN, 1909]. Axis of shell curved, last whorl occupying much more than half of total shell height. *M.Ord.-U.Sil.,* N.Am.-Eu.——FIG. 212,4. **S. (C.) tortilis* (ULRICH), M.Ord., Tenn.; ×2.

S. (Fusispira) HALL, 1872 [**F. ventricosa;* SD S.A.MILLER, 1889]. Fusiform; aperture narrow, acuminate above and narrower below than in *S. (Subulites). M.Ord.-L.Dev.,* N.Am.-Eu.-NE.Asia.——FIG. 212,3. **S. (F.) ventricosus* (HALL), M.Ord., Wis.; ×0.7.

Bulimorpha WHITFIELD, 1882 [*pro Bulimella* HALL, 1858 (*non* PFEIFFER, 1854)] [**Bulimella bulimiformis* HALL, 1858]. Fusiform, with gently arched whorls, final whorl more than half of total height; well-developed siphonal fold seen in broken specimens. *Miss.,* N.Am.——FIG. 212,2. **B. bulimiformis* (HALL), M.Miss., Ind.; apertural view with window showing columellar features, ×4.

Leptoptygma KNIGHT, 1936 [**Auriptygma virgatum* KNIGHT, 1931]. Fusiform but with rounded base, sutures deep; labral inductura with low fold not covering parietal lip; siphonal channel below fold very wide and diffuse; ornament lacking or consisting of fine collabral threads. *Miss.(L.Carb.)-Penn.(U.Carb.),* N.Am.-NE.Asia.——FIG. 212,1. **L. virgatum* (KNIGHT), M.Penn., Mo.; apertural view with window showing columellar features, ×4.

?Sinospira YIN, 1932 [**S. ornata*]. Naticiform, with protruding spire and moderately deep sutures; ornament of fine collabral threads; apertural features unknown. [May prove to be senior synonym of *Leptoptygma.*] *U.Carb.,* E.Asia.——FIG. 212,5. **S. ornata,* China; ×1.3 (153).

Ceraunocochlis KNIGHT, 1931 [**C. fulminula*]. Very small, subulate, whorls of spire, low, first whorl button-like; sutures very shallow; entire labrum covered by inductura, with small anterior notch; without ornament. *Miss.-Penn.,* N.Am.——FIG. 212,6. **C. fulminula,* M.Penn., Mo.; ×10.

Subfamily SOLENISCINAE Wenz, 1938

[*nom. transl.* KNIGHT, BATTEN & YOCHELSON, herein (*ex* Soleniscidae WENZ, 1938)]

Parietal fold present, in some genera appearing as diffuse thickening on parietal inductura. *M.Dev.-M.Perm.*

Ianthinopsis MEEK & WORTHEN, 1866 [**Platyostoma? tumida* MEEK & WORTHEN, 1861] [= *Plectostylus* CONRAD, 1842 (*non* BECK, 1837);

Strobeus DEKONINCK, 1881; *Sphaerodoma* KEYES, 1889; *Strobaeus* COSSMANN, 1909 (*pro Strobeus* DEKONINCK, 1881, obj.)]. Form variable, globular with pointed apex to high-spired fusiform; without ornament but exceptionally with faint spiral ridges; strong columellar siphonal fold barely visible in unbroken apertures but well developed just within it, resorbed in all but last 1 or 2 whorls; an obscure parietal fold may appear as broadly arched thickening of parietal inductura; labrum thin but thickening as growth proceeds until outer shell wall is very massive and earlier whorls completely filled, with whorl partitions and columella much reduced by resorption. *M.Dev.-M.Perm.,* N.Am.-S.Am.-Eu.-NE.Asia-SE.Asia-NC.Asia. —— FIG. 213,4. **I. tumida* (MEEK & WORTHEN), U. Penn., Tex.; apertural view with window showing development and resorption of columellar fold and filling of earlier whorls, ×1.3.

Soleniscus MEEK & WORTHEN, 1861 [*pro Macrocheilus* PHILLIPS, 1841 (*non* KIRBY, 1838)] [**S. typicus*] [*Duncania* BAYLE, 1879; *Macrochilina* BAYLE, 1880 (*pro Duncania* BAYLE, 1879, *non* DEKONINCK, 1872); *Macrochilus* LINDSTRÖM, 1884]. Fusiform; with small siphonal notch visible externally; small siphonal canal present internally with more or less elevated parietal fold somewhat above it; ornament lacking. *Miss.(L. Carb.)-M.Perm.,* N.Am.-Eu.-NE.Asia-SE.Asia.—— FIG. 213,3. **S. typicus*, M.Penn., Ill.; *3a*, apertural view with window showing columella, ×1.3; *3b*, apertural view with broken lip exposing columella, ×2.7.

?Procerithiopsis MANSUY, 1914 [**P. ambigua*; SD COSSMANN, 1918]. Small, minutely phaneromphalous, with rather strong collabral ribs; seemingly with small siphonal notch and columellar folds as in *Soleniscus*. *L.Perm.,* SE.Asia—— FIG. 213,6. **P. ambigua*, Cambodia; apertural view with window showing columellar folds, ×6.

Cylindritopsis GEMMELLARO, 1889 [**C. ovalis*; SD COSSMANN, 1909] [=*Ankorella* DELPEY, 1941 (29, p. 272)]. Ovoid, with shallow sutures and small spire; base produced anteriorly with deep siphonal notch and heavy siphonal fold, higher parietal fold in middle of parietal lip being set off by deep groove; parietal inductura well developed. *M.Perm.,* Eu.-Asia.—— FIG. 213,2. **C. ovalis*, Sicily; ×2 (46).

Labridens YOCHELSON, 1956 [**L. shupei*]. Form much as in *Cylindritopsis* but with relatively higher spire; base produced anteriorly with small siphonal fold, a stronger fold above it low on parietal lip and still higher a very low obscure fold bordered by shallow groove; labium thin, with prominent sharp lira or internal fold approximately opposite 3rd low fold on parietal lip; surface without ornament (156, p. 45). [This is a unique Paleozoic genus in having a well-developed labral lira, which, with the parietal folds, suggests that the Jurassic and Cretaceous Nerineacea may have had

their origin here.] *M.Perm.,* N.Am.——FIG. 213,1. **L. shupei*, Tex.; ×3.

Family MEEKOSPIRIDAE Knight, 1956

Without columellar fold and anterior notch; *?U.Sil., L.Carb.(Miss.)-M.Perm.*

?Auriptygma PERNER, 1903 [**A. fortior*; SD COSSMANN, 1909]. Very similar to *Leptoptygma* but columella thin and gently spiral about pseudumbilicus, without columellar fold. *U.Sil.,* Eu.—— FIG. 214,3. **A. fortior*, Czech.; ×1.3.

Meekospira ULRICH, in ULRICH & SCOFIELD, 1897 [**Eulima? peracuta* MEEK & WORTHEN, 1861] [= COSSMANN, 1920 (20, p. 83); *Cambodgita* STRAND, 1928]. Slender, sharply acuminate; columellar lip somewhat arcuate, reflexed, inductura not covering upper part of parietal lip. *L.Carb.(Miss.)-L.Perm.,* N.Am.-S.Am.-Eu.-SE.Asia.——FIG. 214,2. **M. peracuta* (MEEK & WORTHEN), M.Penn., Ill.; ×1.3.

Girtyspira KNIGHT, 1936 [**Bulimella canaliculata* HALL, 1858]. Small, fusiform, with relatively high final whorl which has narrow ramp or is adpressed, columellar lip arcuate. *L.Carb.(Miss.)-M.Perm.,* N.Am.-Eu.——FIG. 214,1. **G. canaliculata* (HALL), M.Miss., Ind.; ×6.7.

Subclass OPISTHOBRANCHIA Milne Edwards, 1848

[*nom. emend.* BRONN, 1862 (*pro* Opisthobranchiata, *nom. correct.* WOODWARD, 1851, also MORRIS & LYCETT, 1851 (*pro* 'opisthobranches' MILNE EDWARDS, 1848, invalid vernacular name)), *nom. auct. conserv.* proposed COX, 1958 (ICZN pend.)]

Shell tending to be reduced or absent; if present, either aciculate (Pyramidellidae) or more commonly low-spired, involute or convolute, and commonly covered largely by expansions of the mantle or foot which cannot always be entirely withdrawn into it; columellar folds frequent; protoconch commonly heterostrophic, ornament absent

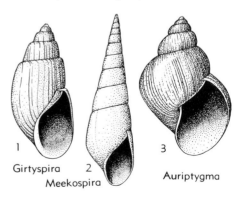

FIG. 214. Subuliticea (Meekospiridae) (p. 1321).

or if present commonly confined to spiral elements, operculum commonly absent in adult, tentacles ear-shaped or flattened; eyes sunken, mantle cavity becoming shallow, commonly rotated to face more or less to the right and finally lost with shell; gills in mantle cavity foliobranch, not filamentous, absent in some genera, replaced in others by pallial outgrowths; ciliated strips present on right side of mantle cavity to help exhalant current, tendency to concentrate all ganglia on dorsal side of esophagus with consequent elongation of pedal and parapedal commissures and shortening of visceral loop, leading to euthyneury (except Acteonidae and *Toledonia*); ventricle anterior to auricle (except Acteonidae, Pyramidellidae, Ringiculidae); hermaphrodite; penis invaginable (except Acteonidae), commonly armed; reproductive ducts tending to be sunk in haemocoele and to split into separate vas deferens, oviduct, and vagina; esophagus without glands, its opening into stomach adjoining that of intestine, with stomach tending to be reduced to a caecum; histology of digestive gland comparatively elaborate. Marine only, eggs hatch to free-swimming veligers showing torsion and operculum. *?Dev., Miss.-Rec.*

Order UNCERTAIN
Superfamily PYRAMIDELLACEA d'Orbigny, 1840

[*nom. transl.* WENZ, 1938 (*ex* Pyramidellidae D'ORBIGNY, 1840)]

Small, aciculate; with or without columellar fold, protoconch orthostrophic, heterostrophic, or deviated. *?Dev., Miss.-Rec.*

The work of THORSON (1946) and FRETTER & GRAHAM (1949) has demonstrated that the Pyramidellidae are opisthobranchs and that some (if not all) living species are highly specialized ectoparasites. The presence and size of the heterostrophic or deviated protoconch found in most species may be a measure of time spent as free-swimming larvae. Living species lack radulae. There is no evidence of parasitism or lack of a radula in the other families (Streptacididae, Mathildidae) that may be included because of form and protoconch. The reported radula of a living species assigned to the Mathildidae, as well as the assignment itself, should be reinvestigated.

Family STREPTACIDIDAE Knight, 1931

High-spired, with moderately deep labral sinus that culminates roundly high on whorl; protoconch with initial discoidal whorl that caps spire flatly or is deviated either simply or at top of a variably long segment of disjunct whorls. *?Dev., L.Carb. (Miss.)-M.Perm.*

The shell form in this family and particularly the labral sinus remind one strongly of the Loxonematacea, from which they probably were descended. The protoconch is very similar to that found in the Mathildidae to which they may be closely related.

Donaldina KNIGHT, 1933 [**Aclisina grantonensis* DONALD, 1898]. Ornament of spiral threads confined generally to lower part of whorl. *?Dev., L. Carb.(Miss..)-L.Perm.,* N.Am.-Eu.——FIG. 215,3. **D. grantonensis* (DONALD), L.Carb., Scot.; *3a,* apertural view, ×10; *3b,* heterostrophic apex, ×25.

Platyconcha LONGSTAFF, 1933 [**P. dunlopiana*]. Ornament of strong collabral costae. *L.Carb.-U. Carb.,* Eu.——FIG. 215,2. **P. dunlopiana,* L.Carb., Scot.; apertural view showing flat apex, ×9.

Streptacis MEEK, 1872 [**S. whitfieldi*]. Very slender, ornamented only with growth lines. *U. Carb.(Penn.)-M.Perm.,* N.Am.-Eu.——FIG. 215,1. **S. whitfieldi,* M.Penn., Ill.; apertural view showing heterostrophic apex, ×10.

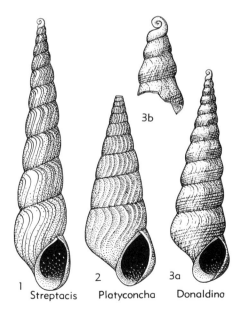

FIG. 215. Pyramidellacea (Streptacididae) (p. *1322*).

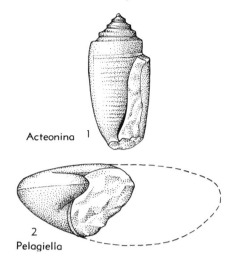

FIG. 216. Acteonacea (Acteonidae); Pelagiellacea (Pelagiellidae) (p. *1323*).

Order PLEUROCOELA Thiele, 1925

Commonly with dextral shell and mantle cavity but both tending to become obsolete; shell commonly involute, nearly so, or convolute. *Miss.-Rec.*

Superfamily ACTEONACEA d'Orbigny, 1842

[*nom. transl.* WENZ, 1938 (*ex* Acteonidae D'ORBIGNY, 1842)] [=Cephalaspidea FISCHER, 1883]

Shell commonly external but in many forms enclosed by mantle. *Miss.-Rec.*

Family ACTEONIDAE d'Orbigny, 1842

Shell spiral, external, commonly with spiral ornament, columella commonly with 1 or 2 folds; with corneous operculum and cephalic shield; soft parts completely retractable into shell; streptoneurous; auricle in front of ventricle. *L.Carb.-Rec.*

Acteonina D'ORBIGNY, 1850 [*Chemnitzia carbonaria* DEKONINCK, 1843; SD MEEK, 1863] [= *Actaeonina* FISCHER, 1883 (obj.)]. Small, cylindrical, with high narrow aperture and very short gradate spire; protoconch seemingly a single deviated whorl, partly immersed; with collar-like structure above suture; probably a fold low on columella; fine spiral striae. *L.Carb.,* Eu.——FIG. 216,*1*. **A. carbonaria* (DEKONINCK), Belg.; ×4.

?GASTROPODA INCERTAE SEDIS

The genus *Pelagiella* is classed tentatively as belonging to the Gastropoda because shell form suggests this assignment, but it is not possible to reach conclusions about its relationships within the class. If *Pelagiella* is a gastropod, its remoteness from others is indicated by such features as the presence of fine spiral striae inside the shell, gerontic thickening inside the aperture, filling of apex by solid shell matter, variable position of apertural sinuses, and common occurrence of dextral and sinistral individuals in a single species. Each of these characters is found in some very much later gastropods but few of them appear in Paleozoic forms. Comprehensive studies based on large collections have never been made.

Superfamily PELAGIELLACEA Knight, 1956

Shell comprising 0.5 to 3 whorls, rather flattened on top and arched below or rotelliform above and umbilicate below, with sharply rounded periphery; initial whorl (protoconch) wider than thick, with faintly bulbous beginning; shell relatively thick and may be filled completely near apex so as to produce short blunt curved steinkerns; with one or more labral sinuses (indicated by growth lines) that vary in shape, depth and position in different species; with numerous very fine spiral grooves inside of shell in some species; external ornament wanting or consisting of fine spiral and collabral markings. *Cam.*

This little-known assemblage is difficult to study and to place systematically. Some authors (WENZ, 1938; KNIGHT, 1952) have doubted that they are gastropods.

Family PELAGIELLIDAE Knight, 1956

With characters of superfamily. *Cam.*

Pelagiella MATTHEW, 1895 [*Cyrtolites atlantoides* MATTHEW, 1894] [=*Parapelagiella, Proeccyliopterus, Protoscaevogyra* KOBAYASHI, 1939 (77, pp. 286-287); *Semicircularia* LOCHMAN, in LOCHMAN & DUNCAN, 1944 (91, p.44)]. Dextral or sinistral, with broad blunt apex and rapidly expanding helicocone; shallow sinus culminating at periphery or with one or more sinuses above or below periphery; interior marginal thickening of gerontic shell indicated by steinkerns. [*Parapelagiella* was proposed for forms without the supposed constricted apertural margin of *Pelagiella,* but this is a gerontic feature of *Pelagiella* itself, though seen rarely; *Proeccyliopterus* was proposed for forms with a ridge on the upper shell surface and *Protoscaevo-*

gyra for sinistral forms. In so-called *Proeccyliopterus* sinuses above and below the periphery generate ridges, and there are both dextral and sinistral individuals in the type species. *Semicircularia* is based on steinkerns of a sinistral form, the supposed short blunt uncoiled spire denoting apical filling of the shell. All these forms are considered to be congeneric with *Pelagiella*.] Cam., N.Am.-NE.Asia. —— Fig. 216,2. **P. atlantoides* (Matthew), L.Cam., N.B.; ×4.

GENERIC NAMES ASSIGNED TO PALEOZOIC FOSSILS IMPROPERLY REGARDED AS GASTROPODA AND MONOPLACOPHORA

Anticalyptraea Quinstedt, 1867 [=*Autodetus* Lindström, 1884] (worm).

Archaeonassa Fenton & Fenton, 1937 (trail).

Barella Hedström, 1930 (hyolithid operculum).

Charruia Rusconi, 1955 (problematical organism).

Chuaria Walcott, 1899 (carbon scale).

Coleolus Hall, 1879 [*pro Coleoprion* Hall, 1876 (*non* Sandberger, 1847)] (hyolithid).

Conchopeltis Walcott, 1879 (scyphozoan).

Conularia Miller (1818) in Sowerby, 1821 (Scyphozoan).

Halophiala Koken, 1925 (?pelecypod).

Harttites Howell & Knight, 1936 [*pro Harttia* Walcott, 1884 (*non* Steindachner, 1877)] (not a mollusk).

Hercynella Kayser, 1878 [*pro Pilidium* Kayser, 1878 (*non* Müller, 1846; *nec* Forbes, 1849; *nec* Middendorff, 1851); *Pilidion* Perner, 1911 (*non* Wagler, 1830)] (pelecypod).

Hyolithellus Billings, 1871 (hyolithid) and *Discinella* Hall, 1871 (its operculum).

Hyolithes Eichwald, 1840 (hyolithid).

Matthevia Walcott, 1885 (possibly extinct class of unknown affinities).

Mobergella Hedström, 1923 (hyolithid operculum).

Paoshanella Yin, 1937 (problematical organism).

Polyopea Clark, 1925 (hyolithid).

Rectogloma Van Tuyl & Berckheimer, 1914 (coprolite).

Salterella Billings, 1865 (hyolithid).

Scenellopsis Resser, 1938 (probably not a mollusk).

Stenotheca Salter, 1872 (crustacean).

Stenothecoides Resser, 1938 (?crustacean).

Tentaculites Schlotheim, 1820 (?worm).

Watsonella Grabau, 1900 (conchostracan).

REFERENCES

Archiac, Adolphe d' & Verneuil, E. P. de
  (1) 1842, *On the fossils of the older deposits in the Rhenish Provinces:* Geol. Soc. London, Trans., v. 6, p. 303-410.

Baker, H. B.
  (2) 1922, *Notes on the radula of the Helicinidae:* Acad. Nat. Sci. Philadelphia, Proc., v. 74, p. 29-68, pl. 3-7.
  (3) 1923, *Notes on the radula of the Neritidae:* Same, v. 75, p. 117-178, pl. 9-16.

Batten, R. L.
  (4) 1952, *The type species of the gastropod genus Protostylus:* Washington Acad. Sci., Jour., v. 42, p. 355.
  (5) 1956, *Some new pleurotomarian gastropods from the Permian of west Texas:* Same, v. 46, no. 2, p. 42-44.

Böhm, Johannes
  (6) 1895, *Die Gastropoden des Marmolatakalkes:* Palaeontographica, v. 42, p. 211-308, pl. 9-15 (Stuttgart).

Boucot, A. J.
  (7) 1956, *Gyrospira, a new genus of bellerophontid (Gastropoda) from Bolivia:* Washington Acad. Sci., Jour., v. 46, no. 2, p. 46-47, fig. 1-5.

Bowsher, A. L.
  (8) 1955, *Origin and adaptation of platyceratid gastropods:* Univ. Kansas Paleont. Contr. Mollusca, Art. 5, p. 1-11, pl. 1-2, fig. 1.

Bridge, Josiah, & Cloud, P. E., Jr.
  (9) 1947, *New gastropods and trilobites critical in the correlation of Lower Ordovician rocks:* Am. Jour. Sci., v. 245, p. 545-559, pl. 1-2 (New Haven).

Broili, Ferdinand
  (10) 1907, *Die Fauna der Pachycardientuffe der Seiser Alp. Scaphopoden und Gastropoden:* Palaeontographica, v. 54, p. 69-138, pl. 6-11 (Stuttgart).

Brösamlen, Richard
  (11) 1909, *Beitrag zur Kenntnis der Gastropoden des schwäbischen Jura:* Same, v. 56, p. 177-322, pl. 17-22.

Campbell, K. S. W.
  (12) 1953, *The fauna of the Permo-Carboniferous Ingelara Beds of Queensland:* Univ. Queensland Papers, Dept. Geol., v. 4, no. 3, p. 3-43, pl. 1-7 (Brisbane).

Chronic, B. J.
  (13) 1949, *Invertebrate paleontology (excepting fusulinids and corals):* in Newell, N. D., Chronic, B. J., & Roberts, T. G., Upper Paleozoic of Peru, p. 46-173, pl. 5-35, Columbia Univ. (New York).

Chronic, Halka
  (14) 1952, *Molluscan fauna from the Permian*

Kaibab Formation, Walnut Canyon, Arizona: Geol. Soc. America, Bull., v. 63, p. 95-166, pl. 1-10 (New York).

Clarke, J. M.

(15) 1904, *Naples fauna in western New York:* New York State Museum, Mem. 5, pt. 2, 454 p., 20 pl. (Albany).

Cobbold, E. S.

(16) 1921, *The Cambrian horizons of Comley, and their Brachiopoda, Pteropoda, Gasteropoda:* Geol. Soc. London, Quart. Jour., v. 76, pt. 4, p. 325-386, pl. 21-24.

Cossmann, Maurice

(17) 1885, *Contribution à l'étude de la faune de l'étage bathonien en France. (Gastropodes):* Soc. géol. France, Mém., sér. 3, v. 3, p. 1-374 pl. 1-18 (Paris).

(18) 1895-1925, *Essais de paléoconchologie comparée:* livr. 1-13 (1, 1895; 2, 1896; 3, 1899; 4, 1901; 5, 1903; 6, 1904; 7, 1906; 8, 1909; 9, 1912; 10, 1916 ("1915"); 11, 1918; 12, 1921; 13, 1925 (Paris).

(19) 1913, *Contributions à la paléontologie française des terrains jurassiques. III. Cerithiacea et Loxonemoatacea:* Soc. géol. France, Paléont., Mém., no. 46, 263 p., 18 pl. (Paris).

(20) 1920, *Rectifications de nomenclature:* in Revue critique de Paléozoologie et Paléophytologie, v. 24, p. 81-83 (Paris).

Cox, L. R.

(21) 1949, *Moluscos del Triasico Superior del Peru:* Inst. geol. Peru, Bol. 12, 50 p., 2 pl.

———, & Arkell, W. J.

(22) 1948-50, *A survey of the Mollusca of the British Great Oolite Series:* Palaeontogr. Soc. Mon., xiii+105 p., revised explanations of 15+38 pl. (London).

Cresswell, A. W.

(23) 1893, *Notes on the Lilydale limestone:* Royal Soc. Victoria, Proc., new ser., v. 5, p. 38-44, pl. 8-9 (Melbourne).

Crofts, D. R.

(24) 1955, *Muscle morphogenesis in primitive gastropods and its relation to torsion:* Zool. Soc. London, Proc., v. 125, pt. 3-4, p. 711-750.

Cullison, J. S.

(25) 1944, *The stratigraphy of some Lower Ordovician formations of the Ozark Uplift:* Univ. Missouri, School of Mines and Metallurgy, Bull. tech. ser., v. 15, p. 1-112, pl. 1-35 (Rolla).

Dahmer, Georg

(26) 1925, *Die Fauna der Sphärosideritschiefer de Lahnmulde. Zugleich ein Beitrag zur Kenntnis unterdevonischer Gastropoden:* Preuss. geol. Landesanstalt, Jahrb., v. 46, p. 34-67, pl. 3-4 (Berlin).

Dawson, J. W.

(27) 1880, *Revision of the land snails of the Paleozoic Era, with descriptions of new species:* Am. Jour. Sci., ser. 3, v. 20, p. 403-415 (New Haven).

Delpey, Geneviève

(28) 1941, *Gastéropodes marins. Paléontologie-stratigraphie:* Soc. géol. France, Mém., new ser., v. 43, no. 1, p. 5-114, pl. 1-27 (Paris).

(29) 1941, *Les gastéropodes permiens du Cambodge:* Jour. Conchyliologie, v. 84, p. 255-278 (Paris).

Diener, Carl & Kutassy, Endré

(30) 1926-40, *Glossophora triadica:* Fossilium Catalogus 1, Animalia, pars 34 & 81, 477 p. (Berlin).

Dietz, Bugen

(31) 1911, *Ein Beitrag zur Kenntnis der deutschen Zechsteinschnecken:* Kön. preuss, geol. Landesanstalt, Jahrb., v. 30 (for 1909), p. 444-506, pl. 13-15 (Berlin).

Donald, Jane

(32) 1889, *Descriptions of new species of Carboniferous gastropods:* Geol. Soc. London, Quart. Jour., v. 45, p. 619-625, pl. 20.

(33) 1892, *Notes on some new and little known species of Carboniferous Murchisonia:* Same, v. 48, p. 562-575, pl. 16-17.

(34) 1898, *Observations on the genus Aclisina De Koninck, with descriptions of British species and of some other Carboniferous Gastropoda:* Same, v. 54, p. 45-72, pl. 3-5.

(35) 1905, *On some Gasteropoda from the Silurian rocks of Llangadock (Caermarthenshire):* Same, v. 61, p. 567-577, pl. 37 (part).

Dubar, Gonzague

(36) 1948, *Études paléontologiques sur le Lias du Maroc. La faune domérienne du Jebel Bou-Dahar, près de Béni-Tajjite:* Service géol. Maroc, Notes et Mémoires, no. 68, 248 p., 30 pl. (Rabat).

Eichwald, Eduard d'

(37) 1860, *Lethaea rossica ou paléontologie de la Russie, décrite et figurée:* v. 1, 681 p., 59 pl. (St. Petersburg).

Etheridge, Robert, Jr.

(38) 1917, *Descriptions of some Queensland Palaeozoic and Mesozoic fossils. 3. A remarkable univalve from the Devonian limestone of the Burdekin River, Queensland:* Queensl. Dept. Mines, Geol. Survey Queensl., Pub. no. 260, p. 13-16, pl. 3, fig. 1-2 (Brisbane).

(39) 1921, *Palaeontologia Novae Cambriae Meridionalis - Occasional descriptions of New South Wales fossils, No. 8:* Geol. Survey New South Wales, Records, v. 10, pt. 1, p. 1-11, pl. 1-7 (Sydney).

Eudes-Deslongchamps, J. A.

(40) 1842, *Mémoire sur les patelles, ombrelles,*

calyptrées, fissurelles, émarginules et dentales fossiles des terrains secondaires du Calvados: Soc. linn. Normandie, Mém., v. 7, p. 111-130, pl. 7, 8, 11 (Caen).

(41) 1849, *Mémoire sur les pleurotomaires des terrains secondaires du Calvados:* Same, v. 8, p. 1-151, pl. 1-18.

Finlay, H. J.

(42) 1926, *A further commentary on New Zealand molluscan systematics:* N.Z. Inst., Trans., v. 57, p. 320-485 (Wellington).

Fleming, C. A.

(43) 1952, *Notes on the genus Haliotis (Mollusca):* Same, v. 80, p. 229-232, pl. 50.

Frech, Fritz

(44) 1894, *Ueber das Devon des Ostalpen. 3. Die Fauna des Unterdevonischen Riffkalkes:* Deutsch. geol. Gesell., Zeitschr., v. 46, p. 446-479, pl. 34 (Berlin).

Fretter, Vera & Graham, Alastair

(45) 1949, *The structure and mode of life of the Pyramidellidae, parasitic opisthobranchs:* Marine Biol. Assoc. United Kingdom, Jour., v. 28, p. 493-532 (Plymouth).

Gemmellaro, G. G.

(46) 1889, *La fauna dei calcari con Fusulina della valle del Fiüme Sosio nella Provincia di Palermo. Nautiloidea & Gastropoda:* Giornale di Scienze Naturali ed economiche, v. 20, p. 37-138, pl. 11-19 (Palermo).

Girty, G. H.

(47) 1939, *Certain pleurotomariid gastropods from the Carboniferous of New Mexico:* Washington Acad. Sci., Jour., v. 29, p. 21-36, fig. 1-27.

Grabau, A. W.

(48) 1936, *Early Permian fossils of China, Part 2, Fauna of the Maping Limestone of Kwangsi and Kweichow:* Paleont. Sinica, ser. B, v. 8, fasc. 4, p. 1-441, pl. 1-31 (Peiping).

Greco, Benedetto

(49) 1937-38, *La fauna permiano del Sosio conservata nei musei di Firenze e di Padova, Parte Secunda, Gastropoda, Lamellibranchiata:* Paleont. Italica, v. 37 (new ser., v. 7), p. 57-114, pl. 3, 4 (Pisa).

Haas, Otto

(50) 1953, *Mesozoic invertebrate faunas of Peru:* Am. Mus. Nat. History, Bull., v. 101, p. 3-328, pl. 1-18 (New York).

Haber, G.

(51) 1932, *Gastropoda, Amphineura et Scaphopoda jurassica:* Fossilium Catalogus, 1, Animalia, pars 53, 400 p. (Berlin).

Hall, James

(52) 1879, *Containing descriptions of the Gastropoda, Pteropoda, and Cephalopoda of the Upper Helderberg, Hamilton, Portage, and*

Chemung groups: Nat. History New York, Paleontology, v. 5, pt. 2, 113 p. (Albany).

———, **& Whitfield, R. P.**

(53) 1872, *Notice of two new species of fossil shells from the Potsdam sandstone of New York:* New York State Cab. Nat. History, Ann. Rept. 23, p. 241-242, pl. 11 (Albany).

Hayasaka, Ichiro

(54) 1939, *Spiromphalus, a new gastropod genus from the Permian of Japan:* Fac. Sci. Agric., Taihoku Imperial Univ., Mem., v. 22, p. 19-23, pl. 3 (Sendai).

Heller, R. L.

(55) 1956 ("1954"), *Stratigraphy and paleontology of the Roubidoux Formation of Missouri:* Missouri Bur. Geol. Survey & Water Resources, ser. 2, v. 35, 118 p., 19 pl. (Rolla). [Heller's publication did not appear in 1954 as shown on title page; it was delivered to the Missouri State Geologist on December 20, 1955, but distribution was not begun until January, 1956 - J. B. Knight.]

Holzapfel, Eduard

(56) 1887-88, *Die Mollusken der Aachener Kreide (Einleitung, Cephalopoda, Glossophora):* Palaeontographica, v. 34, p. 29-180, pl. 4-21 (Stuttgart).

Horný, Radvan

(57) 1953, *Několik nových gastropodu ze středočeského siluru [New gastropods from Silurian of central Bohemia]:* Sborník Uśtředního ústavu geologického oddíl paleontologický [Service géologique de Tchecoslovaquie, Sec. de paléontologie], v. 20, p. 189-195 (Czech), 196-205 (Russ.), 206-211 (Eng.), pl. 22-24 (Praha).

(58) 1955, *Palaeozygopleuridae, nov. fam. (Gastropoda), ze středočeského devonu [from Devonian of central Bohemia]:* Same, v. 21, p. 17-74 (Czech), 75-118 (Russ.), 119-143 (Eng.), pl. 2-11.

Hudleston, W. H.

(59) 1887-96, *A monograph of the British Jurassic Gasteropoda. Part 1. The Inferior Oolite Gasteropoda:* Palaeontogr. Soc. Mon., 509 p., 44 pl. (London).

Huene, Freidrich von

(60) 1900, *Über Aulacomerella, ein neues Brachiopodengeschlecht:* Kais. russ. mineral. Gesell. zu St. Petersburg, Verhandl., ser. 2, v. 38, no. 1, p. 209-237, pl. 4.

Ikebe, Nobuo

(61) 1942, *Trochid Mollusca. Calliostoma of Japan, fossil and Recent:* Jap. Jour. Geol. Geogr., v. 18, p. 249-282, pl. 26-28 (Tokyo).

Jahn, J. J.

(62) 1894, *Neue Thierreste aus dem böhmischen Silur:* Kais. -kön. geol. Reichsanstalt, Jahrb., v. 44, p. 381-388, pl. 7 (Wien).

Kayser, F. H. E.

(63) 1889, *Über einige neue oder wenige gekannte Versteinerungen des rheinischen Devon:* Deutsch. geol. Gesell., Zeitschr., v. 41, p. 288-296, pl. 13-14 (Berlin).

Kittl, Ernst

(64) 1891-94, *Die Gastropoden der Schichten von St. Cassian der südalpinen Trias:* Kais. -kön. naturh. Hofmus., Ann., v. 6, p. 166-277, pl. 1-12 (Wien).

(65) 1894, *Die triadischen Gastropoden der Marmolata und verwandter Fundstellen in den weissen Rifkalken Südtirols:* Kais. -kön. geol. Reichsanstalt, Jahrb., v. 44, p. 99-182, pl. 1-6 (Wien).

(66) 1899, *Die Gastropoden der Esinokalke nebst einer revision der Gastropoden der Marmolatakalke:* Kais. -kön. naturh. Hofmus., Ann., v. 14, p. 1-237, pl. 1-8 (Wien).

Knight, J. B.

(67) 1930-34, *The gastropods of the St. Louis, Missouri, Pennsylvanian outlier:* Jour. Paleont., v. 4 (1930), Suppl. 1, The Pseudogopleurinae, p. 1-88, pl. 1-5, fig. 1-4; v. 5 (1931), *Streptacis* and *Aclisina*, p. 1-15, pl. 1-2, fig. 1; v. 5 (1931), The Subulitidae; p. 177-229, pl. 21-27, fig. 1-3; v. 6 (1932), The Pseudomelaniidae, p. 189-202, pl. 27-28; v. 7 (1933), The Trochoturbinidae, p. 30-58, pl. 8-12; v. 7 (1933), The Neritidae, p. 359-392, pl. 40-46; v. 8 (1934), The Euomphalidae and Platyceratidae, p. 139-166, pl. 20-26; v. 8 (1934), The Turritellidae, p. 433-447, pl. 56-57 (Menasha, Wis.).

(68) 1940, *Gastropods of the Whitehorse Sandstone:* in Newell, N.D., Invertebrate Fauna of the Whitehorse Sandstone, Geol. Soc. America, Bull., v. 51, p. 302-315, pl. 4-9 (New York).

(69) 1941, *Paleozoic gastropod genotypes:* Same, Spec. Paper 32, 510 p., 96 pl., 32 fig.

(70) 1942, *Four new genera of Paleozoic Gastropoda:* Jour. Paleont., v. 16, p. 487-488 (Tulsa).

(71) 1945, *Some new genera of the Bellerophontacea:* Same, v. 19, p. 333-340, pl. 49.

(72) 1945, *Some new genera of Paleozoic Gastropoda:* Same, v. 19, p. 573-587, pl. 79-80.

(73) 1947, *Some new Cambrian bellerophont gastropods:* Smithson, Misc. Coll., v. 106, no. 17, p. 1-11, pl. 1-2 (Washington).

(74) 1947, *Bellerophont muscle scars:* Jour. Paleont., v. 21, p. 264-267, pl. 42 (Tulsa).

(75) 1948, *Further new Cambrian bellerophont gastropods:* Smithson, Misc. Coll., v. 111, no. 3, p. 1-6, pl. 1 (Washington).

(76) 1952, *Primitive fossil gastropods and their bearing on gastropod classification:* Same, v. 117, no. 13 (Pub. 4092), 56 p., 2 pl.

Kobayashi, Teiichi

(77) 1939, *Restudy of Lorenz's Raphistoma broggeri from Shantung with a note on Pelagiella:* Jubilee Pub. in Commemoration of Professor H. Yabe's 60th Birthday, p. 283-288 (Tokyo).

(78) 1955, *The Ordovician fossils from the McKay group in British Columbia, western Canada, with a note on the early Ordovician palaeogeography:* Fac. Sci., Univ. Tokyo, Jour., sec. 2, v. 9, pt. 3, p. 355-492, pl. 1-9.

Koken, Ernst

(79) 1897, *Die Gastropoden der Trias um Hallstadt:* Kais. -kön. geol. Reichsanst., Abhandl., v. 17, no. 4, 112 p., 23 pl. (Wien).

(80) 1925, *Die Gastropoden des baltischen Untersilurs:* Acad. Sci. Russie Mém. (J. Perner, ed.), Classe physico-mathématique, ser. 8, v. 37, no. 1, p. 1-326, pl. 1-41 (Leningrad).

Koninck, L. G. de

(81) 1842-44, *Description des animaux fossiles qui se trouvent dans le terrain carbonifère de Belgique:* 651 p., 54 pl. (Liége).

(82) 1881, *Faune du calcaire carbonifère de la Belgique, 3ᵉ partie, Gastéropodes:* Mus. roy. Histoire nat. Belgique, Ann., sér. paléont., v. 6, p. 1-170, pl. 1-24 (Bruxelles).

(83) 1883, *Faune du calcaire carbonifère de la Belgique, 4ᵉ partie, Gastéropodes (suite et fin):* Same, v. 8, p. 1-240, pl. 22-54.

Kutassy, Endré

(84) 1937, *Triadische Faunen aus dem Bihar-Gebirge:* Geologica Hungarica, ser. palaeont., v. 13, p. 1-18, pl. 1, 3 (Budapest).

Lamont, Archie

(85) 1946, *Some Ashgillian and Llandovery gastropods from the Girvan District, Scotland:* Quarry Managers' Jour., v. 29, p. 635-644, pl. 1-3 (London).

———, & Gilbert, D. L. F.

(86) 1945, *Upper Llandovery Brachiopoda from Coneygore Coppice and Old Storridge Common, near Alfrick, Worcestershire:* Annals & Mag. Nat. History, ser. 11, v. 12, p. 641-682, pl. 1-5 (London).

La Rocque, Aurèle

(87) 1949, *New uncoiled gastropods from the Middle Devonian of Michigan and Manitoba:* Contr. Museum Paleont., Univ. Michigan, v. 7, no. 7, p. 113-122, 1 pl. (Ann Arbor).

Laube, G. C.

(88) 1868, *Die Gastropoden des braunen Jura von Balin:* K. Akad. Wiss., Denkschr., v. 28, pt. 2, p. 1-28, pl. 1-3 (Wien).

(89) 1869-70, *Die Fauna der Schichten von St. Cassian. Abt. III-IV, Gastropoden:* Same, Band 28, Abt. 2, p. 29-94, pl. 21-28; Band 30, Abt. 2, p. 1-48, pl. 29-35.

Lindström, Gustaf
(90)   1884, *On the Silurian Gastropoda and Ptero-*
poda of Gotland: Kongl. Svenska Vetenskaps-Akad., Handl., v. 19, no. 6, p. 1-250,
pl. 1-21 (Stockholm).

Lochman, Christina & Duncan, Donald
(91)   1944, *Early Upper Cambrian faunas of cen-*
tral Montana: Geol. Soc. America, Spec.
Paper 54, 181 p., pl. 1-19, fig. 1-2 (New
York).

Longstaff, J. D.
(92)   1912, *Some new lower Carboniferous Gas-*
tropoda: Geol. Soc. London, Quart. Jour.,
v. 68, p. 295-309, pl. 27-30.
(93)   1933, *A revision of the British Carboniferous*
Loxonematidae with descriptions of new
forms: Same, v. 89, p. 87-124, pl. 1-12.

Loriol, Perceval de
(94)   1874, *Monographie paléontologique et géo-*
logique des étages supérieurs de la formation
jurassique des environs de Boulogne-sur-
Mer - Description des fossiles (Pt. 1): Soc.
Phys. Hist. nat. Genève, Mém., v. 23, p. 261-
407, pl. 1-10.
(95)   1886-88, *Études sur les mollusques des*
couches coralligènes de Valfin (Jura): Soc.
paléont. suisse, Mém., v. 13-15, 369 p., 37 pl.
(96)   1889-93, *Études sur les mollusques des*
couches coralligènes inférieurs du Jura ber-
nois: Same, v. 16-19, 419 p., 37 pl.

Mansuy, Henri
(97)   1912, *Étude géologique du Yunnan oriental,*
2ᵉ partie, Paléontologie: Service géol. Indo-
Chine, Mém., v. 1, fasc. 2, 146 p., 25 pl.
(Hanoi-Haiphong).
(98)   1914, *Nouvelle contribution à la paléontol-*
ogie du Yunnan: Same, v. 3, fasc. 2, 190 p.,
10 pl.

Meek, F. B.
(99)   1873, *Descriptions of invertebrate fossils from*
the Silurian and Devonian Systems: Ohio
Geol. Survey, v. 1, pt. 2, Paleontology, p.
1-243, pl. 1-23 (Columbus).

——, **& Worthen, A. H.**
(100) 1866, *Descriptions of invertebrates from the*
Carboniferous System: Illinois Geol. Survey,
v. 2, Paleontology, p. 143-410, pl. 14-32
(Springfield).

Miller, A. K., Downs, H. R., &
Youngquist, W.
(101) 1949, *Some Mississippian cephalopods from*
central and southern United States: Jour.
Paleont., v. 23, p. 600-612, pl. 97-100
(Tulsa).

Moore, R. C.
(102) 1941, *Upper Pennsylvanian gastropods from*
Kansas: State Geol. Survey of Kansas, Bull.
38, pt. 4, p. 121-163, pl. 1-3 (Lawrence).

——, **Lalicker, C. G., & Fischer, A. G.**
(103) 1952, *Invertebrate fossils:* 766 p., McGraw-
Hill (New York).

Morris, John & Lycett, John
(104) 1851, *A monograph of the Mollusca from*
the Great Oolite. Part 1, Univalves: Palaeontogr. Soc. Mon., 130 p., 15 pl. (London).

Nelson, L. A.
(105) 1947, *Two new genera of Paleozoic Gas-*
tropoda: Jour. Paleont., v. 21, p. 460-465,
pl. 65 (Tulsa).

Newell, N. D.
(106) 1935, *Some Mid-Pennsylvanian inverte-*
brates from Kansas and Oklahoma: II. Stro-
matoporoidea, Anthozoa, and Gastropoda:
Same, v. 9, p. 341-355, pl. 33-36.

Norwood, J. G. & Pratten, H.
(107) 1855, *Notice of fossils from the Carbonifer-*
ous series of the western states, belonging
to the genera Spirifer, Bellerophon, Pleur-
otomaria, Macrocheilus, Natica, and Loxo-
nema, with descriptions of eight new char-
acteristic species: Acad. Nat. Sci. Philadelphia, Jour., ser. 2, v. 3, p. 71-78, pl. 9.

Oehlert, D. P.
(108) 1888, *Descriptions de quelques espèces dé-*
voniennes du département de la Mayenne:
Soc. d'Études sci. d'Angers, Bull., 1887,
p. 65-120, pl. 6-10.

Öpik, A. A.
(109) 1953, *Lower Silurian fossils from the "Il-*
laenus band," Heathcote, Victoria: Geol.
Survey Victoria, Mem., no. 19, 42 p., 13
pl. (Melbourne).

Orbigny, Alcide d'
(110) 1842-43, *Paléontologie française, terrains*
crétacés: v. 2, 456 p., atlas, pl. 149-236 *bis*
(Paris).
(111) 1850-60, *Paléontologie française, terrains*
jurassiques: v. 2, 621 p., atlas, pl. 235-428
(Paris).

Perez-Farfante, Isabel
(112) 1943, *The genera Fissurella, Lucapina and*
Lucapinella in the Western Atlantic: John-
sonia, v. 1, no. 10, p. 1-20, pl. 1-5 (Cambridge, Mass.).
(113) 1943, *The genus Diodora in the Western*
Atlantic: Same, v. 1, no. 11, p. 1-20, pl.
1-6.

Perner, Jaroslav
(114) 1903, *Patellidae et Bellerophontidae:* in
Barrande, Joachim, Système silurien du
centre de la Bohême, v. 4, Gastéropodes,
tome 1, texte p. 1-164, pl. 1-89 (Praha).
(115) 1907, [No title]: Same, tome 2, text, pl.
90-175.
(116) 1911, [No title]: Same, tome 3, text, pl.
176-247.

Picard, Edmund

(117) 1904, *Beitrag zur Kenntniss der Glossophoren der mitteldeutschen Trias.*: Kön. preuss. geol. Landesanst., Jahrb., v. 22, p. 445-540, pl. 9-14 (Berlin).

Pilsbry, H. A.

(118) 1934, *Notes on the gastropod genus Liotia and its allies:* Acad. Nat. Sci. Philadelphia, Proc., v. 85, p. 375-381, pl. 13.

Pitcher, B. L.

(119) 1939, *The upper Valentian gastropod fauna of Shropshire:* Ann. & Mag. Nat. History, ser. 11, v. 4, p. 82-132, pl. 1-4 (London).

Powell, A. W. B.

(120) 1937, *The shellfish of New Zealand:* 100 p., 18 pl. (Auckland, N.Z.).

(121) 1951, *Antarctic and Subantarctic Mollusca: Pelecypoda and Gastropoda:* Discovery Reports, v. 26, p. 47-196, pl. 5-10 (Cambridge).

Quenstedt, F. A.

(122) 1881-84, *Petrefaktenkunde Deutschlands:* v. 7, Gastropoden, 867 p., atlas, pl. 186-218.

Reed, F. R. Cowper

(122a) 1920-21, *A monograph of the British Ordovician and Silurian Bellerophontacea:* Palaeontograph. Soc. Mon., p. 1-48, pl. 1-8, 1920; p. 49-92, pl. 9-13, 1921 (London).

Roemer, C. F. von

(123) 1876, *Lethaea geognostica oder Beschreibung und Abbildung der für die Gebirgs-Formationen bezeichnendsten Versteinerungen, 1 Theil, Lethaea palaeozoica:* 323 p., 61 pl. (Stuttgart).

Roemer, F. A.

(124) 1850-66, *Beiträge zur geologischen Kenntnis des nordwestlichen Harzgebirges:* Palaeontographica, v. 3, p. i-viii, 1-67, pl. 1-10 (1850); v. 3, p. 69-111, pl. 11-15 (1852); v. 5, p. 1-44, pl. 1-8 (1855); v. 9, p. 1-46, pl. 1-12 (1860); v. 13, p. 201-235, pl. 33-35 (1866) (Cassel).

Rusconi, Carlos

(125) 1952, *Fosiles cambricos del Cerro Aspero, Mendoza:* Mus. Historia Nat. Mendoza, Revista, v. 6, no. 1-4, p. 63-122, pl. 1-6.

(126) 1954, *Fosiles Cambricos y Ordovicos de San Isidro:* Bol. Paleont., no. 30, 4 p. (Buenos Aires).

Saito, Kazuo

(127) 1936, *Older Cambrian Brachiopoda, Gastropoda, etc., from northwestern Korea:* Fac. Sci. Imperial Univ. Tokyo, Jour., sec. 2, v. 4, p. 345-367, pl. 1-3.

Salter, J. W.

(128) 1859, *Figures and descriptions of Canadian organic remains:* Geol. Survey Canada, decade 1, p. 1-46, pl. 1-10 (Montreal).

Sandberger, Guido & Sandberger, Fridolin

(129) 1850-55, *Die Versteinerungen rheinischen Schichtensystems in Nassau:* Atlas, pl. 1-39 (Wiesbaden).

Sieberer, Karl

(130) 1907, *Die Pleurotomarien des schwäbischen Jura:* Palaeontographica, Band 54, p. 1-68, pl. 1-5 (Stuttgart).

Simroth, Heinrich

(131) 1906, *Mollusca:* in Bronn, H. G., Klassen und Ordnungen des Tier-Reichs, ed. 2, v. 3, Lief. 85-89, pl. 59-62.

Spitz, Albrecht

(132) 1907, *Die Gastropoden des Karnischen Unterdevon: Beiträge zur Paläontologie und Geologie Österreich-Ungarns und des Orients:* Geologischen und paläontologischen Inst. Universität Wien, Mitteil., v. 20, p. 115-190, pl. 11-16.

Spriestersbach, Julius

(133) 1942, *Lenneschiefer (Stratigraphie, Facies, und Fauna):* Reichsamts für Bodenforschung, Abhandl., Neue Folge, Heft 203, 219 p., 11 pl., 19 fig. (Berlin).

Stache, Guido

(134) 1877, *Beiträge zur Fauna der Bellerophonkalks Südtirols, Nr. 1, Cephalopoden und Gastropoden:* Kais. -kön. geol. Reichsanstalt, Jahrb., v. 27, p. 271-318, pl. 5-7 (Wien).

Stoyanow, Alexander

(135) 1948, *Molluscan faunule from Devonian Island Mesa Beds, Arizona:* Jour. Paleont., v. 22, p. 783-791, pl. 120-121 (Tulsa).

Talent, J. A. & Philip, G. M.

(136) 1956, *Siluro-Devonian Mollusca from Marble Creek, Thompson River, Victoria:* Roy. Soc. Victoria, Proc., v. 68, p. 57-71, pl. 6-7 (Melbourne).

Tasch, Paul

(137) 1953, *Causes and paleoecological significance of dwarfed fossil marine invertebrates:* Jour. Paleont., v. 27, no. 3, p. 356-444, pl. 49 (Tulsa).

Thiele, Johannes

(138) 1924, *Revision des Systems der Trochacea:* Zool. Mus. Berlin, Mitteil., v. 11, p. 47-74, 1 pl.

(139) 1929-31, *Handbuch der systematischen Weichtierkunde:* Band 1, 778 p. (Jena).

Thomas, E. G.

(140) 1940, *Revision of the Scottish Carboniferous Pleurotomariidae:* Geol. Soc. Glasgow, Trans., v. 20, p. 30-72, pl. 2-4.

Thorson, Gunnar

(141) 1946, *Reproduction and larval development of Danish marine bottom invertebrates, with special reference to the planktonic larvae in the Sound (Øresund):* Kommissionen for

Danmarks Fiskeriog Havundersøg., Meddel., ser. Plankton., v. 4, 523 p. (København).

Ulrich, E. O. & Scofield, W. H.
(142) 1897, *The Lower Silurian Gastropoda of Minnesota:* Minnesota Geol. Survey, v. 3, pt. 2, p. 813-1081, pl. 61-82 (Minneapolis).

Vologdin, A. G.
(143) 1955, *Cambrian Solenopora and mollusks of the northern Tyan-Shan:* Akad. Nauk SSSR, Doklady, v. 105, no. 2, p. 354-356 [all Russ.] (Moskva).

Vostakova, V. A.
(144) 1955, *Ordovician gastropods of the Leningrad and Baltic Sea region:* Leningrad Universitet Nauchnoissledovate'skii Institut-Zemnoi Cory Paleontologischeskaia Laboratoriia, Voprosy Paleontologii, v. 2, p. 82-123, pl. 1-8 [all Russ.] (Moskva).

Waagen, W. H.
(145) 1880, *Productus Limestone fossils:* Geol. Survey India, Mem., Palaeont. Indica, ser. 13, Salt Range fossils, pt. 2, v. 1, p. 73-183, pl. 7-16 (Calcutta).

Wanner, C.
(146) 1942, *Neue Beiträge zur Gastropodenfauna des Perm von Timor:* in Geol. Exped. Univ. Amsterdam to Lesser Sunda Islands in the southeastern part of the Netherlands East Indies, 1937, under leadership of H. A. Brouwer, p. 133-208, pl. 1-3 (Amsterdam).

Wenz, Wilhelm
(147) 1938-44, *Gastropoda. Allgemeiner Teil und Prosobranchia:* in O. H. Schindewolf, ed., Handbuch der Paläozoologie, Band 6, 1639 p.; Teil 1, p. 1-240, 1938; Teil 2, p. 241-480, 1938; Teil 3, p. 481-720, 1939; Teil 4, p. 721-960, 1940; Teil 5, p. 961-1200, 1941; Teil 6, p. 1201-1506, 1943; Teil 7, p. 1507-1639, 1944 (Berlin).

(148) 1940, *Ursprung und frühe Stammesgeschichte der Gastropoden:* Arch. Molluskenkunde, v. 72, p. 1-10 (Frankfurt a. -M).

Whidborne, G. F.
(149) 1891, *A monograph of the Devonian fauna of the south of England. The fauna of the limestones of Lummaton, Wolborough, Chircombe Bridge, and Chudleigh.* Gastropoda: Palaeont. Soc. Mon., p. 156-250, pl. 16-24 (London).

Wilson, A. E.
(150) 1951, *Gastropoda and Conularida [Conulariida] of the Ottawa Formation of the Ottawa-St. Lawrence Lowland:* Geol. Survey Canada, Bull. 17, 149 p., 19 pl. (Ottawa).

Winters, S. S.
(151) 1956, *New Permian gastropod genera from eastern Arizona:* Washington Acad. Sci., Jour., v. 46, no. 2, p. 44-45.

Yen, T.
(152) 1949, *Review of Palaeozoic nonmarine gastropods and a description of a new genus from the Carboniferous rocks of Scotland:* Malacol. Soc. London, Proc., v. 27, p. 235-240, pl. 12A.

Yin, T. H.
(153) 1932, *Gastropoda of the Penchi and Taiyuan Series of North China:* Palaeont. Sinica, Ser. B, v. 11, fasc. 2, p. 1-53, pl. 1-3 (Peiping).

Yochelson, E. L.
(154) 1956, *Permian Gastropoda of the southwestern United States: I. Euomphalacea, Trochonematacea, Pseudophoracea, Anomphalacea, Craspedostomatacea, Platyceratacea:* Am. Mus. Nat. History, Bull., v. 110, pt. 3, p. 173-276, pl. 9-24 (New York).

(155) 1953, *Jedria, a new subgenus of Naticopsis:* Washington Acad. Sci., Jour., v. 43, no. 3, p. 65.

(156) 1956, *Labridens, a new Permian gastropod:* Same, v. 46, no. 2, p. 45-46, fig. 1.

Zittel, K. A. von
(157) 1873, *Die Gastropoden der Stramberger Schichten:* Palaeontographica, Supp. 2, p. 193-373, atlas, pl. 40-52 (Cassel).

SOURCES OF ILLUSTRATIONS

(Supplementary to works cited in the preceding list of references)

(158) Abbott, R. T.
(159) Adams, Henry
(160) Ammon, Ludwig von
(161) Bartsch, Paul
(162) Bayle, Emile & Coquand, Henri
(163) Beets, C.
(164) Böhm, Johannes
(165) Buvignier, Amand
(166) Cantraine, F. J.
(167) Chavan, André

(168) Chenu, J. C.
(169) Clark, B. L. & Durham, J. W.
(170) Cossmann, Maurice
(171) Cossmann, Maurice & Pissarro, G.
(172) Dall, W. H.
(173) Dautzenberg, Philippe & Fischer, Paul
(174) De Gregorio, Antoine
(175) Dell, R. K.

(176) Delpey, Geneviève
(177) Deshayes, G. P.
(178) Di-Stefano, Giovanni
(179) Dunker, Wilhelm
(180) Eames, F. E.
(181) Emerson, B. K.
(182) Eudes-Deslongchamps, Eugène
(183) Finlay, H. J. & Marwick, John

(184) Forbes, Edward & Hanley, Sylvanus
(185) Galkin, Y.
(186) Gardner, Julia
(187) Gemmellaro, G. G.
(188) Gerhardt, K.
(189) Greco, Benedetto
(190) Guiscardi, Guglielmo
(191) Habe, Tadashige
(192) Hertlein, L. G. & Strong, A. M.
(193) Jeffreys, J. G.
(194) Jekelius, Enrich
(195) Kittl, Ernst
(196) Koken, Ernst
(197) Kolesnikov, V.
(198) Kuroda, Tokubei & Habe, Tadashige
(199) ———, & Hirase, Shintaro

(200) Kutassy, Endre
(201) Loriol, Perceval
(202) Lycett, John
(203) Martin, G. C.
(204) Marwick, John
(205) Moore, Charles
(206) Müller, Georg
(207) Munier-Chalmas, Ernest
(208) Oppenheim, Paul
(209) Palmer, K. v. W.
(210) Pethö, Julius
(211) Philippi, R. A.
(212) Picard, Edmund
(213) Pilsbry, H. A.
(214) ———, & McGinty, T. L.
(215) Raincourt, Marquis de & Munier-Chalmas, Ernest

(216) Reeve, L. A.
(217) Rehder, H. A.
(218) Rolle, F.
(219) Sowerby, G. B.
(220) Stephenson, L. W.
(221) Stewart, R. B.
(222) Stoliczka, Ferdinand
(223) Strong, A. M.
(224) Terquem, Olry
(225) Vokes, H. E.
(226) Wade, Bruce
(227) Watson, R. B.
(228) White, C. A.
(229) Wilckens, Otto
(230) Williamson, M. B.
(231) Wood, S. V.
(232) Woodward, Henry
(233) Zittel, K. A. von

ADDENDUM

Since the manuscript was prepared the following generic names proposed for Paleozoic gastropods have come to the attention of KNIGHT, BATTEN and YOCHELSON. The suggested systematic placement of these genera is given below, but in order not to delay publication of the *Treatise* volume, no illustrations or diagnoses are given.

Acevina RUSCONI, 1952 [*?*Helcionella (Acevina) cuyunchensis*] ?Archaeogastropoda, incertate sedis. *M.Cam.,* S.Am.(Arg.).

Cycloscena FLETCHER, 1958 [*C. anomphala*] Anomphalacea, possibly Anomphalidae. *Perm.,* Austral.

Elkoceras LINTZ & LOHR, 1958 [*E. volborthi*] Euomphalacea, Euomphalidae, a junior synonym of *Straparollus (Phanerotinus)*. *L.Miss.,* USA (Nev.).

Hampilina KOBAYASHI, 1958 [*H. goniospira*] Helcionellacea, Helcionellidae. *Cam.,* NE.Asia (Korea).

Lacunospira BATTEN, 1958 [*L. alta*] Pleurotomariacea, Eotomariidae. *Perm.,* USA(Tex.).

Lamellopspira BATTEN, 1958 [*L. conica*] Pleurotomariacea, doubtfully Phymatopleuridae. *Perm.,* USA(Tex.).

Mourlonopsis FLETCHER, 1958 [*Pleurotomaria strzeleckiana* MORRIS, 1845] Pleurotomariacea, Eotomariidae. *Perm.,* Austral.

Planikeenia FLETCHER, 1958 [*P. minor*] Pleuromariacea, Sinuopeidae, a junior synonym of *Keenia. Perm.,* Austral.

Pleurocinctosa FLETCHER, 1958 [*Pleurotomaria trifilata* DANA, 1947] Pleurotomariacea, Eotomariidae, a junior synonym of *Peruvispira. Perm.,* Austral.

Rhabdocantha FLETCHER, 1958 [*Pileopsis alta* DANA, 1849] Platyceratacea, Platyceratidae, a junior synonym of *Platyceras (Orthomychia)*. *Perm.,* Austral.

Randomia MATTHEW, 1899 [*R. aurorae*] Possibly Monoplacophora or Helcionellacea. *M.Cam.,* Newfoundland.

Strotostoma FLETCHER, 1958 [*S. rylstonensis*] Possibly Platyceratacea, possibly Platyceratidae. *Perm.,* Austral.

Walnichollsia FLETCHER, 1958 [*Pleurotomaria subcancellata* MORRIS, 1845] Pleurotomariacea, not assigned to family. *Perm.,* Austral.

REFERENCES

Batten, R. L., 1958, *Permian Gastropoda of the Southwestern United States: 2. Pleurotomariacea: Portlockiellidae, Phymatopleuridae, and Eotomariidae:* Am. Mus. Nat. Hist., Bull., v. 114, art. 2, p. 153-246, pl. 32-42.

Fletcher, H. O., 1958, *The Permian gastropods of New South Wales:* Australian Mus. Records, v. 24, no. 10, p. 115-164, pl. 7-21.

Kobayashii, Teichii, 1958, *On some Cambrian gastropods from Korea:* Japanese Jour. Geol. Geog., v. 29, no. 3, p. 111-118, pl. 8.

Lintz, Joseph, Jr. & Lohr, L. S., 1958, *Two new invertebrates from the Mississippian of Nevada:* Jour. Paleont., v. 32, p. 977-980, pl. 128.

Matthew, G. F., 1899, *Preliminary notice of the Etcheminian fauna of Newfoundland:* Nat. Hist. Soc. New Brunswick, Bull., v. 4, art. 18, p. 189-197, pls. 1-3.

Rusconi, Carlos, 1952, *Varias especies de trilobitas del Cambrico de Canota:* Mus. Hist. Nat. Mendoza, Revista, v. 6, p. 5-17, pl. 1.

INDEX

Names included in the following index are classified typographically as follows: (1) Roman capital letters are used for suprafamilial taxonomic units which are recognized as valid in classification; (2) italic capital letters are employed for suprafamilial categories which are considered to be junior synonyms of valid names; (3) morphological terms and generic family names accepted as valid are printed in roman type; and (4) generic and family names classed as invalid, including junior homonyms and synonyms, are printed in italics. Page numbers printed in boldface type as **(I254)** indicate the location of systematic descriptions.

Sericea, I286
Sericominolia, **I260**
Serpularia, I192
Serpulospira, **I192**
sexual dimorphism, I128
Shansiella, **I212**
shoulder, I115, **I133**, I134
shoulder angle, **I133**
Shwedagonia, **I204**
side, **I133**, I134
sigmoidal, **I133**, I135
Siliquariidae, I87
Siluriphorus, **I298**
Simochilus, I273
SIMROTH, I151
Sinezona, **I221**
Sinistracirsa, **I187**
sinistral, I110, **I133**, I134
Sinospira, **I320**
Sinuella, **I175**
Sinuites, I122, **I177**
Sinuitidae, I157, **I175**
Sinuitina, **I175**
Sinuitinae, I157, **I175**
Sinuitopsis, **I177**
Sinum, I88, I106
Sinuopea, **I198**
Sinuopeidae, I158, **I198**, I331
Sinuopeinae, I158, **I198**
Sinus, **I133**, I134, I135
Sinusigera, I138
Sinuspira, **I291**
Sinutor, **I258**
Sinutropis, **I192**
Sinzowia, **I258**
Sipho, I229
Siphodentalium, I40
Siphoentalis, I40
siphon, I91
siphonal canal, **I91**, I116, **I133**, I134
siphonal fasciole, I118, **I133**, I135
siphonal fold, I121, **I133**, I134
siphonal notch, I116, **I133**, I134
Siphonaria, I95
Siphonariidae, I21, I86, I145, I151, I153
Siphonella, I228
SIPHONOBRANCHIA, I147, I311
SIPHONOBRANCHIATA, I153
Siphonodentaliidae, **I40**
Siphonodentalium, **I40**
Siphonodontum, I40
Siphonopoda, I40
Siphonopodidae, I40
SIPHONOSTOMATA, I148, I149, I153
siphonostomatous, I116, **I133**, I134
Sisenna, **I202**
Skenea, **I271**
Skeneinae, I159, **I271**
Skeneopsis, I88
Sklerochiton, I66
Slerochiton, I66
slit, **I46**, **I133**, I134
slit band, I119, **I133**, I135
slit ray, **I46**
Smaragdella, **I285**

Smaragdia, **I285**
Smaragdiinae, I159, **I285**
Smaragdinae, I285
Smaragdista, **I285**
SMITH, I137
Solanderia, I261
Solaricida, **I262**
Solariconulus, I249
Solariella, **I261**
Solariellinae, I159, **I261**
Solariellopsis, I250
Solarioconulus, **I249**
Solemyidae, I28
Solenacea, I23
Solenidae, I25, I26
Soleniscidae, I320
Soleniscinae, I121, I165, I320
Soleniscus, I321
Solenocaris, **I74**
SOLENOCONCHIA, I37
SOLENOGASTRES, I41, I42, I74, I86
Solenospira, I291
Solivaga, I56
Sophismalepas, I230
Sororcula, I303, **I305**
Sosiolytes, **I245**
Sosiospira, I277
Spanionema, **I317**
Spectamen, **I262**
SPENGEL, I144, I149, I150
spermatheca, I99
Sphaerochilus, I280
Sphaeroconia, I286
Sphaerocyclus, I182
Sphaerodoma, I321
Sphenosphaera, **I180**
Spicator, **I258**
spicules, **I46**
spine, I46, I120, **I133**, I135
spiral, **I133**, I134, I135
spiral ornament, I120
Spiratellidae, I46
spire, I107, **I133**, I134
spire angle, I127, **I133**, I134
Spirina, **I300**
Spirocirrus, **I305**
Spiroecus, **I311**
Spiromphalus, **I315**
SPIRONOTIA, I171
Spiroraphe, I204
Spiroraphella, I203
Spiroscala, **I204**
Spirotomaria, **I223**
Spirula, I30
Spondylas, I22, I125
Spongiochiton, I69
Spongioradsia, I56
spout, I133, I134
Squamophora, I65
Squamopleura, **I66**
squamose, **I133**, I135
squat, **I133**, I134
Stachella, **I179**
Staffinia, **I280**
Staffola, **I288**
Staurospira, I239
Stectoplax, I69

Steganomphalus, **I274**
Stegocoelia, **I293**
Stella, I265
Stenochiton, **I56**
STENOGLOSSA, I105, I153, I154, I311
Stenoloron, **I210**
Stenoplax, **I56**
Stenopoma, I284
Stenoradsia, **I56**
Stenosemus, **I55**
Stenosemus, I58
Stenotheca, I324
Stenothecoides, **I83**, I324
Stephanocosmia, I315
Stephanozyga, **I313**
Stereochiton, I58
Stereoplax, I55
Steromphala, **I257**
Stilifer, I86
Stimpsoniella, I63
stirpes, I150
Stoastoma, **I287**
Stoastomatinae, I159, **I287**
Stoastomidae, I287
Stoastominae, I287
Stoastomops, **I288**
STOLICZKA, I143
stomach, I98
Stomatella, **I263**
Stomatella, I250, I263
Stomatellidae, I159, **I263**
Stomatia, **I264**
Stomatiidae, I263
Stomatolina, **I264**
Stomax, I264
Straparella, **I244**
Straparollina, **I239**
Straparollus, I109, **I192**
Strecochiton, I69
Strepsodiscus, **I174**
Streptacididae, I145, I165, **I322**
Streptacis, I145, **I322**
Streptochiton, I63
STREPTONEURA, I148, I149, I150, I151, I153, I171
STREPTONEURA AZYGO-BRANCHIA, I311
Streptotrochus, **I243**
Stretochiton, I69
stria, **I133**, I135
Strianematina, I313
Striatemoda, **I286**
Strigichiton, **I56**
Strigosella, **I254**
Strobaeus, I321
Strobeus, I321
Strombacea, I98, I117, I141, I144
Strombidae, I18, I89, I141, I143
strombiform, **I133**, I134
Stromboli, **I230**
Strombus, I18, I124, I125
Strophella, I318
Strophites, I318
Strophostylus, **I242**
Strotostoma, **I331**
Struthiolaria, I18, I124
Struthiolariidae, I87

Date Due

NOV 1 0 1970		
DEC 1 0		
MT. UNION		
MAY 2 3 1972		
Mt. Union		
APR 2 4 1991		
APR 2 6 1995		
	PRINTED IN U. S. A.	

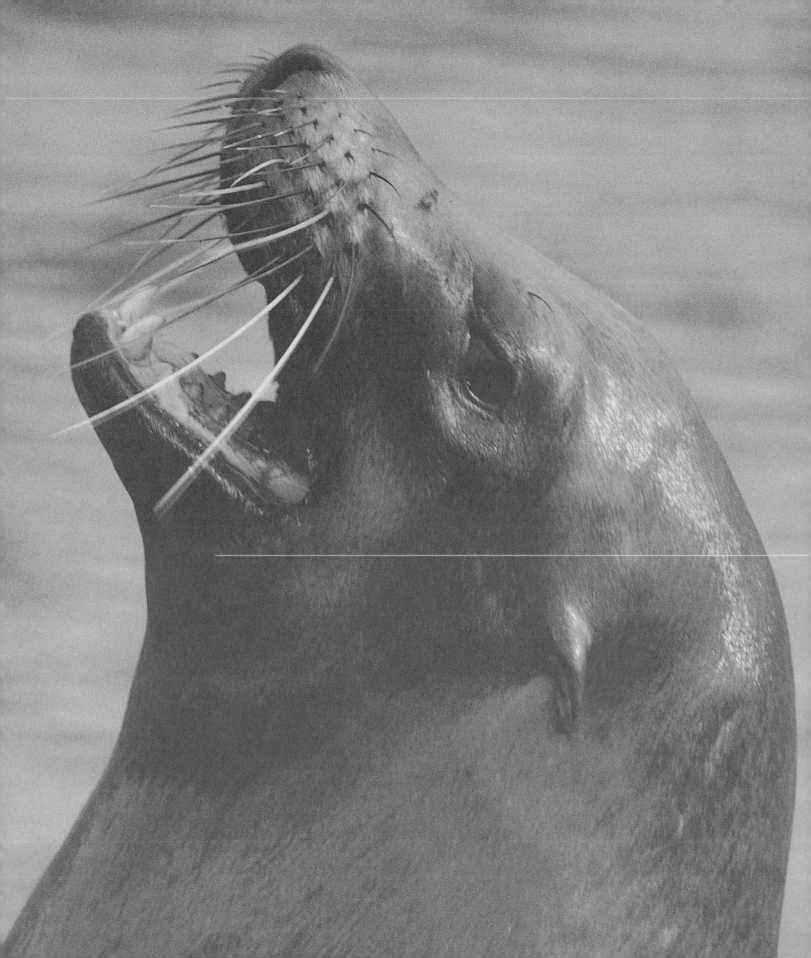